Essential Papers on Addiction

ESSENTIAL PAPERS IN PSYCHOANALYSIS
General Editor: Leo Goldberger

Essential Papers on Addiction

Edited by
Daniel L. Yalisove

∏ NEW YORK UNIVERSITY PRESS
New York and London

NEW YORK UNIVERSITY PRESS
New York and London

Library of Congress Cataloging-in-Publication Data
Essential papers on addiction / edited by Daniel L. Yalisove.
p.   cm. — (Essential papers in psychoanalysis)
Includes bibliographical references and index.
ISBN 0-8147-9672-9 (cloth : alk. paper). — ISBN 0-8147-9677-X
(pbk. : alk. paper)
1. Substance abuse.   2. Psychoanalysis.   3. Substance abuse—
Treatment.   4. Psychodynamic psychotherapy.   I. Yalisove, Daniel
L.   II. Series.
RC564.E776   1977
616.86'0651—dc20   97-10332
                    CIP

New York University Press books are printed on acid-free paper,
and their binding materials are chosen for strength and durability.

Manufactured in the United States of America
10   9   8   7   6   5   4   3   2   1

Contents

PART VII: PSYCHIATRIC ILLNESS AND ADDICTION

Introduction

THIS BOOK is a collection of the most clinically relevant psychoanalytic writings on addiction. I have chosen papers based on their historical importance, clinical relevance, and clarity of presentation. Many of these papers have guided my clinical work in the addiction field for the past twenty years. While I am convinced these papers will be an invaluable source for those interested in the psychology and treatment of addiction, a complete understanding requires consideration of biology, adolescent development, psychopharmacology, neuropsychology, genetics, the study of natural recovery, and cognitive/behavioral psychology. The course I have taken is to follow the psychoanalytic papers, giving the reader an overview of the addiction field including a brief history of specialized addiction treatment in the Introduction, and to make reference to other disciplines in my commentary.

PSYCHOANALYSIS AND ADDICTION

We can trace two major themes in the psychoanalytic understanding and treatment of addiction. First, the psychoanalytic view of addiction has been influenced by the evolution of psychoanalytic theory. Second, from the beginning, psychoanalysts have recommended modifications in psychoanalytic technique to treat addictions. Because Freud developed psychoanalysis by treating neurotic patients, Freud and most psychoanalysts have viewed neurosis as their primary interest.[1] When psychoanalysts have ventured beyond the treatment of neurosis, it has been referred to as "widening the scope."[2]

The first widening scope occurred when the earliest psychoanalysts treated patients outside the neurotic range, including addicts. This early interest made psychoanalysis the first modern discipline to study addiction. The papers reprinted in the historical part are from this period. Early analysts used psychoanalytic drive theory to explain addictive behavior by suggesting that addicts had become fixated in the oral phase of psychosexual development and used the drug to obtain substitute infantile sexual gratification. Thus the addiction was seen as an oral perversion (Chafetz, part V). Even in this early phase of psychoanalysis, Simmel (part I) modified psychoanalytic technique to treat addicts in one of the first psychoanalytic inpatient sanatoria.

With the publication of Radó's classic paper, "The Psychoanalysis of

Pharmacothymia," in 1933 (part I), the modern psychoanalytic understanding of addiction was launched. Radó and most subsequent analysts viewed the drug taking as an effort at adaptation, although often ultimately destructive. In the same period, Glover (part I) observed that addicts often used drugs to suppress aggressive impulses. These two observations mark the beginning influence of ego psychology on the understanding of addiction.

The second widening of scope occurred with the publication of Stone's oft-cited paper, "The Widening Scope of Indications for Psychoanalysis," in 1954[3] and coincided with the increasing application of ego psychology. In this period there were several significant changes in psychoanalytic technique; most consequential was the development of psychoanalytic psychotherapy. Specialized treatments for the borderline condition were being developed at the Menninger Clinic[4] and specialized treatment for the psychosomatic disorders was being developed at the Chicago School.[5] In this period, Chafetz at Cambridge Hospital used psychoanalytic principles to develop a comprehensive alcoholism program (part V).

In the 1950s psychoanalysts like Brown (part IV) began to apply an understanding of transference and countertransference to addicts. Gustafson (part III), among other self-psychologists, suggested that while the transferences of addicts and countertransferences induced by them have unique features, they could often be analyzed in a relatively traditional manner. A contrasting view is that addicts do not develop analyzable transferences and induce countertransference reactions that are more intense than in traditional treatments. The latter view understandably recommends dramatic modifications in treatment of the addict (Silber and Chafetz [part V]).

Another phase of widening scope came in the 1960s and 1970s with the short-lived period of community psychiatry/psychology. During the drug epidemic of the 1970s, several psychoanalysts devoted their energies to treating and understanding addiction. Certainly addiction is the perfect vehicle to consider the cultural, social, spiritual, and adaptive as well as psychodynamic and biological factors in the causation of a syndrome. Ego psychologists in this period posited that addicts have defects[6] in specific ego functions that make them vulnerable to addiction (Krystal, part II).[7] Controversy remains regarding whether these defects in the premorbid character of the addict are the result of conflict (Wurmser, Krystal, part II) or failure of internalization of parental functions (Gustafson, part III).[8] Zinberg (part II) notes that active addiction compromises ego functions, which may account for the ego defect rather than premorbid problems. The psychoanalytic ego psychologists reasoned that the ego defects made it difficult for the addicts to tolerate the rigors of psychoanalytic therapy and thus recommended a number of significant modifications in treatment. Though written in the same period, the case studies (part III) illustrate the application of a relatively unmodified psychoanalytic technique in the treatment of an alcoholic and drug addict. The reader will note the ensuing technical difficulties.

The present is a phase of widening scope[9] where economic exigency is the operating potent force, where the realm of managed care and competition from increased numbers of mental health workers have led psychoanalytically-trained clinicians to broaden their expertise in areas not traditionally addressed by them. There are three current psychoanalytic views of addiction. Some psychoanalysts, like Krystal and Wurmser (part II), adhere to the traditional view that addicts have premorbid psychopathology that predisposes them to addiction. Disturbances in early infantile development, variously conceptualized as separation-individuation, self-formation, or prestructural issues, are considered to be the primary factors that leave individuals vulnerable to addiction. Treatment consists of a relatively unmodified psychoanalysis or psychoanalytic therapy. Other contemporary psychoanalytic therapists like Brickman and Zweben (part VI) feel that psychoanalytic technique must be combined with the concepts of specialized addiction approaches. The third group believes that an emergent psychoanalytic model is needed to integrate the treatment of addiction syndromes and psychiatric syndromes. Richards (part VII) has created an excellent foundation for this model.

THE HISTORY OF SPECIALIZED ADDICTION TREATMENT IN AMERICA

While psychoanalytic treatment of addiction began in the twentieth century, the history of addiction treatment in America extends back to our Founding Fathers. Benjamin Rush, a signer of the Declaration of Independence and the Surgeon General of the American Revolutionary Army, was a physician who treated alcoholics and wrote at length about alcoholism.[10] The Temperance Movement, with its large and committed following, reflected the first major social concern about alcoholism and other addictions in the United States.[11] This largely Protestant religious movement, popular in the nineteenth century subscribed to the moral view of addiction and helped addicts who had lost their moral compass to find their way back to the fold. Thousands took the pledge and became abstinent. The culmination of the Temperance Movement was the establishment of Prohibition in 1920, after which, ironically enough, efforts to treat addicts ceased. The situation did not change when the great expansion of psychiatric services occurred in the 1940s and 1950s. Alcoholics and drug addicts were discouraged from gaining admission to mental health hospitals or outpatient treatment programs.[12] They were viewed as having poor prognoses and poor motivation.[13] If admitted to mental health hospitals, little treatment was provided.[14] Hence, it is not surprising that addicts rarely sought treatment in mental health services and had a negative view of them.

Alcoholics Anonymous (AA), founded in 1935,[15] provided help for alcoholics not available in hospitals or clinics. It is a spiritual, nonprofessional self-help fellowship of alcoholics. One of the cofounders, Bill W., wrote the Twelve Steps and Twelve Traditions (reprinted in part VI). The former are a form of spiritual instruction, which if followed, assure abstinence and a restoration of self-respect and self-esteem[16] and the latter are the principles by which AA chapters function. The spiritual appeal of AA is reminiscent of the Temperance Movement. AA grew rapidly and its philosophy was popularized by the National Council on Alcoholism.[17] AA members volunteered in hospitals to introduce alcoholic patients to the principles of AA.[18] Gradually recovering alcoholics were hired by treatment facilities as lay therapists, then as paraprofessionals, and finally as alcoholism counselors. They now comprise the bulk of treatment personnel in alcoholism.[19] The influx of recovering alcoholic alcoholism counselors into the treatment system has had a dramatic impact on the treatment model that has developed.[20] The self-help principles of AA became incorporated into professional, nonpsychiatric treatment and became known as the disease concept.[21] (See Pattison et al., part VI.)

Specialized heroin and other illicit drug addiction treatment burst upon the scene in the 1970s as a response to the epidemic of illegal drug use and abuse in the United States.[22] Most of the treatment staff, as in alcoholism treatment programs, were recruited from the ranks of ex-addicts. The philosophy of these programs was often antiprofessional[23] and antipsychological.[24] While this antagonism has abated, residues of these attitudes remain.

These specialized addiction treatments have grown enormously and represent the preponderance of treatment services available to addicts today. The specialized alcoholism treatment programs include medically supervised inpatient detoxification,[25] inpatient rehabilitation programs,[26] and outpatient treatment. The specialized heroin addiction treatment programs include medically supervised inpatient detoxification,[27] inpatient therapeutic communities (TC),[28] outpatient methadone maintenance programs,[29] and drug-free outpatient programs. Both TCs and outpatient drug-free programs treat cocaine dependence and polysubstance dependence. In all of the specialized addiction programs there is extensive use of toxicology testing to verify compliance with abstinence from psychoactive substances. These specialized addiction treatments remain largely outside of the mental health system.[30]

COGNITIVE/BEHAVIORAL APPROACHES TO ADDICTION

Cognitive/behavioral approaches, like those of psychoanalysis, have mostly remained outside the realm of specialized addiction treatment programs. Yet these techniques, in the form of conditioned reflex therapy pioneered at Shandel Hospital,[31] reach back to 1940. Like specialized addiction programs, their focus is on surface behavior. In the cognitive/behavioral model, addictive behavior is viewed as a habit, which is subject to the laws of learning. It is viewed as occurring on a continuum rather than the presence or absence of a unitary disease.[32] In the 1970s cognitive/behaviorists researched the goal of teaching alcoholics to control their drinking,[33] which led to a great deal of acrimonious criticism from the disease-concept advocates, who have maintained that abstinence from all mood-altering drugs (except tobacco) is the only acceptable goal for addiction treatment.[34] Recently, however, there has been a movement toward a middle ground. While still offering controlled-drinking training to problem drinkers, cognitive/behavioral psychologists have ceded that chronic alcoholics cannot safely return to controlled drinking[35] and specialized addiction programs have begun to use some cognitive/behavioral techniques.[36]

Cognitive/behavioral theorists have researched the problem of relapse and have developed techniques for relapse prevention.[37] They utilize a variety of behavioral techniques to treat addictive behaviors and have devoted a great deal of effort to empirically test them.[38]

THE CONTRAST BETWEEN PSYCHOANALYSIS AND SPECIALIZED ADDICTION TREATMENTS

Psychoanalysis was founded on the premise that unconscious repressed infantile wishes were the basis of adult neurosis. Freud developed the technique of psychoanalysis to decipher these conflicts, to impart knowledge of the conflicts to the patient through insight, which in turn allowed the patient to gain mastery over the conflicts.[39] Freud employed free association and interpretations of dreams, transference, and resistance to achieve this end. In order to foster the the optimal level of transference, Freud[40] developed the principle of abstinence, which required the analyst to refrain from gratifying many patient wishes that in other social contexts would be gratified.

The specialized addiction treatments and the cognitive/behavioral approaches start from the opposite pole. The counselor begins and remains on the surface of consciousness and behavior. Education, persuasion, and advice giving are common while insight and inner exploration are rare. The counselor in specialized addiction programs, often in recovery himself, expresses identification with the patient in specific ways and discloses information about his own recovery that he feels will aid the patient. The relatively free and self-revealing manner of the alcoholism counselor contrasts sharply with the traditional restraint of the psychoanalyst. The readings of part VI attempt to reconcile these divergent approaches.

Since psychoanalysis was developed for the treatment of neurosis, modifications in technique could reasonably be expected to successfully help addicts. On the other hand, Wurmser (part II) argues that the specialized addiction treatments themselves may reflect the tendency for addicts to minimize the experience of their inner lives. In any event, some addicts require and many can benefit from some exploration of unconscious factors to ameliorate otherwise intractable symptoms. Such interpretive work is generally recommended only after addicts become stably abstinent (Brickman, Zweben, part VI).

Addiction specialists, aside from ideological objections,[41] can criticize psychoanalysis for its neglect of addiction concepts. While psychoanalysts have primarily viewed addiction as a mental phenomenon, addiction specialists view it as a bodily phenomenon. Thus physiological dependence, the withdrawal syndrome, and postacute withdrawal effects were not generally understood by the early psychoanalysts as physiologically based.[42] For those not acquainted with the field of addiction, I review the major addiction concepts in the next part. Addiction specialists also criticize psychoanalysts for assuming that all addicts have premorbid psychopathology, which in essence labeled the addict psychiatrically ill as well as addicted and thus doubly stigmatized. Later in this Introduction I suggest a more neutral assumption regarding addict psychopathology.

OVERVIEW OF ADDICTION CONCEPTS

Classification of Drugs

Drugs may be classified on the basis of their chemical structure, their plant source (e.g., cannabinoids are from the cannabis plant), their site of action in the brain, their effects, their acceptance in the community (e.g., legal or illegal),[43] their relative harmfulness, and their degree of addictiveness. While the different drugs cannot be neatly categorized, generally they are classified according to their effects on consciousness and the sensorium. Opioids, including heroin, morphine, codeine, and methadone, are analgesics (alleviate pain). Barbiturates, minor tranquilizers, and alcohol are depressants, depressing the activity of the central nervous system (CNS). Amphetamines, cocaine, caffeine, and nicotine are stimulants, increasing the activity of the CNS. LSD, psilocybin, and mescaline are hallucinogens. Phencyclidine (angel dust) has analgesic, depressant, and hallucinogenic properties. Cannabinoids, including marijuana, have depressant and hallucinogenic properties. Inhalants, like model airplane glue, create a dizzying and intoxicating effect and are generally considered depressants.[44]

Drug effects occur in withdrawal as well as during intoxication, both of which can mimic psychiatric symptoms. The fourth edition of the *Diagnostic and Statistical Manual of Mental Disorders* (DSM-IV) takes this into account by including the following diagnoses: Substance-induced Psychotic, Mood, and Anxiety Disorders with Onset during Intoxication or Withdrawal.[45] In addition there is postacute alcohol withdrawal syndrome, which affects sleep patterns, emotional state, concentration, memory, and other cognitive functions. While most recovery of function occurs in four to six weeks, subtle effects can last longer.[46] For these reasons, accurate diagnostic assessments cannot be obtained until the patient is abstinent for several weeks.

It is widely accepted that drug effects (intoxication, sedation, etc.) are in large measure caused by the effect of the drug on the neurotransmitters and that the degree of addictiveness of a drug may be due to effects on the neurotransmitter system.[47] The simplest explanation of drug addiction would be that some substances are so highly addictive that most people would be unable to regulate their use. However, this is clearly not the case since many individuals use alcohol and other drugs safely.[48]

Different Substance Addictions

Writings on addiction tend to focus on a specific psychoactive substance or activity. While there has been relatively little effort made to integrate the results of studies on separate substances, there is much to suggest underlying processes in all addictions (Jacobs, part II).[49] Hence an assumption of the book is that there is significant generalizabilty among all addictions. While addiction to some substances may have special features, it is unlikely that each substance carries with it an entirely different process. Some modest evidence to support this commonality is that addiction to multiple substances is common today.[50] It is unlikely that such addicts are suffering from multiple addictive diseases. Further many addicts shift from one addiction to another.[51] Since most of the psychoanalytic writings have focused on alcohol or heroin, most of the selections in this volume focus on one or the other of these substances. For a basis of comparison between substance and nonsubstance addictions, I have included Rosenthal's (part II) review of the psychoanalytic writings on gambling.

The Acquisition of an Addiction and the Addictive Process

Rarely is addiction acquired instantaneously. For example, it takes two to three years to become addicted to cigarettes.[52] Jaffe and Kanzler suggest the following stages of acquisition: initiation, regular use, accelerated or heavy use, and addiction.[53] Additionally, I subscribe to the cognitive/behavioral view that addiction occurs on a continuum from use to addiction. An individual may remain at any of the stages that Jaffe and Kanzler have postulated or go back and forth between them. Once the individual becomes psychologically and/or physiologically dependent, the addiction impacts on the adjustment of the individual (Zinberg, part II). The addictive process is superimposed on a personality organization, which may interact with the addictive process. Premorbid factors, both physiological and psychological, may increase the vulnerability to addiction. Nicotine addiction most clearly illustrates that an addiction is process that can be superimposed on a large variety of personality types. Attention to the process of acquiring an addiction has been neglected both in theory and research. To wit, the extensive data on adolescent use of alcohol, nicotine, and other drugs has not been integrated into addiction theory.[54]

Prevalence of Mental Disorders in Addictions

The readings in the part VII review the prevalence rates of mental illness in addiction and the addiction rate in mental illness. While there is a high rate of comorbidity, 37.4 percent among treated patients,[55] it would be a mistake to think that every addict suffers from a psychiatric illness, let alone a specific type. Zinberg (part II) makes a strong case that drug effects and the drug lifestyle adversely affect ego functioning and can thus account for many of the symptoms associated with psychiatric illness manifested by addicts.

I feel it is best to view addiction and psychiatric illness as two separate syndromes, each having varying degrees of intensity, which may interact in a variety of ways. To illustrate my point, let me continue with nicotine dependence.[56] Would we say there is a nicotinic personality? We know that millions of smokers have stopped on their own while others cannot.[57] We also know that depressed patients have more difficulty giving up smoking[58] and that schizophrenics have the highest rate of smoking of all diagnostic categories.[59] I don't think we have any difficulty seeing this addiction cutting across all diagnostic categories, knowing full well that some smokers may be severely psychiatrically compromised but others relatively normal. We can see clearly that the addiction can take on a life of its own through physiological dependence. While other substances differ from nicotine in the degree to which they alter consciousness and impair ego functioning, I would argue that other substance addictions can be best understood in generally the same way, that the addiction can adhere to and interact with any personality organization. Richards (part VII) elaborates on this theme in his chapter.

GLOSSARY

Unfortunately there is no uniform terminology in the addiction field. In order to avoid any confusion that might arise over terminology, I have defined the basic addiction concepts below. The reader should keep in mind that writers often use different terminology to describe the same processes and, most annoyingly, they can apply different meanings to the same term.

Acquired tolerance means that more of the psychoactive substance must be taken to achieve the same effects previously received on lower doses. Most addicts can tolerate amounts of their drug of choice that would be lethal to the nonphysiologically dependent.

Addiction originally meant physiological dependence on a psychoactive substance.[60] The term *addiction* has come to include phenomena beyond physiological dependence. First, some psychoactive substances like cocaine and marijuana do not induce physiological dependence but can bring about psychological dependence. Second, some authors have included nonsubstance habits like pathological gambling as addictions (Rosenthal, part II).[61] The term *addiction* generally implies a repetitive activity that produces a rapid, powerful, short-lived reward, followed by a longer-lasting dysphoric state, which initiates a new round of the addictive behavior. It includes loss of control over the habit and negative consequences attributable to the habit. (Similar to *substance dependence*. Different from *compulsive behavior* in that the latter is not pleasurable.)[62]

Addictive potential refers to both the reinforcing properties of the drug (degree of euphoria created) and the ease with which physiological dependence is established. (E.g., cocaine has a strong addictive potential in that it is highly euphoric but does not cause physiological dependence. Heroin, on the other hand, induces physiological dependence fairly rapidly as well as inducing moderate euphoria, accounting for its high addictive potential.)

Compulsive drug use is a term used by psychoanalysts to describe pathological, uncontrolled use of a substance or behavior. (See Richards [part VII] and Wurmser [part II]) This term implies a psychological loss of control (i.e., a psychodynamically driven urge).

Craving refers to the urges to take the drug or engage in the addictive behavior. The concept has been criticized for its circular definition and subjective meaning. One component of craving is addicts' wishes to alleviate withdrawal symptoms (e.g., the need for active alcoholics to drink or nicotine addicts to smoke upon awakening, after the drug levels have decreased during sleep). Another component of craving is the conversion of a painful or uncomfortable affect to a wish to take the drug.

Loss of control is a key concept of addiction. (1) The most common meaning of this phrase is that once addicts have ingested a certain amount of the addictive substance, they cannot stop and must continue using the substance until they become unconscious or is otherwise prevented from continuing. The extent to which addicts truly have loss of control is not clear. Alcoholics, for example, have shown the ability to control their drinking in hospital settings.[63] Today, addiction specialists speak of relative loss of control or impaired control[64] rather than absolute loss of control. Thus Keller states addicts cannot predict when taking the substance will lead to loss of control.[65] (2) *Loss of control* has a second meaning, referring to the instigation of addictive behavior after a period of abstinence.[66] It is usually viewed as a physiological phenomenon.

Physiological dependence is indicated by an acquired tolerance of the substance and manifestation of a withdrawal syndrome. It was once thought that this physiological dependence created powerful cravings and thus accounted for addictive behavior. However, most addicts quickly relapse after detoxification, suggesting that other factors than the physiological dependence are primary in maintaining the addiction.

Progression is the concept that the addiction increasingly takes over the addict's life, disrupts his/her functioning, and ultimately kills him/her. While addictions often do show a progression in many individuals, evidence does not indicate that it is inevitable.[67]

Psychological dependence: (1) A substance or habit used in order to function or deal with psychological problems. For example, an addict may use alcohol or cocaine to overcome shyness, to be assertive, to reduce conflict, and to be able to perform sexually. (2) Craving for the drug without physiological dependence.

Substance abuse: This term has had many usages over the years. It is best thought of as a diagnostic category as outlined in DSM-III onwards. Substance abuse is the less severe of the two substance disorders, requiring only that the taking of the drug have problematic consequences for at least a month's duration.[68] *(Alcohol abuse* is similar to *problem drinking.)*

Substance dependence: Similarly this term has had many usages over the years. It is best thought of as a diagnostic category as outlined in DSM-III onwards. It is the more severe condition, which includes combinations of symptoms of physiological dependence, loss of control, and problems resulting from the drug taking for over a month's duration[69] (similar to *drug addiction* and *alcoholism*).

Withdrawal or abstinence syndrome: Some drugs, like alcohol, tobacco, and heroin, have a characteristic withdrawal syndrome. This occurs after prolonged and heavy use when abstinence is suddenly initiated. Depending on the drug, the amount ingested, and the biological condition of the individual, this syndrome can be very dangerous and in some cases fatal.

NOTES

1. Stone, 1954.
2. Stone, 1954.
3. Stone, 1954.
4. Knight, 1937a, 1937b.

5. Alexander and French, 1946.

6. I follow Pine's distinction between defect and deficit (1990, p. 200).

7. Khantzian, 1981.

8. Kohut, 1977.

9. Pine, 1990.

10. Levin and Weiss, 1994.

11. Lender and Martin, 1987.

12. Most hospitals did not treat alcoholics in this period (Strachan, 1971; Hayman, 1966). Nace (1993) comments, "From the 1930's through the 1960's, hospitals either overtly rejected alcoholics or subtly deterred them by negative attitudes" (p. 430). The institutions where the bulk of alcoholics were treated were the state mental hospitals (Plaut, 1967; Cahn, 1970; NIAAA, 1972).

13. Blume (1986), recounting her early experiences at a State Psychiatric Hospital, notes that the alcoholics were not viewed as treatable and were given the diagnosis "Without mental disease, alcoholism, chronic"; they were supposed to be discharged. As she developed the alcoholism unit in this hospital, the stigma attached to the patients rubbed off onto her and her staff, what Straus (1976) calls derived stigma.

14. Glasscote et al., 1967; Chafetz and Yoerg, 1977; NIAAA, 1972; Hayman, 1966; McCullogh, 1952.

15. Alcoholics Anonymous World Services, 1957.

16. Alcoholics Anonymous World Services, 1976.

17. Shortly after AA was founded, the National Council on Alcoholism was created (1944) to promote the notion that alcoholism was a disease and to advocate for alcoholism treatment (M. Keller, 1986).

18. "[T]he around the clock twelfth step work of AA members represents the largest continuing army of unpaid volunteer workers ever mobilized for a health or social problem in the United States" (Cahn, 1970, p. 140).

19. Saxe, Dougherty, Esty, and Fine 1983.

20. Kalb and Propper, 1976; Tournier, 1979.

21. Cook, 1988a, 1988b.

22. During this period, drug addiction treatment evolved from the legal and criminal justice system (DeLeon, 1990). See B. S. Brown (1990) for additional history of drug addiction treatment.

23. Freudenberger, 1976.

24. Wurmser, 1984a.

25. Gallant, 1987.

26. Cook, 1988a, 1988b; Gallant, 1987; Stuckey and Harrison, 1982.

27. Margolin and Kosten, 1991.

28. DeLeon, 1986.

29. Dole and Nyswander, 1967.

30. Wiener (1981) has shown how the NIAAA and other agencies have worked to maintain a separate identity for alcoholism treatment. State agencies for alcohol and drug abuse treatment have their own separate regulations for operating treatment facilities which are quite different from regulations for operating mental health facilities. For example, in New York State the Division of Alcoholism and Alcohol Abuse and the Division of Substance Abuse Services were created in 1978. Eventually

they created their own regulations for the operation of treatment facilities and the credentialling of counselors (New York State Office of Alcoholism and Substance Abuse Services, 1996).

31. Voegtlin, 1940.

32. Lewis, Dana, and Blevins, 1994.

33. Peele, 1984.

34. See Armor, Polich, and Stambul, 1978, for a sampling of the criticism.

35. Sobell and Sobell, 1993.

36. Rotgers, Keller, and Morgenstern, 1996. Morgenstern and McCrady (1992) surveyed addiction professionals and found that behavioral techniques were being integrated into disease model framework.

37. Martlatt and Gordon, 1985.

38. Hester and Miller, 1995.

39. Freud, 1919.

40. Freud, 1919.

41. The ideological positions are that addicts cannot use drugs ever (the requirement of abstinence), that AA is essential in recovery, that only an addict can understand another addict, that active addicts are necessarily in denial (Milam and Ketcham, 1981).

42. Neither Fine nor Gustafson seem to be aware of these effects in their case studies reprinted in part III.

43. Lewis, Dana, and Blevins, 1994.

44. Hofmann, 1975.

45. American Psychiatric Association, 1994, p. 191.

46. Bean, 1981; Becker and Kaplan, 1986; DeSoto et al., 1985; Gallant, 1987; Gorski, 1986; Grant and Reed, 1985. As yet, there is little documented evidence for this syndrome in other addictions.

47. See Milhorn, 1990, for current understanding of how specific drugs disrupt neurotransmission and account for drug effects.

48. Of course, we know that many people drink alcohol safely; furthermore, Zinberg (1984) found controlled users of opiates, marijuana, and LSD.

49. Orford, 1985.

50. According to a recent epidemiolic survey, 69% of those with a drug use disorder also had an alcohol use disorder (Grant and Pickering, 1996). About 30% of treated drug addicts report heavy alcohol and marijuana use (Simpson and Sells, 1982; Hubbard et al., 1989). Chan (1991, p. 87) states, "The majority of persons entering drug treatment facilities all over the country are multiple drug users."

51. Johnson, 1993.

52. Orford, 1985.

53. Jaffe and Kanzler, 1979.

54. Adolescence and early adulthood are typically when alcohol and drug use is initiated. Adolescence is a critical period in the formation of coping behavior and responses, such as using drugs to deal with stress, peer pressure, and emotional distress (Kandel and Logan, 1984; Orford, 1985). Yet theories of addiction in general ignore adolescent development. Longitudinal research regarding adolescent acquisition of substance use and abuse has been conducted for several years by Kandel,

1978; Jessor and Jessor, 1978; Brook et al., 1992; and Newcomb, Maddahian, and Bentler, 1986, among others. The multiple factors shown affecting acquisition and use of drugs include deviance, peer drug use, poor relationship with parents, and sensation seeking (Newcomb, Maddahian, and Bentler, 1986); aggression (Cadoret, 1992); high behavioral activity level (Tarter and Mezzich, 1992); lack of parent-child mutual attachment (Brook et al., 1992); stress (Wills, 1985); and absence of bonds to social institutions in African American males (Brunswick, Messeri, and Titus, 1992). Sadava (1987) gives a good review of these theories and some of the findings. Research is continuing in this area in the Michigan State University–University of Michigan longitudinal study of child health and family development (Fitzgerald, Zucker, and Yang, 1995)

On the clinical side, there has been a paucity of studies on adolescent drug and alcohol abuse. For example, in the *Psychoanalytic Study of the Child* through 1993, there have only been five articles on adolescent substance abuse (Editor's tabulation).

55. The Epidemiologic Catchment Area Program's estimate (Regier et al., 1993). This program is summarized by Richards (part VII).

56. While nicotine is a moderately addicting substance, it has a relatively modest and adaptive effect on consciousness. Although smoking is generally not considered as serious a problem as alcoholism or opiate addiction, it accounts for 300,000 deaths per year, more than all other addictions combined (U.S. Department of Health and Human Services, 1988). Like alcohol it is a legal drug. Smokers report both calming and stimulating effects when they are the desired effects (Jaffe and Kanzler, 1979; Orford, 1985). It is an addiction in that regular smokers develop tolerance and report withdrawal symptoms and cravings (Jaffe and Kanzler, 1979; Orford, 1985; N. S. Miller, 1991). Were there no negative health consequences, it would probably not be a cause for concern.

57. While Coletti, Payne, and Rizzo (1987, p. 243) state "the large majority of smokers who attempt to quit have little long-term success, regardless of of how they try to stop," several million people have stopped smoking since 1968 (P. M. Miller, 1987).

58. Glassman, 1993; Hall et al., 1993.

59. Glassman, 1993.

60. Hofmann, 1975.

61. Orford, 1985

62. See Hofmann, 1975, for history of addiction terminology.

63. Pattison, Sobell, and Sobell, 1977.

64. Wallace, 1996.

65. Keller, 1972.

66. Keller, 1972.

67. Pattison, Sobell, and Sobell, 1977.

68. American Psychiatric Association, 1994, pp. 182–83.

69. American Psychiatric Association, 1994, p. 181.

PART I

Historical Papers (1929–1937)

FREUD

Most of Freud's comments on addiction were written very early on in his career and predate the development of psychoanalytic theory. His first acquaintance with addiction came through his study of cocaine. A thorough and sympathetic treatment of this period of Freud's career is chronicled in the *Cocaine Papers* by Byck.[1] He suggests that Freud should be considered one of the first psychopharmocologists. Freud published several papers on cocaine, the most ambitious being "Uber Coca."[2] He advocated research to explore cocaine's potential for treating psychiatric illnesses and recommended its use for withdrawal from morphine.[3] Freud treated a morphine-addicted friend and colleague, Fleishal, with cocaine for withdrawal. Unfortunately, Fleishal became addicted to the cocaine and his life ended tragically. This difficult episode is thoroughly discussed in Jones's biography of Freud.[4] The idea of treating an addiction to a substance with another substance continued long after Freud's efforts with Fleishal. Freud was attacked for advocating the use of cocaine, which was identified as "the third scourge of mankind" by Erlenmeyer, a contemporary German psychiatrist.[5] By 1887, he had given up promoting its use. Freud himself used cocaine from 1884[6] until 1896.[7]

Freud in a letter to Fleiss referred to masturbation as the primary addiction.[8] Shortly thereafter, he published some remarks on masturbation and addiction, indicating that the source of the addiction problem must be dealt with as well as instituting abstinence to effect lasting change.[9] He continues, "these narcotics are meant to serve—directly or indirectly—as a substitute for a lack of sexual satisfaction; and whenever normal sexual life can no longer be re-established, we can count with certainty on the patient's relapse."[10] These comments derive from his early theory that an unhealthy accumulation of sexual excitation caused "actual neurosis" and neurasthenia.[11]

Freud made very few remarks regarding addiction in his subsequent writings. The reprinted passage is from *Civilization and Its Discontents*. One is struck by Freud's strong repudiation of religion here. By contrast, AA relies heavily on spiritual elements to help the alcoholic. Freud's discussion occurs in the context of conducting one's life rather than a discussion of symptoms. Hence, Freud may have viewed addiction as a condition quite separate from psychiatric illness. In the reprinted passage, Freud suggests that intoxication may be used to ward off external pressures and disappointments. This is interesting because it suggests that he viewed external problems as an etiological factor in addiction while the subsequent hallmark of psychoanalytic thinking has been that addiction is caused by internal factors. This theme is taken up again by Zinberg (part II). Presciently, Freud notes in passing that the body must have substances that have intoxicating effects, anticipating by many years the discovery of the endogenous opioids. Freud's comments on gambling are discussed in Rosenthal's paper (part II).

OTHER EARLY HISTORICAL PSYCHOANALYTIC CONTRIBUTIONS TO ADDICTION

Abraham's "The Psychological Relations Between Sexuality and Alcoholism"[12] was the first psychoanalytic essay entirely devoted to a discussion of addiction. His paper and all those written in this time period are based largely on the drive theory of psychoanalysis. This theory held that many human motives were based on gratifications sought after or received in childhood (infantile wishes). Infantile sexuality suppressed or overindulged was repressed and later emerged in compromise formation as partially gratified in a neurotic symptom or directly gratified in perversion. Abraham noted an analogy between perversion and alcoholism in that the drinking could be said to represent the sexual activity of the alcoholic rather than a prelude to it. Others viewed addiction as a perversion in that pleasure is obtained not through adult genitality but through gratification of an infantile wish.[13] Simmel[14] presents the most complete exposition of the drive theory of addiction.

Glover, a follower of Melanie Klein,[15] made the important observation that not only were libidinal drives implicated in addiction, but in his view, even more important were the sadistic (aggressive) drives. He hypothesized that drugs mitigated sadistic impulses for addicts. Glover also argues that preoedipal as well as oedipal problems are etiological factors in addiction. Both he and Radó note that affect tolerance problems are common in addicts and that the drug can provide a protective function to compensate for this deficit. This attention to the adaptive function signals the introduction of ego psychology into understanding addiction. Radó's article is notable in that he considers pharmacologic and organic effects of drugs, unusual among psychoanalysts, and anticipates the psychoanalytic view of addiction held for many decades. The highlight of the article is a description of the "psychothymic regime" which describes the effects of the cycle of drug-taking and temporary abstinence on the addict's narcissistic equilibrium and ego.

In Schloss Tegel, perhaps the first psychoanalytic sanatorium, Simmel devised a treatment for those suffering from morbid cravings (an archaic term for addiction) based on drive theory, offering the patient substitute gratifications to help them renounce the symptom of addiction. As such, this is the first modified psychoanalytic technique for the addictions. Knight, like Simmel, worked in a psychoanalytic sanatorium, the Menninger Clinic. He recommended further modifications in the treatment of addicts, especially the development of a warm, trusting relationship with the patient. His remarks in the reprinted paper are refreshingly clear and straightforward, recognizable to the current practitioner as good practical advice on building a treatment alliance with these patients.[16]

In many psychoanalytic writings, including two in this part (Radó, Simmel), withdrawal phenomenon is interpreted psychologically without due consideration to its somatic origins.

NOTES

1. Byck, 1974.
2. Freud, 1884, reprinted in Byck, 1974.
3. Freud, 1885, "On the General Effect of Cocaine," reprinted in Byck, 1974.
4. Jones, 1953.
5. Byck, 1974.
6. Byck, 1974.
7. Freud, "Letters to Fleiss," Oct. 26, 1896, in Masson, 1985, p. 201.
8. Freud, "Letters to Fleiss," Dec. 22, 1897, in Masson, 1985, p. 287.
9. Freud, 1898, pp. 275–76.
10. Freud, 1898, p. 276.
11. Freud, 1895, p. 108, and Freud, 1898, p. 268.
12. Abraham, 1908.
13. Clark, 1919; Simmel, 1948; Chafetz, 1959.
14. Simmel, 1948.
15. Rosenfeld, 1960 and 1964, develops the Kleinian view of addiction.
16. In the Knight article, "Keely cures" refer to a inpatient alcoholism treatment popular in the early twentieth century. It was based on the curative value of injections of double chloride of gold. Subsequently it was shown that there was no such substance and the treatment was discredited (Lender and Martin, 1987).

1. *From* Civilization and Its Discontents

Sigmund Freud

In my *Future of an Illusion* [1927c] I was concerned much less with the deepest sources of the religious feeling than with what the common man understands by his religion—with the system of doctrines and promises which on the one hand explains to him the riddles of this world with enviable completeness, and, on the other, assures him that a careful Providence will watch over his life and will compensate him in a future existence for any frustrations he suffers here. The common man cannot imagine this Providence otherwise than in the figure of an enormously exalted father. Only such a being can understand the needs of the children of men and be softened by their prayers and placated by the signs of their remorse. The whole thing is so patently infantile, so foreign to reality, that to anyone with a friendly attitude to humanity it is painful to think that the great majority of mortals will never be able to rise above this view of life. It is still more humiliating to discover how large a number of people living to-day, who cannot but see that this religion is not tenable, nevertheless try to defend it piece by piece in a series of pitiful rearguard actions. One would like to mix among the ranks of the believers in order to meet these philosophers, who think they can rescue the God of religion by replacing him by an impersonal, shadowy and abstract principle, and to address them with the warning words: "Thou shalt not take the name of the Lord thy God in vain!" And if some of the great men of the past acted in the same way, no appeal can be made to their example: we know why they were obliged to.

Let us return to the common man and to his religion—the only religion which ought to bear that name. The first thing that we think of is the well-known saying of one of our great poets and thinkers concerning the relation of religion to art and science:

> Wer Wissenschaft und Kunst besitzt, hat auch Religion;
> Wer jene beide nicht besitzt, der habe Religion! [1]

Translated by James Strachey, pp. 74–78. Translation copyright © 1961 by James Strachey, renewed 1989 by Alix Strachey. Reprinted by permission of W. W. Norton & Company, Inc. and Hogarth Press.

This saying on the one hand draws an antithesis between religion and the two highest achievements of man, and on the other, asserts that, as regards their value in life, those achievements and religion can represent or replace each other. If we also set out to deprive the common man, [who has neither science nor art] of his religion, we shall clearly not have the poet's authority on our side. We will choose a particular path to bring us nearer an appreciation of his words. Life, as we find it, is too hard for us; it brings us too many pains, disappointments and impossible tasks. In order to bear it we cannot dispense with palliative measures. "We cannot do without auxiliary constructions," as Theodor Fontane tells us.[2] There are perhaps three such measures: powerful deflections, which cause us to make light of our misery; substitutive satisfactions, which diminish it; and intoxicating substances, which make us insensitive to it. Something of the kind is indispensable.[3] Voltaire has deflections in mind when he ends *Candide* with the advice to cultivate one's garden; and scientific activity is a deflection of this kind, too. The substitutive satisfactions, as offered by art, are illusions in contrast with reality, but they are none the less psychically effective, thanks to the role which phantasy has assumed in mental life. The intoxicating substances influence our body and alter its chemistry. It is no simple matter to see where religion has its place in this series. We must look further afield.

The question of the purpose of human life has been raised countless times; it has never yet received a satisfactory answer and perhaps does not admit of one. Some of those who have asked it have added that if it should turn out that life has *no* purpose, it would lose all value for them. But this threat alters nothing. It looks, on the contrary, as though one had a right to dismiss the question, for it seems to derive from the human presumptuousness, many other manifestations of which are already familiar to us. Nobody talks about the purpose of the life of animals, unless, perhaps, it may be supposed to lie in being of service to man. But this view is not tenable either, for there are many animals of which man can make nothing, except to describe, classify and study them; and innumerable species of animals have escaped even this use, since they existed and became extinct before man set eyes on them. Once again, only religion can answer the question of the purpose of life. One can hardly be wrong in concluding that the idea of life having a purpose stands and falls with the religious system.

We will therefore turn to the less ambitious question of what men themselves show by their behaviour to be the purpose and intention of their lives. What do they demand of life and wish to achieve in it? The answer to this can hardly be in doubt. They strive after happiness; they want to become happy and to remain so. This endeavour has two sides, a positive and a negative aim. It aims, on the one hand, at an absence of pain and unpleasure, and, on the other, at the experiencing of strong feelings of pleasure. In its narrower sense the word "happiness" only relates to the last. In conformity with this dichotomy in his aims, man's activity develops in two directions, according as it seeks to realize—in the main, or even exclusively—the one or the other of these aims.

As we see, what decides the purpose of life is simply the programme of the pleasure principle. This principle dominates the operation of the mental apparatus from the start. There can be no doubt about its efficacy, and yet its programme is at loggerheads with the whole world, with the macrocosm as much as with the microcosm. There is no possibility at all of its being carried through; all the regulations of the universe run counter to it. One feels inclined to say that the intention that man should be "happy" is not included in the plan of "Creation." What we call happiness in the strictest sense comes from the (preferably sudden) satisfaction of needs which have been dammed up to a high degree, and it is from its nature only possible as an episodic phenomenon. When any situation that is desired by the pleasure principle is prolonged, it only produces a feeling of mild contentment. We are so made that we can derive intense enjoyment only from a contrast and very little from a state of things.[4] Thus our possibilities of happiness are already restricted by our constitution. Unhappiness is much less difficult to experience. We are threatened with suffering from three directions: from our own body, which is doomed to decay and dissolution and which cannot even do without pain and anxiety as warning signals; from the external world, which may rage against us with overwhelming and merciless forces of destruction; and finally from our relations to other men. The suffering which comes from this last source is perhaps more painful to us than any other. We tend to regard it as a kind of gratuitous addition, although it cannot be any less fatefully inevitable than the suffering which comes from elsewhere.

It is no wonder if, under the pressure of these possibilities of suffering, men are accustomed to moderate their claims to happiness—just as the pleasure principle itself, indeed, under the influence of the external world, changed into the more modest reality principle—, if a man thinks himself happy merely to have escaped unhappiness or to have survived his suffering, and if in general the task of avoiding suffering pushes that of obtaining pleasure into the background. Reflection shows that the accomplishment of this task can be attempted along very different paths; and all these paths have been recommended by the various schools of worldly wisdom and put into practice by men. An unrestricted satisfaction of every need presents itself as the most enticing method of conducting one's life, but it means putting enjoyment before caution, and soon brings its own punishment. The other methods, in which avoidance of unpleasure is the main purpose, are differentiated according to the source of unpleasure to which their attention is chiefly turned. Some of these methods are extreme and some moderate; some are one-sided and some attack the problem simultaneously at several points. Against the suffering which may come upon one from human relationships the readiest safeguard is voluntary isolation, keeping oneself aloof from other people. The happiness which can be achieved along this path is, as we see, the happiness of quietness. Against the dreaded external world one can only defend oneself by some kind of turning away from it, if one intends to solve the task by oneself. There is, indeed, another and better path: that of becoming a member of the human community, and, with the help of a technique guided by science, going over to the attack against nature and subjecting her to the human will. Then one is working with all for the good of all. But the most interesting methods of averting suffering are those which seek to influence our own organism. In the last analysis, all suffering is nothing else than sensation; it only exists in so far as we feel it, and we only feel it in consequence of certain ways in which our organism is regulated.

The crudest, but also the most effective among these methods of influence is the chemical one—intoxication. I do not think that anyone completely understands its mechanism, but it is a fact that there are foreign substances which, when present in the blood or tissues, directly cause us pleasurable sensations; and they also so alter the conditions governing our sensibility that we become incapable of receiving unpleasurable impulses. The two effects not only occur simultaneously, but seem to be intimately bound up with each other. But there must be substances in the chemistry of our own bodies which have similar effects, for we know at least one pathological state, mania, in which a condition similar to intoxication arises without the administration of any intoxicating drug. Besides this, our normal mental life exhibits oscillations between a comparatively easy liberation of pleasure and a comparatively difficult one, parallel with which there goes a diminished or an increased receptivity to unpleasure. It is greatly to be regretted that this toxic side of mental processes has so far escaped scientific examination. The service rendered by intoxicating media in the struggle for happiness and in keeping misery at a distance is so highly prized as a benefit that individuals and peoples alike have given them an established place in the economics of their libido. We owe to such media not merely the immediate yield of pleasure, but also a greatly desired degree of independence from the external world. For one knows that, with the help of this "drowner of cares" one can at any time withdraw from the pressure of reality and find refuge in a world of one's own with better conditions of sensibility. As is well known, it is precisely this property of intoxicants which also determines their danger and their injuriousness. They are responsible, in certain circumstances, for the useless waste of a large quota of energy which might have been employed for the improvement of the human lot.

NOTES

1. ['He who possesses science and art also has religion; but he who possesses neither of those two, let him have religion!']—Goethe, *Zahme Xenien* IX (Gedichte aus dem Nachlass).

2. [It has not been possible to trace this quotation.]

3. In *Die Fromme Helene* Wilhelm Busch has said the same thing on a lower plane: "Wer Sorgen hat, hat auch Likör." ["He who has cares has brandy too."]

4. Goethe, indeed, warns us that "nothing is harder to bear than a succession of fair days."

> [Alles in der Welt lässt sich ertragen,
> Nur nicht eine Reihe von schönen
>   Tagen.
>   (Weimar, 1810–12.)]

But this may be an exaggeration.

2. On the Aetiology of Drug-Addiction

Edward Glover

THERE ARE three main sources of psycho-analytic interest in drug-addiction. In the first place its aetiology is still obscure; consequently the treatment of drug-addiction lags behind that of the psycho-neuroses. It is true the psycho-analyst is justified in asserting that the only radical approach to drug habits is through psycho-analytic treatment; but he cannot remain content with such a general recommendation. He ought to be in a position to direct his psycho-analytic energies with more precision. There is a considerable difference between "analysing" a drug-addict and analysing "drug-addiction."

A second source of interest lies in the correlation of drug-addiction with various other psychopathological states. Owing to the close connection on the one hand between drug-addiction and the psychoses, and on the other between drug-addiction and social or sublimatory defence-reactions, it is probable that drug states will prove an essential link in the understanding of such different phenomena as paranoia, obsessional neuroses, open-air cults or even an addiction to scented soap.

The third source of interest is mainly domestic. Study of psycho-analytic views concerning alcoholism and other drug-addictions seems to me to illustrate very clearly the different tendencies which from time to time have dominated psycho-analytical research or doctrine. Those whose interest in psycho-analysis is comparatively recent, dating, say, from the publication of *Beyond the Pleasure-principle,* might be excused for thinking that sadism and the aggressive instincts are new discoveries. In a sense this view is not entirely without justification. Wider historical reading shows however that whereas in earlier times the importance of sadism was recognized clinically, its aetiological significance was to some extent obscured by a preoccupation with more predominantly libidinal factors. Indeed, there are some grounds for the view that psycho-analysts can be divided into those who, as it were, have been brought up on the doctrine of sadism and the aggressive impulses

Reprinted by permission from *International Journal of Psycho-analysis* 13 (1932): 298–328. Copyright © Institute of Psycho-Analysis.

and those who are still strongly under the influence of earlier discoveries concerning libidinal impulses and frustration.

Now it is interesting to note that the first stage in investigating drug-addiction coincided with a period when the tendencies of psycho-analytical research were more or less convergent. Psycho-analysis bore down on the problem armed with experience of transference neuroses, holding closely to traditions of libidinal disturbance, in particular, castration anxiety dating from the phallic phase of libidinal development. The result was a standard reconstruction of psychic events, originally sketched by Abraham[1] in the case of alcoholism and added to piecemeal by later investigators. The details of this reconstruction require no recapitulation. I need only recall the emphasis laid on fixation of libido at oral or anal levels, on the comparative weakness of adult heterosexual interest, the importance of unconscious homosexuality, the significance of alcohol and other drugs as symbols of the procreative power of the male (father, God), the secondary breakdown of sublimation, and the symbolic castration represented first by impotence and later by physical and mental deterioration.

Even in this short summary the bias of libidinal interest is unmistakable. But another equally important tendency is liable to escape attention. The approach to drug-addiction was (and still is) profoundly influenced by the concept of *regression*. The opposite view of a *progression* in psychopathological states has never been exploited to the same extent. The idea of progression implies that psycho-pathological states are exaggerations of "normal" *stages in the mastering of anxiety* and can be arranged in a rough order of precedence. It is, of course, implicit in Freud's[2] original pronouncement regarding paranoid states: namely, that the symptom is in part an attempt at restitution, i.e. an advance from the unconscious situation it covers. Not only does it restore some link with reality, however inadequate, it performs also a protective function. The protective and restitutive aspects of other psycho-pathological states have not been given the same attention. For example, we have long known that obsessional mechanisms function comparatively well in the remissions of melancholia: nevertheless we are inclined to look askance at an obsessional neurosis *per se,* "severe regression." We think and talk of this neurosis as the result of a defensive flight backwards from the anxieties of an infantile genital system of relationships; rather than a remarkable impulsion forwards, a striking advance on the discomforts of an unconscious paranoid organization. Indeed it has been left to the psycho-analytical anthropologist and in more recent years to the child-analyst to administer a corrective to the clinical pessimism which goes with a bias in favour of regression.

As a matter of fact, if we study the numerous drug-habits which, owing to absence of dramatic individual or social consequences, are called "idiosyncrasies" or "indulgences" rather than addictions, we can see that drug-addiction is frequently a successful manoeuvre. The point is of considerable therapeutic interest. Obviously if we can grasp the progressive relations of psychogenetic states, our therapeutic energies can be directed with greater accuracy. For example, the cure of an addiction or even of a severe obsessional state may depend more on the reduction of an underlying paranoid layer than on the most careful analysis of the recognized habit-formation or obsessional superstructure.

To return to our historical survey, the first discoveries concerning addiction were followed by a phase of stalemate. This deadlock coincided with the realization that what had been regarded as almost a specific libidinal factor could no longer be so regarded. The element of unconscious homosexuality had never accounted satisfactorily for variations in the structure of different addictions and it was gradually found to be non-specific. Flight from unconscious homosexuality had already been advanced to account for the systems of paranoia; it was regarded as an important factor in obsessional states; it was discovered to be a source of violent resistance in characterological analyses and it gave considerable trouble in the analysis of normal people. The attempts made to emphasize regressive libidinal aspects of homosexuality, in particular the reassurance obtained by flight from genital anxiety were not satisfactory: reassurance mechanisms alone do not constitute a complete aetiology. Other efforts to maintain a purely libidinal aetiology were not any happier, as for example, Schilder's[3] view that intoxicants brought about changes in the libido and artificially increased homosexual components.

On the other hand, fresh progress seems to have been made by paying more attention to the associated element of sadism and the reactions produced by the aggressive group of impulses. These reactions were first of all studied directly in the form of projections, reaction-formations, regressions or inhibitions of psychic and motor activities, and later indirectly by scrutinizing the super-ego apparatus which is responsible for using up certain sadistic quantities. But in spite of the fact that newer concepts of sadism and of the super-ego have been applied in the study of drug-addiction, and have increased our aetiological understanding, the amount of progress made has not been entirely satisfactory. And I consider this is due in part to a divergence of views as to the actual significance of sadism. The divergences can be detected not only in papers on drug-addiction, but throughout the field of psycho-analytic research. As I have said, sadism is no new discovery. The concepts of hate, aggression and sadism have always been implicit in the concept of ambivalence and an increasing appreciation of its importance can be detected historically in the emphasis laid on negative transferences. The sadistic factor in transference was obscured for a time by the correlation of the negative transference with the inverted Oedipus situation. But this stage did not last, and there must be few analysts who have studied unconscious homosexuality in recent years without forming the conclusion that the problem of unconscious homosexuality is, roughly speaking, the problem of sadism.

In spite of this fact, I maintain that a very clear divergence of opinion can be detected in recent writings on drug-addiction, and also, though less obviously, in papers dealing with the psychoses. For one group sadism is still viewed through transference neurotic spectacles and valued in terms of genital development. The theoretical importance of pregenital sadism is freely admitted, but in practice it is regarded as a potential reinforcement of late Oedipus ambivalence, brought into action by the mechanism of regression. Other workers are not content to trace the development of sadistic impulses from the earliest stages onwards; their aim is to establish definite correlations between a series of characteristic fusions of aggression and certain psychopathological states, pre-eminently the psychoses and addictions and to a lesser extent compulsive formations.

This difference in tendency can be brought out by a comparison of earlier with more recent views on paranoia. It is true that in Freud's latest paper on paranoia[4] the significance of death-wishes is emphasized, and it is true also, as has been stated, that aggression is implicit in the earlier conception of ambivalence. Nevertheless in the Schreber paper no direct mention was made of the aggressive impulses and the mechanism of paranoia was described mainly in terms of libidinal conflict and related to repression of the inverted Oedipus situation. Only a few statements in Freud's more recent writings help to modify the earlier emphasis on libidinal factors in paranoia, e.g. that the mechanism of projection depends on ambivalence,[5] or that in cases of homosexuality an exceedingly hostile aggressive attitude has been not only repressed but *transformed* into a love relationship;[6] implying thereby that a homosexual system can function as a defence against hate and aggression.[7] Considering that for the last fifteen years Freud has constantly emphasized the general importance of hate, aggression and destructive impulses in ego-development, it is all the more remarkable that these teachings have not yet been fully reflected in aetiological formulations concerning paranoia. Yet such is the fact.

A definite contrast is afforded by the views of Melanie Klein.[8] She asserts that the fixation-points of the psychoses are pregenital sadistic fixation-points: that the individual experiences paranoidal anxiety in the early anal-sadistic phase: that the fixation-point of paranoia falls in the phase of phantasied attack on the mother's body; that the individual's aggressive tendencies are transferred to the excretory systems, hence that faeces and urine and all associated organs are unconsciously regarded as possessing dangerous sadistic properties, the projection of which gives rise to anxieties of attack from without; that in particular the fear of poisoning can be related mostly to the individual's original anal and urethral sadism.

I do not suggest that the degree of emphasis laid on sadistic elements necessarily involves any contradiction between the two points of view described. And it has to be admitted that early work of Stärcke,[9] Van Ophuijsen,[10] Abraham[11] and others to a certain extent foreshadowed the views expressed by Melanie Klein (e.g. Stärcke's view of the part played by "negative libido" in the psychoses). But there are definite differences, (a) in respect of the detail with which the sadistic phantasy-systems and defences of the earliest years are outlined (Melanie Klein's being presented with much greater detail), and (b) in regard to the exact nature of libidinal contributions in those early stages. The most important difference can be expressed by saying that if the "genital incest—ambivalence—castration anxiety" nucleus be taken as the model Oedipus situation, one must be prepared, following Klein's work, to discuss the existence of earlier Oedipus situations carrying a higher sadistic charge. It is true that in recent times writers on paranoia refer more frequently to sadistic factors, but they continue to link up those factors with an Oedipus situation of the model genital type (see e.g. Kielholz,[12] Feigenbaum[13] and others). The same applies to studies on delusions of poisoning and other poison phantasy-systems. Although both Kielholz and Fenichel[14] lay considerably more emphasis than usual on the sadistic significance of poisons and excretions, they end on a much milder note of pregnancy and castration phantasy. Here again the difference can be made clear by pointing out that if a representative group of analysts were asked to give a brief interpretation of a poison phantasy, many, including Fenichel himself, would simply describe it as an impregnation phantasy derived from the "classical" Oedipus nucleus; others would regard a poison phantasy as a projection of the sadistic weapon by means of which the primitive ambivalence relating to early frustration at an oral-anal level is expressed, and in which a mainly prephallic view of the Oedipus situation is reflected.

The same divergence can be demonstrated in the case of drug-addiction. If one studies recent psycho-analytic literature on the subject, it is clear that in spite of copious reference to hate and sadism, early fixations, psychotic components, etc., drug-addictions are ultimately assessed in terms of late genital anxieties. Even where attempts are made to establish deeper roots for the fixations of addiction the tendency is to look for them in phases of development when psychic structure must be of the most rudimentary order. Thus Radó,[15] although correlating drug-addiction and abstinence with a manic-depressive sequence, looks for the basic fixation in a phase of "alimentary orgasm" on which a pharmacotoxic orgiastic system is built up. It is true he does not exclude entirely a psychic organization based on this alimentary system, but he has so far attached no specific content to this psychic system. On the other hand he goes on to say that later guilt systems have no specific relation to drug-addictions: that they play no greater part in these addictions than in other pathological states. Simmel[16] in a recent paper shews both tendencies. He ultimately relates drug-addiction to melancholia but only as a secondary regression following a primary obsessional mechanism; as one might gather from his interest in obsessional factors in addiction, he expresses the anxiety factor mainly in terms of castration anxiety. And he follows Radó in seeking for a fixation factor in a phase antedating organized psychic structure, viz. a stage of primal intestinal narcissism. Incidentally, like many other writers, he introduces the "death instinct" as a factor, a course which always seems to me to beg the question of the actual history of sadistic and destructive impulses.

Stimulating as these contributions are, they exhibit an almost reactionary tendency. Pre-structural factors of this type can be adequately valued as "constitutional" or "predisposing" without employing the term fixation. This has always been the practice in estimating the importance of erotogenic zones. Granted that close attention should be paid to dispositional factors in drug-addiction, it seems unduly pessimistic to lay stress on these elements to the exclusion of later guilt-mechanisms. And granted that the latest guilt-systems cannot be regarded as specific, there seems no reason to exclude earlier specific guilt-reactions.

The opposite tendency, viz. search for a specific aetiology of drug-addiction of a kind that is primitive without being pre-structural is hard to find in psycho-analytic literature. Drug-addiction has been treated on the whole as a step-child of the psychoses. I have on previous occasions[17] referred to the mechanism of one type of alcoholism as an "inverted paranoia" and have said regarding drugs in general that they represent the poisons and elixirs wherewith the sadistic aftermath of early libidinal relations is treated. But the only specific reference I can find in the literature is in the form of a speculative suggestion made by Melitta Schmideberg.[18] Writing on psychotic mechanisms, and in particular on the means whereby dangerous "introjected" objects (or their substitutes) can be countered, she describes how a dangerous substance can be transmuted into a beneficent substance, also how friendly substances can be used to neutralize or expel malignant substances. She goes on to link this system with medicinal treatment in general and adds: "Probably this mechanism is at work in morbid cravings; the drug would signify the good father who is to fight against the bad introjected father ... soon it comes to signify the bad father against whom nothing avails but the taking of more drugs." This is "reinforced by the pharmacological effect of drugs as opposed to medicines that really heal."

In the last few years I have had fresh opportunities of studying some drug-addictions and have compared my recent impressions with former experiences of drug-habits. In particular I have tried to find some precise relation between drug-addiction, psychotic states, obsessional neuroses and neurotic character peculiarities. I have also tried to estimate the relative importance of the phallic Oedipus organization and of more primitive types where, it is held, pregenital sadism dominates the picture. The methods of valuation were on the whole empirical, namely, observing the type of mental mechanism employed in different states of anxiety, and the amount of reduction of anxiety that could be effected by following various lines of interpretation.

I am bound to say that as between the tendencies I have described in the earlier part of this paper, recent experience biases me in favour of the second. I agree that interpretations of a nuclear complex existing prior to the mainly genital Oedipus phase are to a certain extent suspect, that they are subject to the charge of being *"rückphantasieren"* products, that they may exploit regression instead of uncovering it. In short, I agree that the onus of proof is on those who attempt to modify existing systematizations. But I cannot find any adequate explanation of drug-addiction which does not assume an active Oedipus situation at a stage when object relations are little more than the psychic reflection of organ relations; when sadistic and libidinal functions overlap considerably and before libidinal systems—chiefly the oral, excretory and early genital systems—have established a stable balance between psychic representation and repression.

The justification for appropriating the term "Oedipus" in this context would take us too far afield. I have the impression that objections to this course are to a certain extent pedantic. A psychic situation contains the essential ingredients of an "Oedipus" complex provided: (1) a state of instinctual frustration exists, (2) this state of frustration is related by the subject to more than one object (or part-object, i.e. organ-object), (3) some degree of genital interest exists (whether directly frustrated or not), and (4) the state of frustration evokes an aggressive reaction to one or more objects (or part-objects). The first and fourth conditions have never been in dispute. The second stipulation has many advantages. By using the term "part-object" or "organ-object," we are able to take cognizance of the fear and conflict brought about by serial frustration of different components of infantile sexuality. And we avoid the necessity of presuming a completely organized set of imagos of both parents. Moreover, it enables us to appreciate more fully the amount of conflict existing at a stage when libidinal interests are almost exclusively directed towards mother-imagos and the drive towards father-imagos is limited to one organ-system (real or phantasied). Thus it makes one particular phantasy-system more comprehensible, viz. the phantasy of the "woman with the (father's) penis." And it meets the case of the posthumous (fatherless) child where the possibility of actual "primal scenes" is excluded: the early stages of the child's conflict (including primal scene phantasies) can then be worked out in reference to different maternal organs or zones of gratification and frustration (real or phantasied). The main objection to adopting this second condition is that it renders the term "inverted Oedipus complex" less precise than is the case at present. The terminological issue rests on the third condition. Genital interest exists from the first year of life in both sexes, and is bound to play a part directly or indirectly in all frustrations. In this sense all frustrations have an Oedipus component. If the argument is advanced that in early stages the genital element is quantitatively negligible, there is no objection to the use of some other term, e.g. "Oedipus prototype," or "fore-runner," "pre-Oedipus," etc. There would, however, be a very definite objec-tion if such terms were used to gloss over the dynamic significance of the earlier conflicts. If we can shew that earlier conflicts play a part in the etiology of, say, the psychoses, similar to the part played by the model genital Oedipus situation in hysteria, why not reduce complications by calling all infantile conflict over frustration "Oedipus" conflict?[19]

In supporting these views, which are in most essentials the views of Melanie Klein, I do not intend to suggest that the importance of later and more organized infantile systems can be glossed over in drug-addiction. It is impossible to neglect, for example, the extremely obvious homosexual phan-tasy-systems observed in, say, cocaine-addictions. It is equally impossible to overlook later "positive Oedipus" anxieties (i.e. typical castration anxiety); or for that matter the importance of stimuli of a much later date. In one case of cocaine-addiction the final determinant of the habit was without any doubt a fascinated interest in Sherlock Holmes, the publication of whose "Adventures" coincided with the addict's pubertal phase of masturbation. Incidentally the patient modified the Sherlock Holmes technique in so far as he injected the drug into the root of the penis. I need not go into all the genital Oedipus determinants of this habit, or enumerate the elements of curiosity, sadism, guilt and punishment represented by identification with a detective. The fact remains that, although interpretation of this familiar type produced signs of anxiety, both in the positive form of discharge and in the negative form of resistance, these reactions could not be compared with the intense resistances shewn when a more primitive reading of the situation was given, viz. in terms of sadistic attack on the parents followed by sadistic counterattack. Only when the situation was reduced to the common ground of a battle between the organs of the parents and the organs of the child, with terrifying excretory substances as weapons, was any adequate response evoked. Only then did an existing compulsive system of inventive and creative work—which had hitherto been singularly unsuccessful and by means of which the patient frittered away time and money—begin to lose some of its compulsive power and at the same time become more effective. I do not say that a quantitative difference in reaction can be invariably detected in giving such interpretations, because of course the factors of timing and dosage must be taken into account. Nevertheless observations of this kind suggest that we are not justified in sticking rigidly to the idea of a *fixed* nuclear system. There is some reason to assume that what in the case of the neuroses has been called the "nuclear complex" could be more usefully described as a "polymorphonuclear" complex. My impression is that in drug-addiction we can detect, perhaps more clearly than in well-defined neuroses or psychotic states, the existence of a *series* of nuclear "Oedipus" situations, to each one of which there is an appropriate symptomatic or para-symptomatic (social) response. In general the changes in the series may be attributed to two factors, (1) a quantitative factor relating to the charge of aggressive impulses carried, and (2) a qualitative factor contributed from erotogenic sources. At different levels one seems to find not only varying confluences of genital with pregenital libido, but different fusions of each libidinal component with aggression. Moreover, the different varieties of drug-addiction seem to suggest that the earliest nuclear formations are not arranged simply in a *consecutive* series but rather in a *cluster* formation. This cluster formation represents a group of component interests and develops into a consecutive series only after what we call the anal-sadistic phase has been established. To express the same idea in terms of anxiety and frustration we might say that drug-addictions are a caricature of the normal processes whereby a number of earlier infantile psychotic (or as Stärcke would call them palaeopsychotic) anxiety states are carried over into and submerged by social adaptations of an "ingestion" order (reading, taking medicines, etc., etc.).

Like all other systematizations, the foregoing has to be judged mainly in terms of descriptive convenience; in other words, the aptness of what Freud has called "the metaphorical expressions peculiar to psychology . . . of the deeper layers." Some apparent differences can be greatly reduced if we consider that earlier psycho-analytical formulations were based on one or two important cross-sectional views of mental development, whereas recent investigation is more in the nature of an examination of longitudinal sections. There are, however, certain theoretical consequences to be considered. Acceptance of an early polymorphous ego-organization involves some recasting of existing rather rigid descriptive views of narcissism; or at least some distinction of the problem of narcissistic *energies* from (a) the problem of narcissistic *topography,* and (b) the clinical problems of narcissistic *feeling* or reaction. For example, a good deal of what has hitherto been considered as belonging to a narcissistic organization would have to be relegated to a system of object-relations. The term "part-object" though to some extent helpful seems to me to beg the question of the narcissistic boundary. On the other hand the term "fixation" would require to be used with more precision. To say that a person has an "oral fixation" is much too vague and throws too much emphasis on the constitutional factor. It would be much more helpful to be able to say that owing to instinctual urges and frustration (occurring at a time to be estimated for each individual) a person is fixated to one or more of a series of nuclear positions. But we must be careful in the use of the term series. It seems to me that difficulties in establishing the fixation-points of psychoses are due in part to a bias in favour of a consecutive series. The complex clinical picture of dementia praecox itself suggests a possible combination of nuclear fixations. And, as I have said, the same appears to be true of drug-addictions.

The following case illustrates some of the points already discussed. A woman came for treatment who appeared at first sight to be suffering from a severe obsessional neurosis with some accompanying anxiety-hysteria and some conversion symptoms mainly affecting the alimentary tract. Preliminary analysis did not alter this diagnosis, although it was noteworthy that the obsessional system seemed to have effected less distortion of ideational content than usual: the ceremonial systems were as to one part almost

unmodified homosexual representations, in which however a phantasy element of hermaphroditism was introduced, e.g. obsessional pictures of possessing a penis, sometimes of fantastic shape, by means of which contact was
made either with a female figure having a fantastic penis or with a male
figure with a fantastic vagina. These pictures provoked typical obsessional
ceremonials. Outside the range of obsessional systems there was no manifest
homosexual interest. It soon became apparent that, under cover of sedative
medicinal treatment, she had established a strong drug-addiction of the paraldehyde type. She had been treated by various doctors for several years
previously, all of whom had either initiated some medicinal treatment or
sanctioned existing hypnotics. One naturally rescrutinised the history for
evidence of earlier addiction tendencies, and found that evidence not only in
the form of medicine-taking but in various social habits concerning eating. A
hunt for paranoidal mechanisms was not successful. Tracing all these elements separately in the subsequent analysis, it became possible to reconstruct
the symptomatic course of events as follows: an active phase of neurosis
formation could be established between the age of 2 and 3½. This corresponded to the period between the birth of the first rival sister and the first
rival brother. Infantile anxiety reactions and tantrum scenes in which the
beating of animals or inanimate objects played a part were followed by a
stage in which it was not clear whether anxiety phobia-formations or obsessional mechanisms would obtain the upper hand. Eventually obsessional
technique won the day; animal phobias gave place to obsessional fears, and
by the age of 3 the child was practically an adult obsessional neurotic
with obsessional fears of contamination and attack together with obsessional
precautions affecting thought, speech and action. For a short period at about
the age of 5, hysterical conversion symptoms dominated the picture and
recurred occasionally in later years. It was clear that the later alternations
corresponded to fluctuations in unconscious homosexual and conscious heterosexual interest, stimulation and frustration. But only for a few months, at
about 25, after an important change in work, emotional relations and social
surroundings, was the neurotic activity effectively suspended. The rest of
the time obsessional systems and defences were constantly increasing, one
contamination fear giving place to another with always an increasing element
of psycho-sexual preoccupation or cover (e.g. masochistic pregnancy-phan-
tasies). At puberty some organic illnesses obscured the picture but, on the
emergence of faint homosexual interests and more intense reactive brooding
over the problem of homosexuality in general, the obsessional systems became more extensive. An alarming cannibalistic element entered into them at

about 18, and from then on to the forties the ego was almost completely absorbed by acute obsessional systems, ringing every possible change on a disguised sadistic contamination theme together with a manifest infantile homosexual theme. As regards the addiction system, the earliest compulsive interest uncovered was concerned with the taste of the first rival baby's bottle feed; that was at the age of 2. Later (at about 8) a phobia of tea made its appearance. Still later (at 10) an anxiety-free ceremonial concerning reading and eating developed, but was soon linked up with contamination-affect concerning teeth and tartar. Still later (at 15) the obsessional hermaphroditic systems became attached to the mouth. Pressure of upper on lower teeth, or of teeth on gums or of tongue on teeth could function as substitutes for more manifest sexual content. Contamination anxiety then spread to anaesthetics. At 18, as has been noted, cannibalistic fears attacked the eating process, and at about 26 the first sedative was given by the father. For some years afterwards, the fears were associated with impulses to take medicine of all sorts in order to combat infections and the patient veered between physical illness requiring medicine and hysterical vomiting. During the first years of addiction, a reduction of the acuteness of ingestion fears coincided with a spread of complicated ceremonial to eating in restaurants.

Applying the usual clinical standards, it could be said that there were no paranoidal formations, although study of the phobia systems both early and late shewed significant reactions; first, the involvement of "pursuing" animals in the phobias and later a tendency to expand obsessional phobias to cosmic dimensions, together with a sense of personal doom in relation to any natural disturbances.

During the course of analysis but particularly in its later phases, the patient voluntarily undertook courses of abstinence which were mostly abortive. Complete reduction of a lesser bromide habit was ultimately effected, but at the cost of great anxiety and followed by an increase of obsessional activity, particularly of the more manifestly sexual ceremonials and defences. At this stage it was clear that the original strength of the addiction was due in part to the fact that the drugs were officially prescribed (i.e. benign substances). An increase in the paraldehyde habit then occurred. This developed to such an extent that a formal deprivation course became essential. The deprivation phase was accompanied by the usual hallucinatory manifestations. When these died down, two facts emerged; that the patient had a slight paranoidal system in operation and that *the obsessional neurosis had for the time disappeared.* As the paranoidal system slowly vanished, the obsessional system returned in full swing. The paraldehyde deprivation was complete, but on occasions of acute anxiety the patient was allowed small doses of non-habit-forming hypnotics. These she herself supplemented with doses of sal volatile. Of the various changes observed I will note here just one. The drugs had previously always been employed in a ceremonial way, not as a direct hypnotic. Now they were used less obsessionally as sedatives and more for their hypnotic effect, but the same drug was definitely regarded as a "good" or "bad" drug depending on whether the amount conformed to or exceeded the prescribed amount. The amount over the prescribed dose was a bad, evil, dangerous substance. The same differentiation applied to the person of the prescriber. Increases sanctioned by the physician who had regulated the deprivation were good; those sanctioned in emergency by myself were dangerous. A pseudo-paranoid mechanism had made its appearance in the drug system. Incidentally the phase following deparaldehyding shewed an immediate transference alteration in which I became more dangerous; first of all the lessened defence to sadistic phantasies increased reactions of anxiety during any absence, and in the sexual part of the obsessional phantasies I was made to play a more direct rôle.

Casting back to the open paranoid features that were manifested immediately after deprivation, it became clear that the mechanism was not purely paranoic. At first sight they had appeared to be pure delusions of reference, but that was not quite accurate. The jeering voices and hostile reproaches, or attacks, which were supposed to damage the patient and at the same time to remove something from her were linked on to a conspiracy system. For example, certain hostile individuals were conspiring to take away some good substance from a clergyman. There was however a hint that the patient herself might somehow be in the conspiracy—or at least that she was being used by others as a tool in order to effect their designs. But by dint of identifying herself with the clergyman she could restore the damage provided she took drugs. The clergyman was a not very effectively disguised mother-figure. This system of identification was on ordinary occasions concealed by the manifest homosexual content of the obsessions, e.g. active or passive contamination or destruction effected by the "fantastic penis" systems.

Here was a case that shewed historically a gradual crescendo of symptoms rising to a paranoid crisis, but including elements of reaction to every stage of development from primitive oral reaction down to infantile genital and adult genital anxiety systems. In the next place the most dramatic and permanent feature, the severe obsessional system, appeared in the rôle of a defence formation, guarding against anxiety of a paranoid type. The homosexual system which had played an obvious part in the obsessional formation was still present in the early hallucinatory phase of deprivation, but gave place to more direct phantasies of incestuous attack by the father; this suddenly gave place to the delusions of persecution. The homosexual element thus showed its "regressive" aspect in relation to the incest phantasies and its "progressive" aspect in relation to paranoid fear of the mother. Moreover in the phase prior to actual deprivation the increase in drug-addiction corresponded directly with an increase in the destructive aspects of obsessional thinking and ceremonial; after the deprivation there was a more manifest connection between ceremonial habit and destructive impulse.

A similar compromise-mechanism could be detected in the Sherlock Holmes case I have mentioned. The castration elements appeared to be mostly concerned with later genital systems. The homosexual organization was kept under effective repression and there was no clinical sign of paranoid reaction; nor was there any notable paranoid reaction after deprivation. The melancholic element in the case was, however, extremely obvious. There was a constant recurrence of manifest depressed oral reactions, and phases of injection of massive doses of cocaine which were practically unsuccessful attempts at suicide. But even in the most acute stages the melancholic mechanisms were not actually pure. The drug habit represented sufficient of a projective system to prevent deeper regression. And after final deprivation it was maintained in the modified form of medicinal drugging for which justification had to be found in every possible source of organic disturbance. For example, a heavy meal would be taken in order to justify all sorts of alimentary medicine drinking. The reduction in projected sadistic charge allowed a substitution of mainly "good" drugs for "bad." Nevertheless the good drugs, by upsetting the patient's internal economy, carried on the work of bad drugs, although in a milder degree. Even the "injection" element was maintained for a time under the guise of vaccine therapy.

Reviewing the paraldehyde case briefly, it could be said that, in spite of the obvious importance of later infantile genital systems (the model Oedipus nucleus), the drug element attached to the obsessional neurosis related to a more primitive Oedipus conflict occurring at the age of 2, and coinciding with the birth of the rival sister. It was an attempt to deal with sadistic charges only slightly more tolerable than those dealt with by purely paranoid mechanisms. It came into action because the later and more developed Oedipus relations (inverted and positive) still maintained a high sadistic charge. No adult derivative from these later systems could be permitted to act as a reassuring system of relations, hence every ordinary fluctuation in libido or aggressive tendency laid the patient at the mercy of an older anxiety system.

While therefore I agree with the tendency of recent attempts to compare drug-addiction with melancholia and obsessional neurosis, I feel that the emphasis laid on the model Oedipus phase and on early constitutional factors has obscured not only an equally close relation to paranoia, but the possibility of establishing a *specific* mechanism for drug-addiction. This specific reaction represents a *transition* between the more primitive psychotic phase and the later psycho-neurotic phase of development. I should have said a *number* of specific mechanisms, because I do not believe in any rigid layering of early psychotic phases. I imagine that different types of drug-addiction represent variations in the amount of original erotogenic sources of libido (and consequently different fusions of sadism): hence that they represent variations not only in the structure of the primitive ego, but in the type of mechanism employed to control excitation. When Simmel claims that drug-addiction is closely connected with both obsessional neurosis and melancholia,[20] I have no objection to offer, except that this applies only to some cases and that it neglects the relation of other cases to paranoia. But in spite of many correspondences of mechanism I cannot confirm his view that the state belongs essentially to the obsessional group, acquiring a melancholic character as a result of regression. Nor do I agree with his general statement that in the first stages the addiction represents a pleasure-toned obsessional state. This description, in my opinion, applies with more accuracy to the medicinal and food idiosyncrasies seen in neurotic-character cases, and particularly to various social habits of normal individuals, e.g. food indulgences and dietetic systems, habits of bodily inunction and inhalation, routine medicinal habit, fresh-air apostledom, and so forth.

A word here about the question of specific phantasies in drug-addiction. In my experience the main phantasy of drug-addictions represents a condensation of two primary systems, one in which the child attacks (later restores) organs in the mother's body, and one in which the mother attacks (later restores) organs in the child's body. These phantasies are also represented in masturbation systems and are still present in later, genital object-relations. In this paper I have not stressed the question of specific phantasies: first, because the condensation I have described seems to be universal, and secondly because I am more concerned for the moment with defining the function of drug-addiction. It is always possible that the main element in any psychopathological state is not so much the actual unconscious phantasy-system as the degree of localization or mastery of anxiety achieved. In any case we cannot estimate the significance of such stereotyped phantasies until we know what organ-substance is represented by the drug.

PROVISIONAL CONCLUSIONS

1. Drug-addiction implies fixation to a transitional Oedipus system—a system lying between the more primitive Oedipus nuclei that produce paranoid (or melancholic) anxieties and the Oedipus nucleus that is responsible for later obsessional reactions.
2. Its defensive function is to control sadistic charges, which, though less violent than those associated with paranoia, are more severe than the sadistic charges met with in obsessional formations. (An alternative formulation would be that the libidinal components found in drug-addiction are stronger and contain more genital elements than those associated with the psychoses, but weaker than those associated with the transference neuroses.)
3. Drug-addiction acts as a protection against psychotic reaction in states of regression.
4. Unconscious homosexual phantasy-systems are not a direct etiological factor, but represent a restitutive or defensive system; on account of their stronger libidinal cathexis (both narcissistic and genital), homosexual systems act as a protection against anxieties of the addiction type. Hence the close association of homosexual interests with drug-addiction implies either the persistence of a defensive system or the ruins of a defensive system.

The next step is to consider what relation exists between drug-addiction and neurotic habits or social usages, in particular habits and customs belonging to an "ingestion" group. Most processes of incorporation, e.g. the processes of eating and reading, are subject to modifications of a more or less pathological stamp. These habits must be correlated with the usual drug-addictions. We must know, for example, why noxious drugs are chosen in certain addictions in preference to less harmful or harmless substances and whether the fixations and defensive systems are identical. Why does an individual swallow, inhale or inject cocaine instead of smoking cigarettes or sucking chlorodyne lozenges or eating ice-cream or drinking almond emulsions or taking nutrient enemata or rubbing in lanoline ointment or chewing bus tickets?

The answer originally given by psycho-analysis was perfectly simple. Study of clinical data confirmed what was already apparent to the student of mythology and anthropology. The drug represented the phallus or semen of the father (God) and the breast—nipple—milk of the mother (Goddess). Less obvious at first—possibly because less attention was paid to this aspect—was the fact the drugs represented other bodily substances of an excretory nature, urine, faeces, etc. Soon it was held that all bodily "ejecta"— breath, sweat, spit, urine, faeces, blood, semen, milk, could be represented by the drug. It was nevertheless believed that the phallic (seminal) symbolism was the most important, and that, through this link, drug-addiction could be traced to the genital Oedipus situation. The other elements were regarded as contributions to genital interest from earlier erotogenic zones (oral, anal, etc.); or simply as disguised displacements of genital interest. The inverted (homosexual) Oedipus aspect was thought to account for the predominance in some cases of anal symbolism.

More careful clinical investigation showed that this apparently water-tight system was inadequate. It had always been known that under conditions of suggestive *rapport,* a comparatively inert substance (injections of salt water, tablets of aspirin, chewing-gum, etc.) could function as a drug-substitute. True, in many cases it was felt to be inadequate but it would tide over phases of deprivation. A more striking observation was to follow.

There is now no doubt that the pharmacotoxic effects of drugs do not play such a specific part in dangerous drug-addictions as is supposed in extra-psychological circles. In certain addiction-cases where a harmless substitute was established (in one case sugar was used in this way), I have observed the same slavish compulsion attach itself to the substitute. And deprivation of the substitute loosened massive charges of anxiety. On the other hand, during the analysis of psycho-neurotics and of neurotic (or psychotic) character abnormalities, I have discovered idiosyncrasies which had the same subjective sense of compulsion and aroused the same anxiety on deprivation as standard drug-habits. These are sometimes connected with food, e.g. a compulsion to eat stewed meat with a highly seasoned ketchup added to the gravy. Compulsive habits of "taking medicine" are even more common. I recall in this connection an addiction to white purgative emulsions, attempts to abandon which invariably induced severe anxiety. In another case the "addiction" was to hot water. Moreover in actual drug-deprivations it is well known that the last and most diluted drop of an addiction substance is as significant to the addict as the last and most trivial ceremonial is to a severe case of obsessional neurosis. It is true that in many cases of neurotic idiosyncrasy, the formation is not a massive one and the emotional reactions are spread over a number of apparently insignificant occasions; but they exert a striking cumulative effect. In one recent case, consuming steak-pie, beer, and reading a newspaper shared equally in an "ingestion" compulsion, by means of which an intolerable state of boredom and depression was periodically relieved. The evidence in other directions is overwhelming. For every contamination-phobia, there is a corresponding compulsion, either social, fetichistic or "perverted." For every cleansing ceremonial there is a corresponding ingestion habit. This fact escapes attention owing to the number of compromise-formations. When a washing maniac must use "scented" soap or an ointment reeking of antiseptic, or when the fresh-air addict with a "fog" phobia insists on living in a pinewood, the mixture of phobia and "counter-addiction" usually escapes notice.

The substitution of psychic "substances" for concrete is not difficult to demonstrate. The activity of reading is perhaps the simplest example and it is clear that systems of "good" and "bad" reading have some resemblances to addictions. In the paraldehyde case I have described the only guilt-free ceremonial was as follows: having drawn the blinds in a particular room the patient removed all objects from the pockets which were then filled with biscuits; she then sat exactly opposite the centre of the fireplace with legs apart and feet raised and proceeded to read "good" books, at the same time munching biscuits. Here again compromise-formations abound: e.g. compulsive reading of "elevating" or "good" books, particularly theosophical literature, during the process of defaecation. Perhaps the most interesting group is that where psycho-neurotic processes and psycho-therapeutic activities function as "drugs." It is easy to observe that obsessional psychic constructions and the affects accompanying melancholia are felt and described in terms of "substance." The obsessional feels that if his neurosis were cured he would be left with a "hole" or "gap" in his mind, and the depressed case very frequently expresses the state of endopsychic conflict and affect in terms of "weights" and "masses" in his "inside." I have recently studied a case in which a very definite drug-addiction was suddenly and spontaneously abandoned in favour of an obsessional neurosis. The patient then reacted to the idea of cure of the neurosis precisely as a drug-addict reacts to the idea of abstinence. She "must have" the neurosis; she "could not give it up," and so forth. The change was not due solely to an alteration in methods of defence; the obsessional psychic construction with its accompanying affect provided a suitable drug "substance." The immediate stimulus to substitution was the establishment of friendly relations with a mothering type of male admirer. A similar valuation of psychotherapeutic activities was suggested by Janet[21] in the case of hypnosis: he pointed out that the stage of somnambulic passion is comparable to the craving of a morphine addict. Ernest Jones,[22] commenting on this observation, linked it up to similar manifestations exhibited in alcoholism. And it is common psycho-analytic experience that patients react to interpretations as if they were either hostile foreign bodies or friendly substances. In short, there is every reason to think (a) that given suitable psychic conditions *any* substance can function as a "drug," (b) that "psychic substances" can function as replacements for ideas of concrete substances, (c) that both types of substance can be subdivided into good or bad, innocent or guilty, beneficent or malignant, restorative or destructive.

It is difficult to resist the conclusion that, however varied may be the contributions to drug-addiction from erotogenic sources, one special interest is represented by all drug-substances, viz. repressed aggressive or sadistic interest. Admittedly it is hard to isolate this interest and therefore to claim that drug-addiction is solely and simply a reaction to sadism. Quite apart from the indisputable importance of libidinal components in drug-symbolisms, there are certain attributes of drugs which represent a combination of libidinal and aggressive components. Thus it is clear that the good and bad elements in some addictions depend on the impregnating and abortifacient powers unconsciously attributed to the drug. Nevertheless it might be inquired whether by accentuating the sadistic element we could establish a specific factor operative in the "noxious" as compared with socially "benign" addictions.

The first step in this investigation is to compare the actual properties of "noxious" with those of "benign" drugs. It is evident that noxious drugs possess certain injurious and destructive properties. And although many non-noxious foods, if eaten regardless of consequences, produce equally disintegrating effects (as in the case of a patient who refuses to follow a prescribed diet), the distinction appears to have some general validity. This would suggest that in the choice of a noxious habit the element of sadism is decisive. The drug would then be a substance (part-object) with sadistic properties which can exist both in the outer world and within the body, but which exercises its sadistic powers only when inside. The situation would represent a transition between the menacing externalized sadism of a paranoid system and the actual internalized sadism of a melancholic system. The addiction would represent a peculiar compound of psychic danger and reassurance. Doubtless the melancholic (internalized) aspects would be increased by an attempt to deal with the externalized menace (drugs) by swallowing, and the fact that drugs actually exist "outside" (in chemists' shops) would encourage a move towards abstinence during the dangers of the exacerbated melancholic phase.

The second group of properties of noxious drugs presents a more difficult problem. These substances have the capacity to produce effects that are usually described in a compromise terminology, partly psychological, partly physiological. They are called stimulants, depressants, hypnotics, narcotics, analgesics, sedatives, intoxicants, etc., and various sensory and psychic disturbances are described in the same terminology. Clinical experience of melancholia, hypochondria and conversion-hysteria warns us, however, that this semi-physiological approach is not only inadequate but misleading; that subjective sensory and affective experiences cannot be understood apart from the existence of conflict between psychic institutions. For example, in one of my cases, the effect of strong doses of a hypnotic was to produce a "tottery" feeling as if the legs were "cut off." Incidentally, the hypnotic was rarely taken at the most appropriate time, i.e. at bedtime. As a rule it was swallowed just before the patient was about to go for a walk. A few associations connected the idea with weakness in the mother's legs. At this time the patient's mother was unable to get about owing to a debilitating illness. So the patient not only carried out a form of self-punishment, but repeated the crime of cutting off the mother's legs. In this case drug-taking was frequently followed by a feeling of "sanity" in the upper parts of the body. This system was illuminated by the discovery that, during obsessional preoccupation with the idea of possessing a penis, one of the ways of ridding herself of this dangerous organ was to imagine it stowed away in one or other of the lower limbs. Evidently not only the legs but the concealed penis was destroyed by taking the drug. The same patient was clear that the compulsion to take a "dose" frequently coincided with worry over the mental images of some person. She felt they were "in her head," and that the drug could "kill them inside her." It could also "dull" (kill) the intensity of certain obsessional "pictures" (organs, persons). Here again there was admittedly a masochistic element: when she was stupified, "little enemies" could steal a march on her, a system which had more obvious representation in conscious rape and pregnancy phantasies.

In this type of case the relief following drug-taking depends to a large extent on the exploitation of sadism to cure sadism, although undoubtedly there is a strong factor of masochistic gratification. In other cases where the immediate effect of the drug appears to be entirely alleviating and gratifying and where no secondary deterioration is apparent, punishment and masochistic aspects are gratified in the abstinence period. This is in keeping with the views of Simmel[23] and many others, viz. that abstinence phases are essential parts of an organized addiction. On the whole the evidence seems to suggest that the narcotic and noxious properties of certain drugs put them in a clinical class by themselves, in so far as they are excellently adapted to the purposes of sadistic expression. The necessary formula appears to be that the individual's own hate impulses, together with identifications with objects towards whom he is ambivalent, constitute a dangerous psychic state. This state is symbolized as an internal concrete substance. The drug is then in the last resort an external counter-substance which cures by destruction. In this sense drug-addiction might be considered an improvement on paranoia: the paranoidal element is limited to the drug-substance which is then used as a therapeutic agent to deal with intrapsychic conflict of a melancholic pattern. In the sense of *localizing* paranoid anxiety and enabling external adaptation to proceed, this may be one of the specific functions of drug-addiction.

On the other hand, there are some considerations which suggest that we should not push this view to extremes. In the first place we find that patients at different times regard the same drug as "good" as well as "bad." Secondly, obsessional neurotics without any manifest addiction tendencies are prone to use food images in "cleansing" as well as in "contamination" systems. "An apple a day keeps the doctor away." Moreover, some drug-addicts exhibit a distinctly obsessional tendency in their dosage and timing of noxious drugs (e.g. taking them when their thoughts are "bad"), thereby suggesting more friendly exploitation of the drug-system. Again, in some noxious addictions the sedative and restorative effects are a prominent feature. On the other hand, in a great majority of "benign" addictions, the restorative and life-giving properties of the substance are clearly manifest. Finally, however important unconscious paranoid and melancholic factors in drug-addiction may be, the clinical fact remains that throughout the greater part of many severe addictions there are no manifest symptoms of this kind. Even allowing for disturbances occurring under the influence of drugs (e.g. intoxication), and for impairment of psychic function during comparative abstinence (e.g. retrograde amnesia), the patient's reality sense is not grossly and obviously distorted. Moreover, as I have indicated, some drug addictions shew an actual refractoriness to paranoid regression. To these clinical views may be added the theoretical consideration that a purely paranoid basis to drug-addiction would suggest a worse prognosis than is actually justified by statistics of permanent abstinence.

Analytic support for the benign aspect of drug-substances is based almost entirely on three groups of observation: (a) the close connection between drug-substances and erotogenic interests, (b) the exploitation of later and more predominantly genital libidinal development as a reassurance against earlier more sadistic phases, (c) the existence of "cancellation" and "restitution" mechanisms.

There is no need to recall the extensive evidence in support of a symbolic relation between drugs and erotogenic interests. The symbolism in many cases requires no interpretation. And there is a good deal to be said for Radó's conception of "meta-erotism,"[24] in the sense of a system of drug-excitation which short-circuits the zonal components of infantile sexuality. I am unable, however, to confirm his assumption of a decisive "alimentary orgasm" based on alimentary erotism. That alimentary erotism is an important factor in most cases I have no doubt. It is in my experience most obvious in addictions of the chlorodyne type (new B.P.). But in still other addictions, e.g. chloroform, ether, etc., it is obvious that nasal and respiratory erotism is picked out. Again, in certain cases of alcoholism it is clear, not only from the symbolism but from actual reports of the patient, that urinary erotism is picked out in preference to the alimentary element. In one instance the first mouthful of white wine, whisky, sherry or beer produced immediate erotic sensations in the bladder which were then referred to the tip of the penis. In any case, whether the important mechanism is "short-circuiting" or a process of direct selection, the guilt or anxiety system involved is not simply a reaction to excitation of one zone. In the alcohol-instance just mentioned, although urinary erotism was obviously the important factor, it was important because the ego-object relations as a whole were expressed in urinary-sadistic terms. Thus wine was a dangerous poison: it could only be cured by taking in more wine; it was an impregnating substance; it was an abortifacient, etc. And ultimately it was a loving and curative substance.[25]

This brings us to the second point, viz. exploitation of later and more genital elements as a reassurance against earlier anxieties of menacing external substances. This aspect of drug-addiction has been emphasized by Simmel and later by Schmideberg. The closer the identification with a comparatively friendly "semen-penis-child" system the more compulsive the benign aspects of addiction. The friendliness is of course only comparative, because in the stage of infantile genital interest a sadistic component is still important, and can be measured by the amount of castration-anxiety.

The third point is also concerned with reassurance. It involves the idea that a good substance can either neutralize a bad substance or can make good any injury caused by an existing bad substance. These mechanisms have now been shewn to play a large part in obsessional neuroses[26] and in many apparently normal activities, e.g. sublimations.[27, 28] So far as my experience goes it is difficult to exclude these factors in drug-addiction. The main difficulty is that, owing to the confused state of identifications of self with object, what appears to be a pure object-restitution is condensed on a system of restitution of the self by the object.

An interesting aspect of this problem of benign elements in addiction is presented by the companion problem of fetichism. The relation between fetichism and some forms of drug-addiction, particularly alcoholism, is well known. But the negative aspects of fetichism have had less attention paid to them, for the reason that they are usually regarded as obsessional phobias of the contamination type. I have observed on several occasions that, after a more than usually anxious phase of abstinence, a type of obsessional phobia makes its appearance which is of this negative fetichistic type. Also that after a more spontaneous abstinence phase the return of the addiction seemed to be delayed by a more positive fetichistic interest, with or without genital masturbation. In the case of the positive fetichistic activities, a feature of the situation was that the interest also obtained narcissistic representation. In one case excitement over the idea of stockings of others could be expressed also by a lesser degree of excitement over the individual's own stockings and shoes. On the other hand, in the phobia system, fears which had originally been attached to contamination ideas concerning the clothes of others later took the form of acute anxiety concerning the destructive powers of the patient's own clothes. Two types of fear-localization could be detected: fear in which the organ-interest was displaced from the genital-abdominal area to stockings and legs, collar and neck, etc., and secondly, fear attached to clothing having close contact with the genital and abdominal area, under-clothes, corsets, etc. The amount of anxiety provoked seemed to depend on whether an early paranoidal system or a later genital system of phantasy predominated. Fear lest part of the patient's knickers should "get into" gluteal or genital folds, and effect some disastrous change, varied in intensity in accordance with the "goodness" or "badness" of the drugs taken. If the drugs were bad, the "getting in" of clothing had no more anxiety than one might expect to accompany a masochistic genital phantasy. When, however, the drugs were reduced or good, the underclothing fear was almost paranoidal in intensity.

Space does not permit more detailed investigation of this subject here. But perhaps two rough formulations are permissible: (1) that in the transition between paranoidal systems and a normal reaction to reality, drug-addiction (and later on fetichism) represent not only continuations of the anxiety system within a contracted range, but the beginnings of an expanding reassurance system. The reassurance is due to contributions from later libidinal stages in infancy which contain a decreasing amount of sadism. (2) That clothing in general is, after food, the next line of defence in overcoming paranoidal reactions to reality. It appears reasonable to suppose that the first paranoid systems of the child attach themselves to food, that these anxieties are modified not only by the appearance of less sadistic impulse but by a determined effort at displacement of anxiety. In this displacement clothes play their part. When subsequently displacement leads to reactions to the clothes of external objects, the foundation of the classical fetish is laid. So that when anxiety is excessive the result is either a typical sexual fetish or the negative form, viz. a contamination phobia. I would suggest that the association of fetichism and alcoholism implies a combined effort to establish friendly relations with external dangerous objects which, at an earlier stage, were thought of as existing within the patient's body, e.g. the sadistic penis of the father which the child has stolen from the mother. *A propos,* the most successful exploitation of a fetichistic principle is to be seen in the mild forms which accompany or merge with the forepleasure of adult genital primacy.

To sum up the position of noxious drug-habits as compared with benign habits: there appears to be no question that noxious addictions represent the reaction to a more acute state of anxiety; that the destructive properties of drugs lend themselves to symbolic and actual expression of sadism, nevertheless that the restitutive and neutralizing effect even of noxious drugs cannot be excluded. In the benign addictions the substance still represents a vehicle of sadism, but the sadism is less heavily charged, and connected with less archaic phantasies. Hence anxiety both as to the state of the body and the dangers of the external world is reduced. Reality has taken on a more friendly aspect, consequently non-injurious foods or their substitutes can function in these milder addictions. With regard to the corporeal element represented by the drug, I have already indicated that we are not in a position to speak with finality on this subject. One or two modifications of earlier ideas are, however, already justifiable. The obvious emphasis laid by drug-addicts on phallic elements must be to some extent discounted. And although in the past I have stressed importance of oral elements, I have come to realize that particularly in the case of noxious drugs, these are sometimes emphasized for defensive purposes. Admittedly in the melancholic types oral elements are the most important, but, taking the average run of noxious addiction, I have the impression that the drug symbolizes excretory substances which in turn represent a primitive and almost uncontrollable form of excretory sadism.

In this paper I have so far deliberately avoided using the term "super-ego." My main aim is to draw attention to the significance of drug-addiction as representing a compromise between projective and introjective processes. And owing to lack of agreement as to early phases of super-ego formation it is advisable to keep to these more general terms. Nevertheless I feel convinced that when Radó says guilt-processes do not play a specific part in drug-addiction, he has in mind the guilt associated with the late Oedipus phase of super-ego formation. Theoretically speaking, however, a super-ego formation can be presumed as soon as an introjective process is sufficiently organized to attach to itself energy which would otherwise strive for more direct discharge on objects. And the whole point about drug-addiction is that it represents a phase of development when primitive part-objects are introjected and absorb psychic energy, but before projection of a massive type has been finally abandoned. It has always been difficult to conceive how the *physiological* effects of alcohol could have a specific effect on *psychic* institutions, e.g. the super-ego. The answer is now apparent: the drug has no more *direct* effect on guilt than a stunning blow on the head. The effect is produced by virtue of a psychological and mainly symbolic manoeuvre, to which the physiological action of drugs adds an element of realism. The physiological action of drugs is exploited by the addict because it saves some expenditure of psychic energy. The same system is seen to operate in the psychoses and neuroses. The remissions of melancholia observed during intercurrent organic illness represent a saving of melancholic energies; and a conversion-hysteric obviously makes the most of any casual organic disturbance, thereby reducing the labour of symptom-formation.

I do not underrate what the physiologist would call the selective action of drugs on or through the nervous system. On the other hand, I maintain that the phenomena of *psychic* inhibition (or relief from inhibition) accompanying drug-addiction cannot be explained along purely *physiological* lines. My view is that the addict *exploits* the "action" of the drug in terms of an infantile system of thinking. In the earliest stages endopsychic appreciation of instinctual stimuli corresponds closely to sensory experience of disturbances in the bodily organs, or, more generally, of disturbing substances in the body. The same is true of the earliest experiences of the operation of primitive psychic institutions (e.g. super-ego conflict leading to frustration). So that when an infant psychically incorporates objects (or important organs of objects) and when a primitive form of guilt ensues, this guilt can be dealt with, as it were, along physiological lines. From this point of view the significance of addiction can be described as follows. By "cutting off" the body (i.e. sensory perceptions) the drug appears to have obliterated instinctual tension or frustration: it can also kill, cure, punish or indulge not only psychic "objects" in the body but the body as "self." By "cutting off" the external world, the drug can obliterate not only actual instinctual stimuli from without but stimuli due to projected instinct. By the same obliteration it can kill or punish external objects with or without projected characteristics: it can also rescue them by keeping them at a distance. This "double action" accounts for the extreme sense of compulsion associated with addiction. It is specially marked in cases where both "self" and "introjected objects" are felt to be bad and dangerous, and the only chance of preserving a good self lies in isolating it in the external world in the form of a good object.

In conclusion, we must inquire what bearing the foregoing discussion of addiction has on the tendencies of psycho-analytic research and in particular on terminological usage. I can imagine that recent emphasis laid on "sadistic" factors might give rise to a temporary undervaluation of libidinal factors, or to a degree of misuse of terms. The phrase "oral-sadistic fixation," for example, is just as inadequate as its fellow, "oral libidinal fixation," or "narcissistic fixation." And its use might foster the tendency to think of a hypothetical "pure sadistic" (aggressive) fixation. Without entering into the actual definition of sadism as a pure culture of instinct or a primary fusion, it may be repeated that the "complexion" of sadism is contributed mainly by its libidinal fusion, whether primary or secondary. As Freud has said on the more general subject of life and death instincts, "we are driven to the conclusion that the death instincts are by their nature mute and that the clamour of life proceeds for the most part from Eros." [29] And in drug-addiction particularly it can be observed that although positive libidinal constructions are used as a cover for and reassurances against earlier more sadistically-charged situations, this very fact gives rise to a compulsive emphasis on libidinal components which is indistinguishable from a fixation effect. In short, there is a great deal to be said for the retention of the term "ambivalence" in etiological essays, provided due emphasis is laid on the primitive and rudimentary nature of the objects towards which the ambivalence is directed, and provided a series of characteristic expressions of ambivalence can be isolated. And, incidentally, Abraham's term "preambivalent" for the first oral phase before dentition is not the happiest way of describing a phase during which the tensions of sadism are very acute.

Any tendency to talk loosely of sadism as the chief aetiological factor without an essential correction for libidinal modification would introduce or emphasize a quantitative element in aetiology. Indeed, Schmideberg [30] has made the suggestion that the differences between various psycho-pathological states are due to quantitative differences in the amount of anxiety. This use of the term anxiety does not seem altogether satisfactory: it neglects the function of anxiety as a "signalling" system and leaves unexplained constitutional and individual factors (instinctual fixations) causing "anxiety intolerance." Indeed, it is difficult to think of an absolute measure of sadistic quantities which would not be complicated by libidinal factors. The difficulty might perhaps be overcome if we could establish characteristic differences between guilt-mechanisms at different stages of development. And it would be still easier if we could combine a characteristic guilt-mechanism with the factor of "localization." In the case of drug-addictions, although the introjective mechanisms are not very markedly localized (e.g. the phantasy-effects of swallowing the drug are not limited to one phantasied system of internal organs), the projective systems are definitely circumscribed (i.e. concentrated on drug substances). For this reason the latent paranoid aspects of drug-addiction are more prominent aetiological factors than the (introjective) guilt-systems alone. Even so we should still be compelled to introduce libidinal factors in order to account for the comparatively stable organization and resilience of some psychoses and neuroses. Admittedly, boundaries between psychopathological states are not very clearly defined and can be temporarily or permanently effaced in any flood of regression. On the other hand, experience of drug-addiction suggests that there are more of these boundaries than we are in the habit of thinking and that they shew a remarkable capacity to reassert function after grave regressional injury.

NOTES

1. Abraham, "The Psychological Relations between Sexuality and Alcoholism," *Selected Papers,* London, 1927.

2. Freud, "An autobiographical Account of a case of Paranoia," *Collected Papers,* Vol. III, 1925.

3. Schilder, *Entwurf zu einer Psychiatrie auf psychoanalytischer Grundlage,* Wien, 1925.

4. Freud, "Certain Neurotic Mechanisms in Jealousy, Paranoia and Homosexuality," *Collected Papers,* Vol. II, 1924.

5. Freud, *The Ego and the Id,* London, 1927.

6. Freud, "Certain Neurotic Mechanisms in Jealousy, Paranoia and Homosexuality," *Collected Papers,* Vol. II, 1924.

7. Later, in *The Ego and the Id,* Freud takes the view that this transformation does not imply a transformation of hate into love, but is the result of a transfer of neutralized energy to the love aim. This later view does not detract from the defensive significance of the manoeuvre.

8. Klein, *The Psycho-analysis of Children,* Chap. IX (appearing shortly).

9. Stärcke, "The Reversal of the Libido-sign in Delusions of Persecution," *International Journal of Psycho-Analysis,* 1920, I, 231; "Psycho-analysis and Psychiatry," *ibid.,* 1921, II, 361.

10. Van Ophuijsen, "On the Origin of the Feeling of Persecution," *International Journal of Psycho-Analysis,* 1920, I, 235.

11. Abraham, "A Short Study of the Development of the Libido," *Selected Papers,* London, 1927.

12. Kielholz, "Giftmord und Vergiftungswahn," *Internationale Zeitschrift für Psychoanalyse,* 1931, XVII, 85.

13. Feigenbaum, "Paranoia und Magie," *Internationale Zeitschrift für Psychoanalyse,* 1930, XVI, 361.

14. Fenichel, "Uber respiratorische Introjection," *Internationale Zeitschrift für Psychoanalyse,* 1931, XVI, 234.

15. Radó, "The Psychic Effects of Intoxicants," *International Journal of Psycho-Analysis,* 1926, VII, 396; "The Problem of Melancholia," *ibid.,* 1928, IX, 420.

16. Simmel, "Zum Problem von Zwang und Sucht," *Bericht über den fünften allgemeinen ärztlichen Kongress für Psychotherapie,* 1930.

17. Glover, "The Etiology of Alcoholism," *Proceedings of the Royal Society of Medicine,* 1928, XXI, 45; "The Prevention and Treatment of Drug-Addiction," *ibid.,* 1931, XXIV.

18. Schmideberg, "The Rôle of Psychotic Mechanisms in Cultural Development," *International Journal of Psycho-Analysis,* 1930, XI, 387; "A Contribution to the Psychology of Persecutory Ideas and Delusions," *ibid.,* 1931, XII, 331.

19. Since this was written Freud has made an important pronouncement on the question of terminology ("Female Sexuality," *International Journal of Psycho-Analysis,* p. 281): he says, *a propos* of pre-Oedipus stages, that there is no objection to attaching a wider significance to the term Oedipus complex; it can be regarded if need be as including all the relations of the infant to both parents.

20. See note 16.

21. Janet, *Néuroses et idées fixes,* 1898, p. 429.

22. Ernest Jones, "The Action of Suggestion in Psychotherapy," *Papers on Psychoanalysis,* 3rd Edition, 1923.

23. See note 16.

24. See note 16.

25. Although there is general agreement as to the importance of oral, excretory and genital interests in the aetiology of drug-addiction, we are not yet entitled to make any final pronouncement on their relative importance. No deep analyses of "respiratory (inhalation) addictions" have yet been published, and until this has been done an open-minded attitude seems indicated.

26. Freud, *Hemmung, Symptom und Angst,* Wien.

27. Sharpe, "Certain Aspects of Sublimation and Delusion," *International Journal of Psycho-Analysis,* 1930, XI, 12.

28. Klein, "Early Anxiety-Situations Reflected in a Work of Art," *International Journal of Psycho-Analysis,* 1929, X, 436.

29. See note 5.

30. See note 18.

3. The Psychoanalysis of Pharmacothymia (Drug Addiction)

Sándor Radó

1. THE CLINICAL PICTURE

Clinical psychiatry regards the disorders known as alcoholism, morphinism, cocainism, etc.—for which, as an inclusive designation, we may provisionally use the term "drug addiction"—as *somatic intoxications,* and places them in the classificatory group "mental disorders of exogenous origin." From this point of view, the process of mental dilapidation presented in the clinical picture of the addiction would appear to be the mental manifestation of the injury to the brain produced by the poisons. The investigation of the addictions has imposed upon it by this theory, as its first task, the determination in detail of the cerebral effect of the noxious substance. Ultimately, its goal would be the exact correlation of the course of the mental disorder with the toxic processes in the brain. But this investigation, especially in its experimental aspects, is disturbingly complicated by the fact that the poisons in question attack not only the brain but the rest of the organism as well; therefore, injurious effects may be exerted upon the brain by changes in other organs through an impairment of the general metabolism. The problem thus includes not only the direct influence of the poison on the brain, but also its indirect influence. It is, consequently, not remarkable that the notion that the problem of addiction is a problem of somatic intoxication has borne so little fruit.

How did it happen, then, that psychiatry became so wedded to this idea? The obvious answer is that the idea was developed because infectious diseases were used as paradigms. To be sure, one could not ignore the fact that alcohol, for example, does not "cause" alcoholism in the same sense as the spirochaete causes luetic infection. The pathogenic microörganisms attack a person quite regardless of what his wishes or purposes in the matter may be. But the drugs in question attack him only if he purposely introduces them into

Reprinted by permission from *Psychoanalytic Quarterly* 2 (1933): 1–23.

his body. This distinction, however, has not sufficiently affected psychiatric thinking. In psychiatry, the idea was promulgated that a certain type of "uninhibited," "weak-willed" or "psychopathic" individual happens to develop a passion for using these drugs—which means, to read between the lines, that how these substances get into the body is of no importance: the problem is scientific and worth touching only after they are inside. It must be admitted that after the drugs have made their entry, there is, unquestionably, a certain similarity to the infections. But in so far as psychological questions, such as the susceptibility of an individual to develop a craving for drugs, were broached at all, one was groping in the dark. The intoxication theory furnished no point of departure for any solution of this type of problem. Indeed, even if all the problems relating to somatic intoxication were solved, there would still be no answer to this type of question.

The psychoanalytic study of the problem of addiction begins at this point. It begins with the recognition of the fact that not the toxic agent, but the impulse to use it, makes an addict of a given individual. We see that this unprejudiced description focusses our attention on the very feature, which, under the influence of premature analogical reasoning, was permitted to fall by the wayside. The problem then presents a different appearance. The drug addictions are seen to be psychically determined, artificially induced illnesses; they can exist because drugs exist; and they are brought into being for psychic reasons.

With the adoption of the psychogenetic standpoint, the emphasis shifts from the manifoldness of the drugs used to the singleness of the impulse which unleashes the craving. The ease with which an addict exchanges one drug for another immediately comes to mind; so that we feel impelled to regard all types of drug cravings as varieties of *one single* disease. To crystallize this theory, let me introduce the term "pharmacothymia" to designate the illness characterized by the craving for drugs. We shall have occasion later to explain our selection of this term.

The older psychoanalytic literature contains many valuable contributions and references, particularly on alcoholism and morphinism, which attempt essentially to explain the relationship of these states to disturbances in the development of the libido function. Reports of this type we owe to Freud, Abraham, Tausk, Schilder, Hartmann and others in Europe; and in this country, Brill, Jelliffe, Oberndorf and others. Two definite conclusions could be drawn from these studies, namely, the etiological importance of the erotogenic oral zone and a close relationship to homosexuality. Several years ago, I outlined the beginnings of a psychoanalytic theory which aimed to include the whole scope of the problem of drug addiction.[1] Further, as yet unpublished, studies have led me to introduce the conception of pharmacothymia, to the preliminary description of which the present paper is devoted.

Since, for our purposes, suggestions derived from the theory of somatic intoxication are of no avail, we ourselves must select a suitable point of departure, taking our bearings from psychoanalysis. Our notion that despite the many drugs there is only one disease, suggests where we may begin. We must separate out of the abundant clinical findings those elements which are *constant* and determine their interrelationships empirically, and then from this material, formulate the general psychopathology, that is to say, the *schematic structure* of pharmacothymia. Generalizations which we can make in this way concerning the nature of the illness will discover for us the viewpoints and conceptions needed for the study of individual phenomena. If our outline is well founded, the more new details are added, the more will it reproduce living reality.

Pharmacothymia can occur because there are certain drugs, the "elatants," to give them an inclusive designation, which a human being in psychic distress can utilize to influence his emotional life. I have given a description of this influence in a previous communication *(loc. cit.).* Here I need only say that there are two types of effects. First, the analgesic, sedative, hypnotic and narcotic effects — their function is easily characterized: they allay and *prevent "pain."* Secondly, the stimulant and euphoria-producing effects — these promote or *generate pleasure.* Both types of effect, the pain-removing and the pleasure-giving, serve the pleasure principle; together they both constitute what may be called "the pharmacogenic pleasure-effect." The capriciousness of the pharmacogenic pleasure-effect is well known; it vitiates the best part of the experimental work of the pharmacologists. I have found that in addition to the pharmacological factors (nature, dose and mode of administration of the substance), the pleasure-effect depends essentially on a *psychological* factor — a certain active preparedness with which the individual approaches the pleasure-effect.

The thing which the pharmacothymic patient wishes the toxic agent to give him is the pleasure-effect. But this is not to be obtained without cost. The patient must pay for his enjoyment with severe suffering and self-injury — often, indeed, with self-destruction. These are assuredly not the effects desired. If, notwithstanding this fact, he clings to the use of drugs, it must be either because the pleasure gained is worth the sacrifice of suffering, or he is in a trap and is forced to act as he does.

Then we must ask: What is the nature of the psychic situation which makes acute the demand for elatants? What is the effect of this indulgence upon the mental life? What is there in it that makes the patient suffer? And why, in spite of the suffering, can he not cease from doing as he does?

The previous history of those individuals who take to the use of elatants, in a general way reveals the following. There is a group of human beings who respond to frustrations in life with a special type of emotional alteration, which might be designated "tense depression." It sometimes happens, too, that the first reaction to the frustration takes the form of other types of neurotic symptoms, and that the "tense depression" appears only later. The intense, persistent suffering due to a severe physical illness may also lead to the same emotional state. The tense depression may change into other forms of depression; since pharmacothymia originates from the tense depression, let us designate it the "initial depression." It is marked by great "painful" tension and at the same time, by a high degree of intolerance to pain. In this state of mind, psychic interest is concentrated upon the need for relief. If the patient finds relief in a drug, in this state he is properly prepared to be susceptible to its effects. The rôle of the initial depression, then, is to *sensitize* the patient for the pharmacogenic pleasure-effect. It is immaterial whether the drug comes into his hands by accident or whether it is prescribed by his physician for therapeutic purposes, whether he was induced to use it or made the experiment on his own responsibility: he experiences a pharmacogenic plea- sure-effect, which is in proportion to his longing for relief, and this event frequently, therefore, determines his future fate. If the substance and the dose were well chosen, the first pharmacogenic pleasure-effect remains as a rule the most impressive event of its kind in the whole course of the illness.

We must consider the pharmacogenic pleasure-effect, particularly this maiden one, more intensively. That which makes it so outstanding, when viewed from without, is the sharp rise in self-regard and the elevation of the mood—that is to say, elation.[2] It is useful to distinguish conceptually be- tween the pharmacogenic elation and the pharmacogenic pleasure-effect, although they merge in the course of the emotional process. The elation would then represent the reaction of the ego to the pleasure-effect. After therapeutic medication, we observe countless instances of the pharmacogenic pleasure-effect which do *not* set up an elation in the patient. It is evident that in the evolution of a pharmacothymia, it is essential that an elation should be developed. In our outline, we must confine ourselves to a description of the outspoken forms, yet we should like to emphasize that the pharmacogenic elation is a protean phenomenon. It may remain so inconspicuous, externally viewed, that a casual observer could overlook it, and nevertheless be an experience which is psychologically an elation. The elation also need not appear immediately after the first contact with the poison. The important thing is not, when it is experienced, but whether it is experienced.

What happens in a pharmacogenic elation can be understood only on the basis of further circumstantial discussion.

This individual's ego was not always so miserable a creature as we judge it to be when we encounter it in its "tense depression." Once it was a baby, radiant with self-esteem, full of belief in the omnipotence of its wishes, of its thoughts, gestures and words.[3] But the child's megalomania melted away under the inexorable pressure of experience. Its sense of its own sovereignty had to make room for a more modest self-evaluation. This process, first described by Freud,[4] may be designated the reduction in size of the original ego; it is a painful procedure and one that is possibly never completely carried out. Now, to be sure, the path to achievement opens for the growing child: he can work and base his self-regard on his own achievements. Two things become evident. In the first place, self-regard is the expression of self-love — that is to say, of narcissistic gratification.[5] Secondly, narcissism, which at the start was gratified "at command" with no labor (thanks to the care of the infant by the adults), is later compelled to cope more and more laboriously with the environment. Or we might put it, the ego must make over its psychology from that of a supercilious parasite into that of a well adjusted self-sustaining creature. Therefore, a complete recognition of the necessity to fend for itself becomes the guiding principle of the mature ego in satisfying its narcissistic needs, that is to say, in maintaining its self-regard. This developmental stage of the "narcissistic system" we may call the "realistic regime of the ego."[6]

There is no complete certainty that one can attain one's objectives in life by means of this realistic regime; there is always such a thing as bad luck or adversity. It is even worse, certainly, if the functional capacity of the ego is reduced through disturbances in the development of the libido function, which never fail to impair the realistic regime of the ego. The maladapted libido can wrest a substitute satisfaction from the ego in the shape of a neurosis, but then the self-regard usually suffers. An ego whose narcissism insists on the best value in its satisfactions, is not to be deceived in regard to the painfulness of real frustration. When it perceives the frustration, it reacts with the change in feeling we have described as "tense depression." Of interest to us in the deep psychology of this condition is the fact that the ego secretly compares its current helplessness with its original narcissistic stature,[7] which persists as an ideal for the ego, torments itself with self-reproaches and aspires to leave its tribulations and regain its old magnitude.

At this pass, as if from heaven, comes the miracle of the pharmacogenic pleasure-effect. Or rather, the important thing is that it does not come from heaven at all, but is *brought about by the ego itself.* A magical movement of the hand introduces a magical substance, and behold, pain and suffering are exorcized, the sense of misery disappears and the body is suffused by waves of pleasure. It is as though the distress and pettiness of the ego had been only a nightmare; for it now seems that the ego is, after all, the omnipotent giant it had always fundamentally thought it was.

In the pharmacogenic elation the ego regains its original narcissistic stature. Did not the ego obtain a tremendous *real* satisfaction by mere wishing, i.e., without effort, as only that narcissistic image can?

Furthermore, it is not only an infantile wish but an ancient dream of mankind which finds fulfilment in the state of elation. It is generally known that the ancient Greeks used the word "φάρμακον" to mean "drug" and "magical substance." This double meaning legitimates our designation; for the term "pharmacothymia," combining the significations of "craving for drugs" and "craving for magic," expresses aptly the nature of this illness.

At the height of the elation, interest in reality disappears, and with it any respect for reality. All the ego's devices which work in the service of reality—the ascertainment of the environment, mental elaboration of its data, instinctual inhibitions imposed by reality—are neglected; and there erupts the striving to bring to the surface and satisfy   either by fantasies or by floundering activity—all the unsatisfied instincts which are lurking in the background. Who could doubt that an experience of this sort leaves the deepest impression on the mental life?

It is generally said that a miracle never lasts longer than three days. The miracle of the elation lasts only a few hours. Then, in accordance with the laws of nature, comes sleep, and a gray and sober awakening, "the morning after." We are not so much referring to the possible discomfort due to symptoms from individual organs as to the *inevitable alteration of mood.* The emotional situation which obtained in the initial depression has again returned, but exacerbated, evidently by new factors. The elation had augmented the ego to gigantic dimensions and had almost eliminated reality; now just the reverse state appears, sharpened by the contrast. The ego is shrunken, and reality appears exaggerated in its dimensions. To turn again to real tasks would be the next step, but meanwhile this has become all the more difficult. In the previous depression there may have been remorse for having disregarded one's activities, but now there is in addition a sense of guilt for having been completely disdainful of real requirements, and an increased fear of reality. There is a storm of reproaches from all sides for the dereliction of duty toward family and work. But from yesterday comes the enticing memory of the elation. All in all, because of additional increments in "pain" the ego has become more irritable and, because of the increased anxiety and bad conscience, weaker; at the final accounting, there is an even greater deficit. What can be done, then? The ego grieves for its lost bliss and longs for its reappearance. This longing is destined to be victorious, for every argument is in its favor. What the pains of the pharmacogenic depression give birth to is, with the most rigorous psychological consistency, the craving for elation.

We obtain, thus, a certain insight into fundamental relationships. The transitoriness of the elation determines the return of the depression; the latter, the renewed craving for elation, and so on. We discover that there is a cyclic course, and its regularity demonstrates that the ego is now maintaining its self-regard by means of an artificial technique. This step involves an alteration in the individual's entire mode of life; it means a change from the "realistic regime" to a *"pharmacothymic regime"* of the ego. A pharmacothymic, therefore, may be defined as an individual who has betaken himself to this type of regime; the ensuing consequences make up the scope of the manifestations of pharmacothymia. In other words, this illness is a narcissistic disorder, a destruction through artificial means of the natural ego organization.[8] Later we shall learn in what way the erotic pleasure function is involved in this process, and how the appreciation of its rôle changes the appearance of the pathological picture.

Comparing life under the pharmacothymic regime with life oriented towards reality, the impoverishment becomes evident. The pharmacothymic regime has a definite course and increasingly restricts the ego's freedom of action. This regime is interested in only one problem: depression, and in only one method of attacking it, the administration of the drug.

The insufficiency of this method, which the ego at first believes infallible, is soon demonstrated by sad experience. It is not at all the case that elation and depression always recur with unfailing regularity in a cyclic course. The part that puts in its appearance punctually is the depression; the elation becomes increasingly more undependable and in the end threatens complete non-appearance. It is a fact of great importance that the pharmacogenic pleasure-effect, and particularly the elation induced by repeated medication, rapidly wanes. Thus, we encounter here the phenomenon of "diminishing return" in terms of elation. I cannot promise to explain the dynamics of this fall. It is doubtless ultimately dependent on organic processes, which are referred to as the "development of a tolerance" but which cannot as yet be given an accurate physiological interpretation. During the past years an extensive study of this problem was initiated in this country. A comprehensive report of the results arrived at so far, has been published recently by the pharmacologists A. L. Fatum and M. H. Seevers in *Physiological Reviews* (Vol. XI, no. 2, 1931). A reading of this report shows that such an explanation has not yet been found. I should like to contribute a point in relation to this problem from the psychological side; namely, the assurance that in the phenomenon of "diminishing return" in elation a *psychological* factor is involved: the patient's fear that the drug will be inefficacious. This fear is analogous to the fear of impotent persons, and, similarly, reduces the chances of success even more. We shall learn, below, which deeper sources give sustenance to this fear.

The phenomenon of "diminishing return" intensifies the phase of depression, inasmuch as it adds to the tension the pain of disappointment and a new fear. The attempt to compensate the reduction of the effect by increasing the dosage proves to be worth while in the case of many drugs; a good example of this is morphine-pharmacothymia. With this develops the mad pursuit of the patients after the constantly increasing doses which become necessary. Moral obligations, life interests of other kinds are thrown to the winds, when it is a question of pursuing the satisfaction of this need,—a process of moral disintegration second to none.

Meanwhile, crucial alterations occur in the sexual life of the patient. In order to remain within the limits of this presentation, I must restrict my remarks to the most fundamental ones. All elatants poison sexual potency. After a transient augmentation of genital libido, the patient soon turns away from sexual activity and disregards more and more even his affectionate relationships. In lieu of genital pleasure appears the pharmacogenic pleasure-effect, which gradually comes to be the dominant sexual aim. From the ease with which this remarkable substitution is effected, we must conclude that pharmacogenic pleasure depends upon genetically preformed, elementary paths, and that old sensory material is utilized to create a new combination. This, however, is a problem which can be postponed. What is immediately evident is the fact that the pharmacogenic attainment of pleasure initiates an artificial sexual organization which is autoerotic and modeled on infantile masturbation. Objects of love are no longer needed but are retained for a time in fantasy. Later the activity of fantasy returns, regressively, to the emotional attachments of childhood, that is to say, to the oedipus complex. The pharmacogenic pleasure instigates a rich fantasy life; this feature seems especially characteristic of opium-pharmacothymia. Indeed, struck by this fact, the pharmacologist Lewin suggested that the "elatants" should be named "phantastica." The crux of the matter is, that it is the pharmacogenic pleasure-effect which discharges the libidinal tension associated with these fantasies. The pharmacogenic pleasure process thus comes to replace the natural sexual executive. The genital apparatus with its extensive auxiliary ramifications in the erotogenic zones falls into desuetude and is overtaken by a sort of mental atrophy of disuse. The fire of life is gradually extinguished at that point where it should glow most intensely according to nature and is kindled at a site contrary to nature. Pharmacothymia destroys the psychic structure of the individual long before it inflicts any damage on the physical substrate.

The ego responds to this devaluation of the natural sexual organization with a fear of castration only too justifiable in this instance. This warning signal is due to the narcissistic investment of the genital; anxiety about the genital should then compel abstention from the dangerous practice, just as, at one time, it compelled abstention from masturbation. But the ego has sold itself to the elatant drugs and cannot heed this warning. The ego, to be sure, is not able to suppress the fear itself, but it perceives the fear consciously as a dread of pharmacogenic failure. This switching of the anxiety is, psychologically, entirely correct. Whoever secretly desires to fail because he is afraid of succeeding, is quite right in being in dread of failure. The effect of the fear is naturally in accordance with its original intent; as we have learned, it reduces the pleasure-effect and the intensity of the elation.

By frivolously cutting itself off from its social and sexual activities the ego conjures up an instinctual danger, the extent of which it does not suspect. It delivers itself over to that antagonistic instinctual power within, which we call masochism, and following Freud, interpret as a death instinct. The ego had an opportunity to feel the dark power of this instinct in the initial depression; partly for fear of it then, the ego took flight into the pharmacothymic regime. The ego can defend itself successfully against the dangers of masochistic self-injury only by vigorously developing its vitality and thus entrenching its narcissism. What the pharmacothymic regime bestowed upon the ego, was, however, a valueless inflation of narcissism. The ego lives, then, in a period of pseudo-prosperity, and is not aware that it has played into the hands of its self-destruction. The ego, in every neurosis, is driven into harmful complications by masochism; but of all methods of combating masochism, the pharmacothymic regime is assuredly the most hopeless.

It is impossible for the patient not to perceive what is happening. His friends and relatives deluge him with warnings to "pull himself together" if he does not wish to ruin himself and his family. And at the same time, the elation diminishes in intensity continuously and the depression becomes more severe. Physical illnesses, unmistakably due to the use of the poison, afflict him with pains. Since the first temptation the picture has completely changed. Then, everything was in favor of the elation, whereas now the hopes set upon it have been revealed as deluding. It might be supposed that the patient would reflect on this and give up the drug—but, no; he continues on his way. I must admit that for many years I could not grasp the economics of this state of mind until a patient himself gave me the explanation. He said: "I know all the things that people say when they upbraid me. But, mark my words, doctor, *nothing* can happen to *me*." This, then, is the patient's position. The elation has reactivated his narcissistic belief in his *invulnerability,* and all of his better insight and all of his sense of guilt are shattered on this bulwark.

Benumbed by this illusion, the ego's adherence to the pharmacothymic regime is strengthened all the more. The pharmacothymic regime still seems to be *the* way out of all difficulties. One day, things have progressed so far that an elation can no longer be provided to combat the misery of the depression. The regime has collapsed, and we are confronted by the phenomenon of the *pharmacothymic crisis.*

There are three ways out of this crisis: flight into a free interval, suicide and psychosis.

By voluntarily submitting to withdrawal therapy, the patient undertakes a flight into a free interval. It is out of the question that he is actuated by any real desire to recover his health. In those rare instances in which the patient really wishes to be delivered from his pharmacothymia, as I have occasionally been able to observe in my analytic practice, he sets great store upon executing his resolve by himself, and it does not occur to him to seek aid from others. But, if he submits to a withdrawal cure, as a rule, he wishes only to rehabilitate the depreciated value of the poison. It may be that he can no longer afford the money for the enormous quantity of the drug that he needs; after the withdrawal treatment he can begin anew with much less expense.

Since the withdrawal of the drug divests the ego of its elation—its protection against masochism—the latter can now invade the ego. There it seizes upon the physical symptoms due to abstinence and exploits them, frequently to the point of a true masochistic orgy; naturally with the opposition of the ego, which is not grateful for this type of pleasure. As a result, we have the familiar scenes which patients produce during the withdrawal period.

Suicide is the work of self-destructive masochism. But to say that the patient kills himself because of a masochistic need for punishment would be too one-sided a statement. The analysis of the suicidal fantasies and attempts of which our patients tell us, reveals the narcissistic aspect of the experience. The patient takes the lethal dose because he wishes to dispel the depression for good by an elation which will last *forever*. He does not kill himself; he believes in his *immortality*. Once the demon of infantile narcissism is unchained, he can send the ego to its death.

Furthermore, in suicide through drugs, masochism is victorious under the banner of a "feminine" instinctual demand. Remarkably enough, it is the deeply rooted high estimation which the male has for his sexual organ, his genital narcissism, which brings about this transformation and transmutes masochism into a feminine phenomenon. This sounds paradoxical but can readily be understood as a compromise. The ingestion of drugs, it is well known, in infantile archaic thinking represents an oral insemination; planning to die from poisoning is a cover for the wish to become pregnant in this fashion. We see, therefore, that after the pharmacothymia has paralyzed the ego's virility, the hurt pride in genitality, forced into passivity because of masochism, desires as a substitute the satisfaction of child bearing. Freud recognized the replacement of the wish to possess a penis by the wish to have a child as a turning point in the normal sexual development of women. In the case we are discussing, the male takes this female path in order to illude himself concerning his masochistic self-destruction by appealing to his genital narcissism. It is as though the ego, worried about the male genital, told itself: "Be comforted. You are getting a new genital." To this idea, inferred from empirical findings, we may add that impregnation biologically initiates a new life cycle: the wish to be pregnant is a mute appeal to the function of reproduction, to "divine Eros," to testify to the immortality of the ego.

The *psychotic episode* as an outcome of the crisis is known to us chiefly—though by no means exclusively—in alcohol-pharmacothymia. This is a large chapter. I can only indicate the framework around which its contents may be arranged.

The failure of the pharmacothymic regime has robbed the ego of its protective elation. Masochism then crowds into the foreground. The terrible hallucinations and deliria, in which the patient believes that he is being persecuted, or threatened—particularly by the danger of castration or a sexual attack—and the like are fantasies that gratify masochistic wishes. The masochism desires to place the ego in a situation where it will suffer, in order to obtain pleasure from the painful stimulation. The narcissistic ego offers opposition to this "pain-pleasure"; it desires the pleasure *without* pain. The wishes of its masochism inspire the ego with fear and horror. It can, to be sure, no longer prevent the eruption of the masochistic fantasies, yet it looks upon them through its own eyes. Thus, the latent *wish* fantasies of masochism are transformed into the manifest *terror*-fantasies of the ego. Now it is as though the danger proceeded from without; there, at least, it can be combated, and the terrified patient attempts to do this in the imaginations of his psychosis.

It is even worse if the anxiety which protects the ego from masochism breaks down. Then, the ego must accede to masochism. If the patient has arrived at this point, he suddenly announces his intention of destroying his genital organ or—substitutively—inflicting some other injury upon himself. He actually takes measures towards the blind execution of the biddings of his masochism; the patient's narcissism, defeated, can only insure that he will literally act blindly. It dims his gaze by means of delusion: the patient is not aware of the true nature of his masochism and refuses to recognize it. Instead, he asserts that he must rid himself of his organ because this organ is a nuisance to him, or has been a source of harm, or the like. If we read, for this statement, "because this organ has sinned against him," a path opens for the clarification of the latent meaning of this delusion. We may now compare it with another type of delusion of self-injury, in which the patient is well aware that he is engaged in harming himself yet persists in his designs nonetheless. This variant of the delusion usually appears in the guise of the moral idea of sin; the ego believes that it must inflict a merited punishment upon itself, in order to purify its conscience. The central feature in this "moralizing" type of delusional state is self-reproach. It may be assumed that in the "unconcerned" type of delusional state, previously described, the ego institutes a displacement of the guilt and directs its reproaches, not against itself, but against its genital organ. Primitive thought finds displacements of this sort very easy. We often hear small children say: "I didn't do it. My hand did it." The life of primitive peoples is replete with instances of this sort. The patient, then, is incensed with his genital organ, dispossesses it of the esteem previously lavished upon it (its narcissistic investment), and wishes to part with it. It is as though the ego said to the genital organ; "You are to blame for it all. First you tempted me to sin." (Bad conscience for infantile masturbation.) "Then your inefficiency brought me disappointment." (Lowering of self-esteem through later disturbances of potency.) "And therefore you drove me into my ill-omened drug addiction. I do not love you any more; away with you!" The ego does not castrate itself; it wrecks vengeance on its genital.[9]

In the "unconcerned" form of delusion of self-injury, the ego obviously is still experiencing an after-effect of the continuous elation; it is still "beclouded by original narcissism." To masochism—that is, to knowledge that it wishes to injure itself and that this is its sole objective—the ego is blind and deaf. It is as though, in the ego's state of grandeur, whether or not it has a genital is of no moment. The genital offended the ego—away with it!

The unconcerned type of delusion of self-injury occurs more frequently in schizophrenia than in pharmacothymia. In schizophrenia, the megalomania is responsible for the fact that the ego, under pressure of masochism, undertakes so easily to inflict the most horrible mutilations upon itself, such as amputations, enucleation of the eyeball, etc. The megalomania of schizophrenia and the megalomania of pharmacothymic elation are related manifestations of narcissistic regression. The former pursues a chronic course, the latter an acute, and they differ in regard to intellectual content and emotional tone; nevertheless, they both are based upon a regression to the "orginal narcissistic stature" of the ego.

Masochism in pharmacothymia may be attenuated into the passivity of a homosexual attitude. This fact gives us deep insight into the dynamics of homosexuality. The pharmacothymic regime has driven eroticism from its active positions and thereby, as a reaction, encouraged masochism. The genital eroticism which is on the retreat can then with the masochism enter into a compromise which will combine the genital aim of painless pleasure with the passive behavior of masochism, and the result of this combination, in men, is a homosexual choice of object.[10] The danger proceeding from the masochistic wish to be castrated, naturally remains extant. If it is of sufficient magnitude, the ego reacts to it with a fear of castration and represses the homosexual impulse, which afterwards in the psychosis may become manifest as a delusion of jealousy, or in the femine erotic quality of the delusions of persecution.

The advantage of homosexuality as compared to masochism is its more ready acceptability to the ego. In overt homosexuality, the ego combats the masochistic danger of castration by denying the existence, in general, of any such thing as a danger of castration. Its position is: there is no such thing as castration, for there are no castrated persons; even the sexual partner possesses a penis. If the ego in pharmacothymia or after the withdrawal of the drug accepts homosexuality, this turn must be regarded as an attempt at autotherapy. The recrudescence of the genital function with a new aim, more readily attainable, psychologically speaking, permits the ego to return to, or fortify, the "realistic regime." After being reconciled to its homosexuality, the ego can subsequently take a new reparative step toward masculinity by progressing from a passive homosexual to an active homosexual attitude. Thus, male heterosexual normality is changed into active homosexuality by a three-stage process: (1) weakening of genital masculinity (because of intimidation due to threats of castration, diversion of the libido into the pharmacothymia, etc.) and a corresponding reactive increase in the antagonistic masochism; (2) the confluence of genital pleasure and masochism in the compromise, passive homosexuality; and (3) the development of homosexuality from the passive to the active form as the result of a vigorous reparative action on the part of the ego. In corroboration of this idea is the finding, hitherto neglected, that the homosexuality which the ego rejects and combats by the formation of delusions (symptoms) is always passive homosexuality. These facts help to clarify clinical manifestations that appeared obscure and complex. Obviously, the ego may have become homosexual, because of analogous circumstances, even before the pharmacothymia began.

These views, as I have presented them here, seem to me to throw new light upon the problem of the relationship between homosexuality and pharmacothymia. The homosexual background became evident to psychoanalysis, first in alcoholism, later in cocainism, and finally in morphinism. Since I attribute homosexuality to the influence of masochism, and since, furthermore, every type of pharmacothymia attacks genitality and by reaction strengthens masochism, the opportunity to effect this compromise must naturally be present in every case of pharmacothymia.

The love life of pharmacothymics may present pathological features other than homosexuality. These all derive from the basic situation described above, in my outline of the development of homosexuality, as "stage (1)." The pharmacothymic whose potency is debilitated by masochism may find ways of preserving his heterosexuality. In the first place, he may choose another compromise solution and become oriented passively towards *women.* This erotic position is quite unstable; but it can be reënforced, by an infusion of fetishism, to withstand the onslaught of castration anxiety. With the aid of the fetishistic mechanism, the beloved woman is in imagination transmuted into the possessor of a penis and elevated to take the place of the "phallic mother."[11] With this alignment of the instincts, the persons chosen as objects are, by preference, women who have a prominent nose, large breasts, an imposing figure, or, too, a good deal of money, and the like. Correlated with this, the emotional tone in regard to the genital region of women is disturbed by a sort of discomfort, and the patient assiduously avoids looking at it or touching it. In mild cases of pharmacothymia, this passive orientation towards women with its fetishistic ingredient often plays a major rôle, but its distribution is by no means restricted to pharmacothymia. A further intensification of the masochistic wish to be castrated, or better, of the fear of castration aroused by this wish, then forces the patient either to be abstinent or to follow the homosexual course and exchange the partner without a penis for one who possesses a penis. (See "stage [2]" described above.) In the second place, the ego may refuse to adopt as a solution the compromise of any passive orientation; it may respond to the danger proceeding from the masochistic instinct by a reaction formation. It is no easy task to divine what special conditions enable the ego to react in this way. But at any rate, the means used by the ego are the strained exertion of its pleasure in aggression. Sadism is rushed to the rescue of imperiled masculinity, to shout down, by its vehemence, fear of castration and masochistic temptation. In this case, too, heterosexuality is preserved, but the ego must pay for this by entering the path of sadistic perversion. In the dynamics of the perversion of sadism, the *vis a tergo* of masochism is the crucial factor; in its construction, infantile and recent experiences are jointly effective, in the usual familiar manner. The appearance of this variant, that is, the production of a true sadistic perversion is not, to be sure, promoted by the pharmacothymia. I recognized this mechanism in non-pharmacothymic cases, and I have mentioned it here only because it may furnish us with the explanation of a conspicuous deformation of the character, which may be considered a counterpart of the perversion of sadism, and which often may be found in pharmacothymia. Particularly in drunkards, we are familiar with aggressive irritability, with unprovoked outbursts of hate or rage against women, and the like, which in apparently unpredictable fashion, alternate with states of touching mollification. We can now understand that the excesses of brutality are the substitutes for potency of the pharmacothymic who is fighting for his masculinity, and that his sentimental seizures are eruptions of the masochism which his pharmacothymia has reactively intensified.

Pharmacothymia is not ineluctably bound to this basic course with its terminal crisis. Many drugs, especially alcohol, admit of combating the recurrent depression by overlapping dosage. The patient takes a fresh dose before the effect of the previous one has ceased. If he does so, he renounces "elation" in the narrower sense of this word; for elation is a phenomenon dependent on contrast. Instead, he lives in a sort of "subdued continuous elation" which differs from simple stupefaction probably only because of its narcissistically pleasurable quality. This modified course leads through a progressive reduction of the ego to the terminal state of pharmacogenic stupor. A flaring up of the desire for a real elation or other reasons may at any time bring the patient back to the basic course with its critical complications.

This sketch of the theoretical picture of pharmacothymia roughly outlines the broad field of its symptomatology. One thing remains to be added. In more severe, advanced cases, symptoms appear which are the result of cerebral damage, and which are consequently to be interpreted with due consideration of the point of view of brain pathology. In this, we may expediently make use of the psycho-physiological point of view introduced into psychopathology by Schilder with the concept of "inroad of the somatic" *("somatischer Einbruch")*.[12] If the poisons consumed have damaged the brain substance, and permanently impaired cerebral activity, this is perceived in the mental sphere as a disturbance of the elementary psychological functions. The psychic organization reacts with an effort to adapt to this fact and correct the result. It is well to differentiate the phenomena which originate in this way, as the "secondary symptoms" of pharmacothymia, from those "primary" ones which we have been considering. The secondary symptoms are more characteristic of the brain lesions which determine them than of the illness in which they appear. This can be seen in the example of the Korsakoff syndrome, which occurs in other conditions as well as in pharmacothymia.

Finally, it might be pointed out that in addition to full-blown pharmacothymia there are obviously abortive forms of this illness. The patient may, generally speaking, retain the realistic regime, and use his pharmacothymic

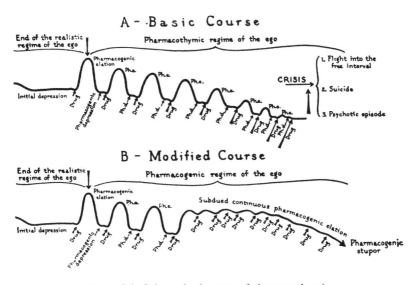

Figure 3.1. Schematized course of pharmacothymia

regime only as an auxiliary and corrective. He desires in this way to make up for the uncertainty in his realistic attitude and cover a deficit by means of counterfeit. By easy transitions we arrive at the normal person who makes daily use of stimulants in the form of coffee, tea, tobacco, and the like.

NOTES

1. "The Psychic Effects of Intoxicants: An Attempt to Evolve a Psycho-Analytical Theory of Morbid Cravings." *Int. J. Ps-A.* VII, 1926. Since this, I have reported the progress of my views in a number of addresses: "Drug Addiction" at the First Congress for Mental Hygiene, at Washington, D.C., May 1930; "Intoxication and 'The Morning After' " at a meeting of the German Psychoanalytic Society in Berlin, November 1930; "Depressive and Elated States in Neuroses and in Drug Addiction," a lecture course at the Berlin Psychoanalytic Institute, Spring 1931.

2. "Elation" = *Rausch*. "Elatant" = *Rauschgift*. TR.

3. Ferenczi, S., "Development of the Sense of Reality." Trans. by Jones, in *Contributions to Ps-A.*

4. Freud, "On Narcissism, an Introduction." *Coll. Papers* IV.

5. Cf. my article, "An Anxious Mother." *Int. J. Ps-A.* IX, 1928.

6. "Regime of the ego" = *Steuerung des Ichs*. TR.

7. "Original narcissistic stature" = *narzisstische Urgestalt*. TR.

8. In my article, "The Problem of Melancholia" (*Int. J. Ps-A IX,* 1928), I first alluded to the narcissistic nature of drug addictions.

9. In Ferenczi's ingenious theory of genitality (*Versuch einer Genitaltheorie,* 1923), the author calls attention to the fact that the relationship of the ego and the genital, in spite of all interests held in common, reflects profound biological antagonisms. The ego is, after all, the representative of the interests of the "soma"; and the genital, the representative of those of the "germ plasm." In so far as the ego feels itself at one with its genital libido, its genital organ impresses it as its most prolific source of pleasure; but for an ego that wishes peace, the genital becomes merely the bearer of oppressive tensions, which the ego wishes to shake off. From these and like premises, Ferenczi infers that—in the male—the act of procreation includes among its psychic qualities a "tendency towards autotomy of the genital."

10. I shall discuss the conditions in women in another article.

11. Freud, "Fetishism." *Int. J. Ps-A.* IX, 1928.

12. Schilder, Paul, "Über die kausale Bedeutung des durch Psychoanalyse gewonnenen Materials." *Wiener klin. Wchschr.* 1921.—The theory of general paralysis formulated by Hollós and Ferenczi is based on a similar idea.

4. *From* Psychoanalytic Treatment in a Sanatorium

Ernst Simmel

AT THIS POINT I should like to say a few words about the sanatorium treatment of morbid cravings in general—a form of disease which constitutes a very large part of our field of work. We have proved in the clinic that there is no special value in allowing patients to struggle alone for a very long time in their efforts to abstain. For in this very struggle lurks an element of pleasure—namely, the pleasure of repeating the battle which took place when the patient was trying to give up his infantile onanism.

The methods of "weaning" adopted by such patients reveal themselves as a defensive ritual, which, like that of the obsessional neurotic, contains possibilities of autoerotic pleasure. For instance, the patient may defer the hypodermic injection in order to enjoy the *craving* for the syringe or the masochistic torment of abstinence.

In patients with morbid cravings, as in obsessional neurotics, onanism has succumbed to the threat of castration, and the subject is compelled to regress to pregenital positions of the libido. These have a characteristic cathexis of dread of loss (removal of anal excrement, loss of the mother's breast). The *form* of the craving is determined by the phantasies which accompany it in consciousness or remain in a state of repression. Having an injection corresponds to an anal-masochistic and drinking to an oral-sadistic phantasy. But the "weaning" process represents a mixture of the processes of giving up onanism, learning habits of cleanliness and weaning from the breast. Ultimately the person whom the toxin poisons in these patients is the person from whom the threat of castration emanates, i.e. in the deepest stratum the introjected object longed for yet hated: the mother, the great castrator of the past on the anal and oral levels.

I will not at the moment enter on a detailed account of the observations we have so far been able to make in the clinic with regard to the pathogenesis of morbid cravings. But as regards their special clinical therapy I will just say here that these observations have shewn me that such patients suffer at bottom from a narcissistic neurosis which they try to ward off by means of the mechanisms of obsessional neurosis. The victim of a craving is a melancholic who makes his guardian super-ego drunk with the poison with which he murders the object in the ego. To outward seeming, however, he is in a state of mania so long as he is indulging in the poison. For a super-ego paralyzed by a toxin (temporarily castrated) ceases to make any demands: it is no longer able to mediate in the interests of self-preservation, between external and internal (psychic) reality.

It is only to be expected that the treatment itself is fraught with the greatest danger to this class of patient—persons who destroy themselves with a double purpose: in self-punishment and in the sadistic gratification of a murderous impulse. In the psycho-analytic clinic, however, we are better able to counter their suicidal tendencies than when we are treating them as out-patients. Our way of protecting them is not so much by careful supervision as by making use of the opportunity which I have already indicated. I mean that in the transference we afford them a possibility of translating into objective reality (for the time being) the destructive tendency directed against ourselves. That is to say, while the treatment is in its perilous phases I agree to the patients going through a stage of killing, devouring or castrating us *in effigie.* At such times I allow them to have the double or treble amount of food which they demand, I let them cut off branches if they want to do so, and I do not reproach them if, when they are in this mental situation, they smash a coffee-service to atoms. Of course the "destructive object-relation" thus established must not be retained: it must be analytically resolved and shewn for what it is—the cathartic relief of tension between ego and super-ego, projected on to the physician.

Thus in the sanatorium we can arrive nearer to the solution of a special therapeutic problem about which we cudgel our brains in ordinary psycho-analytic treatment of the victims of morbid cravings. For, as we see, the peculiar psycho-analytic situation in the clinic enables us to provide the patient with transitory substitute-gratifications in order to help him to re-nounce his symptom. In ordinary treatment the greatest resistance to our carrying-through the cure arises over the question of the manifest gratification derived from the indulgence in intoxicants. Here again, I think that the clinic can provide a suitable substitute, so that there may be the necessary economic compensation.

When we consider that the patient has been sufficiently prepared by analysis to pass on to being treated in a state of complete deprivation of the drug, we order him to stay in bed for a time. A special nurse is assigned to him, whose only charge he is and who is at hand day and night encouraging him and looking after his diet and personal comfort.[1] All the violent manifestations resulting from his abstinence (exaltation, anxiety or depression) are met as far as possible with psycho-analytical help only, i.e. with regular treatment or analytic talks, if necessary several times a day and even in the night. By this change in the psycho-analytic situation the patient's unconscious receives the uttermost fulfilment of his deepest longing, in spite of the torments which he suffers consciously. For the secret of the ultimate unconscious gratification which the victim of morbid craving desires is this: to be quite a little child again, to lie in bed and be allowed to have a kind mother tending and feeding him, a mother whom the father yields to him and who is always there when anxiety seizes him. We *create* the situation of having the mother once more close at hand. This situation in its turn is inevitably transformed back into the analytic situation, for, as the treatment progresses, the infantile phase spontaneously disappears.

NOTES

1. I make use of this phase for the bodily welfare also of the patient. (Baths and the drinking of waters to cleanse the system of toxins; feeding-up and so forth.)

5. The Psychodynamics of Chronic Alcoholism

R. P. Knight

THE NEUROPSYCHIATRIST has always had to deal with what might be called the complications of chronic alcoholism—delirium tremens, hallucinosis, pseudoparesis, pseudoparanoia, Korsakow's psychosis, etc.—but in the last decade or so there has been more and more interest in the problem of simple chronic alcoholism. More frequently than ever the psychiatrist is called upon to treat patients whose excessive drinking has continued in spite of several Keeley "cures," banishments by relatives to ranches, and stays in such institutions as the late Muldoon's men-building resort on the Hudson. In fact the psychiatrist does not usually get the case except as a last resort, when the relatives have become desperate. Among psychiatrists themselves, however, there has been no unanimity of opinion as to either etiology or treatment. Psychiatrists are agreed that the problem is primarily psychiatric and not moral or legal but beyond this point views diverge. As to etiology, some believe on account of easily demonstrable neurological signs in some cases and because of post-mortem brain pathology that the alcoholic's will power must be lessened by damage to the nervous system; others emphasize the habit aspect of the drinking; still others postulate chemical or humoral changes which make the habit persist; and many psychiatrists adopt the orthodox point of view that the chronic alcoholic is a hopeless psychopath *sui generis*. As to treatment, restrictive custodial care, often with attempted re-education of some kind, is the rule among those psychiatrists who are interested in undertaking such a case at all.

Out of the experience gained in studying and attempting to re-educate chronic alcoholics, considerable psychological understanding of them has been gained. It is from the experience gained in treating alcoholics in our institution that I wish today to discuss the psychodynamics of this type of mental illness. I do not believe that such causative factors as habit, humoral changes, and brain damage should be ignored, but for the purposes of this

Reprinted by permission from *Journal of Nervous and Mental Disease* 86 (1937): 538–48.

presentation they may be disregarded. It is recognized that the cases available for study in a private sanitarium such as this one come from a certain social and economic class, and, furthermore, are patients who, for the most part, have come for treatment only after considerable pressure if not actual force has been exercised by the responsible relatives. Such psychological mechanisms as have appeared to us to be regularly found in cases of this sort may not, therefore, necessarily apply to other cases of alcoholics such, for example, as down-and-out wandering drunks who have no funds nor interested relatives to bring them for treatment, or independent, economically successful hard drinkers whom nobody could persuade to seek treatment for their drinking. However, we believe that the group on which this study is based is a fair sample of the alcoholics that finally present themselves to psychiatrists for treatment. I shall be concerned exclusively with men alcoholics as they far outnumber women alcoholics in general and in my experience.

Following an orientation which now has considerable acceptance in psychiatric circles, we regard persistent, excessive drinking as a symptom, rather than as a disease entity. It is, however, a symptom which places the chronic alcoholic on the borderline between neurosis and psychosis. Even in his sober periods, the alcoholic is usually a maladjusted individual with many neurotic traits; but when he is drinking excessively he not only denies and takes flight from reality in significant ways, but seems able, through his alcoholism, to enter upon a temporary psychosis in which his thinking and behavior are distinctly abnormal. We regard alcoholism as a psychogenic symptom, that is, one that is psychologically understandable and psychologically motivated. Anticipating subsequent substantiating arguments for this thesis, alcoholism, like other psychogenic symptoms, represents an attempt at cure, that is, an attempt at some solution of the emotional conflict. In all cases of chronic alcoholism there is a serious, underlying personality disorder. Cessation of the drinking, especially enforced cessation, does not solve the problem, but only throws the personality disorder into bolder relief.

When one studies this underlying personality disorder, it is found that there is no special or typical kind of emotional conflict common to all cases. Any type of neurotic conflict may be present. It is true that most alcoholics whom we have studied exhibit similar superficial character traits and attitudes. They are usually likeable men, often rather glib talkers, and shortly after beginning institutional treatment they are confident that drinking is no more a problem for them. They become irritable under restriction and demand privileges and discharge from the institution. In spite of this typical behavior each one regards himself as different from the usual run and cannot understand the psychiatrist's lack of confidence in his newly made resolutions and assurances.

Aside from these similarities, one finds that each case is quite individual as to the underlying psychology. Since it is true, however, that they all resort to alcohol chronically and excessively in dealing with their individual emotional conflicts, there must be an understandable psychodynamics of the drinking itself. It is the purpose of this paper to present the results of an investigation along this line. The significant questions to be answered are: (1) Why does the alcoholic resort to drinking in the beginning instead of developing another sort of psychiatric picture? and (2) Why does he continue to resort to alcohol in spite of the realization that drinking does not effectively solve his conflict but instead slowly ruins his life? The ultimate answers to these questions are not claimed to be found in this discussion. Infantile material from the deepest layers of the unconscious is difficult to demonstrate, and also there may be some X-factor deriving from constitution or inheritance that plays a part, but it is hoped that some contribution to the understanding of the psychodynamics in alcoholism is contained in this presentation.

Instead of generalizing from all the cases studied (about thirty in number) or attempting any statistical results on so small a group, I decided to select one typical case out of those intensively studied and follow the development of this case, pointing out those findings which are typical for the group.

The case to be described is that of a young man of thirty-four, whose excessive drinking dates back over a period of ten years, much worse in the last two years. He happened to be the youngest of three male siblings, but it is our experience that there is nothing specific at all about the sibling position. The chronic alcoholic may be an only child, the oldest son, or the youngest son, or may have both older and younger brothers and sisters. As a matter of fact, this patient's nine years older brother also was a chronic alcoholic, and his other brother had one known alcoholic episode in which he made a bad marriage that had to be annulled. In the family history a maternal aunt was committed with a diagnosis of dementia praecox, and three paternal uncles were chronic alcoholics for many years. However, we also do not find alcoholism in the family background as a constant factor at all, and we are doubtful that there is an inherited predisposition. In fact, it is usually found that the son of a drunkard father tends to present another type of neurotic reaction, and that the fathers of our alcoholics are for the most part not excessive drinkers if indeed they are not abstainers.

When we come to the question of parental characteristics, however, we notice some striking correlations. First let me describe the patient's mother, for she is absolutely typical; here our observations coincide exactly with a recent statistical study of the mothers of 100 male alcoholics made by Dr. Wall of the Westchester Division of New York Hospital, in a paper read at the 1935 meeting of the American Psychiatric Association. Our patient's mother had always been over-indulgent and protective toward him. She was always trying to shield him from the father's discipline and severity, and consistently acted as intercessor for him in his attempts throughout life to obtain indulgence from the father. If the boy couldn't get money or privilege directly from his father, he would appeal to his mother and have her act as his advocate. Such a situation cannot but have a profound influence in a son's emotional development. The significance of this influence will be discussed a little later. The patient's father was a physician and was always severe and dominating in the family. Furthermore he was unaffectionate and undemonstrative toward both his wife and his children. When he did grant indulgences, he did so sporadically and inconsistently, often only after being swayed by his wife's pleadings. We have frequently found such a father when investigating the family background of an alcoholic patient. Occasionally we find an over-indulgent father, but the cold, aloof, exacting type of father seems to be more frequent. The Bloomingdale study, however, did not bear out this observation.

Realizing, as we now do, how profoundly significant in determining the child's later patterns of interpersonal relationships and attitudes toward life are the early relationships with the parents, let us try to see how such a mother especially would condition her child. It is always extremely difficult to uncover and demonstrate from the history or from the patient's material the actual historical incidents of the mother's early handling of him. But when the patient tells us constantly in his behavior, in his drinking, and in his dreams that he needs to take something into his mouth to soothe him and make him feel better, and when we can logically correlate this finding with the presumptive attitude of such a mother to her infant son, we may be pardoned for indulging in a little speculation as to the unobtainable infantile history of the patient.

Every baby's first experience in having tension and distress allayed occurs when he is nursed. Hunger pains are relieved magically when he takes something into his mouth and fills his stomach. With satiety he becomes contented and free from tension and often passes into peaceful sleep. The nursing experience also brings security in the presence of and contact with the person who is always bringing him comfort with her ministrations. What wonder, then, if the infant is conditioned to expect relief from discomfort and distress in taking something into his mouth, whether it be the nipple, the now fortunately almost obsolete pacifier, or his own finger? If the mother wisely manages to avoid excessive conditioning of the infant by keeping the feeding schedule regular, by adequate feedings, by gently but persistently breaking the finger sucking habit before it becomes established, by tapering off the nursing and intelligently managing the weaning, following up this early rearing by a consistent policy regarding indulgence and denial, the child will normally develop. A contrasting method of management may be presumed in the over-indulgent, over-affectionate mother described. By fostering the pattern of soothing the infant through oral pacifying, she builds in a pattern of tremendous strength. Now when she tries to wean him he is enraged. The mother knows she can quiet his rage — which again means a relief of tension for the infant — by once more gratifying him orally, and, being the type she is, she probably does just that. Eventual weaning for such a child can only mean to him betrayal by the mother. She led him to expect indulgence and he tries by every means to recapture it when it seems to be denied to him. Throughout his life he will try to obtain passive indulgences from people and will develop characteristically oral ways of pacifying himself when his wishes are frustrated. Our patient was the youngest child and hence did not experience further reactions of feeling betrayed by seeing a younger sibling getting the infantile oral satisfactions now denied to him, but with other alcoholics studied who have younger siblings, this factor has been found to have played a part. We can observe its influence in the more or less open resentment against and envy of the younger sibling.

We must continue the story of the patient's development to see how the relationships with both parents added further to his predisposition to later alcoholism (or, we might add, to possible drug addiction in general). The patient's memories of his early childhood are few, but significant. He remembers that he always got, and took it for granted he would get, what he wanted from his mother. She had to continue what she had started, and he did not appreciate her indulgences, but accepted them as his due. He also remembers, however, that when he sought to get things from his father in the same way he was often thwarted. His passive demands were so great, on the basis of his infantile gratifications, that he could not be entirely satisfied even by his mother. This fact, coupled with the feeling of vague resentment and betrayal toward the mother, caused him to turn more and more to the father for proofs of affection in the form of indulgences. Furthermore, since the mother could get things from the father for herself and for him, it was natural for him to identify himself with her in order to promote his own satisfaction. Now it may be that whatever the type of father, a bad outcome for the child is inevitable. If the father also over-indulges him, as have the fathers of some of the alcoholics studied, he is led to expect more passive gratifications from life than this world will ever give him, and more than even an over-indulgent father can later give him. If the father is consistently strict or consistently wise in his gifts, a part of the damage may be undone. But if the father is inconsistently and sporadically lenient, reactions of rage, spite, aggressive taking, and increased identification with the mother ensue. Our patient's father acted in the manner last described. Sometimes he acceded to the boy's demands immediately and without question, to the boy's surprise. Sometimes he denied requests without reason. Sometimes he gave in later when the mother interceded. Often he demanded a rigid accounting of the past money grants before giving out more money. The patient tells a typical and illustrative experience of his fifth year. He was frequently sent to the nearby grocery by his mother to bring home articles of food. She taught him to say "Charge it." To him this came to be a magic phrase. One got food in great plenty and without question by simply saying "Charge it." The store also sold candy. Why not get candy free also? He carried out this idea, getting more and more each time. A rude awakening came at the end of the month when there was ten dollars worth of candy on the grocery bill. His father, without explanation and without understanding, whipped him severely, and the boy became all the more bewildered. The significance of this experience as well as the nondeterring effect of this sort of discipline could be seen when the patient was thirty-four. Although he had earned much money through his own efforts, and had been married and divorced, he was still financially dependent. When he needed money away from home, he would cash a draft on his father. He was still charging candy to his father.

It has been already stated that alcoholics are likeable fellows. They seem to have developed a personality and a technique intended to make people like them and give them what they want. Our discussion so far helps us to understand why this is so. Their wants and demands are so great that they must adopt measures calculated to bring gratifications of these wants. However, because their wishes are so great, they are bound to be frustrated often; and they characteristically react with rage—a rage which is usually felt as a seething discomfort and resentful turmoil within. Because of this reaction, and because of their frequent behavior of getting what they want regardless and forcing their parents to get them out of the consequent trouble, they are problem children and problem adolescents. Our patient, throughout his school life, was always subordinating what was required of him to what he wanted to do, and his father was always getting him out of scrapes. He was sent to military school as a disciplinary measure. He was never able to adjust himself well enough to complete his college work. His father says that he loved a good time too much to ever apply himself. The father tried by increasing severity and frustration to force the patient to be independent. And here we see a typical situation, found in nearly all the cases studied. The father rebels at the mother's indulgence, seeing that the boy is not gaining any independence at all, and demands that his son stands alone. He even reposes confidence in him for a while in order to promote the son's independence, but the experiment seems doomed to failure. Either the son disappoints him repeatedly or else the father himself becomes inconsistent and withdraws the grant of independence. (For example, another alcoholic's father, through wise monetary allowances and payments for odd jobs, permitted his fourteen-year-old son to build up his own bank account of about $100. Then when the family moved to another town, this account was absorbed in the father's and never heard of again by the son.)

When our patient was in his late teens, with the built-in pattern of excessive wants and expectations, rage at frustration, continued indulgence and protection by the mother, and increasing strictness and demands for his independence by the father, he had all the psychological predisposition to become an alcoholic. One might call him at this stage a larval alcoholic. Yet even with all we have pointed out that contributed to this predisposition, there is nothing yet specific for alcoholism. Other children are similarly narcissistic and demanding, expecting gratifications as if they were still under the sway of infantile omnipotence, and these children may become neurotics of other kinds and never develop alcoholism. Barring a constitutional X-factor, or other specific psychological factors so far overlooked, it seems to me that a certain combination of circumstances must play a part in the onset of the drinking. In this case, for example, the physician father made his son take various medicines—tonics, potions to clean out the system, and so on—whether the son seemed to need them or not. These medicines were part of the father's potency as a physician, and the son accepted them as symbolic gratifications. It cannot be fortuitous, for example, that the son, on being brought to the sanitarium for treatment, had this fantasy: He would get better after some treatment, meet an attractive girl whose father would turn out to own a large wholesale drug business, court the girl, through her get a job selling drugs for the father, would be very successful, and would win the girl. It is a strange coincidence, if nothing more, that the patient, after some treatment, actually did meet the wealthy owner of a chemical business and got a job as salesman and agent.

But there are other circumstances which result in the onset of the drinking habit. I have said that the adolescent patient was by his emotional immaturity and passive characteristics incapable of achieving normal masculinity and independence, and that the father, by his demanding, critical attitude, thwarted his own attempts to develop the son's independence. The patient now encountered the opportunity to drink, as does practically every boy, and discovered a certain social situation. He found that a premium of masculinity was put on hard drinking. It was regarded as manly to get drunk. Now the old cravings for gratifications by mouth had a reinforcing influence—the incentive to appear masculine. Thus by defying convention and laws, by spiting and defying his parents, and by emulating the other boys and older men who drank, he hoped to demonstrate he too was masculine and thus overcome the inferiority he had begun to feel on account of his passivity and childishness. That this was a spurious masculinity he was not able to realize. I believe that this combination of previous predisposition, inevitable encounter with drinking, and the incentive to demonstrate his masculinity in this way—a way fatal for him—may be found in most alcoholics. Now under the guise of proving himself a man the old infantile nursing pattern is fulfilled, for the pharmacological effect of the alcohol is such as to relieve his tensions in the same way that nursing and other oral gratifications did when he was a baby. All psychological distress resulting from feelings of inferiority for his passivity, from frustration and rage at thwarting, and from guilt for defiant spitefulness is assuaged by the new pacifier, alcohol. Not only this, but he can also recapture, through the pharmacological effect and through his own expectations, the infantile feeling of omnipotence and euphoria. Through the magic of the drug effect he can develop artificial self-confidence in his abilities along all lines. Our patient, like many other alcoholics, described the warm glow in his stomach which a few drinks would produce, a sensation which made him feel at peace with the world. The infantile satiety is thus repeated. It is not that he loves the taste of the potent alcoholic beverages; very few, if any, alcoholics ever do. He is drinking magic medicine for the psychological effect, an effect which is particularly essential for him, in contrast to normal social drinkers who are able to obtain equivalent satisfaction through achievement and other socially acceptable productive activity, and hence do not *need* alcohol, although they may frequently drink.

It is not necessary to give all the details of this patient's life history. He was typically and continuously dependent on his father financially. He brought incalculable grief and worry to his parents by his drunkenness, unaware that he was thus carrying out his defiance and spite against them for their supposed and actual thwarting and betrayal of him. Except temporarily in his sobering up periods when his parents and friends would plead with him, he did not comprehend how extensively he was debasing and destroying himself. He tried to demonstrate heterosexual potency from much the same motive that impelled him to start drinking, but was always unable to achieve any true affection for a girl because of the typical underlying resentment and contempt for women. He got married but was soon divorced. On his wedding day he dared not get drunk to fortify himself, but he drank a quart of sauerkraut juice because he had heard this beverage conveyed certain sexual potency. (Most of our alcoholics have been married and divorced at least once, illustrating their characteristic maladjustment with women.) Toward men he was consciously friendly and had many boon companions in his drinking bouts but few real friends. He showed the typical behavior of alcoholics toward men friends in drinking and getting tenderly affectionate with them, swearing eternal friendship, and becoming lovingly demonstrative toward them, thus acting out strong and often thinly disguised homosexual attraction. When he was sober, on the other hand, he feared he would be regarded as a "sissy" or a "fairy." After ten years of chronic alcoholism, repeated failures in marital and job adjustments, and several Keeley "cures," he finally came for treatment after strong pressure had been brought to bear on him by his parents. Although he agreed to come voluntarily, he made one last gesture. With the rationalization that he wanted us to be able to observe him at his worst and "drunkest," he drank steadily on his way to the sanitarium and arrived thoroughly intoxicated.

But let us return to the discussion of the psychology of the drinking as it develops into a chronic symptom. Gradually, often sporadically at first, the use of alcohol begins to enmesh itself in the entire emotional life of the alcoholic. Soon he is once more betrayed, as he felt himself betrayed in infancy by his mother—this time by the drug. It becomes increasingly difficult for him to attain just the right sense of well being, freedom from psychic distress, and narcissistic self-esteem, but he always hopes that one more drink will enable him to recapture this feeling. Ultimately the pharmacological effect wins and he passes into a stupor. Many times after such a drinking experience he will realize his betrayal, feel guilty and debased, condemn himself and be condemned by others, and repent and resolve to abstain from liquor forevermore. However, just as he was never able to surmount emotionally the earlier parental betrayal, so now he cannot maintain his resolve. Conflictual situations arise again as life imposes more demands and more difficult situations on him, and again he resorts to drinking. Finally the hangover effects themselves, with the associated guilt and inferiority, become intolerable, and, in desperation, he tries to deal with this unbearable distress in the same way—by more drinking, rationalizing this behavior by telling himself and others he is tapering off or just taking a bracer to put him on his feet. He is now certainly a chronic alcoholic. As he continues, what values—usually very unstable ones at best—he has built up so far in his vocation, in marriage, and in interpersonal relationships, begin to be destroyed. There are brief periods of realization of his plight, but the guilt and inferiority have become so great that further drinking now may be indulged in from motives of masochism and self-destruction to lessen this tension of guilt.

It is quite apparent that the patient has now gotten into a typical neurotic vicious circle, and one which is immensely complicated by the intertwining with it of the alcoholism. Let us describe this sequence. His childhood experiences have given him a personality characterized by excessive demands for indulgence. These demands are doomed to frustration in the world of adults. He reacts to the frustration with intolerable disappointment and rage. This reaction impels him to hostile acts and wishes against the thwarting individuals for which he then feels guilty and punishes himself masochistically. As reassurance against guilt feelings and fears of dangerously destructive masochism and reality consequences of his behavior, he feels excessive need for affection and indulgence as proof of affection. Again the excessive claims, doomed to frustration, arise, and the circle is complete. The use of alcohol as a pacifier for disappointment and rage, as a potent means of carrying out hostile impulses to spite his parents and friends, as a method of securing masochistic debasement, and as a symbolic gratification of the need for affection is now interweaving itself in the neurotic vicious circle.

I wish to conclude this presentation by discussing briefly the implications for treatment contained in the above formulations. It must be obvious that simple confinement and "de-alcoholizing," even though the confinement be prolonged over many months, do not in themselves provide an adequate method of treatment, for confinement only makes the presenting symptom, alcoholism, impossible by artificial means. The immature personality and the neurotic, childish behavior remain, thrown into bold relief by enforced sobriety and restriction. Some method of reeducation and of developing insight must be included in the treatment so that the patient may grow up emotionally. Institutionalization will usually be necessary for the severe cases in order to protect them from further drunkenness while reeducation is begun. In such reeducational treatment, it must early be demonstrated to the patient that his physician is not a critical, severe, moralizing antiliquor fanatic, but a man who understands him, likes him in spite of all past or future excesses, and wants to have him get satisfactions in life, but in a more real and less self-destructive manner. The vicious circle must be broken, and there are several places to break in on it. If the physician takes a condemnatory, moralizing attitude, he breaks in at the reaction of guilt and masochistic self-punishment followed by excessive demands by the patient. If this occurs, reeducation is impossible, and the patient's stay in the institution becomes a siege in which the physician must become increasingly strict and severe to thwart the patient's demands which led inevitably to excessive drinking at the first opportunity. From our experience—and we are confirmed by others who have successfully treated alcoholics—a different, very special type of rapport must be established between patient and physician. Realizing the patient's tremendous needs for indulgence, the physician must adopt a kindly, consistently indulgent attitude, granting those requests which are harmless in their consequences, and in all ways showing him that his physician wants him to have everything that will not harm him. Although liquor is denied him in the institution from the outset, the physician explains that for the time being harmless substitutes will serve much the same purpose, and the patient may have a coca-cola, orange juice, coffee, or milk whenever he wants a drink. Furthermore, the special type of rapport in itself acts as a further pacifier in getting the foothold to begin reeducation.

One of the first tasks in developing insight now can be carried out by skillful questioning designed to make the patient aware of all of the emotional tensions which have previously caused him to need a drink. The investigation of the life history will furnish many opportunities to point out maladjustments, childish behavior, neurotic traits, and fears, so that the patient may come to realize that his cure is much more than a matter of developing sufficient will power to stop drinking. He is then willing to be reconciled to treatment lasting at least a year, for he understands why such a long period is necessary.

As treatment continues, the patient warms up more and more to the physician—this kindly father surrogate—and begins to test him out by making increasing requests for privileges and indulgences; and here begins the most difficult stage of the treatment. Too much frustration will spoil the necessary tender relationship between patient and physician, and too much gratification will lead to experiments in drinking (which by now he feels he has under perfect control). The experiments almost invariably fail, for he drinks too much. However, such episodes are bound to occur, and the physician must never show disapproval or condemnation. We try to avoid having the special psychotherapist of the patient become involved in the granting of major privileges. The patient must go to another doctor with these requests. This doctor is supposed to represent the reality demands of the institutional community, and if the patient's behavior justifies his being granted the privilege, the hospital doctor grants it; if not, he refuses. Many complications are bound to arise in this arrangement, as the patient will try to get his psychotherapist to intercede for him with the hospital doctor. We believe this must be avoided.

When finally the patient is permitted to live outside the institution, get a job, and continue his reeducation, some drinking is likely to happen. Some spells of drunkenness will probably occur. Through it all the psychotherapist remains noncritical, inflicts no punishments, and endeavors to analyze the motives for the drinking. If the drinking becomes excessive and gets out of hand, the patient is brought back to the institution for further protection and the psychotherapy continues as before. If he can be carried through the drinking and continue to live outside, this is probably preferable. As successful treatment proceeds, the need for drinking becomes progressively less intense, and at the same time the patient is gradually growing up. It has been our experience that the form of treatment here briefly outlined, based as it is on an understanding of the psychodynamics delineated in this paper, offers the best chance of "curing" the chronic alcoholic.

PART II

Psychoanalytic Theories of Addiction

$W_{ITH\ THE}$ drug epidemic of the 1970s, there was an upsurge of interest in the study of addiction. Psychoanalysts built upon the theoretical concepts introduced by Radó and Glover regarding the importance of premorbid psychopathology in creating a vulnerability to addiction and the adaptive function of drugs, but moved away from the drive theory of addiction. Some support for these ideas had been provided by *The Road to H,* published in 1964,[1] the first major psychoanalytic investigation of addiction. Chein et al.,[2] studied adolescent heroin addicts and concluded that they had long-lasting, severe personality disturbances and that the addiction was adaptive and functional. Three emergent theoretical trends developed: (1) Wurmser and Krystal worked within a traditional conflict-theory approach (part II). (2) Gustafson (part III) and Khantzian (part VII) followed the deficiency theory of Kohut and viewed addiction as a variant of narcissistic disorder.[3] Both of these views kept the focus on premorbid personality factors of the addict as the cause of addiction. (3) Other psychoanalysts like Zinberg (part II) began to consider factors outside the traditional purview of psychoanalysis to understand addiction.

Wurmser is one of the modern pioneers in addiction treatment and has written extensively on the topic.[4] In the reprinted article, he posits that addicts are predisposed to addiction because of massive narcissistic disturbances in early childhood. In adolescence, these individuals experience a narcissistic crisis that propels an addictive search relieved by the use of the drug, and addiction is rapidly established. The reader will see many of the themes mentioned in the reprinted paper developed by other writers in this volume, including narcissistic problems in addicts, self-treatment of psychiatric problems by addicts (self-medication hypothesis), and hyposymbolization in addicts (problems in affect tolerance).

Krystal is a psychoanalyst with interests in both addiction and survivors of trauma, especially Holocaust survivors. He, as Wurmser, assumes addicts have severe premorbid psychopathology, which predisposes them to addiction. In the reprinted article, he states that addicts have suffered early infantile trauma, which creates difficulties in their affect development and lead to alexithymia. He feels addicts are blocked from exercising self-control in several areas because they cannot integrate the ambivalently held mother introject. He argues persuasively for a conflict explanation of this problem and offers a cogent critique of the self-psychological view of addiction. For a more detailed discussion of the role of affect tolerance in addiction, see his excellent papers, "The Genetic Development of Affects and Affect Regression" and "Affect Tolerance."[5,6,7,8] Zinberg challenges the assumption that premorbid personality problems are a primary cause of addiction. He argues that the lack of stimulus nutriment in addicts' lives causes their egos to regress and interferes with ego autonomy, applying important concepts of Rapaport.[9,10,11,12]

The Jacobs paper is quite different from the others in that it is an effort to forge an etiological theory of addiction from psychodynamic, learning theory, and physiological concepts. The paper has the virtue of linking diverse and relevant factors into an accessible theory of addiction, which in some respects is similar to Wurmser's.

Rosenthal's review of the psychodynamics on gambling provides the reader not only with the major psychoanalytic views of gambling, but offers the reader a history of the psychoanalytic theory of addiction since virtually all theories applied to substance addictions have been applied to gambling. It appears that psychodynamics, however, are more easily applied to this disorder than the substance addictions. Because the relationship between substance and nonsubstance addictions is not yet established, it is left to the reader to consider how similar gambling and other nonsubstance addictions are to the substance addictions.

With regard to contemporary theories of psychoanalysis, I take the stance of Pine[13] that drive theory, ego psychology, self psychology, and object relations theory all play an important role in the understanding and treatment of mental disorders, including addictions, but none is supercedent. Drive aspects of addiction theory relate to the finding that addicts often have a fixation at the oral level (Chafetz, Part V) and have excessive aggressive impulses (Glover, Part I). From the ego aspect of addiction theory, several writers have posited that certain ego functions are impaired in addicts (see Krystal, this part).[14] The self disturbances in addicts are reflected in their self-destructive behavior, their lack of capacity to regulate self-esteem, their extreme self-absorption, and the fragility of their sense of self.[15] Object relations aspects include the tendency for addicts to enact many episodes of their lives over and over again with little or no awareness of the original cause (Rosenthal, this part).

Ironically, it can be noted that the presentation of the addict, described in similar terms by Krystal, Zinberg, and Wurmser, is interpreted differently by each of the authors but in the end the recommended treatment approaches are not that different.

NOTES

1. Chein et al., 1964.

2. Chein et al., 1964, p. 194.

3. Kohut, the father of self-psychology, has two famous quotes on addiction, 1971, p. 46, and 1977, p. 197n. In the latter he explains the addiction as an effort to fill a structural void. In the former, he outlines the early traumatic relationship to the mother that predisposes the individual to addiction. Others writing from this perspective include H. P. Brown (1992), Chelton and Bonney (1987), Dodes (1988, 1990), Goodman (1993), Graham and Glickhauf-Hughes (1992), Levin (1987), Ulman and Paul (1989, 1990), and Van Schoor (1992).

4. Wurmser, 1974, 1977, 1978, 1984a, 1984b.

5. Krystal, 1974, 1975.

6. Krystal and Raskin, 1970, make therapeutic recommendations in *Drug Dependence: Aspects of Ego Functioning.*

7. Antabuse, referred to in the article, is a drug that blocks the metabolism of alcohol. An individual taking antabuse regularly will become violently ill if he drinks alcohol. If is often used as an adjunct to therapy to aid the alcoholic keep his resolve not to drink.

8. Morgenstern and Leeds (1993) compare and contrast the theories of Wurmser, Krystal, Khantzian, and McDougal in a concise and accurate manner. Dowling (1995) has edited an excellent collection of psychoanalytic papers on addiction that includes Khantzian, Wurmser, Krystal, and other contemporary psychoanalysts.

9. Zinberg cites Rappaport's "The theory of ego autonomy." Also relevant is Rappaport's 1951 paper, "The autonomy of the ego."

10. Bean (1986) suggests alcoholics suffer trauma as a result of their drinking, which adversely impacts on their personality functioning.

11. Kaufman, 1978, offers some support for the importance of social setting in the etiology of addiction in his report on opiate addicts from different social classes. He found that addicts from communities where drug use was normative (i.e., impoverished areas) were less psychiatrically disturbed than addicts from communities where it was not (i.e., middle class and higher). The finding suggests that psychoanalysts may be treating the more disturbed, higher social class addicts, and may be a cause of inadvertent bias toward assuming a greater frequency of severe pathology in addicts than is warranted.

12. Blatt et al., 1984, summarize the psychoanalytic theories of opiate addiction and relevant research findings.

13. Pine, 1990.

14. Chodorkoff, 1964, was the first to write about the impaired ego functions in the alcoholic. Khantzian, 1978, 1981; Krystal and Raskin, 1970. See Yalisove, 1992, for summary.

15. Levin, 1987; Van Schoor, 1992.

6. Psychoanalytic Considerations of the Etiology of Compulsive Drug Use

Leon Wurmser

Until now, there has been very little systematic exploration into the etiology of drug abuse. Glasscote et al. (1972) described the situation most aptly:

It may be fruitless to make the effort to identify a group of universal causes of susceptibility. In any case, while there has been some interest in determining what drug users are *like,* by means of interviews and standardized tests, there has been little systematic effort to delineate and quantify causes. On the other hand, there has been much *hypothesizing* about the conditions, events, and circumstances that lead to drug abuse, most of which fall into three categories: the physical, the internal or intrapsychic, and the social and environmental (p. 19).

A study to fill at least part of the gap is envisioned here: viz., to *delineate* in a systematic way the etiology of drug abuse on the basis of large-scale clinical experience with all types of this phenomenon.[1]

Inasmuch as most "drug abusers" are inaccessible to psychoanalysis proper, it is not surprising that, despite the huge upsurge over the last decade of drug abuse in general, and of intensive, compulsive drug use in particular, only a few psychoanalytic studies have appeared which could try to explore in depth the possible etiology of this illness. The contributions of Chein et al. (1964), Krystal and Raskin (1970), Wieder and Kaplan (1969), Dora Hartmann (1969), Savitt (1963), Panel (1970), Zinberg and Robertson (1972), and Khantzian et al. (1974) are notable examples. Earlier works—the essays of Rado (1926, 1933, 1963), Glover (1928, 1932), Savitt (1954), Limentani (1968), and the comments of Fenichel (1945), although still very interesting, seem outdated and barely applicable to most categories of drug abuse seen nowadays.

The question we intend to answer, then, is: What are the causes of drug abuse? This in turn raises the further question of what exactly is meant by

Reprinted by permission from *Journal of the American Psychoanalytic Association* 22, no. 4 (1974): 820–43. Copyright © International Universities Press, Inc.

"drug abuse." The term is so wide and imprecise, contains such a hodgepodge of clinical and social phenomena, and is so dependent on the bias of the observer, that a systematic study of its etiology would be as vast and comprehensive as an inquiry into the etiology of fever. It will therefore be necessary to define what we mean before embarking on our investigation.

SOME BASIC DISTINCTIONS AND DEFINITIONS

The usual definition of drug abuse is based simply on *sociolegal* criteria. According to Jaffe (1965), it is: "the use, usually by self-administration, of any drug in a manner that deviates from the approved medical or social patterns within a given culture" (p. 285). Jaffe narrows this broad definition by focusing on those "drugs that produce changes in mood and behavior." Similarly, Glasscote et al. (1972), apply the term drug abuse "to illegal, nonmedical use of a limited number of substances, most of them drugs, which have properties of altering the mental state in ways that are considered by social norms and defined by statute to be inappropriate, undesirable, harmful, threatening, or, at a minimum, culture alien" (pp. 3–4).

Such sociolegal definitions obviously carry strong connotations of moral judgment and are based on specific ethical values. I believe a further delimitation can be made if the problem is viewed psychiatrically: drug abuse is the use of any mind-altering drug for the purpose of inner change, if it leads to any transitory or long-range interference with social, cognitive, or motor functioning or with physical health, regardless of the legal standing of the drug. Here, the judgment is based on impaired functioning and thus on an observable medical criterion, vague though it might still be.

For most purposes, however, even this definition is unsatisfactory because of its breadth. For a careful study of etiology, we had better set apart all those occasional or irregular drug users in whom the impairment is merely transitory; this latter group seems particularly heterogeneous and contingent. Our starting point is thus the discernment of two groups placed on the two extremes of a continuum. At the one end, we have the _experimenters_ or casual users who represent the vast majority of participants in drug abuse (according to both definitions given above)—probably 90 per cent. They present, medically and psychiatrically, very few and rare problems. Yet, much of the public's attention, the law's concerns and energies, the preventive efforts, are dedicated to these people. The experimenter takes a mind-altering drug a few times and feels he does not really need and require its effect. Out of curiosity, and just as much in order to avoid shame by not conforming with the adolescent peer group, he wants to prove that he has partaken of the initiation, that he knows what it is all about.

At the other end of the continuum, we have the *compulsive* drug abuser. He is the real problem. To him applies the statement that drug use is just a symptom of deep underlying problems. Only those relatively few experimenters proceed to compulsive drug abuse who carry the set of profound deficiencies and conflicts that we are going to explore in this study. It is the compulsive drug abuser who feels that the drug-induced state relieves him of what bothers him and gives him what he is missing, so that he feels unable to renounce the "high," regardless of dangers and threats he is usually fully cognizant of.

In the broad area between these two groups we encounter the so-called *recreational* user of drugs like alcohol or marijuana. For many recreational users the goal is merely relaxation, not intoxication; the amount of the active substance is so small that no interference with motor or mental functioning is noticeable. In many more so-called recreational users, the goal is indeed occasional or frequent intoxication. They usually claim that their temporary abdication of rational controls is an entirely free, noncompulsive activity. I have not reached any final conclusion about this group, but on the basis of my clinical experience, I would associate the first type of recreational users, the relaxers, with the experimenters, the second type, those striving to get "stoned," "high," or "down," with the compulsive users.[2]

COMPULSIVENESS

We turn now to this problem of "compulsive drug abuse" (cf. also Jaffe, 1965; Glasscote et al., 1972).

Of course, the question arises: How far is this compulsiveness of a physical nature? Is that not just what led to the prohibition of these drugs in the first place — that they induce inevitably or at least very often a physiologic dependence which henceforth cannot be broken?

If we carefully study, on the one side, history and treatment experience and, on the other side, the interesting observations in medically and psychiatrically induced addictions, (e.g., when opiates were used to treat melancholics), we are forced to assign very little valence in the long range to this factor of physical dependence. In other words, as Hamlet said, "the readiness is all."

Those who work closely with compulsive drug users observe time and again that if their drug of predilection is taken away (or more precisely, if their drug effect of choice is removed), they sooner or later tend to substitute other symptoms. Neurotic depression and suicidal attempts, acts of violence, stealing, running away, severe attacks of anxiety, found prior to the use of drugs and sometimes accompanying the full-blown drug use, once the resorting to drugs is blocked, frequently reappear in exacerbated form and are often more destructive than drug use itself. Still more frequently, we encounter the replacement of a suddenly unavailable type of drug by a pharmacologically completely unrelated class: i.e., patients deprived of narcotics typically resort to alcohol and sedatives (especially barbiturates), which have no bearing on any physical withdrawal phenomena, but solely on the psychological need for a drug-induced relief. In other words, compulsive drug use is merely one symptom among others, the expression of an underlying disturbance, not the illness itself.

One implication of this observation is, of course, that the really difficult task in treating these patients is not the withdrawal from drugs, but the coping with the emotional need to use a drug, to use any drug, and to use many other equally harmful external means, to find relief. In other words: I have never yet seen a compulsive drug user who has not been emotionally deeply disturbed, who has not shown in his history the ravages of borderline, or even psychotic conflicts and defects. Only secondarily do we encounter the devastations caused by the drugs themselves. We may go one step farther: Not only do we encounter many other signs of pervasive severe psychopathology—most frequently of the borderline type—but the very criterion used to single out this group as compulsive drug users, namely "compulsiveness," leads us straight into the tangled thicket of how to define psychological health and illness, since this observable quality of compulsiveness or peremptoriness has been used by several psychoanalytic theoreticians (notably Waelder, 1936 and Kubie, 1954) to define illness: "The essence of normality is flexibility in all of these vital ways. The essence of illness is the freezing of behavior into unalterable and insatiable patterns. It is this which characterizes every manifestation of psychopathology, whether in impulse, purpose, act, thought, or feelings" (Kubie, 1961, pp. 20–21). Our "habitués" are, without exception, paradigms for people overwhelmed with such "unalterable and insatiable patterns."

HIERARCHY OF CAUSES

Even if we select an apparently homogeneous group, e.g., narcotics addicts, we still are bewildered by the variety of causes and, correspondingly, the vast array of proffered, discussed, and disputed cause-and-effect relationships. We may try to discern layers of causes (or, to be more precise, layers of reasons [Schafer, 1973, p. 268]), ordered according to causative specificity, and start off with a superficial distinction between two factors that always appear to be present: The first is a psychological hunger or "craving," which we might describe as the *addictive search*—an entire group of activities, predating, accompanying, and following the compulsive drug use; they all are used to provide external relief for an internal urge of overpowering drivenness. We refer to activities such as irresistible violence, food addiction, gambling, alcohol use, indiscriminate "driven" sexual activity, or running away. The second factor is the more or less contingent, even accidental entrance of various drugs, in forms of both accessibility and seduction. This factor we shall call the *adventitious entrance of drugs*.

Behind this phenomenological distinction we can perceive a logical and historical structure of causes which we now examine, viewing them as a hierarchy of causes of various specificity. As is very often the case with such differentiations, what in this analysis is torn asunder into various groups and layers of reasons is in reality a continuum, ranging from high to low specificity.

Freud (1895) distinguished four types of causes for an emotional disorder: (a) precondition; (b) specific cause; (c) concurrent cause; and (d) precipitating cause. This distinction seems to have been an original contribution of Freud to the philosophy of causation. With it, he tried to apply the basic concepts of accidental, necessary, and sufficient causes—which had originated with Aristotle and had been developed by d'Alembert, Leibnitz, and Schopenhauer—to the problems of motivation, in particular, to the causation of emotional illness. He used a precursor of this four-part model in Draft B (1893), replacing it later on by the concept of the complementary series (Sherwood, 1969).

I was not able to consider all the philosophical roots, merits, or weaknesses of this model as a basic logical concept, but I feel it may serve us heuristically better than other models of causation. Some of the following layers will be explored more in detail later on.

a. A cardinal, indispensable, but broad layer of reasons is the precondition: "The factors which may be described as *preconditions* are those in whose absence the effect would never come about, but which are incapable of producing the effect by themselves alone, no matter in what amount they may be present" (Freud, 1895, p. 136). Applied to our problem, these inevitable

preconditions can be located in a life history of massive narcissistic disturbances and in a rather specific pattern of family pathology. I describe this in
more detail below (cf. also Wurmser, 1972a, 1972b). Here, it should be only
stated that the narcissistic conflicts referred to pertain to massively overval-
ued images of self and others. The term narcissistic is used in the (precise)
psychoanalytic sense of Freud (1914), Kohut (1971, 1972), Kernberg (1970),
and Pulver (1970), namely, to denote an archaic overvaluation of the self or
of others, a host of grandiose expectations, and the abyssmal sense of frustration and letdown if these hopes are shattered.

b. "The *specific* cause is the one which is never missing in any case in
which the effect takes place, and which moreover suffices, if present in the
required quantity or intensity, to achieve the effect, provided only that the
preconditions are also fulfilled" (Freud, 1895, p. 136).

Most people would now be inclined to seek the specific reason for compulsive drug use in the temptations by peers or pushers. I believe this would be
misleading; it is, though semantically correct, clinically and theoretically
wrong. We earlier differentiated "addictive illness" and "adventitious" appearance of the drug, and can now repeat that we find an emotional illness
brewing independently, whether the drug enters or not. The specificity for its
outbreak in manifest form lies in an experience of overwhelming *crisis,*
accompanied by intense emotions like disillusionment and rage, depression,
or anxiety, in an *actualization* of a lifelong massive conflict about omnipotence and grandiosity, meaning and trust—what we have just described as a
narcissistic conflict. This actualization inevitably leads to massive emotional
disruption and thus to the addictive search. In other words, if we focus on the
illness "addictive syndrome," the specific reason is a more or less acute
external and internal crisis bringing about an exacerbation of a narcissistic
disturbance. We may call this a *"narcissistic crisis."* In contrast, if we focus
on the *symptom* "drug abuse," we are wiser to talk about precipitating, rather
than specific reasons, a category I shall mention shortly. Even without the
advent of the drug itself, we still have the characteristic seeking for a way
out, for an escape, a driven desperate attempt to find a crutch outside of
oneself.

Much vaguer and several steps removed are the reasons ("causes") that
litter the literature, all of which we can put in the next category. Their nature
is very unspecific, broad, of little predictive value. They are shared by many
who do not join in the illness, and vice versa. Yet, they indeed are the only
reasons (and indeed "causes") which epidemiological and sociological studies
are apt to find. The statistical methods employed by these disciplines tend to

bring out the background factors leading to heightened incidence, but not the more specific correlations.

c. "As *concurrent causes* we may regard such factors as are not necessarily present every time, nor able, whatever their amount, to produce the effect by themselves alone, but which operate alongside of the preconditions and the specific cause in satisfying the aetiological equation" (Freud, 1895, p. 136).

The most general of these concurrent reasons are widespread value conflicts in our culture and basic philosophical questions about the limitations of human existence. One crucial element is the conflict between democratic philosophies, postulating the dissolution of most external representatives of the superego, the increasing abolition of the restraining powers of authority and tradition, of external structures and restraints, and totalitarian philosophies, imposing the most tyrannical forms of such authority and power. Drugs are for many the shibboleth of liberation from authority, a symbol of protest and extreme privacy ("doing one's own thing").

A second element is the paradox with regard to mastery and domination of our outer and inner life: most of the ancient dreams of mankind about outer control have been fulfilled, whereas most of the techniques used in the past to gain an (albeit often spurious) sense of inner mastery and control have been discarded. Drugs provide a sense of magical domination and manipulation over one's inner life, analogous to that which science and technique appear to have over the outside.

Another socially more relevant value conflict is that between easy pleasure, immediate material gratification, and indulgence versus the often bizarre harshness of the responses by representatives of punitive and often corrupt authority (the death penalty for some small drug sales, sentences of 25 years for the giving away of one marijuana cigarette, entrapment and degradation of drug users by law enforcement officials). Thus, belonging to a drug-using countergroup can serve as protest against a profound inconsistency in the cultural fabric.

Another such factor may be the changed role of genital sexuality. For many, easily accessible sexuality is a source, not of anxiety, despair, and commitment, but of tedium and routine. The denied, split-off emotions involved in sexual yearnings are sought instead in other avenues, particularly with the help of pharmaca. Moreover, we might wonder how much the shallowness of, and presentation of shortcuts to, gratification by television, viewed for many hours daily from early childhood on and thus substituting a passive form of presentation for the development of an active fantasy life, may contribute to this search for easy stimulation (Grotjahn, 1971).

But most of all, we have to cite the social factors in the slums: social degradation, overcrowding, and overload in stimuli (especially noise and violence); the socially important role of the drug-using peer group as a substitute for the lacking family structure; and the even more relevant function of the drug traffic, and the black market needed to feed it, as an economic equalizer between ghetto and dominant middle-class society. All in all— these are unspecific broad factors—valid as much for occasional and recreational users (if indeed not more so) as for compulsive drug users.

Finally, we have to return to what I described phenomenologically as the "entrance of the drug" and labeled *"adventitious"*:

d. ". . . we may characterize as the *precipitating* or releasing cause the one which makes its appearance last in the equation, so that it immediately precedes the emergence of the effect. It is this chronological factor alone which constitutes the essential nature of a precipitating cause" (Freud, 1895, pp. 135–136).

We would assign the previously mentioned easy availability of drugs and the seduction by peers to this category ("social compliance" [cf. Hartmann, 1939]). The *advent* of the drug suddenly allows the previous desperate search to crystallize around the one object and activity that relieves the unbearable tension. In sum: there is no compulsive drug use without this trigger factor; but there is still an overriding emotional compulsiveness directed toward other activities and objects. It can be assumed that only the latter two sets of factors (concurrent and precipitating ones) are identical for experimenters and compulsive users alike.

CLINICAL OBSERVATIONS ABOUT PRECONDITIONS AND SPECIFIC REASONS

We turn now to a more detailed study of the first two sets of factors: what has been found so far in regard to the essential personality structure predisposing to, and the acute crisis immediately evoking drug use, and how these factors are matched by the pharmacological effect of various drugs.

The psychological factors of impulsiveness and low frustration tolerance are well known and undisputed. I should like to attempt an analysis that goes beyond these sweepingly general characterizations and may open the way to a deeper understanding of some actions and attitudes of these patients (perhaps of "sociopaths" in general?). Much is vague, tentative, even contradictory in what follows. Large gaps need to be filled. Careful longitudinal studies in depth, particularly in psychotherapy, psychoanalysis, and family research are needed to advance our knowledge.[3]

The Defect of Affect Defense

We start with what I believe to be the most important concept in a dynamic understanding of drug use. I consider all compulsive drug use an *attempt at self-treatment.*[4] The importance of the effect of the drug in the inner life of these patients can perhaps be best explained as an *artificial or surrogate defense against overwhelming affects.* Moreover, there evidently exists some specificity in the choice of the drug for this purpose. Patients prefer those drugs which specifically help them to cope with the affects that trouble them most.

In the past, the satisfying, wish-fulfilling aspects of the drug effects have been emphasized. To put this in a catch phrase: drug use was seen as an expensive search for a cheap pleasure. This is certainly the popular and unreflective concept of why people take drugs. Earlier analytic theoreticians (Glover, 1932; Rado, 1926, 1933, 1963) subscribed to this idea, except that they saw in drug use, as in other symptoms, the satisfaction of unconscious wishes.

In other psychological studies of drug abuse, the focus was on the symbolic (again chiefly wish-fulfilling) meaning of drug intake as such (as oral supplies, illusory penis, or its self-destructive, self-punitive aspects) with little regard for the psychodynamic impact of the pharmacological effects themselves.

The view that drug use is an escape has also been popularly held, but largely with regard to intolerable external situations. The concept of the need for drugs as a defense against intolerable internal factors—and, more specifically, affects—has been described but scarcely until a very few years ago. Most tragically, legislation and public policy totally disregard this central factor.

Homer sang of Helena having "drugged the wine with an herb that overcomes all grief and anger and lets forget everything bad."

Freud (1930), too, described narcotics as a means of coping with pain and disillusionment. Glover (1932) was explicit with regard to "drug addiction" (referring to cocaine, paraldehyde, and presumably also to opiate addictions): "Its defensive function is to control sadistic charges, which, though less violent than those associated with paranoia, are more severe than the sadistic charges met with in obsessional formations" (p. 202) and: "Drug addiction acts as a protection against psychotic reaction in states of regression" (p. 203). In turn, he saw in unconscious homosexual fantasy systems "a restitutive or defensive system . . . [acting] as a protection against anxieties of the addiction type" (p. 203).

Rado (1963) named this aspect of affect defense "narcotic riddance" and opposed it to what he called "narcotic pleasure" and "narcotic intoxication" (a climactic sense of triumphant success). Fenichel (1945, p. 380) wrote: ". . . the addiction can be looked upon as a last means to avoid a depressive breakdown. . . ." Similarly, Chein et al. (1964) have described the "opiate's capacity to inhibit or blunt the perception of inner anxiety and outer strain. . . . In this sense, the drug itself is a diffuse pharmacological defense" (p. 233). Dora Hartmann (1969) pointed out that the conscious motivation for the use of drugs was in most cases "the wish to avoid painful affects (depression), alleviate symptoms, or a combination of these factors" (p. 389).

Wieder and Kaplan (1969) describe the drug of choice as "acting as a psychodynamic-pharmacogenic 'corrective' or 'prosthesis' " (p. 401). Their approach is almost identical to the one here suggested. They write:

> Chronic drug use, which we believe always occurs as a consequence of ego pathology, serves in a circular fashion to add to this pathology through an induced but unconsciously sought ego regression. The dominant conscious motive for drug use is not the seeking of "kicks," but the wish to produce pharmacologically a reduction in distress that the individual cannot achieve by his own psychic efforts (p. 403).

Krystal and Raskin (1970) emphasize the dedifferentiated, archaic, resomatized nature of the affect; because of the traumatic nature of affects in such persons, "drugs are used to avoid impending psychic trauma in circumstances which would not be potentially traumatic to other people" (p. 31).

The idea of defense against affects is also a well-known analytic concept and has been elaborated by Jones (1929), Anna Freud (1936), Fenichel (1934), and Rapaport (1953).

In all categories of compulsive drug use, the preeminence of archaic, chiefly narcissistic, conflicts is evident; what changes are some of the affects presenting the most immediate problem to the patient concerned. These affects are close to consciousness, are not really repressed, but cannot be articulated for a reason I shall subsequently describe.

Narcotics and barbiturates apparently calm intense feelings of rage, shame, and loneliness and the anxiety evoked by these overwhelming feelings.[5] In the words of a 22-year-old white heroin addict:

Everything in my life has to have its peak. I cannot accept things for what they are. The actual happening is a letdown compared to the anticipation. It seems then as if all of life comes down on me—in a sense of total despair. Then my first reaction is to get me some dope—not to forget, but to put me farther away from the loneliness, estrangement, and emptiness. I still feel empty and lonely when I am on dope, but it does not seem to matter as much. All is foggy and mixed up.

Heroin, for him, was a cure for disillusionment. He went so far as to say: "Heroin saved my life. I would have jumped out of the window—I felt so lonely." He wants to re-create the feeling of full acceptance and union, a fantasy whose reality he postulates as having characterized his early childhood; "I was given everything. I had a protector. Later, I realized I did not have it anymore: no protector, no shield—only myself" (Wurmser, 1972b).

This effect can be witnessed with particular clarity in patients who are put on methadone maintenance—especially if they are followed in psychotherapy both during periods of abstinence and while on the narcotic. I have seen 19 such patients in intensive psychotherapy, 14 of them for a prolonged period (several months to several years). A summary of these observations (Wurmser, 1972b) follows.

All the patients described feelings of loneliness, emptiness, and depression, of meaninglessness and pervasive boredom preceding drug use and following withdrawal. In all of them, very intense feelings of murderous rage and vengefulness; or of profound shame, embarrassment, and almost paranoid shyness; or of hurt, rejection, and abandonment, were discovered during psychotherapy. In all of them, these feelings of rage, shame, and hurt were reduced as soon as they were on methadone; in a few of them, they disappeared altogether; in some, they still occurred occasionally, but had a less overwhelming quality. Some of the patients said the drug made them feel normal and relaxed—implying that they felt those pervasive feeling states to be abnormal, sick, intolerable. Others said it helped them "not to think of the depression." Several said they felt bored, but that they preferred this to the overwhelming feelings before. The patient quoted above had this to say about methadone maintenance:

At least I do not *feel* that superlonely and excluded; I feel more at ease, although empty and bored. I still cannot be with people, but I can cope with the loneliness better. It keeps me from a showdown with myself; from the dilemma either to destroy myself completely or to move in a new direction without the aid of anything. . . . When I stop methadone, I cannot put up with any frustration. I cannot get enjoyment out of anything. I get frantic about every problem.

It was obvious that in none of these patients were the underlying inner problems resolved, but that the dampening of the mood disorder brought about by methadone was experienced as a great relief. Both the resulting boredom and the insufficient relief from the underlying conflicts led most of them to occasional or habitual use of other drugs while on methadone: mainly cocaine, Ritalin, or alcohol. (Since 1970, when most of these observations were made, the preference has shifted to Quaalude, Valium—and, still, alcohol.) One girl continued using barbiturates and eventually succeeded in killing herself with sedatives (albeit after discharge from methadone maintenance), quite in line, incidentally, with her mother's expectations, who had years before bought a cemetery plot for this, her youngest daughter, then in her late teens.

These patients try to re-establish an omnipotent position wherein either their self is grandiose and without limitations or where the other person ("the archaic self-object" of Kohut [1971]) is treated as all-giving and is required to live up to the highest ideals. As soon as limitations are imposed, the archaic emotions mentioned before emerge; they are uncontrollable and remind us much of those in psychotics. Rage is the most prominent one. Typically, this narcissistic rage is close to murderous or suicidal dimensions: when the ideal self or the ideal world has collapsed, only total devastation remains. Shame is the second one. It is the outcome of the conflict between the limited, disappointing self and the grandiose, ideal self. Hurt, loneliness, rejection, abandonment, the third basic emotion in these patients, is the outcome of the experience that the other person (mother, father, girl friend, boy friend) is not as great and redeeming, as all-giving as expected; anything short of total union with this person is experienced as total isolation and rejection. The importance of narcotics, including methadone, lies in their effect of reducing or even eliminating these basic three affects.

All patients describe states of craving after past or current withdrawal. The real content of this craving (after the physiologic symptoms have subsided) consists precisely in the upsurge of these most disturbing affects. The craving can be equated to a rapid narcissistic decompensation and the breakthrough of those archaic feelings evoked by a most massive sense of narcissistic frustration. In a few, this breakthrough is even experienced as fragmentation. The reinstatement of methadone leads to a prompt recompensation.

Psychedelic drugs counteract the emotional state of emptiness, boredom, and meaninglessness. The drug-induced illusion that the self is mystically boundless and grandiose and that the world becomes endowed with unlimited meaning seems to be a direct antidote to the pervasive sense of disillusionment in the ideal other person. It artificially re-creates ideals and values when they have been irreparably shattered inside and outside. It is important that this artificial ideal formation has a peculiarly passive-receptive ring, most like the identification with a hero in a movie or on TV. Indeed, there seems to be a remarkable similarity between the psychedelic experience and the turning on and tuning in to TV; several patients actually compare it to an inner movie.

Amphetamines and cocaine have superficially much in common with what I just described with regard to psychedelics in that they also eliminate boredom and emptiness. But these more or less conscious affects appear mostly to be caused by repression of feelings of rage, whereas with the compulsive users of psychedelics these moods are induced by the collapse of ideals without the same prominence of aggression. Accordingly, these stimulants provide a sense of aggressive mastery, control, invincibility, and grandeur, whereas the psychedelics impart a sense of passive merger through the senses. But there is more to it: The amphetamine effect serves as a defense against a massive depression or general feelings of unworthiness and weakness. In the few cases of compulsive amphetamine abuse which I was able to treat in intensive psychotherapy, long-term abstinence was accompanied by intense self-directed aggression, in some by suicidal rage and despair, in others by lethargy and self-degradation. Thus, amphetamine abuse can, at least in some patients, be called an artificial normalizing or even manic defense against the underlying affect of depression.

In all three categories, the intended functioning of the pharmacological effect itself as a *defense* against intense affects is quite certain and supported by statements from many other observers. Also, there is good clinical evidence to show some specificity in the correlation between drug choice and affect combatted. But the nature of this *pharmacogenic defense* is less clear. The affects themselves are of heterogeneous origin, but never just of "signal" nature; they are always of massive, "unneutralized," overwhelming character. Their connection with narcissistic conflicts is far more evident than with conflicts in object relations.

Just as the warded-off affects are of global and overwhelming nature, so is the pharmacogenic defense. I do not think that the latter can simply be identified with other well-known defense mechanisms, e.g., denial, or externalization. Yet, is it a defense *sui generis?* Is it a particular form of splitting? Or does it simply support a welter of well-known and individually varying defense mechanisms? The nature of this defense needs a separate, systematic study.

From this most cursory and tentative survey, we recognize the central role of *narcissistic conflicts* in all types of compulsive drug use. The choice of the drug of preference—often found only after long shopping around—is specifically related to the affects engendered by these conflicts: when the inner structures fail as defenses, the pharmacogenic effect has to serve this purpose of inner barrier.

If we suppress this attempt at self-treatment without massive support to the patient's ego, we often force him into more serious forms of decompensation: violent, even homicidal, rage in the narcotics addict, severe suicidal depression in the amphetamine user, a careless apathetic drifting in the user of psychedelics.

What has been described in these thoughts about the artificial defense is consonant with Kohut's (1971) statement: "The drug . . . serves not as a substitute for loved or loving objects, or for a relationship with them, but as a replacement for a defect in the psychological structure" (p. 46), although there are indications that drugs, drug effects, and ambience are not as devoid of object character as Kohut appears to state.

It should be noted, finally, that both defense and wishfulfillment are relative concepts. Gill (1963) pointed out convincingly that every defense is simultaneously the fulfillment of a wish: ". . . a behavior is a defense in relation to a drive more primitive than itself, and a drive in relation to a defense more advanced than itself" (pp. 122–123).

Faulty Formation of Ego Ideal

Another aspect, implicit in some of what I have already described, is the *superego pathology,* the lack of meaning-giving, life-determining, life-guiding values and ideals, or, in their personified form, all-powerful myths. The affects just described usually emerge during or following a crisis wherein such central values, ideals, and myths have been shattered or when the need for such an ideal has become particularly prominent, its absence or unreliability particularly painful. And here the family pathology enters.

The following comments do not do justice to the importance of family pathology as etiological factors; a separate study is in preparation (cf. also Chein et al., 1964). The crucial factors in the family pathology appear, to date, to be consistency, setting of limits, and trustworthiness versus narcissistic indulgence and rage. Parents who did not provide a minimum of consistency, of reliability, of trustworthiness, of responsiveness to the child, especially during his developmental crises, are not usable as inner beacons; instead they become targets of rebellious rage and disdain. Parents who vacillate between temper tantrums and indulgence, who allow themselves to live out their most primitive demands, parents who are more interested in their careers and their clubs and travels than in their children's needs to have them available, or parents who are absent for economic reasons and cannot impart the important combination of love and of firmness—all these parents, unless replaced in their crucial functions by capable substitutes, make it very difficult for their children to accept them as secure models for conscience and ego ideal, to internalize them, and to build them up as inner guardians against transgressions. It is my impression that the ego ideal in patients having such parents has remained archaic, unreliable, global; more mature parts quickly collapse during adolescence or never emerge.

The "high," the relief and pleasure sought with the help of the drug, is a surrogate ideal, a substitute value, a chemical mythology, which normally would be supplied by the internal sense of meaning, goal-directedness, and value orientation. Moreover, peer group, drug culture and, most of all, the "hustling" itself, the whole chasing after the drug, and the ideal of the successful pusher who can beat the hated establishment (particularly in the ghetto), are powerfully determining models and values (cf. Preble & Casey, 1969).

The next aspect is the least secure and most presumptive one; yet, it may prove to be easier to observe and even quantify than the others.

Hyposymbolization

With this, I refer to the frequent observation of a general degradation, contraction, or rudimental development of the processes of symbolization and, with that, of the fantasy life. This curtailed ability or inability to symbolize pertains particularly to the patient's inner life, his emotions, his self-references. One example of this is the inability of most of these patients to articulate feelings. Many, if not all, relevant affects are translated into somatic complaints—e.g., craving and physical discomfort—or into social accusations—"It's all society's fault." They remain preverbal as affects. The same constriction seems to hold true for the entire fantasy life. It is just this lacuna—whether it is a conflict-induced scotoma, or a genuine deficiency—which makes psychotherapy so particularly difficult and frustrating. After all, psychotherapy employs precisely the verbal band out of the spectrum of symbolic processes as its instrument. Tentatively, I dub this defect "hyposymbolization"; I consider it identical with what I found in Blos' (1971) concept of "concretization." Obviously, drugs do not function as a substitute for the lacking symbolization; nor do most enrich the impoverished fantasy life (except for what Louis Lewin [1924] called the Phantastica, i.e., the psychedelic drugs). Rather, their function lies in removing that vague discomfort and tension which replaces the not perceived and not articulated affect and is experienced as "something wrong" in the body or the environment. Thus, the drugs are employed to alter body image and world image into a less unpleasant and more meaningful one.

Archaic Object Dependency

We have so far examined the psychodynamic role of the various pharmacological effects of these drugs. There is a further dynamic implication which is very important and far better known than these three: "Among *the unconscious motivations* (in addition to oral gratification and passive identification with a parent), the need to replace a lost object seemed to play a very important role" (D. Hartmann, 1969, p. 389). Many patients talk about their drug and the paraphernalia and circumstances surrounding it with a loving tenderness, as if it were a love partner. Obviously, it is the *object character* of the drug that assumes a central motivating power here rather than its pharmacological character. Actually, the very term, "drug dependency" reminds us of what we are dealing with, namely an *archaic passive dependency* on an all-giving, sempiternal, though narcissistically perceived—i.e., hugely inflated—object, as is evidenced by the singleminded devotedness and frenzy of the chase after the beloved, in the incorporative greed, the masturbatory and orgiastic aspects of the use, and in the mixture of ecstatic idealization and deprecation vis-à-vis the drug ("star dust," "blue heavens," "white lady" versus "shit," "scag") (Wieder & Kaplan, 1969; Chein et al., 1964). Much of this reminds us of *fetishism.* Dynamic similarities and dissimilarities between these two syndromes need to be worked out: Do we find a similar split of the ego in addictive illness to the one described in fetishism? Glover implicitly raised this question in 1932; ". . . in the transition between paranoidal systems and a normal reaction to reality, drug addiction (and later on fetishism) represent not only continuations of the anxiety system within a contracted range, but the beginnings of an expanding reassurance system" (p. 211). He called fetishism the companion problem of addiction.

The problem raised by Kohut (1959, 1971) remains unsolved: Is this obvious relationship to archaic, easily replaceable part objects only secondary, and is it accurate to explain the dependence on drugs primarily not "as a substitute for object relations but as a substitute for psychological structure" (Kohut, 1959, p. 476)? In many cases this hypothesis seems to be borne out. Yet in others where a symbiotic relation or the dedication to a treatment community completely supplants a former drug dependence, I am quite inclined to see in the latter also an archaic, narcissistically experienced object relation.

Self-destructiveness

Very well known is the self-destructive, self-punitive aspect of drug abuse (Glover, 1932). In some cases, we may observe the direct equivalency of drug use with suicide. If we take the first away, the second may become the menace. Drug abuse in itself can often (not always) be considered a tamed and protracted suicidal attempt, though we have to be cautious not to fall into the pitfall of the teleological fallacy *(post hoc, proper hoc).* In line with the other aspect of superego pathology, described above, where the faulty ideal formation was underlined, we may now add the important role of archaic forms of shame and guilt—as reflected (but not recognized) in many of the vindictive measures used at Synanon and other therapeutic communities, as well as in most of our legislation (Wurmser, 1973a, 1973b; Wurmser et al., 1973). There is no question that very primitive and global fears of humiliation and revenge play a dominant role in the social interaction of these patients; these are usually not simply the consequence of society's reaction, but part of the patient's make-up to begin with. The vindictiveness and corruptibility of the archaic superego is well known and is easily observed among our patients. This dynamic datum, however, is so frequent and general that I assign it a very low specificity for this type of pathology.

Regressive Gratification

This aim of drug use, also mentioned by Homer (*Odyssey,* Book IX, 90–97), has been studied most extensively. My previous emphasis, especially on the notion of the artificial affect defense, has been used to counterbalance the historical emphasis on this aspect. Both are obviously two sides of the same coin.

From all the forms of regressive gratifications attained with the help of the drug, it appears that the increase in self-esteem, the re-creation of a regressive *narcissistic state of self-satisfaction* is the most consistent one. This is partic-ularly relevant when we see this aim of drug use as an integral part of the narcissistic crisis which typically marks the onset of compulsive drug use and to which we now turn.

Narcissistic Crisis

As discussed earlier, the specific reason for the onset of compulsive drug use lies in an acute crisis in which the underlying narcissistic conflicts are mobilized and the affects connected with these conflicts break in with overwhelming force and cannot be coped with without the help of an artificial affect defense.

Such a mobilization quite typically first occurs during adolescence, rarely earlier, and still more rarely later. Often the relapse from abstinence into drug use is regularly marked by the recurrence of such a crisis—which in turn is usually triggered by an external event's setting in motion the juggernaut of pervasive anxieties, rages, and narcissistic demands. This narcissistic crisis is thus the point at which the conflicts and defects converge with a particular external situation and with the availability of the seeming means of solution: the drug. By definition, a "narcissistic crisis" would have to entail a particularly intense disappointment in others, in oneself, or in both—so intense because of the exaggerated hopes, and so malignant because of its history's reaching back to very early times. Precipitating external events of such a crisis can most typically be found in family crises, coinciding with the maturational crisis of adolescence.

CONCLUSIONS: THE ETIOLOGICAL EQUATION

It appears very likely that it is the convergence of at least some, if not all, of six elements—massive defect of affect defense, the defect in value formation, the hyposymbolization, the desperate search for an object substitute, the intensely self-destructive qualities, and the search for regressive gratification—together with the intensity of the underlying narcissistic conflicts that forms the *predispositional* constellation for the "addictive illness" in general and for compulsive drug use in particular. It appears that the most specific of these predispositional factors are the need for affect defense and the compelling wish for regressive gratification; but only further research, including predictive studies, can elucidate the relative relevance of these six factors.

The *specific* reason is the mobilization of the underlying narcissistic conflict in what I called the narcissistic crisis.

The *precipitating* reason is the advent of the drug on stage, functioning only like the crucial though irrelevant messenger in the antique tragedy, a hapless catalyst: "I that do bring the news made not the match" (*Antony and Cleopatra,* II, V, 67).

Some or all of the six predispositional factors described may be *necessary reasons.* The *combination* of the *narcissistic crisis* (specific reason)—viz. a consequence of these predispositions, mobilized by maturational and environmental factors—with the *adventitious entrance* of the drug (precipitating reason) represents the *sufficient reason.*

It appears appropriate to end with two quotations that emphasize the necessity of etiological analysis. The first is from Vergil's *Georgica II: "Felix qui potuit rerum cognoscere causas"* (Fortunate is he who has been able to recognize the causes of things). The second is from Bacon's *Novum Organum, I* (1620) and was in a sense the motto opening up the time of progress in science and technology: *"Scientia et potentia humana in idem coincidunt quia ignoratio causae destituit effectum"* (Human knowledge and power coincide in that regard that ignorance of cause prevents effective intervention).

NOTES

1. During the last nine years, I have seen about 40 patients in intensive, mostly psychoanalytically oriented psychotherapy, many for years and up to 400 hours; I have worked with about a dozen families of such patients, seen close to 1,000 patients (mainly narcotics addicts) in evaluations, group therapy, crisis intervention, while being clinically or administratively in charge of three drug abuse treatment programs (a program of compulsory abstinence from 1964 to 1968, a comprehensive treatment center with several modalities from 1969 to 1971, and a methadone maintenance program from 1971 to the present). For a time I had a small private practice devoted almost exclusively to this type of patient. Notes in shorthand were taken during all individual interviews and treatment sessions, and formed the essential basis for the following attempt to systematize these data.

2. Similar considerations apply to the use of drugs for specific stressful situations: combat, examination, long-distance driving.

3. Explorations with the help of psychoanalytic or psychotherapeutic treatment are the only methods known today allowing a comprehensive recognition of the intrapsychic processes and, with that, an account of the motivational structure (cf. Waelder, 1962, 1970, Wurmser, 1972c). Yet, in this field, the exploration has been disappointingly scanty. The immediate reason is well known: that these patients are very poor candidates for psychotherapeutic approaches.

4. Similarly, Krystal and Raskin (1970): ". . . the drug is not the problem, but is an attempt at a self-help that fails" (p. 11).

5. It is not certain how this pharmacogenic effect comes about. There are three

possibilities: either the drug increases the thresholds of decompensation from narcissistic conflicts; or decreases the intensity of these conflicts; or functions as an artificial dampener on overwhelming affects, a kind of surrogate affect-defense in the narrow sense. Or the effect may consist of all three.

REFERENCES

Blos, P. (1971), Adolescent concretization: a contribution to the theory of delinquency. In: Currents in Psychoanalysis, ed. I. M. Marcus. New York: International Universities Press, pp. 66–88.

Chein, I., Gerard, D. L.; Lee R. S.; & Rosenfeld, E. (1964), The Road to H. New York: Basic Books.

Fenichel, O. (1934), Defense against anxiety, particularly by libidinalization. In: Collected Papers, First series. New York: Norton, 1953, pp. 303–317.

—— (1945), The Psychoanalytic Theory of Neurosis. New York: Norton.

Freud, A. (1936). The Ego and the Mechanisms of Defense. The Writings of Anna Freud, Vol. 2. New York: International Universities Press, 1966, pp. 31–34.

Freud, S. (1895), A reply to criticism of my paper on anxiety neurosis, Standard Edition, 3: 123–139. London: Hogarth Press, 1962.

—— (1914), On narcissism: an introduction, Standard Edition, 14: 69–102. London: Hogarth Press, 1957.

—— (1930), Civilization and its discontents. Standard Edition, 21: 59–145. London: Hogarth Press, 1961.

Gill, M. M. (1963), Topography and Systems in Psychoanalytic Theory [Psychological Issues, Monogr. 10]. New York: International Universities Press, pp. 122–123.

Glasscote, R. M.; Sussex, J. N.; Jaffe, J. H.; Ball, J.; & Brill, L. (1972), The Treatment of Drug Abuse. Programs, Problems, Prospects. Washington, D.C.: American Psychiatric Association and National Association on Mental Health.

Glover, E. (1928), The Etiology of Alcoholism. In: On the Early Development of Mind. New York: International Universities Press, 1956, pp. 81–90.

—— (1932), On the Etiology of Drug Addiction. In: On the Early Development of Mind. New York: International Universities Press, 1956, pp. 187–215.

Grotjahn, M. (1971). The Voice of the Symbol. Los Angeles: Mara Books, pp. 1–23.

Hartmann, D. (1969), A study of drug-taking adolescents. The Psychoanalytic Study of the Child. New York: International Universities Press, 24: 384–398.

Hartmann, H. (1939), Ego Psychology and the Problem of Adaptation. New York: International Universities Press, 1960.

Jaffe, J. H. (1965). Drug addiction and drug abuse. In: The Pharmacological Basis of Therapeutics, ed. L. S. Goodman & A. Gilman. New York: Macmillan, pp. 285–311.

Jones, E. (1929), Fear, guilt and hate. In: Papers on Psychoanalysis. Boston: Beacon Press, 1967, pp. 314–319.

Kernberg, O. F. (1970), Factors in the psychoanalytic treatment of narcissistic personalities. Journal of the American Psychoanalytic Association, 18: 51–85.

Khantzian, E. J.; Mack, J. F.; Schatzberg, A. F. (1974), Heroin use as an attempt to cope: clinical observations. Amer. J. Psychiat., 131: 160–164.

Kohut, H. (1959), Introspection, empathy, and psychoanalysis. Journal of the American Psychoanalytic Association, 7: 459–483.

——— (1971), The Analysis of the Self. New York: International Universities Press.

——— (1972), Thoughts on narcissism and narcissistic rage. The Psychoanalytic Study of the Child, 27: 360–400. New York: Quadrangle Books.

Krystal, H., & Raskin, H. A. (1970), Drug Dependence. Aspects of Ego Functions. Detroit: Wayne State University Press.

Kubie, L. S. (1954), The fundamental nature of the distinction between normality and neurosis. Psychoanal. Quart., 23: 167–204.

——— (1961), Neurotic Distortion of the Creative Process. New York: The Noonday Press.

Lewin, L. (1924), Phantastica, Narcotic and Stimulating Drugs: Their Use and Abuse. New York: Dutton, 1931; reprinted 1964, London: Routledge & Kegan.

Limentani, A. (1968), On drug dependence: clinical appraisals of the predicaments of habituation and addiction to drugs. Internat. J. Psycho-Anal., 49: 578–590.

Panel (1970), Psychoanalytic evaluation of addiction and habituation, W. Frosch, reporter. Journal of the Psychoanalytic Association, 18: 209–218.

Preble, E., & Casey, J. J. (1969), Taking care of business—the heroin user's life on the street. Internat. J. Addictions, 4: 1–24.

Pulver, S. E. (1970), Narcissism: the term and the concept. This Journal, 18: 319–341.

Rado, S. (1926), The psychic effects of intoxicants. Internat. J. Psycho-Anal., 7: 396–413.

——— (1933), The psychoanalysis of pharmacothymia (drug addiction), Psychoanal. Quart., 2: 1–23.

——— (1963), Fighting narcotic bondage and other forms of narcotic disorders. Comprehensive Psychiat., 4: 160–167.

Rapaport, D. (1953), On the psychoanalytic theory of affects. In: Collected Papers, ed. M. M. Gill. New York: Basic Books, 1967, pp. 476–512.

Savitt, R. A. (1954), Extramural psychoanalytic treatment of a case of narcotic addiction. Journal of the American Psychoanalytic Association, 2: 494–502.

——— (1963), Psychoanalytic studies on addiction: ego structure in narcotic addiction. Psychoanal. Quart., 32: 43–57.

Schafer, R. (1973), The idea of resistance. Internat. J. Psycho-Anal., 54: 259–285.

Sherwood, M. (1969), The Logic of Explanation in Psychoanalysis. New York: Academic Press, pp. 172–174.

Waelder, R. (1936), The problem of freedom in psychoanalysis and the problem of reality testing. Internat. J. Psycho-Anal., 17: 89–108.

——— (1962), Psychoanalysis, scientific method and philosophy. Journal of the American Psychoanalytic Association, 10: 617–637.

——— (1970), Observation, historical reconstruction, and experiment: an epistemological study. In: Psychoanalysis and Philosophy, ed. C. Hanly & M. Lazerowitz. New York: International Universities Press, pp. 280–326.

Wieder, H., & Kaplan, E. H. (1969), Drug use in adolescents: psychodynamic meaning

and pharmacogenic effect. The Psychoanalytic Study of the Child, *24: 399–431.*
New York: International Universities Press.

Wurmser, L. *(1972a), Drug abuse: nemesis of psychiatry.* Amer. Scholar, *41: 393–407.*

————— *(1972b), Methadone and the craving for narcotics: observations of patients on methadone maintenance in psychotherapy. San Francisco: Proceedings, Fourth National Conference on Methadone Treatment, pp. 525–528.*

————— *(1972c), Author's reply.* Internat. J. Psychiat., *10: 117–128.*

————— *(1973a), Psychosocial aspects of drug abuse.* Maryland State Med. J., *22: 78–83, 99–101.*

————— *(1973b), Unpolitic thoughts about the politics of drug-abuse treatment.* J. Drug Issues, *3: 178–185.*

————— *Flowers, E.; & Weldon, C. (1973),* Methadone, Discipline and Revenge. *Washington: Proceedings, Fifth National Conference on Methadone Treatment.*

Zinberg, N. E., & Robertson, J. A. (1972), Drugs and the Public. New York: Simon & Schuster.

7. Self Representation and the Capacity for Self Care

Henry Krystal

I. SUBSTANCE ABUSE AND PSYCHOANALYTIC THEORY

Some of the early analysts, especially Abraham (1924, 1926), Simmel (1930, 1948), and Rado (1926, 1933) contributed significant insight into the psychodynamics of alcoholism and drug addiction, and in the process enriched psychoanalysis. As pessimism shrouded over the prospects of individual analytic therapy for these patients, we lost interest in them, and thereby we lost the opportunity to learn from working with them. Symptomatic of this impoverishment of our studies is the absence of a course on problems of alcohol or other drug dependence from the curriculum of all psychoanalytic institutes affiliated with the American Psychoanalytic Association (Handler, 1977). The Board on Professional Standards of the American Psychoanalytic Association does not require or recommend any instruction in the area of the addictions.

Yet I have found this to be a rewarding area to study. Impressed with the vagueness and lack of differentiation of affective states, particularly depression and anxiety in withdrawal states, I pursued a study of affective disturbances in alcoholism and drug dependence (Krystal, 1962). I found an affective disturbance in drug-dependent individuals consisting of affect dedifferentiation, deverbalization, and resomatization (Krystal and Raskin, 1970). These patients showed a severe disturbance in affective forms and function. Their emotions came in vague, undifferentiated, somatic form, i.e., they experienced sensations and not feelings. They were not able to put their emotions into words, and therefore could not use them as signals to themselves (Krystal, 1974). Wurmser (1974) has also reported that in studies of drug addicts he found the coincidence of impairment of symbolization and affect disturbance. "This curtailed ability, or inability to symbolize, pertains

Reprinted by permission from *Annual of Psychoanalysis* 6 (1978): 209–46. Copyright © International Universities Press, Inc.

particularly to the patient's inner life, his emotions, his self-references. One example is the inability of most of these patients to articulate feelings. Many if not all relevant affects are translated into somatic complaints . . ." (p. 837).

The disturbance in affectivity involved verbalization and symbolization and had a double impact upon the problem of addiction: an etiological one and a therapeutic one. For with this disturbance and with what I also found to be an impairment in affect tolerance (Krystal, 1975), it was most unlikely that they could bear the added burden of psychotherapy. In struggling with these challenges I came to the following conclusions:

It is possible to prepare some substance-dependent individuals for psycho-analytic psychotherapy by offering them a preliminary stage of the treatment in which the patient's affective functions are dealt with. I have discussed the techniques of dealing with this type of problem and impairment of affect tolerance elsewhere (Krystal, 1973a, 1975). The emotional disturbances found in alcoholic and drug-dependent patients are not unique to them, but can be found in other patients. I found a very high incidence of the same affective-cognitive disturbance in severely traumatized survivors of Nazi persecutions (Krystal, 1971).

The concentration-camp survivors also showed an extremely high rate of psychosomatic diseases. Whereas the over-all incidence of psychophysiologi-cal disturbances was 30 percent, among the patients who suffered the persecu-tions in childhood and adolescence, the incidence reached 75 percent! (Krys-tal, 1971). The combination of psychosomatic illness and a disturbance in affectivity and cognitive processes was observed early by a group of French psychoanalysts (Marty, de M'Uzan, and David, 1963). Sifneos (1967) has coined the term *alexithymia* for the disturbance of affectivity and verbaliza-tion he found in psychosomatic patients. Sifneos and Nemiah have made many observations and careful descriptions of the patients' inability to ex-press their feelings in words and to link them with fantasies (Nemiah, 1977; Nemiah and Sifneos, 1977). Marty and de M'Uzan (1963) observed the same phenomena; they also reported that many psychosomatic patients were unable to produce fantasies, and that their thoughts seemed preoccupied with mun-dane details and not suitable for symbolizing drive tensions, a phenomenon they labeled *pensée opératoire*.

Our clinical observations on drug-dependent and alcoholic patients coin-cide precisely with those of Sifneos, Nemiah, Marty, de M'Uzan, and others who have studied psychosomatic patients. It has, however, been the drug-dependent group, when compared to my observations of traumatized patients, who made it possible for me to realize that I was observing a regression. The resulting working out of the genetic development of affect (Krystal, 1973a, 1974, 1977) permits us to understand psychosomatic conditions as a regression in regard to affect—in that affects are resomatized and dedifferentiated, with a concomitant impairment in verbalization and symbolization.

The observations derived from patients who represent themselves with a problem of substance dependence or psychosomatic illness apply in various ways to a great number of patients. McDougall (1974) has pointed out that, like it or not, the psychoanalyst ". . . finds himself constantly confronted with psychosomatic behavior of a general kind in all of his analysands, [and] he will also discover that a considerable proportion of his patients, whether he wishes it or not suffer from authentic psychosomatic disorders" (p. 438).

Whether the patients show psychosomatic symptoms, or have addictive tendencies, as long as they show alexithymic characteristics, their capacity to utilize and benefit from psychoanalytic work is seriously impaired (Sifneos, 1973, 1975). De M'Uzan (1974) has stressed that patients showing these characteristics include character neuroses and "normals" and has described them as "anti-analysand, analysis proof" (p. 462). As already mentioned, I have been less pessimistic about the applicability of analysis to these patients. I feel, however, that these problems account for a great number of analytic failures, and for an even greater incidence of impairment of effectiveness of analytic work with primarily neurotic patients. The ongoing explorations of the "alexithymic" disturbance in affectivity and symbolization will continue to yield helpful insights toward the handling of these hitherto ignored problems.

Another area in which the study of drug-dependent and alcoholic patients contributes a helpful view of universal interest is the question of object and self representation, especially with regard to the fantasy of "introjection." For the alcoholic and drug-dependent patient, the nature of their transferences and self representations poses an often insuperable barrier to psychoanalytic psychotherapy, as I hope to demonstrate later. It is precisely because this area is such an obstacle that we must study it. Very likely, our technical weakness stems from a failure to recognize and understand something about those problems.

II. AMBIVALENCE IN OBJECT RELATIONS AND TRANSFERENCE

Let us consider the difficulties resulting from the ambivalence in object relations so frequently noted in the treatment of these patients. What becomes difficult to weather is the early surfacing of aggressive transference. One view of this difficulty relates to the disturbance in affect tolerance. One is inclined to expect that painful (or "emergency") affects present the greatest challenge to the ego, in terms of the management of pain and secondary anxiety. However, drug-dependent individuals are among those who have difficulties with a type of emotion which is commonly experienced as pleasurable. Rado (1969) has called all of those "welfare affects," since they usually favor the well being of an individual. Out of these, Spitz (1963, p. 55) has singled out the "proleptic" group, i.e., the emotions experienced in the process of expecting gratification. However, these emotions are only pleasurable when accompanied by hope and confidence based on previous good experiences. Unfortunately, with these patients, that is not the case. Because of the nature of their transferences, they expect disappointment and rejection, and proleptic affects may represent a "trauma signal" for them (Krystal, 1975).

When exposed to a potential good object, such patients panic and may have to ward off their yearnings for love and acceptance. Such an untoward reaction represents a fear of the positive transference, and has also been observed in psychotherapy with schizophrenic patients (Sechehaye, 1951). These patterns have been described in great detail by Kernberg (1975) and Boyer (1977) in regard to borderline patients. Of course, borderline patients also frequently manifest dependence on drugs and use them defensively to deal with these types of transferences. Kernberg especially has clearly discussed the need to devaluate, even symbolically destroy, the therapist in order to ward off feelings of envy and the resulting rage.

Whether we consider it a manifestation of the transference, or a defense against it, unconscious, hateful, and destructive impulses toward the analyst frequently appear early, and represent a threat to the establishment of a working alliance. Because of the prevalence of magical thinking, fortified by the wish for magical powers, and in harmony with a grandiose self representation, alcoholic and drug-dependent patients in psychotherapy become terrified of their death wishes directed toward the therapist. Relatively early in the treatment they are confronted with their extraordinary envy, and have the need to deal with their poorly mastered narcissistic rages. At this point, they flee from the treatment, because they fear that their death wishes will destroy their therapist. Alternately, they tend to turn their aggression against themselves, and act it out in an accidental injury, suicide attempt, or relapse of drug abuse (Simmel, 1948). This may be one of the major reasons why alcoholics and drug abusers do poorly in *individual* therapy. For this type of drug-dependent patient, for whom individual therapy is desirable, treatment works better in a clinic situation, in which auxiliary therapists are made available. As additional contacts are usually readily available in a clinic setup, these may be observed to be spontaneously sought out by some patients with addictive problems.

The idea of using a team to manage the substance-dependent patient is not new. One of the successful psychoanalytic treatment centers was Simmel's Schloss Tegel Clinic. Simmel was concerned with the alcoholic's tendency to self-punishing ideas and suicide attempts after withdrawal. The patient who was being withdrawn from alcohol was permitted to stay in bed, and a special nurse was assigned to look after him, and supervise his diet. This was a conscious attempt to provide the patient with passive gratification, to provide a gentle "weaning," and prepare the patient for his "regular analysis" (Simmel, 1948).

It has been my observation that when highly ambivalent patients have a therapeutic team available they will use it for the purpose of "splitting" of their transferences. In this way they experience their angry and destructive wishes toward one member of the team while presenting a basically loving relationship toward another, preferably the chief therapist (Krystal, 1964). I believe that this development takes place commonly in treatment clinics and groups. However, most of the time the transferences acted out with various clinic employees are lost from the therapeutic process unless a special effort is made to "gather" them. If everyone in the clinic reports to the chief therapist about every contact and communication with the patient, the picture of the nature of the patient's transference may then be put together. It will be found that the patient is not experiencing a simple splitting of the transference into one love and one hate relation. The picture will be quite complex, and quickly changing. At one moment, the chief therapist may be experienced as the idealized mother whose love and admiration the patient yearns for, whereas another staff member may be experienced as a rejecting, condemning parental image whom the patient dreads, and hates; and still another staff member may be experienced as seductive, intrusive, destructive, or other parental transference object. When the patient feels frustrated by the chief therapist, and needs to experience his rage toward him, instantly he will experience one of the other members of the team as an idealized parent, while he experiences other partial transferences with yet another clinic staff— anybody around, whether they are in a therapeutic role or not. Conversely, when the chief therapist is experienced as kind, concerned, and loving, the patient may be confronted with enormous guilt over his aggressive, envious feelings which may drive him to act out in a self-destructive fashion. He may avert that need if he can justify his feelings by some grievance over a deprivation or slight from someone in the clinic.

In order to demonstrate to the patient the splitting and idealization involved in his transference, it is necessary to bring his projections together, and show that all of these transferences represent various object representations, which he needs to experience toward the *one* therapist. The patient's vacillations and changes in attitudes toward the various staff members can be used to demonstrate his dilemma. Bringing in the ambivalence in the transference is the crucial step in working with such patients, because one of the major forces which propel individuals toward addiction is that they can displace their ambivalence toward the drug in a way which I will discuss in detail later. The very slang names given to alcohol and drugs reflect this ambivalence. Szasz (1958) has emphasized this aspect of drug problems in his paper on the counterphobic attitude in drug dependence.

A special instance of the use of a group of therapists is the situation where the addicted individual is sent to the clinic by a court. The probation officer assigned to the patient becomes an object of transference of a very significant type. The fact that this type of a patient has a characterological disturbance which necessitates that he "externalize" (that is, fail to integrate) his superego function in having others enforce controls for him is a clear indication that these transferences cannot be left out of the treatment (Margolis, Krystal, and Siegel, 1964). Back in 1931, Glover commented that drug-addicted patients are able to give up the drugs up to the very last drop. This "last drop" however, becomes virtually impossible to give up, because it contains the symbolic expression of the fantasy of taking in the love object. The external object which is experienced as containing the indispensable life power that the patient wants to, but cannot, "internalize" illustrated the basic dilemma dominating his psychic reality. This tendency applies to his conscience as well, so that he is unable to experience it as being a part of himself, but arranges for others to exercise it for him. When antabuse is prescribed for an alcoholic, both the doctor and his patient may share the illusion that the pill will replace or repair the alcoholic's failing impulse control. The drug, however does not constitute an insuperable barrier against drinking, as its effect can be abolished by simply skipping it whenever the patient wants to indulge his impulse to imbibe. We can detect in this operation some of the characteristics of the *placebo effect*. The patient becomes able to exercise his hitherto inhibited function, but he denies his part in it, and attributes the activity to the pill. The ingestion of the pill represents a ritual, or symbolic act, through which one gains access to a function which otherwise remains blocked.

The failure to integrate, to be able to own up to one's own functions and aspects such as conscience, and the need to attribute them to others, such as parents, spouses, or probation officers make the drug-dependent individual experience the world in a paranoid way. This pathology was summed up by Glover (1931) when he said that drug addicts are inverted paranoids, and that they are both persecuting and persecuted. Thus, whether there is a probation officer in the picture, or whether antabuse or similar substances (or procedures) are used by the therapist, the transferences involved in the patient's failure to see the self sameness of his superego have to be brought into the treatment by interpretation—if the patient is ever going to be able to accept himself as a whole person. We should note also that these operations in which a patient needs to "take in" some external factor in order to exercise his own function are a mode of behavior paralleling the use of a placebo. I will return to that point later.

III. SELF REPRESENTATION AND VITAL AND AFFECTIVE FUNCTIONS

These observations address themselves to what I consider to be the basic defect and the basic dilemma in the life of a drug-dependent individual such as the alcoholic: He is unable to claim, own up to, and exercise various parts of himself. He experiences some vital parts and functions of his own as being part of the object representation and not self representation. Without being consciously aware of it, he experiences himself unable to carry out these functions because he feels that this is prohibited for him, and reserved for the parental objects. I have studied this and described the clinical evidence for these views elsewhere (Krystal and Raskin, 1970, Krystal, 1975). At this point I would like to consider what prevents the patient from "internalizing" these functions, and indeed, whether the model of taking in such functions from without is a reflection of the patient's fantasy or whether, in fact, functions are "taken over" from parental and later transference objects. A new source of observations in this area has become available recently in biofeedback studies combined with psychotherapy. I would like to consider a certain difficulty which develops sometimes in that setting.

Just as the drug-dependent individual is unable to exercise certain functions for himself, and/or admit that such is the case, so do we all experience those parts of ourselves which are under the control of the autonomic nervous system as being beyond our volition. However, in the last twenty years, a whole literature has become available demonstrating that through the use of biofeedback devices, control over these areas can be acquired. For the most part the reports are exclusively behaviorally oriented, reporting the degree of success in terms of percentages and the number of trials. The concern is with the apparatus, rewards, and results. Rickles (1976) is a rare exception—a psychoanalyst looking at this work and concerning himself with the psychic reality of the patient, and the patient's mental representations and transferences to the machine, the therapist, and his problem. His patients are in psychoanalysis or psychoanalytic psychotherapy while having their biofeedback training. They are also required to speak for five minutes into a tape recorder after each biofeedback session and relate whatever occurs to them. Perhaps it is because of this unusual setting that he relates about one of his patients that "She soon left biofeedback therapy . . . because she was frightened by the depressive feelings which emerged when she relaxed" (p. 5). I have had occasion to treat a few patients who had been undergoing biofeedback treatment. I advised one of these to get it for his severe hypertension. In a couple of other cases, we were dealing with extremely severe manifestations of anxiety: a patient who had a resting pulse of over 110, and several others who suffered from insomnia or severe headaches which had been intractable by all other previously tried methods. The patients responded rather surprisingly. Although most of them cooperated with the instructions of the psychologist, and achieved some desired results in the sessions with him, they developed much difficulty in practicing at home, and most of all in generalizing their newly acquired skills and applying them to their everyday lives. A number of reasons accounted for this, however, including certain of the more usual transference problems. However, one reaction, quite marked in some, and only mild in others, should be highlighted here.

All of the patients showed evidence of guilt and anxiety over gaining control over vital functions and over parts of themselves which they assumed to be beyond their control. Some were conscious of this feeling, and expressed fear that such a Promethean act on their part would be punished severely. Others dreaded that in acquiring such powers they might destroy themselves. Some showed only indications of unconscious reactions in that vein. The patients felt that these major parts of their bodies were proscribed for the incursion of their volition. To assume control over these functions was a forbidden act.

The fact that they did "learn" to exercise a particular action under the direct supervision of the psychologist is consistent with such feelings. While under his tutelage, they were able to do it, as long as they disavowed their responsibility for the act. However, they could not accomplish the same results at home consistently, acting out their denial in various ways, e.g., falling asleep while practicing. Even when they learned to carry out an activity—for example, to lower their blood pressure or relax their muscles while practicing—they had great difficulty in generalizing this act outside of the practice session. To do so would signify a conscious admission that they have taken over the control of the "autonomic" area of their bodies which they felt they were not supposed to do. These feelings are universal, not limited to psychosomatic patients, although they are more problematic to them. A case has been reported, for instance, of a psychoanalyst who learned to relax the spasm of the peripheral blood vessels and thus relieve the symptoms of his Raynaud's disease. After about a year of doing it, he became less successful at it and had to return to the laboratory for "further training" (Schwartz, 1973, p. 672).

Lest we get distracted from our observation that we are dealing with an emotional block to the exercise of our potential functions, let me re-emphasize that we are not dealing with peculiarities of the autonomic nervous system. As I mentioned, for some of the patients who suffered from muscle-tension states or tension headaches, the aim was to relax their muscles. Thus, the area of the body excluded from the self representation does not necessarily coincide with that of the visceral or archipallial areas, but is an individual matter. Frequently, however, it involves all those parts of the body which are importantly involved in a given individual's *affective responses*. When a patient is referred for biofeedback treatment, a significant psychosomatic element is in the picture. Unlike experimental animals or subjects, they are addressing themselves to symptoms of their affective, if not symbolic, disorder.

IV. BODY IMAGE AND MATERNAL TRANSFERENCE

The reason the patients had such guilt and anxiety about learning to control their viscera, or even to relax their muscles, was because their unconscious belief was that organs such as their hearts were under the special care of God (or fate, doctor, hospital, and the like), which guaranteed their survival. This is illustrated in the commonly held theory of sleep—namely, that God causes it by taking away the soul, which He may, by His grace return to us the next morning. This theory of sleep is a transference of the maternal image for whom life-giving powers, as well as nursing, are reserved. This theory is universally shared and incorporated into law. What it means, in effect, is that we do not own our lives, and therefore do not have the right to commit suicide. All basic life-assuring functions are carried out under a franchise, as it were.

This experience has its roots in infancy, and even phylogeny, for certain newborn mammals will not void, but die, unless licked by the mother on the perineum (Lehman, 1961). Abandoned young mammals die, sometimes even when a maternal substitute becomes available, if a personal attachment (object constancy) has been accomplished (Van Lawick-Goodall, 1973). Vulnerability of the human infant is, of course, the greatest, and we could say that the newborn will destroy himself unless rescued by the mother. Much of Melanie Klein's theorizing about the early destructive impulses of the child can be understood in this light. The early mothering is experienced as a *permission* to live. When the biofeedback patients were told that they could learn to control their autonomic functions, some experienced fears that taking over such maternal prerogatives would cause them to destroy themselves. Of course, even dying is experienced as being regulated by the primal mother who takes back her child (e.g., Mother Earth, or the Pieta theme).

It is relevant to remind ourselves again that this area is involved in the "expressive" aspect of affects, because the emotions are similarly experienced as emanating from the object, and the idea of "managing" them, and using them as signals in the patients we are considering, is also experienced as forbidden by many of them (Krystal, 1975). Thus the two areas of disturbance—one in the sphere of affects, and the other in the sphere of self and object and self representations—have their common denominator in the historical sources mentioned. The connection goes even deeper. These patients often have the following definition of love based on the addictive fantasy: "If you love me, you will take care of me, and make me feel good." Therefore, they not only experience their feelings as emanating from the object who carries the whole responsibility for them, but even further compound this construction. Whenever they feel badly, they conclude that they are unloved and rejected by the love object. They become convinced that either the object is bad and dangerous, or they are bad and being punished. Their rage about the "unfair" state of affairs appears to turn either against the object or against themselves. These problems, of course, contribute to the problems of early aggressive transferences mentioned above. Most of all, however, since all the patient's bad feelings are the fault and responsibility of the object, it is up to the love object, and not permissible to the patient, to make themselves feel better.

Behaviorists have overlooked this problem, since it represents, for the most part, unconscious fantasies demonstrable through the analysis of transferences and characterological patterns. They have emphasized that one handicap in acquiring conscious volitional control over viscera lies in the lack of proprioception, which is remedied by the biofeedback apparatus (Stoyva, 1970; DiCara, 1972). But to their credit, behaviorists have questioned the limits of the voluntary control of our selves, as well as the very concept of volition. In a thoughtful review of the problem of volition, Kimble and Perlmuter (1970) pointed out the narrowness and inadequacy of the view of the academic psychologists that volition is equal to conscious intentionality, and proposed to explore the development, initiation, and control of voluntary acts. Implicit in operant conditioning is the conception that an organism will tend to repeat actions that bring it pleasurable consequences (rewards), thus suggesting a broader concept of motivation which goes beyond consciousness or reason.[1]

Their views, however, ignore the psychoanalytic concept of the mind functioning in a state of conflict, and therefore they miss the main point of interest to us: *that volition, intention, or motivation may be opposed by like forces in the opposite direction.* That is the reason why they have not observed the difficulties that subjects encounter within themselves in expanding the limits of their acknowledged function, that is to say, in trying to integrate alienated parts of themselves.

Behaviorists exploring the area of voluntary control of internal states have produced a wealth of evidence that the commonly accepted limits of conscious control of automatic function are not due to absolute anatomic limitations. The following is a good review of their position on these issues:

It is not possible to define in an operational way the meaning of the word "voluntary," but all of us have a *feeling* of voluntary control, at least part of the time, regardless of the psychophysical and metaphysical implications of that feeling. Few people realize, however, that that feeling or intuition of freedom has unusual significance in respect to the autonomic, nervous system, the so-called involuntary nervous system, nor do they realize that the "psychophysiological principle" when coupled with volition makes it possible to regulate a number of important involuntary functions, and at least theoretically to regulate in some degree every psychological and physiological function of one's being.

The psychophysiological principle, as we hypothesize it, affirms that "Every change in the physiological state is accompanied by an appropriate change in the mental-emotional state, conscious or unconscious, and conversely, every change in the mental-emotional state, conscious or unconscious, is accompanied by an appropriate change in the physiological state" (Green, Green, and Walters, 1970, p. 5).

Now, what are some examples which indicate that our inability to control our physiological states is functionally, and not anatomically determined? To start with, some individuals naturally possess the ability to control various viscera. Some people have been found to have conscious control over their heartbeat and blood pressure. One man was even observed to be able to bring his heart to a complete stop for a few seconds, and resume normal function at will (Ogden and Shock, 1939; McClure, 1959). Yogis have also been watched in the exercise of control of various functions through volition alone (Green, Green, and Walters, 1970). Of course, we all exercise control over viscera, but usually we deny it by giving credit to the various devices we use. When, for instance, we select a certain kind of music, in order to calm ourselves, or otherwise modify our affective state, we tend to minimize our own responsibility in this, attributing it to the "external" implements.

The functions so laboriously acquired, apparently through learning, may be gained instantly through the use of hypnosis (Shor, 1962; Marshall, Maslach, and Zimbardo, 1972). Barber (1970) has done a critical review of many reports in this area and concluded: ". . . a wide variety of physiological functions can be influenced directly or indirectly by suggesting to either hypnotic or awake subjects that certain physiological effects are forthcoming" (p. 243). Among these effects were the production of vestibular nystagmus, the production and blocking of pain, the induction and inhibition of labor contractions, modification of vasomotor function in the skin, i.e., blood-vessel dilatation or constriction, cardiac acceleration and deceleration, and the modification of a variety of metabolic and gastrointestinal functions. Another group of researchers concluded: "These experimental results free us from the shackles of viewing the autonomic nervous system with contempt. They force us to think of the behavior of the internal, visceral organs in the same way that we think of the externally observable behavior of the skeletal musculature" (Miller et al., 1970, p. 358).

Beyond the evidence of the potential for the control of physiological states derived from hypnosis and suggestion, the placebo phenomenon should be considered (Krystal and Raskin, 1970). The history of medicine is in essence the history of the placebo, since effective drugs have been a rare and recent development (Shapiro, 1960). As is well known, under the influence of the placebo, patients are capable of exercising a multiplicity of functions in the sphere of their selves over which they usually feel no control (Beecher,

1961). These effects are not necessarily beneficial. A variety of untoward reactions have also been reported—from transient sleepiness, nausea, skin rashes, diarrhea, to urticaria, angioneurotic edema, and others (Roueché, 1960; Beecher, 1956; Wolf and Pinskey, 1942). Why is it, then, that we are unable to exercise control over the parts of our bodies ordinarily controlled by the autonomic nervous system but do so under the influence of biofeedback training, hypnosis, or placebo?

I must address that question by making the outrageous claim that *the usual state of Man in regard to the autonomically controlled part of his body is analogous to a hysterical paralysis.* Since we have the potential to exercise these functions but are prevented from doing it by a psychological cause, we are dealing with a functional or conversion-derived block. This "normal" inhibition of the exercise of volition over the autonomic or affective aspect of ourselves is, like any conversion paralysis, the symbolic representation of a fantasy. The fantasy, however, pertains not to our genital or phallic conflicts, but to the vital functions. In the "normal" state, we dramatize the fantasy that the control of our lives and feelings does not belong to us, and is not a part of the self representation, but is under the sovereignty of mother, doctor, or God—and thus part of the primal object representation.

When one functions under the influence of the doctor's placebo, the behaviorist's biofeedback machine, the hypnotist's suggestion, the shaman's or curandero's magical incantations, one gains access to the functions previously reserved for the object. It is because the needed functions are experienced as part of the object representation that in the ritual of reclaiming them the fantasy of devouring or "introjecting" the object is symbolically acted out. When the symbol of the object is "taken in," whether it is a prescription medicine, alcohol, or illicit drug, or even the ritual of Holy Communion, the evidence of the ambivalence toward the object may become noticeable. Wieder and Kaplan (1969) have pointed out that "drugs" and "potion" both denote at once medicine or poison. They explain:

The earliest prototypes of "druglike" experiences probably are of milk, breast and mother. In the argot of the addict, his supplies are often called "Mother" and his supplies "mood food." . . . The image of the drug may be "good" or "bad" regardless of whether they used pharmaceuticals, caresses, food, laxatives or enemas. Severely or chronically ill children, such as diabetics and asthmatics, relate to their medication as to magic potions, especially during periods of remission (Wieder and Kaplan, 1969, p. 401).

The ambivalence in terms of ill effects from drugs is not limited to "junkies," but is a universal phenomenon. Better than half of all patients never fill their prescriptions. However, this failure to do so is not just a matter of the splitting of the object and taking in of a poisonous object, i.e., "witchmother." The point which is especially made clear in religious beliefs is that the Host is always good, and it is only the taking it by the undeserving which is punishable. Thus it is the transgression of taking in the object for the purpose of acquiring the walled-off, self-soothing, and comforting function which is forbidden and punishable. That is why, if one is still "supposed" to suffer, taking the medicine will cause one to become even more ill (become poisoned or cursed), as we noted above among the adverse reactions to the placebo. This is the reason why psychosomatic patients respond differently to biofeedback than experimental subjects.

What we are confronting, then, are barriers within one's self representation, in which the most basic life-maintaining functions and affective functions are experienced as outside the self representation, and as part of the object representation. The usurping of maternal (God's) privileges is the feared transgression of what is experienced as the "natural" order of things.

What happens, then, under the influence of the placebo or one of the other conveyances is that there is a temporary lifting of internal barriers between the self representation and the object representation, thereby permitting access to, and control of, parts of oneself that were previously "walled off." What are these intrapsychic schisms made of? They represent repressed parts of one's self, repressed by *depriving them of the conscious recognition of selfhood.* This does not pertain only to parts of one's body, but much more so to the spheres of functions.[2]

V. THE BLOCKING OF SELF-CARING FUNCTIONS IN DRUG-DEPENDENT INDIVIDUALS

Alcoholics and drug addicts are among those people who have a great inhibition in carrying out a multitude of "mothering" or self-comforting functions. In studying their difficulties, we gain a chance to observe that we are dealing with an intrapsychic block which prevents them from the consciously exercised use of these functions. They act as if they were forced to repress (alienate) their potential for self care.

These repressions take place at various times in childhood in connection with the various conflicts centered in the psychosexual development. As analysts, we are very familiar with these conflicts and the inhibitions which the neurotic patients show. On the phallic level of development it is very common for us to find the very same kind of structure which I have described in regard to the autonomically controlled-affective part of the body. The neurotic patients often believe that their genitals are not part of their self representation, but belong to their parents, for whom their use is reserved.

A boy finds himself frightened of his competitive strivings with his father because of his fantasies and theories of destroying his father and taking his place; i.e., unconscious identification fantasies related to his theory of becoming *the* father may repress these wishes and fantasies. Thereafter, he sees himself as a boy permanently, with adult masculine modes of action reserved for the father. Unless he finds some way to overcome or get around these repressions, he may never be able to fulfill his masculine ambitions, or consciously own up to, or exercise his masculinity. This may lead to the kind of inhibition in the occupational and sexual goals, with a rise to prominence of homosexual striving, which the early psychoanalytic writers describe so many times in their observations of alcoholics (Simmel, 1930, 1948; Rado, 1926, 1933; Juliusberger, 1913; and Hartmann, 1925). In some homosexuals, the fantasy is that through the sexual act one will regain one's alienated masculinity through the symbolic introjection.

However, in some drug-dependent individuals there is a specific disturbance consisting of the "walling off" of the *maternal* object representation, and within it the self-helping and comforting modes. Thereby, such a person loses his capacity to take care of himself, to attend to his needs, to "baby" or nurse himself when tired, ill, or hurt narcissistically. We have described the resulting deficits in the drug-dependent patient in terms of the impaired ability to comfort and soothe himself (Krystal and Raskin, 1970). I have stressed that one reason the addict yearns for the "nods," or uses drugs to obtain relief from distressing feelings or gain "good" feelings is because he is not able to exercise comforting, mothering functions. Consequently, he may not be able to do the kinds of things that an ordinary person does in order to soothe himself, relax, and go to sleep. In my discussion of the uses of the placebo and other devices, I have also stressed repeatedly that many patients, beyond the group of drug-dependent individuals in whom this is so conspicuous, do not feel free to comfort themselves when they feel bad. In other words, their affect tolerance is impaired because they do not feel free to exercise the kind of comforting, gratifying care that a mother gives to a distressed child. In brief, I have found an inhibition in the substance-dependent patient's ability to take care of themselves physically and emotionally, in the literal sense of that word (Krystal, 1975).

Recently, Khantzian has expanded on these observations, pointing out that they have even wider implications. He showed that the drug-dependent individual had "a type of self-disregard associated with impairments of a multitude of functions related to proper *self-care* and *self-regulation*" (Khantzian, 1978). Khantzian reminds us that many drug-dependent individuals do not take care of their nutrition or general medical and dental care, and that they fail to exercise the usual care and caution to avoid the multiplicity of troubles and tribulations which "befall them." These patients fail to exercise the welfare functions in such a consistent way that we must conclude that they have an inhibition in this essential area. Zinberg (1975) has also commented on the drug addicts' severe impairment in self care. He pointed out that they are not only self destructive, but also "manage almost never to do well for themselves in the simplest life transactions. They lose laundry slips and money, choose the wrong alternative at each instance, and are invariably being gypped at the very moment they think they are the slyest" (p. 374).

Since we have already observed similarities between substance-dependent and psychosomatic patients in regard to affective function, it is relevant to note that psychosomatic patients also frequently fail to take care of themselves, especially in regard to the symptoms of their diseases. McDougall (1974) has commented on this phenomenon, noting that the illness progresses silently:

When once the symptoms break the bounds of silence they still fail to receive much attention in the analytic discourse. Either they are ignored or are referred to in ways which appear to attach little importance to them. This is frequently accompanied by an attitude of blithe disregard for one's physical welfare as though the body were a decathected object even in the face of evident disfunction and physical pain. "I have been having these pains for two years. I didn't know what caused them but I contrived a way of walking which made them bearable. This went on up until the ulcer perforated," reported one patient (p. 458).

The example of the peptic ulcer brings to mind that I found 40 percent of patients admitted for delirium tremens to have peptic ulcer or gastritis (Krystal, 1959). The alcoholic who ignores his ulcer or treats it with more liquor unites these apparently disparate groups for us and helps to emphasize the common denominator.

VI. THE PLACEBO AS A MEANS OF OVERCOMING INTERNAL BLOCKING

The placebo effect is an important element in the development of drug dependence. This was the aspect of addiction we were referring to when we called it "an extreme form of transference" (Krystal and Raskin, 1970, p. 71). Drug-dependent patients are not free to take care of themselves except under the "order" of transference objects or under the influence of a placebo. Again, this is a phenomenon observable in psychosomatic patients as well. McDougall (1974) observed that her psychosomatic patients were extremely dependent on their love object for feelings of "being alive" and that they "tend to fall physically ill when abandoned" (p. 451). But their love objects were "highly *interchangeable*": "The central demand being that someone must be there. This someone is cast in the role of a 'security blanket' and thus fulfills the function as a transitional object" (McDougall, 1974, p. 451). McDougall refers to such object relations in psychosomatic patients as "addictive" and relates how one of her patients with the loss of her mate "lost everything: her sexuality, her narcissistic self-image, her capacity to sleep and her ability to metabolize her food" (p. 452).

In her discussion of the use of objects by psychosomatic patients to enable them to take care of themselves, the same author also stresses that "these patients attempt to make an external object behave like a symbolic one and thus repair a *psychic* gap. The object or situation will then be sought addictively. Basically all addictions from alcoholism and boulimia to the taking of sleeping pills, are attempts to make an external agent do duty for a missing symbolic dimension" (McDougall, 1974, p. 455).

This behavior on the part of the patient represents the dealing with *their fantasy* of a deficiency, or defect, to be repaired by the incorporation of the object. As psychoanalysts, we quite regularly "take over" the patient's fantasies and make them part of our theories, as I have done in a recent paper: "It may be said with Kohut . . . , that the defect in the above patient represented a failure to successfully establish the kind of transmuted internalization that would make it possible for her to exercise certain adult functions" (Krystal, 1975, p. 200).

However, the placebo does not lend the taker the *function,* only the freedom to exercise it. If a drug-dependent, a psychosomatic, or a "normal" individual can exercise a function under the influence of the placebo, drug, hypnosis, love, or inspiration, then he demonstrates that his freedom to exercise it has been blocked by a fantasy. That is why we may conclude that substance-dependent and psychosomatic patients alike experience their self-caring functions as reserved for the maternal object representation, and psychologically "walled off"—inaccessible to them.

It is the child's construction that the mother provides all the comfort for him, and all the good feelings emanate from her, and that when he provides such sensations for himself he is "taking over" her function. This is patently an incorrect perception, for no matter what she did he always *"created"* all his feelings and sensations, including his perceptions and mental representations of her. Based on this childhood theory of the world are many of the difficulties resulting from the attribution of part and function to the object representation.

Here, we are observing the late consequences of the theory that self-comforting and self-soothing functions belong to and are reserved for the primal love object. There is evidence that this fantasy is ubiquitous—notably in the universal blocking of our autonomously controlled parts of the body which I have reviewed above. But drug-dependent individuals and psychosomatic patients have an even broader and more severe proscription of the acknowledged self-directed exercise of self-caring functions. Are there any direct observations of settings in which a child might be likely to develop such attitudes?

VII. THE CHILD'S MENTAL REPRESENTATION OF THE MOTHER AND ITS RELATION TO THE EXERCISE OF VITAL FUNCTIONS

In the introduction to a paper "On the Beginnings of a Cohesive Self," M. Tolpin (1971) explained that it was necessary to study minutely the processes by which autonomous functions are acquired. She used observations on the transitional object to explore the development by the child of self-soothing functions. We are concerned with the problems in this process, particularly since we are concentrating on two groups of patients who show serious psychopathology in this area. We are particularly concerned with the nature of infantile experiences that interfere with the child's gradual development of a freedom for self soothing—in other words, with those situations which retrospectively appear as if a permission for self care was not felt, or a prohibition of it was even experienced.

Our first question involves the kind of mother who, for a number of possible reasons, may act to punish or discourage any self gratification or autonomy on the part of the child. One thinks, offhand, of a mother whose need for a narcissistic unity with the child is so great that she is jealous of other objects, even a transitional object, and prevents the use of it.

I want to stress, however, that I do not imply that such direct causation is a necessary condition for the child to obtain "a message" that his conscious self caring is prohibited. A variety of situations might conspire to give the same result. For whereas some mothers may not favor the child's self integration, and we will discuss some of these types, what concerns us is the child's *psychic reality.* It is the child's mental representation of the object which will cause him to attribute various fantasies and theories to his construction of the object and himself. Thus the child will fuse his perceptions of his mother and his own illness or other distress and come up with a construct of "bad mother" or "bad self being punished" or a myriad of other fantasies. This point has been made previously by Brierly (1945), Angel (1973), and Beres and Joseph (1970).

We find illustrations in Spitz's (1962) observation that where the mother-child relationship is not satisfactory (for the child, we assume) autoerotism is diminished or disappears altogether. But in discussing the kinds of unsatisfactory mother-child relationships, Spitz clearly approaches the issue from the point of the child's experience, as he considers a variety of examples, including Harlow's monkeys. Particularly in our work as adult analysts, it is clear that we are sharing with the patient a reconstruction of his original fantasies regarding his mother and her messages to him.

From her work with adult analysands who only incidently to their main (neurotic) problems were found to also have psychosomatic ones, as well as from direct observations, especially by Fain (1971), McDougall (1974) concluded:

... there are two predominant trends in disturbed baby-mother relationships which are apt to create a predisposition to psychosomatic pathology. The first is unusually severe prohibition of every attempt on the baby's part to create autoerotic substitutes for the maternal relationship, thus initiating the nodal point for the creation of inner object representations and the nascent elements of fantasy life. The second trend is the antithesis of this, namely a continual offering of herself on the mother's part as the only object of satisfaction and psychic viability (p. 447).

Fain and Kreisler (1970) have directly observed children who cannot go off to sleep. One group of infants was unable to sleep unless continually rocked in their mother's arms. These babies, McDougall concluded, were unable to exercise for themselves the psychic activity necessary for sleep, but required the mother to be "the guardian of sleep" (p. 446). Fain (1971) theorized that these babies did not have a *Mère satisfaisante* ("satisfying Mother") but a *Mère calmante* ("tranquilizing Mother"). "The latter, because of her own problems, cannot permit her baby to create a primary identification which will enable him to sleep without continual contact with her" (McDougall, 1974, p. 446). These children can be said to be suffering from a psychosomatic problem as well as an addictive problem. We have here the common root to the affective disturbances and inhibition in self caring which these two groups share.

The child's ability to maintain sleep is the first achievement in regard to exercising the kind of self-caring functions with which we are concerned. In studying sleep disturbances in infants, Fain (1971) describes three patterns: the baby who sleeps with small sucking movements, the baby who sleeps with the thumb in his mouth, and the baby who sucks frenetically and does not sleep. Whereas the first child accomplishes the necessary relaxation by a dream or hallucinatory wish fulfillment, the second infant requires a concrete representation of the breast. The need for the *concrete* external object substitute may be either due to the absence of an internal symbolic "good object," as McDougall (1974) suggested, or it may be the necessary prop which, like the placebo, permits the exercising of functions of "loving" reserved for the object and prohibited to the self. In this sense the placebo like the fetish serves to deny something. For the third child, there is a failure to accomplish relaxation regardless of the continuing sucking. Fain (1971) has explained all of these disturbances by an inability on the part of the mother to grant the child its autonomy. Conceivably, however, the child's inability to gain comfort derives from some inner disturbance, as has been reported by Chethik (1977) from his studies of borderline children.

Fain (1971) also describes the opposite end of the spectrum, where the child engages in a type of autoeroticism which seems to eliminate the mother as an object. This extreme, McDougall (1974) concludes, demonstrates that "instinctual aims and autoerotic activity then run the risk of becoming literally *autonomous,* detached from any *mental representation of an object*" (p. 447; author's italics). However, it may be that in the above cases, babies suffering from merycism, where they constantly regurgitate and swallow the contents of their stomachs, we may see the precursor of an inability to retain the yearned-for supplies which we see in drug-dependent individuals, to which I will return shortly. At this point, I would like to once more quote the conclusions of McDougall (1974) which are so much more impressive when we keep in mind that she was trying to understand the disturbance in psychosomatic patients:

I do not think it would be a misrepresentation of Fain's work to describe the mother of his observational research as performing *an addictive function.* The baby comes to need the mother as an addict needs his drug—i.e. total dependence on an external object—to deal with situations which should be handled by self-regulatory psychological means. In my clinical work I have found similar imagos in patients showing "acting out" behavior other than addictions and psychosomatic symptoms, notably in perversions and in character patterns marked by discharge reactions (p. 448).

The interpretation which McDougall gives to all of these observations implies an absence of good object representations on a symbolic level, which has to be substituted for by the *concrete* supplies. That is, for her, the paradigm for the failure of symbolization that is manifest later in the "operational thinking" which Marty and de M'Uzan (1963) described in psychosomatic patients. McDougall's explanation is attractive as a way of understanding the phenomena of alexithymia. However, it has certain weaknesses. In the first place, I have reported the same findings not only in psychosomatic and addictive patients, but in posttraumatic ones as well, and in this last group it is evident that we are dealing with a regression, rather than with an absence of a symbolic object. Secondly, if we consider the concomitant inhibition in self-caring functions, we cannot relegate it to pure psychopathology. It is in this connection that we need to recall the universal phenomenon of the "hysterical paralysis" of our autonomically controlled parts. The occurrence of this universal inhibition, and the use of the placebo to get around it, forces us to study these problems in terms of the nature of self and object representation. When we say that the transitional object represents the object, we are really saying that, like the placebo, it permits the exercise of functions which, even at an early age, are already experienced as part of the object representation. The impoverishment of the self of self-helping resources and the "walling off" of these as part of the object representation is a most severe form of psychic crippling.

Therein is the source of the need of the oral character to use the drug both as a pharmacological means to manipulate his affective states and as a placebo: to gain surcease from his feelings of depletion which result from the repression[3] of self-helping attributes and functions of his own, making them part of a rigidly "walled-off" object representation. We must recognize them and acknowledge that the kind of person who is likely to become drug-dependent is one who uses the drug to help him carry out basic survival functions which he otherwise cannot perform. People who drink in order to be able to continue to work thus gain access to their assertive, masculine paternal modes of behavior. People who drink for the purpose of surcease and comfort obtain their goal, in addition to the pharmacological effects, by gaining access and ability to exercise their maternal functions. The longing to regain alienated parts of oneself is the real meaning behind the fantasies of fusion with the good mother so clearly discernible in drug-dependent individuals (Chessick, 1960; Savitt, 1963; Krystal and Raskin, 1970).

These yearnings make their appearance in the transference in the analysis of alcoholics and other drug-dependent individuals, and this phase of the treatment, as well as the phenomenon itself, has been termed by Fenichel (1945) "object addiction." This transference needs to be interpreted in the analysis for the very same reason that all transferences are interpreted: so that the patient will discover that the characteristics that he attributes to the analyst are actually his own mental representations, which he first perceived as being part of his mother, and now re-experiences as alienated. The healing principle of psychoanalysis consists of the patient's claiming of his own mind, restoring the *conscious recognition* of his own self.

But, as we know only too well, patients do not feel free to do this. They fight it with all the means at their disposal, as if their lives depended on maintaining the repressions. The drug-dependent individuals often have a terrible struggle with this part of treatment. When we try to understand the nature of their psychic reality which makes the removal of repression from their maternal object representations so difficult for them, we discover that it leads us to the core of the emotional problems that are represented by their infantile trauma.

It is this kind of resistance against establishing the benign object representation, and taking over self-caring functions, which makes me take exception to the view of McDougall and de M'Uzan that in such patients the symbolic function in regard to primary object representations is absent. I will review some findings that suggested to us that drug-dependent individuals have to repress their rage and destructive wishes toward their maternal love object. This need manifests itself in a rigid "walling off" of the maternal love-object representation, together with an idealization of it, and an attribution to it of most life-supporting and nurturing functions. By doing this, the patient manages (in his fantasy) to protect the love object from his fantasied destructive powers, and to assure that "someone *out there*" loves him and will take care of him (Krystal and Raskin, 1970).

VIII. THE ADDICT'S PROBLEMS IN RETAINING A "GOOD INTROJECT"

Probably the most conspicuous indication of the difficulties of the substance-dependent individual has been overlooked because it is too obvious. I am referring to the fact that drug abuse consists in fact, not only of taking drugs, but equally important, of being deprived of drug effect. All the drugs which are addicting are short acting. The longer acting the drug, the greater the likelihood of the user panicking and developing a "bum trip" (Krystal and Raskin, 1970).

The formal withdrawal from drugs is an integral part of the process of addiction (Krystal, 1962). The development of ever-increasing tolerance for the drug is greater and faster in drug-dependent individuals because they have the need to deprive the drug of its power (Krystal, 1966); and at the same time, the moment it does lose its force, they panic (Rado, 1933; Krystal, 1959).

What is the meaning of all these apparent contradictions? It is that *while the drug-dependent yearns for the union with his maternal love object (representation) he also dreads it.* He really can't stand it either way. Schizophrenic patients and some borderline individuals yearn for union with their love object (representation), and once they achieve it (in fantasy), they cling to it passionately, giving up conscious registration of all perceptions or ideas that spoil this delusional fusion.

Drug-dependent individuals are very busy getting the drug, but can feel themselves reunited with the idealized love object only rarely for short periods of time, and only at moments when they are virtually totally anesthetized. Even then, one finds with amazement that many of them—at the very moment of the climactic action of the drug—indulge in acts of riddance, such as moving bowels, vomiting, cleaning their bodies, cutting their nails, or even house cleaning (Chessick, 1960). It may be said that they are *addicted to the process of taking in and losing the drug rather than to having it.* The seemingly bizarre behavior of the drug addict who plays with the drug by "regurgitating" it back and forth between the syringe and vein suddenly falls into place here. And isn't this another version of the "psychosomatic" child with merycism who keeps regurgitating and swallowing the contents of his stomach?

Drug-dependent individuals dread fusion with the love-object representations because of the way they experienced them in the formative period of their lives. The explanations of these difficulties are linked to the problems of aggression, or ambivalence toward the love-object, which we have noted in the beginning of this paper. The ambivalence toward the therapist in the transference is matched by the ambivalence toward the drug, and that in turn is a reliving of the particularly severe ambivalence toward the maternal object representation. Our substance-dependent patients are just like the ones who get very sick upon ingesting the placebo. They even get sick upon hearing an interpretation which is "right on target" in content, form, and timing.[4]

We have previously pointed out that the "hangover phenomenon" was identical with the untoward reactions to the placebo. We explained that these were caused by "[The] inordinate guilt about oral indulgence, related to cannibalistic problems" (Krystal and Raskin, 1970, p. 47). In other words, when the substance-dependent patient tries to regain his alienated functions by swallowing the symbol of the object representation to whom he attributed these powers, he is confronted with his infantile fantasies that caused him the problems originally.

Another clinical observation well known to every worker in this field supports the accuracy of these constructions: that these patients are unable to accomplish normally the work of mourning and the feeling of "introjecting" the lost love-object. The introjection fantasy is a form of partial union of the self representation and object representation, at which most people arrive at the end of mourning. It is a clinical commonplace to say that alcoholics and other drug-dependent individuals cannot tolerate object losses (and that includes therapists) without being so threatened with their affects that they have virtually unavoidable relapse to self-destructive drug use.

This is a dimension of the problem of ambivalence which makes its appearance in the analysis of the drug-dependent individual. In the early stages of the therapy, the very availability of an object creates serious challenges to him. He also suffers from the above-mentioned fear of aggressive impulses and wishes. In addition, as Vaillant (1973) has stressed, when these patients idealize their therapists in the transference, they experience themselves as worthless and bad.

But these are just preliminaries. The greatest difficulties arise because the effective work in the psychoanalytic therapy by which one can give up his attachment to one's infantile object representation and the infantile view of oneself is accomplished by "effective grieving," a process analogous to mourning (Wetmore, 1963).

IX. GRIEVING AND THE EXTENSION OF THE LIMITS OF ACKNOWLEDGED SELF SAMENESS

The very process of mourning spells trouble for the drug-dependent patient, who tends to dread being overwhelmed with depression; he also has a dread of all affects which he experiences as a trauma screen (Krystal, 1977). Raskin and I have found it necessary to postulate, in order to explain this phenomenon, that this type of an individual has had a nearly lethal childhood trauma experience, which he fears may return, and which he experiences as a "fate worse than death" (Krystal and Raskin, 1970). Elsewhere (Krystal, 1974, 1975), I have discussed the technical modifications made necessary by the regression in the nature of the affects and the impairment of affect tolerance. If even that obstacle is overcome, the patient is able to grieve effectively, and he then faces the ultimate challenge: the conscious acceptance of his object representations as his own mental creations.

At the end of a successful analysis one is in the same position as at the end of the hypothetical completely successful mourning. The bereaved person discovers that though the lost person is dead and gone, his love-object continues to exist in the survivor's mind. This gives him the opportunity to discover that as far as he is concerned, that is where the object had been all along—in his mind as an object representation of his own creation. And so one has to face the "return of the repressed." All the "bad" persecutory aspects of the object represent projections. Projections are fantasies, impulses, wishes and feelings that are not integrated. The process of integration of ego-alien wishes represent a loss and has to be accomplished by grieving. Until the grieving, and diminution of the idealized self representation is completed, depression is experienced, or needs to be experienced. There were originally two reasons for the failure to own up to one's death wishes toward the object: the fear of loss of love, and the fear of destroying the object. "Walling off" the object representation as being "external" and "real" provided a protection for it. Attributing all the "goodness" to this "external object" was a bargain in which dependency and helplessness were accepted as preferable to destruction. Thus, the giving up of the repressions, the owning up to the self sameness of one's object representations, confronts one with the aggression that caused one to "wall off" his object representation so rigidly, and subsequently to develop that tragic yearning and dread of the love object.

Earlier I said that the rigid "walling off" of the maternal object representation took place in the face of extreme aggressive impulses toward it. The evidence for that came from this stage of the psychotherapeutic work with drug-dependent individuals. The intensity of the narcissistic rages, the persistence of the aggressive impulses make one wonder if all addiction is, at the bottom, a "hate addiction." The problem of aggression and its apparent threat to the safety and integrity of the self representation and/or object representation sets the limits to the kinds and numbers of drug-dependent patients who can be carried to a completion of analytic work. Along the way, most such patients, when confronted with their aggression, will relapse again and again into the use of the drug and self-destructive activities. Others will be driven to prove that their childhood misfortunes were real, by getting the analyst angry, and provoking abuse. Still others become so terrified of the dangerous, poisonous transference object, that they set out on a panicked, frantic search for the *ideal mother,* in some form—such as drink, love, or gambling.

If the therapist is otherwise equipped to bear the disappointments, provocations, and failures entailed in working with these patients, and if he has the time and patience to permit the patient to do this work by minute steps, then the most helpful thing to keep in mind is that the patient is confronted with problems of aggression that make him experience the transference as a life-and-death struggle. Care and caution must be exercised that the patient not be overwhelmed with his aggressive feelings, or guilt. Emergencies in which the patient's life hangs in the balance will occur, for that may be the way the patient may have to test the therapist.

When Simmel reviewed his lifetime experience with alcoholics in a paper that he never completed, he was very clear about the problems of aggression in the treatment of these patients. He said: ". . . during a state of abstinence under psychoanalysis in a hospital, substituting the addiction to alcohol or drugs was an overt suicidal addiction or an overt addiction to homicide. During this stage the addict's only compulsion is to kill: himself or others. Usually he does not rationalize this urge; he just wants to die or at other times he just wants to kill" (Simmel, 1948, p. 24).

The aggression observable in the self-destructive life style of the drug-dependent individual is, in the process of psychotherapy, traced to its ultimate sources and meanings. In order to do so, the patient has to be able to experience with the therapist that which he has never dared to face—his hatred. Instead of seeing himself as a victim, and claiming *innocence,* now he is confronted with his murderous aggression. To do so, however, requires giving up the treasured view of oneself as the innocent victim, which again, has to be mourned. And so, it can be said that an unavoidable step in the treatment of a certain type of substance-dependent individual in intensive therapy is that he has to go through a depressive stage. During this phase of the treatment the dependence upon the therapist is extreme, and no substitutes are acceptable. Whereas early in the treatment many patients do best in a clinic with multiple therapists, for the few who will be carried to this type of therapeutic completion, the chief therapist has to be the one who will be stationary and available to the very end. The extreme difficulties resulting from the nature of the object representation of addictive personalities determine that those among them treated by psychoanalytic psychotherapy will continue to be the exception, mainly of research interest.

X. THE COMMON ROOT OF IMPAIRMENT IN CAPACITY FOR SELF CARE AND ALEXITHYMIA

Among the problems shared by substance-dependent and psychosomatic patients reviewed in this essay is an impairment in their capacity to take care of themselves. This deficit brings them into the realm of those patients who have deficiencies in strategic functions. This point was made by Kohut (1971), who felt that addicts had an impaired development of "the basic capacity of the psyche to maintain, on its own, the narcissistic equilibrium of the personality." He explained:

The trauma which they suffered is most frequently the severe disappointment in a mother who, because of her defective empathy with the child's needs (or for some other reasons), did not appropriately fulfill the functions (as a stimulus barrier; as an optimal provider of needed stimuli; or a supplier of tension relieving gratification, etc.) which the mature psychic apparatus should later be able to perform (or initiate) predominantly on its own. Traumatic disappointments suffered during these archaic stages of the development of the idealized self object deprive the child of the gradual internalization of early experiences of being optimally soothed, or of being aided in going to sleep. Such individuals remain thus fixated on aspects of archaic objects and they find them, for example, in the form of drugs. The drug, however, serves not as a substitute for loved or loving objects, or for a relationship with them, but as a replacement for a defect in the psychological structure (Kohut, 1971, p. 46).[5]

Kohut goes on to stress that, in the transference, the analysand expects to "have his analyst perform the functions which the patient's own psyche is incapable to provide" (p. 47). In connection with the consideration of these patients, Kohut goes on to discuss the process of *"transmuting internalization."* In it, he spells out the "breaking up of those aspects of the object image that are being internalized" (p. 49), and the depersonalizing of the introjected function, so that an effective internalization can be accomplished which leads to the formation of a psychic structure.

Here we have the basic theory of impairment in function based on deficiency in a psychic structure, due to a failure to appropriately introject an aspect of the maternal image which was the carrier for these functions. The weight of the evidence of the observations on both drug-dependent and psychosomatic patients is that this is the patients' own theory of their problem. The idea that they suffer from a deficiency disease, and that the analyst must supply to them the loving care of which they were cheated is often and despairingly proclaimed by these patients. If only the deficiency can be supplied to them they will love themselves and take good care of themselves. In truth, the patient wants not only his deficiency made up to him, but also wants the analyst to roll back the calendar and "fix" everything that happened to him which was "bad," and even then he would have a grudge left that things did not work perfectly the first time. We see the caricature of our fuzzy thinking when it becomes the rationale of various nonanalytic therapists who do try to supply to their patients the love they had missed.

As psychoanalysts, we deal with distortions in self representation and object (world) representation. So it is a good thing that our patients do not, in truth, suffer from deficiency diseases, or have a deficiency in their ego apparatus.

We have made observations of substance-dependent, psychosomatic and "normal" individuals which suggest that the "deficiency-resulting-from-a-failure-in-internalization" is not the most helpful model to explain the problems:

1. Although the patients are ordinarily not able to perform self-soothing and general self-caring functions, we have observed that they are able to perform them under the influence of placebo, suggestion, or any situation in which they can disavow their doing it. Moreover, the impairments in function are spotty and fluctuating in scope and intensity—and not total and constant as they would have to be if there was a true deficiency.

2. Whereas drug addicts crave to "introject the object" and acquire the function, they have a great deal of difficulty in doing it, often negate the act instantly, and cannot maintain the fantasy of fusion.

3. The frightening and "sickening" effects of introjected objects suggest that the problem of ambivalence toward the object representation is what prevents them from fulfilling the cannibalistically tinged fantasies.

4. In our perusal of reactions to placebo, biofeedback, and other procedures, we found that psychosomatic patients and other people shared the drug addict's attitudes, albeit in a less severe degree. These were based on the infantile fantasy that one's vital functions were part of the object representation, and that the taking over of them would imply an introjection of the maternal object representation which was prohibited.

I have suggested that the child's attribution of soothing and life-giving functions to the maternal object representation becomes firmly established and reinforced as a defensive operation. The greater the problem of aggression resulting from the infantile trauma, the greater the rigidity of "walling off" of the maternal object representation, and the greater the scope of life-maintaining functions attributed to it. The placebo is a means of going around these intrapsychic prohibitions.

My conclusion is that these patients do not have a deficit in either the capacity for self-caring functions or in psychic structures necessary to exercise them. *They have a psychic block; an inhibition in regard to their function of self-soothing, self-caring as well as others.* They are in the same position in regard to these functions as we all are in regard to our life-maintaining and affect-related parts of our bodies. We have the capacity to influence our state, but we dare not, unless we have a placebo-like device handy which makes possible the denial of our usurping these "forbidden" areas.

Although the "internalization-of-maternal-functions" idea has serious weaknesses theoretically (besides my difficulties with it, see also Schafer 1972), it is one of the most important fantasies of mankind, and as such represents important analytic material. But we must deal with it for the purpose of understanding and interpretation that this is the fantasy that caused these patients to develop their inhibitions. It may be recalled, from my early material in this paper, that substance-dependent individuals have a tendency to *"externalize"* their functions in general. I illustrated the difficulties they have in exercising their impulse control, and referred to the use of a team which includes a probation officer of antabuse to deal with that problem. In this context, antabuse may be considered a "superego placebo," as it enables the patient to exercise these alienated functions. In a forthcoming book on drug dependence, Wurmser (1978) puts great emphasis on the tendency of such patients to use externalization as the most characteristic and important defensive pattern underlying substance dependence.

Rather than limiting ourselves exclusively to the model of acquisition of function by the infant through internalization of his perception of his mother's performance, other models may be more applicable in regard to certain aspects of development. Gedo and Goldberg (1973) have demonstrated the advantage of matching the models to developmental lines and types of experiences.

In regard to the problems of life-maintaining and self-caring functions, a Chomskian model of development appears more useful. Just as the innate capacity for the use of language unfolds in every human, so do most of these functions. The favorable environment provided by the mother permits an optimal maturation of these capacities. The problem is not truly with *acquiring* patterns of behavior or structures from outside, but the freedom to extend the boundaries of one's selfhood, and to minimize the areas alienated and turned over to "nonself." If we direct our attention to the process of development of affects as an example, we find that they evolve out of two basic states; those of tranquility and distress, respectively, which are affect precursors. The process of affect development has been worked out through the contributions of a number of authors which, along with my own, I have reviewed in some detail (Krystal, 1974, 1977). The process goes on throughout childhood and adolescence. The developmental lines of affect are verbalization, desomatization, and differentiation out of the common precursor patterns into refined forms of specific emotions.

The development of affects takes place in the context of all the important object relations, and in all phases of psychosexual and psychosocial development. At present, however, I want to focus only on the earliest ones. When the child becomes disturbed, he experiences totally somatic reactions of mounting excitation. As the mother attends to the child's needs, she also becomes attuned to evolving variations in the child's responses and, according to her empathic capacity, recognizes the child's wants and responds to them specifically. This is the beginning of a long process of upbringing in which the children are encouraged to verbalize their affective states as precisely as possible, rather than continuing the mass reaction. Thus a good mother is very attentive to the budding differentiation in the child's affective responses and takes pleasure in guessing their meaning. Every increment in differentiation in affective signals produces more precise responses. This situation favors a continuing differentiation in affective patterns, and the start of the process of desomatization and verbalization. The child has, of course, an innate capacity for it, and as with language in general, unfolds it in response to his love objects. However, in regard to affects there is a hazard which the mother strives to prevent: if she cannot relieve the child's distress, and help him to feel content, he may become flooded with the primitive affect precursors. As long as this possibility is prevented, the child's success with increasingly letting his affective states be known promotes the dawning awareness of a variety of needs, emotions, and signals. If we focus our attention on the *process* of affect differentiation and verbalization—we can observe that the symbolic representation of the child's *needs* goes hand in hand with his ability to experience his narcissistic omnipotence in terms of fulfillment of his wishes. The availability of a good self object not only permits the grandiosity of the child to unfold appropriately but also permits the feeling that it is proper for him to "take care of himself." In other words, the infantile omnipotence permits the fantasy of self-care when the actual capacity for it is nil. In this fashion, because affective expressions are the only form of communication available, the mother's responsiveness and "fine ear" for the evolving nuances of the child's feelings become a crucial aspect of the early developmental milieu. The prompt and gratifying responses on the part of the mother permit the infant to claim credit for the parent's beneficent actions. The early "paradise" of infantile omnipotence, however, is based on the failure to recognize mother as a separate, "external," and hence poorly controlled individual. But this period provides one the conviction that it is all right to will one's gratification and obtain it.

Only when distressed is the child confronted with the external and separate source of his vital supplies. But as one corrects the earlier error and forms the maternal object representation, there is a fatal tendency to confuse the supplies with the *experience of gratification.* The mother feeds the baby, but the baby must suckle, swallow, absorb, digest, metabolize, eliminate, form mental representations of the whole experience, but most of all *enjoy* the food for himself. To lose sight and control of one's authorship of all of his experiences of gratifying, affective and life-preserving functions, and to attribute these to the object representation sets the stage for future proscription of their use. As we have observed earlier, the "hysterical paralysis" of our autonomically innervated organs is virtually universal. We have, to date, no knowledge about influences upon the extent or severity of these inhibitions as related to early experiences.

However, in regard to the capacity for self care, especially for self soothing and obtaining gratification in one's life, there is strong evidence of the influence of the nature of early gratifications and frustrations. Under the experience of "good-enough mothering" the crucial feeling develops that it is *permissible* for the child to exercise a certain measure of self regulation in regard to his affective and hedonic states. One gains the feeling that it is permissible for one to comfort or soothe one's self. Withal, when it is necessary to "baby" one's self, the unconscious fantasy may become manifest that the "benign introject" is doing it, or lending the permission to do it. At times, when "nursing" a sick organ, the identification with the mother taking care of a baby is acted out. All of these are evidences that even in fortunate circumstances of childhood, one grows up with the tendency to attribute these functions to the primal love object. And yet, the principle of psychic reality dictates that from the beginning one had to create for himself, in his mind, all he has ever experienced of comfort or pleasure.

Our observations indicate that *serious frustrations* result in a premature confrontation with the child's helplessness and dependence. The mother is discovered to be the holder of all external supplies, so that sight is lost of the child's active participation in his soothing and comforting. When frustrated or exposed to pain or painful affects, the child becomes dependent upon the mothering parent to protect him from the onslaught of these responses.

The most difficult task of mothering is the recognition of the intensity of affect precursors which the child is able to bear without becoming overwhelmed by them. An essential aspect of mothering related to the affect maturation consists of the gradual allowing of increasing intensity of affects to build up. It is the mother's empathy which directs her judgment as to when she must step in and comfort the child. The failure to interrupt the mounting intensity of affects may lead to the onset of infantile psychic trauma (Krystal, 1975, 1978).

Infantile psychic trauma has serious aftereffects in both spheres which we have identified above:

1. There may be an arrest or regression in the genetic development of affects. This produces the picture of alexithymia, with an impairment in symbolization, and frequently an anhedonia, and a general fear of affects as trauma screens.
2. The premature disruption of the symbiotic unity confronts the child with a dangerous, all powerful external object—that cannot be satisfactorily controlled.

Among the many problems that result from this disruption is the attempt to magically control the object by splitting, idealization, and masochistic modifications of the self representations. It is in this predicament that affective and self-caring functions are relegated to the object representation. The problems of envy and ambivalence prevent the coveted regaining of one's own functions by incorporation. Dorsey (1971) summarized poetically: "In a traumatic living it is my loss of my sense of personal identity that is truly disabling" (p. 125). Khan (1963) described a variety of possible "breaches in the mother's role as a protective shield" (p. 290), which made the child precociously aware of his dependence upon her. To Khan, this development was one of the most harmful aspects of "cumulative trauma."

To recapitulate, then, the interaction between mother and child in the sphere of early affective function vitally affects two areas:

1. Appropriate responses on the part of the mother favor the normal development of affects in the direction of their desomatization and differentiation. They also promote the progressive development of dif-

ferentiated affective responses, modulated in their intensity with increasing vocalization, verbalization, and symbolization. This also involves the development of reflective self awareness, and the use of symbols and fantasy for progressive intrapsychic structure formation.

2. The continuation of the symbiotic relationship without traumatic disruption promotes the attribution of self caring and affective functions to the self representation. With it comes a sense of security and permissibility of striving to attain gratification and comfort.

It follows that disturbances in this process can produce the two problems which we have identified in drug-dependent and psychosomatic patients: (1) an arrest or regression in the disturbance of affect which I have reviewed early in this paper and which Sifneos termed "alexithymia," and (2) an inhibition in the ability to exercise self-caring functions.

Both of these problems represent a serious handicap in regard to the patient's ability to utilize psychoanalytic psychotherapy. In regard to the inhibition in self-caring functions, we have to deal with the fantasies that underlie the distortions in self and object representations. It follows that *the goal of therapy is not to supply to the patients their missing functions or psychic structures, but to enable them to exercise functions blocked by inhibitions.* In the process of therapy one has to work through the transferences as reviewed above, in order to enable the patient to renounce his childhood theory of the world and of himself.

XI. SUMMARY

The nature of the object relations of the drug-dependent patient are such that he craves to be united with his ideal object, but at the same time dreads it. He thus becomes addicted to acting out the drama of fantasy introjection and separation from the drug. There is a corresponding intrapsychic defect; certain essential functions related to nurturance are reserved for the object representation. The objective of the therapy is to permit the patient to extend his conscious self regulation to all of himself, thereby freeing him from the need for the placebo effect of the drug as a measure of gaining access to his alienated parts and function.

Psychosomatic patients show the same kind of inhibition in self-caring functions, especially in regard to their illness. They also share with addictive patients a disturbance in affectivity and symbolization termed "alexithymia." The "operational thinking" characteristic of them shows an impoverishment of imagination, and a blocking of drive-oriented cognition.

Both types of problems seem to have common roots in certain disturbances in object relations that relate to affective communications. These problems are most conspicuous in the lives of substance-dependent and psychosomatic patients, but are present in lesser degrees in every analysand. Our awareness of these problems allows us to address ourselves to these difficulties which otherwise tend to seriously diminish the effectiveness of all of the other therapeutic interventions.

NOTES

1. There is a corresponding effort to review the psychoanalytic conceptions of volition and motivation, notably in the work of Klein (1970) and Holt (1976). For a review see Santostefano (1977).

2. Just what kinds of functions may be among those alienated has long puzzled philosophers and scientists. The view commonly held at present that Laetril represents a placebo which permits some people to mobilize their healing and life-preserving forces renews the question of the extent of these potential powers and the ways to mobilize them.

3. I have discussed elsewhere (1973b) the concept of repression as referred to in this context. It extends the definition of elements repressed from those rendered unconscious, to include those alienated: not consciously recognizable as part of one's self and one's own living.

4. For the purpose of emphasizing a certain view of these patients' reactions, I have avoided discussing the nature of their "introjects" or "internal objects." Although these concepts are useful clinically, we can do without discussing them for present purposes.

5. McDougall (1974) would insist, however, that in psychosomatic and addictive patients there is a lack of the symbolic representation of the good object (breast) too. She sees such a patient as one who "cannot internalize the breast, who cannot create within himself his mother's image to deal with his pain . . ." (p. 458).

REFERENCES

Abraham, K. (1924), The influence of oral erotism on character formation. In: Selected Papers of Karl Abraham. New York: Basic Books, 1954, pp. 370–393.

—— (1926), The psychological relation between sexuality and alcoholism. Internat. J. Psycho. Anal., 7: 2–10.

Angel, K. (1973), The role of internal objects and external objects in object relationships, separation anxiety, object constancy and symbiosis. Internat. J. Psycho-Anal., 13: 541–546.

Barber, T. S. (1970), Physiological effects of hypnosis and suggestion. In: Biofeedback & Self-Control 1970, ed. T. S. Barber et al. Chicago: Aldine, pp. 188–256.

Beecher, H. K. (1956), The subjective response to sensation. Amer. J. Med., *20: 101–103.*

———— *(1961), Surgery as placebo.* JAMA, *176: 1102–07.*

Beres, D., & Joseph, E. D. (1970), The concept of mental representation in analysis. Internat. J. Psycho-Anal., *51: 1–11.*

Boyer, L. B. (1977), Working with a borderline patient. Psychoanal. Quart., *46: 386–424.*

Brierly, M. (1945), Metapsychology and personalogy. In: Trends in Psycho-analysis. *London: Hogarth Press, pp. 124–79.*

Chessick, R. D. (1960), The pharmacogenic orgasm. Arch. Gen. Psychiat., *3: 117–28.*

Chethik, M. (1977), The borderline child. In: Basic Handbook of Child Psychiatry, *ed. J. Noshpitz et al. In press.*

Clark, L. P. (1919), Psychological study of some alcoholics. Psychoanal. Rev., *6: 268.*

De M'Uzan, M. (1974), Analytical process and the notion of the past. Internat. Rev. of Psychoanal., *1: 461–80.*

DiCara, L. (1972), Learning mechanisms. In: Biofeedback & Self-Control 1972, *ed. D. Shapiro et al. Chicago: Aldine, pp. 81–89.*

Dorsey, J. M. (1971), Psychology of Emotion. *Detroit Center for Health Education.*

Fain, M., & Kreisler, L. (1970), Discussion sur la genèse des fonctions représentives. Rev. franc. psychanal., *34: 285–300.*

———— *(1971), Prélude à la vie fantasmatique.* Rev. franc. psychanal., *35: 291–364.*

Fenichel, O. (1945), The Psychoanalytic Theory of the Neuroses. *New York: Norton.*

Gedo, J. E., & Goldberg, A. (1973), Models of the Mind. *Chicago: University of Chicago Press.*

Glover, E. (1931), The prevention and treatment of drug addiction. Brit. J. Inebriety, *29: 13–18.*

Green, E. E., Green, A. M.; & Walters, E. D. (1970), Voluntary control of internal states. In: Biofeedback & Self-Control 1970, *ed. T. S. Barber et al. Chicago: Aldine, pp. 3–28.*

———— *(1972), Biofeedback for mind-body self regulation: Healing and creativity. In:* Biofeedback & Self-Control 1972, *ed. D. Shapiro et al. Chicago: Aldine, pp. 152–66.*

Handler, M. (1977), Oral report of a survey of the American Psychoanalytic Association Affiliate Institutes to the Curriculum Committee. Michigan Psychoanalytic Institute.

Hartmann, H. (1925), Cocainismus und homosexualität. Z. Neur., *95: 415.*

Holt, R. R. (1976), Drive or wish? A reconsideration of the psychoanalytic theory of motivation. In: Psychology vs. Metapsychology: Psychoanalytic Essays in Memory of George S. Klein. [Psychological Issues, *Monogr. 36,*], *ed. M. M. Gill & P. S. Holtzman. New York: International Universities Press, pp. 158–197.*

Juliusberger, O. (1913), Psychology of alcoholism. Z. für Psychoanal., *3: 1. Abstract in* Psychoanal. Rev., *1: 469 (1913–1914).*

Kernberg, O. F. (1975), Borderline Conditions and Pathological Narcissism. *New York: Jason Aronson.*

Khan, M. M. R. (1963), The concept of cumulative trauma. The Psychoanalytic Study of the Child, *18: 286–306. New York: International Universities Press.*

Khantzian, E. (1978), The ego, the self, and opiate addiction. Intern. Rev. Psycho-Anal., *5: 189–198.*

Kimble, G. W., & Perlmuter, L. C. (1970), The problem of volition. In: Biofeedback & Self-Control 1970, *ed. T. S. Barber et al. Chicago: Aldine, pp. 508–31.*

Klein, G. S. (1970), The emergence of ego psychology—the ego in psychoanalysis: A concept in search of identity. Psychoanal. Rev., *56: 511–525.*

Kohut, H. (1971), The Analysis of the Self. *New York: International Universities Press.*

Krystal, H. (1959), The physiological basis of the treatment of delirium tremens. Amer. J. Psychiat., *116: 137–147.*

——— *(1962), The study of withdrawal from narcotics as a state of stress.* Psychiat. Quart. (Suppl.), *36: 53–65.*

——— *(1964), Therapeutic assistants in psychotherapy with regressed patients. In:* Current Psychiatric Therapies, *ed. J. Masserman, New York: Grune & Stratton, pp. 230–232.*

——— *(1966), Withdrawal from drugs.* Psychosomatics, *7: 199–302.*

——— *(1971), Trauma: Consideration of its intensity and chronicity. In:* Psychic Traumatization, *vol. 8, no. 1, ed. H. Krystal & W. G. Niederland. Boston: Little, Brown.*

——— *(1973a), Technical modification in affect regression and impairment of affect tolerance. Presented at the Annual Meeting of the American Psychoanalytic Association.*

——— *(1973b), Psychic reality. Presented to the Michigan Psychoanalytic Society, March 1.*

——— *(1974), The genetic development of affects and affect regression.* Annual of Psychoanalysis, *2: 98–126. New York: International Universities Press.*

——— *(1975), Affect tolerance.* This Annual, *3: 179–219. New York: International Universities Press.*

——— *(1977), Aspects of affect theory.* Bull. Menninger Clin., *41: 1–26.*

——— *(1978), Trauma and affect.* The Psychoanalytic Study of the Child, *33 (in press).*

——— *& Raskin, H. A. (1970),* Drug Dependence: Aspects of Ego Function. *Detroit: Wayne State University Press.*

Lehman, D. S. (1961), Hormonal regulation of parental behavior. In: Sex and Internal Secretions, *ed. W. C. Young. Baltimore: Williams & Wilkins, pp. 1268–1382.*

Margolis, M., Krystal, H., & Siegel, S. (1964), Psychotherapy with alcoholic offenders. Quart. J. Alcoh., *25: 85–89.*

Marshall, G., Maslach, C., & Zimbardo, P. C. (1972), Hypnotic control of peripheral skin temperature. Psychophys., *9: 600–605.*

Marty, P., & de M'Uzan, M. (1963), La pensée opératoire. Rev. Psychanal. (Suppl.), *27: 1345–1356.*

——— *& David, C. (1963),* L'Investigation psychosomatique. *Paris: Presses Universitaires de France.*

McClure, C. M. (1959), Cardiac arrest through volition. Calif. Med., *90: 440–441. Reprinted in:* Biofeedback & Self-Control 1972, *ed. D. Shapiro et al. Chicago: Aldine, pp. 49–50.*

McDougall, J. (1974), The psychosoma and psychoanalytic process. Internat. Rev. Psychoanal., 1: 437–454.

Miller, N. E., et al. (1970), Learned modification of autonomic functions: A review and some new data. In: Biofeedback and Self-Control 1970, ed. D. Barber et al. Chicago: Aldine, pp. 351–359.

Nemiah, J. C. (1977), Alexithymia: Theories and models. Proceedings of the Eleventh European Conference for Psychosomatic Research. In press.

———— & Sifneos, P. E. (1977), Affect and fantasy in psychosomatic disorders. In: Modern Trends in Psychosomatic Medicine, vol. 2, ed. O. W. Hill. London: Butterworth, pp. 26–34.

Ogden, E., & Shock, N. W. (1939), Voluntary hypercirculation. Amer. J. Med. Sci., 198: 329–342. Reprinted in: Biofeedback & Self-Control 1972, ed. D. Shapiro et al. Chicago: Aldine, pp. 34–48.

Rado, S. (1926), The psychic effect of intoxicants: An attempt to evolve a psychoanalytic theory of morbid craving. Internat. J. Psycho-Anal., 7: 396–413. Also in: Psychoanalysis of Behavior. New York: Grune & Stratton, 1956, pp. 25–39.

———— (1933), The psychoanalysis of pharmacothymia. Psychoanal. Quart., 2: 1–23, pp. 25–39. Also in: Psychoanalysis of Behavior, New York: Grune & Stratton, 1956, pp. 64–80.

———— (1969), The emotions. In: Adaptational Psychodynamics, ed. H. Klein. New York: Science House.

Rickles, W. H. (1976), Some theoretical aspects of the psychodynamics of successful biofeedback treatment. Presented at the Seventh Annual Meeting of the Biofeedback Research Society.

Roueché, B. (1960), Placebo. The New Yorker, Oct. 15, pp. 85–103.

Santostefano, S. (1977), New views on motivation and cognition in psychoanalytic theory: The horse (id) and rider (ego) revisited. McLean Hosp. J., 2: 48–63.

Savitt, R. A. (1963), Psychoanalytic studies on addiction: Ego structure in narcotic addicts. Psychoanal. Quart., 32: 43–57.

Schafer, R. (1972), Internalization: Process or fantasy? The Psychoanalytic Study of the Child, 27: 411–438. New York: International Universities Press.

Schwartz, G. E. (1973), Biofeedback as therapy: Some theoretical and practical issues. Amer. Psychologist, Aug.: 666–673.

Sechehaye, M. A. (1951), Symbolic Realization. New York: International Universities Press.

Shapiro, A. K. (1960), Contribution to a history of the placebo effect. Behav. Sci., 5: 109–135.

Shor, R. E. (1962), Physiological effects of painful stimulation during hypnotic analgesia under conditions designed to minimize anxiety. Internat. J. Clin. & Exper. Hypn., 10: 183–192.

Sifneos, P. (1967), Clinical observations on some patients suffering from a variety of psychosomatic diseases. Acta Med. Psychosom. Proceedings of the Seventh European Conference on Psychosomatic Research, Rome, Sept. 11–16, pp. 452–458.

———— (1973), The prevalence of "alexithymic" characteristics in psychosomatic patients. In: Psychotherapy and Psychosomatics, 22: 255–262. Basel: S. Kerger.

Sifneos, P. (1975), Problems of psychotherapy of patients with alexithymic character-istics and physical disease. Psychother. Psychosom., 26: 65–70.

Simmel, E. (1930), Morbid habits and cravings. Psychoanal. Rev., 17: 48–54.

―――― (1948), Alcoholism and addiction. Psychoanal. Quart., 12: 6–31.

Spitz, R. A. (1962), Autoeroticism re-examined: The role of early sex behavior patterns in personality formation. The Psychoanalytic Study of the Child, 17: 283–315. New York: International Universities Press.

―――― (1963), Ontogenesis: The proleptic function of emotions. In: Expression of Emotion in Man, ed. P. E. Knapp. New York: International Universities Press.

Stoyva, J. (1970), The public (scientific) study of private events. In: Biofeedback & Self-Control 1970, ed. T. S. Barber et al. Chicago: Aldine, pp. 29–42.

Szasz, T. S. (1958), The counterphobic mechanism in addiction. J. Amer. Psychoanal. Assn., 6: 309–325.

Tolpin, M. (1971), On the beginning of a cohesive self: An application of the concept of transmuting idealization to the study of the transitional object and signal anxiety. The Psychoanalytic Study of the Child, 26: 316–54. New York: International Universities Press.

Vaillant, G. E. (1973), The dangers of transference in the treatment of alcoholism. Presented to the Symposium on Alcoholism. Boston University.

Van Lawick-Goodall, J. (1973), The behavior of chimpanzees in their natural habitat. Amer. J. Psychiat., 130: 1–13.

Wetmore, R. J. (1963), The role of grief in psychoanalysis. Internat. J. Psycho-Anal., 44: 97–103.

Wieder, H., & Kaplan, E. H. (1969), Drug use in adolescents: Psychodynamic mean-ing and pharmacogenic effect. The Psychoanalytic Study of the Child, 24: 399–431. New York: International Universities Press.

Wolf, S., & Pinskey, R. H. (1942), Effect of placebo administration and occurrence of toxic reactions. JAMA, 135: 339–341.

Wurmser, L. (1974), Psychoanalytic considerations of the etiology of compulsive drug use. J. Amer. Psychoanal. Assn., 22: 820–943.

―――― (1978), Drug Abuse—The Hidden Dimension. New York: Jason Aronson.

Zinberg, N. E. (1975), Addiction and ego function. The Psychoanalytic Study of the Child, 20: 567–588. New York: International Universities Press.

8. Addiction and Ego Function

Norman E. Zinberg

SLOWLY but definitely there is a growing acceptance of the idea that in order to understand what motivates someone to use illicit drugs and what effect these drugs will have on him, one must take drug, set, and setting into account (Brecher, 1972; *Drug Use in America,* 1973; Edwards, 1973; Khantzian et al., 1974; Weil, 1972; Zinberg and Robertson, 1972; Zinberg and DeLong, 1974). That is, for such understanding the pharmacological action of the drug, how a person approaches the experience, which includes an assessment of his entire personality structure, and the physical and social setting in which the use takes place must all be considered and balanced. A not unusual paradox has begun to develop: the concept of drug effect being a product of these three variables is becoming a commonplace among mental health professionals before the implications of the notion for psychoanalytic theory, in particular, and personality theories, in general, have been worked through (Eddy et al., 1963; Jaffe, 1970; Khantzian, 1974; Wurmser, 1973; Yorke, 1970). Thus, existing misconceptions about a one-to-one relationship between personality maladjustment and drug use and addiction continue unabated.

In this essay, building on the work of several psychoanalytic theorists (Gill and Brenman, 1959; Hartmann, 1939; Klein, 1959; Rapaport, 1958; Zinberg, 1963), especially that of David Rapaport, I shall present clinical studies of compulsive drug use, describe how the users' responses to drugs have changed over time, review Rapaport's positions and show how these apply to the clinical states described, and, finally, discuss the implications of all this for dynamic theory and therapy.

THE INFLUENCE OF SOCIAL SETTING ON DRUG USE

Before turning to the clinical studies of compulsive drug use and users, I shall briefly consider the belief that such use almost invariably stems from

Reprinted by permission from *The Psychoanalytic Study of the Child,* vol. 30, Solnit et al., eds. (New Haven: Yale University Press, 1975), 567–88. Copyright © Yale University Press.

severe personality maladjustment or from the individual's being overwhelmed by a powerful chemical. It is true that people described as oral dependent (Rado, 1958), unable to tolerate anxiety (Goldstein, 1972) or aggression (Khantzian, 1974; Wurmser, 1973), or borderline schizophrenics (Radford et al., 1972), do use various illicit drugs to help them deal with their painful affects. Their histories reveal that following the discovery of their drug or drugs of choice, a quick and insistent dependence develops. But it is my contention that these people make up only a fraction, and probably a small one, of even the addict population, let alone the general drug-using population. The idea that certain personality types seek out drug experience because of a specific, early, unresolved developmental conflict, and that such people predominate in the addict group or in the much larger group of controlled users, is based on retrospective falsification. That is, looking at drug users and especially addicts, after they have become preoccupied with their drug experience, authorities assume that these attitudes and this personality state are similar to those the user had before the drug experience, and thus led to it. Then "evidence" from the user's developmental history and previous object relationships is marshaled to show that the addicted state was the end point of a long-term personality process.

This is *not* to say that internal factors are not involved in the decision to use drugs, in the effects of the drugs on the individual, on the rapidity and extent of the increase in drug use, and on the addiction itself and its psychological and social concomitants. But it is to say that there are no psychological profiles or consistent patterns of internal conflicts or phase-specific developmental sequences that can be put forward as the determining factor in the history of drug use and addiction.

Yet, this reasoning persists despite our cultural historical experience with alcohol (Chafetz and Demone, 1962). In the eighteenth century this powerful drug was used very much as heroin is today (Harrison, 1964): 75 or 80 percent of drinkers were alcoholics. Today while there may be 6 to 8 million alcoholics, there are 100 million controlled drinkers of every personality type. Our relative control over alcohol stems from the inculcation of social maxims and rituals (Zinberg and Jacobson, 1974a). "Don't start until sundown," "Know your limit," "Don't drink alone" all serve to minimize excess consumption. There is no consistent effort to select out susceptible personality types, and growing evidence suggests that not even those who do become alcoholics represent specific personality types (McCord and McCord, 1960; Wilkinson, 1970). Hence, it is surprising that there continues to be so much emphasis on the personality of the drug user when there is growing evidence of the power of the social setting to sustain controlled use of a powerful drug among many different personality types (Chafetz and Demone, 1962; Powell, 1973; Zinberg and Jacobson, 1974b).

While the bulk of the clinical work to be presented here will be concerned with the compulsive use of heroin, the history of LSD use over the last decade makes a nice beginning. From about 1965 to 1969 both professionals and the public were terrified by occasional and compulsive use of LSD (Smith, 1969; Tarshis, 1972). Mental hospitals such as Bellevue and Massachusetts Mental Health Center reported that 25 to 35 percent of their admissions resulted from bad trips (Brecher, 1972). The general feeling at that time was that even a single dose of LSD could tip someone who was either seriously disturbed or at a particularly vulnerable life moment, while continued, heavy use, according to this view, would inevitably wear away an individual's psychological capacity to function. Statistics which cited these frequent admissions to mental hospitals, along with lurid accounts in the media of suicides, homicides, and generally bizarre behavior, seemed to justify the fears.

With the passage of just a few years the situation looks quite different. McGlothlin and Arnold (1971) studied 256 subjects who had taken a psychedelic drug *before* 1962, that is, before the enormous publicity of the "Leary era" with its incredible hopes for enlightenment and insight, and the anxiety that inevitably accompanies an act believed to be so daring and potentially disappointing. Although McGlothlin and Arnold's subjects acknowledged that taking these drugs was a powerful experience—indeed some of the subjects thought it had deeply affected their lives—there were no bad trips reported of the kind that lead to mental hospitalization. And today when, according to the 1973 Report of the President's Commission on Marihuana and Drug Abuse, psychedelic drug use is the fastest growing drug use in the United States (*Drug Use in America,* 1973), mental hospitals no longer report bad trips as a factor in admissions. As of July 1974 the Massachusetts Mental Health Center did not know when they last had such an admission, but they were sure that it had been years rather than months ago (Grinspoon, 1974).

Clearly, the pattern of use has changed. The individual taking 200 to 250 trips in one year in a furious search for mystic enlightenment has given way to the two- or three-times-a-year tripper who closely follows countercultural maxims designed to minimize anxiety. To "only trip in a good place at a good time with good people" makes sense with a drug which increases certain perceptual responses. The fact is that the same strong drug is used today by an increasingly wide variety of personality types. Thus the evidence indicates that it was the social setting that got out of hand; before those wild years of the 60s and since, users in a calmer social setting could adapt to and tolerate the experience.

Another excellent piece of work offers further support for this position. The Barr et al. study (1972), which gave LSD to subjects before 1962, strongly suggests that one cannot assume that those people ordinarily diagnosed as significantly disturbed react more severely to these drugs than those considered "healthier." This work shows that a typology of responses to the drug can be constructed, but that they would not be directly determined by the degree of emotional disturbance. Thus personality is a factor in the drug response, just as the drug itself produces unquestioned strong effects, but without a careful understanding of the powerful, and in the case of LSD, almost determining, influence of social setting, many authorities could and did misinterpret what happened in the 60s.

Another example of the power of the social setting to determine drug use and, in this case, the development of drug dependency and addiction comes from our sad experience in Vietnam. Hundreds of thousands of American youths found themselves among people who hated them, fighting a terrifying war they neither understood nor approved, with illicit drugs readily available (Wilbur, 1972, 1974; *Washington Post*, 1971). The Army's misunderstanding of marihuana use led to an "educational" campaign against that drug and the enforcement of penalties. Enlisted men quickly found in heroin an odorless, far less bulky replacement which had the unique property of making time seem to disappear. As almost every enlisted man in Vietnam desired nothing so ardently as to have the year to DEROS (Date of Expected Return from Overseas) pass, many thousands used great quantities of that pure, cheap white powder (Zinberg, 1971, 1972a, 1972b). Data from the rehabilitation centers and from camps processing men returning from overseas leave no doubt that a great many of those using heroin were physiologically addicted. Also, final Army data make it possible to say assuredly (despite the Army's early claims that only those who were heavy drug users before service became addicted) that these young men displayed a wide variety of personality types, that they came from diverse social, ethnic, geographic, and religious backgrounds, and that few were drug users before they went to Vietnam (Robins, 1974). When authorities and professionals alike realized the extent of heroin use in Vietnam, consternation and surprise were expressed that such a variety of people who did not conform to addict stereotypes could become addicts, and fear about what would happen in the United States when these people returned dominated most discussions (Wilbur, 1974). These concerns rested on the traditional view that heroin was so powerful a drug that once one was in its thrall there was no escape. Also, the underlying suspicion remained that, despite the evidence of a variety of personality types using the drug, the users were potential drug-dependents who would have been saved in the United States by the lack of availability of heroin.

Studies of returned Vietnam veterans have shown that for a fraction (under 10 percent) of those who had become drug dependent these fears of continued addiction were realized, but that the vast majority (over 90 percent) gave up heroin upon return to the United States. The determining factor in their heroin use had been the intolerable setting of Vietnam, and once they returned to the United States neither the power of the drug nor a susceptible personality proved to be decisive in keeping them drug dependent (Robins, 1974).

DESCRIPTION OF ADDICTS

The sample of U.S. addicts was obtained from a large detoxification center and two psychological-treatment-oriented methadone clinics. Over a period of 16 months 54 addicts were interviewed for approximately two hours each. They ranged in age from 19 to 34; 35 were male and 14 black. Addicts were chosen solely on the basis of their having applied to the methadone clinic or having gone into the fourth day of detoxification on a day when the investigator had time available. Although each of the addicts studied was as sharply different from the next in presentation and general superficial personality as any other members of the population, a psychodynamic formulation showed them to be remarkably alike in their psychological difficulties.

To begin with, junkies look a lot alike: they are usually thin, their clothing shabby, and their person somewhat unkempt. Initial conversations reveal their almost total preoccupation with heroin or its replacements and the life style that surrounds its compulsive use. Drug effect, drug availability, drug necessity—getting off, copping, hustling—and a concern with the legal, physical, and psychological hazards that go with those interests preoccupy them. As a result of their addiction they see themselves as deviants with little sense of relatedness to the straight world. Their sense of themselves seems to derive from their negative social and psychological responses such as antisocial activities, rebellion, expressed aggression against the "bastards," and from their own victimization. In Erikson's (1959) terms, they depend on a negative identity for a measure of self-esteem and self-definition.

In our conversations the subjects revealed a direct belief in magic, often centering around the drug and its use, but extending to other areas as well.

Junkies frequently tell of how their lives have been star-crossed, with ordinary events being given the power to save or destroy. In these stories frank primary process thinking seems available to consciousness. These thoughts come out as distorted ideas: "I knew if my parents told my grandfather about my sister's marriage, it would kill him, and I was the only one who could stop them." "I knew the train would be late that day before I got on it. There was an aura around the whole station." Or they show an indistinct differentiation between objective reality and a fantasy or magical view: "All it takes is for me to get my shit together, then I can handle all that." The defenses of projection, introjection, and denial are consistently prominent, as is repression, which will be considered separately. As their associations tend to be loose anyway, the combination gives an almost bizarre flavor to most interactions: "I never give in. I'm always fighting the dope and those bastards in the clinic gave me the wrong dope. I know that it doesn't work on me in liquid form and they won't help me cut down by getting the pills."

It must be remembered that despite this presentation of themselves junkies are rarely schizophrenic. Vaillant's 12-year follow-up (1966a, 1966b) found few addicts in mental hospitals, and the clinical impressions of other investigators since then support his work. Since the growth of heroin use in the late 60s, undoubtedly more borderline or schizophrenic people have used heroin as an effort at self-medication, but they remain a small minority—which strikes me as remarkable every time I finish another interview, for it is hard to believe that all addicts are not crazy after talking with them.

There is a general conscious deterioration of the superego. Junkies will tell you fairly frankly that they do what they have to do to survive and get drugs. They know that they cannot be trusted to follow the usual rules, ethics, and codes of social behavior. Tales of stealing from and lying to friends and family abound. Usually there is little real acceptance of responsibility. Their anger and blame for all sorts of troubles are reserved for those circumstances or people that spoiled the perfect deal, the neat setup—often authorities in some form. But always the drug is the basic preoccupation. Their readiness to blame those who interfere with their using the drug so that it works magically is unending. The hours given over in methadone clinics to discussing dosage and whether they are getting enough of the drug, in the right form, by the right person, at the right time, in the right way are literally uncountable. These expressions, while they seem paranoid in flavor and content and carry bitterness and conviction, are nonetheless not paranoid in a paranoid schizophrenic way. The addicts permit their ideas to be more or less susceptible to reality testing if the tester is willing to be subtle, forceful, and extremely patient.

And, as one might expect, while the junkies accept their own unwillingness to play by the rules, they deeply and passionately feel that others, particularly authorities, must. In a way there is no paradox here because their primitive unconscious superego never rests. Junkies are not only self-destructive in the sense that they are incredibly accident prone and constantly arranging to be hurt, but they also manage almost never to do well for themselves in the simplest life transactions. They do lose laundry slips and money, choose the wrong alternative at each instance, and are invariably being gypped at the very moment they think they are slyest. These experiences ostensibly result in an increase in blame for "them" and a feeling that the big strong ones, the doctors, counselors, probation officers, should be more helpful to and more responsible for the poor addict; but this position is invariably accompanied by rigorous and overwhelming self-loathing.

As a result they are argumentative, particularly in a methadone clinic, about matters affecting their precious substance, but very ineffectually so. This need to be unpleasant and to set up struggles that are doomed to defeat arises directly from their insistence on putting and keeping themselves in a weak position. But often if one pushes further into the arcane thought processes surrounding each instance of trouble, fantasy fears that have developed into phobias become apparent. For example, a methadone clinic regulation requires a physical examination; two appointments in a row were missed by several patients, putting them in jeopardy of dismissal from the clinic. Careful questioning revealed that a baseless rumor was circulating that anyone who didn't "pass" the physical would be hospitalized, and since addicts' response to hospitals is truly phobic, they didn't show up for the exam. The development of similar overwhelming fears among junkies is quite common and somehow exaggerated when juxtaposed against the superficial tough (but done in) guy/gal image they try to project.

The breakdown in logical thinking, the disorganization of the ordinary cognitive process above and beyond the difficulty in reality testing is so severe that the inexperienced interviewer fails to understand their educational and vocational accomplishments. Their memories, for example, are terrible, and there seems to be no psychodynamic rhyme or reason to the lacunae. Thinking of repression simply as a defense and an aid to denial and projection does not help one to achieve a dynamic formulation. Neither can one rely for an explanation on conscious dissembling. Certainly the interviewer knows that there is much overt lying to hide real or fancied transgressions and to protect secret pockets of potential gratification. But the forgetting of both significant and insignificant life events and activities often acts more to the addict's detriment on his own terms. Hard as it is to imagine, some even forget a stash of drugs, and they easily manage not to remember addresses, appointments, relevant history, and so on, which could help get them a welfare check or other disability assistance. Running through all this cognitive deterioration is a disorientation of the time sense, which may well be related to the drug experience. Heroin seems to "make time go away," and compensating for that experience may be difficult.

Taken overall, then, this study of addicts shows people whose everyday psychological state seems compatible with a diagnosis of borderline schizophrenia or worse, but who are not schizophrenic; whose current ego functions and cognitive capacities make past accomplishments inexplicable, but who are at times remarkably capable and intellectually able; and who, from this dynamic perspective, appear a lot alike. It is easy to understand the temptation to use this sort of material to work out formulations that would "explain" their seeking drugs and drug dependency. It must be remembered, however, that compared to psychoanalysis or intensive dynamic therapy, these interviews are brief and superficial. Further and more intensive interviewing might disclose more subtle and pervasive evidence of early gross family and individual psychiatric impairment. However, within the severe limitations of this study, the families of these patients were described as consistently different from each other. Only four cases presented frank early histories of emotional disturbance, early school difficulty, and the general sense of oddness associated with early borderline schizophrenia or early severe character disorders.[1]

ADDICTION AND RELATIVE EGO AUTONOMY

Rapaport (1958) delineated the factors that maintain relative ego autonomy. He began by observing that nonliving matter cannot escape the impact of the environment and thus the results of the interaction are invariant and statistically predictable. This is not true of living matter. At times psychoanalytic theory has tried to pretend that inner forces are strong enough to develop some sort of predictability despite the uncounted variables acting through the physical and social environment, but this has not worked out. Using the Berkeleyian and Cartesian positions to develop a dialectic, Rapaport points out that in the Berkeleyian view man is totally independent of the environment and totally dependent on inner forces and drives. He need have little concern for the external world since it is "created" by inherent forces. The cartoon psychiatrist who is shown asking someone who has been hit by a car, "How did you cause this to happen to you?" is an exaggerated clinical version of this position.

Descartes, on the other hand, saw man as a clean slate upon which experience writes. He is totally dependent upon and thus in harmony with the outside world, and totally independent of, autonomous from, internal desires. In essence, Cartesians, like behaviorists, view such drives and the unconscious supposedly containing them as nonexistent. This may well account for the failure of learning machines. Human conflicts over success and failure turned out to be more dominant than the desire for M&Ms.

Rapaport reasons that neither of these totally divergent positions speaks to man's experience: that to understand how the ego, whose functions determine and delineate a sense of self, remains relatively autonomous and copes with the demands of the external environment and of the basic, inborn forces Freud termed "instinctual drives" requires consideration of both and their interactions. The autonomy Rapaport postulated is always relative, and the inside drives and the outside environment carefully balance each other. Drives prevent man from becoming a stimulus-response slave,[2] while the constant stream of stimulus nutriment from the environment mediates and moderates the primitive drives[3] by sustaining primary ego apparatuses such as motor capacity, thinking, memory, perceptual and discharge thresholds, and the capacity for logical communication. In addition, external reality nurtures those secondary ego apparatuses—such as competence, cognitive organization, values, ideals, and a mature conscience, determined by each particular culture as adaptive—and allows these characteristics to become successfully estranged from original drive functions.

Thus the relationship between the ego's relative autonomy from the id and the ego's relative autonomy from the environment is one of interdependence. When drives are at peak tension, as in puberty, the ego's autonomy from the id is in jeopardy. Adolescents try to combat their tendency to subjectivity, seclusiveness, and rebellion by the external reality-related converse of these—intellectualization, distance from primary objects, and efforts at total companionship. But it is an unequal and often painful struggle.

The ego's autonomy from the id can also be disrupted by minimizing the balancing input from external reality. Experiments with stimulus deprivation (Bexton et al., 1954; Heron et al., 1953, 1956; Lilly, 1956) showed how susceptible individuals became autistic and suffered from magical fantasies, disordered thought sequences, disturbed reality testing, primitive defenses, and poor memory under such conditions.

Similarly, conditions which permit only restricted and frightening forms of stimulus nutriment impair the ego's relative autonomy from the external environment. When, as in a concentration camp, external conditions maximize the individual's sense of danger and arouse fears and neediness, the drives no longer act as guarantors of autonomy from the environment but prompt surrender. The deprivation of varied stimulus nutriment and its replacement by insistent streams of instructions in the stimulus-deprivation experiments gave those instructions power and engendered belief. In order to maintain a sense of separate identity, values, ideologies, and orderly thought structures, people require support for existing verbal and memory structures. Not surprisingly, Rapaport used George Orwell's *1984* as a text—one which described in exact and clinical detail how this interdependence functioned under environmental conditions intended to turn the individual into a stimulus-response slave.

Throughout his discussion Rapaport insists that the superego in particular is dependent on consistent stimulus nutriment. The convention, or American Legionnaire, syndrome—when moderate, respectable men and women remove themselves from their usual routines and social relationships and behave in an impulsive and uncontrolled manner—makes it very clear how heavily the strictures of conscience depend on social structure.

The junkies described earlier have lost varied sources of stimulus nutriment. Families have been alienated and previous social relationships severed; or, if contact remains, it consists usually of acrimonious or pleading discussions about giving up drugs. Addicts are declared deviant by the larger society and are referred to as an epidemic, a plague, and the "number one problem" of the country. The social input available to them is thus either a negative view of themselves or the ceaseless patter of their compulsive drug-using groups. Have you copped? When? Where? Was it good? What do I need to cop? What if I can't? Who got busted? Will I get busted? These are conditions, albeit self-arranged, which meet the conditions of stimulus-deprivation experiments. At the same time the addict's desire for gratification from the drug itself, and the memory of the result, a withdrawal syndrome, if the drug is unavailable, keeps drive structures at peak tension.

According to Rapaport's formulation, a regressive state should develop when the ego is unable to maintain its relative autonomy from either the id or the external environment. In such a state the barriers differentiating ego and id processes become fluid. Images, ideas, and fantasies based on primary process thinking rise to consciousness, and there develops a reliance on more and more primitive defenses. The sense of voluntariness and of having inner control of one's actions in relation to oneself and to the external environment disappears. Is that not exactly what I have described as the general clinical picture of the junkie?

The necessity to cop, which excessively increases the addict's dependence on the environment, impairs his ego's autonomy from the id. At the same time, being labeled deviant decreases varied contacts with the usual environmental supports and thus also impairs his ego's autonomy from the id. The addicts' efforts to continue some coherent relationships with whatever objects are left to them make them dependent on external cues. They suffer constantly from doubts about their ability to maintain such relationships, and they cling to stereotyped views of themselves. This clinging to what remains of the external environment maximizes the ego's autonomy from the id, but at the cost of minimizing the conscious input of and trust in affective and ideational signals that usually regulate judgment and decision—that is, at the cost of impairing the ego's autonomy from the environment.

Thus the addicts' relative autonomy from both id and external environment is impaired. They are isolated from their own useful emotions and those views of the world which permit a coherent and integrated sense of self. They are at the mercy of primitive impulses and an overwhelming sense of neediness that invades, or more nearly blocks out, a capacity to perceive and integrate "objective" reality. Filled with doubts, they gullibly respond to those in the external environment who offer schemes or promises that might bring magical succor.

As a result of these impaired autonomies the ego must make do with insufficient or distorted input from both id and external environment. The ego must modify its structures to conform to this new, more restricted, and primitive pattern. It is my clinical impression that the addict's ego fights to retain whatever level of ego functioning can be saved. It is this very struggle to retain some measure of ego functions which is a principal source of the rigidity that therapists working with the addicts, in and out of methadone clinics, find so trying. As long as addicts are classified by the larger culture as deviants, it is hard to imagine that they can see themselves as anything else. And as long as their relationships with the external world continue to supply only restricted stimulus nutriment, the blocking of most affective input not oriented to direct gratification *probably* will continue. Whatever new ego homeostasis the individual has achieved is likely to be rigid and to have a slow rate of change. When threatened, as these people's egos constantly are, by changeable but insistent demands for gratification from drive structures, the new homeostasis of ego functioning cannot easily integrate fresh stimulus nutriment, not even input that is as neutral and sustaining as a therapeutic relationship. Or perhaps it would be more accurate to say: *particularly* the input of a therapeutic relationship because these interactions are *intended* to be at variance with the addicts' usual interpersonal interactions and to make their usual reliance on selective perception, quick repression, projection, and denial more difficult.

There are two other points which stress the importance of the social setting. In showing how the labeling of the addict as a deviant becomes a key factor in impairing his relative ego autonomy I described the extent to which primary process ideation such as interest in magic, belief in animism, generalized unfounded suspiciousness, and acceptance of extremely childish rhetoric become regressively active in regular ego functioning. Junkies often seem to me to be vaguely aware of their own primitive response. But they cannot integrate such thinking sufficiently to make it part of a conscious way of questioning the world, i.e., secondary process, first because the primitive feelings much of the time seem so real. A second interrelated issue is the unconscious effort to retain existing capacity to function no matter how unsatisfactory. In the 60s users of LSD had a similar problem. They too regarded their "trip" as exceptional and at that point found few points of reference between the trip experience and their previous social and psychological experiences. But by the 70s, as a recent study contends (Zinberg, 1974), occasional psychedelic drug users have the same unusual psychic experiences that their counterparts of the 60s had. However, the accumulated and widely dispersed knowledge about the experience prepared them for it. They think about their experiences and discuss them with friends in order to separate out drug effect from essential and usual self-perspectives. Thus the experience is secondary process oriented.

PROSPECTIVE STUDY OF ADDICTION

In 1967–68 I engaged in a large-scale interviewing process to select candidates for a controlled experiment giving marihuana to human subjects (Zinberg and Weil, 1970). Three of those interviewed but not selected for the experiment, who had not used heroin at that time, have gone on to become compulsive heroin users. One is included in the sample of 54 described above, and I have had some lengthy conversations with the other two. They are reluctant to be followed, so I cannot make a full report. Suffice it to say that although all three had many individual quirks and peculiarities in 1967, none was at all like the prototypical junkie then and all three are now. In 1967 the man included in the present sample was rebellious and active in radical politics, intensely intellectual, harshly self-searching, with high standards for himself and others. He had a wide circle of friends and acquaintances which was beginning to narrow at the time I knew him as a result of political disagreements. Nevertheless, his sense of objective reality was not in doubt, his memory was excellent, and his capacity for logical thinking was of the highest order. At that time he had begun to be estranged from his parents, particularly his father, although they too were committed to the political left, and their disagreement was more on method than principle. Previously, despite a lifetime of arguing and concern about economic instability, their relationship had been an enduring one, and he had been quite close to two of his three siblings.

In 1973, while being detoxified for the third time, he had not seen or heard from a family member in over two years. His thought processes were slow and jumpy, and his associations loose. Although he remembered me, he had difficulty in sticking to the subject of the interview, wandering to questions about my hospital function, his medications, and his chances of recovering. When he returned to the subject, his memory was poor, his recall distorted, and his acceptance of responsibility for himself *nil*. At that moment he was on probation for two offenses and had another charge of possession with intent to sell narcotics pending. He gave every evidence of being an impulsive, poorly controlled person. Physically it was hard to recognize him as the same man, and he too said, "I'm not the same person you talked to then."

Both here and in England I have interviewed (Zinberg and Robertson, 1972) many heroin addicts of up to 30 years' standing who showed no emotional or intellectual deterioration. Hence, I do not believe the drug itself was responsible for this man's deterioration, nor can I, on the basis of my previous knowledge of this man, accept the explanation of preexisting addictive personality. I do not at this writing understand what pushed him into addiction. He claims it was fortuity. Following many severe political disappointments and a marked reduction in his social group, he found himself with people whose regular polydrug use, including heroin, was far heavier than his previous standard. They were heavy users of downers (barbiturates), which he had never liked. When they took downers, he used heroin. After a year and a half of chipping (occasional use), he woke up one morning after not using and recognized that the severe stomach cramps, gooseflesh, and sweating meant that he was strung out. He made many efforts to kick, but after that it was essentially downhill all the way.

No doubt somewhere in his psyche the conflicts concerning responsibility, self-sufficiency, and rebellion existed in 1967. But as Freud (1937) argues so persuasively, latent conflicts of all sorts may exist, but whether they will ever become manifest is determined by the subject's life experiences. It is my impression—and I hope to be able to study these three men more thoroughly—that just as with the Vietnam heroin users, it was the changed social setting that was instrumental in impairing their relative ego autonomy.

TREATMENT OF ADDICTS

Mental health workers of all sorts in methadone clinics, detoxification centers, and the like, already have discovered that therapy must be oriented around current reality. Basically it is important for the therapist to point out again and again what his job is. He wants to work with addicts in ways that will help them to find out how their heads work and how they consistently manage to do the worst for themselves. The therapist is friendly, but he is not there to love them, and anyway his love has no special magical healing property. Neither is he a boss, a job counselor, a dispenser of drugs, or the arbiter of dose increases; he has no prescriptions for living with or without drugs. What stops the addicts from using him appropriately, from trying to make sense of what is going on in their lives? How is it that they want him to be anything but a therapist and want so much to bamboozle, provoke, or seduce him? These are the sorts of questions the therapists find themselves asking.

They are keenly aware of the disappointments, deprivations, and social and psychological isolation of a junkie's life, just as therapists are aware of the high excitement to be found in hustling, copping, and shooting up, compared with which a straight life is seen as a conscience-oriented gray straitjacket, and they try to convey their ability to understand this conflict. Therapists point out how the longings for authoritarianism and the clear-cut concepts of what's right and wrong, at least for others, are based on the junkies' lost trust in their own controls, judgment, and awareness of their own wishes. In effect, the therapy aims at understanding how those ego functions which operate do so; how those that might don't; and what makes such ego functioning difficult; also, how the primitive unconscious superego is active but not helpful. The therapy further intends to show how the remaining ego capacity which at times attempts realistically to modify and moderate behavior is ignored.

This therapeutic approach is well known and intended to help restore the lost relative ego autonomy by using the therapist, clinic, and hospital as a source of fresh, diverse stimulus nutriment. These significant social relationships also act to help the subject's embattled ego be less fearful of his drives. Usually, the theory of technique lags behind the formation of a general theory even if individual practitioners learn how to use theoretical concepts intuitively. This essay is intended to add an understanding of what happens to the ego as a result of the changed social condition of the addict and of how this theoretical position can be extended into technique. Hence, if this theoretical view of the patient's problems is accepted, a therapist would not often or forcefully interpret projection or confront denial. It would be useless and actually psychonoxious to point out that the junkie's feeling that the staff of a clinic is hostile and wants to degrade and deprecate him stems from his own destructive preoccupations with himself and others. Rather the staff members consistently explain what they are there for and ask what troubles the addict about their function; that is, therapists provide him with constant, gentle reaffirmation of reality and show how unnecessary much of his difficulty with it is. Thus, the need for the projection and denial becomes less urgent.

Although some discussion of the addict's past and of his or her family relationships may have occasional usefulness, generally speaking this area is of less interest when working with the addict group than in more usual dynamic therapies. For one thing, such discussions often turn into an interest in the motives and interrelationships that may have led the addict to drug use and drug dependency, and this, if the formulations derived in this paper are accurate, is a fruitless area. At least, when one considers the complexity of drug, set, and setting interactions, it is not one that can be worked on until the addict is in better psychological condition. Incidentally, a further complication with most of the 54 addicts studied—and this is again part of the social setting—is that they are "treatment wise." Almost all of them have had experiences in concept houses and with confrontation groups of all sorts. Although they have rarely followed through with these programs, they have developed a patter about what they are feeling and why they are the way they are that serves as armor against reasonable conversation. A therapist following the theory of technique offered here, rather than showing interest in the motivation for drug use and being drawn into discussions of dependency, neediness, anxiety, aggression, and aspects of early development and early family life, would allow that the addict might have had to do many things *then* but could *now* stop and recognize that this or that action might not be as necessary as he experiences it.

It is around therapeutic interactions such as these that this theory of technique becomes important. At times, dynamic therapists who know that they must work toward reestablishing relative ego autonomy and relieving the pressure of the archaic superego feel that unless they uncover and help the patients understand the initial motivations for the behavior, they are not doing their job. When therapists have a concern that they must do both, it creates a duality in the therapy. With people as embattled and desperate as the addicts, it is a subtle and difficult therapeutic problem to remain constant in outlining the therapeutic context and the reduced fields of relationship both to drive structures and to the external environment. Bringing in long-term motivational conflicts is seductive. Maintaining the awareness that such clarifications are both too confusing to the addicts and too frustrating for the therapist is very difficult. The therapist should remember that junkies do not do well for themselves, and the higher the therapeutic hopes of the therapist, if they are excessive, the greater the disappointment. It is no accident that from Synanon on many "therapies" for junkies involved punishing, authoritarian regimens. Most addicts are provocative. They ask to be contained in a way that could easily be translated into a wish to be punished. It is my impression that, whether the addict asks for punishment or not, fulfilling such a wish sets up a vicious cycle. Punishment is followed by a sense of entitlement, followed by guilt, followed by a fresh, unconscious desire to be punished. A therapy that questions the current premises of the addict's behavior and indicates that he has choices and has to accept responsibility for them is containing and limit-setting; and if it is carried out with respect for the dignity of the patient and a precise understanding of his premises, it is neither punishing nor gimmicky.

To sustain such a therapy requires an awareness of the crucial role of the social setting in the current ego state of the addict. And for many professionals that means a shift in their assessment of what has happened to the individual who has become drug dependent. Without that shift the tendency to focus on motivations and unconscious conflicts which could have led to the dependency would be well-nigh irresistible. These factors remain important, as set is as integral a variable as setting, but personality conflict is no longer seen as *the* direct cause of the addict's deterioration.

NOTES

1. There is some further preliminary evidence that tends to point in the same direction but stems from interviews that were even more cursory, done by social workers and with a different intent. Within this sample, 30 families were interviewed by a social worker to decide upon admission to a methadone clinic. Although there were great differences in the family structure and the degrees of difficulty within the family, the workers found that only two of the families thought that the principal disturbances between the addict subjects and their significant others began before serious drug use.

2. Rapaport tells the story of the man who did not march in step to an enthralling military band because he was pondering, and points out how falling in love saved Orwell's Protagonist of *1984,* at least temporarily, from the press of that overwhelming environment.

3. Here, Rapaport uses the story of Moses and the great king who had been told by his seers and phrenologist that Moses was cruel, vain, and greedy. Upon finding Moses gentle, wise, and compassionate, the king planned to put his wise men to death. Moses demurred, saying, "They saw truly what I am. What they could not see was what I have made of it."

BIBLIOGRAPHY

Brecher, E. M., & Editors of Consumer Reports (1972), Licit and Illicit Drugs. *Boston: Little Brown.*

Barr, H. L., Langs, R. J., Hall, R. R., et al. (1972), LSD: Personality and Experience. *New York: Wiley Interscience.*

Bexton, W. H., Heron, W., & Scott, T. H. (1954), Effects of Decreased Variation in the Sensory Environment. Canad. J. Psychol., *8: 70–76.*

Chafetz, M. E., & Demone, H. W., Jr. (1962), Alcoholism and Society. *New York: Oxford Univ. Press.*

Drug Use in America: Problem in Perspective *(1973). Second Report of the National Commission on Marihuana and Drug Abuse. Washington, D.C.: U.S. Government Printing Office.*

Eddy, N. B.; Halbach, H., Isbell, H., et al. (1963), Drug Dependence. Bull. W.H.O. *2: 721–733.*

Edwards, G. (1973), The Plasticity of Human Response. *London: Maudsley Hospital (mimeograph).*

Erikson, E. H. (1959), Identity and the Life Cycle *[Psychol. Issues, Monogr. 1]. New York: Int. Univ. Press.*

Freud, S. (1937), Analysis Terminable and Interminable. S.E., *23: 209–253.*

Gill, M. M., & Brenman, M. (1959), Hypnosis and Related States. *New York: Int. Univ. Press.*

Goldstein, A. (1972), Heroin Addiction and the Role of Methadone in Its Treatment. Arch. Gen. Psychiat., 26: 291–298.

Grinspoon, L. (1974), Personal communication.

Harrison, B. (1964), English Drinking in the Eighteenth Century. New York/London: Oxford Univ. Press, 1958.

Hartmann, H. (1939), Ego Psychology and the Problem of Adaptation. New York: Int. Univ. Press, 1958.

Heron, W.; Bexton, W. H., & Hebb, D. O. (1953), Cognitive Effects of a Decreased Variation in the Sensory Environment. Amer. Psychologist, 8: 366–372.

——; Doone, B. K.; & Scott, T. H. (1956), Visual Disturbances After Prolonged Perceptual Isolation. Canad. J. Psychol., 10:13–18.

Jaffe, J. H. (1970), Drug Addiction and Drug Abuse. In: The Pharmacological Bases of Therapeutics, ed. L. S. Goodman & A. Gilman. New York: Macmillan.

Khantzian, E. J. (1974), Opiate Addiction. Amer. J. Psychother., 28: 59–70.

——; Mack, J. E.; & Schatzberg, A. F. (1974), Heroin Use as an Attempt to Cope. Amer. J. Psychiat., 131: 160–164.

Klein, G. S. (1959), Consciousness in Psychoanalytic Theory. J. Amer. Psychoanal. Assn., 7: 5–34.

Lilly, J. C. (1956), Mental Effects of Reduction of Ordinary Levels of Visual Stimuli on Intact Healthy Persons. Psychiat. Res. Rep., 5: 1–9.

McCord, J., & McCord, W. (1960), Origins of Alcoholism. Stanford: Stanford Univ. Press.

McGlothlin, W. H., & Arnold, D. O. (1971), LSD Revisited. Arch. Gen. Psychiat., 24: 35–49.

Orwell, G. (1949), 1984. New York: Harcourt Brace.

Powell, D. H. (1973), Occasional Heroin Users. Arch. Gen. Psychiat., 28: 586–594.

Radford, P.; Wiseberg, S.; & Yorke, C. (1972), A Study of "Main-Line" Heroin Addiction. Psychoanalytic Study of the Child. 27: 156–180.

Rado, S. (1958), Narcotic Bondage. In: Problems of Addiction and Habituation, ed. P. H. Hoch & J. Zubin. New York: Grune & Stratton, pp. 27–36.

Rapaport, D. (1958), The Theory of Ego Autonomy. In: The Collected Papers of David Rapaport, ed. M. M. Gill. New York: Basic Books, 1967, pp. 722–744.

Robins, L. (1974), A Followup Study of Vietnam Veterans' Drug Use. J. Drug Issues, 4: 62–81.

Smith, D. E. (1969), Lysergic Acid Diethylamide. J. Psychedel. Drugs. 1: 3–7.

Tarshis, M. S. (1972), The LSD Controversy. Springfield, Ill.: Thomas.

Vaillant, G. E. (1966a), A 12-Year Follow-up of New York Narcotic Addicts: I. Amer. J. Psychiat., 122: 727–737.

—— (1966b), A 12-Year Followup of New York Narcotic Addicts: III. Arch. Gen. Psychiat., 15: 599–609.

Washington Post (1971), The U.S. Army: Battle for Survival. 8-part Series, September 12–20.

Weil, A. T. (1972), The Natural Mind. New York: Houghton Mifflin.

Wilbur, R. S. (1972), How to Stamp Out a Heroin Epidemic. Today's Health, July, pp. 9–13.

—— (1974), *The Battle Against Drug Dependency within the Military.* J. Drug Issues, *4: 27–33.*

Wilkinson, R. (1970), The Prevention of Drinking Problems. *New York: Oxford Univ. Press.*

Wurmser, L. (1973), *Psychoanalytic Considerations of the Etiology of Compulsive Drug Use. Presented at the 60th Annual Meeting of the American Psychoanalytic Association, Honolulu, Hawaii.*

Yorke, C. (1970), *A Critical Review of Some Psychoanalytic Literature on Drug Addiction.* Brit. J. Med. Psychol., *43: 141–159.*

Zinberg, N. E. (1963), *The Relationship of Regressive Phenomena to the Aging Process. In:* The Normal Psychology of the Aging Process, *ed. N. E. Zinberg & I. Kaufman. New York: Int. Univ. Press.*

—— (1971), *GI's and OJ's in Vietnam.* N.Y. Times Mag., *December 5.*

—— (1972a), *Heroin Use in Vietnam and the United States.* Arch. Gen. Psychiat., *26: 486–488.*

—— (1972b), *Rehabilitation of Heroin Users in Vietnam.* Contemp. Drug Prob., *1: 263–294.*

—— (1974), "High" States. *Washington, D.C.: Drug Abuse Council Special Studies Series, SS-3.*

—— & DeLong, J. V. (1974), *Research and the Drug Issue.* Contemp. Drug Prob., *3: 71–100.*

—— & Jacobson, R. C. (1974a), *The Social Basis of Drug Abuse Prevention (unpublished).*

—— & Jacobson, R. C., (1974b), *The Natural History of Chipping (unpublished).*

—— & Robertson, J. A. (1972), Drugs and the Public. *New York: Simon & Schuster.*

—— & Weil, A.T. (1970), *A Comparison of Marihuana Users and Non-Users.* Nature, *226: 719–723.*

9. A General Theory of Addictions: A New Theoretical Model

Durand F. Jacobs

SIMILARITIES among different kinds of addicts have long been common knowledge. Clinicians have frequently commented on the similarities in backgrounds, course, treatment, and prognosis among persons with different kinds of addictive behavior patterns. Persons suffering from more than one addictive behavior who join a second (or third) self-help group such as Alcoholics Anonymous, Gamblers Anonymous, Overeaters Anonymous, have been quick to notice striking similarities between themselves and members of these presumably disparate groups. Yet, the tendency among scholarly researchers has been to examine each type of addiction as a separate entity, and to attempt to develop a distinct explanatory schema for each (Walker & Lidz, 1983). As a consequence, reports dealing with alcoholism, heroin and other drug addictions, eating disorders, compulsive gambling, and other addictive forms of behavior, tend to be found in distinct literatures with little cross-reference to one another. When this author first proposed and began testing a general theory of addictions in 1980 (using compulsive gamblers as the prototype subject) there had been little systematic searching for common denominators among various addictions as a unified class of behavior (Jacobs & Wright, 1980). Indeed, the first concerted attempt to present a systematic analysis of the common elements among different forms of addictive behaviors waited until the publication of "Commonalities in substance abuse and habitual behavior" (Levison, Gerstein, & Maloff, 1983). This book reported the outcome of a series of studies that were initiated by the National Institute on Drug Abuse (NIDA) in 1976. The intent was to gather and evaluate relevant scientific evidence that might indicate the extent to which many aspects of excessive substance use and other habitual activities might have common biological, psychological and/or social roots. In a series of meta-analyses a group of distinguished researchers gathered the scattered literature that might reveal underlying common processes in three areas:

Reprinted by permission from *Journal of Gambling Behavior* 2 (1986): 15–31. Copyright © Human Sciences Press, Inc.

sociocultural commonalities, psychological commonalities, and biological commonalities. While a wide range of habitual behaviors were considered, compulsive gambling was not, since "scientific evidence was simply insufficient to warrant intensive committee study" (Levison, Gerstein, & Maloff, 1983, preface). After balancing evidence supporting either similarities or differences among addictive forms of behavior, the editors concluded that, "In general, scientific knowledge does not at present provide the basis for a comprehensive theory of excessive, habitual behavior encompassing the available sociocultural, psychological, and biological evidence" (p. XVI). However, they acknowledged that "compelling and useful regularities do arise when researchers are guided by a coherent scientific frame of reference," and encouraged investigators to follow the research directions that emerged from a commonalities perspective.

Despite the guarded conclusions set forth by Levison et al., this author continues to believe that efforts should continue to explore the utility of theory building and testing regarding addictions as a unified class of behavior (Jacobs, 1982a; 1982b, 1984). Four major objectives have guided the formulation of this author's general theory of addiction. The first is to identify common elements that prevail across different classes of addictive behaviors. Secondly, to identify significant differences that emerge when comparing one class of addicts with another. Thirdly, to highlight and further explore puzzling inconsistencies. Finally, to compare known addicts of a given class with a normative sample including abstainers, users and abusers of that class of substance or activity.

The strategy selected for testing the general theory of addictions set forth in this paper is a matrix approach. Comparable information is being collected from populations of compulsive (pathological) gamblers, alcoholics, compulsive overeaters, drug addicts, and other groups who are characterized by one form or another of substance abuse or habitual behavior over which they have lost personal control (Jacobs, Marston, & Singer, 1985). The matrix design also includes normative samples of adolescent and adult populations who have responded to the same basic survey instrument. To the best of this author's knowledge this approach is the first in which a similar set of indices have been collected and compared across different classes of addicts, as well as normative samples. Hopefully, this strategy will facilitate further refinements in theory building. The ultimate goal is to construct descriptive models that will aid in better understanding the addictive process, as well as facilitate early identification and prompt treatment of persons at high risk for developing addictive patterns of behavior.

An Alternate View of the Etiology and Course of Addictive Behavior

Contrary to the position taken by most other workers, this author places primary emphasis on the presence of two interrelated sets of *predisposing* factors that are held to determine whether or not an individual is at risk of maintaining an addictive pattern of behavior. The first of these two sets of predisposing factors is: *a unipolar physiological resting state* that is chronically and excessively either depressed or excited. This lifelong persistent state of either hypo- or hyper-arousal is believed to predispose the individual to respond only to a rather narrow "window" of stress-reducing, but potentially addictive substances or experiences, and to make the person resistive to other kinds of addictive behaviors. The second set of predisposing factors is of a *psychological nature*. These reactions arise from social and developmental experiences in childhood and early adolescence, and convince these persons that they are inferior, unwanted, unneeded, and/or generally rejected by parents and significant others. Indeed, this author holds that one of the essential reinforcing qualities that maintains the chosen addictive pattern is that, while indulging in it, the individual can escape from painful reality and experience wish-fulfilling fantasies of being an important personage, highly successful and admired. These fantasy states appear to be of a dissociative character and may take the form of frank fugue states in compulsive gamblers (Jacobs, 1982a, 1984) and in alcoholics and compulsive overeaters (Jacobs, Marston, & Singer, 1985).

It is further held that *both* sets of predisposing factors must coexist and be exercising their respective effects before an individual will maintain an addictive pattern of behavior in a conducive environment. Viewed in this light, only a limited segment of the population need be considered at risk for any given addiction. Moreover, even persons in this group may remain latent, *unless* they encounter and perceive the above mix of pleasurable results from a chance triggering event in their daily lives that is of sufficient clarity, novelty, and intensity to motivate them to deliberately arrange future experiences of this type. On the basis of the lawful interaction of these two sets of predisposing factors, the author proposes that one can *predict* the course of any and all addictive patterns, as they progress through three common sequential stages (Figure 9.1) The author suggests further that by applying certain assessment procedures one can estimate an individual's relative position in the progression of stages noted above. With such information in hand, it then becomes possible to predict the *level of readiness* of a given addicted

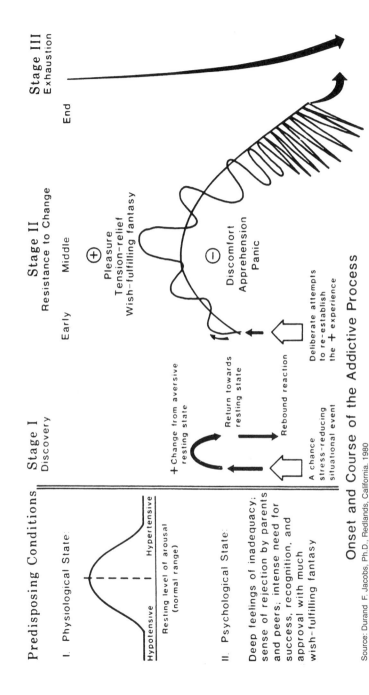

Figure 9.1. A working model of the Addictive Personality Syndrome (APS)

Source: Durand F. Jacobs, Ph.D., Redlands, California. 1980

Onset and Course of the Addictive Process

Predisposing Conditions

I. Physiological State:

Hypertensive

Resting level of arousal
(normal range)

Hypotensive

II. Psychological State:

Deep feelings of inadequacy;
sense of rejection by parents
and peers; intense need for
success, recognition, and
approval with much
wish-fulfilling fantasy

Stage I
Discovery

+ Change from aversive
resting state

Return towards
resting state

Rebound reaction

A chance
stress-reducing
situational event

Deliberate attempts
to re-establish
the + experience

Stage II
Resistance to Change

Early   Middle

⊕ Pleasure
Tension-relief
Wish-fulfilling fantasy

⊖ Discomfort
Apprehension
Panic

Stage III
Exhaustion

End

person to doggedly cling to or consider rejection of the addicted pattern. All such predictions would consider the facilitating or inhibiting influences of situational factors in the addict's here-and-now environment.

Definitions of Addiction

The standard *Medical Dictionary* (Dorland, 1974) defines addiction as "the state of being given up to some habit, especially strong dependence on a drug." Subdefinitions refer to alcohol, drug, opium, and (interestingly enough) polysurgical addiction, i.e., habitual seeking of surgical treatment. In the context of this definition four criteria are listed as being characteristic of an addictive state: "(1) an overwhelming desire or need (compulsion) to continue use of the drug and to obtain it by any means; (2) a tendency to increase the dosage; (3) a psychological and usually a physical dependence on its effects; (4) a detrimental effect on the individual and on society." Peele (1977) has proposed redefining the historical biologically rooted term "addiction," so that it may be dealt with in a much broader, measurable, and socially relevant manner. He proposes (1979) that "an addiction exists when a person's attachment to a sensation, an object, or another person is such as to lessen his appreciation and ability to deal with other things in his environment or in himself so that he has become increasingly dependent on that experience as his only source of gratification" (p. 56). In an article on alcohol addiction Cummings (1979) makes the point that "addiction is not merely popping something into one's mouth, but a constellation of behaviors that constitute a way of life" (p. 1121–1122). Compulsive gambling has been referred to as the "purest addiction," because no external substance is introduced into the biological system (Custer, 1975).

This investigator's approach to addiction tends to espouse the breadth of Peele's approach, the specificity of criteria listed in the medical definition (but without tying the concept to ingested substances), and Cummings' suggestion that addictive behavior constitutes a way of life. In this author's view, addiction encompasses persistent, out-of-control behavioral patterns involving substances such as food, alcohol, other licit and illicit drugs, as well as activities such as gambling.

The function of virtually any obsessive-compulsive behavior as a defense against experiencing *anticipated pain* is an aspect stressed by Jacobs that has been given far less emphasis in other treatises on addiction. In a recent chapter describing what he has characterized as the "Chronic Pain Personality Syndrome," Jacobs (1980) refers to this syndrome as being comprised of "a tightly knit set of learned behaviors directed to defending the patient against the phobic-like fear that his level of pain *may worsen.*" In Jacobs' view, addiction is basically a double-bind phenomenon which may follow the behavioral paradigm of a complex approach-escape-avoidance mechanism. On the one hand it traps the person into an escalating pattern of immediate gratification through greater and more frequent exercise of the "addicted" behavior. (Also see Donegan, Rodin, O'Brien, & Solomon, 1983). More subtly, on the other hand, the addict's extended personal experience with the painful series of ups and downs during his periods of indulgence (and between them) fuels a growing sense of apprehension that even the most extreme exercise of addictive behavior may not prevent the anticipated catastrophe that he dreads will happen when his addictive source is unavailable, or (inevitably) when it fails to produce its previous positive effects. The anticipated catastrophe referred to has nothing to do with a brief period of painful "withdrawal" that may or may not follow sudden cessation of the abuser's or addict's use pattern. Rather, the author has suggested that the termination or collapse of the addictive pattern precipitates a profound and extended anxiety state of debilitating proportions.

THE ADDICTIVE PERSONALITY SYNDROME (APS)

Predisposing Conditions

Addiction is seen as a dependent state acquired over time by a predisposed person in an attempt to correct a chronic pre-existing stress condition. In some predisposed persons under conducive environmental conditions, it can be a matter of one-trial learning because of the novel and dramatic nature of the initial chance encounter with a relief-producing substance or experience. The sheer intensity of perceived tension reduction and psychological release is sometimes expressed as a profound discovery (e.g., "Oh, wow! Where has this been all my life?"). This reaction may be pathognomic of addiction-prone persons who have suffered from extremely high or extremely low resting levels of physiological tension. The literature has referred to this dual minority of persons at either end of the normally distributed range of resting physiological tension (arousal) levels as "reducer" and "enhancer" types (Petrie, 1967; Ogborne, 1974). The "reducers" are characterized by a resting state of chronic overmobilization. The "enhancers" are characterized by a resting physiological state of chronic undermobilization (see Figure 9.1).

Both groups tend to be resigned to their respective lifelong states as being unpleasant, different from other people, and essentially immutable. Many express feelings of being victims of nature in this regard. Not all reducers and enhancers are prone to acquiring an "addictive personality syndrome" (APS). However, the presence of an atypical and persistent physiologic state is held to be one of two necessary predisposing conditions for developing an addiction.

The second essential pre-condition that must prevail before the stage is fully set for acquiring the behavioral pattern that this author has termed the APS is a childhood and adolescence marked by deep feelings of inadequacy, inferiority, and a sense of rejection by parents and significant others. Instead of responding to these circumstances by building success-producing behaviors or reacting with a dominant pattern of anger and aggressive acting out, addiction-prone youngsters generally retreat into wish-fulfilling fantasy where they may find relief from the painful reality of their existence. The combined impact of these physiological and social-psychological disabilities during their early lives conspire to inhibit such persons from interacting freely with their environment and, thereby, reduce their opportunities to learn a range of stress-reducing and coping skills sufficient to offset their inordinate needs for physical relief, freedom from anxiety, and social recognition and approval. As a consequence, such persons are particularly vulnerable during their adolescent years to *chance encounters* with substances or experiences that (for the chronically tense and overmobilized) bring a sense of relaxation and relief, or (for the chronically undermobilized) replaces their sense of being "numb," "empty," or "feeling dead inside" with a scintillating sense of being acutely alive. In either event, when chance occurrences trigger a welcome relief from their unpleasant physiologic state and *also* provide such persons with an opportunity to escape even briefly from the unpleasant realities of everyday life to a world apart wherein they *may actively live out their fantasies* of personal success and of social acceptance, the stage is fully set for such predisposed persons to acquire the Addictive Personality Syndrome. Figure 9.1 attempts to graphically portray the predisposing conditions and progressive stages that, theoretically, characterize the major benchmarks in the course of an addictive career that typically stretches over 20 years or more (Jacobs, 1982b).

A key sign that one is dealing with this particular subclass of persons (Jacobs, 1984) is the striking clarity and completeness with which they recall their very first experience (or the early series of repeated chance occurrences) that led to their discovery that they could change the unhappy conditions they had resigned themselves to endure. Apparently, it is the striking contrast between their aversive, unhappy, non-fulfilling resting state and its dramatic alleviation that creates such a novel, intense and well-remembered experience. From a learning theory point of view this would qualify as one-trial learning. This author has termed this phenomenon the *"Stage I Discovery"* (Figure 9.1). The extremely high level of positive reinforcement produced by this experience virtually assures that the affected person will make efforts to repeat it. Frequently the specific active agents most responsible for producing the pleasurable end results are embedded in a hazy network of co-existing and contingent situational cues so as to escape clear-cut identification. Thus, one finds persons returning expectantly to the general mix of circumstance, situation, associates, etc., that existed at the time of initial discovery. With repeated trials available to them, addiction-prone individuals will gradually eliminate non-essential elements so they may obtain the most intense positive reaction with the least expenditure of time, effort, and resources. In this manner, the addiction-prone individual quickly *overlearns* how to recapture the relief experience through deliberately contrived repetitions. Knowing what to do and having learned how to do it well (to the increasing exclusion of other less rewarding life activities) leads the individual into the planned course of highly motivated, repetitive, and compulsivelike behaviors characterized by Stage II of the APS (Figure 9.1). This has been termed the "Stage of Resistance" because of the dogged insistence of the now clearly addicted person to cling to this behavioral pattern and to evade and reject outside efforts to discourage its practice.

   Thus, one sees that the onset of addiction is triggered by a chance occurrence in the life of an already predisposed individual. The addictive pattern is developed and maintained by a series of learned maneuvers refined over time to maintain and prolong both psychological and physiological relief, and to avoid anticipated pain. As will be elaborated later, only a very limited range of experiences can effectively trigger this type of syndrome in a given predisposed individual. Consequently, one might reasonably speculate that, by far, the greater number of *addiction-prone* persons may go their entire lives without ever encountering an effective triggering event. One can take little comfort from this, if one also believes that today's youth are being exposed to an ever-increasing number and variety of triggering events in their environment. The probability of such an encounter increases in direct proportion to greater geographic mobility and increased contacts with persons and experiences beyond those found in one's home environment, vicarious exposure to new sources of experience offered through the media, deliberate media and street advertising to promote endless ways of instant "feeling better" (uppers, downers, self-actualization, inner peace, etc.), plus permission to explore from an increasingly open and impersonal society.

It is not likely that society will choose to stem the possible emergence of increasing numbers of persons showing one or another kind of Addictive Personality Syndrome by reversing the tide of human affairs. Rather, more addictions in a variety of manifestations appears to be the tragic cost that must be paid among the gains obtained from what society considers to be "progress." Consequently, the documented rise in addictive behaviors, particularly in adolescents and young adults, must be met first by developing improved methods for *intercepting* susceptible persons at the Stage I level of discovery. Those identified would be provided with crash programs to reduce their biologic distress. This would be supplemented with individually targeted stress-management and coping skill training to improve their self-confidence, general adjustments, and psychological state. This in turn would be supported by individual and group management of environmental crises, by family counseling, and by continued contacts with educative self-help groups at the local community level. In the aggregate these actions would serve to reduce the risks of entry into Stage II. Assuming the theory proposed herein finds substantial support in the program of research that already has been initiated (Jacobs & Wright, 1980), one would then venture to mount educational programs aimed at *prevention* among high risk children and youth who would be screened for the presence of the critical combination of physiological and sociopsychological precursors to the APS. This would best be accomplished before a Stage I "discovery" incident occurs.

Unfortunately, clinical impressions suggest that once the course of the APS has moved substantially into Stage II, the likelihood of effective interruption and reversal of this syndrome progressively diminishes until the individual reaches Stage III ("Exhaustion"). The course through Stage II ("Resistance to Change") typically takes years, accompanied by untold personal and interpersonal misery, physical and psychological illness, and crippling economic and social costs. Frequently, the process is aborted by sudden accidental death or death by homicide or suicide, but few spontaneous remissions are reported. Both the morbidity and mortality rates of addicted persons are expected, thereby, to significantly exceed those of their age/sex/socio-economic cohorts in the general population.

Returning to the general course of the APS, the author proposed a combination of three critical factors to explain the marked resistiveness to extinction of such acquired states, *despite* the mounting punishing consequences of their continued pursuit. The first factor is the positive reinforcement obtained during Stages I and II as a result of the high levels of pleasure experienced by those chronically and severely deprived persons. The second factor contributing to the stubborn resistance to change during Stage II is the extensive degree of overlearning that has occurred through deliberately contrived repetitions of the behavior, both in fantasy and in vivo. These real and fancied redentigrations of cues associated with the positively reinforcing experience build up an extremely strong habit strength for the entire behavioral pattern. Were positive reinforcement and mounting habit strength the only factors to be considered, the application of proven counterconditioning principles and methods likely could capture, alter, and eventually eliminate the behavior patterns under consideration. Experience, however, shows that such narrow gauge methods generally have not been successful.

In this author's view, it is the third factor that serves as the linchpin of the Addictive Personality Syndrome, and holds the secret to its extreme resistiveness to extinction. This factor is the addict's phobic-like *avoidance* of a return to the (now well recognized) lifelong aversive resting state that had characterized his unhappy and deprived condition prior to his "discovery" of how it could be altered. With the discovery of relief the individual is confronted by a dramatic contrast effect. He suddenly comes to perceive how *really* terrible his previous existence had been. The release from this long-term prison of deprivation (dramatized by the "Oh, Wow!" reaction) reveals that the individual has realized the impossible dream of feeling so much better. The contrast produced by this feeling of relief serves to deepen the depths of "the pits" from which the individual has emerged. Discovering that there is another, so much better way of feeling changes the whole character of the individual's perceptions about his past life and his expectations for the future. With the discovery of a new goal, (i.e., the unique *combination* of physical and psychological relief) and a rough idea of the instrumental behavior that will achieve it, the nature of the individual's response to his resting state converts radically from one of passive *deprivation* to one of active *frustration*. His reactions henceforth are typical of those shown by frustrated persons, namely, a marked increase in goal-oriented problem solving, anger and resentment at being blocked, substitution of goal-attaining fantasies in the face of continued frustration, increases in regressive behaviors, etc. Perhaps the most lasting of all these reactions is the individual's resolve never to return to the previous aversive resting state. This suggests that the poets were wrong: to have loved and lost is infinitely *worse* than never to have loved at all. With love experienced and then lost, one gains a much deeper awareness of how devastating loneliness was, and how infinite the depths of emptiness can be.

Beginning with the Stage I "discovery," the individual learns to engage in behaviors which prevent the occurrence of internal cues that were associated with his previous aversive resting state. Thus, two extremely potent types of reinforcers combine to maintain the addictive process: (a) *the positive reinforcement* obtained from the memory and expectation of pleasure, and (b) the *negative reinforcement* of escape from and avoidance of anticipated pain. As the addictive process proceeds into the middle and end phases of Stage II, the latter mechanism asserts increasing dominance in the behavior pattern termed the APS. This is illustrated in the statements of long addicted persons that they no longer experience their earlier levels of enjoyment, even as they desperately accelerate their addictive behavior. Their motivation is not to avoid the transient discomfort of physiologic withdrawal, but to buy time before they must face the even greater psychological terror of falling into "the pits" of an ever-worsening reality. This stimulates the addict to build an expanding behavioral repertoire designed to extend gratification and to avoid anticipated pain. These maneuvers, accumulated and systematized over time, inevitably change the entire lifestyle of the affected person, as well as force major modifications on the lives and behavior of other persons and on circumstances in his immediate environment. The workings of this process will be described in detail in the next section.

Onset and Course of the APS: A Working Model for Assessment and Intervention

Figure 9.1 portrays the major structural components of the theoretical paradigm termed the "Addictive Personality Syndrome" (APS). These are: (1) two separate, but interrelated sets of psychosocial and physiological *predisposing factors* which are advanced as necessary prerequisites to acquiring *any* addiction; (2) specification of the two extreme groups on the physiological "resting level of arousal" continuum who are believed to be most at risk for acquiring an addiction; (3) the stimulus: a chance stress-reducing situational event (the "discovery") that sets the stage for acquiring an addictive pattern; (4) the critical "rebound reaction" that follows the triggering episode, and brings the individual back into contact with his previous nonsatisfying physiological and psychological resting states. These four *Stage I* ("Discovery") conditions are the precursors for developing an "Addictive Personality Syndrome."

Stage II reactions represent a subsequent period of building and maintaining the main body of the addictive pattern of behavior. Note that during the course of Stage II, use patterns vary in frequency, duration, and intensity. This is portrayed in Figure 9.1 by a sine-wave progression. Contrary to popular wisdom, this author does not attribute the shape of this progression wholly to habituation and the need for greater amounts of positive stimulation to produce the former effect. Rather, it is proposed that a heretofore over-looked factor contributes significantly to the undulating character of the addictive pattern. This masked (but progressively more potent) factor is comprised of *a set of anticipatory avoidance behaviors directed toward preventing a return to one's previous (and now recognized!) aversive physio-logical and psychological resting states,* i.e., "the pits!" This threat, provoked by perceiving that one is coming down from the "high" or losing the mellow "low," is countered by a frantic overreaction to reinstate the escape mecha-nism of the addictive pattern. The downswing of the sine-wave represents the progressive fading of the positive experience engendered by indulgence in the addictive behavior. Perceiving that one is "falling into the valleys" (be-tween sine-waves) provokes a panic-like "rebound reaction" to escape and to avoid falling further into one's perceived "pits." Thus, the up side of the succeeding sine-wave (i.e., next episode of indulgence) not only represents an approach to greater positive reinforcement, but also signifies a successful escape from and avoidance of threats of anticipated pain and anxiety should such action not be taken. What is described here goes far beyond what might be attributed to avoidance of a physiological "withdrawal" reaction. The reaction described is *internal* to the continuing addictive pattern: the addict is not the least motivated to abort or terminate his use pattern for any extended time.

Clinical observations strongly collaborate the concerted, innovative at-tempts of addicted persons to ensure that they will not be long without the wherewithal necessary to maintain their chosen addictive pattern. These persons have developed ingenious methods for "stashing" substances, so they will be on hand at any hour of emergency. They also squirrel away specially earmarked and otherwise inviolate money (or other negotiables) to purchase same. Similar forms of hedging against the phobic-like anticipatory fear of being without are seen among nonsubstance abusers who demonstrate other types of addictive behavior (e.g., compulsive gamblers). In addition to com-pulsive gamblers, there are several other "psychologically dependent" groups who may fit within the APS conceptual framework. These have been de-scribed as those who cling desperately to star-crossed love relationships, compulsively seek medical attention through complaints of illness or requests for polysurgery, or bask in the notoriety of confessing crimes they did not commit.

Another clinical group who dramatically evidence the building of elaborate avoidant defense strategies against experiencing *anticipated* physical and psychological distress is a small subclass of chronic pain patients. These have been described elsewhere as demonstrating a "chronic pain personality syndrome" (Jacobs, 1980). While much more research is needed, early impressions of this group strongly suggest predisposing conditions of atypical physiological resting state and marked lifelong psychological maladjustment. They attend in a highly compulsive and ever-elaborated manner to the maintenance of a tightly knit set of learned behaviors directed not only to relieve present pain but, particularly, to defending themselves against the phobic-like fear that their level of pain *may worsen*. This syndrome also includes dependency on a variety of physical, health systems, pharmacological, and psychosocial supports. These expand to dominate the person's entire lifestyle and invariably have detrimental effects on the individual and on those in his immediate and extended social circle. This would seem to qualify patients demonstrating the "chronic pain personality syndrome" among the company of other addicts, and would bring them under the broader theoretical rubric of the APS.

It is the author's contention that the heretofore overlooked feature of anticipatory fear of a *future* "catastrophic" event is common, even central, to *all* types of addiction. It is seen as the prime mover that stokes the crescendo of frantic, unmodulated indulgence at the later downhill stages in substance abusers and addicts. This greatly increases the likelihood of *overdose* among those groups. Similarly, where the addiction takes the form of a psychological dependency on the presence of certain activities, supportive relationships or circumstances, the addict's growing realization that he might not be able to obtain or maintain adequate support leads this person to fear-driven excessive demands that go beyond the system's ability or willingness to support, and the individual may be summarily rejected. This in turn usually leads to all manner of psychological, physiological, and social crises that also can reach life-threatening proportions for that person, even though he is not a substance abuser.

The reader is again referred to Figure 9.1. Attention is directed to the changing nature and direction of the sine-wave progression during Stage II. During the "early" phase of Stage II, the area above the baseline of the sine-wave predominates, indicating pleasurable results. As the individual proceeds to the "middle" and "end" phases of Stage II, the area above the baseline (pleasurable effects) progressively recedes, while that below the baseline (negative effects) increases proportionately. Eventually, the addicted person is subjected to a "double whammy." The middle and end phases of Stage II are characterized by a growing and compulsively focused preoccupation, first with maintaining the desired state, and then with avoiding return to the aversive resting state. As this proceeds, the individual shows the typical behavioral manifestations of all addicted persons, i.e., an increased funneling of waking activities to prepare for and support the addictive pattern and a progressive narrowing of or withdrawal from other commitments, producing radical changes in one's lifestyle and causing major disruptions in previously established personal, social, and occupational roles. Common casualties of these middle to end State II activities are alienation from family, friends, and associates who disapprove of or try to stop the addictive behavior, financial disaster and conflicts, both with the law and the criminal infra-system, and seriously diminished physical and mental health. Towards the end of Stage II, pleasure once gained from the addictive pattern has been largely lost, and the build-up of punishing consequences from years of addiction brings the individual, emotionally distraught, dilapidated in mind and body, and bereft of social and economic supports, to the threshold of *Stage III* ("Exhaustion").

The excursion through Stage II usually involves many years. During this time, a heavy toll has been placed on the addict's entire support system, including family, job, associates, economic resources, etc. Not only does he find that his addictive pattern no longer affords him the internal relief it used to but, meanwhile, he has become inundated with everyday environmental troubles of every stripe. Persons in the end phases of Stage II would be expected to show increasing anxiety, reaching phobic proportions, that they will surely fall into "the pits," since episodes of relief have become progressively more short-lived and increasingly more difficult to attain. Indeed, the basic premise of the present theory is that the course of the Addictive Personality Syndrome is shaped by the changing dimensions of the *reciprocal relationship* between positive and negative reinforcement. This essentially is what is represented by the changing sine-curve progression in Figure 9.1. Over an extended period of time, subtle changes occur within this reciprocal relationship. In the entry phase of Stage II the positive reinforcing effects of the "high" or "mellow" states dominate. This leads to attempts to repeat those experiences, since they provide such a rewarding contrast from the individual's former physiological resting state, as well as permit the person's cognitive set to shift from a negative to a positive view of the self. Whether the obtained physiologic state is an excited "high" or a mellow "low," the *psychological* end result is the same: it facilitates complimentary daydreams about the self, blurs reality testing, lowers self-criticalness and, as a consequence, permits acting-out of one's fantasies.

Stage III in the Addictive Personality Syndrome is one of rapid collapse of the entire pattern and a plummeting into a state of physical and psychological exhaustion. It is at this point, however, that the addict is most amenable to treatment. These three stages reflect the onset and course of the Addictive Personality Syndrome once acquired by predisposed persons. This behavior pattern is amenable to modification and reversal almost exclusively during Stages I and III.

The process of acquiring and maintaining an addiction—*any addiction*—is held to follow this basic pattern. One essential difference emerging from the author's theory that distinguishes it from those advanced by others is the author's conclusion that a given addictive behavior can occur *only* in a relatively small proportion of the population. These persons must be predisposed both biologically and psychologically before certain experiences can acquire addictive qualities for them. This theory emphasizes the fact that repeated, intense, and/or prolonged use or abuse of a substance or behavioral pattern *does not of itself* produce an addictive pattern of behavior analogous to the APS. Nor does it necessarily follow that sudden cessation of what appears to be an established use pattern automatically and invariably produce a characteristic set of psycho-physiological "withdrawal" reactions (Custer, 1982: 120; Wray & Dickerson, 1981). A dramatic illustration of this latter point was the tens of thousands of military personnel who admitted to heavy use of heroin and other drugs while in Vietnam. It was anticipated that upon their return the nation would be faced with a massive drug treatment and rehabilitation problem. It is a matter of record that this did not materialize. The overwhelming majority (Robins, David, & Nurco, 1974) abruptly ceased their use of these substances, with few reports of withdrawal problems and with no evidence of resumption upon their return to the United States. This massive unexpected test of the historical hypothesis that addiction is a direct function of use should have sparked a major reexamination and revision of prevailing concepts and theories regarding the precursors, causes, and course of *alleged* addictive behavior. Unfortunately, this was not the case. Not only have the time-honored theories of drug addiction persisted, but dependency on other substances (such as selected foods) and on other activities (such as compulsive gambling) have been prodded to fit into the faulted model. This treatise does not mean to take sides in an idle "mind-body" controversy about whether physiological or psychological factors dominate addictive behavior.

To tilt towards the proverbial Cheshire Cat is really no better nor worse than to lean towards the Headless Horseman! The writer holds that in the final analysis all behavior is the *resultant* of interacting and interdependent biological, psychological, and environmental factors (i.e., $B = P \times E$: *behavior* is a function of the *person* interacting with his here and now *environment*). Historical theories of addiction clearly have overemphasized biological factors and underrated psychological and environmental factors (Glaser, 1974). Unfortunately, this has skewed and often truncated problem definition and limited the range of subsequent treatment approaches. By the same token, psychological theories of addiction have tended to diminish or ignore possible biologic precursors and influences in the onset, course, and treatment of the condition. Both approaches have slighted the impact of situational factors in the current social scene, and the need to deal decisively with them. Exclusive use of either theoretical stance, or adopting the atheoretical position of merely attempting to block and prevent resumption of the pattern, increases the likelihood of misidentifying populations at risk, thereby shortchanging everyone. Such one-sided approaches serve to water down public interest about problems with addiction and delay mobilization of public support for mounting more effective research, treatment, and prevention activities.

SUMMARY

The proposed model of the Addictive Personality Syndrome (APS) has been offered to stimulate efforts to find a comprehensive theory that encompasses the essential characteristics of *any* "addictive" or "psychologically dependent" pattern of behavior. The APS identifies two specific sets of predisposing factors that are held to be characteristic of persons with a high potential for developing an addiction. The theory aims to hasten early diagnosis and to stimulate further research to correct extreme states of physiologic tension or lassitude. Concomitantly, it encourages much broader application of well-validated stress management and coping skill training techniques to alter negative self-concepts, and to increase adaptive and satisfying self-control and problem solving skills. This entire spectrum of approaches must be applied in an integrated manner, if success rates are to increase.

The author offers the challenge that even chronically extreme resting physiological levels may be modified (on an individual basis) by tailored programs of a holistic, rather than exclusively physical or pharmacologic nature. Vigorous research and clinical trials must explore how enduring changes in resting arousal states can be effected and maintained by diet, exercise, controlled breathing, meditation, use of a variety of stress management techniques, including biofeedback, etc. It is hoped that this line of investigation will hasten the discovery of non-intrusive methods for maintaining homeostasis.

REFERENCES

Cummings, N. A. (1979). Turning bread into stones: Our modern antimiracle. American Psychologist, 34, 1119–1129.

Custer, R. L. (1982). "An Overview of Compulsive Gambling," pp. 107–124 in P. Carone, S. Yoles, S. Kieffer and L. Krinsky (Eds.) Addictive Disorders Update. New York: Human Sciences Press.

———— (1975). Characteristics of compulsive gamblers. Paper presented at the 2nd Annual Conference on Gambling, Lake Tahoe, Nevada.

Donegan, N. H.; Rodin, J.; O'Brien, C. P.; & Solomon, R. L. (1983). A learning-theory approach to commonalities. In P. Levison et al. (Eds.), Commonalities in substance abuse and habitual behavior. Lexington, Mass.

Dorland's Illustrated Medical Dictionary (Twenty-fifth Edition). (1974). Philadelphia, Penn.: W. B. Saunders.

Glaser, F. B. (1974) Medical ethnocentrism and the treatment of addiction. International Journal of Offender Therapy and Comparative Criminology, 18, 13–27.

Jacobs, D. F., & Wright, E. T. (1980). A program of research on the causes and treatment of addictive behaviors: Using the compulsive gambler as the prototype subject. Loma Linda, Calif.: unpublished.

Jacobs, D. F. (1980). Holistic strategies in the management of chronic pain. In F. McQuigan et al. (Eds.), Stress and Tension Control. New York: Plenum.

———— (1982a). Factors alleged as predisposing to compulsive gambling. Paper presented at the Annual Convention of the American Psychological Association. Washington, D.C.

———— (1982b). The Addictive Personality Syndrome (APS): A new theoretical model for understanding and treating addictions. In W. R. Eadington (Ed.), The Gambling Papers: Proceedings of the Fifth National Conference on Gambling and Risk Taking. Reno, Nev.: University of Nevada.

———— (1984). Study of traits leading to compulsive gambling. In Sharing recovery through Gamblers Anonymous. Los Angeles, Calif.: Gamblers Anonymous Publishing, Inc.

Jacobs, D. F.; Marston, A. R.; & Singer, R. D. (1985). Testing a general theory of addictions: Similarities and differences between alcoholics, pathological gamblers and compulsive overeaters. Proceedings of the XXIII International Congress of Psychology, Acapulco, Mexico. North Holland Press: The Netherlands (in press).

Levison, P. K., Gerstein, D. R., & Maloff, D. R. (1983). Commonalities in substance abuse and habitual behavior. Lexington, Mass.: D.C. Heath and Company.

Ogborne, A. (1974). Two types of heroin reactions. Brit J Addictions, 39, 237–242.

Peele, S. (1977). Redefining addiction I: Making addiction a scientifically and socially useful concept. International Journal of Health Services, 7, *103–124.*

―――― *(1979). Redefining addiction II: The meaning of addiction in our lives.* Journal of Psychedelic Drugs, 11, *289–297.*

Petrie, A. (1967). Individuality in pain and suffering. *Chicago: University of Chicago Press.*

Robins, L. M.; David, D. H.; Nurco, D. W. (1974). How permanent was Vietnam drug addiction? Am J Pub Health, *64: 38–43.*

Walker, A. L., & Lidz, C. W. (1983). Common features of troublesome habitual behaviors: A cultural approach. In P. Levison et al. (Ed.), Commonalities in substance abuse and habitual behavior. *Lexington, Mass.: D. C. Heath and Company.*

Wray, I., & Dickerson, M. (1981). Cessation of high frequency gambling and "withdrawal" symptoms. British Journal of Addictions, 76.

10. The Psychodynamics of Pathological Gambling: A Review of the Literature

Richard J. Rosenthal

THERE HAVE BEEN three types of theoretical models used to understand the pathological gambler. These have been the psychodynamic, by which has been meant primarily the Freudian; the behavioral; and, most recently, the physiological, or the model of arousal. This chapter will be involved almost exclusively with the first of these, but the third will be broached where relevant. My goal will be to review the literature somewhat chronologically, but emphasizing trends and interconnections; I will summarize what has actually been written, highlighting what I believe to be the positive contributions, and where needed, offering a critical reassessment.

Gambling is a complex activity. The gambling ritual—including the stages of anticipation, playing, and outcome, followed by either triumph or re-morse—is an acting out of a meaningful fantasy, in which someone is doing something to someone else. There are rewards and punishments, with specific meanings, both conscious and unconscious, assigned to winning and losing. These meanings can be multiple and contradictory, i.e., winning may be both good and bad, simultaneously, while the same holds true for losing.

One of the oldest and most fundamental concepts in psychoanalysis is that of *over-determination:* formations of the unconscious (symptoms, dreams, etc.) can be attributed to a plurality of determining factors. There may be several causes, or a multiplicity of unconscious elements organized in differ-ent meaningful sequences, each having its own specific coherence at a partic-ular level of interpretation. Now this does not mean, and Freud (1895, pp. 289–290; 1900, pp. 283 and 569) was very clear on this, that a symptom can be interpreted in an infinite number of ways. Not only must the interpretation be corroborated or verified, but the various interpretations must intersect.

Laplanche and Pontalis (1973), in their discussion of overdetermination,

From *The Handbook of Pathological Gambling,* T. Galski, ed. (Springfield, Ill.: Charles C. Thomas, 1987), 41–70. Courtesy of Charles C. Thomas, Publisher, Springfield, Illinois.

emphasize that it is to be viewed as a positive characteristic, not merely the absence of any one exhaustive meaning. They cite Jacques Lacan's famous phrase about a symptom being "structured like a language." Robert Waelder's (1936) *principle of multiple function* is also relevant; simply put, it states that any psychic act must be understood, not as an effort to solve just one problem, but as an attempt to solve simultaneously a number of different tasks put forth by different parts of the psychic apparatus. These various solutions, he points out, need not be equally successful, since they may be inconsistent and contradictory with each other.

The ultimate test of any clinical theory is not how elegant it sounds but how useful it is in understanding and successfully treating the individual patients. A glaring deficiency in what is to follow is the absence of female gamblers in the various case reports; the exception is in the writing of Edmund Bergler (1935, 1943, 1957). However, my consistent choice of the masculine pronoun was guided as well by considerations of style, and the ease of writing and reading.

REVIEW OF THE LITERATURE

I. Early Contributors

The earliest psychoanalytic study of gambling is by Hans Von Hattingberg (1914); it is often summarized in reviews of the literature, although as far as I know it has never been published in English translation. Von Hattingberg theorized that the tension and fear involved in gambling have been eroticized, and that this is derived from a period of infancy when urethral-anal striving had been thwarted. "Pleasure in fear," or masochism, is central to the gambling situation.

Von Hattingberg's article becomes the forerunner for three different strands in the psychoanalytic literature. First are those contributors who have continued to emphasize the sexual equivalencies of the gambling activity. Laforgue (1930), for example, suggested point by point analogies between the various stages of sexual arousal and the phases involved in the betting process. Simmel (1920) followed up on this idea when he related gambling to masturbation.

The second strand is represented by those authors who have emphasized the role of masochism. Most notably, Edmund Bergler (1935, 1943, 1957) follows up on Von Hattingberg's description of how the infant's urethral-anal strivings are thwarted through the efforts of outside agencies who deny the child pleasure. Bergler spells out how these outside agencies, the frustrating parents, introduce the reality principle, and how it is the rebellion against this which causes guilt, and eventually masochism.

The third and final strand anticipated by Von Hattingberg are authors who have focused on the role of anality. Fuller (1974), for example, view a fixation at the anal level, and anal eroticism, as the primary and most under-appreciated dynamic in pathological gambling.

Ernst Simmel (1920) was the first to discuss the actual psychoanalytic treatment of a pathological gambler. While only a one-page report based on his presentation has come down to us, it is amazing how much insight is crammed into that summary. He begins by noting that there were *multiple meanings* attached to the fortunes his patient won and lost through gambling. There was a vicious circle in which loss must be converted into gain, and gain into loss. The basis for this, Simmel states, was a narcissistic fantasy in which his patient could inseminate and then give birth to himself, and was then able to feed himself, thereby establishing his own independence, having replaced his parents, in fact, having surpassed them. Anality played a role in this fantasy, both in the birth, which was an anal one, and in the notion of the patient's own excrement as a constantly available source of nurturance. Dependency and feelings of smallness were denied; such an individual would be in need of nothing he could not provide for himself.

There are a number of other interesting ideas. Simmel presents a brief survey of the historical development of games of chance. His intention is to show that in the individual development of the gambler is repeated, as it were ontogenetically, the phylogenetic formation of the game. He also discusses the gambler who breaks the law in order to achieve expiation of guilt; the public judge or prosecutor becomes an externalization of the punishing internal parent.

Clearly, however, his delineation of anal omnipotence is far and away the most important of his ideas. Simmel understood, as many who came after him did not, that anality refers not just to a level of psychosexual development at which an individual may become fixated, nor to anatomical functions which have been eroticized, but to a specific group of omnipotent and perverse fantasies. Such fantasies, about the anus as the locus for "false creativity," or about the value ascribed to its contents (heroin and marijuana are commonly referred to as "shit" as a term of approbation), are central to the dynamics of addiction. The addict's withdrawal into an alternative or substitute world is frequently in relation to just such fantasies. More sophisticated variations of the fantasy have been worked out by Meltzer (1966), Chasseguet-Smirgel (1974), and others.

Wilhelm Stekel (1924) begins his contribution by noting the similarity between gambling and alcohol abuse. The gambler is continually challenging fate. *The game is an oracle for him:* "If you win the this game, you will attain also your other secret wish!" As far as I know, this is the first statement of this idea, which will be repeated by Reik (1940), Fenichel (1945), Greenson (1947), Galdston (1960), and others. Stekel emphasizes the importance of superstition. He prefigures Greenson (1947) by referring to the language of gambling in order to show its sexual and aggressive gratifications, as well as some of the partial instincts which are involved, such as exhibitionism. After discussing several literary examples, he presents two case histories.

Stekel's first patient had a potency problem in addition to his gambling, and the material allows him to repeat his theory linking pathological gambling with latent homosexuality. The second patient had, in addition to gambling, a masochistic lifestyle. The analysis, according to Stekel, revealed that winning at the gambling table was equated with the gratification of an incestuous fantasy. The implication is that this would rouse guilt, which would then have to be dissipated by losing.

II. "Dostoevsky and Parricide"

We now come to Freud's famous essay. One would expect there to be a great deal of critical analysis of "Dostoevsky and Parricide" (1928), yet two articles, one by Fritz Schmidl (1965), the other by Joseph Frank (1976), stand almost alone. Both authors note the paucity of critical discussions of Freud's text, as well as of efforts at evaluating the article as a whole. This is something of a surprise, since the essay has been the recipient of such widely divergent opinions. A portion of the psychoanalytic community hail it as a classic, the seminal essay for psychoanalytic studies of Dostoevsky and his work, and the benchmark as well for inquiries into the nature of pathological gambling. Other analysts are considerably less impressed; they find the essay something of an embarrassment, and feel the less said about it the better.

Freud himself did not appear to regard his article very highly. In reply to the comments of Theodore Reik (1940), he wrote, "I think you have applied too high a standard to this trivial essay. It was written as a favor for someone and written reluctantly." This has been interpreted as false modesty on

Freud's part, yet he was not prone to such feelings about his writing. We know how strongly he defended his ideas; about the Dostoevsky piece, he makes clear to Reik, he had no interest in further discussion.

Both of his admissions are correct, the essay was written at a friend's insistence, and Freud kept putting it off; quite clearly he didn't want to write it. In my evaluation of "Dostoevsky and Parricide" (Rosenthal, 1986a), I concur with Frank's assessment of the essay's faulty scholarship, note Freud's hostility towards his subject, and attempt to elaborate what I believe to be the basis for Freud's avoidance of Dostoevsky. Freud chose not to avail himself of the considerable material at his disposal, the biographical information and Dostoevsky's own writings, and most of the ideas about Dostoevsky in the Freud essay had been stated just a few years previously by Jolan Neufeld (1923) in his book on the Russian author. Freud not only had helped publish the Neufeld book, but he acknowledges his indebtedness to it in his essay.

With regard to Dostoevsky's gambling, about which the final third of "Dostoevsky and Parricide" purports to contend, Freud does a most peculiar thing! He introduces the topic by relating the author's gambling addiction to a need for self-punishment: Dostoevsky would need to lose everything in order to expiate guilt. But then Freud seems to turn away from his subject, devoting the remaining four pages of his article to a story by another, Stefan Zweig's "Twenty-Four Hours in a Woman's Life" (1928).

Dostoevsky's novella, *The Gambler* (1866), is the finest and certainly the best known case history of a pathological gambler in or out of literature. Many pathological gamblers have written and spoken about it, acclaiming to its accuracy. Dostoevsky scholars, such as Robert Jackson (1981), regard it as one of his most artistically successful works, and it has always been considered one of his most autobiographical. It is the only one of his works which deals with gambling, indeed the author's own gambling, with passages from the story sounding indistinguishable from some of Dostoevsky's letters.

That Freud, who was obviously quite familiar with *The Gambler,* would pass over it in favor of the Zweig story is incredible. Stefan Zweig was not a gambler, nor was he particularly interested in the subject. However, he was interested in Dostoevsky, whom he idolized (Zweig, 1919), and took as a kind of literary mentor. He consistently misread him, in order to rationalize his own self-destructive tendencies, particularly his idealization of suicide (Rosenthal, 1986a). His short story, as any reading of it will confirm, is derived from *The Gambler,* and, in fact, an important theme in the Zweig story has to do with the subject of imitation. Zweig's relationship with Freud is also relevant, as he took the first psychoanalyst as his other teacher. He read all of Freud's writings, referred to him as his "life-long mentor," and according to Zweig's first wife, did all his own writing with "the great psychologist" looking over his shoulder (Zweig, 1946; Allday, 1972). Thus he wrote "Twenty-Four Hours in a Woman's Life" with Freud in mind! Is it possible then that Freud took to the story so enthusiastically because he recognized in it some of his own ideas?

Does all this mean that "Dostoevsky and Parricide" is to be judged a failure? Certainly with regard to Freud's treatment of Dostoevsky, I find it disappointing. With regard to the gambling, however, Freud does succeed in making a number of important points:

1. That it is not to win money that the gambler gambles, or to be able to pay off creditors; this is mere rationalization. It is for the gambling itself, what we would today refer to as the *action.*

2. In fact, the gambler may gamble *in order to lose.* (Edmund Bergler will popularize this idea, which along with the concept of *psychic masochism,* he will get from Freud.) Out of a sense of guilt, the basis for which is unknown to the individual, he will turn to gambling, and his heavy losses will serve to expedite that guilt, a kind of cure through self-punishment.

3. Pathological gambling is an *addiction.* This is the only diagnostic category which Freud uses—he does not refer to it as an obsessional neurosis, as have a number of analysts both before and after the appearance of this essay. (Freud also refers to Dostoevsky as an "impulsive" or "instinctual character" in whom a neurosis was present.)

4. Freud believed that all the addictions were linked, that alcoholism, and drug abuse and pathological gambling were all manifestations of a *primary addiction.* He believed that underlying primary addiction was masturbation, although it should be stressed that the activity derived its importance as the focus of guilt, not merely because of the masturbatory act, but because of the fantasies which invariably accompanied it.

5. Freud's most significant contribution comes out of his discussion of patricide. A major portion of the essay is devoted to it, and no one could argue that it, and not Dostoevsky, is the major subject of "Dostoevsky and Parricide." There are several immediate reasons why this is so. First, the essay was written specifically as an introduction to a new edition of *The Brothers Karamazov,* Dostoevsky's last work and the only one which features the theme of patricide. Second, Freud was writing for a lay audience, and it was an opportunity to explain his most

important discovery of the nature of the oedipus complex. Third, the subject of patricide had been most dramatically linked to Dostoevsky by the brutal murder of the author's father by some of his own serfs. This had first become public knowledge in 1921, and was still very much on people's minds. Neufeld wrote his book and published it in 1923. "Dostoevsky and Parricide" was begun three years later.

On the subject of patricide, Freud writes, these murderous impulses towards the father constitute "the main source of the sense of guilt, though we do not know if it is the only one." Central to Freud's thesis is the boy's ambivalence towards his father: he hates him as a rival and wants to get rid of him, while, at the same time he feels tenderness and love for him. There is an identification with the father. The boy wants to be in his father's place because he wants to be like him, out of admiration, but also because he wants him out of the way. This desire to remove the father as a rival is punishable by castration, so it is given up, but the wish continues in the unconscious and is associated with guilt.

Freud posits a further complication: bisexuality. Under threat of castration, the boy diverges in the direction of femininity, to put himself in his mother's place and take over her role as the object of father's love. But this brings the threat of castration as well. Therefore, hatred of the father and love of the father both undergo repression.

The giving up of these wishes occurs through a process of internalization. The oedipus complex is not merely an interpersonal conflict—competition with one parent for the love of the other—but intrapsychic, and structural. The relationship between the subject and his father, *as experienced in fantasy,* has been transformed into a relationship between two parts of the personality, the superego and ego. The identification with the father takes place through the formation of the superego. And, if there had been a negative oedipus complex, that is a wish to identify with the mother as the object of father's love, then the relationship between superego and ego is a sadomasochistic one. Superego = father = sadist, and ego = mother or feminine identification = masochist. This is the point at which Freud's thesis becomes most directly relevant for the pathological gambler.

A great need for punishment develops in the ego, which in part offers itself as a victim to Fate, and in part finds satisfaction in ill treatment by the superego (that is, in the sense of guilt). For every punishment is ultimately castration and, as such, a fulfillment of the old passive attitude towards the father. Even Fate is, in the last resort, only a later projection of the father.

It is important to spell out what Freud means here. He is no longer talking about the seeking of punishment to satisfy a sense of guilt—the guilt engendered by the patricidal impulses. No, punishment and mistreatment are sought because that is how the ego, or self, of such an individual experiences being loved by the father. *To be castrated, or, we can add, to be a loser, means to be loved by the father. Another way of stating this is that suffering equals love.* This is the sadomasochistic relationship between the masculine or father-identified superego, and the feminine identification of the ego, as Freud viewed it.

Freud's derivation of masochism here is quite different from that of Von Hattingberg. In fact, he describes two different, but commonly related types of masochism in this essay. The first was what he had called "moral masochism," the unconscious search for punishment as atonement for guilt, while the second kind of masochism, previously called "feminine masochism," refers to the identification with the mother, as love object for the father (Freud, 1924). These do appear to be the crucial dynamics for a number of masochistic pathological gamblers, however, this is not to say that all pathological gamblers are masochistic, or even that all masochists conform to Freud's formulations.

It should be noted that for Freud the association was not just between gambling and sexuality, but, more specifically, between gambling and sadomasochistic sexuality. Since a predominant place in the sadomasochistic world is devoted to the elaboration of beating fantasies, it is pertinent to mention Freud's classic paper, "A Child is Being Beaten" (1919), which studies the significance of such fantasies. Freud's contention was that while the fantasies underwent a series of unconscious changes, in which the identities of the parties shifted, that an important function of the fantasy was to reassure the masturbator (these were essentially masturbatory fantasies) that he, and not a sibling or some other rival, was the preferred love object for the father. In other words, it was another way of ritualizing the question, "Does my father love me?" just as the gambling did. Both methods are unsatisfactory, in that they rekindle guilt, which in turn must be alleviated. A vicious cycle ensues.

Incidentally, beating fantasies play a prominent role in Dostoevsky's writings, just as they do in the mental life, and in the perverse behavior patterns, of the more masochistic pathological gamblers. There is another similarity between Dostoevsky's world and that of our pathological gambler: the preoccupation with power games, with polarities of dominance and submission, shame, and humiliation.

Has Freud then solved the problem of Dostoevsky's pathological gambling? Let me remind the reader of Freud's statement: murderous impulses towards the father constitute "the main source of the sense of guilt, though we do not know if it is the only one." It is not necessary, he adds, for it to be the only one, and he leaves it to future researchers to elicit others and "to establish with certainty the mental origin of guilt and the need for expiation." It is my contention that, while Freud's contribution is an extremely significant one, there is another dimension to Dostoevsky's all-pervasive sense of guilt.

That the author was tortured throughout his lifetime by a profound sense of personal guilt is accepted fact. His long-standing masochism, also, is well known and his life seems to prove Freud's thesis about the individual who, out of a sense of guilt, seeks out "crime and punishment." Most significantly, however, Dostoevsky' pathological gambling was limited to an eight-year period. It began abruptly and ceased just as dramatically; despite multiple opportunities to gamble after that, he was never again tempted.

In my own study of Dostoevsky's gambling (Rosenthal, 1986a), I relate its beginnings to the terminal illness and death from consumption of the author's first wife, an event which undoubtedly echoed his mother's suffering and demise from the same illness. I view his gambling as a manic type of defense against enormous feelings of loss and, especially, of guilt. This theme recurs in all of his writings of the period. For example, Raskolnikov's sense of indebtedness to his mother, financial and otherwise, is persecutory, and causes him to seek escape through an activity which covertly consists of murdering a symbolic mother and her pregnant half-sister (Rosenthal, 1981). While Freud has focused on the crime of patricide, most of the violence in Dostoevsky's fiction is committed against women, frequently mothers or women who are pregnant, and against their small children.

Dostoevsky's mother had given birth to eight children, Fyodor being the second oldest. She was only able to breast feed her firstborn, and because of this he remained her favorite. While pregnant with Fyodor she developed a respiratory infection—if not consumption then some precursor of it—which made her too weak to nurse, and she apparently never sufficiently recovered, as all her other children were also given over to peasant women who functioned as wet nurses. After a long, lingering illness she died of the disease when Dostoevsky was fifteen. The author's mother, I would suggest, is the "absent other" in "Dostoevsky and Parricide" (Rosenthal, 1986a). When Freud asks if we know of any greater guilt than that of patricide, we might reply the guilt of the infant or young child who feels its growth, indeed its very existence, is destructive to its mother.

It would be relevant at this point to momentarily ignore our chronology and mention Richard Geha's (1970) two-part study of Dostoevsky's *The Gambler.* Geha views the preoedipal mother, and more specifically *the mother who refuses to feed,* as the primary determinant in the gambling impulse. The gambler approaches the gaming tables with expectations of satisfying his hunger, and through an identification with the mother (in other words, he displaces and *becomes* her) he imagines himself immune against loss. His storehouse is self-replenishing; he can feed the world. While Geha does not make the connection, this is precisely the narcissistic fantasy delineated by Simmel (1920).

Geha does not stop there, however, and attaches equal importance to the castration complex, as he tries to put oedipal conflicts at the center of both *The Gambler* and all gambling pathology, in order to bring his formulation in line with Freud's (1928) construct. I find his evidence for this, based on his interpretation of the Dostoevsky novella, unconvincing. Other analysts, however, have brought forth clinical material in substantiation of Freud's ideas. There are a number of individual case reports of pathological gamblers successfully treated by psychoanalysis (Lindner, 1950; Harkavy, 1954; Reider, 1960; Comess, 1960; Harris, 1964; Laufer, 1966); the dynamics presented are those of "Dostoevsky and Parricide."

Many analysts writing after Freud have merely elaborated on the contributions of the earlier writers. Theodore Reik (1940), for example, views gambling as "a kind of question addressed to destiny. It is a form of oracle which the modern psyche readily accepts." While this idea is invariably attributed to Reik, it is actually a restatement of a concept initially presented by Stekel (1924).

In 1945, Otto Fenichel, in his classic, *The Psychoanalytic Theory of Neurosis,* summarized the literature to date. Notably, he discusses gambling under the heading of "Perversions and Impulse Neuroses" which he contrasts with compulsion neuroses (p. 324). The actions of the former are pleasurable, or at least are performed in the hope of achieving pleasure. Compulsive acts, on the other hand, are painful and performed in the hope of getting rid of pain. Guilt feelings may disturb a perverse or impulsive action, but there is a difference still in the way the urge is felt. Compulsive gambling, then, is a misnomer; in fact, Fenichel does not use the term.

The conflicts in gambling, Fenichel believes, are those centered around masturbation. However, he reminds the reader, in all conflicts around masturbation, the activity serves as the scapegoat for the objectionable fantasies with which it is associated. Conflicts center around getting the "supplies," hence, an oral fixation. The gambler provokes Fate, which is forced to decide for or against him. Good luck is interpreted as a promise of protection, but what is most important is that the gambler feels *entitled* to ask for special favors. The figure of Fate, with whom the gambler is fighting, is a representative of the father. The battle is one of kill or be killed. While Fenichel refers to the work of Simmel and Bergler, his formulation of the gambling impulse is most heavily drawn from Freud's essay on Dostoevsky.

III. Bergler's Concepts of Psychic Masochism

In the psychodynamic literature on gambling, the most widely quoted after Freud has been Edmund Bergler (1935, 1943, 1957). Bergler published some three hundred articles and twenty-four books during his thirty-five years as a practicing psychoanalyst; today he is known almost entirely for his emphasis on masochism, and for one work, *The Psychology of Gambling* (1957). His has been the only attempt at a complete systemization.

Bergler's starting point is the assumption that the pathological gambler is motivated by guilt, either conscious or unconscious, and that his behavior consists of a series of mechanisms aimed at appeasing his conscience. What is the basis for this guilt? The gambler is rebelling against the reality principal, and against those authority figures, originally, the parents, who instituted it by imposing rules and restrictions on the young child's pursuit of pleasure. This rebellion involves unconscious hostility against the parents, and so there is a retaliatory self-punishment because of that aggression. This self-punishment is always present, but being unconscious is never recognized, except perhaps through therapy.

Even though the pathological gambler's aggression may be unconscious, much of it is superficial and in actuality a kind of pseudo-aggression, that is a defense against something else. What he posits as existing at the deepest level of the gambler's unconscious is a *stabilization on the rejection level,* or what he calls *psychic masochism,* and unconscious craving for defeat, humiliation, pain, rejection.

Bergler doesn't make clear why the gambler is stabilized at this deepest level, but he refers to it as an oral fixation, and does apparently regard it as a "bedrock." He does explain, however, how he conceptualizes the development of masochism. The pursuit of pleasure, being forbidden, has become associated with painful punishments, reproaches, and feelings of guilt. Faced with a series of such punishments, the individual can only submit, to "make the best of it." And the best way to endure unescapable pain, is to follow the

pleasure principle, to produce *pleasure out of displeasure.* Hence the birth of
the psychic masochist. The individual now seeks out situations in which he
can be refused, rejected, unjustly treated, and humiliated. It is an ingenious
device for the nullification of punishment: when punishment becomes pleasure, the whole notion of punishment is reduced to absurdity.

This process must remain secret, however. Why? Because at the first sign
that the victim is deriving pleasure from his torture, the sadist will stop.
Hence the need for the gambler's pseudo-aggression, which is so visible in
his rebellion, an aggression against others *which always leads to defeat and
rejection.* The masochist payoff remains hidden.

Bergler's case histories illustrate how the gambler's behavior is derived
from these dynamics. The patients are involved in an adversary relationship
with the world; their opponents at the poker table, the dealer in the casino,
the roulette wheel or stock exchange are *unconsciously identified with the
refusing mother,* or, in later versions of the fantasy, it is father who does the
rejecting. The conscious conviction he will win masquerades the unconscious
reality, that he "knows" they will refuse him, by making him lose.

It should be immediately apparent that even though *psychic masochism* is
a concept borrowed from Freud, that Bergler's understanding of the masochistic gambler is quite different from the one presented in "Dostoevsky and
Parricide." Von Hattingberg's notion of masochism was different still. This is
one of the difficulties with the concept of masochism—it presupposes more
agreement as to meaning than is there. Freud wrestled with the concept
throughout his entire career; his ideas on the subject underwent major revision at least three times. For Bergler to present *psychic masochism* as a
unitary concept, and as "bedrock," as he frequently insists it is, is simplistic
(so much so that Bergler is totally ignored in all psychoanalytic reviews of
the literature on masochism).

However, much of what Bergler describes is of great clinical relevance.
The pathological gambler, most characteristically, does show a hatred of
reality. Necessity is to be avoided by him at all costs, limitations are to be
denied. As Bergler notes (1957, p. 19), the attacks on reality which occur in
gambling are "vicious and not at all harmless." Particularly relevant, also, are
his descriptions of the pathological gambler's inability to let go of rejection,
how he holds on to his resentment and spite, and makes the world into a
refusing parent, so as to maintain his view of himself as an innocent victim,
full of self-pity and righteous anger.

In attempting to present a general theory for pathological gambling, Bergler offers a typology; he divides his patients into six distinct types: (1) the

classical, (2) the passive-feminine male, (3) the defensive pseudo-superior, (4) the gambler motivated by unconscious guilt, (5) the "unexcited" gambler, (6) the female gambler. I do not find this classification useful, being based as it is on superficial characteristics. There is too much of an overlap between types. If one were to attempt to classify the author, Dostoevsky, for example, or his protagonist, Alexis, from *The Gambler,* one would find that of the five types to which male gamblers are eligible, all fit.

Of approximately two hundred pathological gamblers who came or, more often than not, were sent to him, sixty stayed for treatment and, Bergler reports, more than half of those were cured. By cure he emphasized that does not mean mere cessation of gambling, but a giving up of the whole self-destructive pattern. Should Bergler's method of treatment be considered psychoanalysis? Certainly it has been influenced by analysis and he claims to work with dreams and to analyze the transference. His method, however, seems mostly Bergler.

Treatments lasted for a year, a year and a half at most, and at no point does he mention how often patients were seen and whether they were ever on the couch. Bergler's technique seems very similar to the one August Aichhorn developed for treating juvenile delinquents. He engaged them in argument, challenged their beliefs, and didn't let them get away with anything. Bergler demonstrates a knowledge of the various con games. In a sense, he outmanipulates the manipulator. He sells them. Treatment seems based on getting the patients to accept his theory of psychic masochism. As he told one patient, eight months into therapy, "One of these days, you will pronounce my opinions as though they were your own, forget who had told them to you, and be cured" (1957, p. 160).

IV. Modifications of the Theory

More than anyone else, Bergler popularized the notion of the gambler wanting to lose. His ideas on pathological gambling were picked up by the media of his day, with newspaper articles, and stores in *McCalls,* and *Redbook,* and *Cosmopolitan.* Of the professional contributions which followed his, three in particular—those of Greenson (1947), Lindner (1950), and Galdston (1951, 1960)—tried to modify his theory. Each, we will come to appreciate, while in agreement with the need for self-punishment, will manage to find still other explanations for the unconscious sense of guilt which motivates it.

Greenson's (1947) observations are based on the analyses of five male patients who gambled, as well as his own personal experiences, both in the army and as a civilian among physicians who gambled. He notes the vocabulary (the choice of slang) and behavior patterns of primarily poker players and crap shooters. These activities, he concludes, are derivatives of infantile partial instincts. Gambling, therefore, gratifies these pregenital impulses, and does so with a minimum of guilt since the behavior is accepted by the group and the guilt shared with others. It is understandable why gambling has such universal appeal.

Then he turns from all gambling situations to the problem of the pathological gambler. The neurotic gambler, as he calls him, *mistakes his strong yearning for omnipotence for the feeling he is omnipotent.* Through his gambling he is testing this out, seeking a sign from Fate as confirmation of this omnipotence. What would it mean if he were omnipotent? It would be a way of bringing about a reunion with the nurturing mother of infancy. This kind of oceanic reunion is sought for defensive purposes. *It is an attempt to ward off a severe depression.*

In Greenson's analysis, Chance, Luck, and Fate are equated, and he uses the three terms interchangeably. Each represents the father, although the gambler's approach to this father-substitute may vary, depending upon his attitudes towards his own father. Thus the gambling activity may be a testing of Fate, a battle for supremacy, an act of extreme submissiveness, or an attempt to bribe the father.

There are some cases, he concedes, where Luck may represent a mother-figure, less frightening but still powerful. Lady Luck will then be appealed to, challenged, battled against, begged, and wooed. Bergler, he notes, had stressed that aggression against the mother was the most important unconscious motive in the gamblers he studied. *In all cases, according to Greenson, the image and attitude toward Luck, as it was toward Fate, is determined by the oedipal constellation of the specific gambler.* These fantasies with regard to Luck and Fate, being distorted derivatives of unconscious oedipal fantasies, are, quite naturally, accompanied by guilt. Therefore, neither winning nor losing can bring satisfaction. The gambler must keep playing, since there is no comfortable outcome.

Greenson, himself, does not stop there, and before he has finished he has postulated multiple determinants for gambling from all psychosexual states of development. He insists on the primacy of oedipal conflicts, however, although his clinical material seems drawn more from earlier sources. This disparity between his theory and his clinical observations, in a sense, between what he says he does, and, what he does, weakens his contribution.

Winning, he notes, is equivalent to a triumph, omnipotence having been achieved through reunion with the nurturing mother of earliest childhood. It is an uncomfortable victory, accompanied as it is by guilt. The sources of this guilt, for Greenson, is oedipal, and the superego, he reminds us, is derived from the authority of the father. (This, I would add, is not the only possible explanation for the guilt associated with omnipotence; it is experienced as a triumph over reality, the sense of power associated with it is unlimited and therefore quite frightening, and it is a triumph usually achieved at the expense of others, hence a kind of theft.)

Similarly, for Greenson's typical neurotic gambler, losing is associated with being abandoned by the nurturing mother. This is associated with depression, rather than guilt, although Greenson requires the latter to be present in keeping with his oedipal formulation. In the summary to his article, Greenson stresses his agreement with Fenichel that neurotic gambling is an impulse neurosis, and that the desire to gamble is ego-syntonic. In its dynamics, as in its course, prognosis, and treatment, he believes it similar to the addictions and perversions.

The focus of Robert Lindner's (1950) paper is his two-year analysis of a pathological gambler who had begun gambling shortly following the death of his father. It is of note that the analysis was conducted in a federal prison where the patient was serving a three-year sentence for gambling-related thefts and forgery. It is of interest, also, that Lindner was tempted into accepting the patient for treatment only because he was intrigued by the many close parallels he noticed between the patient's story as it was initially presented and that of the author, Fyodor Dostoevsky. The patient's words, his behavior, the various people in his life, seemed to leap from the pages of *The Gambler,* and from the diaries and letters of the Russian novelist.

Lindner's conceptualization of his patient's psychodynamics appears to be based closely on Freud's emphasis on the oedipal rivalry with the father. However, the basis for the patient's guilt is not so much the long-standing death wishes towards the father, as the confirmation of the patient's omnipotence when the father actually dies. The gambling then becomes a compulsive questioning: Did I (my wishes) actually kill my father? When the patient wins, he experiences it as confirmation of his omnipotence: You can do whatever you like, can succeed at whatever you set your mind on. Winning then is intolerable. Losing not only punishes such wishes, but denies the validity of the patient's omnipotence: You have no such magical powers, cannot influence or control the unknown, cannot make things happen by wishing them. While this is a relief, it is also, as Lindner is perceptive enough to realize, depressing. *To give up the fiction of omnipotence is a painful loss.*

Seemingly following up on the explanation of Reik and Greenson, Lindner understands his patient to be not only addressing a question to the oracle of gambling but attempting to influence the answer. The analysis revealed that the money he was losing unconsciously represented a form of bribery. It was intended to gain for him grace and absolution in the manner of indulgences purchased from the clergy.

Lindner offers an extensive discussion of his patient's chronic compulsive masturbation, a habit which was indulged in from earliest childhood through marriage, but which abruptly stopped at precisely the time the patient began to gamble. There is no doubt in Lindner's mind, and he substantiates this with some observations of other gamblers he has treated, that for his patient, gambling literally took the place of masturbation.

When the patient returned from a gambling bout in which he lost, he had to ask for and obtain his wife's forgiveness. Only then would he "feel clean again." What this means, according to Lindner, is that losing is connected, in the patient's unconscious, with disapproval for masturbation. Thus there is a second question being addressed to the oracle. While the first question was related to the *aggressive* pole of the oedipal configuration (Are my wishes powerful enough to cause the death of my father?), the second question addresses the *sexual* conflict: Will I be rewarded or punished for my secret incestuous desires? Winning, according to this set of meanings, is proof that sexual desires toward mother (the unconscious masturbation fantasy) will be rewarded, while losing means that father disapproves and will punish the patient for his transgression. (The patient's wife, as Lindner notes, then stands as a temporary, and not terribly satisfactory, substitute for the father in her role as forgiver.)

Putting the two poles of conflict together, it is obvious that the gambler is in a real bind. Winning has a positive and negative meaning, and so does losing. The only solution would be to both win and lose at the same time, an impossibility, hence his need to keep playing. Unlike Fenichel and Greenson, Lindner disagrees with the nosological placing of compulsive gambling among the "impulsive disorders," or the viewing of the problem as similar to the addictions and perversions. It is an obsessional neurosis, states Lindner, and while he presented a "pure" case, his point would have been better demonstrated, he claims, by those instances in which the gambling is a temporary stage in the development of a full-blown obsessional neurosis. Lindner certainly would favor retaining the term compulsive gambling rather than the newer designation of pathological gambling. And, in line with this, he argues that "at no time is the compulsion ego-syntonic, that is, a thing which the gambler wants to do and in which he takes pleasure; it is always ego-alien or dystonic." Upon reading such statements, one cannot help wondering whether he is describing the same patients as Fenichel and Greenson.

In reading Lindner's account, I was left with the impression that perhaps the most important determinant in the successful outcome of his treatment was the full uncovering of the patient's omnipotent fantasy, which was gone into great detail during the analysis. Lindner shares little of this, but apparently the patient saw himself as a king, with *unlimited power.* The vast sums he would win gambling would establish him as a philanthropist and benefactor of the race. In other words, everyone would be dependent on him, as a kind of generous parent, while he would remain totally independent and above-it-all. He would be, and would have, everything. A similar fantasy was expressed by Dostoevsky's gambler and of course this was precisely what Simmel (1920) had in mind when he described how the gambler would meet all his own narcissistic needs, thereby shutting out the world. Such fantasies as the one indulged in by Lindner's patient, which often are presented in the most beneficent terms, contain hidden hostility toward the nurturing parents, who are reduced to beggars when the tables have been turned.

Galdston's (1951, 1960) formulation is based on a review of the literature and his unsuccessful treatment of one patient. Gambling is *a question put to Lady Luck, who symbolizes the mother: Do you love me?* Do you approve of me? Do you think I am good, and smart, and strong? Obsessive in his uncertainty, the gambler cannot get a definitive and for all time reassuring answer. By now we are quite familiar with this hypothesis. Galdston's patient, however, a pathological gambler since the age of twelve, presents a kind of natural experiment—a woman has fallen in love with him, and she refuses to be put off. Unlike his previous relationships, which were all casual and superficial—one-night stands, prostitutes—he finds himself getting emotionally involved. She demands nothing from him and isn't even interested in his money. He can not believe his good fortune, has to test her repeatedly, remains tortured by doubts. Could she or anybody love him? *During this period he abstains from gambling.*

The patient keeps testing the woman. Does she care about me? is the question he keeps asking. She passes all his tests and still he is dissatisfied. Eventually he finds his excuse to break off the relationship, after which he returns to his gambling, only now he is totally out of control, and loses heavily. Galdston is correct in his assumption that the dynamics in the man's relationship with his love interest are identical to the ones found in gambling.

Where he falls short, I believe, is in his explanation for why his patient could not be satisfied with an affirmative answer to his question. Such an answer, says Galdston—yes the woman loves—does not square with the facts of his life, and with his memories of childhood deprivation. In other words no one in the present could make up for the loss of the mother's love. "Such a one is doomed to wander through life asking unanswerable questions." Perhaps, but I would suggest a different explanation: *that he is asking the wrong question.* The real question is not "Does she care about me?" but "Can I allow myself to care about her?" All too often the pathological gambler must deny his dependency, and devalue the importance of the other person.

V. More Recent Advances

There is somewhat of a gap between the mid-nineteen sixties and the eighties, although we see the former period giving impetus to certain trends which are first being mined today. One of these is *the consolidation of earlier theories.* Bolen and Boyd (1968) briefly review the literature and then attempt an encompassing statement.

The basic, analytic, psychodynamic formulation is that gambling unconsciously represents a forbidden, guilt activation activity. Reduced to the most abstract components, gambling is forbidden and an unconscious transgression because of the indirect, intrapsychic satisfaction of multiple aggressive and libidinal determinants. Here is the origin of the abundant pervasive guilt feelings which plague the gambler as well as the origin of anticipated, desired punishment in the form of gambling loss.

Their summary seems to cover the main hypotheses about the more neurotic forms of gambling, and is general enough to include the various explanations for the gambler's sense of guilt. I am not sure that it would include Simmel's unique contribution, or the contributions of those who emphasize the defensive functions of gambling, such as the avoidance of depresion (Greenson, 1947; Comess, 1960; and Niederland, 1967). Their summary is even too limited to cover their own contributions, for no sooner do they present us with this summary, than they expand beyond it.

Noting the variety of diagnostic categorizations (compulsive neurosis, obsessional neurosis, oral character, impulse disorder, etc.), they suggest that it is more useful to view pathological gambling as a complex symptom and defensive maneuver present in a wide variety of psychiatric disorders rather than a specific one. For example, they observe that, in their experience, a significant proportion of psychiatric patients afflicted with problem gambling have been schizophrenic. (Today, however, I suspect that many of those patients would be diagnosed as borderline.)

They note that patients frequently began to gamble compulsively after a life crisis or major stress. One of the most common precipitating stresses in their gambling patients had been the breakup of a marriage. According to the literature, one of the most frequent precipitating events for male gamblers has been the death of a father. Other key stresses included the birth of a first child, a business failure, or paradoxically, a career or work-related promotion with features of a success reaction.

In their treatment of pathological gamblers (Boyd and Bolen, 1970), they utilized group therapy with gamblers and spouses. Significantly, they found a preoccupation in the group with the death of the gamblers' parents. This was a frequent and recurrent theme for the group, and they analyze its meaning for one of the pathological gamblers whose gambling behavior had been exacerbated by such a loss. Taking issue with the oedipal interpretation of guilt secondary to the actualization of death wishes towards a rival, with gambling then serving as punishment, they offer an alternative, which for their patient proved to be a more meaningful hypothesis. They suggest that the gambling represented a manic defensive maneuver which, at least temporarily, blotted out the awareness of object loss, the depression secondary to such loss, and the awareness of helplessness in the face of the inevitability which is Death.

Custer, throughout his writings, and other authors as well, have noted the difficulty pathological gamblers have with death. Boyd and Bolen suggest that this is because death confronts us with the inevitable. Their observation reminds me of Dostoevsky, writing "Notes From the Underground" (1864), literally at his dying wife's bedside; the story is a great polemic against Necessity, with the narrator insisting on the freedom of the individual, even if that freedom consists solely of the right to go on against one's own best interest. The painful awareness of one's helplessness, that there is nothing one can do to alter the inevitable, calls for a return to the magical (omnipotent) means of early childhood. Gambling provides the illusion of power, mastery, and control in the face of uncontrollable death. As Boyd and Bolen are quick to note, the illusion is transient, the "solution" has to be repeated, it becomes an addiction.

Nearly all of their patient-gamblers had at least one parent who was a gambler, often a pathological gambler. Several remembered how they had been introduced to gambling by these parents. "One compulsive horse player attended the races frequently with his father during his teenage years and felt this to be the only time he could effectively relate to him." In therapy he commented on how his "gambling father is now a part" of himself. Bolen and Boyd believe that identification with a parent who gambles may play a prominent role in the propensity to gamble. This is not only their most impressive extension beyond their initial attempt at consolidating the psycho-dynamic literature, but it brings us to the second trend I wanted to discuss: the *emphasis on identification.*

According to Custer (1982), the family histories of pathological gamblers reveal problems with alcoholism or pathological gambling in the parents in about one-third of the cases. Custer, Julian Taber (1982), and others working in the field, have been impressed by how often the pathological gambler was first introduced to gambling by a favored relative; the experience of Bolen and Boyd's patient, referred to in the preceeding paragraph, is by no means atypical. This is one of the reasons for concern about the effects of the increased legalization of gambling; the state, and its leaders, viewed as they are as authority figures and parental surrogates, are actively advocating that people gamble. As if that were not problematic enough, entertainment and sports heroes do radio and television commercials urging the public to emu-late them by buying lottery tickets.

A more sophisticated form of parental identification is described in a fascinating article by Philip Weissman (1963). Weissman presents the histor-ies of two of his analytic patients, one of whom he calls the "winner," the other the "loser." He demonstrates how life-long patterns of behavior, ef-fecting every area of their lives, was determined by the early interaction with their fathers, as revealed by the repetitive play between father and son roughly between ages two to five. In each case the father instilled in his son a certain attitude toward the world, and a corresponding set of identifications, through a play pattern which repeated what the father, in turn, had received from his father.

The "loser," whose father was a problem gambler, was programmed to seek out short-lived omnipotent victories alternating with annihilating self-inflicted defeats. What was this game between father and son? The "loser," as a small child, was permitted to greet his father by rushing at him, climbing all over him, messing him up, punching him, and pulling his hair. The father would laugh heartily and at times spur him on; at other times he would permit him to begin his attack, then irritably plead for him to stop. Encouragement and protest would alternate, until suddenly, at a moment's notice, the father would violently detach himself from his son, scream at him, and force him to stand absolutely still until the position became unendurable. This pattern was never modified, and was repeated at a later age through other kinds of interactions between them. As an adult, the "loser" continued and elaborated on the sequence of omnipotent victories followed by annihilating, self-inflicted defeats.

As the article reminds us, the pathology of the parent becomes part of the every-day environment for the child. It was Laius, after all, who first attacked Oedipus. The study of identity formation attributes equal importance to external and internal factors. Our third contemporary trend, then, is the examination of *cultural and societal influences.*

Emmanuel Moran (1970a) takes issue with Fenichel's (1945) conclusion that pathological gambling is always impulsive and that the problem arises from individual abnormalities. He feels that Fenichel ignores the social setting and external pressures which encourage excess. Moran (1970a, 1970b) describes five varieties of pathological gambling: subcultural, neurotic, impulsive, psychopathic, and symptomatic. While the distinctions he makes are not that clear (he does admit that his categories were not meant to be mutually exclusive, that any patient may show characteristics for a number of them) his intention is to distinguish between external, or social, contributing factors, and internal, or what he refers to as individual, ones. He notes, for example, the importance of the opportunity to gamble. It was only after a betting office or gaming club opened up in their neighborhoods that many of the gamblers lost control. In other words, with increased accessibility, a number of social gamblers rapidly became pathological.

Moran's criticism is not quite fair. Greenson (1947), writing almost a quarter of a century before, had been impressed by the social aspects of gambling, how poker players, for example, would share in a community ritual with its own vocabulary and customs; guilt would be deflected away from the individual participant and onto the group. Others have investigated even further these societal and cultural influences on gambling. Charlotte Olmsted (1962), in an extremely interesting work, explores the psychodynamics of the games themselves, thereby suggesting the basis for their attraction for certain types of individuals. First she looks at the development of the playing deck, and of the innovations made at particular periods of history. Then she examines various card games, and how they express the problems intrinsic to various cultures.

An example of her approach would be her analysis of the game of twenty-one, which seems to symbolize mostly dominance-dependency conflicts, and *the attainment of full adult status without assuming the responsibilities.* Twenty-one, the traditional age of attaining adult status, is the goal, but sequences are not valued at all; family ties are not desired or required, simply independent adulthood with no ties. Blackjack, the other name for this game, indicates this also—the single, unattached male, uncertain whether to be aggressive or give way to fear, with the ace an eleven at one moment, a one the next or one time on the top of the pack, the next time at the bottom.

Unlike most casino games, the representative of one house, the dealer, plays a hand in direct competition with the customer. The dealer, according to Olmsted, represents the society or family structure against whom the player is in rebellion and with whom he is in direct, personal conflict. The number twenty-one is played for, but it is even more dangerous to go over this figure than to fall short of it. Independence, by becoming an adult, is aimed for, and without responsibilities. Although the player is in rebellion against his family, he does not contemplate changing the social order in the slightest, only his own role in it. "He does not aspire to become a king, either—he wants the privilege of adult status, but wants to stop right there and remain a jack all of his life."

There is not much direct expression of sexuality in twenty-one, according to Olmsted, but of course dominance-dependency conflicts are by no means confined to father-son duels. Olmsted suggests that it would be interesting to see whether people with a high degree of intersex dominance-dependency conflicts seek out blackjack dealers of the opposite sex.

As one would expect, certain games, and certain types of gambling, seem to correspond with certain kinds of personalities. There is very little systematic inquiry into this, and a need exists for research into why a pathological gambler will be attracted to one form of gambling rather than another, or on the differences between those who are polymorphous or promiscuous in their gambling—they will bet on anything—and those others, no less addicted, who will bet on one type only, poker for example, or horse racing, or the slots, and will not look for substitutes when these are available.

Betting patterns also, within the gambling type, may be extremely variable, or single-minded. An example of the latter is presented by William Niederland (1967), who successfully treated through psychoanalysis a problem gambler whose entire gambling pattern consisted of playing roulette, and betting all combinations involving a single number. The number, thirty-two, held symbolic significance for him; the analysis of its meaning followed an oedipal formulation, and Niederland viewed the treatment as confirming all that Freud had written about incest, masturbation, patricide, and guilt in his study of Dostoevsky.

The most significant trend in psychoanalytic thinking in the past twenty years has been the increasing interest in early development, and, specifically problems of identity; the patient population has both encouraged and reflected this shift, as neurotic symptomatology has been replaced by more character-ological disturbances, and specifically, the narcissistic and borderline disorders. In one sense this emphasis on narcissistic personality traits in relation to pathological gambling has been presaged by the work of Simmel (1920) and some of the other pioneers who emphasized the false sense of self-sufficiency, the feelings of entitlement and grandiosity, the reliance on magical thinking, and other narcissistic features. At the same time it augers something entirely new in that, under the leadership of Heinz Kohut (1971), some psychoanalysts have turned from a conflict model to one which stresses developmental deficiencies. I will have more to say about that in a moment.

The close association between the narcissistic disorders and pathological gambling has been emphasized by a number of clinicians. Julian Taber (1982) has stated that "no less than 50 percent of the gamblers coming to the (inpatient treatment program at Brecksville) fit the criteria for narcissistic personality just as well as they fit the diagnostic criteria for pathological gambling." Robert Custer's composite portrait of the pathological gambler (Custer and Milt, 1985), while it nowhere mentions the narcissistic personality, is unmistakable. He describes the grandiose fantasies of power and success which compensate for the extremely poor sense of self-worth; the rapid and angry withdrawals when the need for constant admiration and attention is not met; the superficial charm which covers up an inability to share meaningfully and feel comfortable with intimacy and affection.

Roston (1961) and Livingston (1974) have also stressed the narcissistic characteristics of the gambling populations they studied, although Henry Lesieur (1979) has questioned whether the gamblers were narcissistic and power oriented before they became compulsive or only afterwards. My own experience in treating pathological gamblers both through psychoanalysis and through intensive psychoanalytic psychotherapy has confirmed, at least to my satisfaction, that these personality patterns are longstanding or precede their involvement with gambling. It is not unusual for pathological gamblers who have remained abstinent for a number of years to continue to manifest these same personality patterns. What will bring them for treatment will be an increased awareness of their self-destructive tendencies, problems in relationships, or continued dissatisfaction with their lives.

I have also treated a number of narcissistic personalities who were not pathological gamblers, yet who demonstrated such strikingly similar behavior patterns involving the taking of risks, the need to test limits and flirt with self-destructive outcomes, that I came to label such behavior as "covert gambling" (Rosenthal, 1986b). These people gambled, not at the racetrack or casino, but with their every day lives. They typically gambled with time, and the meeting of obligations and responsibilities. Nothing was too small or too big to bet on. They would gamble for example, when it came to filling up the gas tank of their car, or paying their bills. There was a need to see how close they could come to some imaginary line, and what would happen should they cross it. As with the pathological gamblers, the outcome was viewed in all-or-nothing terms; one could win or one could lose, but invariably at stake was a rather fragile sense of identity.

In my work with these covert gamblers I came to appreciate what it meant for them to be challenging fate, or needing to test their luck. There has been a tendency to confuse these terms, and, along with chance, and destiny, to use them interchangeably. I proposed a hierarchy (Rosenthal, 1986b), based on the continuum of developmental conflicts which need to be solved on the way to adulthood, with a progressive sense of mastery in moving from Chance, through Luck, and then Fate, to Destiny.

Being dependent on others for that which should reside within himself, the narcissistic individual is always testing, challenging, in order to find out where he stands, or has the right to stand. He is not seeking punishment out of some sense of guilt, although there is plenty of that too, so much as he is involved in a kind of omnipotent provocation (Rosenthal, 1981, 1984), a deliberate flirting with danger in order to test his power and prove that he is in control. In a sense, he is trying to control the uncontrollable, very much like the gambler who is seeking certainty. There is another similarity between the narcissistic personality and the problem gambler; both are preoccupied with the need to find loopholes, to be exceptions to the law. Breaking the law, and getting away with it, is equated with a kind of moral superiority (Rosenthal, 1981, 1984).

Hence we find strikingly similar dynamics between the narcissistic personality and at least some of our pathological gamblers. Both Taber (1982) and myself (1984) have discussed this more extensively. In our treatment approaches, we have focused on the various methods of self-deception: the lying, the power games, the idealization of destructiveness and other value reversals, and the vicissitudes of omnipotence. However, other therapists working with narcissistic patients have viewed the fragile sense of self-identity, not as a result of primitive defense mechanisms, as used for the resolution of specific conflicts, but as the result of some inherent weakness of deficiency. According to this line of reasoning the narcissistic personality is psychologically vulnerable to unregulated swings of central nervous system-autonomic nervous system arousal or depression. The patient then turns to a variety of stimulating and numbing activities (and substances) in a desperate attempt at self-regulation. These are chosen, not for any symbolic meaning, but for their energy-regulating potential. Such activities, in addition to gambling, would include the usage of alcohol and various drugs, overeating, excessive sleeping and television watching, jogging and physical exercise, sex, or other stimulating and numbing activities.

Rickles (1983) summarized four common symptom clusters found in the narcissistic personality disorders: (1) *the under-stimulated self* who is consistently occupied with stimulating activity to avoid internal emptiness; (2) the *fragmenting self* who loses a sense of continuity or self in time and cohesiveness in space, resulting in profound anxiety and hypochondriacal concerns; (3) the *over-stimulated self* who constantly harbors tension-producing, grandiose fantasies but guards against involvement with longed-for merger experiences because of a threat to self-equilibrium; and (4) the *over-burdened self* that lacks the self-soothing capacity that protects one from the traumatic spreading of unchecked disturbing emotions. In each of these situations, he noted, one finds a precarious system for the modulation of arousal and dependency gratification. This deficiency in self-regulation leads to a variety of somatic disorders, as well as the attempts at self-cure listed above.

A parallel is to be found in the arousal model for pathological gambling being investigated by Iain Brown (1984) and others. Brown's evidence suggests that some form of arousal or excitement is a major reinforcer of gambling behavior, and he postulates that individual differences with regard to sensation-seeking are secondary to this need for arousal control. Arousal, in these experiments (Anderson and Brown, 1984; Brown, 1984), was measured by heart rate changes, although other researchers are beginning to look at the electrical and chemical activity of the brain (Carlton, 1983).

Summary

How do we summarize such a complicated and complex subject? It should now be obvious that it simply will not do to say that Freudians equate gambling with masturbation, or that pathological gambling is "explained" by the oedipus complex. Even within the psychoanalytic literature there is not one, but at least several models at work.

Gambling may involve a transgression (of boundaries) and with attendant guilt, the need for punishment. The crime may be oedipal, but this is not the only possibility; omnipotence may be viewed as an attack on reality, or a transgression of the limits of self, gender, and generation; the fantasy may involve a robbery or theft, most likely against the nurturing mother, with a reversal of roles as a way to deny dependency; primitive projective mechanisms may be viewed as intrusive and therefore morally reprehensible; any combination of transgressions may be present. Guilt may be appeased through a complex activity which affords both covert satisfaction (the re-enactment of the crime) as well as punishment.

There may be conflict with a dominant parent: competition and hatred, but also the need or desire to be loved. Such feelings frequently alternate. Subsumed under this would be the fights with Fate, and the appeals for approval to symbolic parental surrogates personified as Lady Luck or "the gods." There are multiple variations and permutations on this, including the one expressed by Freud in "Dostoevsky and Parricide": *To suffer, i.e., to lose, means to be loved.* For men this means being loved by the father, and is one of the central dynamics found in masochism. The negative oedipus complex is by no means as uncommon as was initially believed, and is a part of normal development which extends into and is not usually resolved until well into adolescence (see Blos, 1984).

It is also possible that the parent, due to certain unresolved conflicts of his own, interferes with his son's development, and that the gambler-son is unconsciously responding to the message his father is sending him. "If I am a failure my father will love me." Gambling constitutes "learned" behavior in the sense of identification with a parent or parental attitude. In contrast to this kind of dutiful or *loyal* son is the truly rebellious or *spiteful* son, whose primary motivation is retaliation or revenge. "If I am a failure, my father will be a failure as a father, and that is what is most important to me. I can get back at my father by hurting his son."

Gambling serves multiple defensive functions. There is an illusion of power and control as a way of defending against depression and loss; uncertainty, helplessness, and fragmentation; the inevitability of death; being overwhelmed by the uncontrollable. It may be utilized as a method of self-cure in the struggle to maintain a precarious sense of identity.

REFERENCES

Allday, E. Stefan Zweig: A Critical Biography. *London, Allen, 1972.*
Anderson, G., and Brown, R. I. F. Real and laboratory gambling, sensation-seeking and arousal. Br J Psychology, 75: 401–410, 1984.

Bergler, E. *On the psychology of the gambler.* Am Imago, *22: 409–441, 1935.*

———. *The gambler: A misunderstood neurotic.* J Crim Psychopath, 4: *379–393, 1943. Rpt. in* Selected Papers of Edmund Bergler, M.D.: 1933–1961. *New York, Grune and Stratton, 1969, pp. 687–699.*

———. The Psychology of Gambling. *New York, International University Press, 1957.*

Blos, P. *Son and father.* J Am Psychoanal Assoc, *32: 301–324, 1984.*

Bolen, D. W., and Boyd, W. H.: *Gambling and the gambler: A review and preliminary findings.* Arch Gen Psychiatry, *18: 617–630, 1968.*

Boyd, W. H., and Bolen, D. W. *The compulsive gambler and spouse in group psychotherapy.* Int J Group Psychother, *20: 77–90, 1970.*

Brown, R. I. F. *The integration of arousal and sensation-seeking factors in the explanation of gambling and gambling addictions. Paper presented at the Sixth National Conference on Gambling, Atlantic City (December), 1984. In* Eadington, W. R. (Ed.): The Gambling Papers: Proceedings of the Sixth National Conference on Gambling and Risk-Taking. *Reno, University of Nevada, 1985.*

Carlton, P. *Prospects for clinical research on pathological gambling. Paper presented at The Carrier Foundation Training Conference on Pathological Gambling: The Silent Illness, Atlantic City (June), 1983.*

Chapman, S. R. *An argument against the "unconscious need to lose" concept in the compulsive gambler. Paper presented at the Third National Conference on Gambling, Las Vegas, 1975.*

Chasseguet-Smirgel, J. *Perversion, idealization and sublimation.* Int J Psychoanal, *55: 349–357, 1974.*

Comess, L. *The analysis of the gambler. Doctoral dissertation, Southern California Psychoanalytic Institute, 1960.*

Custer, R. L. *An overview of compulsive gambling. In* Carone, P. A.; Yolles, S. F., Kieffer, S. N., and Krinsky, L. W.: Addictive Disorders Update: Alcoholism, Drug Abuse, and Gambling. *New York, Human Sciences, 1982, vol. VII, 107–176.*

Custer, R. L., and Milt, H.: When Luck Runs Out. *New York, Facts on File, 1985.*

Dostoyevsky, F. M. *Notes From the Underground (1864). In* Coulson, J. (Trans.): Notes from the Underground/The Double. *London, Penguin, 1972.*

———. *The Gambler (1866). In* Coulson, J. (Trans.): The Gambler/Bobok/A Nasty Story. *London, Penguin, 1966.*

Fenichel, O. The Psychoanalytic Theory of Neurosis. *New York, Norton, 1945.*

Frank, J. Dostoevsky: The Seeds of Revolt, 1821–1849. *Princeton, Princeton University Press, 1976, pp. 25–28 and 379–391.*

Freud, S. *The psychotherapy of hysteria (1895). In* Strachey, J. (Ed. and Trans.): The Complete Psychological Works of Sigmund Freud, *Standard Edition, London, Hogarth, 1955, vol. II, pp. 289–290.*

———. *The interpretation of dreams (1900). In* Strachey, J. (Ed. and Trans.): The Complete Psychological Works of Sigmund Freud, *Standard Edition. London, Hogarth, 1953, vol. IV, pp. 283, and vol. V, p. 569.*

———. *"A child is being beaten": A contribution to the study of the origin of sexual perversions (1919). In* Strachey, J. (Ed. and Trans.): The Complete Psychological Works of Sigmund Freud, *Standard Edition. London, Hogarth, 1955, vol. XVII, pp. 177–204.*

————. *The economic problem of masochism (1924)*. In Strachey, J. *(Ed. and Trans.)* The Complete Psychological Works of Sigmund Freud, *Standard Edition. London, Hogarth, 1961, vol. XIX, pp. 157–170.*

————. *Dostoevsky and parricide (1928)*. In Strachey, J. *(Ed. and Trans.)* The Complete Psychological Works of Sigmund Freud, *Standard Edition. London, Hogarth, 1961, vol. XXI, pp. 175–196.*

Fuller, P. *Introduction.* In Halliday, J. and Fuller, P. *(Eds.)* The Psychology of Gambling, *New York, Harper Row, 1974.*

Galdston, I.: *The psychodynamics of the triad: Alcoholism, gambling and superstition.* Ment Hyg, *35: 589–598, 1951.*

————. *The gambler and his love.* Am J Psychiatry, *117: 553–555, 1960.*

Geha, R. *Dostoevsky and "The Gambler": A contribution to the psychogenics of gambling.* Psychoanal Rev, *57: 95–123 and 289–302, 1970.*

Greenson, R. *On gambling.* Am Imago, *4: 61–77, 1947.*

Harkavy, E. *The psychoanalysis of a gambler.* Int J Psychoanal, *35: 285, 1954.*

Harris, H. I. *Gambling addiction in an adolescent male.* Psychoanal Q, *33: 513–525, 1964.*

Jackson, R. L. The Art of Dostoevsky: Deliriums and Nocturnes. *Princeton, Princeton University Press, 1981.*

Kohut, H. The Analysis of the Self. *New York, International University Press, 1971.*

Laforgue, R. *On the eroticization of anxiety.* Int J Psychoanal, *11: 312–321, 1930.*

Laplanche, J., and Pontalis, J. The Language of Psychoanalysis. *New York, Norton, 1973.*

Laufer, M. *Object loss and mourning during adolescence.* Psychoanal Study Child, *21: 269–293, 1966.*

Lesieur, H. R. *The compulsive gambler's spiral of options and involvement.* Psychiatry, *42: 79–87, 1979.*

Lesieur, H. R. and Custer, R. L.: *Pathological gambling: Roots, phases and treatment.* Ann Am Acad Pol Soc Sci, *474: 146–156, 1984.*

Lindner, R. M. *The psychodynamics of gambling.* Ann Am Acad Pol Soc Sci, *269: 93–107, 1950.*

Livingston, J. Compulsive Gamblers: Observations on Action and Abstinence. *New York, Harper Row, 1974.*

Meltzer, D. *The relation of anal masturbation to projective identification.* Int J. Psychoanal, *47: 335–342, 1966.*

Moran, E. *Varieties of pathological gambling.* Br J Psychiatry, *116: 593–597, 1970a.*

————. *Pathological gambling.* Br J Hosp Med, *4: 59–70, 1970b.*

Neufeld, J. Dostojewski: Skizze zu Seiner Psychoanalyse. *Leipzig, Internationaler Psychoanalytischer Verlag, 1923.*

Niederland, W. G.: *A contribution to the psychology of gambling.* Psychoanal Forum, *2: 175–185, 1967.*

Olmsted, C. Heads I Win-Tails You Lose. *New York, Macmillan, 1962. Rpt. in* Herman, D. *(Ed.):* Gambling. *New York, Harper Row, 1967, pp. 136–152.*

Reider, N. *Percept as a screen: Economic and structural aspects.* J Am Psychoanal Assoc, *8: 82–99, 1960.*

Reik, T. *The study of Dostoevsky.* In From Thirty Years with Freud. *London, Hogarth, 1940, pp. 142–157.*

Rickles, W. H. *Self psychology and somatization: An integration with alexithymia.* Paper presented at the Sixth Annual Conference on the Psychology of the Self, Los Angeles, 1983.

Rosenthal, R. J. *Raskolnikov's transgression and the confusion between destructiveness and creativity.* In Grotstein, J. (Ed.), Do I Dare Disturb the Universe? A Memorial to Wilfred R. Bion. *Beverly Hills, Caesura Press, 1981, pp. 199–235.*

———. *Dostoevsky's experiment with projective mechanisms and the theft of identity in* The Double. *In Lazar, M. (Ed.),* Interplay. *Los Angeles, Undena Public, 1983, vol. 2, pp. 13–40.*

———. *The pathological gambler's system for self-deception. Paper presented at the Sixth National Conference on Gambling and Risk-Taking, Atlantic City (December), 1984. In Eadington, W. R. (Ed.):* The Gambling Papers: Proceedings of the Sixth National Conference on Gambling and Risk-Taking. *Reno, University of Nevada, 1985.*

———. *Freud's war with the Russian barbarian: The absent other in "Dostoevsky and Parricide." In preparation, 1986a.*

———. *Chance, luck, fate and destiny: Covert gambling in the narcissistic disorders. In preparation, 1986b.*

Roston, R. *Some personality characteristics of male compulsive gamblers. Doctoral dissertation, University of California (Los Angeles), 1961.*

Schmidl, F. *Freud and Dostoevsky.* J Am Psychoanal Assoc, *13: 518–532, 1965.*

Simmel, E. *Psychoanalysis of the gambler.* Int J Psychoanal, *1: 352–353, 1920.*

Stekel, W. *The gambler (1924). In Van Teslaar, S. (Ed. and Trans.):* Peculiarities of Behavior. *New York, Liveright, 1943, vol. II, pp. 233–255.*

Taber, J. I. *Group psychotherapy with pathological gamblers. Paper presented at the Fifth National Conference on Gambling and Risk-Taking, Lake Tahoe, 1982. In Eadington, W. R. (Ed.):* The Gambling Papers: Proceedings of the Fifth National Conference on Gambling and Risk-Taking. *Reno, University of Nevada, 1982.*

Von Hattingberg, H. *Analerotik, angstlust and eigensinn.* Int Z Psychoanal, *2: 244–258, 1914.*

Waelder, R.: *The principle of multiple function: Observations on overdetermination.* Psychoanal Q *5: 45–62, 1936. Rpt. in Guttman, S. A. (Ed.):* Psychoanalysis: Observation, Theory, Application-Selected Papers of Robert Waelder. *New York, International University Press, 1976.*

Weissman, P. *The effects of preoedipal paternal attitudes on development and character.* Int J Psychoanal, *44: 121–131, 1963.*

Zweig, F. *Stefan Zweig, New York, Crowell, 1946.*

Zweig, S. *Dostoeffsky. In* Three Masters: Balzac-Dickens-Dostoeffsky. *New York, Viking, 1919.*

———. *Twenty-four hours in a woman's life (1926). In* Conflicts. *New York, Viking, 1934.*

PART III

Case Studies

C<small>ASE STUDIES</small> have always been important in psychoanalytic writing because they allow the reader to see how psychoanalytic theory and technique are applied in an actual treatment situation. I have included Fine's report of a traditional psychoanalytic treatment of a man addicted to methadone and Gustafson's self-psychology treatment of an alcoholic.

Fine's case study is the fullest account of the application of a relatively orthodox psychoanalytic technique in the treatment of a drug addict. Though published in 1972, the treatment was conducted in 1951, long before the renewed interest in addiction by psychoanalysts. Despite many pressures, Fine made every effort to preserve a relatively orthodox psychoanalysis. However, many of the techniques and principles of psychoanalysis were of limited use: the couch was tried but not productive, interpretations of libidinal material were not grasped, and insight was secondary to the relationship with the therapist.

He maintained analytic neutrality regarding the drug-taking behavior. In line with psychoanalytic thinking of the time, he felt it was dangerous to confront the drug-taking behavior before understanding the underlying dynamics for fear of psychotic decompensation.[1] Steering this course was difficult since the patient employed illegal means to obtain the drug and possible legal actions impinged on the analysis (in the end, the patient had to choose jail or inpatient treatment at Lexington, Kentucky!). In current practice, the safety of the patient must be established first, which includes establishing abstinence for addicts.[2] The third-night terror reported by the patient, which did not yield to extensive psychological investigation, probably was caused by withdrawal effects of the methadone.[3] It may have been this misplaced psychological focus that led Fine to overextend himself by offering the patient his home to get over the third-night anxiety.

Gustafson reports on the self-psychology treatment of an alcoholic, applying principles of Kohut and Balint. His basic strategy was to use empathy to help induce a mirror transference. The treatment began with a phase of severe resistance followed by the establishment of a mirror transference. Gustafson attributes the change to his awareness of a countertransference reaction that blocked genuine empathy.

An alternate explanation of the two phases of treatment can be attributed to the patient's drinking behavior. In the first phase of treatment the patient was drinking heavily, which had potentially dangerous health and safety consequences toward which Gustafson attempted to take an empathic stance. One may view the patient's resistance and anger as a remonstrance over not being confronted over his dangerous drinking behavior. Anger expressed toward the surgeon and the dream about the father, "my father stands by (doing nothing)," could be interpreted as displaced anger toward the therapist. The improvement in the patient occurred after the near-fatal automobile accident that led him to curtail his drinking. The mastery over the drinking through abstinence may have given him confidence as well as alleviated the need to compensate for a sense of inferiority over not being able to control the drinking and thus allowed him to be less defensive.

The reader will see how both therapists and patients worked hard to effect a positive outcome but struggled within the confines of psychoanalytic theory and technique. In both case studies, similar difficulties in the therapeutic relationship and transference can be noted. In both treatments the relationship to the therapist was more important than the interpretations. Both patients had additional transference relationships with objects other than the psychoanalyst. Both patients initiated termination suddenly before many issues were resolved, yet maintained a superficial but important contact with the analyst afterwards.

Other case studies of interest are Berthelsdorf,[4] successful analysis of a 19-year-old male heroin addict; Daniels,[5] instinct theory discussion of a 33-year-old bisexual male reactive alcoholic; Johnson,[6] 7-year analysis of a 29-year-old male alcoholic returning to controlled drinking; Mannheim,[7] 5-year analysis of 37-year-old female homosexual morphine addict and pathological gambler; Margenau,[8] 1-year psychotherapy of 27-year-old cocaine abuser; Noble,[9] 3-year analysis of 32-year-old female alcoholic; Radford et al.,[10] diagnostic profiles (A. Freud's) of 20-year-old male and female hospitalized heroin addicts; Robbins,[11] 2-year analysis of a 26-year-old male alcoholic begun in inpatient psychiatric unit; Rosenfeld,[12] 22-month broken-off Kleinian analysis of a female barbiturate addict; Savitt,[13] 36-month analysis analysis of 19-year-old male heroin addict; and Shea,[14] 3-year analysis of 50-year-old alcoholic in remission 5 years who became a controlled drinker. Rosenthal discusses psychoanalytic case reports of gamblers in Part II.[15]

NOTES

1. Robbins, 1935; Glover, chapter 2, this volume, "Drug addiction acts as a protection against psychotic reaction in states of regression." This fear appears exaggerated in light of subsequent clinical work with addicts.

2. Khantzian, 1980.

3. Keller, 1992.

4. Berthelsdorf, 1976.

5. Daniels, 1933.

6. Johnson, 1992.

7. Mannheim, 1955.

8. Margenau, 1984.

9. Noble, 1949.

10. Radford, Wiseber, and Yorke, 1972.

11. Robbins, 1935.

12. Rosenfeld, 1960.

13. Savitt, 1954.

14. Shea, 1954.

15. Ornstein and Myers report case material on sexual addiction in Dowling, 1995.

11. The Psychoanalysis of a Drug Addict

Reuben Fine

To CONTRIBUTE to the somewhat sparse literature on the psychoanalytic treatment of drug addicts, the writer will describe here an interesting case from his own practice. The patient, a thirty-three-year-old physician, whom we shall call Peter,[1] was first referred to the writer about a year before he started. His wife, who, as will be seen, dominated his life, objected to the idea that a physician should go to a lay analyst. In deference to her, he went to a man who, she had discovered, was considered the most promising young analyst in New York, even though he had not yet reached the status of institute membership.

In this first analysis, the analyst adopted a vigorous attitude toward the drug. He interpreted the drug as milk, and insisted that Peter take the drug every four hours, as though he were an infant on a rigid feeding schedule. Further, he informed the patient that he would be seen in psychoanalytic therapy three times a week and would sit up, switching to psychoanalysis and the couch when it seemed appropriate. Peter did not understand these reservations, in spite of his medical training.

In three months of this treatment Peter made considerable external progress. When he first went into treatment he had been too depressed to work. His therapy was subsidized by his family. One source of resentment for Peter was that the analyst would not reduce his fee as a professional courtesy: Another was his feeling that the psychiatrist was jealous of his (Peter's) greater medical knowledge.

Nevertheless, the immediate result seemed to be excellent. Peter recovered sufficiently to get back to work. At this point the analyst announced that the sessions would be increased to five per week, that they would switch to analysis conducted on the couch, and that henceforth the patient would have to pay the fee out of his salary. Peter deeply resented this last demand because the increased analytic fee exceeded his entire salary.

Reprinted by permission from *Psychoanalytic Review* 59 (1972): 585–608. Copyright © Guilford Press.

Accordingly he discontinued treatment. The analyst then called him up, offering to take him back for psychoanalytic therapy at three sessions per week and agreeing to let him go on accepting financial assistance from his family. But Peter, angry, would not return.

Instead he went to another analyst, a Horneyite. This shift in theoretical orientation (the first was a Freudian) was significant, since all through the analysis with me he wavered between a Freudian and a Horneyite approach, using this as an intellectual resistance which was very hard to handle. In any case, he distrusted the first analyst's interpretations about the need for mother's milk, preferring to feel that he had resorted to the drug because he could not handle his present-day conflicts. Further, he tended to regard it as a "bad habit," later using this as a rationalization for going to a psychologist.

Unfortunately the second analyst tried to "technique" him too. First he told Peter that he would not accept him for treatment unless he gave up the drug. To this Peter reluctantly agreed. The net result was that he would take the drug in the doctor's toilet (the connection between the drug and the toilet was quite significant, as appeared later), denying that he was still addicted. The analyst would then spend a major portion of the hour telling Peter about other severe cases whom he had helped, particularly alcoholics. Apparently here there was no attempt at interpretation at all. After about three months of this, Peter left, shortly before the summer vacation. In the fall, desperate, he called the doctor to resume treatment, but the latter would not take him back.

In the meantime his addiction became steadily more disturbing. One psychiatrist whom he tried to consult for "medical help," as he put it, wanted him to wait a week for an appointment. This angered him so much that he would not go.

It is understandable that when he finally did come to see me, in January 1951, he was quite desperate. He called on a Saturday at 5:00 p.m. and was given an appointment at 7:00, two hours later. The fee was reduced to a level where he could afford to come three times per week, with the suggestion that it might be best to make it more often, but this was left optional, especially in the light of the experience with the first analyst. During the first session, I commented that he seemed to place great importance on being liked by everybody; to this he responded with great enthusiasm, asserting that it clarified a lot in his life. When he left he said that it was the best session he had ever had.

The analysis was conducted on a three times per week basis at first; later it was increased to four sessions per week, and for the last few months five per week. There were in all 275 sessions, interrupted by one brief hospitalization for an appendectomy and two hospitalizations for withdrawal. Eventually he was able to withdraw from the drug. Sporadic contact was maintained for a period of ten years, in which time he did not relapse into addiction. While it is clear that he did succeed in giving up the drug, the degree to which a basic change in his character structure was effected is less clear.

I. LIFE HISTORY

Inasmuch as a good part of the analytic work, especially after the beginning, centered on his addiction, I could piece together his life history only from occasional comments made in various sessions. To the pressure of the drug must be added his intellectual resistance (Horney) that his childhood really had nothing to do with his troubles. Only the major outlines of his life history came through.

Peter was the youngest of four boys. His father was a tailor who made an adequate living, but his mother was a chronic invalid. His father reacted to her invalidism by going out with other women, virtually deserting his wife entirely. "He never gave a damn about anything," Peter once said, "so he lived hale and hearty to a ripe old age."

As far back as he could remember, Peter was a frightened, insecure little boy. He had been told that as an infant he had had night terrors, but he retained no conscious memory of them. He showed the characteristic pattern of the rejected infant, which would fit in with his mother's chronic invalidism, so oral traumas could be hypothesized, though they were never reconstructed. Then came a period of anal obstinacy, which resulted in lifelong constipation. Even after he had been practicing medicine for many years, he persisted in giving himself enemas.

As a rationalization for his addiction, he held on to the conviction that he suffered from pneumonia and colitis, which were masked by the drug. Were he to give up the drug, they would break out in full force and quite likely kill him. When I questioned these diagnoses, he refused to discuss the matter on the grounds that his medical knowledge was so far superior to mine. (This, incidentally, was one reason he had given for choosing a lay analyst. He had felt that the previous two analysts were jealous of his greater medical expertise, but when they disagreed with his judgment, he found it difficult to prove it to them.) The pneumonia-colitis diagnosis was a somatic delusion which pointed to a severe oral-anal disruption of the body image.

Prior to the virtually complete incapacitation of his mother, which took place when he was about eight and ended with her death about four years later, he was terribly frightened of punishment by everybody else in the house. His brothers regularly tormented him, while his mother often beat him with a rubber hose. He grew into a masochistic, dependent boy who was constantly concerned with gaining other people's approval. This eventually led to a hypomanic front, which was one of his most obvious traits in later life.

During the first period of his illness, when he was unable to work, his brothers had united to support him and finance his analysis. Nevertheless, he was so estranged from them that he never spoke of them during the analysis. The only incident that he did mention with pride was that he had saved the next older brother from abdominal surgery by submitting a questionable x-ray evaluation to a prominent specialist, who had concurred with his opinion that there was no carcinoma so that surgery was contraindicated.

A marked clinging-homosexual component had been present in him from earliest childhood. This was brought out, among other ways, by his two nicknames in childhood: Pesty Peter and passionate Sarah. The role of his homosexuality (it always remained latent) in the later personality formation was quite noticeable.

When his mother's illness became acute, Peter was called upon to nurse her. Since she was completely bedridden and he was alone with her, the nursing was a highly seductive-destructive affair. She was careless about her dress, asking only for relief from her symptoms.

It was obvious that he was highly stimulated by the situation, although he remembered little of what he went through. He did recall dreaming of different parts of her body, both before and after she died.[2] Often he would crawl into bed with her, deriving comfort from the warmth of her body. Once he got an erection, which made him feel very guilty. Another time he gave her codeine instead of digitalis, whereupon she accused him of trying to murder her. This incident tormented him for quite a while.

After his mother's death he entered a new phase, in which the major conscious purpose of his life was to control all his desires. His life goal was to rest, relax, and work. He himself saw this as identical with what he was now trying to do with the drug. Although he had had several early sexual episodes with a girl cousin when he was thirteen and had been approached homosexually by an older man when he was twelve, his determination to control all his desires persisted until he was nineteen. He concentrated on his schoolwork and apparently was a model boy for a number of years. He even frowned upon masturbation.

Unable to get into any of the local colleges because of poor grades, he went off to a college out of state when he was nineteen. There he went through undergraduate college and medical school. Although he was not a brilliant student and did not even have books when he was in medical school, he got through with satisfactory grades.

But once out of town all his controls vanished. While in college and medical school his sexuality was let loose. Since he was an outgoing, handsome young man, he found no shortage of girls. As he remembered this period, it was one of indiscriminate sexuality. Once when he was short of rent money he even had sex with his landlady, some thirty years his senior.

Although he was having a great deal of sex, he remained utterly insatiable. He began to have insomnia at this time, and it never really left him until after the analysis. When he could not sleep, he would go out and find a girl, which would at least give him some relief. His ability to get through school under these circumstances he ascribed to the fact that its standards were much lower than those that he had been accustomed to in New York.

Nevertheless, his struggle for control continued. Two fantasies dominated his thinking in his teens. In one he was a whore, receiving men all the time. The emphasis in this fantasy was that as a woman he would never have to stop feeling the man; there would literally be an endless line of men ready and willing to service her (him). The other fantasy represented the opposite pole. In this he was an English lord, austere, sedate, and completely devoid of any emotion. Obviously this represented the extreme of the control that he had been searching for since he was thirteen.

Although he was having sex all the time, analysis brought out the usual conventional guilt feelings and castration anxiety. The vagina was a "smelly place"; he could never bring himself to kiss it. Fellatio he also avoided. Even as late as the analysis, after he had been practicing medicine for many years, he could not remember the words "fellatio" and "cunnilingus." It was not until he was in France during the war as an Army officer that he allowed a woman to swallow his semen. One effect of the drug, incidentally, was to deaden his sexual desire, at times for weeks on end. He had the usual fear that his penis was too small. However, once he had had a chance to examine many penises in the course of his military duties, he convinced himself by actual measurement that his penis was of about average size. At the time of the analysis the main manifestations of his castration anxiety were a certain disinterest in sex and an inability to love women.

When he was twenty-three, his father remarried. Outwardly, of course, he showed no reaction, but the impact of the marriage was revealed by his reaction to liquor. Before the wedding alcohol had never meant much to him.

As a result of the drinks at the wedding, however, he became deathly ill. Thereafter he never touched alcohol again.

Shortly after graduation from medical school, he married the librarian of the hospital where he was interning. He described her as a warm, motherly person who had taken good care of him. They had two children, a boy and a girl.

After the birth of the children and completion of his residency in internal medicine, he decided to enter private practice. With the help of his family and friends, he opened an office for general practice in a small suburban town. It was then that his surface veneer of happy-go-lucky adjustment collapsed.

In order to build up his practice, he undertook regular social contacts in the community. Since he had always been inept at social gatherings, this public relations campaign proved to be a complete fizzle. His private practice never reached a point where he was self-supporting.

Faced by economic problems, he reacted with a number of somatic symptoms, chiefly persistent headaches. At first he controlled these with codeine. Then, when they persisted, he switched to dolophine,[3] which he continued to use to excess except for the last few weeks of his addiction, when he turned to morphine. On rare occasions he took dilaudid or nembutal.

As usual, he denied the reality of his addiction for a long time. He had long since forgotten the original reason for it, the headaches. After a while he began to take dolophine for any situation that made him anxious—when his wife was angry at him, when some relatives whom he could not stand came to visit, when he felt a pain anywhere. All the while he kept on assuring himself that he could give it up whenever he wanted to.

But whenever he did abstain, even for a day, his anxieties became overwhelming and he experienced the withdrawal symptoms of abdominal cramps and tachycardia. His medical knowledge was useless. Several times he experienced such agony that he called a fellow physician at four in the morning.

After several months of this, on the advice of relatives and friends, he hospitalized himself for withdrawal. Here, without any real medical or psychiatric supervision, he experienced intolerable agony which he afterward would refer to as "that time in Jersey." In less than a week he had signed himself out against medical advice and returned to the drug.

By this time his practice had virtually disappeared. As mentioned above, with the assistance of his family he then went into analysis. The first experience at least got him to the point where he could take a hospital job. This he maintained in one form or another for a number of years. It was not until long after the analysis with me that he was able to re-establish (or, more correctly, establish) himself in private practice.

II. COURSE OF THERAPY

Although the analysis was a stormy one, as might have been anticipated, it was possible to maintain an intensive analytic situation with him for almost two years. In this period Peter was able to acquire some insight into his personality and his addiction. He was anything but an ideal analytic patient, attempting to rely much more on a manipulation than on insight. But he was able to accept the interpretations of his manipulations. Even though his capacity for grasping analytic ideas was quite limited, especially in their libidinal ramifications, he persisted until he had given up the drug.

In view of what had happened previously, I put no pressure on him to withdraw. At one point he asked me point blank: "Should I give up the drug now?" I replied that it was entirely up to him. This made a deep impression on him, since, he said, nobody had ever allowed him so much freedom before.

A Rorschach examination, done about two months after he began therapy with me, was quite revealing. Here are some of the highlights of the report:

Underlying the front of activity, friendliness, and warmth seems to be the probability of strong dysphoric and depressive moods, deep dissatisfaction with himself, feelings of rejection and emotional deprivation which can lead to despondency, resignation, and feelings of hopelessness.

There is considerable support for the view that he feels inadequate as a male, and he displays tendencies to compensate for this by almost adolescent masculinity strivings. Thus, one male figure tries to accentuate his height, another is sinking, another has large, massive boots. There are five sexual responses which focus around the conflict over masculinity. On Card I, "the lower center portion suggests a penis ... the very tip looks like a meatus opening to the urinary tract, or a phallus. It doesn't look like a human penis. ... I think of a dog having such a penis ... thick base and small tip, etc." On Card II, "The eternal phallic symbol *(laughs)* ... can't help but see it." On Card I, "I still see a hidden penis here—that is going to have a connotation—see the head and corona." He goes on to describe these in microscopic fashion as if it were some object he was examining in intellectual fashion and at the same time is defensive about what this might indicate. On Card VI he fails to see the phallic area as a penis, seeing it as a dragon fly stretched out, but he gives a response to an edge detail, "This looks like the rear—buttocks," etc. While on Card IX he responds, "These look like rumps—taking a crap I guess—can't see their faces—posture is as if they were defecating."

The content of the sexual responses, the passivity attributed to the male, and the infantile masculinity strivings, frequent seeing of plant responses, the high number of animal responses . . . and a number of other trends in the record focus attention on what seems to be his basic conflict, possibly latent homosexuality, unconscious identification and envy of the female, unconscious rejection of masculinity, and psychosexual immaturity. Other indications lead to the deduction that this patient may be subject to acute panic states when these trends force their way into consciousness. There is also evidence of infantile fixation at a pregenital level and the failure to achieve adult, mature heterosexuality.

On the conscious level the subject is hostile toward the mother figure who wanted him to be a girl . . . and reacts to his wife as he would to a mother substitute. The maternal figure is considered dominating, difficult to get along with, unable to understand children (meaning him), etc. At the same time he admires her intellect, forcefulness, etc. He periodically rebels against female domination, partly as a rebellion against the mother figure and partly against his own essential passivity. The mature responsibilities of marriage and fatherhood are a problem to him. He would like still to be a child himself. Thus, he gives a number of responses symbolic of the birth process, such as a "snail crawling out of its shell," "a raccoon climbing out of water onto the land," "caterpillars just coming out," "embryonic annuals," etc.

In summary: although there are the possibilities of acute depression and panic states with personality disorganization, on the whole the subject is in sufficient control now and is making a good adjustment in the light of his personality structure. The anxiety level has to be watched in therapy and he will need considerable support at critical periods. He is apt to be very defensive, using intellectualization as a defense and resisting therapy in subtle ways.

It was clearly necessary to let him acquire much more insight before withdrawal could be attempted. Accordingly, as mentioned, I tried to sidestep the topic as long as possible. This could be done for about two months, and it seems in retrospect that this two-month period was decisive for the ultimate favorable resolution.

The *transference* was strongly positive from the very beginning. As will be seen, he soon conceived of the analysis as a struggle between his wife and myself, a struggle in which he was much more tempted to play the role of a child going through a liberation process with me than of an adult male playing the father role with her. Typical of the almost magical quality of the positive transference was his remark in the sixteenth session, when I first suggested that he lie down on the couch. "You must be telepathic. I was just going to suggest that myself." At another point, after a particularly bad fight with his wife, he said: "Now you're the only person I have left in the world."

Nevertheless, almost from the beginning the analysis was characterized by his wish to get more from me, for which he brought into play a variety of manipulative devices. The hours were never satisfactory for him. Hardly a week passed without his trying to shift one or more hours, often on some trivial pretext. As a rule I rejected these requests, and he would accept without protest. All along, however, he continued to express the feeling that there simply were too many demands made on his time, and that the analysis was just another demand. Everybody was exploiting him was the underlying complaint.

At the same time on a number of occasions he showed up at my office several hours before the appointment. He hoped that he could be seen earlier, although he knew that my schedule was so full that this would rarely be possible. But again, reality or no reality, this could be used to reinforce his feelings of rejection.

Except for the fee, which he paid religiously and without complaint, every aspect of the transference, though specifically positive, sooner or later became a source of resistance. When he did finally lie down on the couch, he was unable to produce any associations. When something good occurred to him, he would sit up, saying: "I have something important to tell you."

As has been mentioned before, the fact that I was a psychologist served as an odd form of resistance. He persistently refused to discuss his physical symptoms, since he as a physician could understand them better than I did. But when I suggested that he discuss his physical symptoms with another physician, he objected that there was really nobody in the world he could trust except me. I usually interpreted this as a reflection of his childhood, when he could not rely on anybody, but the interpretation made very little impression on him.

Early Period

For the first two months it was possible to stay away from the addiction question entirely. Thereafter it was always in the forefront of the analysis, especially in the later stages, when the law enforcement authorities were after him. Nevertheless, I made every effort to conduct the treatment analytically, even until the very end.

In the early period, he brought up a number of childhood memories that were of considerable use in unraveling his dynamics. Most of what I described earlier came out in this period. Later the immediate problems were so pressing that it was rarely possible for him to turn the clock back to see how he had come to be what he was.

After about two months came the first significant break in his pattern, an intensification of the transference drama. Without any urging on my part, he announced that he was going to withdraw. A week or so later he announced that he had succeeded. A few days afterward he told me that he had made up the whole story.

This led to a discussion of his *need to please,* which was tied up with the powerful *rescue fantasies* of his childhood. The first time he had had sex with a girl, when he was in his teens, he had bought her a pair of shoes afterward. He was always trying to rescue people in one way or another.

Yet, as so often, the rescue fantasy was strongly ambivalent. At one point he took on a free psychiatric patient who was obviously being neglected by the hospital, but the true purpose clearly was to show what an unfeeling therapist I was. One patient whom he had preserved from his private practice was an elderly, virtually bedridden woman in her seventies. He visited her twice a week to give her "shots," which he frankly admitted had no value. On the surface this was a repetition of his experience with his mother, but at a deeper level there was also hostility involved in his pleasure at the substantial fees he received for the house calls, which he thought of as totally undeserved. Actually he was probably keeping this woman alive, but the whole experience covered up numerous inner conflicts.

His fabrication also brought his withdrawal problem into sharper focus. He could go without the drug for two nights, but the third night filled him with overwhelming terror. It was so horrifying that he could not even verbalize what frightened him so. At best he would refer to "that time in New Jersey," when he had withdrawn in the hospital without adequate supervision. Most often, though, he would say it was just "too awful," and he could not face it. Henceforth we would refer to this as his "third-night anxiety"; as time went on, it and its dynamic elucidation moved more and more into the center of the analysis.

A third outcome of the withdrawal fib was that it brought into focus the *struggle with his wife.* As will be recalled, she had objected to the choice of me as an analyst, resulting in his going to two other analysts first. Once he had started, she evidently became jealous of his strong attachment. She began to badger him for "results"; what difference did it make how good his analyst was, she argued quite rightly, if he did not get better? Even without this, she had reacted to the whole breakdown-drug episode by becoming the carping mother figure. He, in turn, began to treat her as a superego figure rather than a human being, and the battle was firmly launched, to be terminated only by their ultimate divorce.

At this point, however, there was still no talk of divorce. He merely wanted to be freed from her persistent pressure. An interview with the wife was arranged around this time, but it changed nothing.

In the midst of all this a phone call suddenly came in from his girlfriend. It turned out that he had never told me of this girl, a social worker whom he saw on occasion. She was very much in love with him, a feeling that he did not reciprocate. However, she too began to question my capacity as an analyst, and he had to defend me all over again. The relationship with this girl ended fairly soon. No strong sexual or romantic desire appeared in him until toward the end of the analysis.

Dreams

The patient dreamt infrequently, and his dreams were extremely simple, primarily anxiety and masochistic dreams punctuated occasionally by a rescue fantasy. At the beginning he reported two dreams from his previous analyses:

Some kids are beating me up. . . .

I go fishing and am trying to get a kid out of the water who is drowning, but I can't get him out.

In the first few months of analysis he reported the following dreams:

5th session. I reach for the drug and can't find it. . . .

26th session. Breaking glasses. . . .

29th session. I'm in Paris, going from place to place. I didn't seem to fit in with any of the people—I was deficient somehow, uninteresting. I didn't know whether they knew about the medication or not. (This went on all night.)

To the last dream he associated his present situation at the hospital, where he felt so different from the other physicians. He often wondered, angrily, why his colleagues never noticed anything strange about him, particularly the pupillary changes caused by the drug. It was clear from this and other material that the drug merely accentuated feelings of strangeness, inadequacy, and separation that had been with him all his life.

36th session. I'm in a big house like [the one in New Jersey].[4] I run all over looking for the drug. There is a small bottle; it breaks, and the contents run out.

To the theme of the bottle breaking (see the 26th session above as well) he had no special associations. I suggested that this might symbolize his anger at his mother, which currently carried over to his wife and authority figures, but this interpretation aroused no response.

Dynamic Trends

It is impossible to divide this analysis into any clearly demarcated periods after the first few months. Instead I will trace the manifestations of various basic drives as well as possible.

1. Sexuality

Although he had led a very active sex life during his years in college, graduate school, and the Army, not long after the children were born he lost most of his interest in sex. During the time of the analysis he had occasional sex with his wife and other women. These other women were so insignificant emotionally that at times he would not even mention them; what happened would come out inadvertently at a later date.

In intercourse with his wife, the drug apparently had the effect of postponing his ejaculation. Sometimes he would go on for hours without ejaculating; sometimes he would even fall asleep during sex. On occasion he would simulate orgasms in order to have an excuse to discontinue the sex. His wife had relatively little desire at this time, and they had sex only on his initiative. He could go for weeks without any manifestation of sexual desire.

During the earlier withdrawal attempt, he experienced what he called a "continual penile itch" accompanied by a constant desire to urinate. He felt this as excruciatingly uncomfortable, apparently because he refused to recognize its sexual character and the accompanying wish to masturbate. Once his withdrawal attempt had ended and he had returned to the drug, his "penile itch" ended.

It was clear that a major function of the drug was to kill his sexual appetite. This could be traced back to an identification with the suffering, asexual mother rather than the pleasure-seeking sexual father. The drug allowed him to combine the two major fantasies of his adolescence, the whore who received men all the time (through the drug and the paranoid feeling of being looked at constantly), and the English lord devoid of all feeling. But his absence of sexual desire was so ego-syntonic that he did not feel it as a problem.

2. Homosexuality

A strong latent homosexual component was obviously present in him, but it broke through in disguised form only a few times. In the 103rd session, when we actively discussed withdrawal, he dreamed:

I am screwing a woman. Just as I am about to come, I reach down, although it is very uncomfortable, and suck her penis.

In association to the dream he brought out the squeamishness about oral sex which has been mentioned earlier. His search for his mother's penis was obviously one determinant of the inhibition of ejaculation which was such a marked feature of his sex life.

Later on, when he was discussing what the drug was doing to him, he suddenly pulled his pants down to show me the innumerable needle marks in his buttocks. Again my interpretation of the homosexual fantasy fell on deaf ears. It is possible that a good deal of his homosexual libido was sublimated through his medical practice, as in his overcoming his fear of having a small penis by examining the penes of many men, especially in the service. Obviously this involved a degree of attention to the size of his patients' penes that was quite irrelevant to their complaints. Still another aspect of his homosexuality was the small amount of insight he verbalized, even though his transference was so positive. He was deriving so much unconscious homosexual gratification from the analysis that insight was secondary. In fact, it might have spoiled his transference pleasure.

3. Depression, Aggression, and Masochism

It scarcely came as a surprise to find that a severe depressive-masochistic complex formed the core of his personality. He had clearly identified with his dying mother. It was perhaps pure coincidence that his addiction lasted for exactly four years, the same duration as her terminal illness. Or perhaps this too was part of the identification. The point cannot be pushed too far.

It took some time for the depressive-masochistic features to become apparent to him, but he did eventually build up a good deal of insight into them, in contrast to the sexual-libidinal elements, my interpretations of which he dismissed as "too Freudian."

For quite a while he was able to cover up his depression by magical and wishful thinking. He would give up the drug next week—no problem. Or he had already given it up—just a few loose ends to pull together. Once he decided that the drug was really a psychiatric problem, meaning that up to then he had thought of it as purely organic. One day he would just give it up—why all the fuss? Why didn't the authorities leave him alone—he would get over it soon. Why didn't his wife leave him alone? Why did I insist he come to sessions so often (we had just increased to four sessions per week)?

Whatever overt aggression he expressed he directed mainly at his wife. Apparently she had no other complaints about him than the drug, but this she continually nagged him about. He in turn objected that she failed to grasp what he was going through. In one fight he literally twisted her breast, again showing that he was transferring his rage at his mother to her.

As the analysis progressed, his veneer of cheerfulness began to give way to an increasing display of anxiety and depression. In the 40th session he asked point blank: "Am I psychotic?" When I asked him what he understood by psychotic, he could only verbalize vague feelings of unreality. Then he would say from time to time that he was forgetting things more and more, attributing this to the drug.

The dependency and masochism of his way of life also became increasingly clear to him. Once he exclaimed about his marriage: "I married her to suffer—do you realize that?" At times his suffering became so acute that I offered him the interpretation that his masochism was so severe that he had to hit rock bottom before he could start up again. Later, as will be seen, this became quite meaningful to him.

Gradually the depth of his underlying anxiety crystallized out of the analytic material, even though the material produced centered so strongly on the drug and on his wife. Underneath he was truly panicky. He had pneumonia and colitis, the symptoms of which were masked by the drug. He was psychotic. He had cancer. He could not function. Sometimes suicidal thoughts broke through, though he was never actively suicidal.

The few dreams he produced in the second six months of analysis were a mixture of fear and magical thinking. Several were typical examination dreams. In another he was competing with one brother. The most significant came in the 119th hour, when he was recuperating from an appendectomy.

I'm in a war theater. It's very bloody. We go down a hill, pick a soldier up, and come back; we do this over and over again. . . . I'm a wealthy man and move to another place.

The "war theater" referred more to the childhood memories of the battles with his brothers than to any combat experience. The dream brings out the underlying wish to beat out father and brothers which had been so deeply repressed.

When the analysis was in its tenth month (130 hours), three developments combined to force me to attempt a more active role in the withdrawal process. First, he had by now written out so many prescriptions for the drug, with such a meager private practice, that the federal authorities became alerted to his goings-on. It became more difficult for him to get the drug, and he had to resort to a variety of fabrications, such as stories of terminally ill cancer patients with intractable pain, to get a supply from pharmacists. Even at that he had to go to pharmacies outside his area, making up stories about why he was so far away from home.

Second, a mounting sense of futility was becoming apparent in him. For the first time he could even see no point to analysis; why not go out and live? This was similar to the feelings of futility that had come up with the previous analysts. Yet he remembered how, after he had left them, his anxieties had accumulated to a point where he could not handle them.

Third, he had found a physician who had opened a free clinic for addicts. This man's system was to withdraw the addict "cold turkey," merely providing him with companionship and coffee for the night. Here, however, the patient turned physician again, showing more interest in helping the other addicts than in getting any help for himself. However, association with this group exposed him to theft and even one blackmail attempt, when it became known that he was a physician. The self-degradation involved in the addiction became all the more obvious to him.

Since his withdrawal was blocked by his third-night anxiety, which did not yield to ordinary analytic interpretations, I offered to see him through the third night at my apartment, on the assumption that the material that came out in this way would be helpful in the analysis. Up to this point he had never been able to verbalize anything about this third-night anxiety, except that it was too horrible to face.

At first he eagerly assented to my suggestion. We made arrangements for a physician of his choice to be on call and for a night nurse to be present, and I told him he would be free to see me any time during the night that he felt the need. With everything all set to begin at midnight, he called at 10:30 P.M. to cancel the plan. He just could not find the strength to face it, nor could he verbalize what frightened him so.

Accordingly the analysis continued along the lines hitherto followed. Several times we made arrangements again for him to spend the third night at my apartment, and each time he would call it off at the last minute. Once he asked whether he could spend a week at my apartment, but this seemed inadvisable. Hospitalization did effect a withdrawal without consequences, but he would revert to the drug as soon as he was released; he had tried this twice. His efforts to confront his third-night anxiety outside a hospital had failed. Manipulative efforts appeared futile.

However, the continuation of the analysis now came to be increasingly affected by concern about the legal authorities. He never knew whether they had caught up with him or not, so he was perpetually apprehensive. Here for the first time he made bitter complaints about the system, about persecution of addicts, and the like. Though he still hated his wife, whom he was now planning to leave, the "enemy" had now shifted to the government. At an unconscious level this naturally played into his self-punitive trends. Just as he had said at one time that he was taking the drug to spite his wife, now he said he was taking it to spite the government.

After several warnings, which did not lead him to reduce his consumption of the drug, his narcotics license was taken away. This led him to even more illegal activity, such as the forging of prescriptions. Evidence was collected. Finally the government offered him a choice: either he went to Lexington, Kentucky,[5] for rehabilitation, or he would be sent to prison for violation of the medical practices act. In either case his medical license was to be revoked. By then the analysis had been under way for about twenty months (270 hours). It seemed more sensible for him to go to Lexington and resume the analysis when he was released.

The stay in Lexington apparently had some shock effect on him. There he met a number of men to whom addiction and incarceration had become a way of life. One man had been there twenty-seven times; many others had repeatedly come and gone. In spite of the tight security, some managed to smuggle drugs in. One method was to swallow the drug in a condom and then pick it out of the feces.

Withdrawal at Lexington was "cold turkey." He reacted with agonizing abdominal pains. As he was lying on the table in terrible suffering, many of my interpretations came back to him. One that he kept on repeating to himself was: "You've got to hit rock bottom." He saw more plainly than ever before his terrible impulse to degrade himself.

But the third-night anxiety was still there; hospital withdrawal did not affect it. Upon his release from Lexington he came back to New York and to the drug. Still, there was a difference. Instead of dolophine he turned to morphine. And he made an immediate attempt to face the third night.

He looked up an old classmate for assistance, Dr. L. This man had been going through an ordeal of his own. After a promising start in psychiatry, he had begun to act out in the wildest sexual manner. He demanded sex with all his patients, both male and female, justifying the request with the rationalization that since the incest taboo lay at the base of all neurosis, it was only by confronting this taboo directly that the patient could be truly liberated. Most of his patients left. One who remained was Sally, an extremely inhibited, attractive young nurse. She had been through eighteen months of classical analysis on the couch, literally unable to say a word. Finally she left, switching to Dr. L.

When Peter came to Dr. L. for help, he met Sally and promptly fell in love with her. Once he had sex with her in the presence of Dr. L., which made him more aware of his homosexual wishes. It was not repeated.

About two weeks after his release from Lexington, Peter tried withdrawal in Dr. L.'s office. He stayed there day and night, with Sally present all the time. I visited him there four times a day. Finally he lived through the third night uneventfully. None of the dire consequences that he had so long feared came true. He felt liberated.

At this point he was faced with the need for total rehabilitation. He had left his wife, lost his job, and been deprived of his medical license. His first step was to go away for a long rest. He traveled for about two months. Free from the pressures of making a living or taking care of other people, and reflecting on the insights that the analysis had given him, he was able to stay away from the drug.

III. POSTANALYTIC DEVELOPMENTS

The analysis was never resumed systematically. Occasionally he would write or call if he was in New York. Several times he tried to see me again, but the practical difficulties were too great. However, he maintained some contact for about ten years after the end of the analysis.

Although the termination of the analysis was so abrupt that many questions were left unanswered, he seemed to make steady progress with himself, even integrating many of the interpretations that he had fought so vigorously during the analysis. Externally, the changes were striking: he divorced his wife and married Sally, by whom he had three children, one of whom died. This second marriage and family provided much more happiness than the first.

In spite of demands that he would previously have found humiliating, he persisted in the effort to regain his medical license, eventually succeeding several years after it had been revoked. He was put on parole and required to report once a month to a physician and a judge to review his status. With all of this he complied faithfully.

As a result of his own experience, he became interested in psychiatry, which he then practiced together with internal medicine. For a long time he remained in hospital settings, where he felt more comfortable, but eventually he was able to build up a private practice.

As mentioned, he maintained contact with me by correspondence and occasional visits for about ten years after the formal conclusion of the analysis. Although he constantly expressed the hope that he could make arrangements for more analysis, this never materialized. The changes that he consolidated after the analysis, which was concluded in November 1952, can be gauged from the correspondence. Here are some relevant excerpts from a letter he wrote me in May 1954:

> We arrived here Monday, October 12th, in time to see a beautiful sunrise. Despite the exotic atmosphere and beautiful surroundings, the beginning of this new life held much insecurity for me. Would I make good? Be accepted? Get along? Was I running away and kidding myself? Was psychiatric training a way of avoiding analysis? Seeking answers by myself? There are many ramifications of these questions and answers and only time will help solve them. . . .
>
> I started work the same day and pitched in at a rapid pace. I soon had to slow down. I found I couldn't get out of bed in the morning—didn't want to go to work—didn't want to do anything—did only that which was essential. I would leave things up to the time they were due, and then feverishly run through the work. I was bogging down. Sally was her usual permissive and supportive self, but it didn't seem to help. I couldn't blame the drug, because I hadn't taken any for several months. On December 23rd we had a baby girl. . . . When I went to take Sally home from the hospital five days later I took my first dose of Dolophine. I proceeded to take it on and off until I went to a physician and got a prescription for fifty tablets. Until then I had gotten it from the hospital two tablets at a time. The first day I took eight tablets—then got scared of becoming addicted and went to the medical director, turned over the drug to him, told him the story, and asked that he take me on as a patient. He was reluctant at first because of our relationship at the hospital, but because there were no good analysts (available) he agreed. I have been seeing him twice a week since the first of the year and have felt better and have been able to work better. It is interesting too that I have been able for the past two months to take on a few patients in intensive therapy, whereas heretofore I felt too threatened. . . .
>
> I have become more aware of my relationships with people. I try to understand what goes on in me and those with me. I don't always get it right off, but then I'm not thrown. I go over it later on when I am distant and try to tie things up. I don't always succeed, but it is less threatening when you can try to be objective. I am more able to understand my repressed and suppressed hostility. I can even let go now without fear of punishment. This lets me feel hostile without acting out and at the same time not being overwhelmed by it.

In December 1954 he wrote:

> It's been a good year. I'm in better shape than I've been for years. No drug for over a year. Better relationships.... Still too passive and not liking it. Less impulsive. Better endurance and greater tolerance to frustration. Better acceptance and handling of reality. Less masochistic but it is a tough fight because the passive component with fear that aggression means hostility is too frightening, and I'm not too good at sublimating the aggression as yet. But I have succeeded in accepting myself more....
>
> The next six months are critical ones.... At least I shall not be running headlong into a decision which my distorted conscience (superego) usually forced upon me. I'm going to try to play it slow and safe, realizing that circumstances and environment may not be so kind and therefore trying to make the most of the situation and not allow myself to be thrown by disappointment of desire. I am quite anxious to get the necessary training to do analysis but will forego it if it is either 1. inadvisable, 2. too difficult, 3. sacrifices are too great.... I shall be thirty-seven years old this month and have been insecure too long. It is about time I stopped gambling and seeking Nirvana and settled down to living and building a few buttresses.

In 1957 he came in for a few sessions, but since he was living out of town the practical difficulties were too great. In June 1959 he wrote:

> I know I felt mighty sick while seeing you—how sick you probably know better. As far as the drug is concerned, I have not taken any since 1953. A good example of my resistance to it was a recent attack of renal colic, which I lived through, although there was a legitimate reason to ask for opiates for relief. I still have the stone, which is passing slowly down the ureter. I am better able to live with pain, discomfort, and anxiety. I make less demands upon myself, particularly in difficult situations. I relate to people on a much healthier basis. I don't make unreasonable demands in a relationship, but then I am no longer desperate.... I might also tell you that there is less "acting-out" on my part so that the loss of addiction has not resulted in any other serious or evident symptom or syndrome.

In November 1962, just about ten years after the analysis was finished, he again came in for a few sessions and again found the practical difficulties too great. His situation then was pretty much the same as that depicted in the last letter: no drug, fairly happy with his wife and children, working, but still dissatisfied with the passive-dependent-masochistic aspects of his personality, of which he had become acutely aware.

I have had no contact with him since.

DISCUSSION

There is general agreement on the psychodynamics of the drug addict. Rado (9) in an early paper which has been widely quoted, stressed (1) the basic depressive character, early wounded narcissism (defects in ego development); (2) intolerance of frustration and pain (lack of satisfying early object relations); (3) lack of affectionate and meaningful object relations, which adolescent addicts attempt to overcome through the pseudocloseness and fusion with other drug-takers during their common experience; (4) the artificial technique used to maintain self-regard and satisfaction; and (5) the change from a "realistic" to a "pharmacothymic" regime, which may lead to severely disturbed ego functions and to conflict with reality. Other investigations have come to much the same conclusions (2,4,5,7,13). In more modern language the addict is an orally regressed individual who hovers on the brink of a serious break with reality. Only rare exceptions have been noted (5).

Still, one aspect of addiction is unclear: why do some patients with this personality constellation resort to drugs, while others do not? Wieder and Kaplan (13) have hypothesized that the pharmacological effect sets off a specific psychodynamic reaction, which is different with different drugs. This has yet to be confirmed. It is generally believed that the more serious the pharmacological effects (of heroin, morphine, and LSD), the more regressed the individual. The whole question belongs to the still unresolved problem of the choice of neurosis.

Just as there has been widespread agreement about the dynamics of addiction, there has been widespread pessimism about the rehabilitation of the addict. Few problems have attracted more concentrated professional interest, more government funds, and more disappointing results. Of recent years two radically new approaches have captured the professional imagination: the methadone treatment for heroin addiction (1) and the group-living approach (12). While both of these are certainly superior to anything tried previously, their ultimate value is still in dispute. With the methadone treatment the question of withdrawal from methadone remains open (8). It is of interest that the patient in the present case was addicted to methadone, then still referred to as dolophine. The main difference was that he had to take it parenterally, by injection, while now it is administered orally. Nevertheless, his successful withdrawal was a heroic task. What happens in others remains to be seen.

In the methadone treatment devised by Dole and Nyswander (1), the addict is given a maintenance dose of 100 mg. per day. Despite all the claims advanced, this treatment is still regarded as experimental. It has not been approved by the American Medical Association except as an experimental treatment modality (3). The group-living approach, such as Daytop and Synanon, likewise suffers from serious drawbacks. Whether these patients can ever get back to a less artificial way of life remains to be seen (12).

Psychoanalysts have devoted relatively little attention to the problem. Crowley (2) in his 1939 review called it the "step-child" of psychoanalysis. A recent study of drug-taking adolescents was quite pessimistic about the results (5). In the entire psychoanalytic literature I have been able to find only one full-length case history of a successfully treated addict, by Savitt (10).[6] This patient, a nineteen-year-old male student, was addicted to heroin, marijuana, and occasionally cocaine. He was in analysis for thirty-eight months. Later, when he was anxious about his first-born child, he had six more sessions.

Savitt's patient shows some striking similarities to the patient described here. A key dream in the early weeks went as follows:

> I was having intercourse with Helen in Arthur's presence. At the same moment I looked over and saw that Arthur wasn't sleeping. He was annoyed and looked at me sternly. Helen noticed it too and withdrew from me just before I had an ejaculation. Then I went downstairs to the bathroom to wash up.

This is quite similar to the dream given above (p. 229). Dynamically, Savitt also noted the Oedipal situation, the unconscious incestuous wishes for the mother, primal scene material, the frustrating, seductive mother, the castration threat, the sexual-oral longing, the unconscious equation of intercourse with toilet masturbation, and the transference situation in which the analyst was both mother and father. All these features have also been described here.

Since the difficulties involved in treating drug addiction are so formidable, the details of any case history should prove interesting with regard to both the dynamics and the technical problems. As in Savitt's case, the dynamic structure of this patient was not particularly different from that of other orally regressed individuals. His deep-seated oral anxieties were overwhelming: he feared disintegration, both physical and psychological. Consequently he lived in a constant state of terror. In such a state relief is the only solution possible—immediate drastic relief. But the relief is not so much a pleasure as an alteration in the state of consciousness. Nothing is pleasurable to him as long as his present state of consciousness persists; conversely, if his state of consciousness is altered, everything looks good to him. The psychic situation is one in which the only solution is to escape the crushing archaic superego. This could be done either by the drug or by literal flight. If neither of these works, flight can be effected by suicide, a wish which came up occasionally. This is why the addiction can be considered a suicide equivalent and why so many addicts literally kill themselves.[7]

The mother-son symbiosis, typical of the acter-outer, was accentuated here by the accidental factor of her illness and his role as child-nurse-physician to her. The incestuous stimulation was so great that injections came to have an unconscious meaning of incest to him. Hence the drug killed his sexual desire, for he had mother again. The injection came to symbolize incestuous intercourse, treatment of mother, and even possible death (he was a "main-liner") leading to reunion with her.

The symbiotic attachment to mother was repeated in the transference. To be with me became much more important than the insights I offered him. Yet at the same time the relationship was enormously stimulating, especially along homosexual lines. The drug served to keep all these feelings out of consciousness.

While the dynamic picture is familiar, the technical problem requires more extended discussion. Fairly early we were able to crystallize out the "third-night anxiety," and for the major portion of the analysis our efforts were devoted to unraveling the meaning of this fear. Then the analytic work fairly quickly was threatened not by any regressive danger or ego weakness but by external reality: he was in imminent danger of being arrested for obtaining the drug illegally, and in fact the formal analysis was forced into a premature termination by his hospitalization, which he chose as an alternative to prison.

Ideally it would certainly have been best to continue the analysis *lege artis.* Quite possibly then the third-night anxiety would have yielded to patient though necessarily slow analytic exploration. And it is highly probable that if such a slower, more careful unfolding of dynamic resistances had been permitted, the overall personality change might have been much greater.

The technical problem encountered in this analysis, the pressure of external reality, is encountered in varying degrees in every analysis. Often when such cases are reported in the literature, a remark is made to the effect that the patient terminated "for external reasons." Since analysts have no control over these "external reasons" and prefer to work under virtual laboratory conditions, it is understandable that this factor generally receives scant attention, if any at all, in treatises on technique. Yet, as every analyst knows, it is quite important.

Fortunately in the present case we had almost a year of pure analytic work before the external situation forced us to depart from systematic technique. His experiences with the previous two analysts clearly demonstrated the futility of a frontal attack. Yet here too it was the feeling all around that the forced confrontation came too soon.

At the same time the kind of analytic crisis created here, while unusual in content, is not so unusual in structure. In a great many analyses after a variable period of pure analytic work some basic anxiety crystallizes out in such a manner that it inevitably becomes the central focus of the analytic work for a long time. It may even be that this is true of the majority of analyses. In many cases the preoccupation with this focal anxiety eludes attention because it is so pressing for the patient while the analyst, who feels unable to resolve it by a head-on approach, seeks to sidestep it. Nevertheless the patient comes back to it again and again.

What is characteristic of many cases of acting-out disorder, perversions, and schizophrenias is that the reality consequences of the central anxiety cannot be ignored, either because the patient's ego is too weak to handle them, as in schizophrenia, or because there is some really overwhelming outside force, as in the present case. By contrast, in a patient with obsessional preoccupations or some mild phobias, the reality consequences of the central anxiety can be ignored indefinitely. The latter type of case we are apt to think of as pure analysis, while the former is seen as "manipulation" or "supportive therapy," but these terms merely mask the true state of affairs.

The decision as to whether or not to ignore reality is often a difficult one for the analyst, yet a most necessary one, on which the outcome of the analysis may very well hang. It always rests upon clinical judgment, as it did in the following case, rather than upon any technical diagnosis:

A homosexual man had developed an odd method of seducing other men. He would move close to another man in a fairly crowded subway, cover them both with a newspaper, and then proceed to give the other man an erection. As soon as the man had an erection, the patient would get up and leave the train.

His first analyst, alarmed by the possibilities of his being caught, repeatedly stressed the reality danger of being arrested, which the patient pooh-poohed, since he "knew how to approach." When the analyst persisted in the discussion of arrest, the patient left treatment.

When he came to see me after a lapse of many years, I decided to ignore the problem for the time being, on the grounds that since he had been doing this for so many years without being caught he must have developed some special skill for selecting suitable partners. Eventually this practice disappeared in the context of the general analysis of his homosexuality.

In the present case, after the first year the possibility of a sudden interruption of the analysis by an arrest became increasingly imminent. Accordingly I made the third-night anxiety the focus of analysis far more than hitherto, and far more than I would have otherwise. While he reached no resolution of this anxiety before his arrest, the analytic work did leave strong impressions that proved to be of invaluable service in the postanalytic integration.

POSTANALYTIC INTEGRATION

At the time that the analysis was interrupted by his arrest (after some twenty months with 270 hours of analysis), it was by no means clear what the ultimate outcome would be. It was quite possible at that point to regard the whole analysis as a failure.

Yet the subsequent history shows conclusively that the analytic work left a deep imprint that had a marked effect on the course of his life. It seems highly unlikely that he would have been able to withdraw, leave his unhappy marriage for a new and happy one, and go through a whole host of other traumatic experiences without the intensive analysis. It is therefore legitimate in this case to speak of a *postanalytic integration*.

The metapsychology of such a postanalytic integration may be conceived of in this way. In his analysis he was living through a symbiotic, homosexual transference which was largely a repetition of his good experiences with his mother. His oral gratification in the symbiosis was so important that words left little impression; he was basking in preverbal bliss. Yet part of his ego retained enough control to remember the gist of the interpretations, especially those that were less "Freudian" and fairly close to common sense.

Once out of the analysis, he retained the analyst as a fantasy good mother to whom he was some day going to return. This helped him through many trying times and allowed him to avoid the deep regression that he had been through before. On the whole his life situation remained favorable. His ego was then strong enough to accept the new experiences in a pleasure-seeking rather than masochistic manner, because the fantasy-analyst was the core of a new superego, which was gradually replacing the old harsh superego derived from childhood. Return to analysis might very well have led to a regressive break-through of more self-destructive oral wishes, so there was probably some unconscious calculation in his repeated efforts to come back to analysis, followed by quick discontinuation of the attempt. The therapist he saw for a while during the year after he left, when he suffered a mild relapse into addiction, evidently approached him in a supportive manner. A magical transference of the kind that he had developed to me was avoided, probably because his ego had been strengthened to the point where he no longer needed one, and this too helped to integrate some of the previously learned material. But this therapy lasted only a short time. He accomplished the bulk of his postanalytic integration without outside help.

The follow-up period of ten years is sufficiently long to warrant the conclusion that a significant character change was effected by the analysis.

NOTES

1. Names and other identifying data have been disguised.
2. In *The Psychoanalysis of Elation* Bertram Lewin describes similar phenomena in hypomanic personalities.
3. The generic name for methadone.
4. The house where he made his most recent withdrawal attempt. See above.
5. The national center for treatment of drug addiction.
6. In another case, reported by Mannheim (6), the patient died during the treatment, but it was apparently not going well anyhow.
7. In another case which came to my attention, an addict, a young man of twenty-three, took large doses of heroin. Many times after an injection he would lie motionless, pretending to be dead. His girlfriend, alarmed, would then wake him up, whereupon he would say it was all a game. Even to her the suicidal wish involved in this "game" was quite clear.

REFERENCES

1. *Bill, H., Chairman. Progress Report of Evaluation of Methadone.* Journal of the American Medical Association, *Vol. 206, 1968. pp. 2712–2714.*
2. *Crowley, R. Psychoanalytic Literature on Drug Addiction and Alcoholism.* Psychoanalytic Review, *Vol. 26, 1939. pp. 39–54.*
3. *Di Mascio, A., and R. I. Shader. Clinical Handbook of Psychopharmacology.* New York: Science House, 1970.
4. *Harris, P. T., W. M. McIsaac, and R. Schulter, Jr. Drug Dependence. Austin, Tex.: University of Texas Press, 1970.*
5. *Hartmann, D. A. Study of Drug-Taking Adolescents.* Psychoanalytic Study of the Child, *Vol. 24, 1969, 384–398.*
6. *Mannheim, J. Notes on a Case of Drug Addiction.* International Journal of Psycho-Analysis, *Vol. 36, 1955. pp. 166–173.*
7. *Meerloo, J. A. M. Artificial Ecstasy.* Journal of Nervous and Mental Diseases, *Vol. 115, 1952. pp. 246–266.*
8. *Nix, J. T., and G. M. Bates. Letters to the Editor.* Journal of the American Medical Association, *Vol. 207, 1969. p. 2439.*

9. *Rado, S. The Psychoanalysis of Pharmacothymia.* Psychoanalytic Quarterly, *Vol. 2, 1933. pp. 1–23.*

10. *Savitt, R. A. Extramural Psychoanalytic Treatment of a Case of Narcotic Addiction.* Journal of the American Psychoanalytic Association, *Vol. 2, 1954. pp. 494–502.*

11. ———. *Psychoanalytic Studies on Addiction: Ego Structure in Narcotic Addiction.* Psychoanalytic Quarterly, *Vol. 32, 1963. pp. 43–57.*

12. *Shelly, J. A. Daytop Lodge: A Two-Year Report. In* Report of the Institute on Rehabilitation of the Narcotic Addict. *Washington, D.C.: U.S. Government Printing Office, 1966.*

13. *Wieder, H., and E. H. Kaplan. Drug Use in Adolescents: Psychodynamic Meaning and Pharmacogenic Effect.* Psychoanalytic Study of the Child, *Vol. 24, 1969. pp. 399–431.*

12. The Mirror Transference in the Psychoanalytic Psychotherapy of Alcoholism: A Case Report

James Gustafson

INTRODUCTION

There are probably a great variety of separate personality constellations and psychopathologies for which alcoholism serves as the common solution (Devito et al., 1970; Yorke, 1970). Since the broad category of alcoholic patients is generally considered resistant to successful psychoanalytic psychotherapeutic treatment, it becomes important to identify those types that are treatable and by what means. One such type is the patient whose alcoholism represents primarily an expression of a narcissistic personality disorder (Kohut, 1971). Kohut devotes only a few paragraphs to alcoholism and addiction in his monograph, enough to outline the subject, but there have been no case studies in depth reported from this perspective. Balint (1968) describes a similar level of pathology, which he terms "the level of the basic fault," also briefly in relation to the special defensive solutions of alcoholism and addiction. However, to the best of my knowledge, there have been no in-depth case studies of the treatment of an alcoholic patient from this point of view either. Kohut and Balint have recommended strategies of treatment for the narcissistic personality disorder (the basic fault), and reported considerable success based on these strategies, but we do not know to what extent they can be successfully applied to those narcissistic patients whose defensive solutions include addiction to alcohol.

The present case report describes such a successful application of the ideas of Kohut and Balint to the psychotherapy of a very self-destructive alcoholic patient whose core disturbance proved to be that of a narcissistic personality disorder (or a disturbance at the level of the basic fault). How common such patients are within the general class of alcoholics remains to be discovered. Hence how broadly applicable the management of this case may prove to be

Reprinted by permission from *International Journal of Psychoanalytic Psychotherapy* 5 (1976): 65–85. Copyright © Jason Aronson, Inc.

cannot be known at this time. The general plan of this paper is as follows. I will begin with a brief summary of previous psychoanalytic work on the nature of the relationship between the analyst or therapist and the alcoholic patient. Next, I will delineate the views of Kohut and Balint in considerable detail, insofar as they also apply to this relationship between analyst or therapist and alcoholic patient. Finally, I will present and discuss what I took to be the decisive events in my treatment case.

The descriptions of what the alcoholic patient seeks from the therapist have been quite consistent, from Knight (1937) to Chafetz (1959) to Silber (1974). What each writer details is an individual with massive passive-dependent wishes, a need to control the need-fulfilling object, and rage when this is thwarted. Many other motivations are also described, including homosexual gratifications, relief from punitive introjects, and so forth. Yet the patient's wish for a passive-dependent relationship remains a typical finding, and the recommended therapeutic relationship attempts to meet this need constructively. Knight (1937) argues for the necessity of supplying substitutes for alcohol, both literally in the form of other liquids and in the form of a kindly attitude; yet the therapist must also limit these offers: "Too much frustration will spoil the necessary tender relationship between physician and patient, and too much gratification will lead to experiments in drinking (which by now he feels he has under perfect control)." Chafetz (1959) recommends a similar therapeutic relationship, and the therapist's chief consideration again turns upon the limits to gratification: "While the therapist must be an active, continually supporting substitute for alcohol, he cannot help being aware of the insatiable demands of alcoholic patients." Silber (1974) starts from a similar assessment of the patient's impossible wishes and rage at these being thwarted. Silber suggests a method that will gratify the magical wishes, and yet assist the patient with his difficulty with limits. The method is to focus, very early in the treatment, on the patient's anxiety over his rage at important, but secondary, persons in his current environment. The primary relationships, with parent or mate or therapist, are not to be interpreted in this way. "Since this was all initiated early in the therapy, a magical element was introduced: the therapist had a special knowledge about what was going on in the patient's mind, and was thus elevated into the role of a magical, omnipotent figure." Thus, the gratification has a different emphasis from that described by Knight and Chafetz: the therapist provides special understanding rather than literal nurturance.

This difference is a critical one for Balint (1968). The latter thinks that there are many patients who can be treated in a therapeutic relationship which provides the right climate of understanding; he calls this "regression aimed at recognition." Silber's strategy would seem to be suitable for these patients. Others demand a "regression aimed at [literal] gratification." For these patients, it seems that one must manage the gratification as best one can, as suggested by Knight and Chafetz.

Balint's views about how to manage such a "benign regression" (aimed at recognition) and how to recognize patients who require this kind of therapeutic relationship are not easy to summarize, having been developed over several decades and many papers. Balint devoted a small book, *The Basic Fault* (1968), to summarizing his views. We may only outline his major points here and refer the reader to the book for further understanding.

We should emphasize first that the alcoholic patient, in Balint's view, is only one special type of the general category of patients who suffer from narcissistic disorders, but a type that dramatically illustrates the general problem, because of clear and rapid shifts between adult and primitive relationships. The alcoholic, according to Balint, forms shaky object relationships, and is easily thrown off his balance when there is a clash of interest with the love object. The alcoholic withdraws into solitary narcissism, which makes him feel the center of every attention, but forsaken and miserable. "The first effect of intoxication is invariably the establishment of a feeling that everything is now well between them and their environment," that is, a state of "harmony" is reestablished, the yearning for which Balint feels is the most important cause for alcoholism (p. 55). Interestingly enough, Bateson (1971), approaching the subject from an entirely different theoretical tradition, came to a nearly parallel formulation in the terms of general systems theory.

The critical implication for treatment is that this state of "harmony" can be generated in the psychotherapeutic relationship, relieving the patient from the need to seek it through alcohol. The conditions are these: "the absolute demand that one partner—the analyst—must be 'in tune' with the other—the patient—all the time, the absence of conflict, the relative unimportance of the customary forms of interpretation" (p. 58). If there is to be a "benign (therapeutic) regression," given these conditions, it has five primary characteristics, according to Balint: (1) a mutually trusting, unsuspecting relationship is formed without much difficulty, in which the patient feels at peace; (2) the patient has the sense of a "new beginning" in which he discovers new freedom to behave as a child in relation to the analyst, and which in turn allows him freedom in adult relationships; (3) the regression is for the sake of recognition of his internal problems rather than for (4) demands, expectations, and other "needs"; (5) there is an absence of hysterical symptomatology or genital-orgastic elements in the regressed transference.

Kohut (1971) has described very similar regressive relationships which support the therapeutic effort. The vocabulary developed by Kohut is different from that of Balint, but I think the range of phenomena described by each is essentially the same or overlapping in most aspects. Balint's writing is the more poetic and evocative, whereas Kohut's terminology is helpful in defining more precisely some crucial aspects of the therapeutic process.[1] Again, as with Balint, Kohut treats alcoholism as a special type of narcissistic disorder, the special characteristics of which he has given some attention to. In summary, Kohut thinks that the ego of the addict (alcoholic) lacks certain functions that would allow him to soothe himself, insulate himself against overstimulation and supply himself with tension-reducing gratification. For these purposes he requires an archaic object relationship in which these functions are provided by the external object. In a regressive archaic relationship in which the boundaries between self and other are blurred, and the analyst becomes a "self-object," these aforementioned ego functions of the analyst are put in the service of the patient, who has lacked them. Thus, Kohut gives a more precise description of what functions are shared in the "harmony" or "harmonious mix-up" of the patient-analyst relationship. Kohut also describes several important variations on the connection between the more adult relationships of the patient and the archaic self-object relationship: namely, the possibility of either a "horizontal" or "vertical" splitting of these ego states. In "horizontal" splitting, the archaic object relationship is repressed; in "vertical" splitting, these relationships are acted out side by side with the more adult ones, but in different situations, at different times, and with different persons. The use of alcoholic intoxication in order to achieve a state of "harmony" with archaic objects would be an instance of "vertical splitting," the patient alternating between modest, sober adult states and intoxicated grandiose states of involvement in archaic object relationships. This structural formulation fits with Balint's clinical descriptions of the rapid alteration from adult to primitive object relationships.

Furthermore, Kohut describes two important variations of the archaic object relationship, which is mobilized in the transference: namely, the idealizing transference arises from the revival of the idealized parent imago, with which the patient tries to maintain a continuous union. Silber's description of the therapeutic relationship with his group of alcoholic patients is consistent with this paradigm.[2] However, there is another important variation of the archaic relationship which is quite distinct metapsychologically and which requires an entirely different therapeutic strategy: this is the mirror transference, which depends on the mobilization of the grandiose self (as opposed to the idealized parent imago, a self-object). The analyst's function in this relationship is to be an extension of the grandiose self: in the most primitive form, the merger transference, the analyst is experienced as an extension of the grandiose self over which the patient expects unquestioned dominance; a less primitive form, the alter ego transference, involves the analyst as either the same as or very much like the patient; the mirror transference in the narrower sense requires the analyst to mirror the patient's exhibitionistic display and thus to confirm it.

Balint also describes two variations on the archaic narcissistic relationship, for which he has coined two unusual names, ocnophilia and philobatism.

The ocnophil's reaction to the emergence of objects is to cling to them, to introject them, since he feels lost and insecure without them; apparently he chooses to *over-cathect his object relationships*. The other type, the philobat, *over-cathects his own ego functions*, and develops skills in this way, in order to be able to maintain himself alone with very little, or even no, help from his objects. . . . In the philobatic world the objectless expanses retain the original primary cathexis and are experienced as safe and friendly, while the objects are felt as treacherous hazards (p. 68).

These formulations are clearly parallel to those of Kohut, ocnophilia to the idealizing transference, philobatism to the mirror transference. However, in the latter pair of formulations, the emphasis falls differently: both philobatism and the mirror transference involve "overcathexis" of aspects of the self; but in philobatism the description emphasizes the pleasure in objectless expanses, whereas in the mirror transference the emphasis is upon the devoted attachment of an attentive object to the grandiose self. In my own clinical practice, I have found that these two characteristics commonly are shared by the same patients, namely, a pleasure in objectless expanses and a pleasure in mirroring the wanderings of the self through such spaces. Both aspects confirm the grandiose self. Both characteristics are found together in Ernest Jones's description of the God complex (1951).

Finally, Kohut augments Balint's descriptions with a precise formulation of the stages in the analysis of narcissistic patients. The first stage is that of resistance to the mirror or idealizing transference: in the case of the mirror transference, the patient fears isolation or rejection if the extent of his narcissistic aims were known; or he may fear the pain of giving up some aspects of these aims in entering the relationship. Kohut thinks that these early resistances are easily overcome if the therapist is simply empathic with the presentations of the patient. The second stage is that of the mirror (or idealizing) transference itself: the heart of the treatment here is the revelation of the grandiose fantasies of the patient. There are many more complexities of this second phase, to which Kohut has devoted several long chapters ("The Therapeutic Process in the Mirror Transference"; "Some Reactions of the Analyst to the Mirror Transferences") in his monograph (1971), which may only be summarized here. Two important factors in therapeutic change are these: the mirroring of the grandiose self helps to keep it mobilized in the therapeutic relationship, despite the fact that its infantile aims are frustrated. "Under the pressure of the renewed frustrations the patient tries to avoid the pain (1) by recreating the pre-transference equilibrium through the establishment of a vertical split and/or of a (horizontal) repression barrier; or (b) through regressive evasion" (p. 198). These two undesirable escape routes are blocked by transference interpretations and genetic reconstructions which assist the cooperative ego: "In view of the fact that all regressive roads are blocked while the infantile wish for mirroring is kept alive without being gratified in its infantile form, the psyche is forced to create new structures which transform and elaborate the infantile need along aim-inhibited and realistic lines" (p. 199).

Having reviewed the work of Kohut, Balint, and others, we may turn to considering the alcoholic patient whom I saw in outpatient psychotherapy for approximately one year. The work divided very clearly into two phases, the first a phase of severe resistance, during which I saw the patient twice a week for six months, and the second phase, in which a mirror transference was established, during which I saw the patient three times a week for six months.

CASE MATERIAL

The patient, Mr. A, forty-two years of age, married for twenty years, with no children, had been a heavy drinker since the age of sixteen when he left home. Briefly the major events that emerged in his history were as follows: His mother had a stroke when he was three, leaving her with a severe aphasia, but nevertheless she remained the parent who took daily care of the patient. She and the patient fell to yelling and fighting continually with each other. The patient felt continually misunderstood by his mother, whose use of language was restricted to short phrases, and who, thus, probably *did* continually misunderstand the intentions of the child or failed to convey her understanding. In a personal communication, Dr. Kohut has suggested that the language impairment accounts for only one aspect of the disturbance in the relationship between this patient and his aphasic mother: "I would assume that without a broader disturbance in empathy (perhaps as a consequence of emotional dulling due to an organic defect in the basal ganglia) the language disturbance would not have been (equally) traumatic." A sister, three years older, and his father left him at the mercy of his mother. The father continually worked, including evenings and weekends, at his office, and rarely took the boy anywhere. When he did appear, it was to lecture the boy and berate him for his halting replies: "Come out with it, why do you take so long to say things?" He slept in his father's bed until age twelve, and again when he returned from the army at age nineteen.

Eight years prior to starting psychotherapy, he had a myocardial infarction and subsequent open heart surgery on the coronary vessels. He was *abstinent* for the next three years. Four years prior to therapy, he fell in love with a beautiful, narcissistic woman, with whom he had a tumultuous affair. Their relationship, at first ecstatic and very gratifying sexually, became more and more revengeful, that is, like his relationship with his mother. The surgical bypass of occluded coronary vessels, two years prior to therapy, shut down a few weeks later in the midst of more retribution between the patient and his mistress. The patient's father died about this time as well. The angina became so severe that he was operated on again one and a half years prior to therapy, and a Weinberg procedure was performed.

Thus, there was strong evidence for a sudden, traumatic disturbance in the mother's capacity to mirror the intentions and capacities of the three-year-old child. According to Kohut, such a complete and sudden shift in the mother's involvement in the child is a typical history for patients who will develop a mirror transference in the psychotherapy (pp. 253–254).

At the time of therapy Mr. A was taking over a hundred nitroglycerin tablets per week for angina. He had been involved in several automobile accidents while drunk, nearly costing him his life. He was drunk more days than not. He had broken off the relationship with his mistress, but thought of little else but her. He had seen one psychiatrist while in his twenties for a few visits. He came for psychotherapy, he said, because he was destroying his life. He had always been considered "no good" and felt compelled to "fuck up." He was referred by a physician friend.

The first six months we met twice a week. The themes were consistent: (1) on the one hand, how bitterly disappointed he had been by his cardiac surgeon, his mistress, an encounter group leader, his wife, and so on; all had used him to make themselves look good, and with no consideration for his needs; (2) his own remarkable power of recuperation and his power to "fuck up" whatever was going well.

An example of our hours together in this period went, briefly, like this: I (therapist) was right in the last hour about his pride. He delighted in being able to see into customers, selling them articles they didn't want, or in keeping his mistress under his thumb. He didn't want to let anyone "help" him; he would do the opposite of what doctors told him. (A brief episode of angina at this point.) He hated his surgeon, and envied him his confidence; he resented the doctor's view of the failed operation and regarded it as a great technical failure for the doctor! (The patient's failure to get better not appearing to matter.) Yet he made the "fastest recovery ever seen." He thought of running in the Boston Marathon. He could drink because his body "can take anything." The next hour was missed; he got drunk and ended up in the state hospital. He said, on returning, that he felt "defenseless" after the last hour, markedly exposed to criticism from me. During the drunk, he had pulled a coup, which he reported with an air of triumph: walking into a bar without money, he claimed that he had to have a loan or the lady cab driver outside would beat him up. His audience roared with laughter and gave him money.

My responses to these accounts were intended to be empathic, to reflect accurately that I understood the pleasure and anxiety of his performances and his anger and anxiety over being used by the surgeon or others. For many months, however, this seemed to make little difference, save that he did keep coming regularly. The pattern, exemplified by this last hour, was one of narcissistic display, or rage at those who used him, followed by drunkenness. The anxiety, reported in this last hour as his feeling "defenseless," seemed to be based on the fear of alienating me by his displays or his rage and causing me to retaliate. This anxiety, which was frequently manifested in the hours as angina, seemed to be relieved temporarily by the drunkenness, in which he seemed to be able to mobilize his grandiose self with some sense of triumph, as in the example in which he compelled others to appreciate his wit and provide for him. This would be a very clear example of vertical splitting (Kohut, 1971), through which the patient keeps the intense archaic object relationship separate from the therapeutic relationship. Of course, as Kohut has emphasized, this is not only motivated by the anxiety of alienating the therapist by the manifestations of the grandiose self, but also by the secondary gains of continuing a pleasureful acting out. Such secondary gain may contribute importantly to lengthening this phase of resistance to establishing the mirror transference, which lasted six months, rather than yielding easily to the empathy of the therapist, as would be typical of most narcissistic patients described by Kohut.

This pattern of the first several months was interrupted by an automobile accident, in which the patient nearly lost his life, but escaped serious physical harm. The patient had lost control of his car while drunk. He was very frightened by this, and he resolved to stop drinking for several months, until New Year's, which he managed to do. I then began to hear, regularly, bitter and detailed criticism of the mistress and the surgeon. The theme was their devotion to their own selfish aims, with utter disregard for the patient himself. He became very incapacitated by angina during this phase, feeling empty and as if he were "locked in a vise." The transference implications of his position seemed to be that a close relationship with me would also be a hell of being used by me and entailing bitter and vicious attacks and counterattacks. This became quite clear when he told me that he had decided to quit psychotherapy. He said that he had decided to be responsible for himself, and that he was tired of being a "case" for doctors. I urged him to continue, inasmuch as we were getting to the point of intensity where I might be useful to him. In the next hour, he poured out a wealth of material about how he was treated by the surgeon and how helpless and enraged he felt. He then made his own transference interpretation about confusing me with the other doctor (the surgeon). In retrospect, it has seemed to me that my countertransference during this period had resulted in my treating him somewhat distantly as a "case." The intensity of his rage and his displays led to a subtle withdrawal, which was hidden from me by my idea that I was being consistently and strategically empathic concerning his situation. In fact, I was being empathic from a considerable and cool distance. This, according to Kohut, is a typical countertransference reaction:

The most common dangers to which the analyst is exposed vis-a-vis the twinship and merger are boredom, lack of emotional involvement with the patient and precarious maintenance of attention (including such secondary reactions as overt anger, exhortations, and forced interpretations of resistances, as well as other forms of the rationalized acting out of tensions and impatience) (1971, p. 273).

After this crisis, subtle signs of a new climate in the therapy began to appear with increasing frequency over the next two months. These would take the form of a quiet, peaceful smiling after he had recounted certain kinds of incidents: for instance, how he had talked to his wife at length and she had listened ("I talk. She listens."). My own capacity to respond with more warmth also was recovered in this period. For instance, when I reflected to him how it must feel to be confined in the narrow space of his house by the angina, he also seemed to relax and smile with appreciation. These were harbingers of the mirror transference that was to become clear after about two months of oscillation between incidents like these and further descriptions of bitterness with his mistress. Both of these incidents show the patient's appreciation for warm and accurate mirroring of the patient's self and his predicament. A more decided change in tone occurred during a very quiet hour which the patient began by saying that he didn't have much to say and didn't know what he had accomplished. I commented on the smile which followed this statement, to which he replied, smiling again, that he could spend his time as well drinking coffee. He then said that he had come to the conclusion that his bitter brooding was some kind of avoidance of looking to the future. I agreed that his blaming of others or of himself did seem to leave him in the same place. In the next hour, he continued, wondering thoughtfully, "How do I get out of all this blaming?" He said that he continually swung between blaming others and then blaming himself: "When I blame myself I can keep the same thing going because there is nothing to do about it and I'm still not responsible." "But then pride enters in—if I begin to take responsibility—then I'd have to admit I was wrong before." He then began to laugh aloud, for the first time since I had known him, and said: "There's no humiliation in this—People I'm close to *know* I've been wrong about a few things!" I then reflected to him in the same spirit, "Then it wouldn't exactly be a new idea for your friends to think, 'A (the patient's name) surely is wrong about this or that.' " He continued to laugh heartily, which was a dramatic change for a man who had been little but grimly serious for the first six months of our work. I then said, "But it would be a new kind of relationship with them to be open about your shortcomings?" to which he replied that he had induced so much tension and hatred in himself by the previous way he related with them.

These several sessions had the quality of a "new beginning" as described by Balint: the emergence of new behavior and energy in the context of an unsuspecting, trustful relationship. The next session he reported he had been drinking again, but the tone with which he reported it was altogether different: while drinking at home, he had listened to records of Barbra Streisand, his adolescent love, with satisfaction. In the subsequent sessions, a quiet, slow, but moving conversation took the place of bitter, rapid accusation. He said he was relieved not to feel so full of hate. He was relieved not to be hurried. His father had always impatiently said, "Get to the point." Now he felt I could wait for him to express himself as he needed to. I probably had begun to appreciate his need for this unhurried relationship in the month previous and probably did slow down the pace of my own interventions, letting him finish his thoughts without interruption, and so forth. It did seem to me that this slow tempo and quiet was more important than the content of what I said to him in providing the right conditions for his "new beginning." Why is this the case? In the first place, we have the patient's direct statement that hurried interruption reminds him of his relationship with his father, and is thus tantamount to inducing a negative transference. In the second place, we know from his history that his mother continually yelled at him from the time that he was three years old, when she had had a stroke and had become aphasic. Perhaps prior to this traumatic disruption, he had had a peaceful, unhurried, satisfying relationship with his mother. We do not know, but his acute sensitivity to the nonverbal qualities of the climate provided in my office would be consistent with this hypothesis: that is, when I left him in peace to express himself slowly and carefully, I was being like his mother in the first years; when I inadvertently conveyed to him that he should move along or when I jumped in with my thoughts, I was reminding him of the traumatic years that followed with both mother and father. According to Balint, this nonverbal or preverbal sensitivity is one of the central qualities of these patients who are capable of a new beginning, once the sensitivity is appreciated and adjusted to by the analyst. Generally, with these patients, when one does not yet appreciate the specific requirements of the necessary "climate," one does well to provide an environment with as few irritants as possible. The classical analytic setting usually is suitable:

the quiet, well-tempered room, a comfortable couch, unexciting environment, the analyst not interrupting the patient unnecessarily, the patient being given full opportunity to speak his mind, and so on. On the whole, this kind of satisfaction might be described also as looking-after, or even as a kind of psychological nursing (1968, p. 186).

This patient seemed to have great difficulty soothing and calming himself: that is, he tended to become overstimulated, tense and bitter, and contentious, as he continually demonstrated in the first six months of treatment. As Balint would say, when I became "attuned" to this and began to respond to his occasional smiling, his pauses, his need for a very slow unfolding, I helped him to calm himself. It does seem clear in reviewing my notes, and the occasions for them, that I made many fewer responses to the exciting, irritating aspects of his presentation and more responses to his smiling and pleasure and thoughtfulness as the case went on. Thus I mirrored the patient's capacity to soothe and insulate himself against overstimulation, which seemed to have the effect that he could then do this better for himself when he was away from me and on his own.

What then was the nature of this mirroring relationship which helped the patient to calm himself? How did the mirroring help him to provide this for himself? The reader will perhaps remember Kohut's formulation: the alcoholic lacks these ego functions, that would allow him to soothe himself, insulate himself against overstimulation, and supply himself with tension-reducing gratification. In a regressive archaic relationship in which the boundaries between self and other are blurred, and the therapist becomes a "self-object," these aforementioned ego functions of the therapist are put in the service of the patient who lacks them. Kohut's formulations about the alcoholic or addict are made in one of his chapters on the idealizing transference, as if all alcoholic or addictive patients would require an idealizing transference to be able to control their internal tension. In fact, as I am demonstrating here, Kohut's formulation is easily modified: the patient has the ego functions to soothe himself, etc., but is unable to use them until they are mirrored or confirmed in the context of an archaic relationship with the therapist in which the boundaries between patient and therapist are blurred. The patient's situation is like that of a young child who has acquired the capacity to soothe himself, through thumb-sucking, holding onto a favorite blanket, or some other use of a transitional object. However, this child often needs the mother's support for these self-comforting activities, which is given by the mother's confirming smile or pat on the head or even a reminder to go get the blanket. Or the child may need to come away from the exciting situation that is making him too tense, so that he may administer his self-calming help to himself. In these ways, the mother gives invaluable aid to the child's capacity to calm himself and is thus part of his system for doing this. She has to be quite in tune with his level of tension and also with his capacity to do something helpful for himself. In this sense of intimate rapport and confirmation of the child's capacities, there is a blurring of the boundaries between child and mother, who together constitute one tension-reducing system. This is the way in which the mirror transference with the alcoholic patient revives an archaic relationship and functions as such to help the patient calm himself and thus have less need for alcohol to help him perform these functions.

What was unmistakable was that a rather dramatic change in the climate of the therapeutic relationship, from one of hurried bitterness to unhurried calm, took place at the same time as many manifestations of the mirror transference appeared. I have explained how the mirror transference would accomplish this calming effect; now I would give the further evidence that such a mirror transference was established at this point in our relationship. Several hours after the "new beginning" I have described, in which the patient had felt he could leave off blaming and had begun to laugh so heartily, he asked if he could come three times a week, and I agreed after some discussion. Within the same hour that this request was made, the patient compared himself with Stewart Alsop, the columnist who had died of cancer; however bleak his situation, he had gotten something out of the treatment, which was a new interest in reading newspapers. This sense of common fate, and thus a common bond, with Stewart Alsop, seemed to have enabled him to take an interest in Alsop's field. Quiet references to this fantasy relationship with Alsop continued through several hours after the "new beginning." This sense of alter ego or twinship relations of a grandiose nature continued to be observable in dream and fantasy material, and I will return to it later. These materials would suggest the "alter ego" version of the mirror transference was present, but generally I felt that his expectations from me were for mirroring in the strict sense rather than for my being just like him. That is, he began to tell me directly how much he wished to be approved of and admired, how he had felt impelled to swim across the lake alone, to walk the parapets of a ten-story hotel, to be admired in the bar, and so forth. Yet these solo honors never had satisfied him and he had ended up damaging himself. He often wept in telling me about these exploits, and seemed very grateful that I understood how his wish to be admired had driven him. Kohut comments on this characteristic phase of treatment as follows: "Hand in hand with the increasing acceptance of his archaic narcissism, and with the increasing dominance of his ego over it, the patient will grasp the inefficacy of the former narcissistic display in the split-off sector" (1971, p. 185). As is evident from Kohut's accounts, it is not uncommon for a patient to show some evidence for an alter-ego transference, but yet to move into a mirror transference in the stricter sense (Kohut, p. 250).

I have devoted considerable detail to the first six months of the treatment and the overcoming of the severe resistance to the mirror transference relationship, since, in this aspect, the case of this alcoholic patient differs so clearly from the majority of cases of narcissistic personality described by Kohut. Such resistance is also unusual for those patients described by Balint as capable of a new beginning. In summary, my findings concerning this period were as follows: (1) Contrary to the typical case of narcissistic personality, the "appropriately attentive, but unobtrusive and noninterfering behavior of the analyst" did not suffice to remove the initial resistance to the regression into a mirror transference (Kohut, p. 29). (2) "Vertical splitting" of the grandiose states of mind (experienced while intoxicated) from the sober analytic relationships was the initial form of the resistance. (3) The next form of the resistance (after a nearly catastrophic auto accident persuaded the patient to quit drinking and blocked his expression of the grandiosity in the drinking) was a bitter, tense several months in which the patient seemed to be saying that any close relationship would be a hell of mutual recriminations. This was partially relieved by a transference interpretation, made essentially by the patient, about how he had confused me with the surgeon who had hurt and used him. (4) A countertransference problem, that had kept me at a rather cool and detached distance was overcome after the transference interpretation had been made. (5) I gradually became attuned to the patient's need for a very slow and quiet unfolding of his thoughts without interruption and for mirroring of his smile and "small" pleasures. This resulted in the patient's increasing capacity to calm himself and thus change the bitter, contentious climate of the treatment. Balint's formulation about the preverbal needs of the patient and Kohut's formulation concerning the need for an archaic relationship to provide the basis for the exercise of tension-reducing functions were found to be applicable to the events of this phase. (6) A "new beginning" of a relatively unsuspecting, trustful relationship in which the patient felt it no longer necessary to restrict himself to blaming others or himself relieved the patient of the "viselike" constriction that had held him for the previous several months. (7) This new climate of unhurried calm in the treatment coincided with the clear establishment of a mirror transference relationship, in which the patient brought forward directly his wish to be thought well of and the perilous exploits he had performed in order to be admired previously.

A very recent contribution by Anna Ornstein provides a theoretical bridge for connecting these findings (1–7). She suggests that the *characterological* defenses often block the emergence of the therapeutic narcissistic transferences:

One obvious difference between optimal infantile conditions and the narcissistic transferences is the presence of character features in the patient that may resist the perception of the analyst's empathy. The analyst's empathy and the patient's increased ability to perceive it are the conditions that constitute the *sine qua non* for the establishment of relatively stable narcissistic equilibria in the transference (pp. 238–239).

In her case illustration, she shows how a patient's masochistic-paranoid character defenses distorted the perception of the analyst: the latter was believed to be only interested in the patient when she felt bad; feeling good was believed to lead to loss of interest and desertion by the analyst, as it had with her mother. The analyst's real interest and warmth could not be perceived, and, hence, a mirror transference could not be established, until this masochistic merger transference was worked through.

This hypothesis would also explain the long period of resistance to the mirror transference in the present case we are discussing. As the patient himself stated, closeness for him meant a hell of mutual recriminations, such as he had had with his mother following her stroke, and such as he had repeated later with his mistress. However, this intense masochistic-paranoid merger with the mother was all he had to hold onto, as long as his father remained unavailable to him. The earlier archaic mirroring object relationship that was later mobilized was both disavowed and repressed (vertical and horizontal splitting). As Ornstein suggests, the character defenses (merger) act as " 'fortifications' of the primary modes of defense—disavowal and repression" (p. 234). Thus, our patient would hold onto the masochistic-paranoid merger with me, perceive my interest in masochistic and paranoid terms, look elsewhere for empathy (vertical splitting), and gradually involve me in the masochistic-paranoid relationship, for which distance and coolness would be one countertransference reaction (1–4). The transference interpretation (3) allowed the patient to begin to hear my interest as genuine, in contradistinction to that of the mistress and the surgeon. My overcoming my countertransference reaction, appreciating his need for a very slow and quiet unfolding and mirroring (4–7) provided him with the new beginning of the narcissistic equilibrium that he needed. Both aspects, I think, were crucial: overcoming the "viselike" masochistic-paranoid merger, and offering "the appropriately attentive, but unobtrusive and noninterfering behavior of the analyst."

The next major shift in the treatment that needs explanation occurred about three to four months after this clear establishment of the mirror transference and consisted of the patient's cessation of all drinking and a reduction in his need for nitroglycerin (for angina) by one-third. I cannot explain this second major change as clearly as the first. In general, what I could observe is that the lesser need for alcohol and nitroglycerin signified a major reduction in his state of bodily tension and that this reduction in tension followed revelations to me of the intense need he had had for a close relationship with his father. He had needed to be rescued by the father from the terrible burden of being left alone with his aphasic mother. Being left alone with her had filled him with tension, rage, and guilt. The recall of these very painful memories, in the safe, buffering context of the mirror transference relationship, seemed to result in a general reduction of bodily tension.

I will describe only two incidents from the long series of hours in which painful memories were recalled, to give the reader some sense of this period. In the first incident, the patient told me about how he had gone to the bar on Saint Patrick's Day in a green vest, green tie, and green shirt, with a figurine leprechaun. He was having a good time, as he said, talking with his leprechaun, when he accidentally dropped it and it broke. He ended up hurling the remains of the leprechaun at a wall. When he got to this point in his narrative, he began sobbing and then later said that the only other time he had felt this way was when his father died. When I asked him in the next hour about the leprechaun and what it had meant to him, he told me that it reminded him of the song he had always loved and which he had listened to before he had gone to the bar that day. The song was "Danny Boy," which he went on to explain was a song about a father saying good-bye to his son, sending him to war. When I asked the patient what the father says to the son, he replied that the father says, "I love you so much," and then the patient began to sob again and shake. In these two hours, the patient clearly brought forward the intensity of his need to be loved, and began to grieve over the loss of his father or the loss of the father that he had imagined for himself, that was represented by the leprechaun.

The second incident, several months later and just prior to his report of having ceased drinking and having reduced his need for nitroglycerin, began with an hour in which the patient reported himself in a rage with me, feeling an urge to break up my office. In the next hour, he reported the following dream: "My dad and a lawyer are sitting at the kitchen table. I am filling a black bag—with trash . . . hangers are sticking out—I am falling off a curb with the weight of it. My father stands by (doing nothing)—It's the same bewilderment." His associations were that the black bag represented all his difficulties, for which his father offered no help, that the father had even resisted his seeing a psychiatrist early in his twenties because the father was afraid of being criticized. I did not interpret or explore the connection between his rage at me in the previous hour and the dream which would seem to explain the transference (from father to me). In retrospect, this seems like an oversight, but in any case I did not make transference interpretations concerning the patient's rage at me, in the last few months of treatment. Instead, I said that I appreciated from the dream how intensely bereft he must have felt and how this explained more clearly than before his anger at his father. Whether or not it was an error, the effect of not interpreting this aspect of the transference was twofold: (1) the patient began to experience his anger at other people in his present life who had let him down, and he began to defend himself quite appropriately in relation to these people; (2) within a month, he had decided he had gotten what he had needed from me and was ready to terminate. An agreed-upon termination followed after yet another month. I will return to this last phase, but, in regard to the second major shift in the treatment, that of the reduction of bodily tension and cessation of the need for alcohol and reduction of the need for nitroglycerin, my main point is that this was preceded by the intense emergence of memories and affects concerning the patient's father. The patient seemed able to tolerate these painful memories because of the stability of his mirror transference relationship with me. Kohut explains this phase of treatment as follows:

The transference, however, functions here as a specific therapeutic buffer. In the mirror transference in the narrower sense the patient is able to mobilize his grandiose fantasies and exhibitionism on the basis of the hope that the therapist's empathic participation and emotional response will not allow the narcissistic tensions to reach excessively painful or dangerous levels (Kohut, p. 191).

Some of my explanation then is that the tension that had been generated by the need to repress these memories and affects was reduced. In addition, he became able to discharge narcissistic tensions more directly in his current relationships. Why was this the case? I do not think my answer is complete, but, in part, he overcame his intense shame and embarrassment over his intense need to be loved by his father and to be more adequately taken care of by him by presenting these needs to me, with their genetic antecedents and affects, and having them confirmed and appreciated. He subsequently began to act as if he had accepted these needs himself and was thus able to reduce his own tension over them appropriately. When he began to be able to do this for himself, he no longer needed alcohol and had much less need for nitroglycerin. In other words, as the intensely charged unconscious narcissistic aspirations (to be loved and taken care of) were brought into awareness and into contact with the central reality ego, they became progressively more neutralized and capable of being channeled into daily, realistic pursuits, thus enabling the patient to reduce his own tension (Kohut, 1971, p. 187 and p. 248).

In a personal communication, Dr. Kohut suggested that the shift of the transference, in this case from the mother to the father, represents a typical event in the successful treatment of narcissistic personality disorders. The child turns from a frustrating self-object to the other self-object; . . . narcissistic psychopathology occurs only when both attempts to gain the response of the two self-objects fail; . . . in treatment the cure seems to hinge on the re-establishment of empathic contact with the less damaging of the two early self-objects, i.e., often with the father. This movement is in general from mirroring toward idealization. In your case—a more rare sequence—it seems to go from maternal to paternal mirroring.

This perspective explains the first and second phases of treatment and the shift from one to the other most clearly and simply. The first, as previously discussed, consisted of a very frustrating pathological merger with the mother self-object, while the relationship with the paternal self-object was disavowed (vertical splitting) and repressed (horizontal splitting). The second phase was entirely concerned with material concerning the patient's father, his intense wish to be loved, protected, and faithfully mirrored by his father, as represented in the story of Danny Boy and reexperienced in the transference, and the terrible disappointments that had interfered with his getting this from his father, as represented in the dream of the black bag that his father left him with. When these disappointments were to some extent worked through within the protection of the paternal mirroring transference, the patient, in the third phase of treatment, turned back again to the material concerning his mother and was able to reduce his guilt about her and stop injuring himself.

The third and last major event of the treatment, for which we had advanced a preliminary interpretation, was the patient's decision that he had gotten what he needed from the treatment and was ready to terminate. In the last several months of treatment, the patient took a much more active role in relation to the external circumstances of his life and felt free to assert his own wishes where they might conflict with those of other people (which he had not been able to do previously): free not to talk about his problems with other people when he felt this was inappropriate; free to disagree with the police (regarding an alleged traffic violation); free to criticize an official of the Motor Vehicle Division who wanted him to "confess" his alcoholism; free to differ with his priest. He successfully took over the defense of a legal matter in which his lawyer had been dallying. These new capabilities reflect an area of progressive neutralization of narcissistic aims. As Kohut states, "the (new) structures built up in response to the claims of the grandiose self appear in general to deal less with the curbing of the narcissistic demands but with the *channeling and modification of their expression*. (Kohut, p. 187) Thus, the patient made fewer empty grandiose claims, but rather argued in the service of realistic demands. My role in these matters was usually to notice his anxiety as he brought up the issue and to comment on it, and he would proceed to analyze his fear that his demands were not legitimate, etc.

What had prevented him from defending himself previously was most clearly revealed in a series of dreams. I will first summarize the manifest content of these several dreams, which concerned injury to his mother (or his mistress). In the first of this series, he imagined himself locked up in a prison, while watched by his mother. In the second he found himself digging out an area under the floor which revealed a big slab with his mother on it covered by a white sheet. A large white horse then jumped through the opening that had been dug. In the third dream, he brought his mother to me on a hospital bed, and I said I had a colleague directly above who could heal her speech problem. In a fourth, he dreamed that the woman with whom he had had the bitter affair had been dismembered by a gang of teen-agers. He found her in a black bag and reported this to the police. He emerged from this last dream with a great sense of relief that he had not actually committed the crime, even though he might have wanted to. After the discussion of this last dream in the series, he said that he felt free of the pervasive guilt that had prevented him from defending himself and that he now felt he could lead his life without injuring himself or allowing himself to be injured by others. Indeed his conviction about this has been borne out by one year's follow-up in which he has been remarkably free of the self-destructive incidents that had been daily or weekly occurrences.

His associations to these dreams usually took the form of recalling very disturbing memories about his relation to his mother: a bewildered, "profound" feeling about not understanding what he was doing with her; being an unwanted child, continually told that his birth had caused his mother's stroke; being left all alone in the house with his mother, and then having his father refuse to take him for a walk because he had wanted to take along a doll; and finally, the enormous relief of getting the distinction clear between having wanted to hurt her (and also his mistress and also his father) and not actually having done it. In these dreams and a number which followed, there were frequent references to a fatherly figure (a copilot in one dream) who did not leave him alone with his terrible burden.

The manifest content of these dreams suggested various ways in which he could be exculpated: he was a pure white horse leaping free from his mother's bed; I could arrange for God (the colleague directly above) to heal his mother's stroke; some teen-agers had mutilated the woman and he had only come upon her on the road. The latent content concerned his memories and feelings of bewilderment, terror, and guilt over being left alone with her and left with the (felt) responsibility for her condition. Finally, he seemed to emerge with a sense that he no longer had to carry these feelings alone, that a fatherly figure was with him, and that this father appreciated the distinction between his criminal feelings and actual crimes. There are probably several ways of explaining how these several factors relieved him of his self-destructive pattern. First, one could argue that the manifest content represented denials of his criminal intent, and that these defenses were not challenged by the therapist and thus remain part of his defensive structure. Second, the recall of bewildering states of mind in relation to his mother and the sharing of these with the psychotherapist helped to give them some shape and this dispelled some of their terror. This calming relationship with the therapist helped him to distinguish his wishes and fantasies of destructive intent toward his mother from the reality that he had actually not committed the crimes. This help is like that given a very frightened child who wakes from a terrible dream, whose dream is then not minimized but rather appreciated by the parent; yet the child is reassured that the dreadful acts have not been committed. The patient was thus helped to integrate regressive states of mind in which fantasy about his mother and reality had not been distinguished, but which had been split off from the central reality ego, because his father had not made himself available to help the boy with them. As these regressive states were understood, the patient felt a great deal more confidence in being able to use his aggression constructively, confident that he could distinguish real wrongs from those he might imagine. Of course, mirroring of his capacity to make these judgments remained crucial, and became the essential working-through process of the last two months of treatment. Thus, he became able to dispute a traffic violation (he had not just imagined he was driving properly) and so forth, as I have described.

Clearly, the analytic work was not completed. The patient left treatment with a powerful unanalyzed transference of a very special relationship with me. Within the year following our termination he returned twice for a few sessions to discuss difficulties concerning not being appreciated by a teacher (he had returned to college part-time), and later, concerning the death of another cardiac patient whom he had felt was his "twin," and, indeed, I expect I may see him again. In sum, he still tends to form mirror transference relationships outside of psychotherapy, which can get him in some difficulty. However, he has remained free of drinking problems and other self-destructive activities and has been much more able to defend his interests in disputes with other people.

In summary, the principal difficulty in this case was the prolonged resistance to the establishment of a positive transference, which finally after six months took the form of a mirror transference as described by Kohut. The largest part of this paper has been devoted to describing the work of Balint and Kohut concerning the treatment of the narcissistic personality and then to demonstrating how this work could be applied to these problems of severe resistance in this case of an alcoholic patient who was successfully treated in twelve months of outpatient treatment (2–3 visits per week). Once this positive transference was established, the patient brought forward intense, disturbing memories that permitted him to be relieved, in turn, of severe bodily tension and regressive states in which fantasy and reality were poorly distinguished and had led to considerable guilt. As the bodily tension was reduced, he no longer needed alcohol and reduced his nitroglycerin usage by one-third. As his regressive states were controlled and guilt was reduced, he ceased the pattern of injuring himself or allowing himself to be injured by others. The mirror transference was a necessary precondition for the recall of these disturbing memories and states of mind, for some working through of the rediscovered grandiose aims, and their adaptation to realistic ends. Thus, the principal contribution of this paper lies in describing how the work of Balint and Kohut offered a new way of working with a very difficult and resistant alcoholic patient. The principal question for the future is to what extent mirror and idealizing positive transference relationships can be mobilized with other alcoholic patients and so facilitate progress in one of the most difficult areas of psychoanalytic psychotherapy.[3]

NOTES

1. Since my primary task is to discuss the application of Balint's and Kohut's ideas to the problems of alcoholism, I will limit here what could be a lengthy paper comparing their points of similarity and difference. Certainly a case could be made for the importance of certain differences, but I think that the therapeutic implications of each of their views are the same or complementary.

2. Kohut argues that the active encouragement of an idealizing transference (such as recommended by Silber) may be a necessary emergency measure to keep the patient in treatment. A similar active technique to that recommended by Silber with alcoholic patients was that employed by Aichhorn with juvenile delinquents (see Kohut, 1971, p. 162).

3. I would like to acknowledge my debt to Harold Sampson, Ph.D., and Joseph Weiss, M.D., who first introduced me to psychoanalytic psychotherapy that would emphasize understanding the object relationship that the patient requires in order to bring forward new themes and capabilities. In the terms of Weiss (1971), the mirror

transference would be a special case of the "conditions of safety" required by the patient for the emergence of new themes or for a "new beginning" (Balint, 1968).

REFERENCES

Balint, M. (1968). The Basic Fault, Therapeutic Aspects of Regression. London: Tavistock.

Bateson, G. (1971). The cybernetics of "self": a theory of alcoholism. Psychiatry 34:1–18.

Chafetz, M. (1959). Practical and theoretical considerations in the psychotherapy of alcoholism. Quarterly Journal of Studies on Alcohol 20:281–91.

Devito, R. A.; Flaherty, L. A.; and Mozdzierz, G. J. (1970). Toward a psychodynamic theory of alcoholism. Diseases of the Nervous System 31: 43–49.

Jones, E. (1951). The God complex, the belief that one is God, and the resulting character traits. Essays in Applied Psychoanalysis. London: Hogarth and Institute of Psychoanalysis.

Knight, R. P. (1937). The psychodynamics of chronic alcoholism. Journal of Nervous and Mental Disorders 86: 538–548.

Kohut, H. (1971). The Analysis of the Self. New York: International Universities Press.

Ornstein, A. (1974). The dread to repeat and the new beginning: A contribution to the psychoanalysis of the narcissistic personality disorders. Annual of Psychoanalysis 2:231–248.

Silber, A. (1974). Rationale for the technique of psychotherapy with alcoholics. International Journal of Psychoanalytic Psychotherapy 3:28–47.

Weiss, J. (1971). The emergence of new themes in psychoanalysis: A contribution to the psychoanalytical theory of therapy. International Journal of Psychoanalysis 52:459–468.

Yorke, C. (1970). A critical review of some psychoanalytic literature on drug addiction. British Journal of Medical Psychology 43:141–159.

PART IV

Transference and Countertransference

PSYCHOANALYTIC WRITINGS highlight the difficulties addicts have in forming therapeutic transferences in terms of their difficulties trusting, cooperating, and suspending their daily concerns to investigate their inner lives. While the active addiction contributes greatly to these problems (Zinberg, part II), the abstinent addict often continues to struggle with forming a therapeutic transference. For many of these addicts, co-morbid character disorders contributes to this difficulty. The transferences that addicts develop are shallow. Davidson refers to them as transference phenomena because they are not the deep transferences of the neurotic patient, which can be successfully analyzed. Rather, addicts tend to project onto others, including their therapists, with little awareness. She also notes that addicts are subject to psychotic transference reactions.[1]

C. L. Brown (1950) worked at the Winter VA Hospital in Topeka, where psychoanalytic treatment of the alcoholic patients was tried for a time,[2] no doubt influenced by the nearby Menninger Clinic. In his paper, Brown emphasizes the importance of developing a positive transference for these patients and notes the minimal insight they can utilize. Brown's depiction of the presentation of the alcoholic is wonderfully drawn and I believe stands up well today. He refers to Harry Tiebout, the psychiatrist who treated the cofounder of AA, Bill Wilson.[3] Tiebout wrote a number of papers on alcoholism enlightened by AA principles, displaying a talent for explaining psychodynamic concepts relevant to alcoholism such as pathological narcissism in palatable layperson's terms.[4]

Selzer presents a very different view of alcoholics in his paper in which all of their negative traits are brought out for inspection. The great value of the article is the open consideration of the countertransference feelings that can be evoked by these patients, particularly the anger. Of special interest is that Selzer and Brown present vignettes of alcoholic men with similar traits.

Davidson depicts the difficulties treating heroin addicts in methadone maintenance programs and countertransference reactions that are likely to ensue.

Imhof, Hirsch, and Terenzi survey the literature on countertransference and addiction. They make several provocative observations about addicts and therapists' reaction to them. Their discussion of countertransference in ex-addict counselors reminds us of the differences between the traditionally trained mental health professional and the recovering alcoholic or ex-addict counselor. Each has a different tradition and treatment philosophy. Since most clinics have a mixture of both mental health professionals and counselors, cooperation between the two is a key element in a successful program, which is not necessarily easy because of these differences.[5]

While not noted in the readings, two sources of additional countertransference problems need mentioning. A majority of treated addicts are coerced into treatment.[6] While this will profoundly affect the therapeutic alliance for these patients, very few writers have commented on this parameter of treatment. Steiner[7] has written a cogent discussion of the "patsy" or "persecutor" therapist who either "protects" the coerced patient from the referring source, or "joins" the referring source in "persecuting" him.

Finally, one obvious countertransference issue is treating someone who does not respond to our usual technique. I think most professionals are frustrated when hard-learned techniques "fall on deaf ears." Insight is not valued by these patients. Our key concepts are often ridiculed or belittled by them! Hence our very training is challenged. We are tempted to engage in a fruitless debate over the merits of insight, autonomy, and the sense of responsibility, cherished values of psychoanalysis.

The reader will find transference additionally discussed in the case studies (Part III), the Krystal (Part II) and the Chafetz (Part V) articles. Other articles on countertransference include Selzer,[8] Moore[9] and Imhof.[10]

NOTES

1. Little, 1981.
2. Wallerstein, 1957.
3. Kurtz, 1979, pp. 126–27.
4. Tiebout, 1953, 1954, 1961.
5. Kalb and Propper, 1976; Freudenberger, 1976.
6. For example, Fillmore and Kelso (1987) state, "the majority of clients in alcoholism treatment in the United States are referred from the criminal justice system." Panepinto and Simmons (1986) note that in New York City in 1984, 70% of

all people in alcoholism treatment were mandated as a condition of obtaining welfare benefits.

7. Steiner, 1971.
8. Selzer, 1957.
9. Moore, 1961.
10. Imhof, 1991.

13. A Transference Phenomenon in Alcoholics: Its Therapeutic Implications

Claude L. Brown

THE TREATMENT of those who habitually drink to excess, with deleterious consequences, is in general as unsatisfactory as is the attempt to classify them within the current diagnostic nomenclature. Their treatment ranges from the nostrum which the long-suffering wife surreptitiously places in her husband's coffee to the ultima Thule of therapy, the couch of the psychoanalyst. It is also increasingly recognized that successful results in treating alcoholics may come as a surprise to both the patient and the therapist. Sometimes considerable improvements are seen after but a short interval: bothersome somatic complaints disappear, confidence and self-esteem are restored, and drinking may cease—all for no readily comprehensible reason. Although almost every method of treatment can claim some successes, one wonders whether the diverse therapeutic procedures which seem to yield favorable results do not have a common denominator.

In a recent article Tiebout (1) presented the observation that successful results in treating alcoholics sometimes follow a conversion, i.e., a spiritual and moral change accompanying an impressive change in belief. He postulated that such a conversion is motivated by the patient's vivid awareness of the reality of the distressing situation in which he finds himself, so that, prompted by this realization, he can relinquish his former position of grandiosity and defiance. Once this step is taken, he can rebuild his position realistically without the utilization of alcohol.

Leaving aside the process of surrendering to the demands of the situation, a conversion experience has often been observed in successfully treated alcoholics. One even wonders whether this experience is not the principal therapeutic vehicle in the majority of cases that turn out well, regardless of

Reprinted by permission from *Journal of Studies on Alcohol* (formerly *Quarterly Journal of Studies on Alcohol*) 11, (1950): 403–9. Copyright © by Journal of Studies on Alcohol, Inc., Rutgers Center of Alcohol Studies, New Brunswick, N.J. 08903.

the method of treatment. Certainly this seems true of many alcoholics who really "buy" the Alcoholics Anonymous program, of the few who become abstainers in response to some moral exhortation, and of those who quit drinking for no other conscious reason than that they "just saw the light." Even in the "aversion" method of treatment it is quite possible that the person administering the conditioning drug is actually more important to the patient than the drug itself. In other forms of psychotherapy, such a "conversion" can frequently be seen in cases with a favorable outcome; this conversion, however, is best viewed as a transference phenomenon.

It is possible that a prevalent and unfortunate attitude of those undertaking the care of alcoholic patients may be a major obstacle to favorable results. Those acquainted with the individual alcoholic generally tend to view him as a rather enigmatic fellow, as a person unable to exert his will power, as one who somehow seems to take a strange satisfaction in being an Ishmael, and sometimes, perhaps, as even reeking of depravity. This is the usual attitude of the layman, and although the therapist phrases it in more technical euphemisms he, too, often displays similar feelings. The common saying, "Only an ex-alcoholic can help an alcoholic," illustrates the well-nigh universal rejection which the alcoholic experiences, and explains his resultant feeling that only one who has shared a similar loneliness could possibly sympathize with him. Since the patient, from unconscious motivations, does frequently manufacture situations in which he suffers retaliations from others, it is true that, in reality, the alcoholic has an exceedingly difficult time in finding any real, consistent acceptance and understanding. Is it surprising, then, that by this combination of unconsciously fantasied and realistically confirmed frustrations and rejections the alcoholic is eventually reduced to the human prototype of the Flying Dutchman?

That alcoholism has profound socioeconomic effects, that it is to some degree a manifestation of various cultural influences, that the ingestion of alcohol causes various physiological responses—all these and other factors are important in the over-all picture of a person who is a problem drinker; but of what practical moment are they in treatment? I believe that a familiar tool of therapy, the transference relationship, is not being utilized for all its worth. The crying need of the alcoholic is for acceptance; upon that everything hinges: the resolution of emotional conflicts, the attainment of better insight into the goals of his behavior patterns, the working through of disturbing or perplexing reality matters. All too frequently the zealous therapist attempts to deal with these latter elements before the prime catalyst has been developed. In many cases the actual necessity of alleviating deep-rooted conflicts is problematical; alcoholism is admittedly but a symptom of a subjacent emotional disturbance, and it is conceivable that this symptomatic behavior can be removed with the substitution of more felicitous adaptive ones. The example of Alcoholics Anonymous confirms this, since here the alcoholic can really feel that his acceptance by the group is unfaltering, that here are men who, regardless of the pitfalls into which he has stumbled, will nevertheless extend sincerely helpful, sympathetic hands to him. Also, in the case of the alcoholic who has been rehabilitated by the aid of the Alcoholics Anonymous program, there usually has been no probing into unconscious factors.

The potential value of an ameliorative emotional experience has been occasionally mentioned for many years, and by many people other than psychiatrists. General Booth, from his experience in the Salvation Army, believed that before any person could be helped he had to have assurance that there was someone who was really interested in him. (Conversely, this mechanism is displayed in Faust's willingness to allow Mephistopheles to take his soul if the Devil could even furnish him one moment of sufficiently heightened satisfaction.) It is not necessary that such an experience be a prolonged one. What is essential is that the experience include the absolute conviction of the patient that he is truly accepted by the therapist. Such an acceptance can apparently be highly meaningful to the patient, probably because of the alcoholic's inordinately great need of, and correspondingly great lack of, real acceptance.

In essence, then, the alcoholic, who has an excessive need for acceptance, receives it in the relationship with the therapist. Once this need is fulfilled, previous patterns of behavior which were operative either because of, or concomitantly with, this old need, no longer have to be in effect since the exigency has been removed. Indeed, one wonders whether or not most conversions are actuated by similar experiences—i.e., a great unconscious need is fulfilled with resultant transformation of the personality by such fulfillment.

It is remarkable how often patients who have benefited from psychotherapy maintain some kind of contact with the physician, telephoning him, writing letters, or occasionally visiting the office briefly. Such contacts usually serve no obvious or specific purpose; the former patient says that he "just happened to decide to write," or "was just going by and thought I'd say 'Hello.' " These contacts, transitory but repeated as they usually are, are definitely meaningful. Once the alcoholic has known such an emotional relationship he becomes unconsciously eager to learn, again and again, that it really is true;

he must be reassured constantly that the therapist's acceptance, which was once all-important to him, still exists. For other successfully treated patients such repeated contacts are unnecessary; presumably these people, by virtue of their better adjustments and the new strength obtained through relationships made possible by their more salutary attitudes, are able to dispense with this previously important but now less significant acceptance. In brief, although the precise dynamic interpretation of the phenomenon is not clear, it appears that the relationship with the therapist is of major importance and that the nature of the therapy itself is of much less significance. In every case successfully treated by this writer there was a clearly discernible positive transference. This observation is confirmed by the experiences of two co-workers at Winter Veterans Administration Hospital (2), as well as by that of Devereux (3).

How does the therapist convey to the patient that he has been accepted? He neither overwhelms the patient with personal friendliness, nor alienates him by too detached an attitude. He inquires into the realistic problems of the patient, evincing an interest in them and a willingness to help with their solution. He neither asks questions exclusively about "why do you drink?"; nor does he allow too lengthy and irrelevant intellectualizations. Furthermore, since the attainment of considerable insight by the patient is not always a practical desideratum, the therapist gives fewer interpretations to the alcoholic than to some other types of patients. Often the management of these patients in the hospital requires some firmness. There should be no vacillation in this regard, and after an explanation to the patient the attitude of firmness should be pursued with consistency, the therapist being careful never to become moralistic or punitive. An austere bearing is to be avoided in practically all cases. A smile or a laugh can go much further toward establishing friendly feelings than a countenance of unmitigated reserve. Whatever else he may be, the therapist nearly always represents a figure of authority, and as such he is in a strategic position to dispense approval and acceptance. Above all—and the validity of this statement is not impaired by its triteness—the psychiatrist must be a warmly human individual.

By no means can all alcoholics be treated by this approach. Those with more or less pronounced psychotic trends, those for whom alcohol is the last resort before a much more devastating psychiatric illness, those who have no real motivation, and those who are fixated at a stage where their narcissism is so marked that object relationships can be established only with great difficulty—these probably can but rarely benefit by the use of such a method. Those most accessible are the ones suffering from either a neurosis or a neurotic character disorder in which alcoholism is a habitually prominent symptom. The most significant prognostic indication seems to be the degree of reality-testing that the patient displays. It has been observed that the outcome of therapy is generally poor in the case of those alcoholics who, despite the hard fact that their relationships with their family and associates are markedly deteriorated, that their financial condition is poor, and that they face a quite strenuous struggle in the attempt to rehabilitate themselves, can still blithely assert that the rainbow's gold is but a few steps away. Such a pronounced utilization of denial by these patients makes it necessary to view them as having regressed to the stage of at least a partial belief in their omnipotence—which, being indicative of a much weakened ego, augurs unfavorably.

The case material for this article comes from the "alcoholic" ward of the Winter Veterans Administration Hospital. An excellent description of this ward and its program has been given in another publication (4). The following is a summary of a case in which a definite conversion, presumably springing from a positive transference, was readily apparent.

Case Report

The patient was the youngest son of hard-working, rigid, German immigrant parents, and recalled but little pleasure in his childhood and youth. Although his family was of moderate means he was forced to work hard on the farm, receiving no praise for a job well done, and much censure for one poorly done. As a child he was "the runt," and the butt of his older brother's jibes. As he grew older he sought attention through athletic feats, but these evoked only scoffing from his parents. He soon turned to committing minor misdemeanors, and instead of receiving notice for socially acceptable acts, he obtained notoriety. After graduating from high school he worked as a clerk and occasionally did bookkeeping. Although he was intelligent and diligent, his jobs were always short-lived because of his irascibility; the pattern that he was establishing was one of a brief satisfactory progress, ended abruptly by an inappropriate outburst of anger directed at his employer for some real or fancied minor injustice. In the Air Corps, in World War II, his adjustment seemed satisfactory until he was "washed out" of cadet training for reasons which were unknown to him. Shortly thereafter he was in a jeep accident, in which he sustained lacerations of the face. His drinking, which previously had been within socially acceptable limits, now became more pronounced. He also became more irascible, felt that his Commanding Officer was treating him unjustly, and developed headaches, backaches, insomnia, restlessness, anorexia, and a general feeling of dissatisfaction. Eventually he was hospitalized and given a medical discharge with the diagnosis of anxiety reaction.

For the next 3 years this embittered, complaining man was unable to work except for short periods of time; drank excessively, with few days of sobriety; sometimes wrote worthless checks; and was sustained principally by the financial support and care given by his wife. He had entered this hospital twice before the last admission; during his two earlier hospitalizations he had become dissatisfied with the treatment received and left against medical advice after short stays. During his last hospital stay he was transferred to the alcoholic ward after several episodes of intoxication on another ward.

Physically, he was of medium size, appearing to be about his stated age of 36 years. He complained often and at length of headaches, backaches, irritability and insomnia, and thought that these symptoms were referable to some obscure but grave organic disorder. His drinking he explained as a necessary evil to relieve these symptoms. For about 10 days he continued to complain at every opportunity, was invariably sullen and sarcastic, demanded medical or surgical attention, and alienated several of the other patients by his irascibility. During the third office interview he delivered himself of a long tirade of hostility and ended by saying, "I guess you think I'm just a chronic complainer." He was then told that since physical and laboratory examinations had failed to disclose any basis for his complaints, the examiner felt that his symptoms were probably mainly due to emotional factors. A brief explanation was given him as to how such factors could give rise to symptoms, and he was assured that the reality of such symptoms was not in question. He was told, further, that although the examiner was willing to take cognizance of the symptoms as such, he was nevertheless rather weary of functioning as a sounding board and could perhaps be of greater service to the patient by investigating the cause of the symptoms.

The description of what followed is necessarily inadequate, but the therapist had a vivid impression that the patient's attitude underwent a transformation within a few minutes—this was certainly not an anticipated reaction. He smiled sheepishly, appeared a bit uncertain of just what he was trying to express, and then, with no trace of his former hostility, began to speak of his earlier frustrations with his parents, employers and Commanding Officer. From then on a change was apparent; he became more sociable, his somatic complaints disappeared in 2 weeks, and he became a willing participant in ward activities. Simultaneously, a genuinely warm relationship with the examiner became evident. Later interviews, totalling about 12 hours, were filled with an elaboration of his excessive hostility toward his parents and brother, and some attempt was made to enable him to understand that he was repeating these patterns with his employers and associates. Still later he was given passes to seek employment, and was proud of himself when he succeeded in obtaining a good job. During the 9 months which have elapsed since his discharge he has not had a single drink, he has been promoted several times at his job, and both he and his wife are happier than they have been in years. He maintains regular contact with the examiner, calling him about once a month merely to say "Hello" or to report concerning his job, his proposed new car, or his wife's health.

In this case, it seems that any real insight attained was minimal and that few, if any, emotional conflicts were actually worked through. I believe that the change in behavior took place because of a highly significant emotional experience, and that the principal instrument of this experience was the third office interview. The patient, by his provocative behavior, was inviting retaliation which would confirm his feeling of rejection; when this retaliation did not ensue he was dumbfounded. The warm relationship that he was then able to develop served as the basis for the furtherance of his successful extramural adjustments. He does not yet, however, feel able to get along without this acceptance, and must be reassured monthly that it actually exists. Certainly in the majority of cases no such clear-cut conversion will be apparent. The experiences of the author indicate, however, that the "something" that happens when the alcoholic quits drinking is probably closely related to, if not identical with, such a conversion process, either in its surprising clarity or (as more often happens) in a more attenuated and therefore less clearly discernible form.

Further observations are needed to confirm the views advanced in this communication; the cases studied have been too few to allow statistical analysis, nor has enough time elapsed for the full evaluation of the status of former patients. If these views can be validated, the treatment of alcoholism, and particularly its short-term therapy, might be furthered by the finding of the common basis of divergent methods of treatment.

REFERENCES

1. Tiebout, H. M. The act of surrender in the therapeutic process, with special reference to alcoholism. Quart. J. Stud. Alc. 10: 48–58, 1949.
2. Personal communications from M. J. Hornowski and E. H. Knight.
3. Devereux, G. The function of alcohol in Mohave society. Quart. J. Stud. Alc. 9: 207–51, 1948.
4. Haber, S., A. Paley, and A. Block. Treatment of problem drinkers at Winter Veterans Administration Hospital. Bull. Menninger Clin. 13: 24–30, 1949.

14. The Personality of the Alcoholic as an Impediment to Psychotherapy

Melvin L. Selzer

PSYCHIATRISTS are often censured for their reluctance to treat alcoholic patients. This reluctance, if not outright refusal, is found throughout the medical profession. Although it has been discussed (1) and psychiatrists are generally pessimistic about the results of psychotherapy for the alcoholic (2), relatively little has appeared regarding the feelings that the alcoholic engenders in those attempting to treat him with psychotherapy. The purpose of this paper is to point out incompatibilities which are often present between the alcoholic's personality and treatment demands on the one hand, and the value systems and therapeutic expectations of the psychotherapist on the other.

Given the behavior and personality of many alcoholics, and statements in the literature about the attributes which the psychotherapist who treats the alcoholic is *supposed* to have, one is left to wonder if psychotherapy alone can be the treatment of choice for alcoholism. Indeed, there is some evidence that psychotherapy by itself has yielded less worth-while results with alcoholic patients than have other treatment methods (3, 4).

The alcoholic has been variously described as dependent, hostile, provocative, suspicious, manipulative, egocentric, depressed, and self-destructive. To cope with this formidable array, the psychotherapist who treats the alcoholic is told he may have "no hidden or overtly critical attitude toward the symptoms" (5), be "protective, understanding, accepting, regardless of how the alcoholic is behaving" (6), and have "no appreciable degree of difficulty in the healthy management of his own hostility" (7). The psychotherapist is also cautioned that he will experience many frustrations in treating alcoholics, but must nevertheless establish a positive, warm relationship with the patient (6). One wonders if psychotherapy for the alcoholic often falls short of its goal because of the difficulty, if not impossibility, of maintaining these benign attitudes in the face of the alcoholic's psychopathology and behavior. Is it possible that when treating the alcoholic, the physician is often thrust into

Reprinted by permission from *Psychiatric Quarterly* 41 (1967): 38–45. Copyright © Human Sciences Press, Inc.

confrontations that do such violence to his own concepts of right and wrong that the feelings evoked make effective psychotherapy unlikely?

In an earlier paper on psychotherapy for alcoholism, the author attributed the psychotherapist's hostility toward his patient entirely to the therapist's counter-transference feelings and unrealistic expectations regarding his patient (8). Briefly re-stated, these feelings were: (a) unconscious envy of the hedonistic aspects of the alcoholic's behavior, and (b) a tendency to regard the patient's relapses as the therapist's personal failures. In retrospect, these views appear valid but limited, because any discussion of the hostility engendered in others by the alcoholic patient must include consideration of the provocative personality and behavior of many alcoholics.

THE ALCOHOLIC PERSONALITY AND PSYCHOTHERAPY

As noted earlier, a plethora of adjectives are used to describe the alcoholic's psychological deviations which lie predominantly in four areas. These are dependency, egocentricity, depression, and hostility (9). Although discussed separately in this paper, these traits are, of course, intimately related.

Dependency

The least obviously provocative trait encountered in the alcoholic is also the most difficult to deal with in psychotherapy. Some idea of how burdensome the alcoholic's dependency can be to the therapist is gained from the vivid terminology clinicians use to describe this aspect of the alcoholic patient's personality: terms like "infantile," "greedy," "sucking," and "insatiable" appear in the literature and certainly suggest strong feelings and attitudes toward the alcoholic patient.

The alcoholic's dependency poses a formidable therapeutic barrier for many reasons, but not least for its effect upon the therapist. Halpern (10) has pointed out that the alcoholic is satisfied with the passive role in the majority of instances and seeks a passive way of handling his difficulties, a way that will put the problem entirely in someone else's hands. This is explicitly stated by other investigators: ". . . the alcoholic manifests dependency needs in the sense of wanting some authority figure, parental figure, or surrogate to take over the responsibility of guiding him, directing him, and making decisions for him" (11). Once the alcoholic has placed himself in the care of a therapist, the doctor becomes that authority figure and the alcoholic often settles down to the grim business of thwarting the therapist's efforts, since the patient cannot tolerate the threatened loss of dependency. The therapist, in turn, attempts to deal with the patient's pathological dependence in a manner dictated by his professional training and personal experience. Regardless of the approach he uses, whether it is to interpret the dependency, point it out to the patient, or indulge the patient's demands, the chances are that initially the patient's dependency will increase or remain static. Hence, the alcoholic's demands, which can be quite subtle and non-verbal, will continue to exert pressure on the therapist. The patient's persistent orientation to the therapist as a provider of something which he is unable to provide engenders both anger and discomfort in the therapist. Granted that therapists with unresolved dependency needs may succumb more readily to anger in the face of the alcoholic's persistent seeking for an all-giving, all-sacrificing parent, can any therapist remain free of exasperation in the face of constant demand and rebuke? The following case illustrates problems posed by the alcoholic's demanding and dependent behavior.[1]

A., a 37-year-old alcoholic salesman, was admitted to the psychiatric services of University Hospital directly from jail where he was serving a sentence for driving while intoxicated. Before admission, he discussed his severe alcohol problem frankly and intelligently, acknowledging that his illness had made a shambles of his social and economic life. He was genuinely interested in arranging for his admission. After several days, it became apparent to the patient that his psychotherapist expected him to play an active role in his rehabilitation. The patient, who had started complaining of mild pain in his left wrist during his third hospital day, thereupon began to complain much more vehemently about the pain and was referred to the orthopedic clinic. A diagnosis of a mild arthritic condition was made, the wrist was placed in a cast and analgesic medication was prescribed.

Despite this, the patient's demands that something more be done about his wrist pain became increasingly strident and manipulative. He felt he was being medically neglected and it was impossible to satisfy his demands for more than a few hours at a time. He loudly informed anyone who would listen that the ward was run by a bunch of quacks, and that if his doctor weren't careful, he would find himself involved in a malpractice suit. To make matters worse, the patient's pain seemed of dubious authenticity because it appeared to fluctuate with the different situations in which the patient found himself. The resident psychotherapist attempted to remain objective but it was apparent that he was becoming increasingly angry about the patient's slanderous statements and unprovoked attacks upon him. Ultimately, the therapist, perhaps too guilty about his resentment of the patient, decathected the treatment situation and became increasingly indifferent toward the patient and his demands.

Reference is frequently made to the alcoholic's vulnerability to frustration. Yet we ignore the fact that the therapist also has a frustration threshold. When this is exceeded, he can no longer function in an optimal way and successful psychotherapy becomes less likely. The overdependent, demanding patient can provoke considerable anxiety, and ultimately frustration and irritation in the therapist. It is the persistently dependent patient who most readily arouses the psychotherapist's doubts about his abilities. It would be helpful to acknowledge that such patients threaten his need to be successful, fully recognizing that the patient's illness plays an important role in this threat.

Egocentricity

The alcoholic has been succinctly described as selfish and infinitely more concerned with his own real or imaginary needs than about the happiness and well-being of those about him (11). This description barely conveys how devastating the alcoholic's selfishness can be to those persons who must look to him to meet their needs.

B. was an alcoholic who often boasted about his four children. Otherwise, he hardly recognized their existence, harshly insisted that they make no demands of him; while he demanded they stay out of his way when he was feeling irascible—which was virtually all the time that he was at home. He was inconsistent in his demands, often administered cruel beatings which were unprovoked, and was proud of his callousness and coldness toward them. He rarely exerted himself to do anything for any member of his family, but nevertheless demanded displays of loyalty from them.

How does this interaction in the family life of the alcoholic affect the psychotherapist? Is it possible to listen to a story of emotional deprivation and psychological mutilation, particularly where the victims are small children, without negative feelings? There are limits to human objectivity, and it may be asking too much of any therapist that he remain "accepting" in the face of behavior that would normally evoke anger toward the patient and sympathy for the patient's victims. (Indeed, the author does not believe he would like to see psychotherapists who remain unmoved by such events.) Admittedly, the case cited is extreme, but egocentricity and narcissism to a pathological degree are present in many alcoholics. Their families almost always suffer because of it, and this must be recognized as an important factor that can negatively influence the therapist's feelings.

(There is an unfortunate tendency to label all of a psychotherapist's feelings about his patients as "counter-transference," particularly when these feelings are negative. The term counter-transference should be reserved for those irrational feelings of the therapist which are the result of repressed psychic phenomena originating in the therapist's own life. To illustrate the misuse of this term, let us say the patient abuses the therapist and the therapist becomes angry at him. Is this necessarily counter-transference? The anger here may be a realistic response and we need not conjure up unconscious displacements to explain it. Although the alcoholic may not directly abuse the therapist, his verbal and psychic assault on others can be provocative.)

Depression: The Suicide Threat

The self-destructive tendency of alcoholic populations is well documented with a suicide frequency ranging from 7 per cent to 21 per cent (12). If one includes alcoholics who are often seriously preoccupied with thoughts of suicide, the figure rises to 50 per cent (13).

What is the potential effect of chronic depression, suicide preoccupation, and suicide threat upon the therapist? In a frank paper, Tabachnick (14) points out that the suicide attempt or threat is often a manipulative and demanding action—as well as a rebuke to the therapist which implies that the therapist has failed in his job: "What more signal sign of failure . . . than the patient's announcing a decision to end his life?" The therapist often senses the patient's anger and rejection in the suicide threat and may respond negatively and nontherapeutically.

Even if the therapist does not respond negatively, treating a seriously suicidal out-patient can be a severe drain on the therapist's psychic energy. Knowing this, the depressed alcoholic patient may refuse hospitalization with the result that a disproportionate amount of the therapist's time is devoted to preventing the patient's demise. Here the therapist's anxiety may impede an objective approach to the patient's illness.

Hostility

Since the alcoholic's insatiable oral demands cannot be gratified, the resultant feelings of deprivation leave him chronically angry at the world and its inhabitants. Usually too fearful and guilt-ridden to express his anger overtly, his behavior is often unconsciously designed to provoke negative feelings and retaliation (15). If he can succeed in making others retaliate, the alcoholic can be angry at them without realizing his own provocative role. His guilt feelings are thus minimized or avoided. Chafetz and Demone (15) acknowledge that "few human beings can long endure alone the pressures, hostility, and acting out of conflicts of alcoholics."

Patients' provocative hostility may emerge in any psychotherapeutic situation and is not unique to the psychotherapy of alcoholics. However, the alcoholic's provocation often manifests itself in ways that are incompatible with successful psychotherapy. The most common and, of course, most disruptive form of hostile acting out occurs when the alcoholic terminates therapy prematurely—often before it has really begun. Less drastic variants are missing appointments or appearing for interviews in a highly intoxicated state. Too impulse-ridden to control his acting out, the alcoholic, during psychotherapy, may proceed to create even more havoc than usual in many areas of his life, thus forcing the therapist to spend considerable time in the discussion of "current events." This can effectively block any insightful exploration of the patient's emotional life. Another form of provocation is the alcoholic's vehement denial of the seriousness of his drinking problem. It can be exasperating to attempt treating an individual while simultaneously trying to convince him he has the illness for which the therapist is supposed to be treating him.

To treat the alcoholic, it may be necessary to recognize and accept one's anger at the patient. Conversely, it is inimical to the treatment process to pretend good-humored acceptance of the alcoholic's vexatious and destructive verbalization or behavior (16). The therapist will be unable to cope with his own feelings, or with his patient, if he attempts to be warm and giving in such situations. He must recognize his own anger as a logical response if impossible demands are made and share this recognition with the alcoholic patient.

DISCUSSION

It is obvious that when one discusses "alcoholics," he is describing a group of people encountered in his own professional experience who may differ markedly from alcoholic groups found in other settings. A description of alcoholics treated by a psychiatrist in private practice may bear little resemblance to alcoholics seen in a state mental hospital. The remarks in this paper are based largely on observations made of the treatment of alcoholics in state-financed hospitals and clinics. Most of these patients were classified as having character disorders in addition to their addiction to alcohol. Many alcoholics seen in these settings lack motivation for overcoming their alcohol problems, have difficulty relating to the psychotherapist, and not infrequently regard their alcoholism as an impersonal accident.

Although psychotherapy alone does not constitute effective treatment for most alcoholics, it nevertheless remains an invaluable treatment modality when used in conjunction with other therapies.

SUMMARY

The personality traits and behavior of the alcoholic patient and their role in provoking negative feelings in the psychotherapist are major factors in the reluctance of mental health personnel to accept alcoholic patients for psychotherapy, and in the persistent failure of psychotherapy alone to become a significantly successful form of treatment for alcoholism. When used in conjunction with other types of treatment, psychotherapy remains a useful approach to the rehabilitation of the alcoholic.

NOTES

1. The case material in this paper is drawn primarily from observations made while supervising the psychotherapeutic work of psychiatric residents. This offered the possibility of observing both the behavior of the alcoholic patient and the attempts of the resident therapist to deal with the feelings aroused within him by the patient.

REFERENCES

1. *Strauss, R. Medical practice and the alcoholic.* Ann. Am. Acad. Polit. Soc. Sci., *315: 40–47, 1958.*
2. *Hayman, M. Current attitudes to alcoholism of psychiatrists in Southern California.* Am. J. Psychiat., *112: 485–493, 1956.*
3. *Moore, R. A. Who is qualified to treat the alcoholic?* Quart. J. Stud. Alc., *24: 712–718, 1963.*
4. *Gerald, D. L.; Saenger, G.; and Wile, R. The abstinent alcoholic.* Arch. Gen. Psychiat., *6: 83–95, 1962.*
5. *Powdermaker, F. The relation between the alcoholic and the physician.* Quart. J. Stud. Alc., *5: 245–249, 1944.*
6. *Chafetz, M. E. Practical and theoretical considerations in the psychotherapy of alcoholism.* Quart. J. Stud. Alc., *20: 281–291, 1959.*
7. *Graves, J. H. Suicide, murder and psychosis in relation to alcoholism. 26th International Congress of Alcohol and Alcoholism. Stockholm, Sweden. 1960.*

8. Selzer, M. L. *Hostility as a barrier to therapy in alcoholism.* Psychiat. Quart., *31:* 301–305, 1957.

9. Zwirling, I., and Rosenbaum, M. *Alcohol addiction and personality (nonpsychotic conditions).* In: American Handbook of Psychiatry. *Silvano Arieti, editor. Basic Books. New York. 1959.*

10. Halpern, F. *Studies of compulsive drinkers. Psychological Test Results.* Quart. J. Stud. Alc., *6: 468, 1946.*

11. Korman, M., and Stubblefield, R. L. *Definition of alcoholism.* J.A.M.A., *178:* 1184–1186, 1961.

12. Kessel, N., and Grossman, G. *Suicide in alcoholics.* Brit. Med. J., *2., 1671–1672, 1961.*

13. Selzer, M. L., and Payne, C. E.: *Automobile accidents, suicide and unconscious motivation.* Am. J. Psychiat., *119: 237–240, 1962.*

14. Tobachnick, N. *Counter-transference crisis in suicidal attempts.* Arch. Gen. Psychiat., *4: 572–578, 1961.*

15. Chafetz, M. E., and Demone, H. W.: Alcoholism and Society. *Oxford University Press. New York. 1962.*

16. Moore, R. A. *Reaction-formation as a counter-transference phenomenon in the treatment of alcoholism.* Quart. J. Stud. Alc., *22: 481–486, 1961.*

15. Transference Phenomena in the Treatment of Addictive Illness: Love and Hate in Methadone Maintenance

Virginia Davidson

INTRODUCTION

Wilfred Bion observed that "society, like the individual, may not want to deal with its stresses by psychological means until driven to do so by a realization that at least some of its distresses are psychological in origin" (Bion 1959). After more than a decade of experience in methadone maintenance, there is now widespread acknowledgment—even if it is belated, often grudging, and sometimes obscure—that attempts to treat heroin addiction by chemical means alone have failed. This admission of failure has crept stealthily into the literature, seemingly unnoticed at any given time because of the lack of emphasis on its presence. Terms such as "ancillary services," "social, personal, or vocational rehabilitation," and "supportive counseling" camouflage the fact that some meaningful psychological intervention has to take place in the treatment of addicted patients, or they will relapse to heroin use. Each time we read these phrases, we assume we know what they mean. They are as expectable by now, and are about as brief and meaningful as the complimentary close at the end of a business letter. Recent, typical examples from the March 1976 *Archives of General Psychiatry* include this statement from one author's summary about the effectiveness of the narcotic antagonists (Meyer et al. 1976): "Blocking drugs may be very usefully applied as *adjuncts* [italics mine] to psychologic intervention." From another article (Goldstein 1976) in the same journal we learn that: "Alternative satisfactions have to be developed to substitute for those previously obtained from heroin. Experiences that are better and more satisfying than heroin use have to be built into a new behavioral repertoire. Self-image has to be improved, a new sense of worth has to be developed." The author goes on to say that *without*

From *NIDA Research Monograph* 12 (1977): 118–25.

this accomplishment, relapse to heroin use is virtually certain. Who with experience in treating addicts would disagree with such a sensible observation? Yet there is little in the literature of the treatment of the addictions which indicates that we understand what such claims imply about the necessity for accomplishing such massive personality change in addicted patients.

If the allegations are taken seriously that psychologic intervention will be necessary in conjunction with whatever chemical remedy is offered to treat addictive illness, it is curious that no coherent body of literature has developed that addresses the problems of psychologic treatment even after there is agreement that it is necessary.

Rather, the introduction of each new chemical is associated with an eagerness to discard the previous experience gained concerning the need for psychologic intervention, and hope emerges for a brief time that the new drug alone will produce a cure. This cycle has operated through the introduction of methadone, long-acting methadone, and each one of the narcotic antagonists, by turns. The wish to locate the cure for addictive illness *outside* the patient's psyche is obviously very strong in the persons who have been engaged in drug abuse research and treatment over the past 10 years. It probably exists in a stronger form only in the addicted patient him- or herself, where it is called "denial." Yet it is interesting to note that the same process exists in patients and researchers alike, though with perhaps varying degrees of intensity.

BACKGROUND

In this paper I shall describe certain recurring patterns of behavior which I observed in methadone maintenance patients during a 34-month period I worked in the setting of a methadone maintenance clinic. I shall relate these patterns to the descriptions in the psychoanalytic literature of ego defense mechanisms, and draw certain parallels between the behavior I observed in the clinic setting with the descriptions of transference phenomena which have been observed in the psychoanalysis of patients with so-called borderline personality organization (Kernberg 1975). Other writers, notably Khantzian, Mack, and Schatzberg (1974) and Vaillant (1975) have called attention to the primitive nature of the defenses in addicted patients. The defenses which Vaillant refers to as "immature"—splitting, denial, and projective identification—correspond to those which characterize patients with borderline personality organization, best described by Otto Kernberg (1975). Khantzian, in his study, notes an *absence* of neurotic defenses in his patients, but does not go on to describe the existence of more archaic patterns. Leon Wurmser (1974) has added much to the understanding of compulsive drug use by relating it to "narcissistic crises" in the lives of the individual drug abusers. Wurmser states that he has never seen a compulsive drug abuser who was not emotionally deeply disturbed, and he links this disturbance to the borderline type of psychopathology. In spite of observations such as these by persons who have had considerable experience in treating addicted patients in individual psychotherapy, most of the psychological treatment of addicts will be left to those persons in the treatment hierarchy who have the least knowledge and experience in psychotherapy. There are no serious attempts to gain—for addicts—access to the best forms of psychotherapy available, partly because of the process that involves denying that addictive illness has psychological origins, but also because of the extremely trying nature of therapy with borderline patients (Leibovich 1975; Pines 1975), even if they are not addicted to heroin.

TRANSFERENCE PHENOMENA AND COUNTERTRANSFERENCE BEHAVIOR

Transference is a term which implies that the patient's behavior at a given moment in treatment is determined more by his very early experiences with significant others than by the reality stimulus of the present setting.

I use the term transference phenomena to refer to observable patterns of behavior in patients' transactions with clinic staff members and the clinic itself, as well as in their relationships with individual therapists. Whenever there are rapid shifts in the way patients perceive others, whenever strong affective states such as love or hatred are predominant (and especially when there is rapid alternation between the two), and whenever there is a powerful projection of hostile, aggressive impulses from the patient to someone else, it is safe to say that transference phenomena are present. These responses I have just described are not perceived by the patient as being unusual or strange, in fact they are natural for him or her, and characterize the styles of relating to others that he/she has developed from early life.

Countertransference, as used in this paper, will refer to the totality of the therapist's response to the patient. It includes reality factors such as the setting and the working alliance with the patient, plus the internal response of the therapist to the patient.

CHARACTERISTIC PATTERNS OF BEHAVIOR IN THE CLINIC AND RELATED MANAGEMENT PROBLEMS

The behavior of methadone patients in the clinic setting is remarkable in several respects, when compared with the behavior of other groups of psychiatric patients whose treatment utilizes the outpatient clinic format. I shall focus on three major observable differences in the clinic behavior of methadone patients, and comment on the kinds of difficulties each one presents for staff management in the outpatient methadone maintenance clinic. I believe that these patterns of behavior are roughly equivalent to the ego defense mechanisms of splitting, projective identification, and denial, which have been described in the psychoanalytic literature dealing with the treatment of borderline patients (Kernberg 1975), even though the behavior described is occurring in the context of an outpatient clinic.

1. Analogous to splitting are *manifestations in the clinic setting of extreme affects,* which appear to be inappropriate to the reality stimulus of the moment. These affective states are usually characterized by extreme rage; for example, murderous hatred can be expressed by a patient toward a dispensing nurse who does not ready the medication as soon as the patient expects it. This expression of rage is limited to the situation in which it emerged—the patient does not carry the feeling over to everyone else he/she encounters. Feelings of contrition and remorse are likely to follow closely the expression of hatred and rage. What is familiar to workers in methadone is the rapidity with which patients can oscillate between extreme states of feeling. The patient has diminished capacity to modulate feelings, so must swing back and forth between strong positive and strong negative affects.

Problems for staff in relating to this aspect of the addicted patient's personality are enormous. Expression of strong hostility, anger, and blamefulness in patients arouses equally powerful emotions in staff, whose most common response is to retaliate—overtly or covertly—against the patient. In physicians, this is most commonly expressed through the dosage of methadone, since this is the powerful medium through which most patient contacts occur. All of us know patients who manage to alienate the staff one by one, then find themselves removed from the program for violations of one sort or another. The staff is usually not aware of this process, and will deny—if asked—feeling hostility and suppressed rage toward the patient. In a well-run program this process of retaliation against the patient can be minimized by enlightened supervision, ideally by someone *outside* the treatment system.

Related to retaliation as a means of coping with the patient's tendency to experience strong emotions separately and intensely (splitting), is pairing. Patients "select" a staff member with whom they establish a dependent, demanding, and clinging relationship. Few negative emotions are channeled into this relationship, but rather are expressed in strong dislikes for and refusals to deal with other staff. The "chosen" staff person becomes the patient's advocate in all matters relating to progress and performance, and may at times jealously protect the patient from having contact with other staff. While patient-staff pairing is less destructive than retaliation, in that it allows some patients to remain in treatment through thick and thin, it cannot be therapeutic for the patient unless it carries some generalizability to other relationships. As long as the therapist is obtaining gratification from the "specialness" of the relationship, this is not likely to occur.

2. Analogous to projective identification is the *expectation on the part of patients that they will be unfairly dealt with by treatment personnel, and an associated tendency to perceive the external environment as hostile and threatening,* regardless of what the actual circumstances are. Because of the fact that addicts live dangerous lives in their search for drugs, and because they are frequently incarcerated or are being implicated in criminal activities, we assume it is reasonable for them to behave in a suspicious, guarded, and untrusting manner when they come to treatment. While this kind of explanation might possibly account for the addict's initial problems in relating to the staff, it cannot begin to account for the persistent incapacities in forming trusting relationships that exist for years after the patient has begun treatment.

For any staff, the task of providing the qualities that are necessary for a therapeutic alliance to be established with the patient is difficult when the patient's problems are manifest in qualities that appear to make this primary task impossible. Staff members, to be effective, must maintain the capacity to be empathic toward the patient; the patient, however, behaves in such a way toward "helping" people that this empathic quality in staff is always undermined and jeopardized. All therapists must maintain a sense of their own worth and value; they must have self-esteem and a sense that the work they do with patients "matters." Yet when the patient's style of relating involves projecting onto others the intensely aggressive, hostile, and negative impulses felt inside, the other person (in this case, the therapist) receives constant messages that he/she is being aggressive, hostile, and unsympathetic toward the patient. In my experience, most methadone patients are not capable of distinguishing the origin of these hostile impulses except after years of exposure to a person who can remain relatively neutral in the face of these sorts of accusations.

With therapeutic problems of this magnitude, not to become locked into an equally hostile countertransference relationship is a monumental task for the best-trained and most talented of therapists; for the untrained, unskilled, and uninitiated, it is virtually impossible.

3. *Denial of entire segments of reality, especially involving behavior concerning drug usage* is typical; related forms of denial are evident in the need patients demonstrate to appear impervious to the impact methadone maintenance has on their lives. Patients commonly express the belief that *they* are in control of their drug usage—they maintain that they will be able to withdraw from methadone at a future time of their own choosing, even after previous attempts have resulted in quick relapse to heroin. Years of compulsive drug use have not altered the psychic reality of many patients— namely, disbelief in the reality of the psychologic component of their addictive illness. Denial of feelings of anxiety and depression in addicted patients has been discussed by other writers (Vaillant 1975), as well as the return of these feelings during attempted withdrawal from methadone and the necessity for psychological support during withdrawal (Chappel et al. 1973; Lowinson and Langrod 1973). Denial, in the psychological sense, is most often confused by staff with conscious lying and manipulation. While addicted patients certainly have in common with other patients the habits of lying and manipulation, it is impressive to what extent the latter explanations are used by staff members to account for patients' behavior.

The gruff, loud, and complaining behavior that patients exhibit toward appointments often covers up the desperate fear these patients have about emotional contact with another person. Their apparent superficial involvement in counseling is often interpreted by staff as "low motivation." Grumbling about having to keep appointments, complaints about the time lost in the clinic, and especially assertions that the counseling relationship is a waste of time, may mask the patient's terror of involvement.

Many times I have had the experience of hearing vituperative protests from patients that keeping their appointment with me would cause them to be fired from the job; that they simply could not afford the time to discuss their medication, and so on. Yet these same patients, once in the office, shed their belligerence like an unwanted skin, and want to discuss more than their medication. So what masquerades as a devil-may-care attitude toward the clinic frequently represents massive denial of the importance of the clinic in the patient's life. Sometimes only during withdrawal from methadone does this attachment to the clinic enter the patient's awareness.

CONCLUSION

By describing typical patterns of behavior that can be observed in methadone maintenance patients in the outpatient clinic setting, I have attempted to demonstrate that this behavior is markedly different from that observed in other groups of psychiatric patients who are treated in outpatient clinics. Much of the "difficult" behavior is often seen as part of a constellation of undesirable social characteristics attributed to addicted patients. Staff may try to eradicate this behavior (usually through elaboration and enforcement of clinic rules) with the associated hope that the patient will become more compliant, and then amenable to therapy. This is somewhat akin to stating that if the patient did not have psychological problems he/she would be easier to treat.

I am suggesting that the behavior we see in the patient *is* the manifestation of his/her problems in living, and not an artifact of either the clinic setting or of the addicted patient's sociocultural background. This behavior makes sense, so to speak, if it is related to the ego defense mechanisms which have been delineated in the psychoanalytic study of borderline patients. The problems which this behavior presents for the outpatient psychotherapy of addicted patients are considerable, as I have attempted to show, and are similar to the problems encountered whenever the treatment of any borderline patient is undertaken. Understanding why (and when) patients establish negative transferences can lead to effective management, and to the prevention of transference psychoses, which are not infrequent in this population of patients. It is crucial to protect and nurture the positive transference relationships that develop; for many patients it is easier first to establish a positive bond with the clinic than with a counselor. Whenever clinics are structured in such a way that this is an unreasonable expectation, treatment prospects remain glum.

REFERENCES

Bion, W. Experiences in Groups, *New York: Basic Books, 1959. p. 22.*
Chappel, J.; Skolnick, V.; and Senay, E. *Techniques of withdrawal from methadone and their outcome over six months to two years.* Proceedings of the 5th National

Conference on Methadone Treatment, *Washington, D.C., 1973, pp. 482–489.*

Goldstein, A. *Heroin addiction.* Arc Gen Psychiatry, *33(3): 353–358, 1976.*

Jackman, J. *A hypothesis concerning the difficulty of withdrawal from maintenance of methadone.* Proceedings of the 5th National Conference on Methadone Treatment, *Washington, D.C., 1973, pp. 471–475.*

Kernberg, O. Borderline Conditions and Pathological Narcissism. *New York: Jason Aronson, 1975.*

Khantzian, E.; Mack, J.; and Schatzberg, A. *Heroin use as an attempt to cope: Clinical observations.* Am J Psychiatry, *131(2): 160–164, 1974.*

Leibovich, M. *An aspect of the psychotherapy of borderline personalities.* Psychother Psychosom, *25: 53–57, 1975.*

Lowinson, J., and Langrod, J. *Detoxification of long-term methadone patients.* Proceedings of the 5th National Conference on Methadone Treatment, *Washington, D.C., 1973. pp. 256–261.*

Meyer, R.; Mirin, S.; Altman, J.; and McNamee, B. *A behavioral paradigm for the evaluation of narcotic antagonists.* Arch Gen Psychiatry, *33: 371–377, 1976.*

Pines, M. *Borderline personality organization.* Psychother Psychosom, *25: 58–62, 1975.*

Vaillant, G. *Sociopathy as a human process.* Arch Gen Psychiatry, *32: 178–183, 1975.*

Wurmser, L. *Psychoanalytic considerations of the etiology of compulsive drug use.* J Am Psychoanal Assoc, *22: 4, 820–843, 1974.*

16. Countertransferential and Attitudinal Considerations in the Treatment of Drug Abuse and Addiction

John Imhof, Robert Hirsch, and Rickard E. Terenzi

INTRODUCTION

Within the past 50 years, a vast amount of literature has explored the issue of drug abuse and addiction from a variety of distinct vantage points: etiologic, demographic, criminological, socioeconomic, and psychological causation. In addition, a significant degree of attention has been given to the myriad of treatment approaches dealing with drug abuse and addiction. For example, Lettieri, Sayers, and Pearson (1980) have detailed 43 separate and distinct theories of drug abuse, just one indicator of the disparities inherent in the management and treatment of the drug-involved individual. Furthermore, Austin, Macari, and Lettieri (1979) have summarized 1,326 major research and treatment studies, while Dupont, Goldstein, and O'Donnell (1979) have developed an extensive guide and handbook for drug abuse treatment practitioners. Yet in the majority of all treatises reviewed, scant attention is given to one factor that may affect the positive or negative outcome of any treatment provided: the countertransferential and attitudinal posture of the treatment provider. While outcome studies in drug abuse (Anderson, O'Malley, and Lazare, 1972; Renner and Rubin, 1973; Simpson and Savage, 1980) point to either the failure of the treatment methodology itself or to lack of motivation on the part of the patient, all major reviews consistently omit the role of the therapist.

The therapist in a position to provide a particular treatment and/or rehabilitative service to a drug-involved patient may, in fact, possess such a significant amount of negative feelings and/or attitudes, whether conscious or

Reprinted by permission from *International Journal of the Addictions* 18, no. 4 (1983). Copyright © Marcel Dekker, Inc.

unconscious, that any hope for objective and effective diagnosis and treatment becomes diminished, if not completely eliminated. It is not the purpose of this treatise to offer a complete review of the topic of countertransference and its evolutionary history. Rather, this paper seeks to explore the concept of countertransference specifically in relation to its presence, utilization, and impact in the evaluation, diagnosis, and therapeutic management of the drug-involved patient.

For the purposes of this presentation, "countertransference" is conceptualized as the total emotional reaction of the therapist to the patient, with consideration of the entire range of conscious, preconscious, and unconscious attitudes, beliefs, and feelings in the therapist who comes in contact with a psychiatric patient who is also a drug abuser. "Therapist" is defined as any individual charged with the professional responsibility of providing drug abuse treatment and rehabilitation services to a drug-involved individual. Such a category would essentially include psychiatric social workers, psychologists, psychiatrists, psychiatric nurses, and former substance abusers, commonly referred to as "ex-addict counselors."

In summary therefore, this paper seeks to present the following:

1. A brief overview of the pertinent literature related to countertransference in the treatment of drug abuse and addiction
2. A discussion of the drug-involved patient as a psychiatric patient, with special consideration to the underlying psychopathological condition that may potentiate countertransferential reactions in the therapist.
3. Manifestations of countertransferential and/or attitudinal derivatives in the treatment of the drug patient

LITERATURE REVIEW

There is a marked paucity of psychiatric and medical literature specifically addressing the issue of countertransference and its relation to the treatment of drug abuse and addiction. Rather, the majority of authors considered here have described specific behavior patterns associated with addictive behavior that might activate within the therapist the potential to counterreact in an antitherapeutic manner. However, it is primarily left to the reader to draw inferences concerning the effect that these patient behavior patterns might have on the therapist, the patient, and the treatment outcome.

In 1929 Simmel indicated that because of murderous impulses and the need for self-punishment, the treatment of the drug addict carries several risks, especially the heightened possibility of the patient's suicide. Rado (1933), a pioneer in describing the psychological status of the drug-dependent individual, was able to conclude after 30 years of investigation that, in general, "the prognosis of drug addiction is quite unfavorable" (p. 34). Fenichel (1945) urged against the treatment of addicts in any location other than an institutional setting, in particular because of the tendency of the drug addict to act out while in treatment. Meerloo (1952) cautioned against the patient who will attempt to bribe the analyst with passive, compliant, and limited drug-free behavior, while waiting for the first perceived error by the therapist as justification for falling back to a pattern of drug use.

Despite references to suicidal behavior, "danger," "acting out," and "bribery," these writings omit exploration of the actual personal, subjective, and objective experience of the therapist in treating patients with such descriptions of their symptomatology. And in those selections where writers do give caution regarding the problems inherent in the treatment of addiction, few have used those cautions as a springboard from which to further evaluate the role of the therapist in the outcome of the treatment for drug-dependent individuals.

Ausubel (1948) wrote that "drug addiction constitutes more than a rare and isolated phenomenon of behavioral maladjustment (which psychiatrists and other medical men approach with disinterest, dread and despair) . . ." (p. 219). This parenthetical reference to the causal relationship between patient and treatment provider was further explained by Ausubel (1958) 10 years later:

. . . Yet despite the need for the establishment of rapport and positive transference the physician only too frequently, even in the best institutions, openly displays a cynical, unrealistic and hostile attitude towards the addict; he is indifferent to the latter's genuine complaints, assumes in advance that he is a liar, and maintains that it is a waste of effort and money to attempt a cure. Such an attitude must be deplored as . . . contributing toward the resentment and lack of personality reintegration that helps pave the way for relapse. In the case of the voluntary patient, it leads to his immediate discharge (p. 61).

In writing of countertransferential difficulties in the treatment of alcoholism, Selzer (1957) noted that "when hostility enters the picture as part of the defensive armor, not of the patient, but of the therapist, and is directed against the patient, the chances for the establishment of a positive therapeutic relationship are markedly diminished. If anything, this situation will intensify the patient's difficulties and make recovery more unlikely" (p. 301). Selzer further states that such countertransference "often perpetuates the drinking pattern." Furthermore, "the hostility may be expressed on an overt or conscious manner, or may operate so that both patient and therapist are unconscious of its presence" (p. 305).

In his article "Reaction Formation as a Countertransference Phenomenon in the Treatment of Alcoholism," Moore (1961) postulates that "because of renounced infantile cravings, the therapist is angered by the constant seeking of indulgence by the alcoholic patient. He may express this directly by rejection of the patient. Because the therapist is often made anxious by any awareness of anger at his patients, he may defend himself by establishing a reaction formation in the form of an overly indulgent and permissive attitude. . . . This attitude is destructive of the patient's chance of recovery as it impairs his reality testing and encourages denial of the severity of the drinking problem. Thus, the therapist's unconscious hostility ultimately finds its mark" (p. 485).

In an expansive review and summary of the major psychoanalytic contributions to the understanding of the etiology and treatment of drug addiction, Rosenfeld (1964) acknowledges that "only a few of the authors mentioned in the review have discussed the technical difficulties which arise in the treatment of both alcoholics and drug addicts" (p. 242). Wurmser (1972) has written that "drug abuse is the nemesis to haunt psychiatry itself. The enormousness of emotional problems dwarfs our skills, more than our knowledge; we understand far more than we can actually influence . . ." (p. 406). We are again led to inquire, therefore, as to the resultant treatment implications for mental health practitioners who might approach such a challenge that "dwarfs our skills."

Merry (1967) noted that due to both personality disorders and the tension and urgency frequently associated with (heroin) addiction, physicians often have to contend with nonconformist behavior such as lateness, bad manners, and bad tempers. To deal with this situation, Merry calls for a "tolerant and sympathetic staff" (p. 206).

In exploring the management of the drug-addicted patient in treatment, Rosenfeld (1964) states that the "drug addict is a particularly difficult patient to manage because the analyst has not only to deal with a psychologically determined state but is confronted with the combination of a mental state and the intoxication and confusion caused by drugs" (p. 128). Here again it is important to note the absence of countertransferential consideration in exploring major management issues regarding the drug patient.

It is only in the mid to late 1970s that more specific attention is given to the therapist's role in the treatment of addiction. Wurmser (1978) has written a scholarly and insightful book on drug abuse, a total of 635 pages of which, interestingly, only 2 pages specifically address the topic of countertransference in the treatment of the drug abuser. Davidson (1977) is one of the few authors that have begun to explore drug abuse treatment outcomes as requiring careful consideration of the impact of the patient's defensive constellation on the therapist, and the ensuing manner in which this issue is managed on a therapeutic level. In writing of the transference and countertransference phenomena regarding the treatment of methadone maintenance patients, she notes that often extreme affects of methadone patients present enormous problems for staff. "Expressions of strong hostility, anger and blamefulness in patients arouse equally powerful emotions in staff, whose most common response is to retaliate—overtly or covertly, against the patient" (pp. 121–122).

This survey of the literature leads to some interesting observations in regard to the relationship between countertransference and the treatment of drug abuse and addiction, including alcoholism: First, as noted by Yorke (1970) "the majority of writers do not distinguish between addiction of different kinds of drugs, tending to treat them as identical and including alcoholism too as part of the same pathology which may or may not be the case" (p. 143). Today we have a far more diverse population of individuals who might categorically be classified as "drug abusers": recreational marijuana users, prescription drug misusers, individuals who use hallucinogens and similar mind-altering substances, and alcohol abusers. Therefore, the application of the majority of historical writings related to the treatment of drug abuse must be tempered with the reality of a far more diverse and clinically demanding patient population. Also, the majority of writings are physician oriented and primarily conceived and presented within a framework of classical psychoanalysis. This is in stark contrast to the fact that of all full-time mental health professionals and paraprofessionals currently providing drug abuse treatment services in the United States as of 1980, less than 1% are psychiatrists. Consequently, the authors of the majority of drug abuse treatment articles are, from a specific professional affiliation, those proportionately least likely to be involved in direct and continuing drug abuse treatment and rehabilitation services (see Table 16.1).

The authors are impressed by the marked absence of any substantial references to countertransferential and attitudinal considerations throughout the 50 years of drug abuse literature. Might such an absence in itself suggest a veiled countertransference—a hesitancy and/or unwillingness, whether conscious or unconscious, to address one's own interaction in the dyadic

Table 16.1. Number of Full-Time Paid and Volunteer Employees for All Units Providing Drug Abuse Treatment Only: National Drug and Alcoholism Treatment Utilization Survey, April 30, 1979[a,b]

| | Full-time employees | | | | Part-time employees | | | | | | |
| | Paid | | Volunteer | | Paid | | | Volunteer | | |
Staff category	N	%	N	%	N	FTE[c]	% (FTE)	N	FTE[c]	% (FTE)
Psychiatrists	107	0.6	0	0.0	650	133.1	6.0	59	5.0	0.8
Other physicians	150	0.8	5	2.4	801	213.0	9.6	124	11.4	1.8
Psychologists—doctoral level	232	1.3	0	0.0	462	98.0	4.4	55	9.4	1.5
Psychologists—master's level	494	2.7	4	1.9	318	103.8	4.7	89	16.5	2.6
Nurse pract./physician's asst.	136	0.8	2	1.0	81	31.0	1.4	20	2.7	0.4
Reg. nurses, MS and above	110	0.6	2	1.0	73	21.8	1.0	12	1.5	0.2
Other reg. nurses	1,176	6.5	4	1.9	486	172.3	7.8	75	8.3	1.3
LPN and vocational nurses	631	3.5	0	0.0	223	84.1	3.8	21	7.5	1.2
Social workers, MS and above	1,004	5.6	4	1.9	451	155.0	7.0	101	12.8	2.0
Social workers, bachelor level	796	4.4	5	2.4	118	46.0	2.1	75	8.9	1.4
Other degreed counselors, BA and above	3,157	17.5	21	10.1	515	199.0	9.0	455	72.7	11.6
Degree counselors, AA level	653	3.6	1	0.5	60	25.7	1.2	32	6.9	1.1
Nondegreed counselors	3,404	18.8	63	30.4	445	161.7	7.3	1,639	187.8	29.9
Voc./recreational therapists	429	2.4	5	2.4	282	72.7	3.3	84	10.0	1.6
Other admin./support staff	5,434	30.1	27	13.0	1,561	600.4	27.0	469	75.4	12.0
Student trainees	156	0.9	64	30.9	309	102.9	4.6	844	191.7	30.5
Totals	18,069	100.0	207	100.0	6,835	2,220.5	100.0	4,154	628.5	100.0

[a]This table is based on 2,192 units.
[b]From Final Report, National Drug and Alcoholism Treatment Utilization Survey, April 1979, National Institute on Drug Abuse, Rockville, Md., Series F, No. 8, p. 16.
[c]Full-time equivalent (FTE) is defined as the total number of part-time worker-hours per week divided by 35 hours per week.

relationship? Or might it reflect a widespread view that perhaps the drug abuser is not a psychiatric patient, but rather a sociological phenomenon better left to examination and scrutiny by statisticians and theoreticians, rather than front-line treatment providers?

THE DRUG ABUSER: A PSYCHIATRIC PATIENT

Perhaps nowhere in the entire spectrum of mental health practice is the issue of countertransference more relevant than in the treatment of the drug-dependent person. Individuals already laden with a social outcast imagery, who are given such labels as "addict" and "junkie," often unwittingly find themselves in the care of therapists who, while meaning well and attempting to sincerely offer a positive rehabilitative framework, find themselves experiencing a sudden and often formidable array of feelings, reactions, and attitudes toward their patients. Such reactions by the therapists are not at all uncommon in working with the drug-dependent individual, and a greater understanding of why treatment of the drug abuser is so difficult suggests further review of the emotional status of the drug abuser and his true status as a psychiatric patient.

The individual with a serious, compulsive drug abuse symptom arrives for treatment in a relative state of psychological, social, biological, and/or economic decompensation. As with any individual who experiences a major destabilizing and stressful crisis, he is desperate for immediate relief. The drug abuser who presents himself for professional help is often terror stricken, anxiety ridden, depressed, and demanding, and is often attempting to communicate his helplessness and hopelessness in a pleading and pathetic manner. The clinical picture is one of relative ego regression, with demonstrable states of fragmentation, depersonalization, and, most commonly, a deep, immobilizing depression which is in itself a protective defense for a patient who can no longer utilize, exploit, or manipulate the environment to gratify his primitive oral needs. The drug-dependent patient is concurrently dependent upon the external world for survival, yet terrified of this dependency because of his basic mistrust and rage (Hirsch, Imhof, Terenzi, and Fried, 1980).

The individual drug-abusing patient abuses himself in a most vengeful and ultimately masochistic manner. In this regard, Stolorow (1975) notes that

by actively producing his own failure and defeat and actively provoking humiliation, abuse and punishment, the masochistic character experiences the illusion of magical control and triumphant power over his object world. . . . Such illusions of magical control enable the masochist to deny his narcissistic vulnerability by retaining his fantasies of infantile omnipotence (p. 445).

The attendant psychological and physiological pain is enormous, and the drug(s) serves as the analgesic. In effect, the patients ask: "What can you offer me that is better than heroin [or whatever drug of choice]?" Knowing this patient's life-style, level of immaturity, social milieu, psychopathology, family dynamics, and the paucity of available treatment facilities, it is indeed a difficult question to answer.

Therefore, a fundamental programmatic and operational definition of severe drug abusers is that they are psychiatric patients with varying ranges of psychopathology, and that the drug use is symptomatic of the basic, underlying pathological state. The absence of this conceptual view in the continuing development, refinement, and application of drug abuse treatment modalities would perpetuate the historical status of the drug abuser: a nonpsychiatric patient, a sociomedical outcast viewed as untreatable and unmanageable. It has not been uncommon that these patients have traditionally been shunned by mental health professionals and agencies, not only as a result of professional abdication but perhaps more often by the therapist's subjective feelings of ineffectiveness and impatience.

It has been the authors' experience that with regard to diagnostic considerations, the majority of these patients fall into the categories of narcissistic and borderline personality disorders. Further acceptance, understanding, and appropriate clinical management of the drug abuser as a psychiatric patient may be obtained in considering the defensive constellation of the borderline and narcissistic patient, the most pronounced components of which are splitting and projective identification. These defense mechanisms serve to unconsciously induce the therapist to experience the intense range of negative and hateful emotions that exist within the patient. The therapeutic significance of splitting and projective identification is further explained by Grotstein (1981), who writes that

Powerful feelings are more often than not expressed by giving another person the experience of how one feels. . . . All human beings seem to have the need to be relieved of the burden of unknown, unknowable feelings by being able to express them, literally as well as figuratively into the flesh, so to speak, of the other so that this other person can know how one feels.

We each are projections and ultimately wish the other to know the experience we cannot communicate or unburden ourselves or until we have been convinced that the other understands. We cannot be convinced that they understand until we are convinced that they now contain the experience (pp. 201–202).

Masterson (1976) provides further illustration when he writes of this phenomena:

... the borderline patient projects so much and is so provocative and manipulative, particularly in the beginning of therapy, that he can place a great emotional stress on the therapist. Unless the therapist can understand both what the patient is doing and how it is affecting his own emotions, he will be unable to deal with it therapeutically. It is important to keep in mind that the patient is a professional at provocation and manipulation while the therapist is an amateur at the use of these mechanisms (p. 105).

Altschul (1980) has noted that "unless a psychiatrist has extensive experience in the exploratory psychotherapy of borderline . . . patients, he will tend to have difficulty understanding or conceptualizing the eruption of primitive feelings in the transference or countertransference; and, he will tend to underdiagnose them" (p. 15).

In addition to considering a borderline patient with all his or her attendant intense transference reactions (for which any therapist must not only be prepared, but clinically seasoned and astute), the diagnostic label of "drug abuser/drug addict" is now imposed *over and above* the already complicated clinical composite. The drug abuser—who by that label alone may evoke an entire range of feelings, attitudes, and stereotypes within the therapist— presents a therapeutic challenge that is indeed awesome. While intellectual debates will continue regarding the sociocultural, demographic, and criminological aspects of drug addiction, the individual compulsive drug abuser presents a therapeutic challenge of immense proportions, the eventual outcome of which cannot be ascribed to anything other than interactional psychological dynamics and determinants on the part of both patient and therapist. As stated by Davidson (1977):

... the behavior we see in the patient *is* the manifestation of his/her problems in living, and not an artifact of either the clinic setting or of the addicted patient's sociocultural background. This behavior makes sense . . . if it is related to the ego defense mechanisms which have been delineated in the psychoanalytic study of borderline patients. The problems which this behavior presents for the outpatient therapy of addicted patients are considerable . . . (p. 124).

Krystal (1977) underscores this point by noting that "it is helpful to keep in mind that the (drug abusing) patient is confronted with problems of aggression that make him experience the transference as a life and death struggle" (p. 97).

In consideration of countertransference viewed as "totalistic," involving the total emotional setting, it is essential to consider that, like the patient's range of transference reactions, the therapist may also experience a range of countertransferential reactions, "a continuum . . . ranging from those related to the symptomatic neurosis on one extreme to psychotic reactions at the other, a continuum in which the different reality and transference components of both patient and therapist vary in a significant way" (Kernberg, 1975, p. 179).

Unless the therapist is both emotionally and clinically prepared, the initial transference reactions of the patient may be of such an intense nature that the therapist is overwhelmed by the ensuing assault. It is not uncommon for the therapist to rather immediately experience hateful feelings for such a patient. Such dislike is ego dystonic, certainly not what "good and loving" therapists should feel toward their patients. With the therapist's understanding of the patient's utilization of splitting and projective identification, the therapist's experience of such initial countertransferential feelings may be directly turned toward therapeutic advantage, enabling the therapist to become sensitized and therapeutically responsive to the massive turbulence within the patient.

THE PSYCHOTHERAPEUTIC ENCOUNTER

This section concerns the manifestations of countertransferential and attitudinal factors in the treatment of the drug abuser.

The drug-abusing patient, with his sense of worthlessness, self-hate, and destructive rage, now meets his obverse—the "good" therapist, a "paragon of virtue," and essentially everything the patient is not. The resultant good–bad dichotomy is a serious threat to the ego identity of the patient, and the first order of psychic business for the patient is to reverse the imbalance. More specifically, the patient (unconsciously) begins to employ any strategy available to provoke, cajole, humiliate, and deceive the therapist—in essence to make the therapist more like himself, or worse than himself. Without the concurrent presence of the therapist's skill and understanding of the dynamics at work, including his own countertransferential and attitudinal postures, the proposed treatment may be short-lived, and the probable negative results all too frequently ascribed to the patient alone.

As Krystal and Raskin (1970) noted regarding the treatment of drug abusers:

With these patients the problems of countertransference are especially difficult because of the aggression they include. Because patients are very demanding, expressing insatiable, 'endless' oral fantasies, the analyst has to deal with their fears of being devoured or destroyed, and often becomes concerned with giving too much or too little with them" (pp. 103–104).

In considering the personality patterns of drug patients and their implications for therapy, Cohen, White, and Schoolar (1971) have noted that the therapist "must be ready to assume a position which allows him to empathize with the drug abuser's feeling of isolation and impotence." Therapy will of necessity involve a

long term commitment. Not only is this inherent in severe identity problems but there will be many resistances to involvement combined with acting out, designed at some point to test the genuineness and stability of concern exhibited by the therapist. In some respects, the challenge to the mental health treatment community seems almost overwhelming. How does one move unflinchingly into an arena where he is made to feel unwanted, incompetent and even malevolent? (p. 358).

Without an awareness of countertransferential and attitudinal responses, in addition to a thorough understanding and appreciation of splitting and projective identification, it is postulated that continuing and effective therapy with a drug-abusing patient is virtually unmanageable. However, with their appropriate recognition, analysis, and application, they may be used to facilitate and enhance the therapeutic process. Lack of awareness and clinical naivete may often result in negative countertransferential and attitudinal messages, acted out in derivative forms, the specificity of which is a function of the therapist's own unconscious.

There are therapists who may be chronically late, cut sessions short, fantasize during the treatment hour or get drowsy, and refuse to return phone calls to patients within a reasonable amount of time. These are but a few brief examples of a negative countertransference induced by the patient and acted out by the therapist.

While occasional lapses in the continuing treatment frame may occur, be recognized, and corrected, continuation of such acting out by the therapist must be viewed as part of the antitherapeutic, countertransferential posture either consciously or unconsciously assumed by the therapist to guard against what is perceived to be unpleasant and unwanted feelings and reactions induced by the patient in the dyadic relationship.

As the presenting pathology of the drug abuser may vary from neurotic to overly psychotic, so too may the countertransferential reactions of therapist vary in marked degrees—at times becoming overt and transparent, at other times quite subtle and camouflaged. Following is a sample of various groupings of countertransferential and attitudinal reactions based upon experiences of professionals involved in the treatment of psychiatric patients who have serious drug-abusing components. It should be noted that these comments are intended for communication and reflection in a nonjudgemental manner, and hopefully will be viewed in a spirit of clinical and academic examination.

1. The therapist who assumes the role of "good parent rescuing the bad impulsive child": Such a therapist may become overinvolved, protective, maternal, permissive, and, at times, literally feeding ("how about a cup of coffee?"), hoping that this outpouring of "love" and "goodness" will prove curative.

One must naturally question this behavior in terms of one's need to be viewed as all-giving and all-loving. It is suggested that such a (anti)-therapeutic posture is ultimately a re-creation of the unhealthy primary relationship, wherein love was provided to the child to the extent that the child serviced the needs of the parent (Miller, 1981; Spitz, 1965). The antitherapeutic effect of such behavior may be clinically validated when the drug-abusing patient, having initially "accepted" the all-giving and maternal therapist, suddenly regresses and resorts to serious acting-out behavior, including overdose, criminal behavior, or suicide attempt. The therapist often then becomes both furious and hurt at this betrayal, labels the drug patient as "resistant" and "acting out," and may proceed with plans to discharge the patient as untreatable on an outpatient basis.

It is further considered that while such acting-out behavior by the patient evokes negative countertransferential reactions, it may not be unrealistic to also view such precipitous acting out by the patient as an unconscious attempt to end what Langs (1975) refers to as a "therapeutic misalliance."

2. It has been the experience of the authors, and has been documented in the literature, that a few but still significant number of physicians are unaware of the implications of their prescribing patterns (Stolley, 1971). Patients may seek to dethrone the perceived omnipotent authority of the physician by surreptitiously obtaining and abusing prescription medications, thereby perpetuating a drug-using habit. This antitherapeutic complicity serves not only to reaffirm the patient's narcissistic grandiosity, but furthermore perpetuates the vicious cycle of what has to date been the patient's therapeutically unchallenged, ego syntonic pathological behavior.

An example is offered here of a clinic patient who deftly maneuvered two staff psychiatrists into providing neuroleptic medication, which was constantly abused, twice resulting in life-threatening overdoses. The patient, a

47-year-old woman, was described as extremely demanding, whining, cling-ing, guilt ridden, and chronically ill. She presented as very pathetic, longing for any kind of relief to her miseries, and she expressed open and caustic criticism of the more than two dozen prior treatment providers from various mental health clinics, drug programs, and hospitals throughout the metropoli-tan area. As stated by the first staff psychiatrist she saw at the drug clinic, "I had to give her something. I felt sorry for her." Supervisory sessions revealed that countertransferential issues centered around both protective feelings and an intense loathing of the unceasing barrage of complaints. When this patient was finally presented with firm therapeutic guidelines, and the doctor was able to stand his ground and not be threatened or intimidated by the patient's massive bombardment of verbal abuse, there began a slow but steady im-provement in this patient's demeanor, appropriate dyadic interaction, and a decrease in drug abuse.

3. Perhaps one of the most classic scenarios to unfold in a drug treatment setting is when a substance-abusing patient demonstrates initial and remark-able signs of improvement. Within days to just a few weeks, the patient looks and feels better, has urines free of any drugs, and to an untrained observer might appear on the road to recovery. The inexperienced therapist may immediately attribute this to the "effectiveness" of his therapeutic approach until the patient, suddenly and without warning, begins acting out through renewed drug use, overdosing, getting arrested, or missing sessions. The result is a shattering of the illusion that the therapist is in complete control of the therapy. Both depressive and rage reactions may be quite common re-sponses to such patient actions, and the therapist's guilt in such a situation may be tied to the unconscious dynamic that "I have failed in rescuing the bad, impulsive child, and now I feel like a bad therapist." It is not uncommon in such situations to perceive the therapist's responses as a reaction formation induced by the patient's behavior.

4. One type of countertransferential mechanism that has been observed from time to time is the "you and me against the unjust world" approach to treatment. Such a mechanism may be observed in a therapist who perhaps identifies with the patient's antiauthoritarian strategies, or vicariously roman-ticizes or dramatizes the life-style of the substance abuser. Also, such a therapist may have unresolved conscious and unconscious impulse fantasies which are activated and subsequently fulfilled through the acting-out behavior of the patient, who perceives the therapist's approval of his self-defeating behavior as gratifying and inspirational.

5. Mental health professionals and paraprofessionals working with drug

abusers are quite familiar with the concept of "burnout," yet are perhaps unaware of the resultant countertransferential and attitudinal implications of this syndrome. The clinical picture of such a staff member generally centers around a withdrawal mechanism—a self-protecting, narcissistic distancing which manifests itself as indifference, tiredness, boredom, and in general, a separation from the therapeutic interaction. Such burnout features are not uncommon when considering the consistent and intense demands that the patient makes, and the recidivistic and chronically relapsing manifestations of the addictive disorders.

6. It must be noted that countertransferential and attitudinal reactions are not confined to the dyadic experience of individual therapy, or for that matter, to group and/or family therapy alone. We must acknowledge milieu countertransference, which is not uncommon on inpatient psychiatric or detoxification units. Here the frightened, provocative substance abuser with severe character pathology can evoke intense countertransferential staff reactions. While the provocation by the substance abuser can be explored in regard to its characterological and dynamic implications, it may be of greater importance to emphasize the necessity of retaining a limit-setting posture, rather than therapeutic abdication and laxity in the hope of forestalling or averting what may be perceived as dangerous and manipulative behavior.

7. Societal countertransference corresponds with the social outcast imagery of the compulsive drug abuser. Staff personnel working with drug abusers at times may feel that they are being "tarred with the same brush" as their patients are. Drug workers may be quite familiar with phrases such as "Do you ever help them?" or "How can you treat people like that—isn't it dangerous?" In such situations, the therapist must be cognizant in terms of his own potential to act out—viz., identifying with the "victimized" patient and joining forces in a "you and me against the world" scenario.

Stereotypical classifications by therapists of drug patients as "addicts" or "junkies" serve not only to perpetuate the nontreatable outcast status of the drug abuser, but furthermore may reduce, if not eliminate, the opportunity for a drug-involved patient to emerge from treatment with a feeling of wholeness as a person, rather than carrying a permanently affixed stigmatizing label (Imhof, 1979).

PRACTICAL APPLICATIONS

It is suggested that a number of factors be considered if the therapist is to recognize, analyze, and intervene in the dyadic relationship with a psychiatric patient who is also a drug abuser. Therefore, the following comments may be viewed in regard to their application to program policies and procedures, especially as they relate to staff selection and training.

As noted earlier, the social outcast imagery of the drug abuser cannot be underestimated, and its recognition by the therapist is essential to the subsequent outcome of the treatment interaction. Furthermore, there must exist a knowledge of, and attunement to the dynamics of severe character pathology, and the subsequent feelings that can be induced in the therapist by patients who manifest this pathology. Optimally, the therapist should be emotionally and cognitively receptive to receiving, recognizing, and analyzing the intense feelings generated by such patients. In particular, it is incumbent upon the therapist to continuously examine his/her verbal and nonverbal interventions for the presence of antitherapeutic countertransferential indications. Special attention needs to be given to overly solicitous or hostile remarks, self-serving interventions, or premature and/or unnecessary interpretations by the therapist, in addition to an entire potential array of affective reactions.

Following are some brief suggestions and considerations for therapists and program personnel:

1. Historically, the field of drug abuse treatment has been one in which former patients have been accepted as treatment providers. In some instances, prior drug abuse experience has been viewed as a prerequisite for provision of treatment services. Given the significant number of individuals providing drug abuse treatment services who were themselves formerly compulsive drug abusers, it would seem appropriate to indicate specific countertransferential and attitudinal issues that may be germane to this treatment-provider community. Sometimes stereotypically referred to as "ex-addicts," former drug abusers now serving as therapists may in fact experience many feelings and attitudes, both conscious and unconscious, toward individuals who currently use drugs. Specific areas of concern may relate to an identification with the drug abuser, or perhaps to a dissociative reaction that might unconsciously serve to assist the therapist to deny his own past, unresolved pathological behavior. The drug patient may serve as a constant and perhaps uncomfortable "reminder" of the therapist's past, and the termination of such cases can be explored in relation to this possibility. Also, it is worth noting that the therapist who is a former compulsive drug abuser might inadvertently seek to utilize the identical therapeutic framework with the patient that the therapist himself experienced, and currently views as being responsible for his own successful rehabilitation. In such cases, a "what worked for me will

work for you" attitude may result in unreasonable therapeutic expectations, often leading to premature treatment termination.

The authors further wish to consider the countertransferential implications for an area of mental health treatment (i.e., drug abuse) that in varying degrees has placed equal emphasis on prior personal drug experience in relation to clinical training. The authors are unaware of any other areas of mental health treatment where having had the illness is a requirement for treating the illness. This would seem to indicate the status of the compulsive drug abuser as a sociological phenomenon, rather than a psychiatric patient.

The authors are well aware of the extensive numbers of former residents of therapeutic communities who have been given responsibility as primary therapists. However, it would appear that the growing professionalism of the therapeutic community attests to the recognition that clinical skills far outweigh the requirement of personal drug experience in order to provide effective rehabilitation services to the compulsive drug abuser. Naturally, the use of the "ex-addict" treatment model also calls into question a number of technical procedural issues, one of which is the extent to which the patient should have knowledge of his/her therapist's personal life. Use of the "ex-addict" as role model therefore presents contradictory statements in this regard, and clinicians might benefit from further exploration and discussion in this area. It would, furthermore, seem appropriate that these issues be examined in the interview process when considering the recruitment of former drug abusers in the position of treatment providers.

2. The importance of one's own personal therapy must be highlighted. While the authors recognize the existence of debate regarding whether or not having personal therapy is a prerequisite to providing therapy, we maintain that only through an examination of one's own emotional development can the therapist most effectively recognize, tolerate, and begin to sort out the infinite range of countertransferential and attitudinal considerations inherent in the treatment of such patients.

3. For the appropriate recognition and management of all countertransferential and attitudinal considerations in the treatment of drug abuse, the role of clinical supervision continues as a most necessary and effective mechanism.

4. The continuing education of the therapist is also reviewed as a prerequisite to the effective management and treatment of the drug-dependent individual. To what extent does the therapist continually familiarize himself with a greater understanding of the psychopathological factors that precipitate compulsive drug use? Workshops, seminars, grand rounds, graduate pro-

grams, and training institutes are but a few of the continuing education alternatives available to the therapist.

5. What are the therapist's own personal values and attitudes toward individuals who knowingly and willingly inject or ingest life-threatening chemical substances? If a therapist possesses a strong dislike (or perhaps even repulsion) for the behavioral manifestations of a drug patient, these attitudes would require both recognition and understanding if effective treatment is to take place.

It has been the not infrequent experience of the authors to encounter well-trained, seasoned, and sensitive clinicians who have openly indicated a preference not to work with a drug-abusing population. Rather than taking a judgmental position toward therapists who maintain this view, such acknowledgment may be both heroic and mature. If it is accepted that certain behavioral areas of mental health treatment are beyond the preferences of some therapists (e.g., working with individuals who are criminally insane, severely retarded, sex offenders, brain injured, child abusers), it is not at all unreasonable to accept one's admission of preference not to work with a compulsive substance-abusing population.

6. Given the endemic and epidemic nature of substance abuse in society today, it is no longer unlikely that a member of a therapist's family may have a serious problem with drug abuse, including alcoholism. In such instances, there is an even greater need for heightened awareness of countertransferential and attitudinal derivatives emanating from the therapist's personal life. It is imperative to recognize to what extent, if any, a therapist's own personal issues become intertwined with the separate treatment issues of the patient, and in this area clinical supervision can again play a most significant role.

SUMMARY

It has not been the intent of this paper to offer a complete overview and analysis of the myriad of countertransferential and attitudinal features inherent in the treatment of the compulsive drug abuser; rather, it has been the authors' intention to highlight the inclusion of countertransferential and attitudinal factors in the consideration of failures in the treatment of drug abuse and addiction. Too often such failures are ascribed to a multitude of factors that exclude the therapist's contribution to the treatment situation.

The transference-countertransference matrix has many variations and clinical manifestations that can enhance, or destroy, a therapeutic relationship and treatment plan. The personal differences in patients and therapists make for a multitude of transference-countertransference responses which must be examined if therapy is going to be a functional and viable modality in the rehabilitation of the compulsive drug abuser.

It is hoped that this discussion will serve as a springboard for further review and analysis of this dimension of clinical treatment in regard to drug abuse and addiction. The myth of the conflict-free, aseptic, neutral mirror therapist ultimately creates unrealistic and unattainable therapeutic expectations. As Langs (1980) has noted, "While expressions of countertransference, when excessive, constitute an unconscious exploitation of the therapeutic situation by the therapist, it is this reality which also provides him, as long as he becomes insightful, a unique opportunity for at least some measure of cure in his interaction with every patient . . ." (p. 372).

As noted earlier, the instinctual side of addiction has received the greatest share of attention, and in the majority of all treatment outcome studies reviewed, the cause of treatment failure is viewed as a failure within the patient, resulting from his own psychopathology, rather than from any negative derivatives of the patient-therapist interaction. Self-reflection and self-analysis into one's participation and impact on the treatment relationship and outcome may not necessarily be a pleasant task, but it is hoped that such an undertaking will enhance one's knowledge and awareness, and ultimately lead to increased effectiveness with a population that has traditionally been considered by some to be all but untreatable.

REFERENCES

Altshul, V. A. *The hateful therapist and the countertransference psychosis.* Natl. Assoc. Private Psychiatric Hosp. J., *11(4): 15–23, 1980.*

Anderson, W. H.; O'Malley, J. E.; and Lazare, A. *Failure of outpatient treatment of drug abuse: II. Amphetamines, barbiturates, hallucinogens.* Am. J. Psychother. *128(12): 122–125, 1972.*

Austin, G. A.; Macari, M. A.; and Lettieri, D. J. Guide to the Drug Research Literature *(NIDA Research Series No. 27). Rockville, Md.: NIDA, 1979.*

Ausubel, D. P. *The psychopathology and treatment of drug addiction in relation to the mental hygiene movement.* Psychiatr. Q. *22(2): 219–250, 1948.*

———. Drug Addiction: Physiological, Psychological and Sociological Aspects. *New York: Random House, 1958.*

Cohen, C. P.; White, E. H.; and Schoolar, I. *Interpersonal patterns of personality for drug abusing patients and their therapeutic implications.* Arch. Gen. Psychiatry *24: 353–358, 1971.*

Davidson, V. *Transference phenomena in the treatment of addictive illness: Love* and hate in methadone maintenance. In J. D. Blaine and D. A. Julius (eds.), Psychodynamics of Drug Dependence *(NIDA Research Monograph No. 12). Washington, D.C.: NIDA, 1977.*

Dupont, R. L.; Goldstein, A.; and O'Donnell, J. Handbook on Drug Abuse. *Washington, D.C.: U.S. Government Printing Office, 1979.*

Fenichel, O. The Psychoanalytic Theory of Neurosis. *New York: Norton, 1945.*

Grotstein, J. Splitting and Projective Identification. *New York: Jason Aronson, 1981.*

Hirsch, R.; Imhof, J. E.; Terenzi, R. E.; and Fried, M. The drug treatment and education center: An overview. North Shore Univ. Hosp. Clin. J. *3(1): 8–16, 1980.*

Imhof, J. E. "Addicts," "addicts," everywhere: But has anyone seen a person? Contemp. Drug Probl. *8(3): 289–290, 1979.*

Kernberg, O. Borderline Conditions and Pathological Narcissism. *New York: Jason Aronson, 1975.*

———. Object Relations Theory and Clinical Psychoanalysis. *New York: Jason Aronson, 1976.*

Krystal, H. Self and object representation in alcoholism and other drug-dependence: Implications for therapy. In J. D. Blaine and D. A. Julius (eds.), Psychodynamics of Drug Dependence *(NIDA Research Monograph No. 12). Rockville, Md.: NIDA, 1977.*

Krystal, H.; and Raskin, H. Drug Dependence: Aspects of Ego Functions. *Detroit: Wayne State University Press, 1970.*

Langs, R. Interactions: The Realm of Transference and Countertransference. *New York: Jason Aronson, 1980.*

———. Therapeutic misalliances. In R. Langs (ed.), *International Journal of Psychoanalytic Psychotherapy. New York: Jason Aronson, Vol. 4, 1975.*

Lettieri, D.; Sayers, M.; and Pearson, H. W. (eds.). Theories on Drug Abuse *(NIDA Research Monograph No. 30). Rockville, Md.: NIDA, 1980.*

Masterson, J. F. Psychotherapy of the Borderline Adult. *New York: Brunner and Mazel, 1976.*

Meerloo, J. A. M. Artificial ecstasy: A study of the psychosomatic aspects of drug addiction. J. Nerv. Ment. Dis. *115: 246–266, 1952.*

Merry, J. Outpatient treatment of heroin addiction. Lancet *1(7483): 205–206, 1967.*

Miller, A. Prisoners of Childhood. *New York: Basic Books, 1981.*

Moore, R. A. Reaction formation as a countertransference phenomenon in the treatment of alcoholism. Q. J. Stud. Alcoholism *22: 481–486, 1961.*

Rado, S. The psychoanalysis of pharmacothymia. Psychoanal. Q. *2: 1–23, 1933.*

Renner, J. A.; and Rubin, M. L. Engaging heroin addicts in treatment. Am. J. Psychiatry *130(9): 976–980, 1973.*

Rosenfeld, H. A. Psychotic States. *New York: International Universities Press, 1964.*

Selzer, M. L. Hostility as a barrier to therapy in alcoholism. Psychiatr. Q. *31: 301–305, 1957.*

Simmel, E. Psycho-analytic treatment in a sanitorium. Int. J. Psychoanal. *10: 70–89, 1929.*

Simpson, D. D.; and Savage, L. J. Drug abuse treatment readmissions and outcomes. Arch. Gen. Psychiatry *37: 896–901, 1980.*

Spitz, R. The First Year of Life. *New York: International Universities Press, 1965.*

Stolley, P. D. Physician prescribing habits. In G. I. Wadler, J. E. Imhof, and D. F. Buckley (eds.), The Federal Challenge to the Community: A Health and Education Program for the Prevention and Treatment of Drug Abuse and Addiction. *New York: Crafton Graphic Company, 1971.*

Stolorow, R. The narcissistic function of masochism (and sadism). Int. J. Psychoanal. *56: 441–448, 1975.*

Wurmser, L. Drug abuse: Nemesis of psychiatry. Am. Scholar *41: 393–407, 1972.*

———. The Hidden Dimension: Psychodynamics in Compulsive Drug Use. *New York: Jason Aronson, 1978.*

Yorke, C. A critical review of some psychoanalytic literature on drug addiction. Br. J. Med. Psychol. *43: 141–159, 1970.*

PART V

Modifications in Psychoanalytic Technique

THIS PART outlines major modifications in psychoanalytic technique to treat alcoholism by authors who worked in psychoanalytically oriented outpatient alcoholism clinics. Their observations are drawn from several hundred patients, and therefore they have a broader perspective of the range of alcoholics who present for treatment than the earlier psychoanalysts who saw only a few addicts in private practice.

Chafetz was the director of the first psychoanalytically-oriented outpatient alcoholism clinic. He went on to become the first director of National Institute of Alcoholism and Alcohol Abuse. Chafetz subscribes to the drive theory of addiction, which he summarizes in the article reprinted here. He then details a modified psychoanalytic approach for treating alcoholism. Key aspects of the specialized therapy take into account the preverbal disturbance of the alcoholic and the sensitivity of the alcoholic to slights and disappointments. This provides the rationale for an action therapy, the need for a positive relationship, and self-disclosure by the therapist. The distinction between reactive alcoholic and alcohol addict was devised by Knight, using the term "essential alcoholic" rather than "alcohol addict."[1] The reader may compare Chafetz's description of the alcoholic with Davidson's depiction of the heroin addict. Chafetz offers one of many psychological explanations of AA.[2]

Silber writes from the ego psychological point of view. Silber begins by noting that therapy of alcoholics often concludes without an understanding of the drinking, an implied criticism of those who had focused exclusively on drive theory explanation of addiction. He elaborates a supportive, ego psychological approach to therapy with the alcoholic. Silber introduces the concept of the therapeutic working compact, derived from the working alliance of psychoanalysis. The latter evolves without special considerations in psychoanalysis.[3] The alcoholic patient, however, requires a detailed explanation of the process of therapy, the benefits of the treatment, and the usefulness of mutual cooperation.[4] By moderating transference reactions, the difficulties alluded to by Krystal and Davidson can be minimized. The treatment can be likened to a "transference cure," where positive transference aspects are internalized but not interpreted and result in lasting change. Silber's observation that these patients often have a severely disturbed parent with traumatic consequences has clinical utility, but one must keep in mind it is based on a small sample. Additionally it should be noted that a high percentage of addicted patients report childhood sexual abuse.[5] He describes the alcoholic as being open to suggestion and guidance, which may be a factor in his or her receptiveness to AA. The fact that only 5 percent of the clinic population was suitable for this type of treatment should be kept in mind. The interested reader may trace the evolution of this therapy in Silber's papers of 1959 and 1970.[6]

NOTES

1. Knight, 1938.
2. Simmel, 1948, Mack, 1981, and Dodes, 1988, have written about AA from a psychoanalytic perspective. Bateson, 1973, offers a fascinating cybernetic interpretation in an essay "The Cybernetics of Self: A Theory of Alcoholism."
3. Greenson, 1967.
4. Silber, 1970.
5. Rohsenow, Corbett, and Devine, 1988.
6. Silber, 1959, 1970.

17. Practical and Theoretical Considerations in the Psychotherapy of Alcoholism

Morris E. Chafetz

ALCOHOLISM is a growing medical problem toward which the medical profession has only recently directed any sustained energies. Present-day thinking views alcoholism as a symptom of an underlying personality disorder; psychological factors are seen as leading to the self-destructive use of this toxic agent. The maintenance of the psychological dependence on alcohol is seen as hinging upon a combination of emotional, physiological and pharmacological factors and the end result for the individual is usually illness or oblivion. The psychiatric implications of alcoholism have led to the assumption by psychiatrists of a more active role in the search for more efficient methods of dealing with this immense problem. The purpose of the present report is to present some of the psychodynamic hypotheses and therapeutic implications derived from long-term psychotherapeutic relationships with alcoholics.

An outpatient clinic for the treatment of alcoholism was established under state auspices in 1953 at the Massachusetts General Hospital. The purpose of the clinic was twofold: (a) to study the effectiveness of long-term psychotherapy with alcoholic subjects and (b) to utilize the therapeutic relationship to investigate further some of the underlying psychodynamic factors generally associated with alcoholism.

The following data concerning the results of treatment are presented with full recognition of the limitations within which behavioral evaluations must be scrutinized. These limitations include the lack of universality of criteria for "success" in treatment and the bias of the interpreters who apply the criteria adopted.

Out of 600 patients referred to the clinic in the 5 years of its operation, 25

Reprinted with permission from *Journal of Studies on Alcohol* (formerly *Quarterly Journal of Studies on Alcohol*) 20 (1959): 281–91. Copyright © by Journal of Studies on Alcohol, Inc., Rutgers Center of Alcohol Studies, New Brunswick, N.J. 08903.

per cent developed and maintained a continuous therapeutic relationship. These 125 patients were studied during long-term psychoanalytically oriented psychotherapy, by social service anamnesis, and by psychological testing methods. Of the cases treated, over 62 per cent achieved satisfactory results. By satisfactory results we mean that the drinking was brought under greater control than the patient had ever achieved prior to treatment. The patients' behavior patterns were more mature in dealing with day-to-day living, and their response to anxiety was considered to be more realistic by the patient and by the therapist. While the remaining 38 per cent of the patients in this series did not meet these criteria for satisfactory results, many of them achieved what we considered to be some beneficial alteration of their drinking patterns.

Review of the literature reveals many theories based on dynamic formulations. Freud (1, pp. 43–74) alluded to strong oral childhood influences as a cause of excessive drinking and considered change of mood the most valuable contribution of alcohol to the individual. His thesis was that under the influence of alcohol the adult regresses to a childhood level in which he derives pleasure from thinking which is unrelated to logic. In later papers (2, 3) Freud spoke of a reactivation of repressed homosexual traits and considered this to be the reason why men disappointed by women frequented bars.

Brill (4) considered alcoholism as a flight from homosexual impulses, incestuous thoughts and masturbatory guilt. Jones (5) suggested that alcoholism is a symptom of epilepsy and psychosis, while Glover (6) related addiction to sadistic drives and oedipal conflicts. Sachs (7) viewed alcoholism as the compromise between hysterical and obsessive-compulsive neuroses, while Radó (8) suggested that alcohol addiction is mainly a problem of depression, the alcohol producing pharmacologically a magical sense of elation which the patient craves. Menninger (9) emphasized the self-destructive drives of the alcoholic and termed alcoholism "chronic suicide." Feelings of inadequacy, internalized fears of failure and deficiencies in social relationships are the main forces operating in the alcoholic according to Klebanoff (10). Tiebout (11) believes that the alcoholic has an unconscious need to dominate, together with feelings of loneliness and isolation, while Knight (12) considers that the addictive alcoholic suffers basically from a character disorder distinguished by excessive demands, an inability to carry out sustained effort and feelings of hostility and rage, alcohol being utilized to satisfy and pacify the alcoholic's frustrated needs.

In our clinic alcoholic patients are classified into two broad categories: the reactive and the addicted. While we recognize the limitations of classification systems, we have utilized these categories as a means of aiding us in the definition of the problem presented by each patient.

The reactive or neurotic alcoholics have relatively normal prealcoholic personality structures. They utilize alcohol to excess when temporarily overwhelmed by some external stress. Retrospective examination of their life patterns reveals reasonable adjustment in the areas of the family, education, work and social demands. There is a reasonably progressive movement toward realistic goals. Drinking, for patients in this group, is usually associated with observable, external stress situations, usually of long duration. An episode of excessive drinking has a determinable onset, runs a course consistent with tension release, and may terminate through some measure of control exercised by the individual. Some of the reactive alcoholics may become so involved in their neurotic drinking that they regress to a state approximating that of the malignant or addicted alcoholic, and this makes differentiation of the two groups extremely difficult. Reactive or neurotic alcoholics can be treated with psychotherapeutic techniques similar to those used in other neurotic disorders.

The alcohol addict, on the other hand, presents a somewhat different picture. Examination of the life history of the addict shows gross disturbances in his prealcoholic personality. Difficulties in adjustment during the early years are manifested in the relationships within the family, school, work and attempts at marital adjustment. There is no clearly defined point at which the loss of control over drinking occurred, and there is usually minimal observable external stress associated with the onset of a drinking episode. Needs for drinking arise from within the individual and, to the casual observer, these needs seem to have no rhyme or reason. Drinking bouts of the addict usually continue until sickness or stupor ensues; the drinking and the events surrounding it are usually self-destructive.

While each patient must be studied individually to understand the personal dynamics behind his addiction, certain dynamic factors are common to alcohol addicts and are related to the psychotherapeutic approach which is proposed in this paper.

The evidence from the present study suggests that by psychoanalytic classification addictive alcoholism is an oral perversion (13). An oral perversion results from traumas which occur during the earliest stage of psychosexual development, at the time when the individual's means of achieving security and release from tension was through stimulation of the oral cavity. The tendency to fixation of the oral level may be heightened by constitutional factors tending toward increased intensity of oral drives. Much energy is directed toward excesses in drinking, eating, smoking, pill taking and the like; there is emphasis on the mouth in sexual activity; and there is a predominance of orality in fantasy production. One patient who had been in therapy for 5 years, when asked by a friend what her therapist looked like, could only remember that he had a beautiful mouth, and could describe no other feature. Because the addictive alcoholic gratifies his instinctual oral wishes directly and without anxiety, we view addictive alcoholism as a perversion rather than as a neurotic mechanism which is the disguised anxiety-ridden converse of a perversion.

In our patients, the fixation at this early level of emotional development seems to have been the result of deprivation in a significant emotional relationship during the early years of life. This deprivation usually involved the death, or the emotional or physical absence, of a key figure during the early period of development. Many of the addicted alcoholics were abandoned, illegitimate children. Others were children of psychotic mothers. Still others had had a parent die shortly before or after their own birth, while some were the progeny of parents who were severely alcoholic during the patient's early years. A few addicted alcoholics were the children of excessively indulgent or overly protective mothers, with underlying disguised hostility existing in both cases.

Fundamentally, the common thread running through these patients' early relationships was the absence of a warm, giving, meaningful relationship with a mother-figure during this period of development. A very similar situation is frequently observed in the early relationships of schizophrenics. Certainly, with respect to the primitive fantasies and the behavioral patterns and responses of addicted alcoholics, the similarity to those of the schizophrenic cannot be readily dismissed. Sherfey has reported that up to 68 per cent of the case histories of some groups of alcoholics reveal a significant family figure who depended on alcohol in an unhealthy way (14, pp. 39–40). It might be proposed that one of the main reasons the addictive alcoholic does not use frank schizophrenic mechanisms to escape unpleasant reality is because the significant members of his environment with whom he relates and identifies handle their desire to escape via alcohol. Possibly, therefore, the symptom choice in these two primitively deprived classes is environmentally and culturally determined.

The loss or lack of a meaningful relationship with a mother-figure may help us to understand some of the motivating unconscious drives of the alcoholic. Just as the infant seeks through ingestion to quiet the emptiness and soothe the pangs which threaten his security, so does the alcoholic seek this gratification by stimulation of the oral mucosa, by imbibing massive amounts of ethanol and by seeking peaceful oblivion, symbolically attempting to achieve the blissful infantile state. Many patients, after their drinking has become controlled, express their envy of their intoxicated brethren who continue to achieve alcohol-induced oblivion. Therefore, the main devastating unconscious wish with which the alcoholic must deal seems to be his passive-dependent wish for reunion with an all-giving mother-figure.

The loss of an object relationship early in life may be responsible for the depression which is the main affect present in the addictive alcoholic. This severe underlying depression, expressed through feelings of emptiness, loneliness, "something important is missing," and so forth, results in the utilization of the main defense mechanism seen in alcoholism—denial. There is no more striking example of denial to be seen than the intoxicated alcoholic denying that he has any problem. If asked whether he has had a drink, the reply is "a little,"—another denial. When confronted by his intoxicated state the familiar response is, "I can stop any time I want to." Denial constitutes the main method which alcoholics use in dealing with life. They deny their feelings of inferiority, depression, lack of self-respect and dependence on alcohol.

The severe, ever-present, deeply penetrating depression pervades all of the alcoholic's personality and all of his reactions in the search for oblivion. Alcohol for the addict is a simple, easy method of achieving control over feelings of helplessness and deprivation. At the same time it symbolically substitutes as an object something which he feels he can control. The object loss during the oral stage results in primitive, excessive demands which are ultimately insatiable. Consequently, almost all interpersonal relationships eventually result in a rejection to the patient, reawakening the original loss and rejection he experienced as an infant. The pain, depression and loss of self-esteem which alcoholics experience reproduce the rage experienced by a deprived infant, a rage so intense and all-consuming that the infant will seemingly destroy himself rather than relent. So it is with the alcoholic. The rage is of murderous ferocity and intent, and rather than destroy another, the anger is internalized and consumed in drink. As one patient succinctly put it, "It is more socially acceptable to get stinking drunk than to murder someone."

The alcoholic's fixation at the oral stage suggests a possible explanation for the alcoholic's lack of satiation. In mature love, the instinctual wish is gratified but the object is preserved. In the oral stage, the instinctual wishes are gratified by incorporation and the love object is destroyed. Each drink, therefore, gratifies the instinctual wish but destroys the love object and hence a new one must be found; satiation is never achieved. Hence, the continued consumption of alcohol is a symbolic acting out of the oral conflict; satisfaction of the instinctual wish is achieved by means of the destruction of a love object which must continually be replaced.

If one accepts the preceding psychodynamic formulation for the addictive alcoholic, the difficulties of treating him become apparent. Most primitive disorders are treated within the protective and supportive confines of an institution. Not only does the addicted alcoholic suffer from a primitive psychological disorder, but there is a great tendency to act out conflict situations. Hence, the attempt to treat him psychotherapeutically on an ambulatory basis can be fraught with danger. The danger, we believe, lies in two main failings on the part of therapists. The first is the tendency of most psychiatrists to maintain a rather rigid therapeutic approach; their training has emphasized the limits of their role and their behavior. The second is in the overgeneralized classification of alcoholics as patients who suffer from hopeless character disorders and, hence, are untreatable.

The psychotherapist who is prepared to deal with the alcoholic must be prepared to be a pioneer in his approach to each case. Fundamentally, he must be a warm, kind, interested individual who can at the same time set and maintain reality-oriented limits. He must not and cannot assume moralizing and punitive attitudes. Since we are dealing with a disorder of the early personality development, words are of little use. It is not what we say to the alcoholic but what we really feel and do that will determine the outcome. Alcoholism, as a preverbal disorder, must be treated by action—by "doing for the patient." These primitive individuals want to be loved, want to be treated, and want to grow emotionally. Yet all of their emotional life experience warns and threatens them against entering into relationships where rejection is the inevitable outcome.

Action or "doing" therapy means, for example, that if the patient requires physical treatment, then hospitalization and medical care should be readily provided. Prescriptions for vitamins or disulfiram may be meaningful when the patient is seeking evidence of tangible support. In other words, in the early relationship one must be a very active therapist, since the passive, nondirective therapist of alcoholics who follows his usual therapeutic approach usually has no patients to treat after awhile.

In all therapeutic situations dealing with primitive problems a positive relationship is of prime importance. Without this firm bond between therapist and alcoholic no exploratory approach can hope to succeed. This bond may take a few interviews or several years to develop but it cannot be bypassed.

When it appears to be firm the patient will test it again and again, and even when the tests are passed the bond will be tested further. To ensure such a bond the patient must be offered help again and again, no matter how often he fails and resorts to alcohol.

Since the addictive alcoholic patient is fundamentally hostile, his behavior is unconsciously designed to arouse negative feelings and to invite retaliation. Hostility and retaliation must be constantly guarded against by all treatment personnel. Counterhostility is frequently expressed by being nice or excessively permissive. The absence of controls by the therapist is poorly tolerated by, and threatening to, the patient who is already leaning heavily toward loss of control. It indicates to the patient a lack of understanding of his basic problem, and intensified the identification of loss of control with loss of contact with reality, resulting in disintegration of personality.

Anxiety in the therapist is interpreted by the patient as evidence of insecurity and uncertainty of control. The hostility present in the therapist who is rigid, harsh and punitively controlling is self-evident. The attitude of tolerant acceptance with consistent firmness is healthy and reassuring. The therapist must maintain a position of constancy and absolute honesty, acknowledging to the patient mistakes, errors and feelings arising within him as soon as he becomes aware of them. When the patient makes a demand, an over-simplified but safe question to ask oneself is: "Am I doing this really for the patient's good, or to make him like me?" This question will be especially pertinent when the patient, besides inviting punishment, attempts to seduce the therapist to prescribe drugs or other dependency gratifications.

While the therapist must be an active, continually supporting substitute for the alcohol, he cannot help being aware of the insatiable demands of alcoholic patients. Few human beings can long endure the pressures, hostility and acting out of conflicts which are commonly endured in treating alcoholics. Thus these patients are most appropriately treated within a team setting which includes the psychiatrist, the social worker and the psychologist. The all-important social worker should be available to help with the financial, family and social pressures that commonly arise to interfere with treatment. The psychologist, with his particular way of understanding people, makes his contribution to the team's formulation of problems and predictions. Medical facilities should be readily available so that the patient can be prevented from utilizing physical symptoms and demands for medical treatment as a weapon against the therapist. A division of labor brought about through the team approach aids in the delineation of the physiological needs, the socioenvironmental demands and the underlying emotional upheavals with which the therapist works. Thus the task of the therapist becomes somewhat more manageable and the possibilities for arousal of his counterhostility are minimized. By this delineation the patient is more readily confronted with reality. The therapist who must dominate his patients to compensate for his own insecurity, and the one whose motivation is to be loved by all, will rarely deal successfully with the addictive alcoholic.

When a satisfactory relationship has been successfully developed, the therapist must gradually wean the alcoholic from his dependency needs to a recognition and acceptance of reality factors. Once the drinking is controlled, the therapist must avoid the tendency to continue his now outgrown protective attitude. He must be prepared to encourage his patient to carry out tasks, make decisions and, consistent with the patient's abilities, to meet and deal with reality in a mature manner. Situations which reactivate emotional reactions associated with the patient's original rejection are common pitfalls which therapists must avoid. These pitfalls include missing or canceling appointments without adequate warning to the patient, tardiness, making promises and not keeping them, and telling the patient untruths. Such events tend to be interpreted as rejection; they can lead to a catastrophic setback in the progress of therapy and to renewed acting out.

In formulating a course of psychotherapy for a patient, one must establish realistic goals. For some patients a supportive relationship and the provision of external aid in control over drinking is all that can be tolerated. Others may require partial custodial care and more continuous support. For many others, however, an intensive, exploratory, uncovering psychotherapeutic approach with resolution of the transference may be tolerated. The goals must be set within the abilities and the capacities of the patient; they should be based upon a team evaluation of the patient's make-up and many clinical hours of amending and confirming the preliminary formulations.

Denial must be dealt with quickly and as often as it becomes recognizable in the treatment setting, since the recognition of denial allows the patient to be more aware of his problem and his role in its causation. Denial mechanisms must equally be confronted and handled when they appear among caretaking personnel. For example, for years the Alcoholism Clinic at Massachusetts General Hospital was called "Psychiatry A." This name was an inadvertent means of strengthening the patient's denial and no objection was evoked when the clinic was truthfully renamed the "Alcoholism Clinic."

An important aspect of the psychotherapy of the addictive alcoholic involves the first contact with him. This contact is not usually made by the therapist but by either a secretary, a social worker or a house officer in an emergency ward. Here the battle may be won or lost. Initial rejection is a constant hazard. Permitting the patient to be treated as a second-class citizen who waits around, or handling him gruffly and with little interest, are major examples of rejection. Also, merely pushing some medication at the patient and discharging him outright hinders the establishment of a supporting therapeutic relationship. The importance of early contacts was strikingly illustrated by a patient who had come to the emergency ward on many occasions while she was intoxicated but who had refused to accept follow-up care in the clinic. A turning point came on the occasion that a volunteer worker, while serving coffee to the employees in the emergency ward, included the patient in her distribution. As a result, the patient made an appointment in the clinic, which was kept, along with subsequent appointments, and she was successfully treated. She frequently expressed the association to her therapist that the turning point for her had been the fact that someone had considered her as an equal, as shown by including her in the coffee service. This incident also underlines again the action or "doing" aspect of the early treatment of the addictive alcoholic.

Alcoholics Anonymous has shown itself to be a helpful adjunct in our work. Since we and others have conceived of alcoholism as the result of an object loss, the loss of a mother-figure which must be symbolically replaced by alcohol, we have looked at A.A. in this frame of reference. A.A. is an uncritical, accepting group, since all members are themselves alcoholics. It is an action or "doing" group and evokes a spiritual conversion with its implied maternal reunion. In other words, it tends toward being a "good," nonrejecting object. A. O. Ludwig[1] has pointed out that the compulsiveness of A.A. workers to help other alcoholics not to drink resembles the compulsiveness they formerly exhibited in their drinking pattern. Thus the effectiveness of A.A. is understandable within our psychodynamic formulation of alcoholism.

SUMMARY

Alcohol addiction has been described as a result of early emotional deprivation in relation to a significant parental figure, the symbolic and physiological replacement of which is achieved through alcohol. The symptom-choice of alcoholism seems to be culturally and environmentally determined. It is proposed that treatment is most effective when managed so as to establish a warm, giving relationship within the limits of reality.

NOTES

1. Personal communication.

REFERENCES

1. *Freud, S.* Three Contributions to the Theory of Sex. *4th ed. Washington, D.C.; Nervous & Mental Disease Publishing House; 1930.*
2. *Freud, S. Contributions to the psychology of love. The most prevalent form of degradation in erotic life. [1912.] In:* Collected Papers; *Vol. 4, pp. 203–216. London; Hogarth; 1925.*
3. *Freud, S. Mourning and melancholia. [1917.] In:* Collected Papers; *Vol. 4, pp. 152–170. London; Hogarth; 1925.*
4. *Brill, A. A. Alcohol and the individual.* N.Y. Med. J. *109: 928–950, 1919.*
5. *Jones, E.* Papers on Psychoneurosis. *Baltimore; Ward & Co.; 1938.*
6. *Glover, E. The etiology of drug addiction.* Int. J. Psycho-Anal. *13: 298–328, 1932.*
7. *Sachs, H. The genesis of perversions. Abstract in:* Psychoanal. Rev. *16: 74, 1929.*
8. *Radó, S. The psychoanalysis of pharmacothymia.* Psychoanal. Quart. *2: 1–23, 1933.*
9. *Menninger, K. A.* Man Against Himself. *New York; Harcourt, Brace; 1938.*
10. *Klebanoff, S. G. Personality factors in symptomatic chronic alcoholism as indicated by the Thematic Apperception Test.* J. Consult. Psychol. *11: 111–119, 1947.*
11. *Tiebout, H. M. The role of psychiatry in the field of alcoholism. With comment on the concept of alcoholism as symptom and as disease.* Quart. J. Stud. Alc. *12: 52–57, 1951.*
12. *Knight, R. P. The psychodynamics of chronic alcoholism.* J. Nerv. Ment. Dis. *86: 538–548, 1937.*
13. *Ludwig, A. O. Some factors in the genesis of chronic alcoholism and their bearing on its treatment. In:* Papers Presented at the Physicians Institute on Alcoholism of the National States Conference on Alcoholism, *March 9–10, 1956. Boston; [1957.]*
14. *Sherfey, M. J. Psychopathology and character structure in chronic alcoholism. In: Diethelm, O., ed.* Etiology of Chronic Alcoholism; *pp. 16–42. Springfield, Ill.; Thomas; 1955.*

18. Rationale for the Technique of Psychotherapy with Alcoholics

Austin Silber

For ANALYSTS and therapists, it has always been of primary importance to understand the meanings of various psychological questions. The most intriguing question, and the one that has led most of us on this perhaps chimerical quest, has been that of individual motivation and behavior.

It has been somewhat startling for me to realize, after devoting many years to supervising the psychotherapy of alcoholic patients, that rarely if ever do I recall understanding the meaning that the drinking really had for the patient. At the same time, however, this drinking behavior was frequently modified and often, during the course of therapy, given up entirely. For some, the drinking turned out to be of negligible importance in the course of the therapy. It was much easier completely to alter the drinking pattern, to bring about a profound change in behavior, which, incidentally, brought satisfaction to both patient and therapist, than to gather any basic understanding of what this drinking meant to the patient. Although the patient and the therapist were content, I found myself troubled. The fact that the therapy brought about a change in behavior in relation to drinking was most conclusive. However, our results were not very different from, perhaps even less effective than, those effectuated by the exhortatory methods indulged in by other groups, especially A.A., which also seemed able to manipulate drinking behavior without ever being troubled by the fact that they did not understand why.

At the same time, during the course of several analyses, the meaning of a particular kind of drinking became quite clear. In each instance the patient involved would only mention in passing that he enjoyed a cocktail at home prior to dinner. He was frequently joined by his spouse and it was a time for conversing and relaxing. This kind of drinking has almost been institutionalized by its prevalence in our society, and it is precisely this behavior that upon analysis readily leads to an understanding of the meaning the drink has to the individual.

Reprinted by permission from *Journal of Psychoanalytic Psychotherapy* 3 (1974): 28–47. Copyright © Jason Aronson, Inc.

It turns out that this kind of drinking is a compulsive symptom, extremely complex and overdetermined even though of little consequence. It appears that not only the drink itself, but also the environment in which the drinking takes place, have significant meaning to the individual. On the other hand, where there is a need to drink and the drinking absorbs more and more of the interest and attention of the drinker, it will be much more difficult to understand what the drinking means to the individual, but it will be much easier to have him completely abstain from the ingestion of alcohol.

It is, of course, a not infrequent finding that symptoms disappear during the course of therapy. However, it is most rare that the primary symptom, which is instrumental in motivating the patient to seek help, disappears without a whimper and without a whit of understanding.

What kind of patient is seen in this clinic setting, and how does he get to us? What is he looking for from us? How can we go about attempting to explain our results? Is it in some way dependent on our orientation and our goals? What modifications have been introduced into our therapeutic approach and what is their rationale?

As we attempt to answer these questions, we hope to describe both the workings of the clinic (The State University Alcohol Clinic, S.U.N.Y.) that are relevant to our individual psychotherapy program and the modifications we have evolved in our attempts to treat most effectively our particular type of patient. We believe that the knowledge gleaned from our therapeutic efforts has a general applicability to the psychotherapy of the alcoholic patient.

My own understanding has gradually evolved during many years of supervision of both psychiatric residents and social work staff and students. Since my immediate contact was with the therapists, my awareness of the patient and the patient's problems was filtered through their communications to me. Supervision lasts from one to three years, and the therapy is most often conducted on a once weekly basis.

My own primary interest has been in attempting to devise and communicate varied methods of approaching the patient that will utilize as much psychoanalytic understanding and information as can be assimilated and translated into an effective psychotherapeutic encounter. Of course, this has meant modifying certain goals not only because of the needs of the patient, but also because of the limitations of the therapist.

This paper will represent, then, a distillate of a particular type of clinical experience, to which has been added my experience as a practicing psychoanalyst and as a teacher on a psychoanalytic faculty.

Patients are referred to our clinic from a variety of sources, including: private practitioners who convince the patient that his drinking is a problem; the local psychiatric hospital (Kings County) after discharge following admission for many different reasons; various social work agencies and out-patient clinics, when it comes to the attention of the staff there that the patient also has a drinking problem; the Department of Welfare, because the drinking has interfered with gainful employment; the court system, where a condition of parole is the treatment of the drinking; present or former patients of the clinic.

It can be readily understood that these many different sources of referral have a variety of expectations about the clinic's performance. All have in common an expectation that the patient will be helped to either curb or give up his drinking.

The patients also have various expectations of the clinic. Some come either fulfilling an obligation to their referring agency, or because of prodding from various interested relatives, friends, colleagues, and other concerned parties. The patient's recognition or acceptance of a drinking problem cannot be assumed from his mere presence at the clinic. A fair number of the patients come from the kind of background where being able to drink as much as one wishes is considered an accomplishment rather than a disaster. In some occupations, continual drinking is considered a normal part of the day's endeavor, and those who do not drink are looked upon as being somewhat suspect. Clearly it is necessary to ascertain from the patient just what service he is expecting the clinic to provide.

The patient is first seen by a social service worker. What the worker views as the clinic's function, how he or she regards drinking—from a personal frame of reference, from his social frame of reference—both in an individual and group sense, in relation both to himself and to his patient, represent important background factors that will affect the initial contact with the patient. This is of especial significance in those instances where it is felt that an ex-member of a particular group who has experienced the situation in question has a unique advantage in dealing with the patient. The same questions have to be considered in terms of the other members of the clinic team who will be involved in the screening of the patient. This might involve the psychiatric consultant and, finally, the patient's therapist. These rather obvious factors of motivation, expectations, social background, and social orientation will affect the attitude of both the patient and the therapist.

The patient's attitude to drinking as it affects himself and others will vary. Many patients do not regard the alcohol itself but the unpleasant consequences of the drinking as a problem: losing time at work, unpleasant physical symptoms, disruption in family relationships.

We have learned that only about five percent of our patient population will even consider the possibility that the drinking they are involved in may be related to some problem that may arise from within themselves. The vast majority of the alcohol patients coming to our clinic are either not suitably motivated nor interested in psychotherapy of any sort. The small percentage of patients amenable to therapy are generally considered the healthier, psychologically speaking, segment of our alcoholic population. It is from our experience with this very select group that we draw the relevant observations about psychoanalytic psychotherapy.

Alcoholism has most generally been regarded as an addiction in the psychological sense (Glover, 1932). Thus, an alcoholic develops a dependence upon alcohol with the expectation that it will function in a twofold manner: it is expected to help him to avoid pain, which is usually experienced as an unpleasant mood or feeling, and it is anticipated that it will bring about instead a feeling of satisfaction and comfort (pleasure). Alcoholism, which involves persistent or excessive drinking, can also be viewed as a symptom, a compromise effort to deal with a host of conflicts that use the drinking as the common vehicle of expression. A very general definition of this sort encompasses within its confines the many psychologically descriptive diagnostic entities that happen to share in this one common feature. It thus prepares us for the known fact that alcoholic patients fall into many diverse diagnostic categories, ranging from the neurotic to the psychotic, with very many varied etiological factors predominating in different instances. A symptom also has another function—it helps to bind anxiety. Once we, as therapists, establish our interest in relation to anxiety and its vicissitudes, and in symptom formation with its many possible meanings and functions, we feel on more secure ground. It is helpful, in supervising or teaching psychotherapy with alcoholic patients, to deal with concepts, such as symptom formation or the function of anxiety, with which the therapist has ready familiarity.

There are certain general features, in a psychodynamic sense, that are consistently found to form part of the psychological background of patients suffering from the symptom of alcoholism. As a group, they are strikingly dependent and immature. The dependency can be defined, in libidinal terms, by the attribution of strong pregenital needs with the accompanying aggressive component most easily demonstrated by any thwarting situation. The immaturity is stressed by the quality of their object relations, which are most generally shallow, fragile, and tenuous. This group is noteworthy for the ease with which they develop seemingly new attitudes that seem to be based on primitive identificatory mechanisms. They imitate readily and display a somewhat chilling "as if" propensity. All of this points to basic problems in the development of a stable sense of identity. As a group, they are prone to behavior which is frequently impulsive, and seems dominated by drive rather than restraint. Their behavior has a primitive cast, with seemingly casual strictures exerted upon their aggressive and libidinal impulses. Thus, sexual activity seems poorly integrated, and is frequently perverse. Aggressive discharges are ill-restrained and unpredictable. In conjunction with the failure to exert certain restraining functions in situations that might be conflictual, there is also a relative failure of adequate performance in the so-called autonomous functions of the ego, which generally develop outside the realm of conflict. The impaired usefulness of the autonomous functions is of especial significance, since they are so crucially operative in the optimally structured psychotherapeutic situation.

The importance of the family constellation of the alcoholic patient has been stressed by many authors. The almost invariable finding that psychotic behavior was manifested by the parents of our patients has markedly affected our therapeutic approach.

I am limiting myself to this rather brief description of the general features of alcoholism that seem ubiquitous in our patient population, so as to be free to concentrate on the techniques gradually evolved for treating our alcoholic patients and the rationale for their evolution and development.

In the early years of therapy at our clinic, the therapists were encouraged to attempt to deal as rapidly as possible with the expressed anxiety of their patients. The prevalence of anxiety was a constant, and its intensity frequently was the most important factor leading to the selection of patients for therapy. It was decided to try to deal with this anxiety as though its manifestation indicated a fear of the aggressive impulse on the part of the patient's ego (Silber, 1959). With our knowledge of the almost invariable prevalence of frustration and thwarting behavior by the parents during the early years, we felt that excessive aggression would be a natural consequence. This aggression, manifested as anger or rage, is in turn defended against, and anxiety, either ill-defined or formidably discrete, is consciously experienced.

The therapist, early in treatment, would attempt to objectify the anxiety in relation to a contemporary and probably important figure in the patient's current environment. A friend or a superior could rather readily be seen as the object currently functioning in a thwarting capacity. The therapists were encouraged to focus on objects of secondary rather that of primary significance, e.g., friend or boss, rather than mate or parent. The patient was informed that he was fearful of experiencing rage in relation to these objects, but felt anxious instead. The therapist, by thus using his knowledge of the general dynamics of the alcoholic patient, was rapidly presenting himself as an all-knowing figure in a psychological sense. Practically all these patients are full of aggressive impulses, and frequently they would be fearful of consciously recognizing their extent. By interpreting the fear rather than the wish, the therapist operated from the vantage point of the ego and in alliance with the patient's ego. Since this was all initiated early in the therapy, a magical element was introduced: the therapist had a special knowledge about what was going on in the patient's mind, and was thus elevated into the role of a magical, omnipotent figure.

With this newly acquired authority, an educational approach was propounded. The patients were encouraged to begin to recognize, experience, and accept their feelings. At the same time however, feelings were clearly differentiated from actions. To experience feelings is the essence of life, to act upon them is another matter, requiring the exertion of judgment, and to be clearly differentiated from what one feels. Feelings, wishes, thoughts—all these are given a positive valence. Actions are to be avoided as a natural consequence of feelings—these feelings must first be reflected upon, actions must be restrained and, if deemed necessary, executed only after suitable reflection.

Through this approach some of the super-ego's primitiveness and punitiveness is mitigated, and a better appreciation of reality is enhanced by making explicit the differences among feeling, thinking, and doing.

In those instances where it was noted that the depressive affect rather than anxiety was the most prominent, the sense of guilt was highlighted, as being related to the need to be punished because of aggressive impulses and wishes. Once again, it was necessary to differentiate between wishes, feelings, and actions. All wishes are reasonable and desirable. It is only in relation to actions that guilt is an appropriate response. The attempt was made to help the patients recognize the fact that they had been attacking themselves for their aggressive wishes because they had failed to distinguish among feeling, thinking, and acting.

The same approach was followed with masochistically provocative behavior, which stems from the wish to be punished because of one's aggressive impulses. Once again, the therapist reiterated the need to accept all impulses, feelings, thoughts as reasonable and permissible. Actions, on the other hand, are unreasonable, and need to be defended against. Thus, the patients were encouraged to experience more of their inner life, and exhorted to accept this aspect of themselves. This positive educational effort also helped to diminish the severity of the superego's demands and strengthened the ego's ability to control. The differences between inner and outer reality were promoted as these patients were helped to separate and differentiate feelings from actions.

This initial approach, which is basically manipulative, using knowledge of dynamics in a magical sense, made for an initial strong bond between patient and therapist. As treatment progressed, the therapist attempted to shift from playing the role of an omnipotent figure to that of a more benign, consistent parental type, benevolent in so far as wishes and feelings were concerned, firm in eschewing action, and consistent in clarifying the distinction among wishes, feelings, and actions.

Over a period of years, it became more apparent that the attitudes that the therapists harbored toward both the alcoholic patient and his symtomatology frequently had a more significant effect upon the course of the treatment than the particular technique employed by the therapist. Thus, emphasis in supervision was shifted from delineation of the fears of aggressive behavior, with the resulting magical effect exerted by the therapist, to efforts to help the therapist quickly recognize and appreciate the essential helplessness of his patients. By attempting to modify the therapist's attitudes, which were frequently latently antagonistic, it was hoped to facilitate the successful treatment of these patients.

The therapist is urged to view lack of sobriety as a symptom in a similar dynamic sense to other familiar symptoms, such as those compulsive or phobic symptoms that are recognizable entities in all psychotherapy encounters, and are generally approached with circumspection until their function in the psychological life of the patient is adequately appreciated. What frequently gives the symptom of alcoholism a special significance is that, as it absorbs more and more of the attention and concern of the patient, it assumes more and more importance in his life. Concurrent with this increased absorption in the process of drinking itself is the gradual impairment of certain ego functions, which cease to function autonomously, and are caught up in the conflicting forces that in a dynamic and economic sense affect the structure of the symptom. The perception of reality and the interest in, meaning of, and constancy of this perception can all be affected to varying degrees. The ego's integration and utilization of this precept is also compromised. Other autonomous ego functions affecting judgment, anticipation, thinking, object comprehension, recall, language, capacity for self-observation, delay of action, motility, can all in a similar way lose their autonomy as they are embroiled in a conflict. The manner in which the patient's ego will be able to handle operations dependent upon optimal ego autonomy is thus affected. Moreover, one psychological consequence of the ingestion of alcohol is frequently the illusion that the impaired autonomous functions have been restored to optimal functioning as a consequence of the drinking.

The loss of ego autonomy has an immediate effect upon any kind of psychotherapy. The autonomous functions are the medium through which the patient communicates with the therapist (Loewenstein, 1972), and through which it is possible to make inferences about the functioning of the psychic apparatus itself. The psychotherapeutic situation, which by its very nature accentuates the importance of certain of these autonomous functions, e.g., self-observation and verbalization, is dramatically altered as a consequence of impairment. Thus, it should become apparent that it will be the therapist's function to recognize the deficits inherent in this psychotherapeutic situation, and that the therapist's ego must supply the necessary reparative ingredients—in this sense, he must be prepared to do more talking and be prepared to make observations about the patient that one would ordinarily expect the patient to be able to make unaided.

This "indoctrination" of the therapist takes place prior to the inception of therapy. At the same time and in an accompanying series of lecture-seminars alcoholism is discussed as a symptom. The therapists are given an intellectual grasp of the function of symptoms as before described: a compromise formation between drive derivative and opposition to it in a situation of conflict, with the consequent binding of anxiety.

Signal anxiety, the hierarchy of danger situations described from the genetic point of view (S. Freud, 1959), and the hierarchy of responses available to the ego are also discussed. The importance of the ego's biphasic response to anxiety, e.g., the evaluation of the danger and its magnitude, imminence, and pertinence, as well as the ego's reaction to this evaluation (Schur, 1964), is sketched in for the therapists, and the differences between feeling and acting reemphasized—since it is here that the ego's biphasic response is of such importance and of such immediate clinical use.

These elements are all specifically emphasized so that the therapist will not initially concentrate all interest upon the drinking per se, but will begin to recognize that the drinking itself represents an attempt to deal with many conflicting ideas and impulses, as yet unknown both to the patient and the therapist. It is important to stress our fundamental interest in the need to understand the meaning of behavior, even if that satisfaction does not seem probable with our current therapeutic means.

The therapists are familiarized with the alcoholic patient's general need to be given and to be cared for, and also with the fact that these patients constitute an extremely emotionally deprived group. These explanations are necessary to overcome the therapists' reticence in actively explaining to their patients the purpose of the psychotherapy, the particular methods used in this treatment milieu, and the rationale implicit in this psychotherapeutic approach. Such an exposition by the therapist constitutes an early satisfaction granted to the patient within the structure of the therapeutic situation; it is consonant with a psychologically sound initiation of therapy with the alcoholic patient.

In preliminary sessions, these ideas are discussed and, in a way, rehearsed with the therapists, who are explicitly urged to share them with their patients as soon as it is feasible in the treatment.

The object of the psychotherapy is discussed, in terms of helping the patient to function more comfortably and with greater awareness of himself and his surroundings. The patient is made more aware that there are many determinants to his illness, and he will gradually become more aware of some of their meanings and the effects that they exert upon him and the manner in which he lives his life. As the patient verbalizes his complaints and concerns, the therapist will, with time, be able to help him view these concerns from many different vantage points, most of them quite novel to the patient, and helpful in alleviating some of his pain and discomfort. The more he is able to understand about his life and his difficulties, the more control he will be able to exert over the concerns that cause him pain. In this endeavor, the therapist can be helpful by listening, remembering, and aiding the patient to learn to deepen his own awareness of himself. The patient is offered the expectation that through increased knowledge and understanding comes increased control over his person and his functioning. Such increased control becomes the touchstone of the therapy.

Actually, this preliminary work orients both the therapist and the patient toward regarding the therapeutic situation as the cornerstone of a joint venture. The expectations of the patient and the functions of the therapist have been outlined, and the psychotherapeutic equivalent of the "working alliance" has been fostered. In psychoanalysis, the working alliance has been defined as "that part of the therapeutic alliance related to the healthy portions of the patient's ego. This involves the reality relationship between doctor and patient" (Dickes, 1967). "Therapeutic alliance" is a more inclusive term, bringing into consideration positive transference, in addition to the rational relationship between the patient and the analyst (Greenacre, 1959; Greenson,

1965; Zetzel, 1956). The psychotherapeutic relationship differs, however, from the working alliance which arises with proper tact and technique in the specific analytical climate with a suitable analytical patient. In this psychotherapeutic milieu, an engrafted intellectual construct built around the depiction and description of the psychotherapeutic situation is offered as a common bond with the patient for the joint therapeutic effort. This forms the nidus for the "therapeutic working compact" (Silber, 1970), which incorporates elements in the working alliance (reality relationship between doctor and patient) plus the suggestive element inherent in the engrafted intellectual construct of the psychotherapeutic situation (with its implied promise of relief if the patient cooperates). This added element is necessary because these patients need a more rapid and concrete depiction of the structure of the therapeutic situation to ward off the anxiety that would otherwise accrue from being subjected to the more abstinent, slowly evolving, gradually structured, analytical type situation. The ego of the alcoholic requires nurturing, not judicial neglect.

Thus, it can be seen that the usually less structured approach to therapy has been modified and the "therapeutic working compact" introduced. It should be noted that the reality considerations between therapist and patient, as these involve the therapeutic situation, are openly and clearly discussed. The area similar to the working alliance in an analysis is also defined. Transference meanings or implications are avoided. In making confrontations or observations to the patient, the same order of priorities is followed. First, reality considerations, which also include the delineation, definition, and use of those ego functions germane to this concern with reality. Second, the elements similar to the working alliance—here the therapeutic working compact. Transference meaning and implications are brought in only as a last resort, and only if it is felt necessary to maintain the therapeutic working compact.

It has already been noted that many of the so-called "autonomous ego functions" (Hartmann, 1959) of the alcoholic patient are impaired in their functioning, as one result of the alcoholic's increasing preoccupation with the drinking itself, with the consequent deflection of available attention cathexis from those functions. The therapist lends his own autonomous functions as a temporary prosthesis (Dickes, 1967) for the patient. This might involve supplying help in the recognition of a judgment the patient was making—in testing the reality of that judgment, in determining the meaning and meaningfulness of the judgment in the patient's present and past life situations, in helping the patient to integrate the judgment in a psychologically useful sense. In the same manner perceptions, observations, ideas, and feelings have to be scrutinized. The patient must be helped to learn to use the many evaluative functions that are necessarily operative prior to making a decision or becoming involved in an action. As the therapist "lends" the alcoholic his ego functions in the area where the alcoholic's are defective, it is the therapist's ego functions which tend to replace the reliance on alcohol, which, as previously mentioned, has given the alcoholic the illusion of adequate functioning.

It becomes very clear that this approach to the psychotherapy of the alcoholic patient is at great variance with the traditional analytic method. The rationale for this different approach, of course, comes from knowledge originally obtained from psychoanalysis and modified to fit our particular objective in psychotherapy. Thus, in the psychotherapy of the alcoholic, we deal with reality problems, impaired reality functioning, and the altered autonomy of ego functions in a reparative sense first. The "therapeutic working compact" will next come in for repeated scrutiny—interpretations will be offered for any attempts to infringe upon its viability. Transference interpretations, as a rule, will be avoided. The transference relationship will be interpreted as a last resort in order to maintain the therapeutic working compact. In the interpretation, the therapist will first be described as representing the wished-for parent from the past. Also the therapist will be seen as supplying those attributes and attitudes that the parents never supplied, but which the patient so desperately missed.

Practically, this means that only those negative transference reactions that threaten the viability of the therapy will be interpreted. The same goes for erotic positive transference features. Transference interpretations are eschewed to avoid bringing genetically earlier determinants into the forefront of the therapy, which is emphasizing present functioning. The genetic elements that do emerge are recast into a perspective that highlights our intellectual knowledge relating to the continuity of and evolvement of individual psychic development (thus, making general the specific element learned, as well as isolating its unique emotional significance). This is done in lieu of concentrating upon specific libidinal fixations and the actual consequences of regressive tugs. The defense of isolation is being energetically fostered.

Symptoms are noted and respected, and will generally come into the center of the therapeutic arena when ample knowledge of their defensive significance has been understood and the importance of these compromise formations for the functioning of the patient has been absorbed by the therapist. Only symptom formation that seems manifestly deleterious for the patient's well-being and ability to continue the therapy will be circumspectly probed (e.g., denial). Defenses, and certain character traits, are usually reinforced rather than attacked. Reaction formations and some counterphobic activities frequently are reinforced rather than analyzed.

As a generalization, it would be fair to say that attempt is made to strengthen existing defenses (Gill, 1967; Knight, 1953), with some of the binding substance being contributed by the therapist's ego functions temporarily lent to the patient. These functions are offered to enable the patient to gain greater recognition of his own inner world and greater awareness of his person and his environment. They are also essential to help make the therapeutic situation, which is dependent for its stability upon the intactness of these autonomous functions, viable. These autonomous functions act as a prism in focusing the communications between patient and therapist, and for sharpening the patient's ability to grasp his own inner world. The therapeutic approach is both manipulative and seductive. It takes as much advantage as can be derived from our knowledge of the general psychological backgrounds of patients suffering from alcoholism. Their need to be given and cared for is exploited by our detailed explanations, which begin to offer a structure of some stability within which the treatment will be conducted. Suggestion is used in a psychologically sound sense that takes advantage of the basically unstable sense of identity these patients demonstrate. They are psychologically open, looking for precepts, guidance, information, and general help in learning how to function. They are searching for the parent who can be consistent, fair, and informative, and who will employ all his pertinent knowledge in the patients' interest. We take advantage of the neglect and omissions and attempt to help supply, in a genetically general rather than specific sense, what we suspect is developmentally wanting. We help to build up a picture of an inner world which has some psychological fidelity and lend ourselves and especially our attitudes and knowledge for them to use, in structuring a consistent and accurate depiction of general psychic reality. We are trying to make do by providing a synthetic endo- and exopsychic structure that represents them, others, and their new-found psychic world, which now provides a consistent generalized reflection through which these essentially unstable and identity-less individuals can view themselves.

Another important observation, whose delineation will help round out this discussion, also helps explain why these patients are so open to change if the therapy is conducted by a reasonable, benign, knowledgeable, and consistent therapist. In practice, every alcoholic patient seen had at least one parent who manifestly displayed psychotic behavior. Such behavior was especially pronounced during the early developing years and as such exerted a profound and far-reaching effect upon the development of these rather vulnerable individuals.

The significance of the family constellation in the etiology of alcoholism has been stressed by many authors, Knight (1937 a, b; 1938) indicated that both parents affect the development and elaboration of the illness. Simmel (1948) described mothers who overtly seduced and manipulated their children. When the child, as a result of this marked overstimulation, responded to the seduction with a sexual response of its own, it was unmercifully attacked by the outraged parent. This behavior is similar to that of parents of sexually delinquent children described by Litin et al. (1937), Johnson (1949), and Szurek (1942). These workers noted that the children in their delinquent sexual behavior were acting out the unconscious impulses of their parents. Chafetz (1959) felt that "the common thread running through these patients' early relationships was the absence of a warm, giving, meaningful relationship with a mother figure during this period (early years) of development." Schuckit et al. (1969) stressed that "both the clinical psychiatric concomitants and the family history of the psychiatric illness are important factors in the nosological grouping of alcoholics." Ferenczi (1955) notes that pathological adults, especially if they have been disturbed in their balance and self-control by some misfortune or by intoxicating drugs, mistake the play of children for the desires of a sexually mature person. They allow themselves to be carried away. "The real rape of girls who have hardly grown out of the age of infants, similar sexual acts of mature women with boys, and also enforced homosexual acts, are more frequent occurrences than has hitherto been assumed."

One resident described an alcoholic stepfather who insisted on sleeping in the same bed with his ten-year-old stepson. The other son and the mother were banished from the bedroom. The boy developed an anal tear with some moderate bleeding which required some suturing at a local hospital emergency room. The stepfather attacked the boy for having irregular bowel habits and was reinforced in his verbal and physical abuse by the mother and the spared stepbrother. I had some difficulty convincing the resident that it was necessary to try to intervene with the mother of this boy (she was the alcoholic patient in treatment) and to help rescue him from the bedroom and the activities of this stepfather.

This type of tale is frequently reported by alcoholic patients about parents. The bizarre actions can take place when the parents themselves are in an alcoholic state, at which point there is minimal control of impulses and reality testing by the ego. In other instances, there is no question of the temporary toxic influence of alcohol; rather, the strange behavior is an expression of the chronic psychological disturbance of the parent. Chafetz (1959), in enumerating factors contributing to the emotional deprevation of alcoholic patients, listed the fact that as children they had psychotic mothers and that some parents were severely alcoholic during the patient's early years.

Parenthetically, it is interesting to note that I was first alerted to the nature of this pathology not by supervising the therapy of alcoholic patients, but during the course of the prolonged psychotherapy of a schizophrenic young man. He was living with an elderly mother and frequent attempts were made to encourage him to move from this apartment and to begin to function more independently. All attempts were fruitless. If I persisted in indicating that he should "free himself from his mother," he would respond to this suggestion by saying "now I have breasts"—indicating to me that he appropriated part of her body to interfere with any attempt to free himself from her.

One day, he was recounting how his mother was looking out of the window, reporting to the patient on some of the neighbors leaving the apartment house. "Now Mrs. Smith is going to the meat market; she is going to buy roast beef—Mrs. Jones is going to the grocery store for rolls and butter." It occurred to me to point out to the patient that his mother could not possibly know where Mrs. Smith or Mrs. Jones were going or what they intended to buy. I stated that his mother's behavior indicated that she was suffering from a severe mental illness that had impaired her ability to make proper judgments about reality events and this illness must have affected her relationship with the patient. The patient responded to my observation by indicating for the first time that he felt himself separate from his mother. He became more and more aware of his own body and experienced more clearly his various body parts. During several subsequent years, the technique of "cleaving" the parent and then other members of the family away from the patient continued. The patient has noted an increasing sense of reality in relation both to his own body and environment. He repeatedly scolded me for my earlier attempts to have him free himself from his mother. He never understood what I meant. It was only after he was able to "see" his mother defined in terms of her confused ideas and these ideas defined in terms of illness that he could gradually feel himself becoming separate from her and then gradually more aware of himself as a separate person. It was this fortuitous clinical observation that alerted me to listen more attentively to the patient's description of his immediate environment (parents), and note that one or sometimes both parents were suffering from severe mental illness of psychotic proportions. Thus, in treatment, small discrepancies in behavior were focused upon and pursued until they were fully understood. I recognize that, in the past, details of the parents' behavior would have been overlooked. That my experience with a schizophrenic patient served as a factor in my ability to make a similar observation in relation to alcoholic patients may be more than a matter of chance. Sugarman et al. (1965) notes the similarities between the reactive and essential alcoholics (as defined by Knight, 1937a), and the reactive and essential schizophrenics as indicated by Langfeldt (1937). Chafetz (1959) observed that the meaningful relationship with the mother that was absent in the alcoholic was similar to the relationship of schizophrenic patients with their mothers. One is struck by the frequency with which alcoholic patients report incidents describing the parents' eccentric behavior without any realization that there is anything strange about it. It was also interesting that frequently the therapist would report the material with an equal lack of awareness of the abnormalities involved. When the incidents were further pursued, it became apparent that the judgment of the patient was compromised to the extent of being unable to determine what constituted abnormal behavior on the part of the parent.

In doing therapy, the reality of the parents' abnormalities is pointed out and worked over. Since the bizarreness had been part of the developmental reality of the patient's background, the ability to see the parents' disturbed behavior against the background of an average environment may be emerging for the first time. This approach, if successful, gives rise to a great sense of relief on the part of the patient. It helps him to see not only the parent, but himself: as Shengold (1963) noted, "to see and not to be" the parent.

This atypical parental behavior is enmeshed within the family structure. Attempts at clarification evolve into a problem of ferreting out those aspects of the family situation that are pathological in the psychological sense from those that are more consistently normal. This understanding then provides a background against which the symptomatology of the parent can be judged more accurately. The extensive identification with the parents' abnormalities still affects the patient's character and behavior in the present. These pathological identifications represent a bond with the parent and compromise the patient's separate identity. There is special damage to one's sense of identity and a satisfactory integration of disparate aspects of the personality when the attitudes and actions of the parents are contradictory, confused, bizarre, or psychotic.

We note that the therapist, who is placed in the role of an ideal, can be substituted in the patient's mind for the parental figures with the disturbance, so that the possibility for new identifications with a healthy, reality-oriented figure is possible. This is a process that can take place slowly and silently as therapy progresses. It is actually responsible for the rather marked changes in behavior that can be observed in the psychotherapy of the alcoholic. Sudden shifts in comportment are frequent. Some patients will precipitously give up drinking. They might start to work more steadily or suddenly become aware of very positive feelings toward their spouse. They become willing to listen to the judgment of the therapist and will readily substitute his attitudes for their own. Many alcoholic patients seem easily to form rapid although shallow and diffuse temporary identifications. These may be based upon the tentative acceptance of the therapist's criteria for reasonable behavior as being consonant with their own newly evolving values. The standards of the therapist are gradually absorbed by the patient, the guidelines of the disturbed parent and, by identification, that of the disturbed patient are reevaluated against the new models held forth by the therapist. The patient, with his therapist's help, learns to reevaluate attitudes that are based on superego identifications, and functions that are dependent upon ego tendencies. As internalized elements of the disturbed parent that are represented in both the ego and the superego of the patient are gradually critically evaluated, they can be replaced by features that are now derived from the therapeutic working compact between therapist and patient. This process is frequently expedited by the patient's ease in resorting to imitation and mimicry. The sense of identity in these patients is tarnished and burdened by the pathological parental attitudes, and they have a marked "as if" propensity (Deutsch, 1942). They vicariously adopt attitudes of others easily and adeptly. Thus, an attempt is made to exploit this pathological ego tendency therapeutically, by fostering attitudes based on the therapeutic working compact with the therapist.

An example is in order. A patient reported that from childhood on his mother would hide small quantities of food in various unlikely places in the house. When occasionally these caches were discovered, the mother would remark, "The world is always so unsettled, perhaps we'll lose our money, or dad will lose his job—it's important to prepare for any eventuality." If the patient would protest about the odor or the insects attracted by the food, the mother would in a fury attack him with the statement, "You want us to be unprepared, to be at the mercy of anyone who has money and food; you don't want us to be a free and independent family, etc." The patient would succumb to the harangue, feel guilty because he really did not have the family's best interests in mind, and come away from the confrontation with the idea that his mother was prudent and he was thoughtless. His mother was extolled by his father, the rest of the family and many neighbors as a thoughtful, pleasant person—the patient in a general way shared their views.

During treatment, the mother's distortion of reality was emphasized, noting the fact that this was symptomatic of a rather marked disturbance on her part. The patient was then helped to see the unrealistic nature of the mother's thinking. The therapist here helps the patient's shaky reality testing by pitting his (the therapist's) knowledge of reality against that of the mother, and in this way gradually frees the patient sufficiently to be able first to question and in some instances actually oppose the mother's ideas. This is not as easy a task as may seem at the outset. If what we can see as a delusional element is held to be true by the patient's parent, the patient will need to accept the parent's view of reality in order to preserve the sometimes desperately needed relationship to that parent. This is especially true of the child. By identification, denial of reality or distortions of reality become almost automatic. Since delusions are attempts to solve basic psychological conflicts, those aspects of the parent's behavior that are sickest and most trauma-producing are likely to be hidden from the patient.

In a therapeutic sense, one is first setting oneself up in opposition to the parent by highlighting his or her unrealistic attitude. The patient will frequently be pleased to have the therapist as an ally who acts as an extension of his ego for reality testing, and who serves as an opponent of his parents. Therapists have continually found themselves in this role in opposition to some of the traditional views of the parents. The difference in this instance is that the focus is on the pathology of the parent. The parent's disturbed behavior is made alien from the rest of the parent's functions. This helps the patient to recognize aspects of the parent's disturbed behavior within himself, and then to make this ideation or behavior alien to the rest of his personality. The therapist, by offering his views as representative of a different reality from the parent's now discredited and objectively faulty perception and depiction of reality, offers the patient the opportunity to compare and to choose his view of reality with a freedom heretofore denied him by virtue of the early pathological identifications.

One can trace the vicissitudes of the parents' pathology as seen in the alcoholic patient. Frequently, these patients act out in relation to their own children certain traumata inflicted upon them as children. The action is frequently carried out in a fury, during which there may be some subtly altered state of consciousness, so that the patient gives the impression of being momentarily "lost." In this instance, a hypnoid state (Dickes, 1965) wards off the patient's awareness of certain drives and affects. This defective ego control permits an "acting out" of primitive impulses. In one instance, the same hairbrush that was used on a patient was saved and used in exactly the same manner on the patient's child.

Another very frequent manifestation of irrationality that also must be interpreted involves the patient attacking himself the way he was attacked by a disturbed parent. This is an example of identification with the aggressor (A. Freud, 1937), whose actions are internalized and made syntonic. The element of identification with the parent must be pointed out, made alien, and interpreted. Further vicissitudes of the pathology of the parent can then be followed by noting externalizations of elements of behavior onto other figures in the environment, with a quasi-delusional effect. For instance, every superior is seen as a demanding, irrational, tormenting object—this has often little to do with his actual behavior for, by using primary process mechanisms, especially *pars pro toto,* and displacements, a slight element in the behavior of the superior becomes "the" behavior of the superior. All of this can be profitably traced back via patient to parent. It is also manifestly obvious that elements of this kind of distortion will be perceived by the patient in relation to the person of the therapist.

I think then that it becomes even more clear why the delineation of the pathology of the parent strengthens in the psychotherapy the entity analogous to the working alliance in analysis, that most important element in the patient-therapist relationship, in its "real" rather than the "transference" implications. The therapist becomes an understanding ally in dealing with a frequently overwhelming and shattering experience (the experience of the patient with his disturbed parent). In a sense, the therapist is initially acting like an auxiliary ego and one that is anchored in reality, rather than the parental ego that was rooted in pathology. The therapist thus allies himself with the healthy portion of the patient's ego against the ill parts. This joint effort, involving the highlighting of the pathology of the parent, contributes to a rapid and early welding of the therapeutic working compact. It provides necessary ingredients for withstanding some of the transference reactions that may arise in the course of therapy, and also helps blunt the intensity of the pathological projections onto the therapist of the internalized parental attributes.

After the pathology of the parent is clearly defined as constituting a major problem in the way the patient views his person, one that alters in a most deforming way his sense of self, and thus his sense of identity, this part of the therapeutic task can recede in its emphasis. My supervisory experience has shown that this technique, which alerts the therapist to look for rather typical pathological behavior as indication of parental disturbance, is a most valuable addition to the therapeutic armamentarium helping to facilitate the successful psychotherapy of the alcoholic patient.

Thus, basic psychoanalytic information derived from our increased knowledge of the sequence and importance of early development, and especially the skewing effect of the severe parental pathology upon this development, provides the background of data through which we view our alcoholic patient.

We know that maturation took place in an environment that would not be considered a generally expectable one, and that these patients have needs that were not met during phase-appropriate periods of their development. They are literally bound to their primary objects by virtue of unsatisfied needs, and have great difficulty moving on to more suitable objects. Their frustration tolerance is minimal, as is their ability to bear anxiety. They were not adequately helped to differentiate their wishes from their actions by the imposition of proper parental restraint. Self-control is minimal, pleasure in experiencing feelings, evaluating these and making decisions in regard to actions has to be learned in the present therapeutic situation. The therapist is viewed and in a way acts as the wished-for and needed parent, who in reality was too psychologically disturbed to be developmentally helpful, but instead left the patient with a residue of distorted notions and fragmented ego functions, and a lasting object hunger. As a group, these patients lack an inner psychological structure that is either stable or consistent. Their sense of identity is unjelled, as is any stable sense of self. They eagerly seize upon any suggestive information supplied by the therapist that will provide support for their most porous inner being. They need precepts and dicta, and are readily open to psychologically sound information and knowledge that has relevance to their own growth and development. They need help in being able to evaluate what they observe in others—frequently they need to be taught how to evaluate their self-observations as well. It is their openness to suggestion, by virtue of their extensive psychological disturbance and vulnerability, that makes the strongly suggestive approach outlined in this paper such an effective tool for therapy. Suggestions, in the form of information and knowledge, are imparted in an intellectual manner with the object of fostering the defense of isolation.

The therapist supplies a new psychological matrix in the form of intact ego functions that are lent out to the patient to make up for those functions that are found to be developmentally deficient because of the instances of parental pathology. In therapy, the parents' deficiencies are clearly highlighted so as to help the patient separate his attitudes, ideas, and functioning from theirs. As the therapist helps in this process, he permits his attitudes, ideas, and methods of functioning to be substituted for those of the degraded and psychologically deformed parent. The readiness and openness to change that these patients demonstrate frequently leads to dramatically effective therapeutic results, but this is not because of any real understanding or insight into motivation for either the drinking or for giving it up. The patients are responding to sound suggestion which they may view as a beloved order from a longed-for and needed parent who has been essentially absent in a developmentally helpful sense, but is now experienced as present in the form of the therapist.

This technique utilizes insight in the form of increasing knowledge of certain functions of the ego, which may be initially defined and offered by the therapist and finally may be utilized by the patient. The patient is increasingly familiarized with his inner life and its differentiation from his external world and is also supplied with more general information about the norms of development. Insight is thus offered in a more selective sense—less emphasis on the more traditional transference and resistance—with more emphasis on defining and explicating various ego functions and general developmental knowledge. The main vehicle for change revolves around new identifications with the ideas and attitudes of the therapist, which replace the identifications with the pathological parents.

We can use this method of approach outlined with some understanding of its rationale as a welcome supplement to the many efforts to understand and treat the alcoholic patient. This psychotherapeutic technique, using psychoanalytic tools and knowledge, provides a welcome addition to our therapeutic repertoire.

REFERENCES

Chafetz, M. E. (1959), Practical and theoretical considerations in the psychotherapy of alcoholism. Quarterly Journal of the Study of Alcohol, 20: 281–291.

Deutsch, H. (1942), Some forms of emotional disturbance and their relationship to schizophrenia. Psychoanalytic Quarterly, 11: 301–321.

Dickes, R. (1965), The defensive function of an altered state of consciousness: a hypnoid state. Journal of the American Psychoanalytic Association, 13: 356–403.

——— (1967), Severe regressive disruptions of the therapeutic alliance. Journal of the American Psychoanalytic Association, 15: 508–533.

Ferenczi, S. (1955), Confusion of tongues between adults and the child. In Final Contributions to the Problems and Methods of Psychoanalysis. New York: Basic Books.

Freud, A. (1937), The Ego and the Mechanisms of Defense. London: Hogarth.

Freud, S. (1959), Inhibitions, symptoms and anxiety. In Standard Edition 20: 77–175. London: Hogarth.

Gill, M., ed. (1967), The Collected Papers of David Rapaport. New York: Basic Books.

Glover, E. (1932), On the etiology of drug addiction. International Journal of Psycho-Analysis 13: 298–328.

Greenacre, P. (1959), Certain technical problems in the transference relationship. Journal of the American Psychoanalytic Association, 7: 484–502.

Greenson, R. R. (1965), The working alliance and the transference neurosis. Psychoanalytic Quarterly 34: 155–181.

Hartmann, H. (1959), Ego Psychology and the Problem of Adaptation. New York: International Universities Press.

Johnson, A. M. (1949), Sanctions for superego lacunae of adolescence. In Searchlights on Delinquency, ed. M. K. Eissler, 225–245. New York: International Universities Press.

Knight, R. P. (1937a), The dynamics and treatment of chronic alcohol addiction. Bulletin of the Menninger Clinic, 1: 233–250.

——— (1937b), Psychodynamics of chronic alcoholism. Journal of Nervous and Mental Disorders, 86: 538–548.

——— (1938), The psychoanalytic treatment in a sanitarium of chronic addiction to alcohol. Journal of the American Medical Association, 111: 1443–1448.

——— (1953), Borderline states. Bulletin of the Menninger Clinic, 17: 1–12.

Langfeldt, G. (1937), Prognosis in schizophrenia and factors influencing course of disease. Acta Psychiat Neurol Scand, 13: 1–288.

Litin, E. M.; Griffin, M. E.; and Johnson, A. M. (1937), Parental influence in unusual sexual behavior in children. Psychoanalytic Quarterly, 25: 37–55.

Loewenstein, R. M. (1972), Ego autonomy and psychoanalytic technique. 41: 1–22.

Schuckit, M.; Pitts, F. N., Jr.; Reich, T.; King, L. J.; and Wanokur, G. (1969), Alcoholism. Archives of General Psychiatry (Chicago), 20: 301–306.

Schur, M. (1964), Symptom formation and character formation. International Journal of Psycho-Analysis, 45: 147–150.

Shengold, L. (1963), The parent as sphinx. Journal of the American Psychoanalytic Association, 11: 725–751.

Silber, A. (1959), Psychotherapy with alcoholics. Journal of Nervous and Mental Disorders, 129: 477–485.

——— (1970), An addendum to the technique of psychotherapy with alcoholics. Journal of Nervous and Mental Disorders, 150: 423–437.

Simmel, E. (1948), Alcoholism and addiction. Psychoanalytic Quarterly, 17: 6–31.

Sugarman, A. A.; Reilly, V., and Albahary, R. S. (1965), Social competence and essential reactive distinction in alcoholism. Archives of General Psychiatry (Chicago), 12: 552–556.

Szurek, S. (1942), Genesis of psychopathic personality. Psychiatry, 5: 1–6.

Zetzel, E. R. (1956), Current concepts of transference. International Journal of Psycho-Analysis, 37: 369–6.

PART VI

The Disease Concept and Psychoanalysis

Pattison, sobell, and sobell set out a brief formulation of the disease concept taken from a part of their classic book *Emerging Concepts of Alcohol Dependence* (1977). Pattison was a passionate advocate for scientific research in the study of alcoholism. In this book the authors review the evidence against the disease concept. Despite their and others' criticism,[1] the disease concept has flourished as a treatment model,[2] and there are a number of passionate defenders of the disease concept,[3] which has been extended to all chemical dependency (all addictive substances),[4] gambling,[5] and nicotine.[6]

Disease concept treatment consists of education, exhortation, and confrontation.[7] If the patient does not acknowledge his addiction, he is confronted by the counselor and the peer group. Once acknowledging the problem, the patient is taught that he must abstain and encouraged to attend AA, get a sponsor in AA, and work the twelve steps of AA.[8]

The objectives of the disease concept of treatment are to abstain, to become and remain active in AA (or Narcotics Anonymous [NA], a twelve-step program for narcotic addicts) as a form of aftercare (for several years, but not necessarily forever), and to resume normal functioning in the community. Insight is generally limited to understanding that most of the alcoholic's problems are caused by active addiction and can be alleviated by adherence to AA/NA principles. Since most alcoholism counselors and many addiction counselors are members of twelve-step programs, they are role models and often employ self-disclosure as a treatment technique. An excellent depiction of this treatment can be found in Nowinski and Baker.[9, 10]

The two reprinted papers combining psychoanalytic therapy and disease concept are on opposite poles. The Brickman paper retains the focus on psychoanalysis, while Zweben's applies some psychoanalytic concepts to a basic disease concept model.

Brickman notes the failure of traditional psychoanalysis to successfully treat additions, and he offers an explanation. My analysis of the addicted patients in the Menninger Research Project supports his conclusion.[11] Brick-

Table VI.1.

The Twelve Steps of Alcoholics Anonymous	The Twelve Traditions of Alcoholics Anonymous
1. We admitted we were powerless over alcohol—that our lives had become unmanageable.	1. Our common welfare should come first; personal recovery depends upon A.A. unity.
2. Came to believe that a Power greater than ourselves could restore us to sanity.	2. For our group purpose, there is but one ultimate authority—a loving God as He may express Himself in our group conscience. Our leaders are but trusted servants; they do not govern.
3. Made a decision to turn our will and our lives over to the care of God *as we understood Him.*	
4. Made a searching and fearless moral inventory of ourselves.	3. The only requirement for A.A. membership is a desire to stop drinking.
5. Admitted to God, to ourselves and to another human being the exact nature of our wrongs.	4. Each group should be autonomous except in matters affecting other groups or A.A. as a whole.
6. Were entirely ready to have God remove all these defects of character.	5. Each group has but one primary purpose—to carry its message to the alcoholic who still suffers.
7. Humbly asked Him to remove our shortcomings.	6. An A.A. group ought never endorse, finance, or lend the A.A. name to any related facility or outside enterprise, lest problems of money, property, and prestige divert us from our primary purpose.
8. Made a list of all persons we had harmed, and became willing to make amends to them all.	
9. Made direct amends to such people wherever possible, except when to do so would injure them or others.	7. Every A.A. group ought to be fully self-supporting, declining outside contributions.
10. Continued to take personal inventory and when we were wrong promptly admitted it.	8. Alcoholics Anonymous should remain forever non-professional, but our service centers may employ special workers.
11. Sought through prayer and meditation to improve our conscious contact with God, *as we understood Him,* praying only for knowledge of His will for us and the power to carry that out.	9. A.A., as such, ought never be organized; but we may create service boards or committees directly responsible to those they serve.
12. Having had a spiritual awakening as the result of these steps, we tried to carry this message to alcoholics, and to practice these principles in all our affairs.	10. Alcoholics Anonymous has no opinion on outside issues; hence the A.A. name ought never be drawn into public controversy.

11. Our public relations policy is based on attraction rather than promotion; we need always maintain personal anonymity at the level of press, radio, and films.
12. Anonymity is the spiritual foundation of all our traditions, ever reminding us to place principles before personalities.

The Twelve Steps and Twelve Traditions are reprinted with permission of Alcoholics Anonymous World Services, Inc. Permission to reprint the Twelve Steps and Twelve Traditions does not mean that A.A. has reviewed or approved the contents of this publication, nor that A.A. agrees with the views expressed herein. A.A. is a program of recovery from alcoholism *only*—use of the Twelve Steps and Twelve Traditions in connection with programs and activities which are patterned after A.A., but which address other problems, or in any other non-A.A. context, does not imply otherwise.

man suggests that the addiction be viewed as a serious medical condition that disturbs the psychoanalytic situation and thus must be confronted, and once successfully dealt with, the analysis can resume. He discusses the integration of AA and psychoanalytic treatment, finding no essential conflict. [12, 13] The reader may note in the first clinical vingette the transformation of the patient's attitude after the cessation of drinking bears a resemblance to that of Gustafson's case example.

Zweben has coined the term "recovery-oriented psychotherapy." This therapy is much more specialized addiction treatment than psychoanalytic therapy. In the paper here, she discusses the addiction-specific tasks that must be addressed before conventional psychoanalytic therapy can be applied. She discusses the treatment contract, popular in treatment programs, which can be viewed as a concretization of the therapeutic compact. Additionally, Zweben discusses the use of some cognitive/behavioral approaches in combination with the disease concept and the dynamic approach.[14, 15] In another paper,[16] she discusses how basic psychoanalytic concepts can be used in specialized addiction programs. Zweben's approach draws upon the work of Stephanie Brown, whose book[17] presents a developmental epistemological view of addiction recovery. Brown's treatment approach is based on incorporating the principles of AA into psychotherapy.

Other writers who combine psychoanalytic therapy with the disease concept include Bell and Khantzian,[18] Kaufman,[19] Levinson,[20] and Vanicelli.[21]

NOTES

1. Peele, 1984, 1989; Fingarette, 1988.
2. Rotgers, Keller, and Morgenstern, 1996, p. 7.
3. Blume, 1983; M. Keller, 1976; Miller and Toft, 1990; Wallace, 1993.
4. Milhorn, 1990.
5. Blume, 1987.
6. N. S. Miller, 1991.
7. Cook, 1988a; Laundergan, 1982; Mann, 1991; Stuckey and Harrison, 1982.
8. Nowinski and Baker, 1992.
9. Nowinski and Baker, 1992.
10. Other useful sources include Nace, 1987; Rogers and McMillan, 1989; and Wallace, 1996. Milam and Ketcham, 1981, have written the most radical version of the disease concept, called the dispositional disease model.
11. Yalisove, 1988.
12. Dodes, 1988; Rosen, 1981; and Spiegal and Mulder, 1986, also discuss combining therapy and AA.
13. S. Brown, 1985, illustrates potential conflicts between traditional therapy and AA. In my view, the difference in values between traditional psychoanalytic therapy and AA is perhaps the most important consideration. AA values spirituality, inspiration, common communal purpose, depending on others, self-disclosure, giving service by helping other alcoholics. Psychoanalysis values independence, insight, judicious self-disclosure, and rationality. See also Humphreys, 1993.
14. Keller, 1996, combines cognitive/behavioral and psychodynamic techniques for relapse prevention strategies.
15. "Euphoric recall," a term used in Zweben's article, refers to the drug user's selective memory of the euphoric effects of the drug as opposed to the dysphoric effects. The negative effects are forgotten or ignored (Washton and Gold, 1987).
16. Zweben, 1989.
17. S. Brown, 1985.
18. Bell and Khantzian, 1991.
19. Kaufman, 1994.
20. Levinson, 1985.
21. Vanicelli, 1992.

19. The Traditional Model of Alcoholism

E. M. Pattison, M. B. Sobell, and L. C. Sobell

D EFINING traditional concepts of alcoholism is an extraordinarily difficult task, because they derive from multiple sources—Alcoholics Anonymous, books relating individual struggles with alcoholism, the disease concept of alcoholism formulated by E. M. Jellinek, and public interpretations of these ideas. The traditional model, as we shall consider it, can best be described as a "folk science" model. It is an accretion of beliefs, values, and ideologies. In large part, its development was intended to meet sociopolitical needs rather than to synthesize scientific findings. This brief summary of traditional concepts provides a context for understanding why it is necessary to develop new concepts of alcohol dependence. We have identified the following basic elements as comprising the traditional model of alcoholism; we acknowledge that not everyone working in the field of alcoholism will agree with this exact formulation.

1. *There is a unitary phenomenon which can be identified as alcoholism.* Despite its variations, alcoholism can be considered a distinct entity which can be described and recognized.
2. *Alcoholics and prealcoholics are essentially different from nonalcoholics.* Some of those persons who are not already alcoholics are predisposed to develop alcohol problems if they drink at all. The alcoholic reacts differently to alcohol than the nonalcoholic. This difference may be pre-existing or developmental and probably has a physiological basis, perhaps genetically determined. A nonalcoholic may experience drinking problems but does not become a true alcoholic.
3. *Alcoholics may sometimes experience a seemingly irresistible physical craving for alcohol, or a strong psychological compulsion to drink.* They often appear to begin drinking against their own volition.

4. *Alcoholics gradually develop a process called "loss of control" over drinking, and possibly even an inability to stop drinking.* By Jellinek's definition, this "loss of control" happens even when the alcoholic has ingested only a small amount of alcohol; physical dependence on alcohol becomes established and somehow compels the alcoholic to continue drinking. By popular definition, "loss of control" has been extended to mean that once an alcoholic has begun to drink, that person has no voluntary control over further drinking behavior during that episode — "First drink, then drunk." These two versions of "loss of control" should not be confused with one another.

5. *Alcoholism is a permanent and irreversible condition.* As alcoholism develops, permanent biological changes occur in the alcoholic. Even after a number of years, ingestion of only a small quantity of alcohol by a person who was once physically dependent on alcohol will reinitiate physical dependence. Since the physiological consequences of alcoholism are enduring even when the alcoholic is not drinking, alcoholism can be arrested but never cured in the sense of the alcoholic ever being able to drink in a nonproblem manner. "Once an alcoholic, always an alcoholic."

6. *Alcoholism is a progressive disease which follows an inexorable development through a distinct series of phases.* For most alcoholics, alcoholism is a disease process which develops gradually over a ten- to fifteen-year period. If the alcoholic's drinking is not arrested, this progression will lead to ultimate deterioration and death.

The components of the traditional model are not necessarily interdependent. Some major elements could be modified or omitted without affecting all of the remaining components. Overall, however, the traditional model has had clear implications for the design of alcoholism treatment services. Specifically, it dictates that alcoholism treatment should emphasize making alcoholics aware of their permanent physiological abnormality and the necessity for them to be permanently abstinent. Further, it implies that treatment should be largely concerned with problems which result from learning to live without alcohol.

However, in recent years many fundamental assumptions of the traditional model of alcoholism have been seriously challenged by new clinical and experimental evidence. Because these data conflict with traditional concepts, the evidence has often been ignored or dismissed by those working in the field. Taken as a whole, this recent evidence indicates that substantial changes in the heretofore popularly accepted "facts" about the nature of alcohol dependence are inevitable. We shall find, for example, that there appears to be no separately definable entity which can be identified as "alcoholism." Rather there appears to be a variety of situations which have in common that persons suffer adverse consequences as a result of using alcohol. Eventually, certain factors—physiological, psychological, sociocultural, and/or environmental—which increase the susceptibility for persons to incur drinking problems are likely to be identified. However, the breadth of such determinants and problems already appears so encompassing that the post hoc labeling of individuals as "alcoholic" has little utility and may even precipitate a worsening of some persons' drinking problems. Physical dependence on alcohol has been repeatedly demonstrated not to occur merely from the ingestion of a few drinks, even by the most chronic of "alcoholics." Further, the "progressive" nature of the development of alcohol problems has been seriously challenged by recent epidemiological and longitudinal data. Finally, there exist a multitude of demonstrations that alcohol problems are reversible, at least for some individuals. This accumulation of evidence conflicts with traditional concepts to such a degree that the two cannot be reconciled. The resulting problems threaten to restrict the range of available treatment and prevention services, and to hinder the development of new and more effective treatment methods.

Having recognized the present failings of traditional concepts, we must develop new concepts of alcohol dependence which are more consonant with contemporary research findings. While it would be premature to specify a formal revised model of alcohol dependence, we can suggest the characteristics of such a model based on the present state of knowledge. The sociopolitical objectives of earlier concepts have in large part been satisfactorily achieved, and the need for providing services to individuals who have alcohol problems has been generally accepted and legislated in most cases. It is now time to move in the direction of developing a better quality of service, both in terms of effectiveness and efficiency.

20. Psychoanalysis and Substance Abuse: Toward a More Effective Approach

Bernard Brickman

INTRODUCTION

The purpose of this paper is to advance the thesis that chemical dependency encountered in psychoanalytic practice is frequently mismanaged due to a failure of psychoanalytic theory to integrate more recent biobehavioral and neurophysiological research findings during the past two or three decades. I shall propose that psychoanalytic treatment of chemically dependent individuals frequently fails as it is informed by theories that have suffered serious methodological flaws in their inception. The basic misconception is that substance abuse is a secondary phenomenon to underlying psychopathology *and thus amenable to being influenced through psychoanalytic insight.*

I shall review major psychoanalytic contributions to the understanding of drug and alcohol addiction that both reflect and shape the above concept. Then I shall cite findings from other biobehavioral disciplines that support the idea that drug dependency constitutes a separate disease syndrome in itself, requiring a direct nonpsychoanalytic intervention strategy leading to total chemical abstinence if analysis is to succeed.

The role of Alcoholics Anonymous and related mutual-help groups will be discussed as potential allies to the psychoanalyst wishing to expand his/her effectiveness in treating substance abuse.

DEFINITION

Drug dependence can be defined as "a state psychic and sometimes physical, resulting from the interaction between a living organism and a drug, characterized by behavioral and other responses that always include a compulsion

Reprinted by permission from *Journal of the American Academy of Psychoanalysis* 16 (1988): 359–79.

to take a drug on a continuous or periodic basis in order to experience its psychic effects and sometimes to avoid the discomfort of its absence. Tolerance may or may not be present" (World Health Organization, 1964). I would like to stress that the syndrome can be a continuous or periodic one.

Classically, what we term addiction consists of two properties: (a) tolerance, and (b) withdrawal symptoms (manifestation of altered function as a result of deprivation of the required drug as an essential metabolite). Some researchers (Bejerot, 1980) have felt that this definition is too restrictive and have preferred to consider addiction to be present when there is compulsive use, inability to stop, and continued use despite adverse consequences.

I shall use terms such as "chemical dependence," "drug addiction," "drug abuse," "substance abuse," and "alcoholism" interchangeably.

THE CLINICAL PROBLEM

Persons who are dependent on drug and other chemical substances in order to maintain their psychic equilibrium are frequently found in psychoanalytic practice. The technical difficulties that they present to the psychoanalyst are impressive and at times overwhelming. Consequently, most psychotherapists tend to avoid the treatment of patients who present addictive disease as a prominent presenting feature of their complaints. However, it is not unusual for the analyst to recognize previously undisclosed drug dependence in their analysands during the unfolding of a psychoanalytic treatment. The explanation for this type of picture can be two-fold: On the one hand, chemical abuse may be revealed as the patient develops greater trust in the analyst's capacity to accept egodystonic aspects of the patient's personality. On the other hand, it may be occasioned by the patient's increased reliance upon chemical substances because of the intensification of dysphoric affect states stimulated by the treatment itself.

A systematic review that I have recently conducted of the successes and failures in the 20 years of my own psychotherapeutic and psychoanalytic practice has demonstrated that alcohol and drug dependence (alcohol, cannabis, cocaine, opiates, and various prescription drugs such as benzodiazepines) were significantly implicated in over 60% of cases that either unilaterally interrupted treatment because of little or no improvement or in which stalemated treatment was terminated by mutual consent. One completed suicide in my practice involved a patient who seriously abused drugs and alcohol. In that case, substantial use of alcohol was one of the major presenting complaints along with other self-destructive activities. However, in most of the other cases the extent of the patient's use of chemical substances came to light incidentally during the unfolding treatment process. Whenever it eventually became clear that substance abuse was a significant issue in the patient's life, it turned out to be a serious impediment to successful treatment. Retrospectively, I was able to see that successful treatment was precluded by a major theoretical misconception that I harbored based on inadequate information regarding the nature of chemical dependence. Simply stated, it was that chemical dependence is always a symptom of an underlying personality disorder. My working hypothesis had been: treat that disorder and the secondary chemical dependence will fade and disappear.

Growing clinical experience over the years has led me to reject the above assumptions as they had not led to successful results. In the next section I will attempt to indicate how the psychoanalytic literature has contributed to shaping my previous assumptions.

Prior to proceeding with that section, however, I would like to present a revised viewpoint that relates to more recent data from the literature of genetics, toxicology, addictionology, biobehavioral medicine, and neurophysiology.

More recent data bring into focus the importance of genetics and the sociocultural-historic context in which drug addiction is spawned. They suggest that observed psychopathology is often a secondary phenomenon rather than a primary one. Furthermore, they support the notion that drug and alcohol addiction is a primary illness or syndrome in its own right. One can observe the entire spectrum of psychopathology as a result of drug and alcohol intoxication. Included are: anxiety and panic attacks, depression, psychotic states, and suicidal behaviors. The treatment implications of these findings will be discussed.

REVIEW OF PSYCHOANALYTIC LITERATURE

As one might expect, the psychoanalytic literature on drug addiction in particular tends to reflect the status and historical evolution of psychoanalytic thinking in general. The early literature, particularly Freud's (1897) emphasized fulfillment of libidinal wishes. Freud considered masturbation the primal addiction. He felt that it is only a substitute and replacement for it that the other addictions to morphine, alcohol, tobacco, etc., came into existence. Rado (1926) stressed the orgasmic effects of intoxicants. Simmel (1929) emphasized the role of fulfillment of aggressive wishes. Glover (1932) called the addictions "circumscribed narcissistic neuroses" and further stressed the importance of aggression. Fenichel (1945) emphasized the libidinal aspects. In his view, addicts represent the most clearcut type of impulsives. Fenichel stressed the importance of treating the addict in an abstinent state following withdrawal. However, he did not expect the addict to remain abstinent throughout the treatment as he believed that relapses would inevitably occur at times of increased resistance.

The defensive function of drug use was stressed in many works from 1930 onward as ego psychology began to replace id psychology. Freud (1930) saw in narcotics a means of coping with pain and disillusionment, keeping misery at a distance. Glover emphasized that drug addiction functioned to control sadism, also as a protection against psychotic reaction and states of aggression. Rado (1927) viewed drugs as acting as a shield against stimulation from within. He also raised the issue of drugs supplying that which the mental organization was deficient in, a view that was seemingly echoed by Kohut (1971). Fenichel believed that addiction could be seen as a last means of avoiding depressive breakdowns. Rosenfeld (1960) emphasized manic mechanisms used by the addict to control paranoid anxieties and identification with the ideal object and the omnipotent control of the objects which may be part or whole objects. Little (1966) discussed the relevance of addiction to patterns of defense against anxiety and to object relations. She stressed the substance abusers' attempts to avoid the necessary addiction to the analyst in the transference by resorting to drugs, food, sex, cigarettes, etc.

More modern, in-depth explorations include those of Anna Freud (1965) who considered addiction as a complex structure in which the action of passive-feminine and self-destructive tendencies are added to oral wishes. The case for drug use being secondary to personality structure is most clearly made by Krystal and Raskin (1970). They emphasized the view that the etiology of drug use resides in the psychological structure and function within a human being rather than in the pharmacological effect of the drug and that the drug is not the problem but is an attempt at self-help that fails. The work of Khantzian (1985) stressed the use of narcotics as self-medication of the patient's underlying problems centering mainly around aggression. "Rather than simply seeking escape, euphoria, or self-destruction, addicts are attempting to medicate themselves for a range of psychiatric problems and painful emotional states."

Kohut (1971) stressed the importance of traumatic disappointments suffered by the child in archaic stages of relating to the idealized self-object leading to fixation on aspects of archaic objects and finding them in some cases in the form of drugs. However, he posited that the drug serves not as a substitute for loving objects or for a relationship with them, but as a replacement for a defect in the psychic structure.

Adams (1978) in an extensive review of the psychoanalytic literature on addiction concluded that one does not find much reference to effective treatment approaches of patients who are dependent upon chemical substances. He summed up the various attitudes of the treatment of addicts expressed in psychoanalytic literature as follows: these patients are too difficult, if not impossible, to treat because of serious, underlying narcissistic, pregenital pathology. He believed that the underlying problem is their pathological narcissism of which their dependency on a chemical substance is but a symptom. Adams's concept closely parallels Kernberg's in relationship to pathological narcissism. Wurmser (1978) stressed the severity of the underlying psychopathology of drug addicts. He believed that the preconditions of drug addiction were to be found in the life history of massive narcissistic disturbances in drug addicted patients. His view of compulsive drug use as an attempt at self-treatment was similar to Adams's and Khantzian's view. He believed that the compulsive use of drugs guarded against the outbreak of more serious debilitating and underlying psychopathology. He stated that drugs are not the problem. Even drug abuse is not really the core, but solely the symptom.

REVIEW OF LITERATURE FROM PSYCHIATRY, ADDICTIONOLOGY, AND OTHER BIOBEHAVIORAL FIELDS

These studies tend to emphasize other etiological theories regarding drug dependence. Some are derived from genetic studies that clearly suggest that drug dependence is a primary rather than a secondary disease. Schuckit (1979) differentiates primary from secondary alcoholism. Secondary alcoholism is diagnosed in cases where the use of alcohol is secondary to an underlying psychiatric illness, which can occur in the midst of any psychiatric picture. He believed it is most likely seen in the antisocial personality and in individuals with primary affective disorder. He described primary alcoholism which he thought of as "the disease of alcoholism." He pointed to evidence from genetic studies of a higher rate of concordance for alcoholism in identical twins than in nonidentical twins. He cited important information from separation and adoption type studies done in the United States and Denmark demonstrating that the children of alcoholic biologic parents separated from their parents early in life and raised without the knowledge of their natural parents have markedly elevated rates of alcoholism. However, the children of nonalcoholics adopted into the homes of alcoholics do not show elevated rates of alcohol problems as adults. He concluded that alcoholism is a genetically influenced disorder with a rate of heritability similar to that expected for diabetes or peptic ulcer disease.

Meyer and Mirin (1981) showed much evidence derived from the research of Davis (1971), Mendelson and Mello (1966), Fraser et al. (1963), Haertzen and Hooks (1969), as well as their own studies (Mirin et al., 1976) that strongly supported the notion that psychopathology could be secondary to drug and alcohol addiction rather than the opposite view as suggested by the psychoanalytic literature. They cited the above experimental studies of alcoholics and heroin addicts that have consistently identified dysphoric mood states, increasing psychopathology, and regressive and withdrawn behavior consequent to chronic alcohol and opioid use in addicted individuals.

A significant contribution to our knowledge of the natural history of alcoholism was made by Vaillant (1983), who made a prospective study of 200 college men, 400 socially underprivileged men in a core city sample who had been followed from adolescence into middle life, and 100 hospitalized alcoholics that had been followed for eight years. His findings were startling in that they contradicted many popularly held beliefs about alcoholism. For instance, he found that the addictive or alcoholic personality was much more likely to be secondary to long-term use of alcohol rather than the other way around. Most future alcoholics do not appear different from future asymptomatic drinkers in terms of premorbid psychological stability. He discovered that alcoholics were selectively personality disordered as a consequence, not as a cause of their alcohol abuse. Schuckit (1986) stressed, after carefully reviewing the data from the literature, that alcoholism and affective disorder appeared to be independent diseases with some overlap in clinical symptoms.

Bejerot (1980) cited the work of Olds and Milner (1954) on applied electrical stimulation to the pleasure center of rats to construct a biological and social psychological theory of addiction. He made a very convincing case for the theory that addictions represent newly acquired drive states that oftentimes overpower natural drive states such as hunger and sex. They arise, he maintained, from exposure to chemical substances that affect the pleasure centers of the brain and one need not invoke psychological etiologies in order to explain them.

DISCUSSION OF THE LITERATURE

It should be mentioned at the onset, that the psychoanalytic literature is rich in psychodynamic formulations but unfortunately poor in favorable outcome studies. The most comprehensive outcome study of psychotherapeutic techniques in the treatment of alcoholism between 1952 and 1963 is found in Chafetz et al. (1970). He pointed out the ineffectiveness of psychotherapy in the treatment of the alcoholic as reflected in the general literature during that period.

How does one account for the observation that psychoanalytic literature is so dominated by the theory that substance abuse is secondary to underlying psychopathology in light of these findings? I am reluctant to conclude that psychoanalysts are disinterested in the findings of other biobehavioral disciplines or simply uninformed by them. It is more likely that psychoanalysts fail to integrate these findings for other reasons.

The vantage point of the psychoanalytic observer is retrospective. In examining the psychopathology of his patient, he is often unable to sort out cause and effect relationships, primary from secondary factors. A good example of this is Garma's (1958) etiological theories regarding peptic ulceration. Garma found that one of his patient's peptic ulcerations was caused by a fantasy of an internalized oral/aggressive biting maternal imago. I would consider that notion to be a confusion between what is primary and what is a secondary fantasy elaboration of the patient's experienced epigastric pain. Freud (1920) demonstrated his awareness of this hazard of confusing cause and effect when he wrote the following:

So long as we trace the development from its final outcome backwards, the chain of events appears continuous and we feel we have gained an insight which is completely satisfactory or even exhaustive. But if we proceed the reverse way, if we start from the premises informed by the analysis, and try to follow them up to the final result, then we no longer get the impression of an inevitable sequence of events. . . .

I believe that much of the research in psychosomatic disorders has been flawed by this methodological problem. An outstanding example of this is how progress in the understanding of endocrinological, neurological, metabolic, and circulatory causes of male sexual impotence during the past two decades has completely reversed our conceptions of the contributions of organic versus psychogenic causes.

In a 12-year follow-up of 100 drug addicts, Vaillant (1966), using a prospective approach, suggested that except for continued dependency on drugs and alcohol, addicts remained remarkably free from psychopathology, including those who became abstinent. In the latter situation, these findings failed to support Wurmser's and Khantzian's contention that drugs protected the addict from severe underlying psychopathology.

AN INTEGRATED VIEW OF THE FIELD

It seems reasonable to look upon chemical dependence as multifactorial in etiology. These factors would include genetics, sociocultural factors, histori-cal, sociological, and psychological ones, interacting in complex cause and effect relationships to one another. Furthermore, there are undoubtedly many different types of drug addicts and alcoholics. One need only consider how differently one would have to assess the etiological factors in the case of a skid row alcoholic whose final pathway resulted from the convergence of genetic, familial, social, psychological, ethnic, and medical factors from a chronically anxious, upper-middle-class accountant who became addicted to Valium through a prescription given him by the family doctor or psychiatrist.

It seems likely that all the above studies are looking at one piece of the puzzle. However, in order to deal with these disorders adequately, one must be provided with an integrated concept.

TREATMENT IMPLICATIONS

The most effective treatment approach in most cases is informed by the concept that the chemical dependency is a disease entity in its own right and must be treated as such. This statement holds as well for those instances in which the condition is originally secondary to underlying psychopathology. To attempt to treat the "underlying" condition first would in my opinion be analogous to undertaking the treatment of a bleeding peptic ulcer through psychoanalysis alone without the help of a gastroenterologist or surgeon, based on the theory that the ulcer is caused by a specific conflict over the patient's oral dependency needs (Alexander, 1950). Even though the latter may be indeed a significant etiological factor, that approach would be tanta-mount to malpractice.

Whether chemical dependency in a given case is primary or secondary, it makes sense to deal with it from the start. Cohen (1985) recommends, "Treat the alcohol disorder first. Then treat the depression, the schizophrenia, the borderline state or the attention deficit disorder if it exists. Little can be accomplished before detoxification and abstinence. Diagnosis becomes more precise after the ethanol has been eliminated."

In practice, I believe that Cohen's approach is sound in most cases in which the alcoholism or drug addiction is one of the chief complaints, particularly when it is coupled with severe anxiety or depression. In such cases, the only way to make an adequate differential diagnosis is to require detoxification first.

In my experience, however, this is not the most common scenario. In a psychoanalytic practice, a much more frequently encountered situation is that of covert chemical dependence. In such cases, the magnitude of the problem eventually is uncovered during the evolving psychoanalytic process. Furthermore, it is often the case that the substance abuse intensifies as the stress of uncovering painful, underlying affect states increases. Treatment is then often stalemated unless the analyst requires total abstinence.

How the issue is dealt with is, of course, a matter of judgment on the part of the analyst as would be the case for any other serious medical problem that interferes with the unfolding analytic process. As I shall point out through the clinical examples in the next section, the ideal situation is one in which both the analyst and the analysand agree that the substance abuse is a serious issue that must be faced independently of the analysis and that a mutually agreed upon course of action is arrived at. In such favorable cases, there is no reason in my experience why the analysis cannot continue as the patient agrees to do whatever is necessary in order to achieve and maintain chemical abstinence.

For reasons that I shall elaborate upon in a later section, I almost always suggest that the patient become involved with Alcoholics Anonymous, Narcotics Anonymous, or some other 12-step program. Experience obtained in various drug rehabilitation programs (McLellan et al., 1982; Vaillant, 1983) has shown that adherence of the recovering addict or alcoholic to a 12-step program modeled after A.A. is a useful model for recovery. I have found that my psychoanalytic approach and style are fully compatible with the patient working an A.A. program. It is indeed essential that there be no conflict created by the analytic situation that would interfere with the A.A. program, and I believe the converse is also true. There is no position intrinsic to the A.A. program that conflicts with the patient's continuing to engage in intensive analytic therapy.

CLINICAL VIGNETTE

A 45-year-old attorney sought analytic treatment because of marital dissatisfaction, depressive suffering, and severe anxiety states of several years' duration. He had grown up the youngest child of a large family that emigrated to the United States from a Middle European country. He was told that he had been a "cute kid" who attracted much attention through his singing and dancing. However, the analytic work showed that he had suffered significant deprivation of love, guidance, and support as he grew up. His major authority figures were older brothers and sisters whose chief function was to discipline him as his parents were by that time older and worn out. At the age of eight or nine, he began to gain weight, do poorly in school, and suffered from the taunting of his peers. Compulsive overeating, the use of alcohol and tobacco as well as gambling became habitual means of coping with dysphoric affect states from his adolescence on.

In the second year of the analysis, a core conflict regarding success began to emerge as his business markedly improved. His fear that this success would certainly cause surrogate brother figures to become envious and withdraw from him or ridicule him became intense and manifest, gradually finding its way into the transference. It became clear that these conflicts were occasioned by his realistic perception of himself as being more gifted with shrewdness and boldness than his older siblings who had raised him. This view was supported by the inevitable comparisons he made between his considerable financial achievements and their relative lack of success. As the underlying fears of being isolated and ridiculed intensified, his compulsive overeating, imbibing alcohol, and smoking increased as well. The drinking pattern was usually nocturnal, whenever he spent an evening at home alone after a particularly successful day. It became the subject of repeated analytic attempts. This pattern was gradually understood to have an extensive role in affect regulation. In particular, drinking increased considerably in order to help maintain psychic equilibrium during states of narcissistic overstimulation and threatened expansiveness and grandiosity. Other roots lay in self-destructive impulses, dampening of anxiety, and combatting depressive states.

Ironically, these depressive states were part of a vicious cycle. It was impossible to separate their primary from their secondary relationship to alcohol intake. As we continued to meticulously analyze the various affect states that preceded the increase in alcohol intake, we found that we learned a great deal about the dynamics of his alcoholism. However, after two years of continuous and compulsive use of alcohol, the patient began to question my approach. He recognized that his alcoholism was increasing rather than decreasing, he was gaining weight through his compulsive bingeing, and he was growing increasingly concerned about his excessive use of cigarettes. He expressed the fear that these conditions would "do him in" and wondered if my approach, which consisted of analyzing the underlying conflicts and psychic deficits, would be adequate to deal with these addictions: "By the time we straighten my head out, I'll die of diabetes, high blood pressure, lung cancer and cirrhosis of the liver." This comment was made in a jocular tone, but I could see that it had much merit.

In a long overdue reassessment of our work, he and I then discussed a more direct approach to his addictions. In the course of our discussion I suggested that he consider attending some A.A. meetings. "Do you think I'm an alcoholic?," he asked with evident concern. I suggested that he attend a few meetings and decide for himself. After some initial difficulty in finding an A.A. group that he could identify with, he was finally convinced that the program could be useful for him, and he formed an intense attachment to it. In order to do so, he had to overcome significant obstacles created by his longstanding atheism. However, he was rapidly able to become completely abstinent with the support of the program. During this time, there was a considerable upsurge in his well-being. His self-esteem improved, he felt free of the toxic effects of the alcohol, and found himself perhaps for the first time in his life in a peer environment that was largely nonjudgmental and accepting.

This, however, was a mixed blessing for him. He experienced a tremendous upheaval in his life as the maintenance of his sobriety required that he shun most of his former companions who relied heavily on alcohol. Shortly thereafter, he was able to stop smoking and to control excessive food intake with the help of Overeaters Anonymous, another 12-step program, where he immediately felt a greater sense of identification. His former addictions to substances were replaced by an intense preoccupation with and dependence upon the abstinent peer group of A.A. and the analysis. He began to comment upon the feeling of a new beginning in relationship to his own affect states as he began to realize that he had been terrified of all feelings, good or bad, an awareness that had eluded him because of his previous reliance upon various substances to dampen those feelings. He both marveled at and was frightened by the experience of facing life sober.

He noted for the first time how difficult it had been for him to allow the analyst to be important and needed by him as it meant being exposed to feeling unmanly and weak. "I feel like the analysis is just beginning," he said after about three months of sobriety, but he added, "I can't say that I'm happy about facing all these fears. I'm terrified of everything known to man: success, failure, feeling good, feeling bad, you name it!" The analysis of his former womanizing was gradually revealed, with much resistance, as a bravado that covered painful feeling states of weakness, inadequacy, and terrors of being rejected by women. There was no question in my mind, or in his for that matter, that we had opened up important new areas that lay beneath his former alcohol-bolstered narcissistic invulnerability and superiority. The entire analysis took on a much deeper affective coloration.

REGARDING ALCOHOLICS ANONYMOUS

I believe A.A. is currently the most effective means of dealing with the addictions. This opinion is based upon my own professional experience which is supported by several major investigators in the field (Zimberg et al., 1985; Vaillant, 1983; Chafetz, 1970; McLellan, 1982; and Tiebout, 1961).

The experience of A.A. is that the most effective source of help, support, and understanding for a newcomer is another recovering alcoholic who has been through the experience and understands exactly what it is like.

Alanon and Naranon are outgrowths of Alcoholics and Narcotics Anonymous respectively. By attending regular meetings, family members of substance abusers can be helped through the support and understanding of those who have had similar experiences. They learn to accept their powerlessness to control or change the addict. They are also exposed to the valuable concept of "enabling," which consists of the various ways that family members and friends unwittingly support the addict's illness through monetary means and the like. This support is eventually understood as interfering with the person's recovery through the necessary experiencing of the adverse consequences of their addiction and drug-related behavior.

The psychotherapist can learn much from this type of group about the disease and a kind of psychotherapeutic "enabling." This term refers to keeping an addict in analysis despite the stalemating effect of the addiction, thus nurturing the myth that further therapy will help. This postpones the inevitable realization that the disease can only be arrested through the establishment of total abstinence.

An example of how this situation can arise is the following vignette from my own practice.

A young married woman in her early thirties, whom I shall call Jane, was referred to me by a colleague for a severe agitated depression of some two weeks' duration. She had just returned from a lovely overseas vacation with her husband. Coming back to work in the entertainment industry, she fell into a depression for no accountable reason. With the possible exception of feeling insecure and somewhat anxious about some work-related issues, the search for a precipitant cause for her suffering was at first fruitless. In the second interview, she began to open up an area that was frightening to her. She expressed a growing sense of dissatisfaction in her five-year marriage which centered around her perception of her husband's poor communication with her. It came out also that she had been absorbing considerably more alcohol during the preceding month or so than was her usual practice. My attempts to determine duration and quantity of alcohol intake were met with rather vague and equivocal responses. She told me that her mother had been an alcoholic, that her drinking was aggravated by her divorce from the patient's father when Jane was sixteen, at which time Jane was required to take over the care of both her mother and younger sister. Jane's mother eventually died of cirrhosis, vehemently denying her alcoholism to the bitter end. I suggested an exploratory conjoint session with her physician husband in order to ascertain the nature of the communication difficulty. She readily accepted. The husband, a somewhat frightened but sensitive man, with great trepidation broached his anger about her drinking. It embarrassed him socially and disgusted him to the point of avoiding her sexually. He admitted that he had trouble communicating with her. He explained that he withdrew because his complaints about her drinking "made her fall apart."

I told her that she would have to stop drinking in order to help clarify the nature of her depression (primary vs. secondary) and asked her if she could. She replied that since she was sure that her drinking was under her control, she would abstain. There was a prompt lifting of her depression within a week or so, and we were able to explore her deep feelings of insecurity and fear of rejection by people if she did not do everything to please and entertain them. She found that she was always "on" socially and that it was very difficult to be without a drink in those situations. In fact, total abstinence was impossible since her friends might suspect that she had been an alcoholic and would lose respect for her. It was predictable that she relapsed twice during the next two months to the point of missing two or three sessions because of blackout spells. The marital conflict worsened. Each time Jane relapsed, she was filled with shame, her depression returned, and she vowed that this time she would surely be able to control herself.

At this point, I believed that I was engaging in a kind of enabling by going along with her denial, and I recommended a more active approach to manage her drinking problem. We discussed both hospitalization to help her detoxify and A.A. meetings. She was frightened by the idea that I thought her an alcoholic and insisted that she could handle the situation without A.A., again expressing fears that her friends might find out that she was attending meetings and she would fall in their esteem. Finally, I offered her a choice: either to go into a recovery program or we would have to stop treatment, as I believed that the latter without the former would be a waste of time. She held to the belief that she could manage her drinking and wanted the chance to prove it. We parted amicably with the understanding that I would be happy to reconsider treatment if she ever decided to enter into a recovery program.

Nine weeks later, her husband called to tell me that she had entered on her own into a local inpatient chemical dependency unit, and he requested my opinion of the facility. I was able to endorse it without qualification and suggested that he attend Alanon meetings himself.

Vaillant (1983), Zimberg et al. (1985), and Chafetz (1970) stress the importance of A.A. in alcoholism recovery, yet it is surprising how few psychoanalytic authors even mention A.A. I suspect that the most likely explanation lies in the spiritual orientation of the program which is felt by those steeped in the scientific tradition as alien to them or perhaps even antagonistic to psychoanalysis. The psychoanalytic and the spiritual approach do in fact appear to be two separate realms of human experience. However, they can be bridged successfully for the benefit of our patients. William James's classic work, *The Varieties of Religious Experience* (1902), provided a psychology of religion applying the scientific method to the understanding of such religious experiences as conversion of the type that A.A. seems to foster. James believed that individual religious experiences, rather than precepts of organized religion, were the backbone of the world's religious life.

Some psychoanalytic observers suggest that the A.A. member has substituted one compulsion (that of A.A.) for another (alcoholism). Such charges are not ill-founded in light of the intense preoccupation with A.A. and its activities observed in the recovering addict. However, A.A.'s admonition to "use people, not drugs" recognizes and responds to the recovering alcoholic's enormous need for a substitute for a chemical substance that uniquely responded to a newly acquired drive state (Bejerot, 1980). The A.A. member's relationship to his/her sponsor is crucial in this regard. The sponsor is another alcoholic who has successfully maintained at least one to two years' sobriety and places him/herself at the disposal of the A.A. member's need for support and guidance on a 24-hour, 7-day-a-week basis.

The psychotherapist can learn a good deal by attending a few open A.A. or N.A. meetings. One can hardly fail to be impressed by the atmosphere of nonjudgmental acceptance and warmth that is so much a part of the A.A. tradition. Furthermore, it increases the therapist's understanding of how A.A. has many different groups and facets to fit the needs of the individual, who should be cautioned to try several different groups before deciding whether or not the program is appropriate for his/her needs.

Another objection to A.A. that is traditionally raised by psychiatrists is that A.A. opposes not only psychiatry but the use of psychotropic drugs. There is nothing in the A.A. literature that supports this idea. However, it is true that individual zealots within A.A., especially having been disappointed by unsuccessful attempts by psychiatrists to treat their own alcoholism, may reactively attack and condemn all of psychiatry. Indeed, some groups have a low tolerance for individual needs for psychotropic drugs such as lithium, antidepressants, or antipsychotics and display a blanket condemnation of all exogenous substances out of ignorance of the nonaddictive properties of some drugs. Since the essence of the program is personal honesty, it is best for such an individual to find another group which is more flexible in its attitudes toward prescribed medication.

It is advisable for the psychoanalyst or psychodynamically oriented psychotherapist to become familiar with the principles and operation of A.A. as one would the use of any form of adjunctive help as it promotes overall effectiveness in the treatment of the substance abuser.

Last but not least, some psychoanalysts might be reluctant to actively suggest or recommend A.A. out of a concern that it would violate principles of analytic neutrality. I do not take this objection lightly. However, the concept of neutrality ought not be used, in my opinion, as justification for an attitude of passive inaction in the face of a real threat not only to the forward progress of the analytic work, but more importantly to the maintenance of health and life itself. I hold that it is better to err, whenever in doubt, on the side of active intervention, and then be fully prepared to analyze the transference implications of one's actions. This stance seems to work well to maintain the forward momentum of the analytic work, in my experience.

CONCLUSIONS AND SUMMARY

I have outlined what I believe to be an effective approach to the psychoanalytic treatment of chemical dependence, either as one of the presenting complaints or as an incidental but complicating factor that emerges during the course of an analysis.

In so doing, I have mentioned the psychoanalytic literature from Freud to the present time and demonstrated that traditional approaches have suffered from certain serious conceptual flaws stemming from the inherent methodology of psychoanalytic investigation. I have suggested that these deficits in psychodynamic thinking as regards the treatment of drug addiction and alcoholism arise from a retrospective stance in which primary and secondary factors cannot be easily differentiated. Secondly, that psychoanalysis has failed to integrate more recent findings from other biobehavioral disciplines that broaden our understanding of the nature of the addictions. These conceptual errors and deficits have in my opinion led to the incorrect and overly narrow position that the addictions are entirely secondary to underlying serious psychopathology which must be addressed if the addiction is to be cured. The inevitable clinical observation of serious psychopathology in substance abusers without the understanding of how the addiction itself can produce secondary symptoms has tended to reinforce and self-validate incomplete theoretical approaches. Furthermore, psychoanalytic literature traditionally abounds in dynamic formulations about substance abuse without the support of necessary outcome studies to verify those formulations. I have shown the disappointing results of traditional psychodynamic approaches in most outcome studies.

I have then reviewed more recent findings from other biobehavioral disciplines and have shown how they tend to support the notion of the addictions as constituting a disease entity in their own right. With this documentation, I have outlined an integrated approach to the treatment of the addictions that is more likely to be effective, as it no longer rests solely on isolated psychological data but on a demonstrated sound biological base as well.

I have devoted a section of this paper to describe the vital role of Alcoholics Anonymous and related groups to the furthering of the addict's recovery. I have pointed out that A.A. has not gotten the recognition that it deserves in terms of its effectiveness in the process of the addict's rehabilitation. I have suggested some of the possible explanations for this fact.

My conclusion is that the scope of psychoanalytic treatment can be extended through the development of the described integrated approach in order to effectively treat this most difficult and vexing syndrome.

REFERENCES

Adams, J. W. (1978), Psychoanalysis of Drug Dependence: The Understanding and Treatment of a Particular Form of Pathological Narcissism, Grune and Stratton, New York.

Alcoholics Anonymous (1976), The Big Book, A.A. World Services, Inc. New York.

Alexander, F. (1950), Psychosomatic Medicine, Norton, New York.

Bejerot, N. (1980), Addiction to pleasure—A biological and social psychological theory of addiction, in Theories on Drug Abuse: Selected Contemporary Perspectives, National Institute Drug Abuse Research Monograph 30, March 1980.

Chafetz, N. E., et al. (Eds.) (1970), Frontiers of Alcoholism, Science House, New York.

Cohen, S. (1985), Forward, S. Zimberg et al., Practical Approaches to Alcoholism Psychotherapy, 2nd ed., Plenum Press, New York.

Davis, D. (1971), Mood changes in alcoholic subjects with programmed and free choice drinking, in N. K. Mellow and J. Mendelson (Eds.), Recent Advances in Studies of Alcoholism, U. S. Public Health Service, Vol. HSN 719045, Bethesda, Maryland.

Fenichel, O. (1945), The Psychoanalytic Theory of Neurosis, Norton, New York.

Fraser, H. F., et al. (1963), Effects of addiction to intravenous heroin on patterns of physical activity, Men. Clin. Pharmacol. Ther., 188.

Freud, A. (1965), Normality and Pathology in Childhood: Assessments in Development in the Writings of Anna Freud, *Vol. 6, International Universities Press, New York.*

Freud, S. *(1897), Masturbation, Addiction and Obsessional Neurosis,* Standard Edition, *Vol. 1, Hogarth Press, London, p. 272.*

Freud, S. *(1920), The psychogenesis of a case of homosexuality in a woman,* Standard Edition, *Vol. 18, Hogarth Press, London, 1955, p. 167.*

Freud, S. *(1930), Civilization and Its Discontents,* Standard Edition, *Vol. 21, Hogarth Press, London, p. 86.*

Garma, A. *(1958),* Peptic Ulcer in Psychoanalysis, *Williams and Wilkins, Baltimore.*

Glover, E. *(1932), The Etiology of Alcoholism, in* On The Early Development of the Mind, *International Universities Press, New York, pp. 187–215.*

Haertzen, C. H., and Hooks, N. T. *(1969), Changes in personality and subjective experience associated with the chronic administration and withdrawal of opiates,* J. of Nervous and Mental Diseases, *148, 606.*

James, W. *(1902),* The Varieties of Religious Experience, *Penguin, Middlesex and New York, 1982.*

Khantzian, E. J. *(1985), The self-medication hypothesis of addictive disorders,* Amer. J. Psychiatry, *142, 11.*

Kohut, H. *(1971),* The Analysis of the Self, *International Universities Press, New York.*

Krystal, H., and Raskin, H. A. *(1970),* Drug Dependence: Aspects of Ego Functions, *Wayne State University Press, Detroit.*

Little, M. *(1966), Transference in borderline states,* Int. J. Psa, *47, 476–85.*

McLellan, A. T., et al. *(1982), Is treatment for substance abuse effective?,* J. Am. Med. Assoc., *March 12, 137.*

Mendelson, J. H., and Mello, N. K. *(1966), Experimental analysis of drinking behavior of chronic alcoholics,* Annals of the New York Academy of Sciences, *133, 828, Sept. 23.*

Meyer, R. E., and Mirin, S. M. *(1981), A psychology of craving: Implications of behavioral research, in J. H. Levinson and P. Ruiz (Eds.),* Substance Abuse, Clinical Problems and Perspectives, *Williams and Wilkins, Baltimore, 1981.*

Mirin, S. M., et al. *(1976), Psychopathology and mood during heroin use: Acute vs. chronic effects,* Arch. Gen. Psychiatry, *33, 1503.*

Olds, J., and Milner, P. *(1954), Positive reinforcement produced by electrical stimulation of central areas and other regions of rat brain,* J. of Comp. and Phys. Psychology, *47, 419–427.*

Rado, S. *(1926), The psychic effects of intoxicants: An attempt to evolve a psychoanalytic theory of morbid craving, in* Psychoanalysis of Behavior, Collected Papers, *Vol. I, Grune and Stratton, New York, 1956.*

Rado, S. *(1927), The problem of melancholia, in* Psychoanalysis of Behavior, Collected Papers, *Vol. I, Grune and Stratton, New York.*

Rosenfeld, H. A. *(1960),* On Drug Addiction in Psychotic States, A Psychoanalytical Approach, *International Universities Press, New York, 1965.*

Schuckit, M. A. *(1979),* Drug and Alcohol Abuse, A Clinical Guide to Diagnosis and Treatment, *San Diego V.A. Medical Center, University of California School of Medicine.*

Schuckit, M. A. (1986), Genetic and clinical implications of alcoholism and affective disorders, Am. J. of Psychiatry, 143, 140–147.

Simmel, E. (1929), Psychoanalytic treatment in the sanitorium, Int. J. of Psychoanal., 10, 70–89.

Tiebout, H. M. (1961), Alcoholics anonymous, An experiment of nature, Quart. J. Stud. Alcohol, 22, 52–68.

Vaillant, G. E. (1966). A twelve year followup of New York narcotic addicts I, The relation of treatment to outcome, Amer. J. Psychiat. 122, 727–737.

Vaillant, G. E. (1983), The Natural History of Alcoholism, Harvard University Press, Cambridge.

Wilson, B. (1958), Alcoholics anonymous: Beginnings and growth, Presented to the New York City Society on Alcoholism, April 21.

Wilson, B. (1944), Basic concepts of A.A., in Three Talks to Medical Societies, A.A. World Services, Inc., New York (originally presented to the Medical Society of the State of New York, Section on Neurology and Psychiatry, Annual Meeting, New York, May 1944).

World Health Organization (1964), Expert Committee Report on Mental Health, Technical Report Series Number 273, Geneva.

Wurmser, L. (1978), The Hidden Dimension, Psychodynamics of Compulsive Drug Use, Aronson, New York.

Zimberg, S., et al. (1985), Practical Approaches to Alcoholism Psychotherapy, 2nd Edition, Plenum Press, New York.

21. Recovery Oriented Psychotherapy

Joan Ellen Zweben

INTRODUCTION

The role of psychotherapy in the treatment of substance abuse has long been subject to dispute. The failure of conventional mental health therapists to appropriately diagnose and address these problems has created a gulf which leads many practitioners, especially in short term chemical dependency programs, to advise their patients to steer clear of psychotherapy for at least a year. Others take the position that a psychoanalytically oriented psychotherapy, with additions and some modifications, can be appropriate to drug and alcohol abusers (Khantzian, 1981, 1982, 1985; Wurmser, 1984, 1985). The many meanings of the term psychotherapy contributes further to the problem. In certain geographical areas, psychotherapy means psychoanalytically oriented therapy, and in others an eclectic approach is assumed. There is as yet no commonly agreed upon knowledge base in substance abuse (Shaffer & Milkman, 1985), and hence no clear criteria for systematic training or even selection of a therapist competent to deal with these problems.

Another source of controversy over the utility of psychotherapy is that the substance abuse field itself has several disparate approaches and is rapidly changing. The recovery model based on the disease concept has dominated the field of alcoholism, and views involvement in 12 step programs as an integral part of treatment. Chemical dependency programs built on this model frequently discourage clients from entering or remaining in psychotherapy. The two major modalities for treating opiate dependence, methadone maintenance and the therapeutic community, have different historical antecedents, different methods, and different treatment goals (Deitch, 1973; Lowinson, 1981; Newman, 1982). The increasing prominence of the cocaine and alcohol abuse cycle has drawn treatment providers with very different backgrounds together, highlighting some contemporary problems in the field. For example, a therapeutic community client whose primary drug of abuse is cocaine may

Reprinted with permission from *Journal of Substance Abuse Treatment* 3 (1986): 255–262. Copyright © Elsevier Science, Ltd., Pergamon Imprint, Oxford, England.

be advised to abstain from alcohol while the client preferring heroin may not. The different modalities have distinct philosophies and approaches, leading to an absence of consensus about what constitutes effective treatment. The result is that practitioners with many years experience in the drug and alcohol field may speak different languages, and may be in conflict about what is appropriate.

This paper uses a sequential stage model to clarify the progression of tasks and the strategies for achieving them, in an attempt to highlight commonalities and provide a framework to think about effective treatment. Although its reference point is outpatient treatment, the stages and many of the strategies can be readily applied to inpatient treatment as well. Models describing stages are becoming more visible (Brown 1985; Washton & Gold, 1986) and permit a different kind of dialogue among those of differing theoretical persuasions. In some cases, apparent conflicts disappear when the question of timing is considered. The role of insight oriented exploration is an obvious example. What may be ineffective with the client who is struggling to break the abuse cycle may be very useful with the client who is three months abstinent. Dynamically oriented insight is not irrelevant in the early stages, but it must be clearly focussed in its purpose.

Individual therapy is generally underutilized in most areas of chemical dependency treatment, partly for economic reasons, partly from a sense that the group process offers unique and powerful possibilities that dyadic interaction does not. However, individual attention may be the key to keeping the client in treatment through the tempestuous early stages in which the major dropout occurs. This paper will focus on the treatment tasks themselves from a vantage point that permits application to individual, family, and group work, all of which are valuable in effective substance abuse treatment.

THE STAGES OF TREATMENT

The Client in the Active Abuse Cycle

When clients come to treatment they are usually in the midst of an active abuse cycle which may take extensive time and effort to break. Unfortunately, the relationship between retention and treatment outcome has been poorly understood and appreciated, resulting in a common practice of terminating clients who do not cease using within a relatively short period of time. This is especially likely in Health Maintenance Organizations and government funded settings where there is pressure to see more people and "show results." Economics can have subtle and covert impact on clinical decision making and program policy, and it is common for such programs to make a virtue out of "being tough" and to label anyone who operates differently as an enabler. In certain settings, being described as an enabler is tantamount to an accusation of naivete or incompetence, and serves to deter examination of how to reduce dropout.

The drug treatment outcome literature would suggest different policy. Studies of several different modalities have indicated that the longer people stay in treatment, the better they do on a variety of outcome measures (Cooper, Altman, Brown, & Czechowicz, 1983; De Leon, 1984; Washton, Gold, & Pottash, 1986). Hence if we can improve retention, we can probably improve outcome. Also, in a variety of modalities, the most significant dropout occurs within the first thirty days (Craig, 1985). Thus attention paid to keeping the client in treatment through the difficult early stages has the potential of high payoff. Experienced therapeutic community personnel comment repeatedly about how many times they are surprised by who does poorly and who does well in treatment; impressions of behavior during the early stages are often misleading.

Brown (1985) offers similar data. In her Stanford Alcohol Clinic research sample, an average of twenty months elapsed between initial contact and acknowledged membership in AA, and another eight months passed before the average respondent achieved abstinence. This can be interpreted to mean that over two years passed between the time an individual recognized enough of a drinking problem to check out AA, and the time he embraced AA membership, with its corresponding acknowledgment of being alcoholic and unable to drink. And even after that, abstinence took another eight months to achieve (Brown, 1985). Seen in this perspective, terminating the client who does not achieve abstinence within a matter of weeks hardly seems clinically appropriate. The goal of the therapist, then, is to facilitate the commitment and transition to abstinence.

The tasks at this point are to break down the denial about the consequences of use and explore the barriers to an abstinence commitment. Since the symptoms of drug and alcohol problems imitate everything else, the therapist can take any presenting complaint and demonstrate how a period of abstinence is necessary to clarify the diagnostic picture (Bean, 1981). For example, the client seeking treatment for low self-esteem and depression can be shown how his or her alcohol use, or cocaine use, might play a role in the problem. Obtaining even a time limited commitment to the goal of abstinence is a workable place to begin.

Images of what it means to be an addict/alcoholic, both in terms of the stigma and in terms of the renunciation to be undertaken, are profoundly influential. Brown (1985) has pointed out that the therapist may not be able to tolerate the depression and pain that accompany the drive toward surrender and abstinence. The therapist who intervenes to salve the client's battered self-esteem may interrupt the move towards despair that facilitates surrender. This surrender is a key transformation, in which the user gives up the prolonged attempt to control both the consumption of drugs or alcohol, and acknowledges that his or her life is unmanageable (Alibrandi, 1978). It is the beginning of a transformation with profound consequences, including not only behavior modifications but a complete identity shift as well (Brown, 1985).

The Crisis

For clients who enter treatment in a crisis, either a naturally occurring one or one precipitated by an Intervention (Wegscheider, 1981), it is important to use the opportunity to structure a comprehensive treatment contract, as devoid of loopholes as possible. Again, this is an area of difference from conventional psychotherapy, in which the therapist usually has some leisure to formulate priorities. Clients often lose motivation once they start feeling better, and it is important that the commitments necessary for the early stage of recovery be made clear.

A treatment contract needs to include specifics about the time frame: the frequency, type (e.g., individual sessions, family work, groups) and duration. The commitment and involvement of the family or significant others should be established immediately, as they are usually harder to engage once work with the user is underway and the crisis situation is relieved. Engaging them at the point of intake often results in improving retention of the user (Zweben, Pearlman, & Li, 1983). The consequences of relapse (e.g., hospitalization, termination from job) need to be spelled out. Urinalysis can be a crucial element of the initial treatment structure, in which case the frequency of testing and consequences of a positive urine need to be specified. Appropriate releases of information need to be secured: these may cover the possibility of relapse, premature termination, or general progress. In cases where the user is not paying for the treatment, or another is paying some of the fee, it may be desirable to obtain a release in order to disclose no-shows.

It is also important to establish the cessation of all intoxicants as a treatment goal (Smith, 1984). Clients are usually aware that they need to be committed to abstaining from their primary drug of abuse, but many do not realize that elimination of other intoxicants is necessary as well. This can be recommended on pragmatic grounds, because it offers the widest margin of safety. The clinician often sees the use of another intoxicant preceding a relapse to the primary drug of abuse (either by hours, or even weeks in people who have been abstinent for some time). Substitution of one drug problem for another is also common. Unfortunately, there is currently a practice among disease model proponents of predicting inevitable relapse and even death for those who do not sustain this commitment indefinitely. We certainly have abundant clinical observation to support this position, but we do not yet have a *single* systematic study of the phenomena, so we do not know the frequency with which it occurs. This is one area in which it seems especially hazardous to generalize from the population in treatment. Statements which compromise our credibility do not enhance our effectiveness. It is important in early recovery to be unambivalent about our recommendations, but we must do so without making unsubstantiated claims. Abstinence from all intoxicants is advisable because it provides the widest margin of safety, not because we can accurately predict the fate of all who do not comply.

A plan for assessing the presence of a major psychiatric disorder, or an anxiety or eating disorder, and treating it appropriately is another important element in the treatment contract (Brisman & Siegel, 1984; Mirin, 1984; Schuckit, 1985). Since even the symptoms of a major psychiatric disorder may be either intoxication or withdrawal effects, it is often difficult to make this distinction at the point of intake. The current gap between mental health and substance abuse has created a situation in which drug and alcohol problems are grossly underdiagnosed in the mental health system, and psychiatric disorders are often missed in the substance abuse treatment setting. A client with serious psychopathology which is not adequately treated is unlikely to be able to remain abstinent. The same is true for persons with severe anxiety disorders. Eating disorders are another example of an entity too hazardous to be ignored until abstinence is securely established; they also tend to be closely interwoven with the substance use pattern. Treatment personnel are sometimes excessively cavalier in suggesting all problems can be reduced to recovery issues and therapy should not be instituted until someone has been abstinent for a year. Often programs do not have ready access to professionals capable of making complicated differential diagnostic decisions. The area of dual diagnosis and related issues is likely to continue to receive increasing attention, as it is one of the serious weaknesses in our current treatment system. In the meantime, we must attempt to address these issues, because relapse in one area usually results in relapse in the other.

Breaking the Addiction Cycle

A strong educational component is one of the things that distinguishes substance abuse treatment from other kinds of psychotherapy. Giving information, clarifying misunderstandings, provides the framework necessary to interpret resistance. The wife of a cocaine using client who has never been told about the importance of his abstaining from alcohol cannot be confronted about sabotaging her husband's recovery if she offers him wine at a celebration. Information is important for a variety of reasons, in this example because it clarifies treatment expectations and creates a common understanding.

The educational process needs to include a review of intoxication and withdrawal effects, the disease concept, and other ways of understanding addiction (e.g., learning theory models which alert clients to the power of environmental triggers). In particular, clients and their families or significant others need to understand the recovery process and the commitments it requires. Education should cover the hows and whys of abstinence; denial and enabling; what to do in the event of relapse. The transmission of information can be done in groups, even large groups, but this alone is not sufficient. Clients need the opportunity to apply the concepts to their unique situation, giving specific and concrete examples of what they observe, and identifying areas which need to be worked on. The therapist seeking a chemical dependency program should thus distinguish between family education and family therapy. Many programs offer education only, and more work is needed to insure that the family has adequately grasped and integrated the concepts.

Programs need to have screening and protocols for problems which require medical attention. Detoxification does not usually require much medical intervention, except when sedative hypnotic drugs are involved, or the client has a history of delerium tremens when withdrawing from alcohol, or when the client has major medical problems. Psychotic, homocidal, or suicidal behavior may indicate a need for hospitalization. Otherwise, the major strategy is to generate a tight structure of activities, and passing on information about what staff and other clients have found helpful. This includes specifying appropriate dietary and exercise practices and generating a firm interpersonal support structure through the difficult period. Attention to diet is important because clients with long histories of drug use, or clients using appetite suppressing drugs such as cocaine, are usually nutritionally imbalanced. Also, the common client practice of overeating starches and sweets appears to stimulate the rushes and crashes of drug use, and hence can stimulate drug hunger. Exercise seems beneficial as a way of accelerating the rate at which the body chemistry normalizes. It is also useful as an index of the commitment to self-care. More details of an outpatient detoxification plan have been described elsewhere (Zweben, 1986).

Both the client and the family should have appropriate expectations of what to expect; what the difficulties are likely to be, and within what time frame discomfort is likely to abate. The major dropout is generally within the first thirty days, much of it closely related to withdrawal phenomena. Frequent treatment contacts and solid interpersonal support is especially important to weather this period. Explaining how surges of drug hunger relate to the body's adapting back to a drug free state, giving some estimate of when the worst is likely to be over, can be immensely reassuring to the client. Clients in this phase are not very amenable to psychodynamically oriented work, so their therapists often become frustrated, label them as unmotivated or unworkable, and miss the opportunity to address their needs in a way that bonds them to the treatment process.

Work in this stage focusses on the *behaviors* of abstinence (Brown, 1985). Insight oriented work is useful in identifying the major circumstances (e.g., parties, conflict with spouse) and internal states (e.g., boredom, increased job pressure) that are likely to trigger the desire to use (Gorski & Miller, 1982; Marlatt & Gordon, 1985; Zackon, McAuliffe, & Ch'ien, 1985). The therapist's skills at clinical inquiry are a major asset in eliciting the key issues and prioritizing their importance. However, the effort at this time is not in resolving these issues, but in generating an action plan with practical alternatives to using. Clients who have achieved a solidly abstinent lifestyle are much more able to come to grips with major anxiety provoking issues. The therapist needs to be firm that psychological problems do not have to be solved for clients to refrain from using drugs and alcohol, but rather, abstinence is the foundation of therapeutic progress.

Many therapists use journals to help clients identify patterns of craving and develop ways to cope with it. Journal assignments involve noting when these occur, who they were with, what were the circumstances, what were they feeling, what did they do, what did they wish to do differently. Examination of successful handling is instructive to establish new patterns; often people have little understanding of why something worked well, what exactly they did to make for a successful outcome. Simple modifications like temporarily changing the physical surroundings during key times can be important in breaking the cycle. For example, the client who longed for a drink at 5:30 P.M. upon returning home from work may benefit from introducing an exercise session during that time. Redoing the family dinner ritual in a more satisfying manner can accomplish the same purpose. Going to 12 step meetings is another behavior change which serves multiple functions. The key is to fill the vacuum left when drug use is discontinued with something concrete and specific (Brown, 1985).

Introducing 12 step programs has many benefits during this time, as they offer a wealth of survival skills as well as generous support. So great are the potential benefits of involvement with these programs that it is useful for the therapist to facilitate the client's ability to make use of them in whatever way possible (Gitlow, 1985). Typical resistances at this stage revolve around unwillingness to admit "I am an alcoholic/addict," fear of losing identity and individuality, discomfort at being the outsider, irritation at "that religious stuff" or at the language. The therapist who has checked out the meetings in the community is in a better position to work with these obstacles. Clients need not introduce themselves as an addict/alcoholic, or at all for that matter. They can be encouraged to "take what you need and leave the rest," by a therapist insistent that they give it a fair try. Often clients who appear highly resistant become much more receptive once they get past the stage of being a stranger, and find particular meetings that they like. The structure provided by regular attendance at meetings, plus the unfolding understanding which begins to occur, is invaluable, particularly since there are no financial barriers. However, there are clients who cannot or will not use this resource, and it is important not to insist that the 12 step process is the only way to recovery, as is the practice in some chemical dependency programs. One mark of a good treatment system is the existence of alternatives, and a respect for the complexity of the recovery process.

Urinalysis can be a tool with many benefits during this and the next stage of treatment. Clients report that "knowing the counselor (and designated others) will know" often serves as a deterrent to impulsive use during the difficult period of early abstinence. Voluntary clients can increase the stakes by specifying others to be notified in the event of a positive urine test. These may include spouses, parents, licensing boards, employers, etc. (Crowley, 1984). Many clients report urinalysis offers a kind of security, by making the option of using seem further removed. In addition, they usually encounter a fair amount of negative feelings about their behavior during their drug using periods. Urinalysis can be particularly important for restoring credibility with intimates. It relieves anxiety on the part of significant others and protects the client from the discouraging experience of being mistrusted even when doing well. The increasing reliance on urinalysis by industry will likely make it more readily available at reasonable prices.

Consolidating Abstinence and Creating New Lifestyles

The basic task at this stage is to accept the identity of a recovering person, develop support networks, and fill in the social and recreational gaps (Brown, 1985; Zackon et al., 1985). For many, once they break their chronic abuse cycle, they come to see drugs and alcohol as "the problem I used to have" and want to withdraw energy from the recovery process. Part of this comes from the desire to avoid the stigma associated with being an addict or alcoholic. They want to believe that so long as they do not use, they do not have to remain attentive to this area of their lives. Premature termination is a common occurrence at this point.

Some clients begin to convince themselves "I feel better now; I am together in a way I wasn't before. Now I can handle it." Euphoric recall commonly comes into play here, as well as during the detoxification process (Gawin & Kleber, 1986). Some clients report success in using refresher lists of negative consequences at this point. The therapist may invoke this strategy by asking the client in the throes of misery (e.g., as a detox assignment) to write extensively or make a tape of all the negative consequences drugs and alcohol have had in their lives, to be used as a tool when euphoric recall sets in.

One common problem occurs when therapists are perceived as so "hard line" in their opposition to drug or alcohol use that the client becomes reluctant to share fantasies about using or drinking when they occur. Indeed, some outpatient programs will terminate a client for only one slip. This simply drives the problem underground where no discussion is possible. Therapists need to be firm in their recommendations while conveying a realistic acknowledgement that people have given up something they like very much, and will have urges or even try to convince themselves they can use it again. Making these a part of the treatment without making them a focus of a power struggle is a challenging task for the therapist. Many make the error of dealing with these issues by further lectures on the disease model, rather than by clinical exploration. Education provides the basis for interpreting resistance early in treatment, but in the later stages is often misapplied as the remedy. At this stage, the therapist needs to inquire about what factors operate in the client's increasing interest in drugs. These may range from increasing anxiety over emerging psychological or interpersonal problems; social pressure or feelings about "not being normal, like people who drink;" approaching celebrations or vacations; feelings of deserving a reward "for being so good." Clients need to be encouraged to strengthen their behavioral supports for abstinence, for example, increase the number of 12 step meetings attended, while engaging in inner explorations (Brown, 1985).

The issue of use of intoxicants other than the primary drug of abuse is a common arena where this battle is waged. Therapists of all theoretical persuasions have observed: (1) many clients "solve" one drug problem only to substitute another (e.g., former heroin addicts, successfully abstinent, turn up on alcohol inpatient units); (2) use of another intoxicant frequently precedes relapse to primary drug of abuse. Therapists working primarily within the disease model take the firm position that once a person has crossed the boundary of uncontrolled use, he or she can never return to controlled use, and that this principle applies to other intoxicants as well (Smith, Milkman, & Sunderwirth, 1985). What must be examined and renounced is *chemical dependency*, not just the primary drug of abuse.

This area causes conflict among certain treatment providers, and confusion and resistance among clients. For example, the therapeutic community has a history of successful treatment of opiate addiction (De Leon, 1984) despite a long tradition of using drinking privileges as a reward for progress. Attitudes and policies are undergoing substantial revision today (Zweben & Smith, 1986), but the fact remains that there are numerous visible leaders in that field who have been abstinent from heroin for long periods of time and use moderate amounts of alcohol. In these same circles, there are also examples of painful tragedies: deaths in drunk driving accidents, careers destroyed because of alcoholism, relapses to heroin involving alcohol use. The dilemma this poses for the clinician is that clients will not readily accept the notion that anything short of total abstinence leads to inevitable doom, which is how some treatment providers present it.

The dilemma presents itself outside the therapeutic community environment as well. Cocaine users ask if they must forever give up wine with dinner, if "alcohol is not my problem." Disease model proponents, in their enthusiasm for the studies demonstrating a genetic factor in alcoholism (Petrakis, 1985), point to this as support for abstaining from all intoxicants: addiction is a disease, and if you have the disease you cannot use psychoactive drugs. Many are not even aware that there is not a single study which clearly establishes a link between the genetic factors involved in alcoholism, and abuse of other drugs. Clinicians believe it is there, because the frequency with which we see it is very compelling, but it is inappropriate to announce to our clients that it is proven fact.

A more credible position is that abstinence from all intoxicants provides the widest margin of safety, and is justifiable on pragmatic grounds, independent of one's endorsement of the disease model. Certainly the client in early recovery can be asked to examine attachments to other intoxicants (alcohol and marijuana being those favored) and to explore the nature of resistance to the chemical free life style. Often these clients have strong involvement with a secondary drug, which they have come to view as unimportant because their attention was occupied with their primary drug of abuse. The cocaine user often downplays the importance of alcohol and marijuana use, and the alcoholic may rationalize the use of marijuana, which is still seen as harmless in many circles. Working with these denial mechanisms can be very delicate, and it is around these issues that many clients terminate prematurely. In general, asking for a short term commitment (six months) to remain abstinent from all intoxicants usually works better than immediately insisting that total and lifelong commitment is essential for success. Resistance to making this short term commitment can be more easily handled as ambivalence towards the recovery process in general, as most clients view it as a sensible practice. Once abstinent from their secondary drugs, clients are much more receptive to the notion of remaining so. Thus we can *advocate* lifelong abstinence from all intoxicants, but a short term commitment gives a workable place to begin.

Relapse prevention is another area that needs to be addressed early in the recovery process (Gorski & Miller, 1982; Marlatt & Gordon, 1985), as it is common for relapse to occur and important to minimize the destructive effects. In the period during which the abuse cycle is being broken, relapse has more varied causes and is probably more related to changes in brain chemistry than later on, when the client has been abstinent for a while. In the later stages of recovery, the factors are more clearly psychological.

Research on the relapse process (Marlatt & Gordon, 1985) indicates that the precipitants fall roughly into three categories: (1) negative mood states, such as boredom, depression; (2) interpersonal conflict; and (3) social pressure. Identification of the specific vulnerabilities for each client allow the therapist to determine which issues merit high priority attention. Most clients who come to use can describe some periods of abstinence or sobriety which preceded their current treatment attempt. Careful, detailed inquiry as to how these ended yields valuable data on how to focus therapeutic efforts. Specific problems, for example, marital conflict, can be addressed from the standpoint of how to avoid having it lead to relapse, and then as a problem requiring serious attention. Clients need to be alerted to the possibility of flareups of craving or withdrawal symptoms that can occur many months after the last episode of use. Holidays, birthdays, anniversaries, and other celebrations are also times of increased vulnerability. In addition to insight oriented work, structured techniques, such as assertion training, are often useful at this point to deal with known problem areas.

Another way of addressing relapse is through sensitization to the relapse dynamic (Gorski & Miller, 1982). This can be viewed as an independent and free standing syndrome, in which there is progressive degeneration of physical, psychological, and behavioral functioning. Gorski has provided a list of warning signs which aids in defeating denial and identifying changes which merit concern. The client is then in a better position to formulate a plan to disrupt the relapse dynamic. These efforts also serve as a basis for defining the involvement of the significant other, including agreements about concrete behaviors when the significant other observes warning signals.

Addressing Psychological Issues

This stage necessarily overlaps with the previous ones, and involves identifying feelings and old problems obscured by drug use. Clients with long histories of chemical use are often underdeveloped in their ability to identify their feelings and express them appropriately (Khantzian, 1981, 1982, 1985). Tools like those used in Gestalt therapy can be invaluable aids to helping clients notice and track their feelings, as well as develop alternative modes of expression. It is useful to help clients become aware of which feelings are easy and which are more difficult for them to acknowledge and express, as a guide for further exploration. Work on simply tolerating an experience, rather than forcibly changing it with a chemical, can be very valuable at this point.

Another important issue at this stage is helping the client face the disappointment that not everything is fixed by abstinence. Some problems remain; others emerge once the constant preoccupation with obtaining and using a chemical is eliminated. Taking stock and making a new treatment plan may be helpful at this point, to help the client who feels overwhelmed by new sources of problems.

This is also the time of dealing with the interpersonal consequences of drug and alcohol use: the anger, guilt, frustration, blame, and disappointment of others. It is no accident that actually making amends is the ninth step in AA; the task is difficult, complex, and requires a fairly solid base before it can be productively tackled. In any case, taking responsibility for past behavior without self-recrimination is a delicate task. Family therapists who encourage the spouses to express their anger prematurely may precipitate an unnecessary crisis. It is important that therapists working with these families understand that affect expression for its own sake is not appropriate in treatment of substance abuse.

Among the important psychological concomitants of substance abuse are personality distortions created by heavy reliance on denial. Wurmser (1985) makes the point that many patients considered lacking in superego function are in fact defending against superego functions, to avoid the experience of overwhelming shame and guilt. With heavy use of denial comes a split identity; it is as if another personality takes over, for example, the responsible parent and the angry, impulsive drug user. Patients relying on this mechanism often report a sense of uneasiness and depersonalization, presumably generated by unconscious awareness of the walled off identity.

How much a penchant for denial and split identity exists before involvement with substance abuse, and how much develops in exaggerated form as a result of involvement, is difficult to say. Vaillant (1981) argues that much of the pathology observed is developed in the course of the abuse history and gradually clears once abstinence is established. Nonetheless, part of the therapeutic task is to assist the reintegration of part identities, including acknowledgment and coming to terms with past shameful behavior.

Long Term Psychological Issues

In the later stages of recovery, therapy much more resembles conventional insight oriented, psychodynamic therapy. Most practitioners recommend that the therapist wait at least a year before underlying developmental issues or major traumatic events (such as abuse, incest, etc.) are addressed. These issues will of course come up early in the treatment, but serious attempts at resolution must be postponed in order to be effective. Early in recovery the task is to help the client cope with the pain without resorting to drugs or alcohol, and insight oriented approaches are undertaken with the goal of arriving at concrete, practical strategies and behaviors to maintain abstinence. Later in recovery, more uncovering and detailed exploration may be tolerated, but the therapist and client should always remain alert to the possibility of relapse as a way of obscuring painful material. The ability to shift from an exploratory focus to one which addresses the need to strengthen the support system and increase the behaviors of abstinence when the client is particularly troubled is crucial at this stage (Brown, 1985). Those with solid connections with 12 step programs have a great advantage here, as they can simply increase their participation as a way of tightening the structure of treatment. Others who have not made such a connection will have to devise functional equivalents.

There are several exceptions to the guideline of postponing therapeutic work on other issues until abstinence is solidly achieved. Major psychiatric disorders and eating disorders are examples of entities which are so intertwined with the chemical abuse that it is unlikely one can break the abuse cycle without initiating concurrent treatment. This area is receiving increasing attention, and it is likely that our understanding of how to address these challenging problems will improve dramatically within the next few years.

CONCLUSION

This paper has used an evolutionary model in order to clarify the recovery tasks and the nature of the activity of the therapist at this stage. Hopefully, it will resolve some of the existing confusions about the utility of psychotherapy for the treatment of substance abuse problems.

REFERENCES

Alibrandi, L. (1978). The folk psychotherapy of alcoholics anonymous. In S. Zimberg, J. Wallace, & S. Blume (Eds.), Practical approaches to alcoholism psychotherapy pp. 163–80). New York: Plenum Press.

Bean, M. (1981) Denial and the psychological complications of alcoholism. In M. Bean & N. Zinberg (Eds.), Dynamic approaches to the understanding and treatment of alcoholism. (pp. 55–96). Free Press: New York.

Brisman, J., & Siegel, M. (1984). Bulimia and alcoholism: Two sides of the same coin? Journal of Substance Abuse Treatment, 1 113–118.

Brown, S. (1985). Treating the alcoholic: A developmental model of recovery. New York: John Wiley & Sons.

Cooper, J.; Altman, F.; Brown, B.; & Czechowicz, D. (Eds.) (1983). Research on the treatment of narcotic addiction. Rockville, MD: NIDA Treatment Monograph.

Craig, R. (1985). Reducing the treatment drop out rate in drug abuse programs. Journal of Substance Abuse Treatment, 2, 209–219.

Crowley, T. (1984). Contingency contracting treatment of drug-abusing physicians, nurses, and dentists. In J. Grabowski, M. Stitzer, & J. Henningfield (Eds.), Behavioral Intervention Techniques in Drug Abuse Treatment. (NIDA Research Monograph #46). Rockville, MD: National Institute on Drug Abuse.

Deitch, D. (1973). Treatment of drug abuse in the therapeutic community: Historical *influences, current considerations, and future outlook.* Drug Abuse in America: Problem in Perspective. *Washington, DC: U.S. Government Printing Office.*

De Leon, G. *(1984).* The therapeutic community; Study of effectiveness. *Rockville, MD: NIDA Treatment Research Monograph.*

Gawin, F., & Kleber, H. *(1986). Abstinence symptomatology and psychiatric diagnosis in cocaine abusers.* Archives of General Psychiatry, *43 107–113.*

Gitlow, S. *(1985). Considerations on the evaluation and treatment of substance dependency.* Journal of Substance Abuse Treatment, *2 175–179.*

Gorski, T., Miller, M. *(1982).* Counseling for Relapse Prevention. *Missouri: Herald House-Independent Press.*

Khantzian, E. *(1981). Some treatment implications of the ego and self disturbances in alcoholism. In M. Beàn & N. Zinberg (Eds.),* Dynamic Approaches to the Understanding and Treatment of Alcoholism *(pp. 163–189). New York: Free Press.*

Khantzian, E. *(1982). Psychopathology, Psychodynamics, and Alcoholism. In M. Pattison & E. Kaufman (Eds.),* Encyclopedic Handbook of Alcoholism *(pp. 581–97). New York: Gardner Press.*

Khantzian, E. *(1985). Psychotherapeutic interventions with substance abusers—The clinical context.* Journal of Substance Abuse Treatment, *2, 83–85.*

Lowinson, Joyce *(1981). Methadone maintenance in perspective. In J. Lowinsonson & P. Ruiz* Substance abuse: Clinical problems and perspectives *(pp. 344–354.) Baltimore: Williams & Wilkins.*

Marlatt, G., & Gordon, J. *(Eds.). (1985).* Relapse prevention. *New York: The Guilford Press.*

Mirin, S. *(Ed.). (1984).* Substance abuse and psychotherapy. *Washington, DC: Psychiatric Press.*

Newman, Robert *(1982, October).* Evaluating the success of methadone maintenance treatment. *Paper presented to the Second Statewide Methadone Conference, New York.*

Petrakis, P. *(1985).* Alcoholism: An inherited disease. *Rockville, MD: U.S. Department of Health and Human Services.*

Schuckit, M. *(1985). Treatment of alcoholism in office and outpatient settings. In J. Mendelson & N. Mello (Eds.),* The diagnosis and treatment of alcoholism *(pp. 295–324). New York: McGraw Hill.*

Shaffer, H., & Milkman, H. *(1985). Introduction: Crisis and conflict in the addictions. In H. Shaffer & H. Milkman (Eds.),* The addictions: Multidisciplinary perspectives and treatments *(pp. ix–xvii). Lexington, MA: Lexington Books.*

Smith, D. E. *(1984). Substance use disorders: Drugs & alcohol. In H. Goldman (Ed.),* Review of general psychiatry *(pp. 278–297). Los Altos, CA: Lange Medical Publishers.*

Smith, D. E., Milkman, H. B., & Sunderwirth, S. *(1985). Addictive disease: Concept and controversy. In H. B. Milkman & H. Shaffer (Eds.),* The addictions: Multidisciplinary perspectives and treatments *(pp. 145–160). Lexington, MA: Lexington Books.*

Vaillant, G. *(1981). Dangers of psychotherapy in the treatment of alcoholism. In M. Bean & N. Zinberg (Eds.),* Dynamic approaches to the understanding and treatment of alcoholism *(pp. 36–51) Free Press: New York.*

Washton, A., & Gold, M. (1986). Cocaine treatment today. *Rockville, MD: The American Council for Drug Education.*

Washton, A.; Gold, M.; & Pottash, A. (1986). *Treatment outcome in cocaine abusers. In L. Harris (Ed.),* Problems of drug dependence, 1985 *(pp. 381–384). (NIDA Research Monograph #67, pp. 381–384). Rockville, MD: Department of Health and Human Services.*

Wegscheider, S. (1981). Another chance: Hope and health for the alcoholic family. *Palo Alto: Science and Behavior Books.*

Wurmser, L. (1984). *More respect for the neurotic process: Comments on the problem of narcissism in severe psychopathology, especially the addictions.* Journal of Substance Abuse Treatment, 1, 37–45.

Wurmser, L. (1985). *Denial and split identity: Timely issues in the psychoanalytic psychotherapy of compulsive drug users.* Journal of Substance Abuse Treatment, 2, 80–96.

Zackon, F.; McAuliffe, W.; & Ch'ien, J. (1985). Recovery training and self-help. *Rockville, MD: NIDA Treatment Research Monograph Series.*

Zimberg, S. (1982). *Psychotherapy in the treatment of alcoholism. In E. Mansell Pattison & E. Kaufman (Eds.),* Encyclopedic handbook of alcoholism *(pp. 999–1010). New York: Gardner Press.*

Zweben, J., (1986). *Treating cocaine dependence: New challenges for the therapeutic community.* Journal of Psychoactive Drugs, 18, 239–245.

Zweben, J.; Pearlman, S.; & Li, S. (1983). *Reducing attrition from conjoint therapy with alcoholic couples.* Drug and Alcohol Dependence, 11, 321–331.

Zweben, J., & Smith D., (1986). *Changing attitudes and policies towards alcohol use in the therapeutic community.* Journal of Psychoactive Drugs, 18, 253–260.

PART VII

Psychiatric Illness and Addiction

BY FAR the greatest challenge in addiction treatment today is to successfully care for addicted patients with comorbid psychiatric disorders. Data
from the Epidemiologic Catchment Area Study (ECA) indicate that one-third
of those suffering from an addictive disorder have a comorbid psychiatric
disorder[1] and 45 percent of admissions to psychiatric hospitals have comorbid psychiatric and addictive disorders.[2] These investigators specifically point
out the need to develop services for this population.[3] Unfortunately, this area
has been generally neglected by clinicians and researchers.

McLellan's article details a series of outcome studies he and colleagues
conducted with addicts in different treatment modalities. The most striking
finding was that psychiatric severity was the best predictor of treatment
outcome; those patients with greater psychiatric severity had poorer outcomes. He indicates there is no current effective treatment approach for the
15 to 30 percent severely psychiatrically impaired addicts. His research
showed that severely psychiatrically disturbed addicts improved somewhat in
methadone maintenance, but they actually got worse in TC-style treatment.
He found that there was additional benefit derived from adding psychotherapy
to methadone maintenance for this population.

Psychoanalysis has always seen a link between psychiatric illness and
addiction. A current version of this theory is the self-medication hypothesis
developed by Khantzian, which postulates that addicts are attempting to
medicate themselves for a range of psychiatric problems and painful emotional states (Khantzian, this part). Ironically, this is a restatement of the
symptom theory (i.e., that addiction is a symptom of an underlying psychiatric illness) that has been so unpopular with disease concept advocates.[4] The
practical treatment implication of the theory is that addicts should have a
thorough psychiatric evaluation to determine if there is any significant psychiatric illness. If such pathology is found it can be treated with medication or a
special form of psychotherapy.[5] Elsewhere,[6] Khantzian makes clear his view
that the active addiction must be arrested before addressing any underlying
psychiatric disorder. In other papers, Khantzian emphasizes that addicts have

ego deficits predisposing them to addiction.[7] Weiss and Mirin, in their article, provide a balanced review of the self-medication hypothesis and discuss their research on the relationship between psychiatric illness, addiction, and the self-medication hypothesis.

In the chapter reprinted here, Richards sets out a model to integrate the treatment of psychiatric illness and addiction. He suggests there are continua for both addictiveness and psychopathology that can combine in several ways. His approach is to integrate the treatment of the two disorders rather than treat them separately and concurrently. The rest of the book elaborates the paradigm developed in this chapter and outlines a new treatment approach for these patients.

The competing treatment model is the disease concept of addiction combined with a biological view of mental illness, providing a straightforward approach. Treating the addiction involves education, confrontation, AA/NA-involvement, and abstinence. The psychiatric disorder is treated with medication. This model then, is completely medical/biological. Zweben[8] outlines such an approach and Hanson, Kramer, and Gross[9] report results of a specially developed program for this population. Richards calls this a parallel approach because the two disorders are treated separately and concurrently by addiction specialists and mental health professionals.

NOTES

1. Regier et al., 1993.
2. Narrow et al., 1993.
3. Narrow et al., 1993.
4. Leeds and Morgenstern, 1996.
5. Khantzian et al., 1990.
6. Khantzian, 1980; Khantzian et al., 1990.
7. Khantzian, 1978, 1980, 1985, and 1987.
8. Zweben, 1992.
9. Hanson, Kramer, and Gross, 1990.

22. "Psychiatric Severity" as a Predictor of Outcome from Substance Abuse Treatments

A. Thomas McLellan

IN 1979 (McLellan, 1979), I reported the development of a new, multidimensional clinical research instrument for substance-abusing patients, called the Addiction Severity Index (ASI). The design of the ASI is based upon the premise that addiction to either alcohol or street drugs must be considered in the context of those additional treatment problems that may have contributed to and/or resulted from the chemical abuse. The objective of the ASI is to produce a "problem severity profile" of each patient through an analysis of seven areas commonly affected in drug- or alcohol-abusing patients. These include alcohol use, drug use, medical condition, employment, legal problems, family relations, and psychiatric status. My colleagues' and my experience has suggested that these problems combine in a variety of complex ways to create particular treatment needs in each patient. Furthermore, we feel that if these problems are not addressed along with the chemical dependence in a substance abuse treatment, they can leave the patient susceptible to relapse, readdiction, and return to treatment.

In each of the seven ASI areas, objective questions are asked measuring the number, frequency, and duration of problem symptoms in the patient's lifetime and in the past 30 days. The patient also supplies a subjective report of the recent (past 30 days) severity and importance of each problem area. The interviewer assimilates the two types of information to produce seven global ratings reflecting problem severity in each area. These 10-point (0 = "no problem," 9 = "extreme problem") ratings have been shown to provide reliable and valid estimates of problem severity for both alcohol- and drug-dependent patients. The individual objective items offer a comprehensive basis for assessment at treatment admission and at subsequent evaluation periods (see McLellan, Luborsky, O'Brien, & Woody, 1980).

Reprinted by permission from *Psychopathology and Addictive Disorders*, R. E. Meyer, ed. (New York: Guilford Press, 1986), 97–139.

Using this instrument in a 4-year design, we have found that the nature and severity of these associated treatment problems are important predictors of patient outcome from both alcohol and drug abuse treatments. They may also be used prospectively at the time of admission to "match" patients to the most appropriate treatment. In particular, our results indicate that a global estimate of a patient's psychiatric symptomatology (i.e., his or her "psychiatric severity") is the single best overall predictor of outcome across patient types, treatment methods, and outcome measures. The data to be presented relevant to this issue are organized in two parts. In the first part, I present the design and results of our 4-year prediction study. These results show the importance of our global "psychiatric severity" measure in predicting treatment outcome. In the second part, I present a series of subsequent studies targeting the most psychiatrically impaired sample of our substance-abusing patients. We have attempted to determine the most effective and appropriate of the available treatment options for this important subgroup of substance abusers.

PSYCHIATRIC SEVERITY AS A PREDICTOR OF TREATMENT OUTCOME

General Procedure

The 4-year outcome prediction project was carried out using a three-stage design (McLellan, Druley, O'Brien, & Kron, 1980). In Stage I, extensive patient background and 6-month follow-up data were collected on all patients who were admitted to the six programs within the treatment network during calendar year 1978. In Stage II, these initial data were analyzed to determine the nature and extent of patients' improvements within each program and the specific patient factors that were most predictive of optimum improvement within each program. In Stage III, the efficacy of these predictive factors was tested by assigning a 10-month (1980) sample of newly admitted patients to the six programs, using the predictors to "match" patients to the most appropriate treatment. During-treatment improvement and posttreatment (6-month) outcomes were compared between those patients who *were* admitted to the program predicted to be appropriate ("matched" patients) and those patients who were admitted to a program that was not predicted to be appropriate ("mismatched" patients). Results and major conclusions are presented below for each stage of the project.

Treatment Programs

The substance abuse treatment network of the Veterans Administration (VA) in the Philadelphia area consisted of four inpatient (two alcohol, one drug, one combined) therapeutic community programs at the Coatesville VA Medical Center, plus outpatient alcohol and drug abuse clinics at the Philadelphia VA Medical Center. This treatment network has enjoyed cooperative referral arrangements since 1975. Once admitted to substance abuse treatment at either hospital within the network, patients are assigned to one of the six rehabilitation programs on the basis of their personal requests, the clinical judgment of the admitting staff, administrative considerations such as bed census or patient visit criteria, and simple chance.

The following are brief descriptions of the programs; for more complete information, see Gottheil, McLellan, and Druley (1979).

1. The Alcohol Treatment Unit (ATU) is a 60-day therapeutic community based on the principles of Alcoholics Anonymous (AA). The staff conducts small-group therapy four times weekly.
2. Fixed Interval Drinking Decisions (FIDD) is a research program designed to examine and treat alcoholism in the presence of alcohol. The 6-week treatment cycle consists of two 1-week alcohol-free periods and a 4-week drinking-decision phase in which two ounces of 80-proof alcohol are available, and the patients have the opportunity to decide whether to drink. Group and individual therapies are offered daily.
3. Combined Treatment (CMB) is a short-term (45-day) program that delivers intensive addiction management therapy to both alcoholics and drug addicts.
4. Therapeutic Community (TC) offers personal and social drug abuse treatment in a 60-day program designed to "habilitate" the patient to society using individual and group psychological therapy, educational and vocational counseling, and the social structure of a self-governing therapeutic community.
5. Alcohol Outpatient (AOP) is a variable-length treatment program that concentrates on the medical, psychological, and social problems of outpatient alcoholics. Therapeutic goals include alcohol abstinence through referral to AA and the concurrent reduction of medical and psychological problems associated with alcoholism.
6. Methadone Maintenance (MM) offers methadone maintenance, in com-

bination with a full program of psychiatric and social work counseling. Chemotherapeutic and individual therapy interventions are used to treat associated psychological problems of these patients.

Stages I and II

Subjects

All male veterans who presented for alcohol or drug abuse treatment at either the Coatesville or Philadelphia VA Medical Centers during 1978 were eligible for Stage I of the study. There were no significant differences in demographic or background characteristics between patients in the two hospitals, and approximately 90% of all subjects were Philadelphia residents. There were no treatment admission criteria other than eligibility for veterans' benefits.

We initially evaluated 1035 male veterans who were admitted to alcohol ($n = 671$) or drug abuse ($n = 364$) rehabilitation programs at the Coatesville or Philadelphia VA Medical Centers during 1978. Since the aims of the study were confined to patients who had been effectively engaged in the treatment process, we did not follow patients who dropped out of treatment prior to 5 inpatient days or five outpatient visits. We were able to contact approximately 85% of the remaining 879 patients 6 months after admission to treatment, and complete data were therefore available on 742 subjects (460 alcoholics and 282 drug addicts).

Table 22.1 summarizes the pretreatment characteristics of the study population, divided into alcoholics and drug addicts. Immediately noticeable are the distinct differences between the alcohol and drug populations in age ($t = 22.6$, $df = 877$, p < .001), and racial composition ($X^2 = 26.6$, $df = 1$, $p < .001$), while the groups were similar with respect to mean number of previous substance abuse treatments and years of education. In the remaining sections of the table, I have summarized the treatment problems for the total population and for each group by presenting the mean ASI problem severity ratings (see "Data Collection"), as well as additional pertinent background characteristics to clarify the admission status of these patients.

These admission data indicate that the average patient started treatment with severe problems of alcohol or drug abuse, and also had moderately severe employment, family, and psychiatric problems. However, it is obvious that extreme differences existed at admission between the alcoholics and the drug addicts. The alcoholics presented with more severe medical prob-

Table 22.1. Background Characteristics at Admission

Characteristics	Alcoholics		Drug addicts	Total
Demographic factors				
Age	46	**	31	40
% white	60	**	47	56
% black	39		52	43
Years education	11.2		11.7	11.4
Previous alcoholic and drug treatments	6		5	6
Medical problem severity[a]	3.0	*	2.2	2.7
% w/chronic medical problems	48	**	28	40
Medical hospitalizations	5	*	3	4
Employment problem severity[a]	4.1	*	5.2	4.6
% w/skill or trade	56	*	62	58
Longest period of employment (months)	69	**	36	59
Substance abuse problem severity	6.1		6.6	6.3
Years problematic alcohol use	13	**	3	10
Years opiate use	0.5	**	6	2
Years nonopiate use	1	**	4	2
Longest period of abstinence (months)	5		7	6
Legal problem severity	2.2	**	4.0	2.8
% awaiting charges	9	**	22	13
Months incarcerated	7	**	14	10
Family/social problem severity	3.9		4.2	4.0
% divorced, separated	43		36	40
% living alone	30	**	19	26
% friends w/alcohol or drug problems	27		25	26
Psychiatric problem severity	3.8		4.0	3.9
% having previous psychiatric treatment	16	**	8	13
% attempted suicide	17		17	17
Maudsley Neuroticism Scale	27		28	27
Beck Depression Inventory	17	*	14	16
IQ (age-connected)	103		101	102

NOTE. For alcoholics, $n = 460$; for drug addicts, $n = 282$; total $n = 742$.
[a] All severity ratings range from $0 = $ "No problem" to $9 = $ "Extreme problem."
*$p < .05$.
**$p < .01$.

lems, while the drug addicts showed more severe legal and employment problems.

Data Collection

Admission and Follow-up Data. The admission and follow-up evaluations were based upon data from the ASI (McLellan, 1979; McLellan, Luborsky, O'Brien, & Woody, 1980). The ASI is a structured, 30- to 40-minute, clinical research interview designed to assess problem severity in seven areas commonly affected by addiction: alcohol use, drug use, medical condition, employment, legal problems, family relations, and psychiatric problems. In each of the areas, as noted above, objective questions measuring the number, extent, and duration of problem symptoms in the patient's lifetime are asked, and the patient also supplies a subjective report of the recent (past 30 days) severity and importance of each problem area. The interviewer assimilates the two types of information to produce a rating (0–9) of the patient's "need for treatment" in each area. These 10-point ratings have been shown to provide reliable and valid general estimates of problem severity for both alcoholics and drug addicts (McLellan et al., 1985; McLellan, Luborsky, O'Brien, & Woody, 1980).

Follow-up. All follow-up evaluations were done through repeat ASI interviews by an independent research technician 6 months following treatment admission. No information from secondary sources was used, and all data were closely monitored to preserve confidentiality. The validity of the follow-up data was checked through built-in consistency checks within the ASI and through spot checks on subsamples of the outpatient population, by assessing the ASI data against urinalysis, pharmacy, and criminal justice system records. We found less than 5% inconsistency. Similar findings have been reported by many other investigators studying the validity of patients' self-reports. Since the fixed, 6-month follow-up interval produced unequal times between treatment discharge and the follow-up interview, we examined the relationships between time out of treatment and outcome status on all criterion measures. No significant correlations were found for any of the groups (all p's > .10), and there were no differences among the inpatient programs with regard to time out of treatment.

Developing Appropriate and Reliable Measures of Outcome. We felt it was important to develop general measures of outcome in each of the seven problem areas, since assessments based solely on single-item criteria (e.g., days of drug use) offer meager and inherently unreliable estimates of post-treatment status (Nunally, 1967). We therefore constructed composite outcome measures based on combinations of objective items from each of the ASI areas. In this method, which has been used by Mintz and Luborsky in their studies of outcome from psychotherapy (Mintz, Luborsky, & Cristoph, 1979), several of the objective items within each ASI area were intercorrelated to eliminate unrelated items, and the remaining items were standardized, summed, and tested for conjoint reliability using Cronbach's formula (Cronbach & Furby, 1970). In this manner, seven composite criteria were constructed from sets of the ASI objective items, producing highly reliable (.73 or higher) general measures of outcome.

With regard to the number of outcome measures to be used in the analyses, we had originally hoped to be able to factor the seven composites into fewer measures of general improvement. However, an examination of the relationships between these measures (see McLellan, Luborsky, Woody, & O'Brien, 1981) indicated that there were very low intercorrelations between the criterion measures, both for the total population and for the alcohol and drug abuse samples individually. The lack of intercorrelation suggested that the outcome measures were tapping independent aspects of the outcome status, and that it would be important to examine each criterion separately.

What Factors Predicted Response to Alcohol and Drug Abuse Treatments?

We were primarily interested in what type of pretreatment information would predict outcome and in whether certain "types" of patients appeared to have better outcomes in certain programs. However, we knew that the treatment programs and the patients in them were quite different at the outset of treatment; thus it would not be meaningful to compare outcome results directly. We therefore required a statistical procedure that would allow us to account for this pretreatment variation and still detect outcome differences among programs and among patient–program combinations. To this end, we employed the stepwise multiple-regression procedure (Dixon & Brown, 1979).

The multiple-regression analysis permitted us to sequentially enter independent (predictor) variables that we considered important in determining outcome as measured by each of our composite scores. For each of these independent variables, the regression analysis performed two important functions. First, it tested whether the specific independent variable explained a significant ($p < .01$) proportion of outcome variance. Stated differently, the procedure was able to determine whether patients who differed on demographic, admission status, or during-treatment variables (e.g., age, race, years drinking, ASI psychiatric severity score) had significantly different scores on the outcome measure. Second, the regression procedure removed that portion of outcome variance accounted for by all of these variables. In this manner, it was possible to adjust (control) for pre-existing differences in demographic and admission status factors before testing for significant effects due to treatment programs and patient–program matches.

Table 22.2 describes the variables used in the regression equations and the order in which they were entered. Thus, the four demographic variables were entered first, followed by the pretreatment ASI severity scores (depicting the admission status of the patients), and then by the during-treatment measures of days in treatment and type of discharge. Therefore, the criterion measures were adjusted for differences in each of these variables prior to tests for differences among programs and patient × program interactions.

Specific tests for outcome differences between programs were accomplished in the standard manner, by assigning a bivariate (0, 1) variable to each treatment program and then entering each of these variables into regression analysis. Patient–program interaction effects were tested by multiplying each program variable with each demographic and admission status variable, and entering these product variables into the last stage of the analysis.

Thus, in summary, it was possible to determine whether a patient characteristic such as age was a significant determinant of outcome alone, regardless of treatment program, by entering the age variable early in the analysis. Similarly, it was possible to determine whether treatment in a particular program such as the ATU was associated with significantly better outcome by entering the ATU program variable after the demographic and admission status variables had been entered and adjusted for. Finally, it was possible to determine whether older patients had better outcomes when they were treated in the ATU (patient–program interaction) by entering that product variable after all other factors had been adjusted for.

Table 22.2. Accounting for Outcome: Stepwise Multiple Regression

Type of independent variable (in order of entry)	Variables
1. Demographic	Age (years) Education (years) Race (0 = black, 1 = white) Previous treatments (number)
2. Admission status (ASI ratings)	Medical Employment Legal Family Psychiatric Substance abuse
3. During-treatment	Days in treatment Type of discharge (0 = favorable, 1 = unfavorable)
4. Treatment program	Variable for each treatment program
5. Interactions	Demographic × program variables Admission status × program variables

Regression analyses were calculated separately for the alcoholic ($n = 460$) and drug addict ($n = 282$) samples (see "Subjects") on each of the seven follow-up criteria. An examination of the overall results from these first analyses indicated virtually no evidence of significant patient–program interactions in either sample. In short, these initial findings were quite comparable to results of previous national reports (Armor, Polich, & Stambul, 1978; Simpson, Savage, Lloyd, & Sells, 1978) showing no differences in outcome among different treatments or among different patient–program combinations.

Psychiatric Severity as Outcome Predictor

However, the results did show a clear and significant ($p < .01$) relationship between all of the outcome measures and the patients' pretreatment ASI psychiatric severity score. The correlations between admission psychiatric severity and the 6-month outcome measures were calculated for both the alcoholic and drug addict samples. Significant relationships were seen on five of the seven measures for the alcoholics, and on six of the seven criteria for the drug addicts. In every case, *greater* pretreatment psychiatric severity was related to *poorer* 6-month outcome, and this variable alone accounted for an average of 10% of the outcome variance across the seven criteria.

Detailed Description of the ASI Psychiatric Severity Scales. The 10-point ASI rating of psychiatric severity is made without regard for drug use, family problems, employment difficulties, or other problems, which are assessed separately. In the case of psychiatric severity, some of the more prominent items question each patient's experience with "significant periods of" depression, anxiety, confusion, persecution or paranoia, inability to concentrate, inability to control violent tendencies, and so on. It should be clear that this is a very basic, global estimate of symptom severity, psychopathology, or psychological health–sickness. It most resembles the Health–Sickness Rating Scale (Luborsky & Bachrach, 1974), which has now been adapted to the Global Assessment Scale and as such is included in the Schedule for Affective Disorders and Schizophrenia (SADS) (Endicott, Spitzer, & Fleiss, 1976). We have intercorrelated these measures in several studies, and the coefficients are uniformly .70 or above. We have previously published evidence for the high reliability of the ASI psychiatric severity rating (McLellan, Luborsky, O'Brien, & Woody, 1980), and we have since confirmed this at three different treatment sites and with 12 raters (McLellan et al., 1985). Further, we have correlated the ASI psychiatric severity scale with standardized psychological tests, producing the following coefficients: Maudsley Neuroticism Scale, .69; Beck Depression Inventory, .71; total score on the Hopkins Symptom Checklist, .81; and a measure of cognitive impairment or brain damage, .62, but not IQ, .13. In sum, there is evidence that the ASI psychiatric severity scale is a reliable and valid, *global* estimate of the severity of psychopathology, *but does not designate specific psychiatric diagnosis.*

The strength and pervasiveness of the relationships in the present data suggested the possibility of further dividing the alcoholic and drug addict samples into low, middle, and high groups, based upon their pretreatment psychiatric severity scores, under the assumption that qualitatively different results might appear. To this end, we selected the mean value on the psychiatric severity scale, plus and minus one standard deviation, as the score range for the middle group in each sample. The low groups had psychiatric severity scores that were more than one standard deviation below the mean, and the high groups had severity scores more than one standard deviation above the mean. The middle group comprised 60–70% of the patient population, while the low and high groups comprised 15–20% each (McLellan, Luborsky, Woody, Druley, & O'Brien, 1983; Woody et al., 1983). Patients who were rated in the low group were generally asymptomatic or had slight problems of anxiety or minor depression in their past. Middle-severity patients might have had recent symptoms of depression, anxiety, or cognitive confusion, but no clear history of recurring symptoms. Patients in the high group generally reported suicidal ideation, thought disorder, and/or cognitive confusion. Again, it is important to note that the designations were made on the basis of severity, not diagnosis or specific symptom patterns.

Interpretation of Regression Analyses. Since seven regression analyses were computed for each of these six groups, there were obviously a large number of individual predictors for specific criteria. In order to present these results in a clear and interpretable fashion, I have summarized the regression results for the two low groups in Table 22.3, for the two high groups in Table 22.4, and for the two middle groups in Table 22.5. In these tables, the leftmost column indicates the category of independent (predictor) variables and the order in which they were entered into the equations. The variables that are shown were included only if they were significant ($p<.01$) predictors on *at least three* of the seven criteria. This is not to suggest that these were the only important variables, just that they were among the most salient and generally robust. The average zero-order correlation between the predictor variable and these criterion measures is presented in the R column for each

Table 22.3. Outcome Predictors in Patients with Low Psychiatric Severity

Type of variable	Alcoholics (n = 102)		Drug addicts (n = 68)	
	Variable	R	Variable	R
Demographic	No. of previous treatments	.32	—	—
Admission severity	Medical severity	.33	Drug use severity	.30
	Employment severity	.28	Employment severity	.30
During-treatment	Days in treatment	−.20	Days in treatment	−.28
Treatment program	—	—	—	—
Interactions	Legal severity × FIDD	.28	Employment severity × MM	.28
Mean outcome variance explained	34%		32%	

Table 22.4. Outcome Predictors in Patients with High Psychiatric Severity

Type of variable	Alcoholics (n = 82)		Drug addicts (n = 53)	
	Variable	R	Variable	R
Demographic	Age	.30	—	—
Admission severity	—	—	Drug use severity	−.26
During-treatment	—	—	—	—
Treatment program	CMB	.36	CMB	.44
	AOP	.37		
Interactions	—	—	—	—
Mean outcome variance explained	48%		54%	

sample. Since higher scores on the outcome criteria are indicative of greater problem severity, positive correlations indicate that *higher* scores on the predictor variable were related to *worse* outcomes. Thus, in the example of the low/alcoholic group (Table 22.3), the number of previous treatments was significantly (+.32) related to poorer posttreatment status on at least three outcome measures. Similarly, the number of days in treatment was significantly (−.20) related to better status on at least three outcome measures. The significant interaction between legal status and treatment in the FIDD program ("Legal severity × FIDD") indicates that low/alcoholic patients with greater than average legal problems who were treated in the FIDD showed poorer results on at least three outcome measures than low/alcoholic patients with similar legal problems treated in the other alcohol programs.

Table 22.5. Outcome Predictors in Patients with Midlevel Psychiatric Severity

Type of variable	Alcoholics (n = 276)		Drug addicts (n = 161)	
	Variable	R	Variable	R
Demographic	Age	.38		
	No. of previous treatments	.34	Race	.37
			Age	−.27
Admission severity	Family severity	.28		
	Legal severity	.26	Employment severity	.36
	Days in treatment	−.38	Days in treatment	−.35
During-treatment	Type discharge	−.26	Type discharge	−.27
Treatment program	FIDD	.25	CMB	.33
Interactions	Legal service × FIDD	.31	Family service × MM	.37
	Employment service × AOP	.30	Employment service × MM	.34
	Legal service × ATU	.28	Medical service × TC	.30
	Age × CMB	.25	Drug use service × CMB	.28
	Family service × AOP	.24		
	Family service × ATU	.24		
Mean outcome variance explained	44%		48%	

Summary of Findings

When the alcoholic and drug addict samples were divided into six groups based upon the ASI psychiatric severity measure, several specific relationships emerged that had been masked in the ungrouped analyses. For example, the regression results for the low groups were generally similar to the results for the ungrouped data. That is, greater amounts of treatment were associated with better outcomes, but there were no significant differences in outcome between the different programs, and only a few significant patient–program matches. However, an examination of the outcome results indicated that these low-group patients showed the best posttreatment status and the most significant amount of improvement on virtually all measures. These data led us to conclude that low-severity patients have the best treatment prognosis generally, and that they appear to improve significantly in *any* of the treatment programs to which they are assigned. The admission characteristics of these patients and the type of improvement shown are suggestive of the small group of alcoholic patients described in the Rand Corporation study (Armor, Polich, & Stambul, 1978) who were able to return to "social drinking" following treatment. It may be that nonabstinent goals are possible for some members of this more intact group of patients. From a practical perspective, we have recommended that the majority of these low-severity patients be treated in an outpatient setting, since this is the most economical and seemingly equally effective alternative. Despite this general conclusion, the data indicate (consistent with our clinical experience) that even with the generally favorable prognosis for this group, patients with significant family and/or employment problems should be treated in an inpatient setting.

The results of our analyses in the high groups also showed few significant differences in outcome among programs and no significant patient–program matches. However, unlike the low groups, the high-severity patients did not show better outcome with more treatment. These Stage I data and our clinical experience indicated that *none* of the programs currently available within our treatment network were effective with these individuals. Interestingly, although treatment outcome could not realistically be called satisfactory, the MM program appeared to have the most positive impact on the high-severity drug patients, possibly due to the regulatory and weak antipsychotic effects of methadone.

Once the high and low groups (which comprised approximately 40% of the total population) were separated from the remaining (middle) population, it was possible to discern significant differences in outcome associated with specific treatments (i.e., specific patient–programs matches). For example, middle patients (both alcoholics and drug addicts) with more severe family and/or employment problems had poorer outcomes in outpatient treatment. These findings are consistent with our clinical experience and suggest that while severe alcohol or drug use, and even medical or legal problems, may be dealt with effectively in an outpatient setting, family and employment problems appear to be clear contraindications for outpatient treatment. Finally, two of the inpatient alcohol abuse treatment programs showed evidence of poorer outcomes with clients having more serious legal problems. We have suggested that these clients be transferred to the CMB program or (in some cases) the AOP program, which did not show poorer outcome with these patients.

Clinical Implications

The present data, as well as other reports (Armor, Polich, & Stambul, 1978; De Leon, 1984; Simpson, Savage, Lloyd, & Sells, 1978), indicate the importance of making independent pretreatment assessments of patient status in several areas commonly affected by addiction. These addiction-related problem severity measures were the most significant predictors of outcome in all groups. The fact that patients with greater pretreatment psychiatric severity showed the poorest outcome is not surprising. A great deal of research has indicated that it is the best and most reliable predictor of treatment outcome in psychotherapy (Luborsky, Mintz, & Auerbach, 1980), and in substance abuse treatment (De Leon, 1984; Meyer, 1983). What is remarkable is that alcohol and drug abuse severity were *not* generally important in predicting outcome. In fact, pretreatment psychiatric severity was a better predictor of posttreatment drinking than was pretreatment drinking. This finding in particular suggests why previous predictive studies, which have used brief data collection instruments concentrating on demographic and substance abuse variables, have not demonstrated meaningful outcome prediction.

Finally, the demonstration of significant differences in outcome as a function of interactions between patient factors and treatment programs suggests that different forms of substance abuse treatment, like other medical treatments, have specific as well as general effects. Further, the data illustrate how the specific effects of the treatment programs may combine with the particular treatment needs of the patient to produce favorable outcomes, as well as contraindications.

As a test of the validity and utility of these predictors in normal clinical practice, those factors that were statistically significant predictors of outcome in this study were utilized as determinants of treatment assignment in Stage III of the project. Thus, we were able to determine whether these factors were generalizable enough to be of practical value in producing improved treatment effectiveness for the six-program treatment network.

Stage III

The data and analyses from Stages I and II, respectively, of the project formed the basis for several hypotheses regarding the most effective and efficient method for matching substance abuse patients to appropriate treatments. These hypotheses were tested using a new sample of patients admitted to treatment during 1980 to the same programs.

Subjects

Subjects were all male veterans who applied for substance abuse rehabilitation treatment at the Philadelphia or Coatesville VA Medical Centers during the months from February through October 1980. As in the retrospective stage of the project, all patients who completed a minimum of 5 inpatient days or five outpatient visits were considered eligible for the study.

We initially interviewed 649 patients (238 alcoholic and 411 drug-dependent). Approximately 15% of each group dropped out of treatment prior to the eligibility criterion. Follow-up efforts were successful with 94% of eligible subjects, leaving 466 subjects (178 alcoholic, 298 drug-dependent) with complete data.

Programs

The same six programs that were studied in 1978 were again studied in 1980. There were obviously changes in personnel during this period, with three of the six programs changing their directors. However, no program changed either its basic orientation to treatment or its program length.

Data Collection Procedure

Admission and follow-up data were recorded on all subjects by independent research technicians, using the ASI in the same manner as previously described.

All follow-ups were completed 6 months (± 2 weeks) following treatment admission by an independent research technician in the same manner as described in Stage I. Of the attempted follow-ups, 94% were successful, and the completion rates were not different between the alcohol and drug abuse samples or among the six treatment programs (all p's > .10).

Results

Matched and mismatched patients were compared using a range of ASI criteria. Comparisons of improvement from admission to follow-up (paired t tests), as well as adjusted comparisons of 6-month outcome (analysis of covariance), were calculated on all 19 criteria (7 composite scores, 12 single-item measures).

Alcohol-Dependent Patients. Comparisons of improvement from admission to follow-up (Table 22.6) indicate that both groups showed similar types of improvement, predominantly in the areas of employment and alcohol use. However, the matched patients also showed some evidence of significant ($p < .05$) improvement in the areas of medical and psychiatric status, while the mismatched patients did not. Analyses of 6-month outcome status variables for the two groups, adjusted for pretreatment differences in age, number of prior treatments, and the admission criterion score, are presented in the final column of Table 22.6. As can be seen, the matched patients showed significantly better outcomes (accounting for pretreatment differences) in the

Table 22.6. Comparisons of Admission to 6-Month Performance of Matched and Mismatched Alcohol-Dependent Patients

	Matched patients (n = 81)		Mismatched patients (n = 97)		ANCOVA[b] on
Criteria[a]	Admission	Follow-up	Admission	Follow-up	follow-up
Medical factor	22 *	11	18	14	.10
% days medical problems	65	36	56	40	
Employment factor	−20	−15	−14	−14	
% time worked	16 **	27	13 **	32	
Money earned/day	13.37	10.83	5.14	8.65	
Welfare income/day	1.38 *	0.84	2.80 *	1.32	.10
Alcohol use factor	29 **	9	26 **	10	
% days any drinking	69 **	29	60 **	28	
% days intoxicated	60 **	19	50 **	17	
Drug use factor	0	0	1	2	**
% days opiate use	0	0	6	2	
% days nonopiate use	2	2	4	4	*
Legal factor	5	1	10	3	.10
% days of crime	3	0	2	0	
Illegal income/day	0.22	0	2.59	0	
Family factor	12	7	17	12	**
% days of family problems	4	6	16	10	
Psychiatric factor	140 *	91	199	175	*
% days of psychiatric problems	42 *	27	54	52	.10

[a] All criteria were measured during the 30-day period preceding admission and the 6-month follow-up. Higher factor scores indicate greater problem severity.
[b] Covariates in the analysis were age, number of prior alcohol or drug abuse treatments, and the admission criterion score.
* $p < .05$.
** $p < .01$.

areas of drug use, legal status, family relations, and psychological function. In addition, 16 of the 19 comparisons showed better status in the matched patients, although only 8 comparisons were statistically significant.

Thus, the data indicate generally better adjustment to treatment, somewhat more improvement, and better 6-month outcomes in the matched alcohol-dependent patients than in the mismatched group.

Drug-Dependent Patients. Measures of improvement from admission to follow-up on the 19 criterion variables indicated significant and pervasive improvement in the areas of alcohol and drug use, legal status, and family relations for both groups and additional improvements in psychiatric status for the mismatched group (Table 22.7). Thus, the mismatched drug abuse patients showed somewhat more improvement (12 vs. 11) than the matched

Table 22.7. Comparisons of Admission to 6-Month Performance of Matched and Mismatched Drug-Dependent Patients

Criteria[a]	Matched patients (n = 116) Admission		Follow-up	Mismatched patients (n = 182) Admission		Follow-up	ANCOVA[b] on follow-up
Medical factor	8		6	21		10	*
% days medical problems	19		18	57		30	*
Employment factor	−20		−16	−11		−11	**
% days worked	41		42	23		27	**
Money earned/day	20.77		17.99	7.43		9.03	*
Welfare income/day	0.97		1.20	2.06		2.00	
Alcohol use factor	5	**	3	7	**	4	
% days any drinking	39	**	25	39	**	26	
% days intoxicated	15	*	7	14	**	9	
Drug use factor	14	**	4	16	**	7	*
% days opiate use	72	**	10	61	**	20	.10
% days nonopiate use	19	**	4	34		27	*
Legal factor	6	**	2	10	**	3	
% days of crime	24	**	7	33	**	8	
Illegal income/day	12.49	**	2.56	20.12	**	4.81	**
Family factor	11	**	7	14	**	10	*
% days of family problems	5		5	20	**	10	
Psychiatric factor	110	*	78	223	**	131	*
% days of psychiatric problems	21		17	59	**	36	*

[a] All criteria were measured during the 30-day period preceding admission and the 6-month follow-up. Higher factor scores indicate greater problem severity.
[b] Covariates in the analysis were age, number of prior alcohol or drug abuse treatments, and the admission criterion score.
*p < .05.
**p < .01.

group, largely in family relations and psychiatric status, although both groups showed considerable improvement. However, when the 6-month outcome status of these two groups was compared using analysis-of-covariance procedures to adjust for pretreatment differences, the matched drug abuse group showed generally better outcome. In fact, the matched group had better outcomes on all 19 variables, significantly so in the areas of medical status, employment, drug use, illegal income, and psychiatric function. Thus, as in the alcohol-dependent sample, the comparisons indicated better within-treatment and posttreatment adjustment in the matched drug-dependent patients.

Further Analysis Without High-Severity Patients. Although these analyses were quite encouraging in both patient samples, it was possible that the results might be accounted for by differences in the proportion of patients with serious psychiatric symptomatology at admission—the high-psychiatric-severity group that we had identified in the 1978 analyses. The results of our 1978 analyses suggested that these high-severity patients responded poorly to all of the available alcohol or drug abuse treatments (see also Armor, Polich, & Stambul, 1978; Simpson, Savage, Lloyd, & Sells, 1978). Thus, in our treatment assignment strategy, we considered these high-severity patients to be unsuited for *any* program and there were no "matched" patients in the high-psychiatric-severity groups.

Therefore, in an attempt to provide a more fine-grained analysis of the treatment assignment issue, we eliminated all high-psychiatric-severity patients and reanalyzed the data in both the alcohol- and drug-dependent samples, divided into matched and mismatched groups.

Analyses of improvement from admission to the 6-month follow-up point showed generally widespread improvement among both matched and mismatched groups in each subsample. Major improvements for the alcohol-dependent subsamples were seen in the areas of alcohol use and employment. Generally, these groups had low initial levels of drug use or criminality. Thus the only areas that might have been expected to show more significant change were medical condition, family relations, and psychiatric function. Major improvements for the drug-dependent subsamples were in the areas of drug use, illegal activity, and sometimes alcohol use. There was less evidence for significant improvement in medical condition, family relations, psychiatric function, and (surprisingly) employment. In all of the subsamples, there were more improvements at generally higher levels of significance in the matched patients.

Analyses of covariance on the 6-month follow-up data, using age, number of previous alcohol/drug abuse treatments, and the admission criterion score to adjust for pretreatment differences, yielded evidence for significantly better outcomes among the matched patients in all subsamples *except* the middle/alcoholic group. Although 10 of the 19 comparisons showed better outcome among the matched patients in this subsample, there were two significantly better outcomes for the mismatched patients and only two significantly better outcomes for the matched patients. Comparisons in all other subsamples yielded almost uniformly better outcomes (generally significantly so) for the matched patients.

Therefore, we must conclude that even without the potentially magnifying effects of high-psychiatric-severity patients, there was considerable evidence for significantly better during-treatment performance and posttreatment adjustment in the matched patients than in their mismatched counterparts.

Summary and Discussion of Stages I, II, and III

An evaluation of treatment effectiveness in male veteran substance abuse patients was conducted in six treatment programs from two cooperating medical centers. The evaluation study was conducted in three stages over 40 months. In Stage I, all patients admitted to the six programs were evaluated comprehensively at the start of treatment and again, 6 months later, using an instrument developed and tested during this project (see McLellan, Luborsky, O'Brien, & Woody, 1980).

The comprehensive evaluation instrument used in the study allowed us to identify one major predictive factor that was well related to treatment outcome in most of the seven criterion areas. This predictive factor was a 10-point interviewer rating of global psychiatric severity at admission to treatment. This psychiatric severity rating was based upon patients' reports of past and present psychiatric symptoms. The alcohol and drug abuse samples were stratified into low-, middle-, and high-severity groups, and the outcome data were reanalyzed. Results showed evidence of outcome differences among the treatment programs and evidence of significant outcome differences associated with patient–program matching, especially among the middle-severity patients. The results provided the basis for a decision strategy to match incoming alcohol and drug patients to the most appropriate treatment program within the six-program network.

In Stage III of the study, the early data were used to generate *a priori* predictions for each patient regarding appropriate (matched) and inappropriate (mismatched) treatment program assignments. Admission staff were not apprised of the matching strategy; thus Stage III patients were assigned to treatments in the same manner as in Stage I, permitting an experimental test of the matching strategy by comparing the treatment response in matched and mismatched patients. Results of these comparisons indicated generally superior performance during treatment and better 6-month outcomes in the matched patients than in their mismatched counterparts. Furthermore, these results were consistent across the majority of subsamples and all of the treatment programs examined.

Limitations of the Study

Prior to a detailed discussion and interpretation of these results, it is important to examine the design and methodological limitations of the study. The first stage of the design was explicitly nonexperimental, since the patients were not assigned to the treatment programs. Furthermore, it could be argued that since there were no explicit hypotheses suggested or tested, the procedure was simply a "fishing expedition." An experimental design is appropriate for investigating a few key variables in a situation where it is possible to control external variation. In the present study, we were not sure which variables were potentially the most important in determining treatment outcome. Moreover, we felt that strictly experimental procedures were inappropriate for wide general use in evaluation studies of this type (see Bale, Van Stone, Kuldau, & Miller, 1980; Gottheil, McLellan, & Druley, 1981), questionable on ethical grounds, and impractical to implement. The lack of experimental procedures was partially compensated for by the statistical procedures, which adjusted the treatment programs for differences in patient characteristics. We also added rigor to the analysis by using a range of outcome criteria and two types of predictive analyses. It was recognized that these statistical adjustments would not entirely compensate for the rigor of an experimental design; yet we felt that they provided the advantage of a methodology that could be widely applied by other treatment networks without disrupting normal clinical function.

With regard to the methods used to analyze the data, several points are relevant. First, the reliability of the admission and follow-up self-reports of the patients were spot-checked by requesting urine samples and pay stubs, and by checking criminal records. We are satisfied that there was no general tendency for patients to falsify these self-reports, although there was naturally an error rate (less than 10% variance across items), due to difficulties in comprehension and recall. Furthermore, several other investigators have examined this issue with essentially the same conclusions (Ball, 1972; Sobell & Sobell, 1975).

Conclusions

Three project findings suggest several implications with regard to the delivery of health services to alcohol- and drug-dependent patients. First, the data from both the 1978 and 1980 patient cohorts and for both the alcohol- and drug-dependent samples clearly indicated that substance abuse rehabilitation was effective even without modification of treatment assignment procedures. The impact of this finding was given added weight by the consistency in the type, magnitude, and distribution of improvements shown in these cohorts from 1978 to 1980.

A second major finding from the project results is that the effectiveness of this six-program treatment network was improved by more than 37% (across all outcome criteria) by matching patients to the most appropriate treatment program within the treatment network. We were able to determine the patient background and admission status variables that were predictive of optimum outcome in each treatment program within the network. The practical value of these empirically based predictive factors was tested in a new patient cohort, treated 2 years later in the same network. Patients who were assigned and admitted to a program, based upon the predictive factors (matched patients), had significantly better adjustment and performance during treatment, showed more significant improvements, and had generally better 6-month outcomes than patients who were treated in the same programs but had been predicted to have a different treatment assignment (mismatched patients).

The third major finding from the project was that a truly comprehensive patient assessment at admission, probing potential problem areas such as employment, physical health, legal status, family relations, and especially psychiatric function, is absolutely necessary to the process of matching patients and treatments. We feel certain that a key reason for the historical lack of success at predicting outcome and matching patients to treatments lies in the previous focus upon patient demographic factors and quantitative measures of alcohol and drug use as the major predictive factors. The data presented here and by other authors (Luborsky, Minz, & Auerbach, 1980) suggests that patient demographic factors, even when combined with a full range of measures on alcohol and drug use patterns, provide relatively little information regarding treatment responsiveness and/or posttreatment adjustment. Apparently, the use of alcohol and/or street drugs is one of the few things that this otherwise diverse population has in common, thus reducing the value of substance use itself as a differential predictor. It was only after the strong relationship between admission psychiatric status and posttreatment outcome was noticed that we were able to develop the predictive strategy discussed. It should be noted that admission psychiatric severity was a better predictor of posttreatment alcohol/drug use than was alcohol/drug use at the time of admission.

In this regard, the relationship between the severity of patients' pretreatment psychiatric problems and their response to substance abuse treatment had clear implications for the most appropriate and clinically effective match of patients and treatments. For example, low-severity patients (i.e., patients whose psychiatric severity score at admission was more than one standard deviation below the population mean) showed the best outcomes from treatment, regardless of the program to which they were assigned. Because of this, these patients were most suited to the less expensive outpatient programs, at a savings of more than $53 per patient per day, or an average of more than $3000 per patient over the normal course of treatment. The clear contraindications to outpatient treatment for these low-severity patients were significant problems in employment and/or family relations. Such contraindications are quite logical and consistent with clinical observation. When outpatient treatment is hindered by these problems, targeted referral to employment development agencies (inpatient or outpatient) or to family counseling services has been attempted. We have not as yet determined whether these services can be effectively and economically provided by the outpatient programs, or whether they should continue to be provided by targeted referral. This will be the subject of future investigations.

On the basis of findings from the 1978 data, we concluded that high-psychiatric-severity patients, both alcohol- and drug-dependent, had the least improvement and the poorest outcomes, regardless of the program in which they were treated. This conclusion was also borne out in the 1980 data. In the case of the high-severity/alcohol-dependent sample, no rehabilitation program was found to be effective with the majority of special problems found in this group. We have studied this group of patients (McLellan, Erdlen, & O'Brien, 1981) and have recommended that they be detoxified and stabilized, then referred to inpatient psychiatric treatment. This suggestion is not based upon the demonstrated effectiveness of our psychiatric programs with these patients. Rather, it stems from the lack of effectiveness and the profound administrative problems associated with these patients in our alcohol treatment programs. These patients were more than twice as likely to return to hospitalization (often via the emergency room) as the other alcohol-dependent patients during the 6-month follow-up interval.

While the high-severity/drug-dependent patients had the poorest outcomes of all treated drug abuse patients, a series of studies on this group has suggested some potential treatment solutions. The results of these studies and their clinical implications are discussed in the next major section of this chapter.

DETERMINING APPROPRIATE TREATMENTS FOR THE HIGH-PSYCHIATRIC-SEVERITY DRUG ABUSER

Choosing the Best Alternative: TC or MM

Despite the disappointing results of our available treatments for the high-severity group of drug abusers, we were left with the day-to-day decision of what to do with the 15–20% of our drug abuse patients who fall into this group. Staff from both the MM and TC programs recognized their limitations with these patients, and treatment in the inpatient psychiatric units was virtually prohibited by the admitting staffs of those units. Given the limited practical alternatives available, we felt it would be important to compare the effectiveness of our two programs with the high-severity patients, and specifically to examine the issue of treatment duration. We reasoned that this type of patient might respond more slowly to treatment, and might, therefore, require a more extended treatment plan than the conventional 60-day program presently available in our TC program.

Thus, we compared rates of improvement on the ASI criteria of drug use, employment, and criminality for 118 patients admitted to the TC program and 154 patients admitted to the MM program during 1980. Each of these samples was divided into low-, middle-, and high-severity groups in the previously described manner, using the admission score from the ASI psychiatric severity scale. The percent improvement scores were calculated for the three criteria by subtracting the ASI follow-up criterion score from its corresponding admission score and then dividing the result by the admission score. The result was a measure of percent improvement from admission to 6-month follow-up on each of the three criteria.

The Total Sample

Figure 22.1 depicts the relationship between percent improvement on the three criteria and days in treatment for the total sample of patients treated in the TC (left panel) and the MM (right panel) programs. The plotted lines are linear regressions, which represent the best linear estimate of percent improvement, based upon knowledge of the number of days in treatment. It is important to note that these regression lines are *idealized and are not exact measures of patient improvement* at all points along the line. We have analyzed these data in many ways and have developed several methods of depicting the results. All analyses have revealed essentially the same results, and we feel that they are best represented using these linear regressions.

In the Figure 22.1 plot, the solid line in the center of the two panels indicates no change from admission to 6-month follow-up, while the area above the line indicates improvement and the area below the line indicates worsening. In these plots, the approximate midpoint of the line indicates the mean percent improvement for the groups, while the slope of the line indicates the extent to which more days of treatment were associated with greater percent improvement.

As can be seen, there were general similarities among the functions for

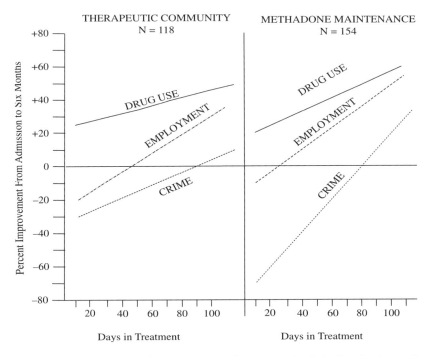

Figure 22.1. Improvement in drug use, employment, and criminality for the total population

both programs. For all measures in each program, there was a direct relationship between time spent in treatment and amount of positive change. Patients who dropped out of treatment early showed less improvement (or worsening, on some measures) than patients who stayed in treatment longer. Clearly, there were some differences in the functions and in the absolute amounts of improvement shown. For both programs, the drug use measure showed the most immediate changes and the greatest absolute amount of improvement. Change in employment was less immediate and showed less total improvement, but equal treatment durations produced greater changes in patient improvement. This is illustrated by the steeper slope of the function and suggests that comparable amounts of treatment had quantitatively different effects on the outcome measures. Legal status showed significant worsening in TC patients with treatments of less than 30 days, but with extended treatment (up to 90 days), there was significant positive change. Similar effects were seen for the MM patients on the legal status measure.

Thus, these initial analyses of the total samples indicated that while there were differences among the measures in the latency, rate, and absolute amounts of improvement, greater lengths of treatment in either program were associated with greater amounts of improvement.

Low-Severity Patients

Figure 22.2 presents the regression plots illustrating the relationships between treatment duration and percent improvement on the three outcome measures for low-severity patients treated in the TC ($n = 29$) and the MM ($n = 38$) programs. It is apparent that the nature of these plots is different from those seen in Figure 22.1. Although there was, again, a direct relation between treatment duration and percent improvement in both treatment modalities, the plots for these low-severity patients indicate that there were more immediate improvements with less treatment. Furthermore, the majority of plots are flatter, indicating that longer treatments were not associated with dramatic improvements. However, the absolute levels of improvement were generally higher, across the three measures, than those depicted in Figure 22.1.

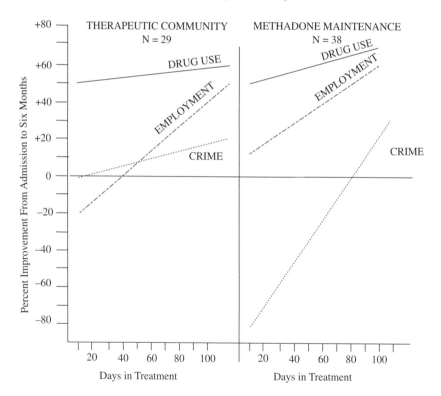

Figure 22.2. Improvement in drug use, employment, and criminality for low-severity patients

Middle-Severity Patients

Figure 22.3 presents the same relationships for middle-severity patients treated in the TC ($n = 52$) and the MM ($n = 86$) programs. The relationships presented here are again similar between the programs, and are quite comparable to those seen in Figure 22.1. The plots for these middle patients are steeper on all measures than those for the low patients, indicating a greater effect of treatment. Further, the plots for the legal status and employment measures in the TC patients, and for the legal status and drug use measures in the MM patients, indicate that shorter treatment durations were associated with worse status at 6 months than at admission.

High-Severity Patients

Figure 22.4 presents the same relationships for high-severity patients treated in the TC ($n = 28$) and the MM ($n = 30$) programs. As can be seen, there were *qualitative differences* in the percent improvement functions be-

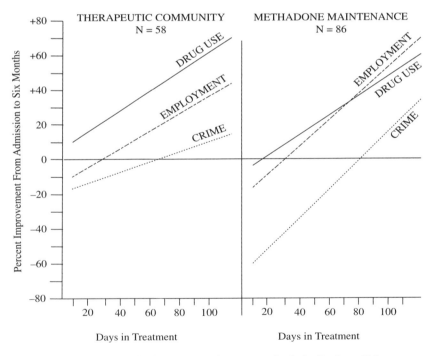

Figure 22.3. Improvement in drug use, employment, and criminality for middle-severity patients

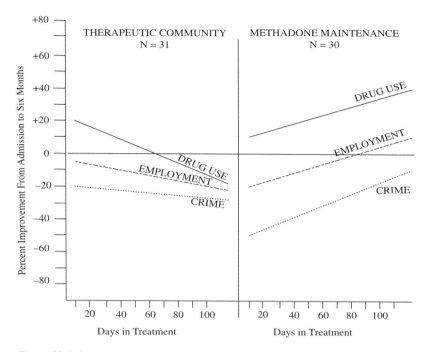

Figure 22.4. Improvement in drug use, employment, and criminality for high-severity patients

tween the treatment programs. The functions for the MM patients are similar to those shown in Figure 22.2, with relatively flat slopes, indicative of an attenuated treatment duration effect. However, the absolute levels of improvement shown were substantially lower than those in the other severity groups, at all treatment durations. In fact, the employment measure did not show a net improvement until after 70 days of treatment, and the legal status measure never showed a net improvement.

The percent improvement functions for the high-severity TC patients were unlike those seen in any other group for either program. For each measure, there was a negative relation between time in treatment and percent improvement, especially in the measures of drug use and criminality. These plots indicated that high-severity patients who stayed in TC treatment for longer durations showed less improvement (in fact, worsening) than those who stayed shorter amounts of time.

Conclusions

Two conclusions can be derived from these results. First, treatment was effective across the majority of patients and outcome measures. We have previously reported on the effectiveness of drug abuse treatment in an earlier sample (McLellan, Woody, Luborsky, & O'Brien, 1982), and these data indicate that treatment continues to be associated with significant positive changes. Further, there was a clear and direct relationship between treatment duration and amount of improvement, with those patients who remained in treatment longest showing the most improvement and the best outcomes.

The second conclusion from these results is that psychiatric severity was an important predictor of treatment response generally and of differential treatment response in the more psychiatrically impaired drug abuse patients. Results of these and previous analyses (Laporte, McLellan, & O'Brien, 1981; McLellan, Erdlen, & O'Brien, 1981; McLellan, Luborsky, Woody, Druley, & O'Brien, 1983) indicate that patients with few psychiatric problems at admission showed the greatest improvement and the best outcomes, while patients with the highest levels of pretreatment psychiatric problems showed the least improvement and the poorest outcomes. The additional finding from these data was that the psychiatric severity measure was also a predictor of a differential treatment response. Specifically, in the case of high-severity patients, longer treatment durations were associated with some additional improvement in the MM program, but this was not the case when they were treated in the TC program. High-severity patients who stayed in the TC program for longer durations had less improvement than similar patients who stayed for shorter periods of time.

It is our opinion that the TC program was counterproductive for these high-severity patients, and that the explanation for this effect lies in the particular therapeutic techniques of the TC modality. Like most other drug-free therapeutic communities, our program was based upon the Synanon model (Biase, 1972) and was implemented in 1971 for the primary purpose of treating heroin addicts. The goals of the program are quite clear: the total elimination of all drugs, including marijuana, and the responsible use of alcohol. Therefore, there is a general sanction against the use of psychotropic medications during treatment, although some antidepressant medications have been prescribed. Therapy is conducted by paraprofessional and ex-addict counselors three to five times per week, and the usual method is group encounter. The primary agent of therapeutic change is, as in most TC programs, the community itself. The self-governing community sets rigorous behavioral guidelines, polices its members strictly, and metes out punishments to offenders; these usually include public admission of guilt, followed by an embarrassing penance.

Evaluations of this particular TC program, as well as other, more general evaluations of the TC modality, indicate that these techniques are generally quite effective, especially for the more intact opiate abuser. However, in the case of the more impaired polydrug abuser, we have reason to believe that these techniques are particularly contraindicated. Our experience indicates that high-severity patients are often younger, generally use fewer opiate but more nonopiate drugs, and have fewer social and personal supports than the patients for which this modality was originally designed. For these patients, the stresses of community living, the absence of potentially appropriate medication, and particularly the group encounter therapy may be countertherapeutic. In this regard, it is interesting to note that we have not found this negative relationship between treatment duration and percent improvement among the high-severity alcoholic patients treated in the ATU, although it too is a therapeutic community. Consistent with our explanation, it is significant that the ATU does not employ group encounter techniques, does not mete out embarrassing punishments, and does approve the more liberal use of psychotropic medications during treatment.

Optimizing Treatment Within the MM Modality

The results of our comparative study had indicated that, relative to the TC program, the MM program was potentially more effective with the high-severity drug abuse patients. However, we recognized that even this level of performance was less than satisfactory. We therefore attempted to determine whether additional services might be added to our existing program that might provide special benefit to these patients.

The Psychotherapy Study: Subjects, Treatments, Hypotheses

To this end, we began a study designed to measure the potential benefits of adding professional psychotherapy to existing drug counseling services within the MM program. In this study, recently admitted opiate-dependent veterans were randomly assigned to receive either supportive–expressive psychotherapy plus counseling, cognitive–behavioral psychotherapy plus counseling, or drug counseling alone (see Woody et al., 1983). All therapy was provided by trained, supervised professionals on a weekly basis over a

24-week period. Drug counseling was provided by rehabilitation workers with bachelor's degrees who had an average of 8 years' experience in the drug abuse field.

Our working hypothesis was that the psychotherapy would be able to reduce drug use and improve overall patient functioning by diminishing the intensity of the psychiatric symptoms. To test this hypothesis, we examined data on the first 62 patients to complete therapy and divided them into four groups, based on ASI ratings of psychiatric severity that were obtained at intake; we felt that this provided a valid estimate of general psychological status. On this basis, we selected two extreme groups: those showing high levels of symptoms ($n = 21$) and those showing low levels of psychiatric symptoms ($n = 21$). A total of 42 patients were included in these two groups, excluding 20 patients who were in the midrange. We selected only the extremes, since we felt that this method would give us the best chance to test our hypothesis.

We then subdivided these groups on the basis of their treatment assignment into high-severity/counseling ($n = 10$), high-severity/therapy ($n = 11$), low-severity/counseling ($n = 11$), and low-severity/therapy ($n = 10$). A summary of the psychological test results for these four groups is presented in Table 22.8. As seen, the groups were distinctly different in terms of the amount of psychopathology.

Pre- to Posttreatment Improvement

We examined pre- to posttherapy improvement for patients in each group using the ASI. The ASI severity scores and other related items are presented in Table 22.9. As seen, the high-severity/counseling group showed improvement only in areas clearly related to drug use. One might expect this, since the patients were on methadone. The low-severity/counseling group demonstrated significant improvement in several areas, indicating that the counselors had a distinctly greater impact on this group than on the high-severity patients. Con-

Table 22.8. Psychological Status of the Four Groups at the Start of the Survey

	High-severity/ counseling	Low-severity/ counseling	High-severity/ therapy	Low-severity/ therapy
n	10	11	11	10
Beck Depression Inventory	18	10	21	9
Maudsley Neuroticism Scale	41	24	37	20
Shipley IQ	100	102	96	104
Shipley CQ	80	87	80	94
ASI psychiatric severity	5.1	2.7	5.6	2.3

Table 22.9. Pre- to Posttherapy (7-Months) Improvement

Criteria	High-severity/counseling		Low-severity/counseling		High-severity/therapy		Low-severity/therapy	
	Pre	Post	Pre	Post	Pre	Post	Pre	Post
Medical severity	3.1	2.4	1.7	3.2	2.5	3.5	1.8	0.7
Days medical problems	4	2	2	4	3	3	1	1
Employment severity	4.5	4.6	5.1	3.2	3.8 *	3.0	3.9	2.7
Days worked	9	11	10 *	13	7	10	9 *	13
Money earned	272	306	242 *	380	309	482	318 **	523
Abuse severity	5.7 *	3.8	3.8 **	1.4	4.9 *	3.0	4.0 **	1.4
Days drunk	4	2	2	1	3	2	2	0
Days opiate use	6	3	10 **	2	5	2	8 *	3
Days nonopiate use	10	8	4	2	7 *	3	3	1
Money for drugs	430 **	190	164 **	47	344 **	65	188 **	8
Legal severity	3.1	3.0	4.5 *	3.1	2.8 *	0.7	2.0 *	0.8
Days crime	6	3	10 *	4	5 *	0.8	1	0.4
Illegal income	216	181	506 *	300	186 **	43	166 **	10
Psychiatric severity	5.1	4.8	2.7	1.8	5.6 *	3.0	2.5 *	1.0
Days psychiatric problems	17	13	8	3	15 *	8	4 *	1

* = p < .05.
** = p < .01.

versely, the high-severity/therapy group demonstrated significant improvement in several areas, equal to that seen in the low-severity counseling group. The low-severity/therapy group had made considerable improvement, perhaps of greater magnitude than that of the low-severity/counseling group.

Drug Treatment Results

The mean methadone doses for each group are seen in Figure 22.5. There was a significantly ($p<.01$) higher mean methadone dose for the high-severity/counseling patients than for any of the other three groups. The low-severity/therapy group received a significantly ($p<.05$) lower dose than any of the other three groups, and the high-severity/therapy and low-severity/counseling groups received comparable intermediate dosages. The mean dosage of the high-severity/counseling group was significantly ($p<.05$) greater than the other groups in both a statistical and clinical sense. Urine drug

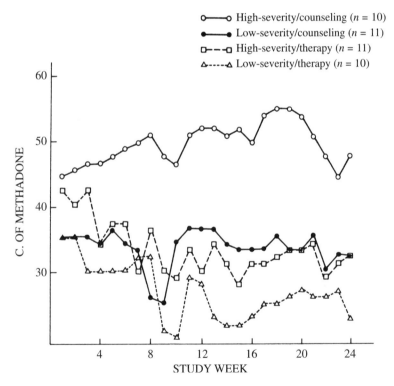

Figure 22.5. Mean methadone dosage by group

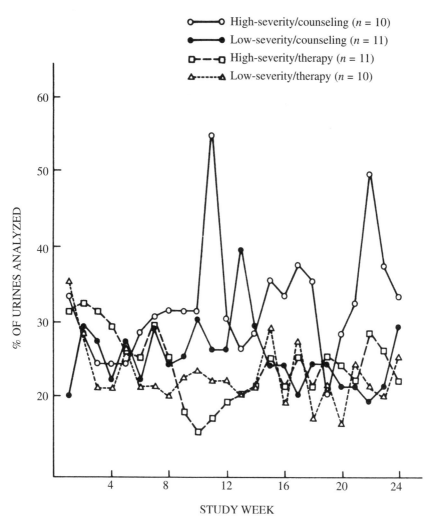

Figure 22.6. Positive urines by group

screening results are seen in Figure 22.6. The high-severity/counseling group had significantly ($p < .05$) more drug-positive urines than either of the other three groups, which had about the same frequency of positive urines.

Comments on the MM Study

Prior to discussing the potential role of psychotherapy with these patients, it is important to mention a design limitation in this project. Patients treated in the therapy groups saw a helping person (therapist or counselor) an average of 23 times, whereas those in the counseling-alone group saw their counselors an average of 17 times. Thus, the patients in the therapy groups spent about 30% more time with a helping person. This design was deliberate and was instituted to determine whether the addition of professional therapy to counseling services would provide extra benefits. This question was the major practical issue addressed by the project. We never considered it reasonable that therapists could be used to replace counselors. However, we do think it may be practical and even cost-effective for psychotherapy to supplement the important role of counselors with certain patients.

Despite the design limitations, the results of this study offered convincing evidence that traditional drug abuse counseling was able to provide significant benefit to the low-severity patients. In fact, the overall results for the low-severity/counseling patients were comparable to those for the low-severity/therapy patients. However, the data also indicated that counseling alone was only marginally effective with the high-severity patients, despite the use of significantly greater average doses of methadone. The supplemental therapy did provide significant benefit to the high-severity patients, especially in the areas of drug abuse, legal status, and psychiatric function. It is important to note that these improvements were brought about while concurrently lowering the average methadone dose—an important consideration for therapists concerned about producing high levels of physiological tolerance in patients.

Given the favorable results of adding psychotherapy to drug counseling for these patients, we find it interesting to speculate about why the psychotherapy allowed for a reduction in drug use without the need to elevate the methadone. One important factor in this regard was the development of an important relationship between patient and therapist. Authors in the field have theorized that drug dependence is a substitute for important personal relationships. However, we think that the benefits shown were more than simply the results of a relationship. Our observations suggest that the benefits of therapy were a result of the ability to form a relationship, combined with special knowledge and skill about how to use it. We have noticed that many of the counselors form good patient relationships, but have trouble managing them, especially with the very disturbed patients. It is also important to remember that, like other patients who have been treated with psychotherapy, the high-severity patients had significant psychiatric problems especially in the areas of depression and anxiety. To the extent that drug use is an attempt to medicate these problems, and to the degree that psychotherapy can reduce them, psychotherapy can reduce drug use indirectly.

GENERAL SUMMARY AND CONCLUSIONS

The present chapter has reviewed a 7-year program of research at the Philadelphia VA Medical Center investigating the psychiatric factors in determining response to drug abuse treatment. This body of research suggests five conclusions:

1. The severity of a substance abuse patient's psychiatric condition at treatment admission is the single best predictor of response to treatment (see De Leon, 1984; Luborsky, Mintz, & Auerbach, 1980; McLellan, Luborsky, Woody, Druley, & O'Brien, 1983; Meyer, 1983). The psychiatrically severe substance abuser shows less improvement during treatment and much poorer outcome following treatment than other patients, regardless of treatment modality (McLellan, Erdlen, & O'Brien, 1981; McLellan, Woody, Luborsky, & O'Brien, 1982).

I should reiterate here that we have used the term "psychiatric severity" to indicate the seriousness of a patient's overall psychiatric impairment, without regard to specific diagnosis. We have determined psychiatric severity from a structured interview designed to assess the number and intensity of psychiatric symptoms (the ASI), and we have also calculated a measure of psychiatric severity from a standardized combination of widely used psychological tests (e.g., the Beck Depression Inventory, the Hopkins Symptom Checklist—90 Item, and the Maudsley Personality Inventory). Clearly, this severity measure is not meant to take the place of a psychiatric diagnosis. However, we and others have found that a global estimate of overall severity can be easily and reliably judged by a nonprofessional, and can offer a useful supplemental estimate of the potential type and amount of intervention needed.

2. The psychiatrically severe substance abuser (i.e., the patient with clear and concurrent problems of addiction and one or more other psychiatric disorders) represents approximately 15–30% of our primary psychiatric and primary drug-dependent patient populations (see Alterman, Erdlen, & McLellan, 1980; Crowley, Chesluk, Dilts, & Hart, 1974; Hekiman & Gershon, 1968; McLellan, Druley, & Carson, 1978).

3. The psychiatrically severe substance abuser may be reliably identified and evaluated by trained technicians using a brief, structured interview (see McLellan, 1979; McLellan, Luborsky, O'Brien, & Woody, 1980).

4. Given the available drug abuse treatment options, our data indicate that MM is more effective than inpatient, drug-free, TC treatment. This may be due in part to the stabilizing effect of the methadone schedule, in part to the

antidepressant and antipsychotic effects of methadone, and in part to the probable contraindication of encounter therapy and patient self-governance interventions used by TCs.

5. While MM combined with regular counseling and a full program of medical and social services appears to produce some minor benefits for high-psychiatric-severity drug abuse patients, this is usually at great cost of staff time and energy. Furthermore, even these results are less than satisfactory. We have found that these patients in particular are easier to manage and can show significant improvement when professional, weekly psychotherapy sessions are added to the existing program of services. For these patients, the addition of professional psychotherapy over a 6-month period has been associated with significant reductions in drug abuse, illegal activity, and psychiatric symptoms (see Woody et al., 1983).

We conclude that brief psychological assessment of drug-dependent patients at admission may be useful in differentiating those patients who are likely to show sustained benefit from traditional counseling and those who are not. The present data indicate that, despite the modest improvements shown by these high-severity drug abusers, their 6-month outcomes suggest that they are likely candidates for recidivism and rehospitalization. We must, therefore, conclude that primary drug abuse counseling and rehabiliation, as offered in conventional MM or TC settings, is not by itself adequate to bring about enough change to make self-support likely, even for relatively short periods. Drug-dependent patients with more severe psychological problems require more focused and independent interventions to address their psychopathology directly through appropriate medication and psychotherapy. Drug abuse rehabilitation programs may serve as a valuable first step in the extended treatment of these patients. By stabilizing the drug abuse and improving general adjustment, they may provide the necessary prerequisites for effective assessment and subsequent treatment of the psychiatric problems found in this growing population of patients.

REFERENCES

Alterman, A. I.; Erdlen, F.; & McLellan, A. T. (1980). Alcoholic schizophrenics. In E. Gottheil et al. (Eds.), Substance abuse and psychiatric illness (pp. 141–169). New York: Pergamon Press.

Armor, D. J.; Polich, J. M.; & Stambul, H. B. (1978). Alcoholism and treatment. Santa Monica, CA: Rand Corporation.

Bale, R.; Van Stone, W.; Kuldau, J.; & Miller, R. (1980). Therapeutic communi-

ties versus methadone maintenance. Archives of General Psychiatry, *37, 1434–1449.*

Ball, J. C. *(1972). The reliability and validity of interview data obtained from 59 narcotic addicts.* American Journal of Sociology, *72, 26–40.*

Biase, D. J. *(1972). Phoenix Houses: Therapeutic communities for drug addicts. In L. Kemp (Ed.),* Drug abuse: Current concepts and research *(pp. 210–230). Springfield, IL: Charles C. Thomas.*

Cronbach, L. J., & Furby, L. *(1970). How should we measure "change"—or should we?* Psychological Bulletin, *74, 187–198.*

Crowley, R. J.; Chesluk, D.; Dilts, S.; & Hart, R. *(1974). Drug and alcohol among psychiatric admissions.* Archives of General Psychiatry, *30, 172–177.*

De Leon, G. *(1984). The therapeutic community: Study of effectiveness (NIDA Treatment Research Monograph, DHHS Publication No. ADM 84-1286). Washington, DC: U.S. Government Printing Office.*

Dixon, W. J., & Brown, M. D. (Eds.). *(1979). BMDP-79:* Biomedical computer programs. *Los Angeles: University of California Press.*

Endicott, J.; Spitzer, R. L.; & Fleiss, J. L. *(1976). The Global Assessment Scale: A procedure for measuring overall severity of psychiatric disturbance.* Archives of General Psychiatry, *33, 766–771.*

Gottheil, E.; McLellan, A. T.; & Druley, K. A. (Eds.). *(1979).* Addiction research and treatment: Converging trends. *New York: Pergamon-Maxwell.*

Gottheil, E.; McLellan, A. T.; & Druley, K. A. *(1981). Reasonable and unreasonable standards in evaluation of substance abuse treatments. In E. Gottheil, A. T. McLellan, & K. A. Druley (Eds.),* Matching patient needs and treatment methods in substance abuse *(pp. 371–388). New York: Pergamon Press.*

Hekimon, L. J., & Gershon, S. *(1968). Characteristics of drug abusers admitted to a psychiatric hospital.* Journal of the American Medical Association, *205, 119–126.*

Laporte, D.; McLellan, A. T.; & O'Brien, C. P. *(1981). Treatment response in psychiatrically impaired drug abusers.* Comprehensive Psychiatry, *22, 411–419.*

Luborsky, L., & Bachrach, H. *(1974). Eighteen experiences with Health–Sickness Rating Scale.* Archives of General Psychiatry, *31, 292–304.*

Luborsky, L.; Mintz, J.; & Auerbach, A. *(1980). Predicting the outcomes of psychotherapy: Findings of the Penn Psychotherapy Project.* Archives of General Psychiatry, *37, 471–481.*

McLellan, A. T. *(1979, June). The Addiction Severity Index. Paper presented at the meeting of the Committee on Problems of Drug Dependence, Philadelphia.*

McLellan, A. T.; Druley, K. A.; & Carson, J. E. *(1978). Evaluation of substance abuse problems in a psychiatric hospital.* Journal of Clinical Psychiatry, *39, 425–430.*

McLellan, A. T.; Druley, K. A.; O'Brien, C. P.; & Kron, R. *(1980). Matching substance abuse patients to appropriate treatments: The Addiction Severity Index.* Drug and Alcohol Dependence, *5, 189–195.*

McLellan, A. T.; Erdlen, F. R.; & O'Brien, C. P. *(1981). Psychological severity and response to alcoholism rehabilitation.* Drug and Alcohol Dependence, *8, 23–35.*

McLellan, A. T.; Luborsky, L.; Cacciola, J.; Griffith, J. E.; Evans, F.; & Barr, H. *(1985). New data from the Addiction Severity Index: Reliability and validity in three centers.* Journal of Nervous and Mental Disease, *173, 412–423.*

McLellan, A. T.; Luborsky, L.; O'Brien, C. P.; & Woody, G. E. (1980). *An improved evaluation instrument for substance abuse patients: The Addiction Severity Index.* Journal of Nervous and Mental Disease, *168, 26–33.*

McLellan, A. T.; Luborsky, L.; Woody, G. E.; & O'Brien, C. P. (1981). *Are the "addiction-related" problems of substance abusers really related?* Journal of Nervous and Mental Disease, *169, 68–74.*

McLellan, A. T.; Luborsky, L.; Woody, G. E.; Druley, K. A.; & O'Brien, C. P. (1983). *Predicting response to drug and alcohol treatments: Role of psychiatric severity.* Archives of General Psychiatry, *40, 620–625.*

McLellan, A. T.; Woody, G. E.; Luborsky, L.; & O'Brien, C. P. (1982). *Is treatment for substance abuse effective?* Journal of the American Medical Association, *247, 1423–1427.*

Meyer, R. (1983, May). Sociopathy as a negative predictor of treatment for alcohol abuse. *Paper presented at the annual meeting of the American Psychiatric Association, New York.*

Mintz, J.; Luborsky, L.; & Cristoph, P. (1979). *Measuring the outcomes of psychotherapy: Findings of the Penn Psychotherapy Project.* Journal of Consulting and Clinical Psychology, *47, 319–334.*

Nunally, J. (1967). Psychometric theory. *New York: McGraw-Hill.*

Simpson, D. D.; Savage, L. J.; Lloyd, M. R.; & Sells, S. B. (1978). Evaluation of drug abuse treatments based on first year follow-up *(NIDA Research Monograph, DHHS Publication No. 78-411). Washington, DC: U.S. Government Printing Office.*

Sobell, L. C., & Sobell, M. B. (1975). *Outpatient alcoholics give valid self-reports.* Journal of Nervous and Mental Disease, *161, 32–42.*

Woody, G. E.; Luborsky, L.; McLellan, A. T.; O'Brien, C. P.; Beck, A. T.; Blaine, J.; Herman, I.; & Hole, A. (1983). *Psychotherapy for opiate addicts: Does it help?* Archives of General Psychiatry, *40, 639–645.*

23. The Self-Medication Hypothesis of Addictive Disorders: Focus on Heroin and Cocaine Dependence

Edward J. Khantzian

D EVELOPMENTS in psychoanalysis and psychiatry over the past 50 years have provided enabling new insights and approaches in understanding mental life and in treating its aberrations. In psychoanalysis, there has been a shift from a focus on drives and conflict to a greater emphasis on the importance of ego and self structures in regulating emotions, self-esteem, behavior, and adaptation to reality. In psychiatry, we have witnessed the advent of psychotropic medications, a more precise understanding of the neurobiology of the brain, and the development of standardized diagnostic approaches for identifying and classifying psychiatric disorders. Such developments have had implications for understanding and treating addictions, especially given the recent dramatic rise in drug abuse in all sectors of our society and our growing inclination to treat our drug-dependent patients through private practice, in community mental health centers, and in methadone-maintenance or self-help programs, in close proximity to the surroundings in which their addictions evolved.

Popular or simplistic formulations in the early 1970s emphasized peer group pressure, escape, euphoria, or self-destructive themes to explain the compelling nature of drug dependency. In contrast, the work of a number of psychoanalysts in the 1960s and 1970s has led to observations, theoretical formulations, and subsequent studies representing a significant departure from these previous approaches and explanations. On the basis of a modern psychodynamic perspective, these analysts succeeded in better identifying the nature of the psychological vulnerabilities, disturbances, and pain that predispose certain individuals to drug dependence. This perspective, which has spawned a series of diagnostic studies over the past decade, emphasizes that heavy reliance on and continuous use of illicit drugs (i.e., individuals who become and remain addicted) are associated with severe and significant

Reprinted with permission from *American Journal of Psychiatry* 142 (1985): 1259–64.

psychopathology. Moreover, the drug of choice that individuals come upon is not a random phenomenon.

On the basis of recent psychodynamic and psychiatric perspectives and findings, I will elaborate on a self-medication hypothesis of addictive disorders, emphasizing problems with heroin and cocaine dependence. This point of view suggests that the specific psychotropic effects of these drugs interact with psychiatric disturbances and painful affect states to make them compelling in susceptible individuals.

PSYCHODYNAMIC FINDINGS

An extensive review of the psychoanalytic literature on addiction goes beyond the scope of this paper. I have reviewed elsewhere the early psychoanalytic literature on addiction, which principally emphasized the pleasurable aspects of drug use (1, 2). Psychoanalytic reports that pertain most to this thesis date back to the work of Chein et al. (3) and the earlier related work of Gerard and Kornetsky (4, 5), who were among the first groups to study addicts in the community (inner city, New York addicts) and attempt to understand the psychological effects of opiates and how they interacted with addicts' ego, superego, narcissistic, and other psychopathology. They emphasized that individuals use drugs adaptively to cope with overwhelming (adolescent) anxiety in anticipation of adult roles in the absence of adequate preparation, models, and prospects. Because they did not have the benefit of a modern psychopharmacologic perspective, they referred to the general "tranquilizing or ataractic" properties of opiates and did not consider that the appeal of narcotics might be based on a specific effect or action of opiates. In addition, their studies were limited to narcotic addicts, thus providing little basis to compare them to addicts dependent on other drugs.

Around 1970, a number of psychoanalysts began to report findings based on their work with addicts, who were coming in increasing numbers to their practices and to a variety of community treatment settings. In contrast to the early emphasis in psychoanalysis on a drive and topographical psychology, their work paralleled developments in contemporary psychoanalysis and placed greater emphasis on structural factors, ego states, and self and object relations in exploring the disturbances of addicts and understanding their suffering. More particularly, this literature highlighted how painful affects associated with disturbances in psychological structures and object relations interacted with the psychopharmacologic action of addictive drugs to make them compelling.

Despite a superficial resemblance to earlier formulations that stressed regressive pleasurable use of drugs, work by Wieder and Kaplan (6) represented an important advance and elaboration of trends set in motion by Gerard and Kornetsky in the 1950s. Wieder and Kaplan used recent developments in ego theory, which enabled them to appreciate that individuals self-select different drugs on the basis of personality organization and ego impairments. Their emphasis on the use of drugs as a "prosthetic," and their focus on developmental considerations, adaptation, and the ego clearly sets their work apart from earlier simplistic formulations based on an id psychology.

On the basis of this and other recent work that considers ego and adaptational problems of addicts, and following lines pursued by Weider and Kaplan, Milkman and Frosch (7) empirically tested the hypothesis that self-selection of specific drugs is related to preferred defensive style. Using the Bellak and Hurvich Interview and Rating Scale for Ego Functioning, they compared heroin and amphetamine addicts in drugged and nondrugged conditions. Their preliminary findings supported their hypothesis that heroin addicts preferred the calming and dampening effects of opiates and seemed to use this action of the drug to shore up tenuous defenses and reinforce a tendency toward withdrawal and isolation, while amphetamine addicts used the stimulating action of amphetamines to support an inflated sense of self-worth and a defensive style involving active confrontation with their environment.

The work of Wurmser (8, 9) and Khantzian (1, 10–12) suggested that the excessive emphasis on the regressive effects of narcotics in previous studies was unwarranted and that, in fact, the specific psychopharmacologic action of opiates has an opposite, "progressive" effect whereby regressed states may be reversed. Wurmser believed that narcotics are used adaptively by narcotic addicts to compensate for defects in affect defense, particularly against feelings of "rage, hurt, shame—and loneliness." Khantzian stressed drive defense and believed narcotics act to reverse regressed states by the direct antiaggression action of opiates, counteracting disorganizing influences of rage and aggression on the ego. Both these formulations proposed that the psychopharmacologic effects of the drug could substitute for defective or nonexistent ego mechanisms of defense. As with previously mentioned recent investigators, Wurmser and Khantzian also considered developmental impairments, severe predisposing psychopathology, and problems in adaptation to be central issues in understanding addiction. Radford et al. (13) reported detailed case material which supported the findings of Wurmser and Khantzian that opiates could have an antiaggression and antiregression action or effect. They further observed that opiate use cannot be exclusively correlated with any particular patterns of internal conflict or phase-specific developmental impairment.

Krystal and Raskin (14) were less precise about the specific effects of different drugs but allowed that they may be used either to permit or prevent regression. However, their work focused more precisely on the relationship between pain, depression, and anxiety and drug and placebo effects. They explored and greatly clarified addicts' difficulties in recognizing and tolerating painful affects. They proposed that the tendency for depression and anxiety to remain somatized, unverbalized, and undifferentiated in addicts resulted in a defective stimulus barrier and thus left such individuals ill-equipped to deal with their feelings and predisposed them to drug use. Their work also focused in greater depth on the major problems that addicts have in relation to positive and negative feelings about themselves and in relation to other people. Krystal and Raskin believed that addicts have major difficulties in being good to themselves and in dealing with their positive and negative feelings toward others because of rigid and massive defenses such as splitting and denial. They maintained that drug users take drugs not only to assist in defending against their feelings but also briefly and therefore "safely" to enable the experience of feelings like fusion (oneness) with loved objects, which are normally prevented by the rigid defenses against aggression.

DIAGNOSTIC AND TREATMENT STUDIES

Partly as an extension and outgrowth of the psychodynamic studies and partly as the result of the development of standardized diagnostic approaches for classifying and describing mental illness, a number of reports over the past decade have documented the coexistence of psychopathology in drug-dependent individuals. Some of these investigators have also reported on the results of conventional psychiatric treatment, including psychotherapy, with drug-dependent individuals. Although the results of such studies to date have been inconsistently successful or inconclusive, they are suggestive enough to further support the concept that drug dependence is related to and associated with coexistent psychopathology.

In a placebo-controlled study, Woody et al. (15) treated a series of narcotic addicts with the antidepressant doxepin and documented significant symptom reduction. Their study suggested that this group of patients suffered with an anxious depression, and as the depression lifted with treatment, there was a corresponding reduction in misuse and abuse of drugs and an improvement in overall adaptation. More recently, this group of investigators (16) reported longitudinal data on individuals dependent on psychostimulants, sedative-hypnotics, or opiates which suggested that addicts might be medicating themselves for underlying psychopathology. Their study suggested that such individuals might respond to the administration of appropriate psychopharmacologic agents for target symptoms of phobia and depression.

Dorus and Senay (17) and Weissman et al. (18–20) evaluated large samples of narcotic addicts and, using standardized diagnostic approaches, documented a significant incidence of major depressive disorder, alcoholism, and antisocial personality. Rounsaville et al. (19, 20) concluded that their findings were consistent with the clinical theories of Wurmser and Khantzian, i.e., that depressed addicts used opiates as an attempt at self-treatment for unbearable dysphoric feelings.

At a conference sponsored by the New York Academy of Sciences on opioids in mental illness, Khantzian, Wurmser, McKenna, Berken, Millman, Vereby, and others presented clinical findings and theoretical observations that support a self-medication hypothesis of addictions (21). The sponsors of the conference and the participants reviewed the role of exogenous opiates as well as endorphins in regulating emotions. One of the conclusions drawn from these findings was that the long-acting opiate methadone might be an effective psychotropic agent in the treatment of severe psychoses, especially cases refractory to conventional drugs and in instances associated with violence and rage.

Treece and Nicholson (22), using diagnostic criteria from *DSM-III*, published findings indicating a strong relationship between certain types of personality disorder and methadone dose required for stabilization. They studied this same sample and compared "high drug" and "low drug" users (i.e., in addition to their prescribed methadone dose) and were able to show that the high drug users were significantly more impaired in the quality of their object relations than the low drug users (23). In a recent report, Khantzian and Treece (24) studied 133 narcotic addicts from three subject samples (i.e., a methadone program sample, a residential setting sample, and a street sample) and, using *DSM-III*, documented depression in over 60% and a range of personality disorders (that included but was not limited to antisocial disorder) in over 65%. We also explored the possible relationships between the disturbed/disturbing behavior of addicts as reflected by the personality diagnosis, and the painful affects with which addicts suffer as reflected by the diagnosis of depression.

Recently, Blatt et al. (25) used the Loevinger Sentence Completion, the Bellak Ego Function Interview, and the Rorschach to extensively study 99 opiate addicts and compare them to normal subjects. Their findings provide further evidence that opiate addicts suffer significantly in their interpersonal relations and in affect modulation. The authors indicate that addicts use drugs in the service of isolation and withdrawal.

In two carefully executed studies (26, 27) based on the assumption that opiate dependence is associated with psychopathology, the effectiveness of psychotherapy on the psychopathology and presumed related drug dependence of 72 and 110 narcotic addicts, respectively, was tested. Rounsaville et al. (26) found no evidence that psychotherapy appreciably influenced treatment outcome. Woody et al. (27) demonstrated that the addicts receiving psychotherapy had greater improvement than the addicts who received only drug counseling and that the psychotherapy subjects required less methadone and used fewer psychotropic drugs.

Finally, carefully executed studies dating back to the early 1970s document that in selected cases and samples of substance-dependent individuals, target symptoms and psychopathology have been identified and successfully treated with psychotropic drugs (15, 28–31).

CLINICAL OBSERVATIONS – NARCOTIC AND COCAINE DEPENDENCE

Clinical work with narcotic and cocaine addicts has provided us with compelling evidence that the drug an individual comes to rely on is not a random choice. Although addicts experiment with multiple substances, most prefer one drug. Weider and Kaplan (6) referred to this process as "the drug-of-choice phenomena," Milkman and Frosch (7) described it as "preferential use of drugs," and I (32) have called it the "self-selection" process. I believe that narcotic and cocaine addicts' accounts of their subjective experiences with and responses to these drugs are particularly instructive. They teach us about how addicts suffer with certain overwhelming affects, relationships, and behavioral disturbances and how the short-term use of their drug of choice helps them to combat these disturbances.

Narcotic Addiction

Although narcotics may be used to overcome and cope with a range of human problems including pain, stress, and dysphoria (33), I have been impressed that the antiaggression and antirage action of opiates is one of the most compelling reasons for its appeal. I base this conclusion on observations of over 200 addicts whose histories reveal lifelong difficulties with rage and violent behavior predating their addiction, often linked to intense and unusual exposure to extreme aggression and violence in their early family life and the environment outside their homes. These experiences included being both the subject and the perpetrator of physical abuse, brutality, violent fights, and sadism. In the course of their evaluation and treatment these patients repeatedly described how opiates helped them to feel normal, calm, mellow, soothed, and relaxed. I have also observed addicts in group treatment whose restlessness and aggressiveness, especially manifested in their abusive and assaultive use of obscenities, subsided as they stabilized on methadone (1, 10–12). I was also impressed that many narcotic addicts discovered the antirage action of opiates in a context of violent feelings, often of murderous proportion, being released in them by sedatives and alcohol or being manifested as a consequence of amphetamine and cocaine use (34).

Clinical vignette. A 29-year-old ex-felon, admitted to a closed psychiatric ward because of increasing inability to control his alcohol and cocaine use, demonstrated dramatically this special relationship between violence and drug use and why opiates were his drug of choice. I saw this patient in consultation on a day when he had become very agitated and intimidating as he witnessed a very disturbed female patient being placed in four-point restraints. An alert attendant, who was a felon himself on work release, ascertained from the patient that this scene triggered panic and violent reactions similar to those he had experienced when he had been attacked by guards in prison because he had been threatening or assaultive. When I met him I was surprised by his diminutive stature and reticence. I told him I wanted to understand his drug-alcohol use and determine whether our unit was okay (i.e., safe) for him. He immediately apologized for overreacting to the restrained patient and explained how much it reminded him of his prison experience. He quickly launched into his worry that his alcohol and cocaine use was causing increasingly uncontrolled outbursts of verbally assaultive behavior and, as a consequence, an increasing tendency to use opiates to quell his violent reactions. He openly admitted to past overt assaultive behavior, most frequently involving knifings, when he felt threatened, provoked, or intimidated. He kept returning to the confrontation and restraint of the patient, apologizing for his reaction but also explaining how disorganizing and threatening it was for him. He said there had been a time when attack would have been a reflex in such situations, but he wanted to reassure me and the staff that he really understood why we were doing what we were. He seemed to be begging to stay and said he wanted help with his alcohol and drug use. An inquiry about his drug use and its effect on him revealed that he preferred opiates, so much so that he knew he had to avoid them. (He explained that he knew too many people who had become hopelessly dependent on or had died because of opiates.) Whereas alcohol or stimulants could cause violent eruptions, he explained that opiates—and he named them all correctly—countered or controlled such reactions. He said that the only person he had to rely on was his mother but that she was very ill and in the hospital. He complained that he had suffered as a consequence of his father's alcoholism, the associated violence, and his premature death (alcoholic complications) when the patient was in his early teens. His father's unavailability and early death had left him without supervision or guidance. He bitterly lamented that a brother 5 years older had been "useless" in providing any guidance on how to control his drug-alcohol use or his impulsive and aggressive behavior ("he didn't help me to smarten up").

The patient's description of his violent side before prison and once in prison, confirmed by the mental health aide who corroborated his story, was chilling and convincing. He was equally graphic in describing the many attacks he suffered at the hands of sadistic correction officers and other inmates. What was clear was that, whether he was the perpetrator or the victim, the violence was a recurrent, regular, and repetitious part of his adult life. I have concluded (11, 12) that such individuals welcome the effects of opiates because they mute uncontrolled aggression and counter the threat of both internal psychological disorganization and external counteraggression from others, fears that are not uncommon with people who struggle with rage and violent impulses. The discovery that opiates can relieve and reverse the disorganizing and fragmenting effects of rage and aggression is not limited to individuals who come from deprived, extreme, and overtly violent backgrounds.

Clinical vignette. A successful 35-year-old physician described how defensive and disdainful he had become since his early adulthood as a consequence of his mother's insensitivity and his father's cruel and depriving attitude toward the patient and his family, despite their significant affluence. He said he became dependent on opiates when his defense of self-sufficiency began to fail him in a context of disappointing relationships with women and much distress and frustration working with severely ill patients. More than anything else, he became aware of the calming effects of these drugs on his bitter resentment and mounting rage. He stressed how this effect of the drugs helped him to feel better about himself and, paradoxically, helped him to remain energized and active in his work.

I have described (12, 34) similar patients from privileged backgrounds in which sadistic or unresponsive parents fueled a predisposition to angry and violent feelings toward self and others.

Cocaine Addiction

From a psychodynamic perspective, a number of investigators have speculated on the appeal of stimulants and, in particular, cocaine. For some, the energizing properties of these drugs are compelling because they help to overcome fatigue and depletion states associated with depression (32). In other cases the use of stimulants leads to increased feelings of assertiveness, self-esteem, and frustration tolerance (6) and the riddance of feelings of boredom and emptiness (9). I have proposed that certain individuals use cocaine to "*augment* a hyperactive, restless lifestyle and an exaggerated need for self-sufficiency" (34, p. 100). Spotts and Shontz (35) extensively studied the characteristics of nine representative cocaine addicts and documented findings that are largely consistent with the psychodynamic descriptions of people who are addicted to cocaine.

More recently, we have considered from a psychiatric/diagnostic perspective a number of factors that might predispose an individual to become and remain dependent on cocaine (36, 37): (1) preexistent chronic depression; (2) cocaine abstinence depression; (3) hyperactive, restless syndrome or attention deficit disorder; and (4) cyclothymic or bipolar illness. Unfortunately, studies of representative larger, aggregate samples of cocaine addicts do not yet exist to substantiate these possibilities.

Clinical vignette. A 30-year-old man with a 10-year history of multiple drug use described the singularly uplifting effect of cocaine, which he came to use preferentially over all the other drugs. In contrast to a persistent sense of feeling unattractive and socially and physically awkward dating back to adolescence, he discovered "that (snorting) it gave me power—and made me happy. It was pleasant—euphoric; I could talk—and feel erotic." Subsequently, injecting it intensified these feelings, but more than anything else, the cocaine helped him to not worry what people thought about him.

I have been repeatedly impressed how this energizing and activating property of cocaine helps such people, who have been chronically depressed, overcome their anergia, complete tasks, and better relate to others and, as a consequence, experience a temporary boost in their self-esteem (37).

Clinical vignette. In contrast, a 40-year-old accountant described an opposite, paradoxical effect from snorting cocaine. Originally, when I evaluated this man, I thought he was using the stimulating properties of the drug as an augmentor for his usual hyperactive, expansive manner of relating. He finally convinced me to the contrary when he carefully mimicked how he put down several lines in the morning, snorted it, and breathed a sigh of relaxation and then described how he could sit still, focus on his backlog of paper work, and complete it.

This man's story, a recent dramatic and extreme case (38), and two other related reports (36, 37) suggest that cocaine addicts might be medicating themselves for mood disorders and behavioral disturbances, including a pre-existing or resulting attention deficit/hyperactive-type disorder. The extreme case responded dramatically to methylphenidate treatment. I have successfully treated several other patients with methylphenidate. The patients I have treated with methylphenidate provide further evidence to support a self-medication hypothesis of drug dependency. At this point it would be premature to conclude precisely what the disorder or disorders are for which cocaine addicts are medicating themselves. However, the pilot cases and my previous clinical experiences suggest several possibilities. The patients share in common lifelong difficulties with impulsive behavior, emotional lability, acute and chronic dysphoria (including acute depressions), and self-esteem disturbances that preceded cocaine use. All of the patients experienced a relief of dysphoria and improved self-esteem on cocaine; they also experienced improved attention leading to improved interpersonal relations, more purposeful, focused activity, and improved capacity for work. The substitution of the more stable, long-acting stimulant drug methylphenidate provided an opportunity for me to observe these patients clinically and to confirm the stabilizing effect of stimulants on them.

COMMENT

Clearly, there are other determinants of addiction, but I believe a self-medication motive is one of the more compelling reasons for overuse of and dependency on drugs. Clinical findings based on psychoanalytic formulations have been consistent with and complemented by diagnostic and treatment studies that support this perspective, which, I believe, will enable researchers and clinicians to further understand and treat addictive behavior. Rather than simply seeking escape, euphoria, or self-destruction, addicts are attempting to medicate themselves for a range of psychiatric problems and painful emotional states. Although most such efforts at self-treatment are eventually doomed, given the hazards and complications of long-term, unstable drug use patterns, addicts discover that the short-term effects of their drugs of choice help them to cope with distressful subjective states and an external reality otherwise experienced as unmanageable or overwhelming. I believe that the perspective provided by the self-medication hypothesis has enabled me and others to understand better the nature of compulsive drug use and that it has provided a useful rationale in considering treatment alternatives. The heuristic value of this hypothesis might also help us to more effectively understand and treat the most recent elusive addiction, cocaine dependence.

REFERENCES

1. *Khantzian, E. J. Opiate addiction: a critique of theory and some implications for treatment.* Am J Psychother *28: 59–70, 1974.*

2. *Khantzian, E. J.; Treece, C. Psychodynamics of drug dependence: an overview, in* Psychodynamics of Drug Dependence: NIDA Research Monograph 12. *Edited by Blaine, J. D., Julius, D. A. Rockville, Md., National Institute on Drug Abuse, 1977.*

3. *Chein, I.; Gerard, D. L.; Lee, R. S., et al.* The Road to H: Narcotics, Delinquency, and Social Policy. *New York, Basic Books, 1964.*

4. *Gerard, D. L.; Kornetsky, C. Adolescent opiate addiction: a case study.* Psychiatr Q *28: 367–380, 1954.*

5. *Gerard, D. L.; Kornetsky, C. Adolescent opiate addiction: a study of control and addict subjects.* Psychiatr Q *29: 457–486, 1955.*

6. *Wieder, H.; Kaplan, E. H. Drug use in adolescents: psychodynamic meaning and pharmacogenic effect.* Psychoanal Study Child *24: 399–431, 1969.*

7. *Milkman, H.; Frosch, W. A. On the preferential abuse of heroin and amphetamine.* J Nerv Ment Dis *156: 242–248, 1973.*

8. *Wurmser, L. Methadone and the craving for narcotics: observations of patients on methadone maintenance in psychotherapy, in* Proceedings of the Fourth National Methadone Conference, *San Francisco, 1972. New York, National Association for the Prevention of Addiction to Narcotics, 1972.*

9. *Wurmser, L. Psychoanalytic considerations of the etiology of compulsive drug use.* J Am Psychoanal Assoc *22: 820–843, 1974.*

10. *Khantzian, E. J. A preliminary dynamic formulation of the psychopharmacologic action of methadone, in* Proceedings of the Fourth National Methadone Conference, *San Francisco, 1972. New York, National Association for the Prevention of Addiction to Narcotics, 1972.*

11. *Khantzian, E. J. An ego-self theory of substance dependence: a contemporary psychoanalytic perspective, in* Theories on Drug Abuse: NIDA Research Monograph 30. *Edited by Lettieri, D. J., Sayers, M.; Pearson, H. W. Rockville, Md., National Institute on Drug Abuse, 1980.*

12. *Khantzian, E. J. Psychological (structural) vulnerabilities and the specific appeal of narcotics.* Ann NY Acad Sci *398: 24–32, 1982.*

13. *Radford, P.; Wiseberg, S.; Yorke, C. A study of "main line" heroin addiction.* Psychoanal Study Child *27: 156–180, 1972.*

14. *Krystal, H.; Raskin, H. A.* Drug Dependence: Aspects of Ego Functions. *Detroit, Wayne State University Press, 1970.*

15. *Woody, G. E.; O'Brien, C. P.; Rickels, K. Depression and anxiety in heroin addicts: a placebo-controlled study of doxepin in combination with methadone.* Am J Psychiatry *132: 447–450, 1975.*

16. *McLellan, A. T.; Woody, G. E.; O'Brien, C. P. Development of psychiatric illness in drug abusers.* N Engl J Med *201: 1310–1314, 1979.*

17. *Dorus, W.; Senay, E. C. Depression, demographic dimension, and drug abuse.* Am J Psychiatry *137: 699–704, 1980.*

18. *Weissman, M. M.; Slobetz, F.; Prusoff, B., et al. Clinical depression among narcotic addicts maintained on methadone in the community.* Am J Psychiatry *133: 1434–1438, 1976.*

19. *Rounsaville, B. J.; Weissman, M. M.; Kleber, H., et al. Heterogeneity of psychiatric diagnosis in treated opiate addicts.* Arch Gen Psychiatry *39: 161–166, 1982.*

20. *Rounsaville, B. J.; Weissman, M. M.; Crits-Cristoph, K., et al. Diagnosis and symptoms of depression in opiate addicts: course and relationship to treatment outcome.* Arch Gen Psychiatry *39: 151–156, 1982.*

21. *Vereby, K. (ed.) Opioids in Mental Illness: Theories, Clinical Observations, and Treatment Possibilities.* Ann NY Acad Sci *398: 1–512, 1982.*

22. *Treece, C.; Nicholson, B.* DSM-III *personality type and dose levels in methadone maintenance patients.* J Nerv Ment Dis *168: 621–628, 1980.*

23. *Nicholson, B.; Treece, C. Object relations and differential treatment response to methadone maintenance.* J Nerv Ment Dis *169: 424–429, 1981.*

24. *Khantzian, E. J.; Treece, C.* DSM-III *psychiatric diagnosis of narcotic addicts: recent findings.* Arch Gen Psychiatry *(in press).*

25. *Blatt, S. J.; Berman, W.; Bloom-Feshback, S., et al. Psychological assessment of psychopathology in opiate addicts.* J Nerv Ment Dis *172: 156–165, 1984.*

26. *Rounsaville, B. J.; Glazer, W.; Wilber, C. H., et al. Short-term interpersonal psychotherapy in methadone-maintained opiate addicts.* Arch Gen Psychiatry *40: 629–636, 1983.*

27. *Woody, G. E.; Luborsky, L.; McLellan, A. T., et al. Psychotherapy for opiate addicts.* Arch Gen Psychiatry *40: 639–645, 1983.*

28. *Butterworth, A. T. Depression associated with alcohol withdrawal: imipramine therapy compared with placebo.* Q J Stud Alcohol *32: 343–348, 1971.*

29. *Overall, J. E.; Brown, D.; Williams, J. D., et al. Drug treatment of anxiety and depression in detoxified alcoholic patients.* Arch Gen Psychiatry *29: 218–221, 1973.*

30. *Quitkin, F. M.; Rifkin, A.; Kaplan, J., et al. Phobic anxiety syndrome complicated by drug dependence and addiction.* Arch Gen Psychiatry *27: 159–162, 1972.*

31. *Gawin, F. H.; Kleber, H. D. Cocaine abuse treatment.* Arch Gen Psychiatry *41: 903–908, 1984.*

32. *Khantzian, E. J. Self selection and progression in drug dependence.* Psychiatry Digest *10: 19–22, 1975.*

33. *Khantzian, E. J.; Mack, J. E.; Schatzberg, A. F. Heroin use as an attempt to cope: clinical observations.* Am J Psychiatry *131: 160–164, 1974.*

34. *Khantzian, E. J. Impulse problems in addiction: cause and effect relationships, in* Working With the Impulsive Person. *Edited by Wishnie, H. New York, Plenum, 1979.*

35. *Spotts, J. V.; Shontz, F. C.* The Life Styles of Nine American Cocaine Users. *Washington, D.C., National Institute on Drug Abuse, 1977.*

36. *Khantzian, E. J.; Gawin, F.; Kleber, H. D., et al. Methylphenidate treatment of cocaine dependence—a preliminary report.* J Substance Abuse Treatment *1: 107–112, 1984.*

37 *Khantzian, E. J.; Khantzian, N. J. Cocaine addiction: is there a psychological predisposition?* Psychiatric Annals *14 (10): 753–759, 1984.*

24. Substance Abuse as an Attempt at Self-Medication

Roger D. Weiss and Steven M. Mirin

THE RELATIONSHIP between substance abuse and psychopathology has been the focus of a great deal of research. Numerous studies in this area have shown that the presence of either disorder may exert a profound influence upon the development and course of the other (1). For example, chronic administration of heroin (2) and alcohol (3) have been shown to increase certain psychopathological symptoms, including anxiety, depression, and hostility. Conversely, the nature (4) and severity (5) of psychopathology can affect prognosis for drug abuse treatment. Rounsaville and associates (4) found that opiate addicts who were depressed at admission to treatment returned to drug use more frequently than nondepressed patients. McLellan and associates (5) found that the severity of psychiatric symptoms was an important prognostic factor in drug abuse; patients with less severe psychopathology fared better than those with more psychiatric symptoms.

Psychopathology has also been implicated as an etiologic factor in the development of substance abuse. One theory of drug abuse that has generated considerable interest posits that the use of drugs may initially represent a legitimate though misguided attempt to modify intolerable affects or symptoms.

This "self-medication" theory of substance abuse has been proposed in different forms by clinicians and researchers from a variety of perspectives. Psychoanalytic formulations of self-medication have focused on drug use in the face of uncomfortable affect. Early psychoanalytic theorists such as Glover (6) and Rado (7) described drug abuse as an attempt to defend against aggressive and depressive feelings, respectively. More recently, Khantzian (8) and Wurmser (9) have stressed the "adaptive" use of opiates to combat the psychologically disorganizing effects of overwhelming rage. According to this theory, the ability of opiates to quell uncontrollable anger allows certain opiate addicts to function better.

Reprinted by permission from *Psychiatric Medicine* 3 (1987): 357–67.

"Deficiency theories" have provided a more recent basis for some self-medication theories. The discovery of endogenous opioid-like peptides (endorphins) and opiate receptors in the brain has led some researchers to posit that certain individuals may be genetically endowed with a relative deficiency of endorphins or receptors (10); these individuals may experience physical and emotional pain more intensely than others, and may obtain dramatic relief from the administration of exogenous opiates. This response may predispose these individuals to repeated use, and ultimately abuse, of opiate drugs. Indeed, Martin (11) has speculated that many substance abusers suffer from an affective state called "hypophoria," which he defines as "the polar opposite of feelings of well-being produced by drugs of abuse." Martin suggests that an endorphin deficiency may be one risk factor for the development of hypophoria. The recent discovery of benzodiazepine receptors in the brain (12) has led to speculation that certain patients who suffer from a relative lack of these endogenous benzodiazepine-like compounds may analogously be at increased risk to develop dependence upon benzodiazepines.

SUBSTANCE ABUSE AND OTHER PSYCHIATRIC DISORDERS

Overview and Methodologic Concerns

The self-medication theory of substance abuse may also be applied to patients who suffer from other psychiatric disorders in addition to substance abuse. This line of investigation has generated a great deal of interest recently, fueled by the hope that identification and treatment of a concurrent psychiatric disorder in a drug-dependent patient will improve the prognosis of the substance abuse disorder.

One limitation of this theory is the fact that the mere presence of two disorders in the same individual does not imply causality. A variety of disturbances in mood and cognition may occur as a *result* of intoxication and/or withdrawal. Moreover, drug abusers, who are notoriously unreliable informants, may be unable or unwilling to provide a clear chronological history of their substance abuse and other psychiatric symptoms. Indeed, even the clear establishment of the temporal relationship between the two disorders does not prove that the initial illness is "primary" and the other disorder "secondary." For example, if an individual who drinks heavily during the prodromal stage of an affective disorder then develops the latter illness, one cannot necessarily conclude that his alcohol abuse has caused his affective disorder. Conversely, an individual who develops signs and symptoms of an affective disorder in his early twenties and begins abusing cocaine in his thirties may appear to be self-medicating his depression. However, one could also posit that he has developed an independent disorder, and that he might have become a cocaine abuser during adolescence if he had had ready access to the drug at that time.

Depression

Depression and Alcoholism

Nowhere are the above-mentioned methodologic difficulties more clearly illustrated than in the study of the relationship between substance abuse and affective disorder. The coexistence of alcoholism and mood disturbances has been noted by numerous authors (13–16). However, despite the fact that some patients with affective disorder may use alcohol or drugs in an attempt at self-medication, numerous investigators have demonstrated that alcohol itself is capable of producing intense sadness in both alcoholics and nonalcoholics. Mendelson and associates (3) observed that alcoholics become more dysphoric, withdrawn, irritable, anxious, and depressed after heavy drinking. Warren and associates (17) reported low mood in a group of nonalcoholic college students after imbibing alcohol. Vaillant (18) has also cited the adverse effects of chronic heavy drinking on mood and personality. Thus, it can be hypothesized that the depression seen in many alcoholics is often secondary to their drinking rather than vice versa.

The frequent finding of depression in alcoholics interviewed in treatment programs may be related to the fact that the alcoholic who seeks treatment often does so as the result of a recent life stress or crisis which has provoked him to seek help. Thus, looking at alcoholics in treatment may distort the actual prevalence rate of depression in this population.

Another difficulty inherent in elucidating the causal relationship between alcoholism and depression is the wide variety of definitions that have been applied to the term "depression" in previous studies. Keeler and associates (13), for instance, reviewed studies which showed the prevalence rate of "depression" in alcoholics ranging from 3% to 98%. The disparity in these studies can be related to different definitions of depression. Many of these studies reported the frequency of depressive *symptoms,* as measured by rating scales and psychological tests. Hesselbrock and associates (14) demonstrated the disparity between rating scale data and diagnoses based upon DSM-III criteria. She found that although 54% of her sample of alcoholic inpatients were "depressed" based on their scores on the Beck Depression Inventory, only half of those patients met DSM-III criteria for a major affective disorder.

The differentiation between depressed mood and affective disorder becomes critical in determining proper treatment. Studies of the use of antidepressants to treat the depressed mood of alcoholics entering treatment (15) have generally been flawed because the mood of these individuals often improves spontaneously as the pharmacological effect of the alcohol abates and as the patient attempts to resolve the crises that have precipitated treatment. Carefully controlled studies have thus shown that although patients on antidepressants usually show mood improvement within two weeks after admission, patients without medication improve to a similar degree (15). The identification of patients at risk for the future development of depression may have prognostic importance, however; in a study by Pottenger and associates (19), the recurrence of depression in a sample of alcoholic outpatients was associated with renewed drinking.

Depression and Drug Abuse

Numerous studies have demonstrated a high frequency of depressive symptomatology in patients who present for treatment of drug abuse problems (20–25); the prevalence rate of these symptoms in various surveys ranges from 30% to 60% (22–25). As in the studies of alcoholics, methodologic problems make these results difficult to interpret. For example, many of these studies measure depression according to rating scale data. Moreover, Mirin and associates (2) have demonstrated that chronic heroin intoxication can produce increased agitation, hostility, and depression. Thus, one can hypothesize that with opiate addicts, as well as alcoholics, the depression seen at the beginning of treatment is related in part to the effects of chronic intoxication. Unfortunately, depression levels are most often measured precisely at this time, when psychosocial stresses are likely to be highest, and when drug effects are greatest. Results from a study by Rounsaville and associates (4), showing that depressive symptoms in opiate addicts generally improve over time without specific antidepressant treatment, lend even further weight to the conclusion that the mere presence of depressive symptoms in a newly admitted opiate addict is insufficient evidence to warrant a diagnosis of an affective disorder.

Rounsaville and associates (25) attempted to refine the diagnostic process in these patients by administering the lifetime version of the Schedule for

Affective Disorders and Schizophrenia (SADS-L) to 533 opiate addicts in treatment; they found that approximately 70% of their sample met diagnostic criteria for a non-drug-related psychiatric disorder at the time of admission. Over 86% met Research Diagnostic Criteria for a psychiatric disorder other than drug abuse at some point in their lives. Thirty percent of the sample met DSM-III criteria for a current diagnosis of major depression, while 73% had suffered from an affective disorder during their lifetimes.

Individuals who abuse nonnarcotic drugs have been studied much less intensively than opiate addicts. Despite the growing popularity of cocaine as a drug of abuse, few studies of chronic cocaine abusers have assigned formal diagnoses to their patients (26,27). The use of cocaine as "self-medication" for depression has been posited since Freud (28) cited the drug's antidepressant activity in 1884. The evidence for this hypothesis comes from several areas: (a) the fact that cocaine induces profound euphoria (29,30); (b) the ability of cocaine, like antidepressant drugs, to increase noradrenergic activity in the central nervous system (31); and (c) the pharmacological similarity of cocaine to amphetamine, which has been used successfully in the treatment of certain depressed individuals (32). Post and associates (31) tested this self-medication theory by giving cocaine to a group of depressed patients. They found that although one-third of these individuals felt better on moderate doses of cocaine, most of them experienced an exacerbation of their depression after receiving higher doses. The results of this study do not rule out the self-medication hypothesis of cocaine abuse; certain individuals who obtain an antidepressant response from the drug in low to moderate doses might continue to abuse cocaine in larger amounts, despite its dysphoric effects. Indeed, other studies have shown that abusers of opiates (2), alcohol (3), and phencyclidine (33) continue to self-administer these drugs despite their eventual adverse effects on mood. Thus, although self-medication of depression may sometimes initiate drug use, other factors, such as conditioned responses to drug-related stimuli and avoidance of abstinence symptoms may later assume increased importance in the perpetuation of addiction.

Bipolar Disorder

The use of drugs and alcohol during manic episodes has been the subject of some investigation. Harding and associates (34) described a series of four patients who demonstrated increased marijuana use following the onset of hypomanic symptoms. Morrison (35) reported that 67% of his sample of bipolar patients admitted to having some difficulties with alcohol; other authors (36–38) have reported prevalence rates of alcohol abuse among manics ranging from 20% to 50%. In addition to hypothesizing that manics use drugs and alcohol as self-medication, we can attribute the increased use of drugs and alcohol during manic episodes in part to impulsiveness, recklessness, and poor judgment. The importance of identifying substance abusers with concurrent bipolar disorder has been highlighted by the promising reports of lithium carbonate treatment in alcoholics (39,40).

Panic and Anxiety Disorders

The use of alcohol and central nervous system depressants in patients with phobias, panic disorder, and anxiety has also been the subject of research. Mullaney and Trippett (41) found that two-thirds of the patients admitted to their alcoholism treatment program suffered from a phobic disorder, which usually preceded the onset of alcohol-related problems. Quitkin and associates (42) reported a group of patients with "phobic anxiety syndrome," characterized by panic attacks and subsequent phobias; these patients had developed depressant or alcohol abuse, which the authors viewed as an attempt to self-medicate chronic anticipatory anxiety. Treatment of these patients with imipramine eliminated their panic attacks and substance abuse. Other studies of patients with phobic, anxiety, and panic disorders have estimated that between 5% and 25% of this population suffer from alcohol and/or depressant abuse (43).

THE McLEAN HOSPITAL STUDY

One aspect of the self-medication theory which has not been addressed by much of the previous literature is the importance of the addict's drug of choice. If one hypothesizes that a patient is using drugs in an attempt to alleviate specific symptoms, then the particular medication he chooses becomes an important variable in understanding his psychopathology. There have thus far been few studies which have compared the psychopathology of groups of patients addicted to different drugs (44). We undertook such a study in order to determine whether patients with specific psychiatric disorders do in fact choose particular drugs of abuse in order to ameliorate their symptoms.

Methods

In order to evaluate substance abusers for other types of psychopathology, we collected extensive clinical information on 160 consecutive admissions to the

Drug Dependence Treatment Unit at McLean Hospital, a private psychiatric hospital. For each patient, we collected demographic data, obtained a detailed substance abuse history, and evaluated current symptomatology and progress by administering the Beck Depression Inventory, the Hamilton Depression Rating Scale, and the 90-item symptom checklist (SCL-90). Patients were diagnosed according to DSM-III criteria by the ward psychiatrist in conjunction with another psychiatrist who was not affiliated with the research project. Because of the difficulty of assessing psychiatric symptoms in the face of drug abuse, patients were not assigned diagnoses other than substance abuse unless they were currently ill and had previously met diagnostic criteria while drug- and alcohol-free. Family history data were gathered by directly interviewing first-degree relatives whenever possible; the relatives were then assigned DSM-III diagnoses when appropriate. Details of the study have been summarized elsewhere (26, 45–47).

Results

Rating scale data revealed a high degree of concordance between the scores on the Beck Depression Inventory, Hamilton Depression Rating Scale, and SCL-90. We found considerable depressive symptomatology in newly admitted patients, with a steady reduction in mean depression scores at two weeks and again at four weeks. When we compared those patients (n = 33) who received a diagnosis of major depression (n = 27) or atypical depression (n = 6) with patients (n = 127) who warranted neither diagnosis, it was difficult to distinguish between the two groups on the basis of their degree of depression at admission. Although the mean admission Hamilton score was 28.7 in the depressed group, the nondepressed patients had similar symptoms, with a mean Hamilton score of 20.0. The differences between the two groups of patients became somewhat clearer at two weeks, with mean Hamilton scores of 18.6 and 11.6, respectively. At four weeks, the mean scores of the affectively ill patients declined much more slowly than the scores of the nondepressed individuals; mean Hamilton scores were 13.7 and 7.5, respectively. Thus, we confirmed findings from other studies by showing a general improvement in mood among substance abusers while in treatment. However, we also showed that the mood of affectively ill patients generally changes more gradually than that of patients whose depressive moods are related to drug and/or situational factors. We also found that the serial measurement of depressive symptoms by means of standardized psychiatric rating scales can be useful in distinguishing drug abusers with affective disorders from patients with transient depressive symptoms.

Diagnostically, 40% of our total patient population met DSM-III criteria for an Axis I diagnosis other than substance abuse. Among this group, approximately three-fourths of the patients suffered from an affective disorder; major depression (n = 27) was the most common diagnosis. Grouping the patients by drug of choice showed some striking differences in the prevalence of specific disorders among different subgroups. Affective disorder, and particularly bipolar disorder, was significantly more common among stimulant abusers than among other drug-dependent patients. Our studies of depressant abusers confirmed the findings of Mullaney (41), Quitkin (42) and others; we found that panic and anxiety disorders were significantly more prevalent in the depressant abusers than in patients dependent upon opiates or stimulants. We also found two stimulant abusers with a childhood history of attention deficit disorder (ADD), who initially began abusing stimulants because the drugs increased their ability to concentrate and sit still. Recent studies have shown alcoholism (48–52) to be a frequent adult complication of attention deficit disorder; more recently, cocaine abuse has also been reported as a sequela of ADD (53). Since our stimulant abusers with childhood attention deficit disorder responded well to the administration of magnesium pemoline (54), it appears that eliciting a careful history for ADD may be an important part of the evaluation of substance abusers.

One striking finding that did not fit the self-medication hypothesis was the frequency of bipolar disorder among stimulant abusers. In fact, we found that the majority of cocaine and amphetamine abusers with bipolar disorder used these drugs far more frequently when already euphoric than when depressed. They generally stated that they enjoyed being endogenously "high," and used cocaine in order to intensify and prolong their hypomanic or manic episodes. The manic patients who abused central nervous systems depressants or opiates, on the other hand, generally described their drug use as an attempt at self-medication, because they found their manic episodes to be dysphoric, and they experienced the use of these drugs as calming. Thus, the coexistence of affective disorder and substance abuse does not necessarily mean that a patient is self-medicating. This finding underlines the importance of taking a careful history in order to understand the significance and context of a patient's drug abuse.

Family studies showed that affective disorder was significantly more prevalent among the first-degree relatives of stimulant abusers when compared to the same sex-relatives of patients who were dependent upon opiates or depressants. When the relatives of affectively ill patients were compared with the relatives of patients without affective disorder, the prevalence rate for affective disorder among the family members was significantly higher among the former group. Thus, obtaining a careful family history may also help identify drug-dependent patients with a coexisting affective disorder.

CONCLUSIONS

The high prevalence rate of other psychiatric disorders in substance abusers makes a careful search for coexisting psychopathology an integral part of the evaluation of these patients. We have found that taking a detailed clinical and family history and observing patients for 2–4 weeks after they have been drug-free allows the clinician to more clearly separate those patients with premorbid psychopathology from individuals with drug-related symptoms. Paying attention to drug of choice may also aid the diagnostic process: a careful search for an affective disorder and attention deficit disorder is particularly warranted in stimulant abusers, while panic disorder should be ruled out in patients dependent upon depressant drugs. It is clear that substance abusers are a heterogeneous group; treating them otherwise does these patients a great disservice. Careful evaluation, followed by individualized flexible treatment planning, is necessary in order to successfully treat this very difficult patient population.

REFERENCES

1. *Meyer, R. E., Hesselbrock, M. N.: Psychopathology and addictive disorders revisited. In Mirin, S. M. (ed):* Substance Abuse and Psychopathology. *Washington, DC, American Psychiatric Association Press, in press.*
2. *Mirin, S. M., Meyer, R. E., McNamee, H. B.: Psychopathology and mood during heroin use.* Arch Gen Psychiatry *33: 1503–1508, 1976.*
3. *Mendelson, J. H., Mello, N. K.: Experimental analysis of drinking behavior of chronic alcoholics.* Ann NY Acad Sci *133: 828 845, 1966.*
4. *Rounsaville, B. J., Weissman, M. M., Crits-Christoph, C., et al: Diagnosis and symptoms of depression in opiate addicts.* Arch Gen Psychiatry *39: 151–166, 1982.*
5. *McLellan, A. T., Luborsky, L. L, Woody, G. E., et al: Predicting response to alcohol and drug abuse treatments: Role of psychiatric severity.* Arch Gen Psychiatry *40: 620–625, 1983.*
6. *Glover, E. G.: On the aetiology of drug addiction.* Int J Psychoanal *13 (Part 3): 298–328, 1932.*
7. *Rado, S.: Psychoanalysis of pharmacothymia.* Psychoanal Q *2: 1–23, 1933.*
8. *Khantzian, E.: Opiate addiction: A critique of theory and some implication for treatment.* Am J Psychother *28: 59–70, 1974.*

9. *Wurmser, L.: Psychoanalytic consideration of the etiology of compulsive drug use.* J Am Psychoanal Assoc *22: 820–843, 1974.*

10. *Simon, E. J.: Recent developments in the biology of opiates: possible relevance to addiction. In Lowenson, J. H., Ruiz, P. (eds):* Substance Abuse: Clinical Problems and Perspectives. *Baltimore, Williams and Wilkins, 1981.*

11. *Martin, W. R.: Emerging concepts concerning drug abuse. In Lettieri, D. J., Sayers, M., Pearson, H. W. (eds):* Theories on Drug Abuse: Selected Contemporary Perspectives. *NIDA Research Monograph 30. Rockville, MD, US Government Printing Office, 1980.*

12. *Braestrup, C., Squires, R. F.: Brain specific benzodiazepine receptors.* British J Psychiatry *133: 249–260, 1978.*

13. *Keeler, M. H., Taylor, C. I., Miller, W. C.: Are all recently detoxified alcoholics depressed?* Am J Psychiatry *136: 586–588, 1979.*

14. *Hesselbrock, M. N., Hesselbrock, V. M., Tennen, H., et al: Methodological considerations in the assessment of depression in alcoholics.* J Clin & Consul Psychol *51: 399–405, 1983.*

15. *Schuckit, M.: Alcoholism and affective disorder: Diagnostic confusion. In Goodwin, D., Erickson, C. (eds):* Alcoholism and Affective Disorders. *New York, Spectrum Publications, 1979.*

16. *Liskow, B., Mayfield, D., Thiele, J.: Alcohol and affective disorder: Assessment and treatment.* J Clin Psychiatry *43: 144–147, 1982.*

17. *Warren, G. H., Raynes, A. E.: Mood changes during three conditions of alcohol intake.* Quart J Stud Alc *33: 979–989, 1972.*

18. *Vaillant, G. E., Milofsky, E. S.: The natural history of male alcoholism: Paths to recovery.* Arch Gen Psychiatry *39: 127–133, 1982.*

19. *Pottenger, M., McKernon, J., Patrie, L. E., et al: The frequency and persistence of depressive symptoms in the alcohol abuser.* J Nerv Ment Dis *166: 562–570, 1978.*

20. *Steer, R. A., Schut, J.: Types of psychopathology displayed by heroin addicts.* Am J Psychiatry *136: 1463–1465, 1979.*

21. *Rounsaville, B. J., Weissman, M. M., Rosenberger, P. H., et al.: Detecting depressive disorders in drug abusers: a comparison of screening instruments.* J Affect Disorder *1: 255–267, 1979.*

22. *Kleber, H. D., Gold, M. S.: Use of psychotropic drugs in the treatment of methadone maintained narcotic addicts.* Ann NY Acad Sci *331: 81–98, 1978.*

23. *Dorus, W., Senay, E. C.: Depression, demographic dimensions, and drug abuse.* Am J Psychiatry *137: 699–704, 1980.*

24. *Weissman, M. M., Pottenger, M., Kleber, H., et al: Symptom patterns in primary and secondary depression: A comparison of primary depressives with depressed opiate addicts, alcoholics, and schizophrenics.* Arch Gen Psychiatry *34: 854–862, 1977.*

25. *Rounsaville, B. J., Weissman, M. M., Kleber, H., et al: Heterogeneity of psychiatric diagnosis in treated opiate addicts.* Arch Gen Psychiatry *39: 161–166, 1982.*

26. *Weiss, R. D., Mirin, S. M., Michael, J. L., et al: Psychopathology in chronic cocaine abusers.* Am J Drug Alcohol Abuse *12: 17–29, 1986.*

27. *Gawin, F. H., Kleber, H. D.: Abstinence symptomatology and psychiatric diagnosis in cocaine abusers.* Arch Gen Psychiatry *43: 107–113, 1986.*

28. *Freud, S.: Uber Coca. In Byck, R. (ed):* Cocaine Papers: Sigmund Freud. *New York, Stonehill Publishing Co., 1974.*

29. *Resnick, R. B., Kestenbaum, R. S., Schwartz, L. K.: Acute systemic effects of cocaine in man: A controlled study by intranasal and intravenous routes.* Science *195: 696–698, 1977.*

30. *Siegel, R. K.: Cocaine: Recreational use and intoxication. In Petersen, R. C., Stillman, R. C. (eds):* Cocaine. *NIDA Research Monograph 13. Washington, DC, US Government Printing Office, 1977.*

31. *Post, R. M., Kotin, J., Goodwin, F. R.: The effects of cocaine on depressed patients.* Am J Psychiatry *131: 511–517, 1974.*

32. *Silberman, E. K., Reus, V. I., Jimerson, D. C., et al: Heterogeneity of amphetamine response in depressed patients.* Am J Psychiatry *138: 1302–1307, 1981.*

33. *Mello, N. K.: Control of drug self-administration: The role of aversive consequences. In Petersen, R. C., Stillman, R. C. (eds):* PCP: Phencyclidine abuse: An appraisal. *NIDA Research Monograph 21. Washington, DC, US Government Printing Office, 1978.*

34. *Harding, T., Knight, F.: Marihuana—modified mania.* Arch Gen Psychiatry *29: 635–637, 1973.*

35. *Morrison, J. R.: Bipolar affective disorder and alcoholism.* Am J Psychiatry *131: 1130–1134, 1974.*

36. *Mayfield, D. G., Coleman, L. L.: Alcohol use and affective disorder.* Dis Nerv Syst *29: 467–474, 1968.*

37. *Winokur, G., Clayton, P.: Family history studies: II. Sex differences in alcoholism in first degree affective disorder.* Br J Psychiatry *113: 973–979, 1967.*

38. *Reich, L. H., Davies, R. K., Hemmilhock, J. M.: Excessive alcohol use in manic-depressive illness.* Am J Psychiatry 131: 83–83, 1974.

39. *Kline, N. S., Wren, J. C., Cooper, T. B., et al: Evaluation of lithium therapy in chronic and periodic alcoholism.* Am J Med Sci *268: 15–22, 1974.*

40. *Fawcett, J., Clark, D. C., Aagesen, C. A., et al: A double-blind, placebo-controlled trial of lithium carbonate for alcoholism.* Arch Gen Psychiatry *44: 248–256, 1987.*

41. *Mullaney, J. A., Trippett, C. J.: Alcohol dependence and phobias: Clinical description and relevance.* Br J Psychiatry *135: 565–573, 1979.*

42. *Quitkin, F. M., Rifkin, A., Kaplan, J., et al: Phobic anxiety syndrome complicated by drug dependence and addiction.* Arch Gen Psychiatry *27: 159–162, 1972.*

43. *Woodruff, R. H., Guze, S. B., Clayton, P. J.: Anxiety neurosis among psychiatric outpatients.* Compr Psychiatry *13: 165–170, 1972.*

44. *McLellan, A. T., Woody, G. E., O'Brien, C. P.: Development of psychiatric illness in drug abusers: Possible role of drug preference.* N Engl J Med *301: 1310–1314, 1979.*

45. *Weiss, R. D., Mirin, S. M.: Drug, host and environmental factors in the development of chronic cocaine abuse. In Mirin, S. M. (ed):* Substance Abuse and Psychopathology. *American Psychiatric Association Press, Washington, DC, pp 41–55, 1984.*

46. *Mirin, S. M., Weiss, R. D., Sollogub, A., et al: Affective illness in substance*

abusers. In Mirin, S. M. (ed): Substance Abuse and Psychopathology. *American Psychiatric Association Press, Washington, DC, pp 57–77, 1984.*

47. *Mirin, S. M., Weiss, R. D., Sollogub, A., et al: Psychopathology in the families of drug abusers. In Mirin, S. M. (ed):* Substance Abuse and Psychopathology. *American Psychiatric Association Press, Washington, DC, pp 79–106, 1984.*

48. *Goodwin, W. G., Schulsinger, F., Hermansen, L., et al: Alcoholism and the hyperactive child syndrome.* J Nerv Ment Dis *160: 349–353, 1975.*

49. *Wood, D. R., Reimherr, F. W., Wender, P. H., et al: Diagnosis and treatment of minimal brain dysfunction in adults: A preliminary report.* Arch Gen Psychiatry *33: 1453–1460, 1976.*

50. *Tartar, R. E., McBride, H., Buonpane, N., et al: Differentiation of alcoholics: Childhood history of minimal brain dysfunction, family history, and drinking pattern.* Arch Gen Psychiatry *34: 761–768, 1977.*

51. *Tartar, R. E.: Psychosocial history, minimal brain dysfunction and differential drinking patterns of male alcoholics.* J Clin Psychology *38: 867–873, 1982.*

52. *Turnquist, K., Frances, R., Rosenfeld, W., et al: Pemoline in attention deficit disorder and alcoholism: A case study.* Am J Psychiatry *140: 622–624, 1983.*

53. *Khantzian, E. J.: Extreme case of cocaine dependence and marked improvement with methylphenidate treatment.* Am J Psychiatry *140: 784–785, 1983.*

54. *Weiss, R. D., Pope, H. G., Mirin, S. M.: Treatment of chronic cocaine abuse and attention deficit disorder, residual type, with magnesium pemoline.* Drug Alcohol Depend *15: 69–72, 1985.*

25. Parallels and Paradigms

H. J. Richards

CONFRONTING THE PROBLEM

Suzanne arrived at the door of a specialty dual diagnosis program from the public hospital's psychiatric screening unit. Her dirty hair was disheveled, and her personal belongings were crammed into a black Hefty bag. She had been on the street for several days. Last year she had taken a housemate's pills in an attempt to kill herself, but nothing had happened. After that, she felt even worse, more desperate, and she began to fear she would do something more dangerous and violent to herself. She went to the screening unit to tell someone about her feelings of self-destruction. In a few minutes she would be interviewed by the dual diagnosis program's intake staff. This was an unusual way for her to gain admission to the program. Fortunately, the central intake psychiatrist had come to recognize over the years the cases that the dual diagnosis program director was apt to admit, and a developing rapport had led to earlier-than-usual specialized help for some patients in the dual diagnosis cycle. The intake psychiatrist was a mature, warm woman with grandmotherly charm who projected a sense of safe haven. Suzanne opened up enough to her to give a fairly candid interview. Despite this, relatively little of her complicated history would be discovered and documented in this one-session assessment.

Six months after this interview, a very detailed understanding of Suzanne's problems and background would emerge. She was 26 years old, from a working class Irish-American family. She had first started having problems in college, where she was studying to become a high school art instructor. In her sophomore year, she had fallen in love with her dormitory roommate. After sending the young woman a typewritten anonymous love letter, Suzanne realized how transparent her act was, since she had mailed the letter while on campus and referred to things that only the two of them would know. So she concocted an elaborate scheme to protect herself and her friendship with her roommate. She mailed several expensive gifts from a nearby town and constructed a note from newspaper clippings claiming to be from male terrorists who threatened Suzanne's own life if she revealed the identity of the imagined anonymous suitor. Suzanne then staged an attack upon herself that left the entire dorm in an uproar along with various rumors floating over campus ranging from a rapist

Reprinted by permission from *Therapy of the Substance Abuse Syndromes* (Northvale, N.J.: Jason Aronson, 1993), 3–39. Copyright © 1993, by Jason Aronson, Inc.

afoot to patent descriptions of her insanity. Before mailing a letter threatening her roommate with death should she attempt to move from the dormitory, Suzanne had carved a line with a letter opener from the nook of her right elbow ending with a flared arrowhead in her open palm. The dorm counselor knew that the wounds were only superficial, but after seeing Suzanne's inept attempts to care for them and realizing that the young woman lied about the origin of the cuts, she had insisted that Suzanne go for formal counseling. The dean of students, who already knew Suzanne because of her failing grades, agreed.

Suzanne had avoided the student counseling center. In her community mental health center, she was diagnosed as having bipolar disorder, based on her history of depressive symptoms and previously contained but somewhat bizarre hypomanic episodes. Suzanne lied about her drinking, although the center took enough of a history to determine that she would have to deal with the problems of having an alcoholic mother. She was started on psychotropics after refusing to enter a hospital voluntarily, although she agreed to a simple contract of not hurting herself in any way.

That was seven years ago. Since then, Suzanne had dropped out of school, performed clerical work in several widely separated cities, was in alcohol detoxification programs twice, and had had four brief psychiatric hospitalizations. She had been raped once while drunk but had not discussed this with anyone. The attack did not appear in any of her scattered records. She had had one debilitating bout with hepatitis after her male lover contracted the disease, probably from IV drug use. A close somatic examination, which she did not undergo at the time of the intake interview, would have revealed a swollen and distended liver. Her HIV status was also unknown.

Besides her hospitalizations and detoxification stints, Suzanne has been in several good outpatient programs for mental illness and others for substance abuse. She has never felt comfortable with the idea of being a psychiatric patient and has never complied consistently with any outpatient treatments for more than a few weeks. The medication has always made her feel bloated and sluggish. The one substance abuse program that engaged her interest (one with daily 2-hour meetings) had discharged her for poor attendance and too many relapses, and had referred her back to the mental health system. In periods of controlled drinking and when not depressed, Suzanne has made friends, lived in apartments or group houses with adults of her own age, and worked at various jobs, sometimes getting very favorable reviews of her typing skills. She had come to view her problems as being due only to her alcohol use, which she realized usually made her feel more depressed. She had also learned to avoid her family because they made her depressed and angry. She now rarely talked of them and rarely thought of them for more than a few seconds at a time, except when she needed something she could not get anyone else to provide.

Most recently, she had lived for several months in a house with three recovering alcoholics. Her AA sponsor of only two months had recently told her in a telephone conversation that she was too demanding and that it was a "selfish program," meaning that Suzanne had to look out for herself and she should get more out of the meetings she claimed to be attending and call her sponsor less often.

After two of the housemates became a couple and began doing things as a separate unit away from the house, Suzanne had started drinking in her room, spending days there watching television. She had received a message that she had been fired from her job. Her rent went unpaid for two months. Her hygiene deteriorated. Soon, her only contact with her roommates was to insist angrily that they leave her alone. Eventually, they asked her to move. She had wandered for several days weeping and trying to hold on to her belongings. Her main contacts with people were from getting drinks and a little food from strangers on the street. She felt miserable, then suicidal.

Now, Suzanne wanted help for these feelings and a place to stay. She did not want to be in another alcohol program by some other name, but this dual diagnosis program sounded better than a "regular" mental hospital.

Although most of this background information about Suzanne was not available to the program intake staff, they recognized that her case had come to their attention relatively early in the dual diagnosis cycle. After only six years of a clear symptom pattern and involvement in the health care delivery system, the constant stream of acute hospitalizations and aborted treatment programs had really just started. Yet, she had already become a treatment failure in three systems: the mental health system, the formal substance abuse treatment system, and the self-help alcoholism recovery community. Her point of entry was a coerced referral to the mental health system, where she was correctly diagnosed as suffering from a mental disorder with primarily affective features. After several forced detox hospitalizations, Suzanne had referred herself to the self-help programs of Alcoholics Anonymous. She had received help and support, but there remained an invisible wall creating distance and absence of real communication with her peers. In AA, her psychiatric problems had often been dealt with either harshly or with deep sympathy that later turned to exasperation and avoidance. People had tolerated Suzanne long enough for her to feel involved and hopeful, but they had always let her down. Even the things she heard in meetings—the life stories, the morals given to the stories, and the elaborations of the Twelve Steps—had confused her.

Sometimes people told her she should see a doctor or therapist; more often they told her that medication for mental problems was an unnecessary crutch, a way of denying a continuing dependence on chemicals. But when she tried to apply the things she heard, they never seemed to work for her, and she had sometimes left meetings wanting to drink more than ever before. Also, she more often than not met people who would exploit her or who seemed to have more emotional problems than she did. Being a treatment failure in this informal system had probably been the most bitter failure yet for Suzanne, because it had been intertwined into her daily life, her thoughts and feelings, and all of her relationships. Now, her denial and ambivalence about her problems with alcohol were returning, bolstered by her delusions.

Without yet having most of this information, the staff admitted Suzanne.

How did they understand what had happened to her? What aspects of her clinical picture, other than the co-existence of her alcohol problem and her emotional symptoms, made her an appropriate candidate for such a program? What should such a program be able to offer her that either mental health nor substance abuse programs could provide? What was her prognosis? Was she apt to be labeled a treatment failure again?

Why does it appear that there are so many more individuals like Suzanne today as compared to two decades ago? The theoretical, clinical, and practical administrative questions and issues posed by the problems of patients such as Suzanne are the primary subjects of this book *[Therapy of the Substance Abuse Syndromes]*. The remainder of this chapter maps out the conceptual ground that must be covered before addressing specific clinical strategies and procedures. This chapter also attempts to provide the reader with an experiential grasp of the effects of mental illnesses and addictions as processes acting upon the total life of the individual, but especially upon the individual's experience of self.

DEFINING SYNDROMES

Suzanne and others like her (and still others very unlike her) suffer from an emergent psychiatric syndrome. A syndrome is a statistical concept. It relies on the probability of the occurrence of a pattern of divergent symptoms. This occurrence may suggest, for the various component symptoms, either common pathogenic mechanisms, common etiological clues, interactive patterns of predisposition, or vulnerability to various disorders. Suzanne's symptom complex is typified by the reciprocally reinforcing effects of psychiatric problems and substance abuse or dependence.

AN EMERGENT SYNDROME

In this [chapter], the reciprocally reinforcing psychiatric and substance abuse syndromes, as they most properly might be named, are described as emergent in several senses. In one sense they are being recognized, dealt with consciously, and written about by professionals in a systematic way, after about a decade of unsystematic contributions. The dual diagnosis syndromes are emergent in that they are becoming more frequently encountered in clinical settings due to improved clinical sensitivity and because larger numbers of patients are developing the syndromes. (The plural is used here, because several different subtypes of the combined pathological processes of addiction and psychopathology will be identified.) In another sense, these syndromes are emergent because of the emerging social and health care environments that both cause more dual diagnosis cases and present opportunities for recognition and treatment. Several of these emerging environmental factors are located in the wider society, others are within the mental health system, still others occur in the boundary between that system and society.

Two contributing factors flow from the success and newly found effectiveness of the mental health system. The first factor is specialization. Growing demand for services and increases in knowledge and competency bases have permitted mental health care to be specialized into several separate training and treatment systems, each with its own particular traditions and cultures. Until recently this specialization had evolved into a pecking order that relegated substance abuse to either low status professionals, paraprofessionals, or self-help groups. These individuals, however well meaning, were the least prepared to deal with any coinciding psychopathology beyond mild character disorders or mild reactive depressions. The relegating of alcoholism and drug abuse cases to lay and paraprofessional attention had the unintended result of de-skilling core mental health professionals in the assessment and treatment of addiction. The division also produced a complex delivery system with more cracks to fall through for those patients whose needs and problems did not fit neatly into any of the specialty lines. The dual diagnosis case was likely to be called a treatment failure and referred out of several of these specialty delivery systems.

The second contributing factor resulting from a strength within the mental health system is the rapid growth of psychopharmacology, which made possible the humane deinstitutionalization of the mentally ill within modern society. Unfortunately, unrelated changes in political and social values put even more stark limitations on the extent to which one is personally or communally the keeper of one's brother. These values were less prevalent early in the deinstitutionalization movement. At that time, only heavy marketing, which presented overly optimistic views about medical maintenance and severe mental illnesses, and promises of sufficient funding to create a new community mental health network persuaded citizens to tolerate the dismantling of the asylum. Such dismantling, which in many areas of the United States was spearheaded by mental health professionals themselves, proceeded like Samson to bring down the temple, with only lip service given to providing community support for newly released patients. Once back in the community, expected to cope under relatively intense demands and stressors, and after being inculcated into a pharmacological model of problem solving, chronic patients participated in the social mores surrounding them and discovered their own drugs of choice. (This is the self-medication hypothesis in dual diagnosis problems, which we later revisit.)

For all members of the community, including the psychiatric patient, the rise of drug and alcohol use in society is an opportunity for addictive processes to be initiated more often. Sometimes increased drug use masks other pathological processes, while the resulting behaviors, because they are understood as drug effects, are met with more acceptance until they reach clearly dangerous levels. This can be seen as the dual diagnosis problem on the societal level, a process that provides a rich pool for the development of more dual diagnosis cases at the clinical level. Taken together, these trends have contributed significantly to the emergence of the syndromes described in this book. Finally, the syndromes described here are emergent in that they come into being and are defined by the new qualities that appear when addictive processes and patterns interact with other pathological processes in a reciprocally reinforcing manner.

DEFINING DUAL DIAGNOSIS POPULATIONS

In the mental health literature, the term *dual diagnosis patient* may refer to several groups of patients with more than one diagnosis on the primary axes of the diagnostic system. Here the term refers to those groups of patients with particular clusters of symptoms, usually resulting in two diagnoses: a psychiatric disorder and a substance abuse disorder. Using dual diagnosis as a population concept underlines the notion that there are possible subpopulations or categories *within* the dual diagnosis group and that the problems in the dual diagnosis subpopulation are, for the most part, continuous with those in the larger mental health population.

This broad population concept-based definition has the advantage of simplicity. Every patient with both a psychiatric and a substance abuse or substance dependence disorder may be easily pigeonholed by the dual diagnosis term. In one sense, it is no more than a shorthand way of describing a group of co-occurring diagnoses. In use, however, the term often implies that these patients have much more in common, either in treatment course, preferred management and treatment techniques, or perhaps etiologically. Defining the term more precisely will help to describe what is implied by this sense of commonality and will be one step toward identifying a treatment population or populations. Identifying meaningful population groups often results in refinements in research, theory, and clinical practice.

The widest definition offered in the literature reflects the view that any use of any psychoactive substance by any psychiatric patient (other than as prescribed) constitutes a dual diagnosis problem. The logic here is that such use may complicate or worsen an already tenuous psychiatric adjustment. More often than not, this may be the case, and this definition provides the heuristic advantage of warning patients and clinicians of the increased dangers of psychoactive drug use among the mentally ill. However, this definition lumps the dysthymic individual who occasionally uses cocaine with the paranoid who has active persecutory delusions, who is a severe alcoholic, and who has odd delusional beliefs about the antidemonic powers of alcohol and other drugs. It becomes obvious that so broad a definition defeats any useful attempt at classifying patients when we realize that the estimates of psychiatric patients with some significant substance abuse or dependence history ranges from 50 to 70 percent (Kosten and Kleber 1988, McKelvy et al. 1987).

The recent NIMH Epidemiologic Catchment Area (ECA) Study should be considered the watershed event in this field of research (Regier et al. 1990). With only limited space to deal with the wealth of statistical information that the ECA study has made available, readers are encouraged to obtain as complete a listing of the detailed statistics as possible and to check the study's findings against the assertions and theoretical speculations made in this text. Using a sample size of over 20,000, the study analyzed base rates of mental illnesses and addictive disorders to provide empirical estimates of their co-morbidity. Lifetime prevalence rates for mental disorders without substance abuse were estimated at 22.5 percent. Alcohol dependence/abuse and substance dependence/abuse had respective lifetime prevalence rates of 13.5 and 6.1 percent. For individuals diagnosed with a mental disorder, the odds ratio (subgroup base rate divided by the general population rate) of having some addictive process was 2.7, with a lifetime prevalence rate of 29 percent, which included a 22 percent overlap of mental illness and alcohol-related disorders and a 15 percent overlap of other drug disorders and mental illness. For persons with an addictive disorder, the odds for also having a mental illness were seven times higher than for the general population; 37 percent of alcoholics were found to have a co-existing mental disorder. Among other substance addictive disorders, 53 percent were found to have another mental disorder (a 4.5 odds ratio).

The ECA findings were even more dramatic for individuals in American institutions. Although the institutionalized population represents only 1.3 percent of the total U.S. population, being in an institution greatly increases the likelihood of having an alcohol, drug, or mental disorder (referred to as ADM by the study authors), with the lifetime rate being 71.9 percent, twice that of the general population. Mental hospitals, as expected, had the highest lifetime rate of 82.2 percent. (That means, of course, approximately 18 percent of hospitalized mental patients had no ADM disorder in their lives, using the NIMH research diagnostic instrument!) Prison inmates had a rate almost as high—82.0 percent. Nursing homes had a prevalence rate of 65.5 percent.

For individuals presenting for treatment in specialty mental health or substance abuse treatment centers, the ECA findings, based on 6-month prevalence base rates, give a closer picture of what clinicians working in these environments might expect. The co-morbidity of alcohol disorders and mental illness was 55 percent. For drugs other than alcohol, the co-morbidity rate was 64.4 percent. Looking at this rather impressive data base and using the wide definition of any co-existing mental illness with any substance use disorder, the majority of psychiatric patients clearly would have to be considered dual diagnosis patients.

A narrower definition than mere clinical and statistical occurrence is more useful. In the author's view, the most useful definition of the dual diagnosis syndrome or patient group must aid in establishing subpopulations based on clinical presentation, response to treatment, course of illness, or suspected etiology. Preferably, such a definition would reflect the relevant symptom dimensions or treatment issues that evolve in working with these patients. Optimally, such a definition would be informed by theoretical notions surrounding the most prominent feature of these cases, that is, the *persistence* of diagnostic occurrence despite active treatment for both disorders and the *interactive,* potentiating relationship between these disorders within the individual.

Several dimensions are key to forming relevant clinical subgroups from the apples-and-oranges population of those with both a substance abuse disorder and another psychiatric disorder. These conceptual dimensions have varying currency and usages in the clinical diagnostic and treatment literature and clinical practice. They are discussed in the next section before we return to refining our definition of the dual diagnosis population and to marking off the subgroups that may best be treated from the perspective offered in this book. The emphasis here is on the intractable patient, or the multiple treatment failure. In addition to patients for whom the approach to dual diagnosis work offered here is optimal, there are others for whom this approach offers only paradigmatic or heuristic value. Other ways of conceptualizing their cases will prove more efficient. The key dimensions discussed below will be useful in sorting cases into either of these two categories.

KEY DIMENSIONS OF DUAL DIAGNOSIS WORK

The concepts discussed in this section are not new. They are part and parcel of the clinician's everyday toolbox. In the current context, however, these concepts are delimited, providing additional connotations, elaborated or integrated with one another in a conceptual grid that helps to clarify and understand dual diagnosis problems. The key concepts are: acuity, chronicity, cyclicity, urgency, severity, and degree of reciprocity. Three of these concepts—acuity, chronicity, and cyclicity—relate to symptoms over time, and a fourth—urgency—relates to the subjective perception of time and priorities. The metaphor *clinical picture* is often used, but in their dependence on time, psychiatric disorders are closer to disturbing musical compositions than to crazed pictures. Psychiatric disorders exist in time; they have predictable courses and phases.

Acuity answers the question of how stable is the problem we are looking at. Did it just start? Has it reached its worst phase? What can we expect next? Often, the dual diagnosis patient reaches the health care system in acute distress from both a severe psychiatric problem (psychosis, suicidality, or dangerousness) as well as a severe substance abuse problems (intoxication, an overdose, or acute withdrawal symptoms). Just as often, in the acute phase the two pathological processes are not distinguishable as parallel or intersecting lines, but rather the lines appear superimposed. The symptom pattern may be explained as totally due to acute mental illness, or substance related effects. Acuity describes the expected acceleration, deceleration, or slope of the illness from where the patient is now, assuming that adequate care will be provided. Acuity often helps us to judge the level of severity.

Chronicity lets us know how long-standing or persistent the presented problems and symptoms are, how resistant they will be to interventions, how ingrained in the lifestyle, social functioning, and personality of the individual. Chronicity allows us to estimate how much anxiety will be produced in the patient and family (and sometimes, unfortunately, in the involved helping systems) should we be successful in changing the pattern. Dual diagnosis cases are usually chronic in either the substance abuse process or the psychiatric deteriorating process, or both.

Chronic illnesses are often cyclical. *Cyclicity* is a normal aspect of most biological processes (Sabelli and Carlson-Sabelli 1989). In periodic illnesses, such as seasonal affective disorder, premenstrual stress syndrome, anniversary depressions, and some levels of substance use disorders, an external driver (biological or situational) of the cyclical process may be easily identified. In other illnesses that demonstrate cyclicity, such as bipolar disorder, recurrent depressions, or cyclical exacerbations of schizophrenic symptoms, an external driver is not apparent and perhaps not present. As we shall see, biological and psychological processes grow out of the combination of opposing (or alternative but linked) processes often demonstrate cyclicity. Each repetition of a cycle, of course, involves differences from previous cycles, as well as the preservation of the basic pattern of illness. The shape of the pattern over time is more of a spiral helix than a circle. Knowing the degree of cyclicity of an illness, estimating where the patient is now in the spiral, and whether it is ascending or descending help in predicting the spontaneous or treatment-induced opening of windows of opportunity for various interventions. This information also provides clues to uncovering the external drivers, internal drivers, or drivers inherent to the pathological process itself, thus suggesting ways to short-circuit or ameliorate the cycle.

Urgency is a matter of perception of priority: what has to be dealt with first. Does the patient or the patient's family see the problem as the first priority? Does the treatment team (given their various disciplinary training backgrounds, countertransference, and preferences) feel that some aspect of the case is really pressing and has to be dealt with now? The reader may notice that the problem of primary–secondary diagnosis has been deemphasized in this discussion by not being listed as a key concept. Although making the primary–secondary distinction in cases where both a substance use disorder and another mental disorder are present has been recommended as a modification of the *DSM* for future revisions; this recommendation was rejected due to the lack of empirical justification of the distinction and to the clinical problems with the required judgment.

To the extent that primary–secondary diagnostic status may be established for any particular case, the case fits less neatly in the approach being offered here. Urgency on the part of the staff in regard to one symptom or problem versus others will usually reflect their judgments of primary versus secondary diagnoses or problems. This sense of urgency may be determined in part by factors somewhat external to clinical considerations, such as a forensic determination requiring proportional judgments of the contribution of the two pathological processes at the time of a crime, for example, or by the relative reimbursements offered by third-party payers for psychiatric versus substance abuse disorders. A clinical factor influencing urgency is the patient's tendency to powerfully engage countertransference issues of the staff. Urgency, at least in part, is a dimension that exists between the patient's needs and perceptions, and the needs and perceptions of involved others, especially family and treatment staff. Without separating urgency from other dimensions offered here and weighing it appropriately in the clinical decision-making process, most dual diagnosis cases will be dealt with almost exclusively in terms of the urgency dimension.

Severity may be described as how extreme the symptom pattern is when one combines the acute picture with the chronic pattern. Severity is a key concept, because it captures so much other data. The current course of the illness, the premorbid adjustment, the psychological structure of the individual, the typical level of functioning, the intensity and duration of continued treatment, and the predicted slope of a relapse are all reflected in an estimate of severity. Because it captures so much information and is a dimension easily traced for both pathological processes, we investigate the distinguishable levels of severity for both processes and project how these levels are apt to be interrelated in most cases. This leads us a fuller discussion of *reciprocity* as the pivotal dimension that reflects the interrelatedness of the severity levels of the two pathological processes and provides the most crucial criterion in defining the reciprocally reinforcing psychiatric substance abuse syndromes.

LEVELS OF SEVERITY FOR TWO PATHOLOGICAL PROCESSES

Life Space and Need-Related Motivation

Discussing abstract conceptual dimensions, population overlaps, and synergisms is a far cry from the heartfelt involvement that is the day-to-day work of the clinician or counselor. To assist the process of involving both the head and the heart in thinking about these issues, let us take a brief excursion into the phenomenology (the experience from the inside) of psychopathology and substance abuse as we discuss their various levels of severity. Two theoretical frameworks familiar to many mental health and substance abuse workers will provide a conceptual and schematic context from which to view the global effects of severity for two pathological processes. Slices of life will be sampled from various points along the addictive cycle and the cycle of breakdown from psychopathology. Kurt Lewin (1936) and Abraham Maslow (1962, 1964, 1970, 1971) both developed theories of motivation and personal-

ity based on need gratification or achievement. Both thinkers used visual
schematics to assist in understanding human behavior based on responses to
needs. Most introductory texts on personality or motivational theory include
chapters or sections on these theories. Here, we outline only a few simple
aspects of these theories in order to make explicit some of the relationships
between the phenomenological effects of various severity levels of the two
pathological processes focused on throughout this book.

Lewin's theories have influenced motivational concepts beyond those that
directly use his terminology and methods. One of his key concepts was that
of the life space. For Lewin, life space is a range of activity for the individual
that can be depicted visually in a simple graph. A person moves toward or
away from objects in his or her life space along vectors, or lines of psychological or motivational force. The strength and direction of these lines are
determined by basic needs and values, or valencies, to use Lewin's terminology. We borrow these ideas and adapt them here to create some useful visual
representations.

Figure 25.1 depicts a normal healthy individual balanced in a life space
that consists of persons (circles), things (rectangles), and ideas or ideals

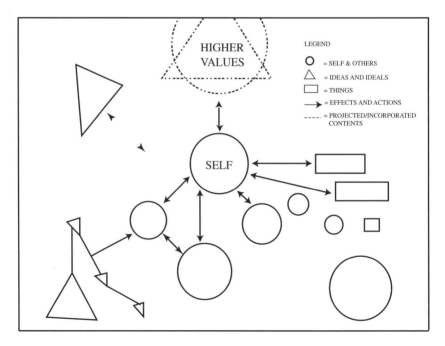

Figure 25.1. Balanced life space

(triangles) connected by vectors (arrows). Size and distance are used here to represent importance and closeness to the self, or intimacy. Here, the vectors are drawn to show only how the individual person (self) perceives the influence or power of the relationship as either exerted toward or coming from him or her, or both.

The healthy individual depicted here is centered in the middle of the life space by his or her dynamic relationships with various objects, persons, things, ideas, or ideals. The life space is organized and meaningfully occupied, not cramped or empty. There is even an equally large other in this individual's life (lower right corner) who is acknowledged as a complete, unique, other person but who has no major significant relationship with the self. Here, the absence of vectors depict the healthy individual's understanding that others have their own autonomy in their own life space. The large broken circle at the top of the figure that partially contains a triangle represents this individual's internalized relationship to higher values, perhaps God, country, or humanity. Most of the vectors show influence or power moving in both directions, indicating mutuality.

An important aspect of the life space that is not easily represented in a paper figure is the aspect of fluidity, or change within continuity. This healthy individual's life space should demonstrate spontaneous change in organization and objects. A hanging mobile might better represent this aspect, if one could occasionally add or subtract objects from the mobile, change the color of the objects, or occasionally make a slight change in the length of the strings and wires connecting them. One might further imagine each hanging object in the mobile as being magnetic with a positive and negative pole, thus exerting attracting and repelling forces of various degrees on other hanging objects, creating dynamic movement. The line from which such a mobile would hang would pass through the higher values and the self.

We will return to this graphic analogue of the individual as we discuss the impact of increasing levels of pathological processes on the person. The concepts depicted in this figure and several related ones that follow it are numerous but simple. Take the time to try empathically to feel how a balanced life like this one is from the inside. (It may be useful to return to the sequence of figures several times while reading this [chapter]. They may also be useful visual aids in educating patients and their families.)

Our healthy individual, in managing the life space to meet his or her needs, has a good chance of beginning to achieve what Maslow called *self-actualization.* Maslow explained human development as a movement from basic need fulfillment (motivation) to the pursuit of higher needs (metamotivation). His view of needs is hierarchical in the conceptual and social senses. Conceptually, the achievement of functioning based on higher needs and values is dependent on achieving those lower on the pyramid. Figure 25.2 shows this stepwise relationship between need achievement and self-actualization as a pyramid, where each level rests on the achievement of lower levels of need-related functioning.

Society has often been compared to a pyramid. From the standpoint of

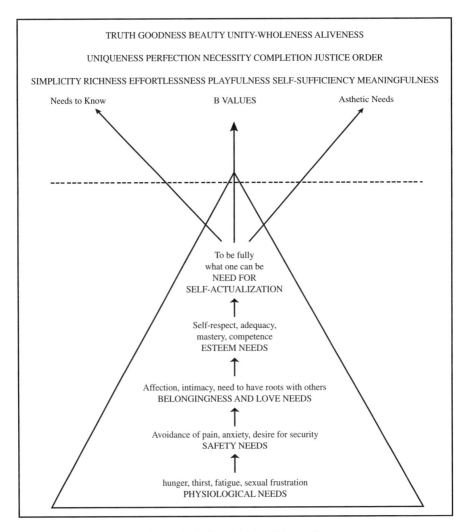

Figure 25.2. Maslow's need hierarchy

need achievement, only a minority of individuals, at the pinnacle of the social pyramid, are able to spend their energies and resources in pursuit of higher goals and values. Most of humanity throughout history has been primarily engaged in meeting basic needs, or what Maslow called *D-needs*, or deficiency needs. Individuals at this level of functioning invest most of their energies in tension reduction, relieving frustration, and avoiding deficiency or pain. In doing this they are highly motivated, pushed, or driven. The ultimate goal of mental health systems should be to turn this social hierarchy on end so that most individuals are able to strive for what Maslow called the *B-values,* or being values. As opposed to survival and self-maintenance, these people would be engaged in self-actualization, which is self-directed and highly individualized. It reverses the direction of motivation, that is, the person will increase tension or stress, often frustrating lower needs, to approach an individual vision or goal (metamotivation).

Along the vertical dimension of the needs hierarchy, one might trace a spectrum of freedom/unfreedom (see Table 25.1).

When a person's need-functioning is optimal, that is, in the self-actualizing arena, the person experiences him- or herself as a prime mover, a source of power, the fountainhead of events in his or her own life. The individual has many high quality, complete objects in his or her world and is fairly well balanced between other persons, useful and valued objects, ideas, and higher ideals. A balance is struck between continuity and change in the organization of the life space, resulting in a fluid order. Such individuals experience both freedom and liberty. They experience freedom in that they have the internal ability to separate themselves to a certain degree from immediate environmental contingency (from the demands of the moment or of persons and situations), thus being able to make choices based on the integrity of their own values. They experience liberty in that they have in mind a virtually limitless number of environmental options that they have the capacity either to act on immediately, or for which they can create life space for future

Table 25.1. Experience of Freedom/Unfreedom

Experience of self	Constraints on freedom
Being a prime mover: rich in objects, fluid order	Freedom limited only by higher values Freedom limited by law and social constraint Constraint by character limits and flaws
Being acted upon: few objects, or objects in disorder	Stuckness Unfreedom: life determined by internal drives and external forces

action. To return to our mobile representing the healthy life space, the self can act or be acted on anywhere in the life space, there is ample room for movement, and the position of the objects may move or shift somewhat, as directed by the self.

Pathological processes such as addiction or mental illness quickly result in lowering the level of needs that an individual can typically strive to satisfy. As need functioning decreases to the basic or deficiency level, the person experiences his or her self as being acted upon, a victim or pawn. Objects become fewer in number, poorer in quality, and there is less of a balance among persons and things. Ideas and ideals become either absent or irrelevant. The order in the life space is either atrophied and rigid, or overly fragile and easily disrupted. Freedom is quickly lost to undermined values and the habit of immediately reacting to or manipulating the current environment for rapid need gratification. Liberty may, ironically, appear to increase at first, due to the loss of prohibitions and inhibitions, but ultimately, at the lower levels of needs-related functioning, no liberty exists. *Stuckness* connotes the sense of being caught, mired down—as if in mud or quicksand—that accompanies the loss of freedom and liberty and the loss of balance in the life space. The parts of the mobile are losing magnetic charge, and no wind is stirring in the room. When a person's sense of agency is stuck, order is perceived as oppressive, allowing little space for free will, or, as the existentialists have pointed out, order is felt to have no inherent sense but is felt to be "thrown" or randomly (and unjustly) determined. The goal of both substance abuse treatment and treatment for psychopathology is to help individuals to move toward higher levels of the experience of freedom and to establish or re-establish balance and fluid change in the life space. This process is called *recovery* and is experienced as a movement up the hierarchy in Table 25.1. Movement down this hierarchy is the experience of the process of relapse.

The Psychiatric Severity Dimension

Let us take a closer look at the two pathological processes from which we are to help our patients to recover in dual diagnosis work and see how this phenomenological picture changes as these processes influence the life space. Table 25.2 outlines the levels of severity of psychopathology ranging from low to high. These are the levels most often referred to in the psychological literature. Although psychodynamic meanings are implied, the severity dimension here is fairly useful across theoretical formulations. The different

Table 25.2. Levels of Severity of Psychopathology

Self experience	Severity of psychopathology
Being a prime mover: rich in objects, fluid order	Self-actualizing
	Normal
	Stress and adjustment reactions
Being acted upon: few objects, or objects in disorder	Neurotic
	Narcissistic
	Borderline
	Psychotic
	Florid psychotic

levels reflect differences in ego strength, adequacy of coping skills and mechanisms, structural level, range of behavioral freedom, and other ways of viewing optimal versus dysfunctional states and behaviors. The different categories reflect the typical psychological functioning of an individual, so that, for example, a person who is typically in the personality disordered spectrum of functioning may be psychotic for brief periods under stress, or display only mildly neurotic symptoms under pacific conditions.

At the top of the hierarchy is the high functioning individual characterized by reason, effective living, creativity and productivity, and spontaneous, modulated emotional reactions. The normal individual is usually described as being adequately adapted, free of crippling emotionality. Neurotics are not so lucky. Psychological factors often intrude on their emotional and cognitive functioning, which is typified by conflict, usually in specific sectors of living. The character-disordered individual demonstrates a pervasive pattern of impaired adjustment, deficient coping skills, and affective disruption or rigidity with usually intact reality testing and unimpaired perception. Such a person usually has a warped or severely limited interpretation of reality. The psychotic individual has lost close tracking of the external and internal environments. Behavior is usually disorganized, inappropriate, and inept. Affect is typically extreme, blunted, or inappropriate. In a florid psychosis, these psychotic traits are extreme, unremitting, and often unresponsive to medication or other intensive treatments.

When we superimpose this hierarchical dimension of increasing psychopathology over Maslow's hierarchy of needs, we find a close parallel between the level of psychopathology and the level of needs to which the individual's functioning is related. In turn, this need functioning level is parallel to the number, organization, and fluidity of relationships to objects in the person's phenomenal world, which together constitute his or her experience of freedom/determinism. As graphically represented earlier, the normal individual lives in a world of many things, persons, ideas, and ideals. The normal individual has a balanced relationship with these objects and with the self. These relationships are orderly, and the individual has a sense of spontaneity, leading to a fluidity or sense of flow among the various aspects of his or her phenomenal field. On the opposite extreme, the floridly psychotic individual's world is populated with few objects rigidly related, or with no really complete objects, but a multitude of distorted shadow objects. Such individuals have great difficulty even achieving a basic deficiency level of need-oriented functioning. We must return to similar descriptions in order to typify the most severe levels of the addictive disorders.

The Addiction Severity Dimension

Table 25.3 outlines the levels of severity of the addictive process disorders. The description, which is my integration of terms often used in the literature on substance abuse with my own experience, follows no single source or authority.

At the lowest level of severity is rational use of substances. The most obvious example is following a physician's orders for a psychotropic medication, or following a physician's or pharmacist's advice in choosing and taking over-the-counter medication. Cannabis use for glaucoma or morphine for hospice care are fairly clear examples.

The next level of severity is controlled, socially appropriate use. On this level, social and emotional factors are strongly present in the type, amount, frequency, and effects of the used substance. Obviously, local sociocultural norms determine what is appropriate to some extent. The qualifier *controlled* is added because when levels and patterns of use are within socially acceptable ranges but beyond an individual's personal control, a different pathologi-

Table 25.3. Levels of Severity of Addictive Processes

Self experience	Severity of addictive process
Being a prime mover: rich in objects, fluid order	Rational use of substances
	Controlled, appropriate use
	Insidious dependence
	One trial dependence
Being acted upon: few objects, or objects in disorder	Substance abuse
	Symptomatic dependence (Characterological dependence)
	Compulsive, accelerating addiction
	Psychotic addiction

cal level has occurred. The two levels discussed so far are subpathological, but they present a context of use that may offer the opportunity for a pathological development. The threats come from three possible sources: external change, internal change, and interactions between external and internal events. External events may cause a change in the individual's physical, emotional, or social status quo. Subtle changes in these spheres may be due almost exclusively to the effects of the substance. More commonly, perhaps, synergistic effects among subtle changes in both internal and external status begin a potentiated emergent process: the addictive process.

Examples of the next level of severity, insidious dependence, are easy to find. An insidious dependence on a drug or substance develops slowly and without blatant early warning signs. The social drinker begins to have occasional party binges more than a few times a year. The cocktail to relax becomes two or three. A pathological process has been switched on that may or may not escalate. A decrease in freedom, perhaps imperceptible at first, has occurred. Dependence on caffeine and nicotine is usually held at this level. Alcohol and cocaine dependencies are less often stabilized indefinitely.

Near this level of severity is a somewhat rare form called one-trial dependence. This kind of dependence fits the age-old stereotype of the heroin addict who injects an unsuspecting victim who becomes immediately hooked for life on the first use or first trial of the drug. This popular view is more relevant to Dr. Jekyll and Mr. Hyde movies than to the typical addictive process, even for most highly addictive substances. One-trial dependence does occur, however, most often in alcoholism and is typified by a family history of alcoholism, early onset, and vivid memories of the first experience with the drug (especially the physiological and arousal level aspects of the effects) usually accompanied by an inability to experience emotion normally. (One-trial dependence often appears in the use of free-base or crack cocaine, although closer examination usually reveals that many trials of the drug occurred within several hours and days of first use, with no perception of an ego-alien addictive process at this early stage). One may hypothesize that this form of addiction has a very strong neuropsychological basis, probably related to the physiology of emotion and arousal. One-trial dependence is the pathological reverse, for example, of learning from one trial not to consume poisonous or emetic substances, and as such may be explainable by basic neuropsychological principles.

Substance abuse is placed further down on the severity scale than these forms of dependence. The rationale is that substance abuse is the lowest level of severity defined by social, personal, or other problems related to the drug.

Any use of an illegal drug that may lead to arrest and loss of freedom and reputation is a form of substance abuse, at least from one point of view. Substance abuse is often a precursor to dependence, but dependence may occur with relatively few effects on the social and psychological functioning of the individual. However, in even mild dependencies a time bomb is often set ticking that may result in devastating physical and psychological effects, sometimes after a decade or more.

Symptomatic dependence is the level of severity that begins clearly to indicate a relationship with the levels of psychopathology already discussed. A dependence that is symptomatic of an individual's emotional problems, persistent conflicts, or pervasive pattern of self-defeating behaviors and thoughts is often qualitatively different from the levels of severity discussed to this point. However, chronic substance abuse is also usually symptomatic of these problems and often results in symptomatic dependence.

Individuals whose psychopathology is in the neurotic or character-disordered spectrum often demonstrate symptomatic dependence or symptomatic substance abuse. In this form of addiction, the uncontrolled, inappropriate use of substances is clearly a psychological defense against, an expression of, or an instrumental reaction to another psychopathological process. Notice that this is not often the case in insidious or one-trial dependence. Physiological factors and the psychophysiology of one-trial learning and allergic reactions are more relevant to these forms of substance dependence than are emotional and psychological factors. Examples of symptomatic dependence are often depicted in movies and novels about addicts and alcoholics who are strong characters. *The Great Santini,* Richard Pryor's *JoJo Dancer, Your Life Is Calling,* and the film *Clean and Sober* may be viewed as depicting individuals suffering from symptomatic dependence.

The difference between these two forms of dependence—symptomatic versus insidious—may be established by a history of accompanying life problems and, more importantly, by response to substance abuse treatment. Because addiction affects judgment through denial, insidious dependencies are often not initially addressed by the individual, but when they are challenged in treatment, the treatment progresses with relatively few obstacles. This is not true with symptomatic dependence; emotional factors independent of withdrawal, deconditioning, and relearning are constant obstacles to sobriety and continued progress. The urge to use the drug of choice does not follow simple, easily identified environmental, physiological, or even emotional cues. The patient's problems involve two related pathological processes. Using a film example noted above, the female character in *Clean and*

Sober has an addiction that is more clearly symptomatic than that of the male character, who responds to treatment and begins to show recovery in social and personal functioning. The female character conforms only temporarily to the demands of the residential treatment setting, but upon discharge returns to her previous lifestyle, where emotional and interpersonal stress are managed through drug use.

Symptomatic dependence is the only category in this typology that by definition is a kind of dual diagnosis problem. Other kinds of addiction, including the two more severe forms discussed below, may not be the result of interactive pathological processes. The term *characterological dependence* might also be considered for what is here called symptomatic dependence. However, symptomatic dependence is preferred because although it usually involves long-standing, personality-based problems in an addictive process, personality disorders are not always present when an addictive process is related to a symptom or symptom cluster. Dependence may be the result of a more isolated symptomatic process such as reactive or endogenous depression, anxiety, or poorly suppressed anger due to adjustment reactions, or other emotional and behavioral patterns. These symptoms or symptom clusters are not necessarily organizing or disorganizing *principles,* or self-reinforcing pathological processes, as is always the case in personality disorders. Of course, although these more isolated symptoms may point to structural weakness in a personality, they do not in themselves constitute a pathological process in the personality. A later chapter [of *Therapy of the Substance Abuse Syndromes*] addresses in depth the role of personality or character disorders in dual diagnosis problems.

Once dependence is established, its slope or acceleration is an important factor to consider. The levels of severity discussed to this point may be remarkably stable over many years. There may be a plateau of symptoms, dosage, and frequency of use. Personal impairment may be stable or may show a gradual, steady, predictable decline. To the nonclinical observer, disruption is apt to be noticeable only in selected areas of the individual's life. In a compulsive, accelerating addiction, the pattern is one of steep increasing decline, a rolling snowball gathering momentum. This may occur after only a brief period of substance use, such as in the case of one-trial dependence on free-base crack cocaine. Such an addictive course may have only a very brief stable period before converting into a rapidly escalating picture. The term *compulsive* reflects this level of an addiction's similarities with the compulsive disorders: the rigidity, absence of freedom, and the counterintentionality of behavior that typifies the compulsions. Needless to say, this level of severity is also accompanied by an obsessive preoccupation with the drug.

The term *addiction* indicates the most severe levels of substance use because of its connotations of loss of control and freedom and its associations with disease, evil, or the demonic, meanings that point to the radical isolation from or disruption of the self that occurs in addiction. Unlike the less severe levels of dependence, with addiction, no aspect of the person's life space is left fully intact. A compulsive, accelerating addiction may grow out of any of the other levels of severity due to an externally or internally based change in the person's life adjustment. It may be seen as the acceleration phase of the other types of addiction. Compulsive, accelerating addictions cause mental health problems but are not necessarily the result of them. Special sensitivity to the drug, constitutional predisposition to addictive processes, or harrowing sociocultural conditions (as seen, for example, in the native American alcoholic) may result in this level of severity without an accompanying level of severe and pervasive psychopathology. Individuals who are typically normal in their psychological functioning do acquire addictions in this compulsive, accelerating range. However, now that our culture is more open to obtaining help and less moralistic about addictions, persons with lower levels of psychopathology may be less apt to allow this pattern to continue uninterrupted without seeking treatment.

If left to continue on this accelerating course, a person may develop what may be called a psychotic addiction. Reality testing, not simply judgments about reality, are grossly distorted. All thinking and emotion are in the service of the addictive process, to the extent that they are not disrupted by the effects of the drug itself. The best example of psychotic addiction is the cocaine addict who continually picks lint from carpets, upholstery, or garments, thinking that these light-colored specks are particles of the drug of choice. The same individual may dream only of drug use episodes. He or she may break down in tears following moments of great excitement and joy after viewing a news report about the confiscation of several tons of the drug in a warehouse as though this event was a great personal find followed by a great personal loss. Also, this individual might become more aroused about using from a bag from which another addict has just overdosed in front of him, thinking that it is "great stuff" and that his "friend" is no longer a competitor for the drug. This extreme distortion of cognition, affect, behavior, and values may be equitably described as psychotic.

This condition does not most often occur with individuals whose typical psychological functioning is psychotic. Individuals suffering from psychotic levels of psychopathology usually do not have the financial resources to maintain this level of drug use, or the interpersonal skills needed to conduct the complex social exchanges required to accelerate to this level. This addiction level is more common in severe character disorders than with normal or neurotic individuals.

In discussing levels of severity in the addictive process, drugs of choice are treated here as equivalent. But, this is only partially true. As noted, some drugs are more apt to lead to certain levels of addictive severity. Some drugs cannot be used in a rational or controlled, appropriate manner. PCP is the best example. Since its cumulative effects are unpredictable and the desired individual dosage and short-term effects are indeterminable, there can be no rational use of PCP. It could be argued that this is true of all hallucinogens.

Another aspect of the nonequivalence of drug of choice has to do with long-term physiological and neurological effects, which differ from drug to drug. Typical courses have been established for various addictions, especially alcoholism (Jellinek 1963). We will return to differences in the effects of drug of choice and some possible reasons why individuals choose different drugs in our later discussion of assessment, treatment, and the personality disorders.

Parallels in Experience and Needs Motivation

When we mentally superimpose this hierarchical dimension of increasing severity of addictive process over Maslow's hierarchy of needs, we find (as we did for psychopathology) a rough parallel between the level of addiction and the level of needs-related functioning. Again, we see the decline in freedom, the increase in being determined and driven, as severity increases. With each level, the number and quality of objects, their orderliness, and the balance between fluidity and rigidity in their interrelations are increasing disrupted. Figures 25.3, 25.4, and 25.5 depict common outcomes of both pathological processes.

They also represent experiential or phenomenological states, or ways of viewing the self from the inside, which often recur cyclically in both the addictive and psychopathology processes. The titles of each of these figures have two adjectives that describe the sense of self from the inside. The first adjective is the *less severe* form of the experience, the second is the *more severe*. The depleted (depressed or debased) self, the inflated (or grandiose) self, and the detached (or schizoid) self are both pathological endpoints and phase components in a pathological process over time. We describe them in the order in which they usually occur in the addictive process, which is somewhat more predictable than for increasing severity levels of psychopathology.

Although these processes and experiences of the self are described in a certain order here, they should be viewed as opponent processes in the manner of those described by Solomon (1977, 1980). In later chapters [of *Therapy of the Substance Abuse Syndromes*] we describe the opponent process theory to discuss the linked and roughly opposite physiological effects of a drug and the cyclical patterns of opposite mental status findings in psychotic conditions (especially bipolar disorder), as well as the learning history involved in the development of addiction and mental illness. At this point, let us describe opponent processes as interactive states, conditions, or processes that are related to each other like the two faces of a coin. When one aspect of the opponent process is dominant or apparent, the others build in intensity until the coin is flipped over and another assumes the dominant role, and the initially dominant process subsides into the background or does not appear at all, blocked from sight by the new dominant process.

We have used movement up and down in Table 25.1, for example, to describe the opponent processes of recovery and relapse, two complex processes each consisting of biological, psychological, and social aspects. The two processes are linked in the individual, who can no more permanently eliminate the unwanted one than a coin can avoid having a flip side. Using these graphs to show an opponent process relationship, the grandiose self (usually accompanied by the drug high) is in the opponent process with the debased self (usually accompanied by withdrawal and craving). They are two sides to the same coin of the addiction cycle. Here, the analogy of the coin faces breaks down, because several processes are in opposition to one another simultaneously in the same individual, much as the six sides of a die are opposed to one another in coming up on each throw.

In addictive processes where other pathological factors are only mildly present these opponent ways of viewing and feeling about the self may be experienced in a rough causal sequence. The usual pattern is for a healthy self first to become depleted or depressed. (This depletion process may be the result of recurrent drug abuse or the long-term effects of an insidious addiction.) In this experience (Figure 25.3), the self is pushed out of the life space by other objects, especially the drug of choice. There is less available space for motion, and fewer well-developed objects are in mutual interaction with the self. In Figure 25.3, the self is smaller in size and being acted on by other objects. The shadow of a sense of higher values is depicted as no longer effective in centering the self.

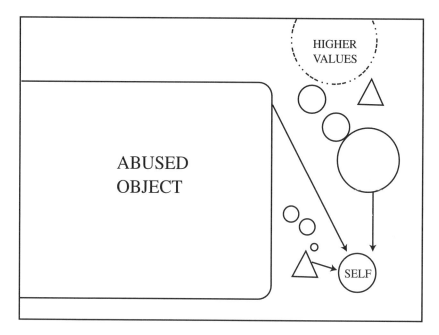

Figure 25.3. Depressed/depleted self

The depleted individual turns to the artificial defense of the drug of choice to avoid, interrupt, or obscure this process. The drug use results in a chemical bolstering of the self, and an inflated sense of self is established. In this experience, depicted in Figure 25.4, the self is primary, although not centered in the space, which may become occupied almost as much as the abused object as by the self. Others are either pushed out of the life space or are perceived as a means to obtaining the drug. The bolstering aspect of the abused object eventually becomes an internalized aspect of the self. This is both partially caused by and has later implications for the object relations (in the psychodynamic sense) and later object choices of the individual.

When the drug's physiological opponent process becomes dominant (creating the opposite effect to why the drug is sought) or when the chemical defense fails for some other reason, the self is left debased. This is not only experiential debasement or depletion but adaptive skills, stability of mood, physical health, and social networks have also been depleted or destroyed. The individual again seeks the abused substance both out of need for a defense against this depletion, and as a result of physiological or psychological craving for the substance that is, for the most part, separate from the drug's psychosocial or defensive function. The inflating process is intensified.

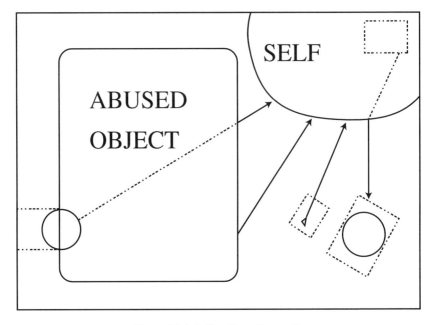

Figure 25.4. Inflated/grandiose self

In the case of the manic, the grandiose schizophrenic, the user of uppers when high, or the manipulative addict or character-disordered individual in a victorious phase, or a gambler on a winning streak, the self has become inflated and overextended, and balance is totally lost. There may be many objects, but they have lost normal object value because of the absence of order or a reasonable sense of relative priority among the objects. The individual becomes grandiose, that is, an unrealistic sense of victory over external threats and/or dysphoric feelings or self-perceptions is established.

Often the pathological experience of detachment (Figure 25.5) is an aspect of grandiosity but just as often it is a separate experience or component that is an opponent to others in the process. The individual separates him- or herself radically from the environment, except for those aspects related to the substance and securing it. Emotional indifference to life experiences, and even detachment from one's own experience—depersonalization—may occur. At times this is a predictable experiential effect of the drug of choice and may provide a motive for preferring it over other substances of abuse. As the addictive cycle repeats, the individual becomes further detached from reality until there is a breakdown in the ability to function, or until the individual is motivated to enter treatment by severe losses or threats of loss. At the worst stage of detachment, the hang wire of our mobile has been severed; the

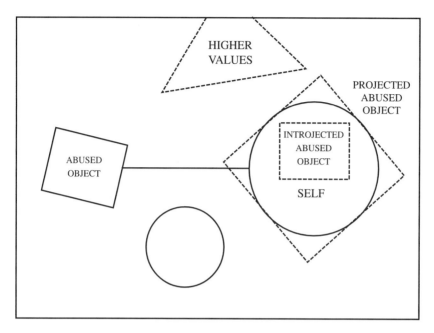

Figure 25.5. Detached/schizoid self

person has become literally debased, that is, the ground or basis for the self to grow and manage the life space has been undermined to the point of collapse.

Of course, the scenarios presented here greatly simplify this single causal path in the addictive process, which in most cases is the result of several causal lines intersecting and interacting, as in all the movements and eventual placements of the faces of two dice tossed in the air and coming up seven. Although the situation is even more complex for the experiential and causal sequences in mental illnesses, nonetheless, similar vicious cycles are clearly present. In Figures 25.3, 25.4, and 25.5, it is easy to recognize experience of the self in the major mental disorders of depression, mania, and schizophrenia. In each of these disorders, an individual resorts to less effective behaviors or less developed levels of psychological functioning in response to perceived threats until the self has become depleted, depressed, grandiose, or detached. Inflation, deflation, and detachment are decompensating processes of both addiction and mental illnesses.

These schematic concepts have been forged in the context of understanding dual diagnosis disorders, that is, treatment failures with severe psychopathology and addiction. For a similar scenario of self experiences that explains normal experience though the dialectical interaction of experience modes, the reader is referred to Ogden's (1989) description of the depressive, paranoid–schizoid, and autistic–contiguous positions as the basis for personality functioning. Ogden builds on the work of both Klein and Bion in his formulation of self states or modes. Klein had identified the paranoid–schizoid and depressive positions as phenomenologically distinct states, which, although tied to developmental stages, continue to exist as two different ways of relating to inner and outer reality throughout the lifespan (Klein 1952, Segal and Bell 1991). Klein viewed the more primitive paranoid–schizoid mode dominant only under stress-induced regression in normal adults. Ogden added a third state or position (the autistic–contiguous mode) to that scenario, to be discussed later at greater length in reference to the schizoid personality and the detached/schizoid position. Although this writer was unaware of Ogden's scenario while developing the addictive cycle positions, a good deal of similarity appears in the two theoretical constructions. Such serendipity does not necessarily indicate validity for the constructs, but it does suggest that both schematic systems reflect a relatively high degree of correspondence to clinical experience with primitive states and also suggests a general coherence of each system within the currently accepted paradigms of psychodynamic understanding and treatment.

A DEVELOPMENTAL VIEW

The experience of the self has so far been examined in its adult manifestation during addiction. The roots of these experiences, however, are in infancy before the development of speech. Wilson and colleagues (1989) have proposed failures in self-regulation as central to what they call the addictive self. These failures have their origin in preverbal experience that is incorporated into the adult person as a preverbal core self. In their view, misattuned caregiver–infant dyads produce the troublesome experiences of self that are later replicated by the addict through use of the drug and for which the drug is a home remedy. As in the model presented by Wilson and co-workers (1989), the life space figures presented here assume that addicts fall less into clear types—for example, the threefold typology by Adams (1978) of addictions based on symbiotic urges, management of rage, and failing self-cohesion—than into cyclical or related experiences of self that are expressed in the addiction. The reader familiar with dynamic views of the self, or the developmental psychology of the self, should view the presented figures as basic pathogenic positions in infant experience, as well as adult manifestations of the self under conditions of addiction. For the depressed self, the drug helps to unify experience after separation from the caregiver. In the grandiose self, the drug pacifies a globalized sense of threatened bewilderment related to traumatic overstimulation of the infant. For the schizoid self, the drug supports denial of interpersonal dependency related to failed attachment and repressed rage. The individual addict will emphasize one of these aspects of self over others, based on the predominant pathological position in the mixture of the addict's early parent–infant experiences. This will have important implications for the course of the addict's illness, its persistence during treatment, and the drug or drugs of choice.

Only the parallels to developmental Self psychology for the most extreme experiences of self are outlined here. For later developmental periods, the experiences may appear similar to the milder pathological views of self portrayed here and may have periodic or helixical relationships to the expression of more primitive infant experience. For example, the grandiose self may be seen in an addict's attempt to manage higher-level oedipal anxieties, that is, as an expression of power–powerlessness in response to disillusionment and defeat from an uncompromising, controlling parent.

Placing the two pathological processes on parallel scales in one table, as in Table 25.4, and keeping Maslow's hierarchy in mind as a contextual backdrop, we can mentally draw the lines across from typical level of psychopathology to typical level of addictive process, with the threatened need being the rough link between the two processes. The lines are not drawn in on the table, however, to remind us that these relationships are only probable or suggestive and that many exceptions are apt to occur, such as the normal individual who gets caught in a chronic, compulsive, accelerating addictive pattern. Having the two processes on one table suggests that there are parallel effects from similar levels of severity on these two dimensions, that the two processes move toward common experiential and clinical endpoints, and that they have similar process components. The table also implies the possibility of interaction, reciprocity, or synergism that is really the key concept in dual diagnosis work. We have seen that at least one type of addiction—symptomatic addiction—must presuppose a related psychopathological condition or process.

WHY THE CHICKEN-OR-EGG-FIRST QUESTION IS ABSURD

One exciting aspect of the dual diagnosis problem is its ability to bring up some crucial theoretical dilemmas and controversies in new, practical, and

Table 25.4. Combined Levels of Severity and Maslow's Hierarchy

Psychopathology	Threatened need	Addiction
Self-actualizing	B-values	Rational use
		Controlled appropriate use
	Self-actualization	
Normal		Insidious dependence
	Efficacy	
Neurotic		
		One trial dependence
	Self-esteem	Symptomatic dependence (Characterological dependence)
Narcissistic		
	Belonging	
		Compulsive, accelerating addiction
Borderline	Identity	
	Emotional regulation	
Psychotic		
	Safety needs	
Florid psychotic		Psychotic addiction
	Physiological needs	
———— General failure of life supports ————		

important ways. For example, dual diagnosis issues have sparked the call for a substance abuse axis as part of the *DSM* diagnostic system and for officially recognized primary-secondary distinctions in dual diagnosis cases. These are both practical expressions of the chicken-or-egg-first discussion that is sometimes introduced in dual diagnosis problems. The question goes: Did the substance use cause the psychosis or depression, or did the psychopathology lead to the addiction? Such questions often seem academic, but the related question of what is the proper primary and secondary diagnosis has significant practical implications for treatment, administration, research, and reimbursement, as well as for theory construction. Some of the habits of thought that go unexamined and become codified in our diagnostic systems, and from there influence case formulation and treatment to the detriment of some cases, are brought to the light of closer examination by seminal problems and recurrent failures such as those found in the dual diagnosis patient group. In the language of Thomas Kuhn (1970), the dual diagnosis problem is useful because it challenges some aspects of our current paradigm of diagnosis, nosology, and etiology.

BIASES IN REASONING

The absurdity and humor in the chicken-or-egg first question come from its ability to point out the limitations inherent in demonstrative reasoning. This mode of thought, as useful as it may be, has led to many of the conceptual dead ends in dual diagnosis work. Demonstrative reasoning has been the dominant mode of thought in Western evidence and argument since Aristotle. Demonstrative thinking is based on premises that are assumed to be true. Their opposites are, therefore, necessarily false. In order to arrive at logical truth through demonstrative reasoning, all of one's premises must be true. Even when this is the case, logical truth may not jibe with reality. As Hegel put it, "The tree of life is greener than the tree of thought."

In the chicken-or-egg-first dilemma, one of the major premises, common to many attempts at demonstrative reasoning, is, in fact, a fallacy. The premise is that what comes first in a line of actions causes the subsequent elements on the line. The first form of the question assumes that temporal priority can determine causal priority and sequence, or, put simply, if the chicken was here first, it laid (caused) the egg, or if the egg was here first, it hatched (caused) the chicken. The tack-on assumption is one of value; the earlier cause takes priority, is more important, and presents the first term in a critical path that flows sequentially. This premise and its tacked-on value can easily be called into question, but that will not be necessary for the purposes of discussing theory building in dual diagnosis problems.

The second major premise in the chicken-or-egg-first question has proved more problematic for thinking about the problems at hand in this discussion, and it is a premise that is essential to demonstrative reasoning per se. The premise is that major categories are discrete and mutually exclusive. A chicken cannot be an egg and an egg cannot be a chicken when we attempt to reason demonstratively about chickens and eggs in a system of causality. Since we are aware that every chicken is in a sense an egg at an end point of development and every egg is a chicken at a starting point of development (and that we can view either alternatively as either end point or starting point), questions of causality in the sense of priority become absurd. Instead of straining at the logical absurdity in which we would be cornered if we had to live with exclusive discrete categories, we can concentrate on the biological process called reproduction (or at a higher level, emergent evolutionism), which defines the developmental relationship between chickens and eggs.

Demonstrative reasoning is preferred for thinking about problems where a small number of premises may be determined to be either clearly true or false and where categories are clearly established. It is at its best in situations where the categories of interest may be considered fixed, discrete, and relatively unchanging, and where all members of a category share the same defining features, that is, situations that meet the requirements of monothetic categorization. Recent revisions in the substance use disorders and personality disorders nosologies presented in the *DSM III-R* demonstrate a movement away from this kind of categorization. The new approach is toward dimensional models that place cases on a continuum or range of severity, and toward polythetic models of categorization, where no single feature or index is required for inclusion in a category. In polythetic models, categorization is accomplished by determining the overall goodness of fit of a case to a prototype description (Cantor et al. 1980). The approach advanced in this book combines dimensional and polythetic–prototypic methods.

Dialectical Thinking: A Corrective Alternative

The kind of thought that is designed to examine causality within process development (where categories are not exclusive or discrete) is called dialectical reasoning. It allows us to see many aspects of the dual diagnosis conundrum as aspects of both pathologies; it allows us to see both pathologies as mutually causal of each other and creating mutual effects in the form of what Bandura (1978) has called reciprocal determinism. From a dialectical point of view, once the dual diagnosis syndrome has emerged, each symptom is part of both processes, although it may be viewed in any given clinical formulation from the alternative perspective of one process or the other.

Another strength of the dialectical way of thinking is that it accounts for the phenomena of emergence. In demonstrative reasoning, a thing cannot be and not be at the same time. If it exists, it cannot be in two discrete, mutually exclusive categories. Dialectical reasoning allows for events and dynamics to be viewed as becoming or emerging. Events and dynamics can be latent, tending toward being in one category or the other, but in neither or both, depending on the emphasis given by the thinker based on the work at hand at the time an idea is struck. For the reader familiar with this century's developments in the world view stemming from modern physics, dialectical thinking will appear as nothing new, although it may not have been considered as applying to the dual diagnosis problem. It should be noted that theory constructed from either mode of thought must be operationalized to have scientific meaning and must be at least in part amenable to empirical tests.

Such tests must result in modifications to the theory, and possibly to total rejection of the theory itself.

The interested reader should view Rychlak's (1981) careful analysis of some of the philosophical issues that influence psychological theory building. Also, Sabelli and Carlson-Sabelli (1989) offer an integrated approach to psychiatry based on a elaboration of dialectical thought that they refer to as process theory. They follow Jung in emphasizing the union of opposites in dialectical change, but they add the general systems theory approach to levels of organization or description by stressing the flow of information from one level of organization to another.

For the current discussion, the point to be made is that cognitive biases related to exclusive reliance on demonstrative reasoning about dual diagnosis problems have influenced how these patients were dealt with clinically, and explain, in part, why theory construction in this area has been so slow getting off the ground. Effort was wasted on deciding whether patients were primarily addicts or primarily mentally ill, reflecting a need for discrete mutually exclusive categories and failing that, attempting to create a neat linear causal line of priority between the two disorders. Now we recognize that for a large group of patients, both disorders are primary, both are mutually causative. Effort had been spent on the order in which the two processes developed to determine treatment priority and etiology, when often both processes emerge from the same biological, psychological, and social vulnerabilities.

Perhaps the best reason for discussing these philosophical issues is that the prior equals primary fallacy has influenced treatment strategies in dual diagnosis work. In early dual diagnosis programs, patients in this population were treated in logical sequences, in part determined by the urgency criteria established by the management demands such patients place on a treatment setting. Patients first were detoxed chemically in a controlled environment, with the expectation that they would turn into normal mental patients. Then they were treated chemically for psychopathology or given psychotherapy. This consecutive or sequential strategy did not work after the acute phase of treatment, because of the interactive–emergent nature of the dual diagnosis problem.

The current dominant treatment strategy is more enlightened since the diagnostic problem has been partially resolved. Psychotic or severely depressed patients are now provided substance abuse interventions after brief detoxification and medication of the most severe psychotic symptoms in a simultaneous strategy. It is as though their two diagnoses were being treated separately but at the same time in the same person. This may at first appear to be an exaggeration of current practice and the criticism of it as a straw man, but the examination of a few treatment plans for the dually diagnosed will reveal this kind of strategy in spades. Addiction-related problems and mental health-related problems are listed separately with sensible, internally coherent interventions aimed at each. Such plans may be comprehensive and built on solid assessments. When all the various players are competent and well trained and communicating optimally, a level of integration of these interventions may approach the kind of reciprocal strategy advanced here. Minkoff (1989), for example, refers to the parallel treatment of the two disorders and parallel recovery processes.

The approach to treatment strategy suggested here and explored later in this book is described as reciprocal treatment for substance abuse and psychiatric disorders. It involves a concerted effort to determine the degree of interaction or reciprocal causality of the two pathological processes, the points of reciprocal origin and reciprocal current effects of the processes, as well as the relative extremity of the two processes on the other key dimensions outlined above. With this information, intervention plans aimed at both utilizing and decreasing the reciprocal interactions are constructed. The two disordering processes are both untangled and resolved simultaneously. The recovery process for one disordering process is used reciprocally to reinforce the other recovery process and to undermine and depotentiate the other pathological process.

Reciprocity as a Key Dimension in Dual Diagnosis Work

At this point, let us take a closer look at the kind of relationships that can exist between the two disorders of interest. Table 25.5 outlines the relatedness of the two pathological processes as a severity dimension in dual diagnosis cases. At the lowest level of relatedness, the two disorders are merely coexistent, presumably noninteractive. The fact that the two disorders are present only serves to give the individual more problems with which to deal. At the next level, the disorders are interactive, but do not spring from a common or related cause. The disorders are more closely related when causally linked in a linear manner (one causes or mediates the other, but not vice versa), or when their influences are additive or geometric in the same direction toward increasing pathology and life problems. At this interactive level, we are more interested in potentiating or catalytic interactions because they result in

Table 25.5. The Relatedness Dimension

Degree of relationship addiction	Qualities of effects/causes
Co-existence	Cumulative impact of effects
Interacting effects	Additive impact of effects
Linear mediation	Catalytic relationships
	Geometric increase in effects
Linear causal paths	
	Shift in thresholds needed for change in quality
Reciprocal mediation	
	Potentiation of effects
	Complementarity
Reciprocal causal paths	
	Emergent qualities
	Synergism
	Cyclicity
Reciprocal reinforcement with reciprocal causal paths	
	Opponent process relationships
Dynamic unity	Union of opposites
	Synthesis
	Stable, self-replicating helix

the most virulent cases; however, inhibiting, moderating, and depotentiating interactions also routinely occur.

When causal paths from origins to effects cannot be clearly separated for the two pathological processes, they are reciprocal in nature, and, again, it is, of course, the reciprocally reinforcing processes that become our focus. In fact, the syndromes discussed in this book could be classified as one set in a class of emergent or synergistic disorders that are typified by potentiating interactions among established disordering processes. If one takes the easily supported position that most psychiatric disorders are primarily due to these synergisms, then the most appropriate class in which to place the disorders might be that of second order psychiatric synergisms.

One way to make the synergism between two processes more tangible is to return to the analogy of the throw of two dice in gambling games and examine some trivia about how dice are constructed and played. We have stated that the two processes are in a sense opponent or alternative processes within the same individual. As with a die or a coin, the alternative sides or processes are not necessarily logical opposites. The numbers on opposing sides of a die are not logical opposites, but they are logically linked, they always sum to a total of seven. When two dice are thrown together, they are so constructed that when seven has been thrown, the side facing down of each die is the value of the face that is up on the other die. In relation to the number seven, the upper faces of the dice are in exact complementarity to the lower faces that are not shown. This bit of trivia provides an analogous route to appreciating opponents, opposites, complementarity, and logical connectedness in interaction of the kind encountered in the relationship among processes discussed in this book. One might further capture the destructive process of addictive and psychopathological vicious cycles together by imagining each cycle of drug use and decompensation as a throw of two dice. When the number seven is thrown, a certain combination, the potentiating effects of the two illnesses, creates a win for illness and a big loss for the individual. In these situations, decompensation is much more severe, more persistent, and the cycle itself is exponentially ingrained. This process is called potentiation, or synergism. The process can most clearly be seen when two drugs interact in the same individual, having a stronger impact than the additive effects of either one alone; in effect, one plus one equals more than two. The dice become increasingly loaded in favor of a loss for the person and an increase in the pathological process.

The analogy to a game of chance, a gambler's game, is more than germane to the issues here. Gambling is addictive in part because of the opponent processes related to winning and losing, and to the illusion of control or predictability involved in games of chance. Both of these factors have impacts on the perception and experience of self that result in an addictive process and relapses from recovery. The disorders discussed in this book have been termed reciprocally reinforcing psychiatric substance abuse syndromes. In the term *reciprocally reinforcing,* reinforcing means both additive in effects as well as denoting the wearing the groove process that the term has in behavioral theory, that is, both processes make behaviors related to the other process more likely to occur and to occur with greater intensity. Finally at the most extreme end of the continuum of relatedness, the disorders become a synthetic unity or negative synergism, a closely tied vicious knot. This is not the usual outcome of increasingly interrelated pathological processes. This is because, as we have seen, at various severity levels on either pathological process, the individual bottoms out, becoming incapable of maintaining the required behaviors to continue an addiction beyond a certain level of severity. Beyond this level, they are likely to suffer a collapse of the self into chaotic behavior and experience and to reenter the health care delivery system in a way that usually restricts their personal liberty. A prolonged synthesis of these two disorders that is allowed to go uninterrupted would probably be terminated by death due to somatic pathology related to drug use, drug overdose, severe withdrawal, severe neglect of self-maintenance behaviors, suicide, or provoked homicide. As in most opponent processes or oppositions, the most intense forms of the processes are incompatible, whereas the mild to moderate forms exist together in helixical stable states.

SYNDROME DEFINITIONS AND SUBPOPULATIONS

Let us return to our attempt to clarify the terms used throughout this book. We outline broad categories of dual diagnosis work. In addition, a tentative typology of dual diagnosis cases is presented. The supportive evidence for this typology is provided in later chapters [of *Therapy of the Substance Abuse Syndromes*], but enough of the required conceptual elements have already been covered to allow a preview in the form of a general typology.

DEFINING CATEGORIES OF DUAL DIAGNOSIS WORK

Programs or approaches to mental health or substance abuse that tend to avoid working with the other set of problems may be called single focus programs, or approaches. Not all approaches with a dual focus will be called dual diagnosis work, that implies at the least an integrated approach. Single focus and dual focus approaches are effective and most cost effective for many, perhaps most, patients. However, this [chapter] primarily focuses on patients who are usually treatment failures without highly integrated, reciprocal approaches, approaches which can profitably inform treatment with less extreme cases in single focus or dual focus programs, but may not be required for their effective treatment.

The term *dual diagnosis work* is broad enough to include the categories of treatment that follow. Within the confines of this [chapter], the term refers to the integrated, reciprocally focused assessment, treatment, or management of patients who have a level of severity on the psychopathology dimension of character disorder or higher, as well as a level of severity on the addiction severity dimension of substance abuse or higher. The term is limited to these cases, primarily because all substance abuse treatment approaches are prepared to deal with the psychological and emotional problems of normal and mildly neurotic individuals. Acknowledging this by way of practice, mental health workers will typically refer normal or mildly neurotic individuals with substance abuse or higher levels of severity of addictive disorders to an addictions professional. At levels of psychiatric severity below the character disordered individual, simultaneous treatment of the individual by two treatment approaches is often effective, even without the coordinated, integrated, reciprocal approach offered here.

Almost in contradiction to the distinction stated above, however, we include in the category of dual diagnosis work the treatment of individuals who have some focal psychological or emotional problem that is not typical of their normal functioning, but that has in effect lowered their typical level of functioning temporarily to a level more common to disturbed individuals. Although patients with one or a few focal problems are usually dealt with successfully in many single focus or dual focus approaches, they may be helped more effectively and in less time by using dual diagnosis strategies. Like their deficits, the dual diagnosis work to be done with these patients is focal and relatively time limited. Table 25.6 outlines the categories of dual diagnosis work with respective sub-populations.

Symptomatic and Characterological Dependence Work

Working with individuals who show either a clear symptomatic relationship between an isolated emotional or psychological concern and a substance use problem (e.g., a brief reactive depression complicating treatment for alcohol binges) can be called symptomatic dependence work, or symptomatic substance abuse work. Symptomatic dependence work is based on an understanding of how the individual's use of substances is related to his or her focal problem or symptom.

The Greek root of the word *character* means to inscribe, as in engraving or carving. It connotes both depth and the signification of unique meaning to a written mark. Characterological problems are more deeply ingrained than isolated focal problems. When characterological problems, or character defects, are more pervasive, are incorporated in the personality, and intertwined in its organization (resulting in narrow, rigid, or invariant ways of viewing, judging, and acting), a personality disorder is present. Usually, distortions in

Table 25.6. Categories of Dual Diagnosis Work

| | | Major symptom clusters | |
| | Anxiety | Cognition and context | |
	Arousal/reward	Dominance of affect	Sociability and identity
N E U R O T I C	Stress-related problems	Anxiety disorders	Socio-cultural problems
	Sexual problems	Reactive depression	Pathogenic beliefs
	Schizoid personality	Dysthymia	Dependent personality
C D H I A S R O A R C D T E E R R E D	Psychopathic personality	Depressive personality	Obsessive compulsive personality
	Organic personality (sensation seeking)	Histrionic personality Passive aggressive personality	Narcissistic personality Avoidant personality Paranoid personality
		Borderline personality	
P S Y C H O T I C	Schizophrenia (negative signs)	Organic personality (affective features)	Organic personality (cognitive disruption or paranoia) Schizophrenia (positive signs)
		Major depression (psychotic features)	Paranoid disorder Paranoid schizophrenia
		Bipolar disorder	

the interpretation of life events and the demonstration of poor judgment surrounding such events have resulted in an accumulation of lost opportunities, undeveloped skills, and self-defeating routines. In addition, these cases have been resistant to routine methods of substance abuse treatment. Characterological dependence work is based on understanding the relationship between the substance abuse or dependence and the focal psychiatric problems and character deficits of that individual. The pathological experiences of the self and their developmental precursors described earlier in this chapter are of special relevance in this kind of work, because the self is essentially impaired and will fuel the addictive cycle more than in other cases where the core self is relatively intact. Obviously, more severe personality disorders and addictive problems will require more intense, longer term interventions. As with the categories of work to follow, the cases that demonstrate a high degree of reciprocity between the two pathological disorders will require the most intensity and length and will require a more reciprocal focus in the treatment.

Dual Diagnosis Work with the Major Mental Disorders

Several major mental disorders may result in psychotic levels of functioning. The most common of these major mental disorders are the schizophrenias, the paranoid disorders, and the major affective disorders, which include bipolar disorder and major depression. (Individuals with a single episode of major depression may be clinically distinct from those with recurrent episodes. These individuals may also not fit the treatment failure context of the usual dual diagnosis case.) Many intoxicants, including drugs of abuse, produce effects that mimic the syndrome patterns of one or several major mental disorders, depending on dose or conditions of administration, thus providing chemical models for these illnesses. As this would lead us to suspect, biological factors often are most prominent in driving these disorders. Working with individuals with major mental disorders is the primary focus of this book. The most severe, chronic forms of the major mental disorders, accompanied by a high degree of reciprocity with an addictive disorder comprise the greatest challenge in dual diagnosis work. This is especially true if, as is often the case, the individual also has a concurrent personality disorder.

Table 25.6 groups the major mental disorders into three categories: those in which regulation of mood is the predominant feature, those in which modulation of arousal level and various stimulus thresholds are implicated, and those in which the dominant features involve the production and quality of thought, especially in regard to the control of both the context and range of associations among mental contents.

Dual diagnosis work with the major mental disorders is based on understanding the relationship between the abused substance and the symptom pattern of the major mental illness, which together often implicate both a biological and a psychosocial function for the drug use. There will often be a complementary or opponent process biological relationship between the major mental disorder and the psychopharmacology of the abused drug, or the addictive function more generally. The escape hypothesis of addiction (that individuals use psychoactive substances to avoid certain feelings and thoughts) and the self-medication hypothesis of drug use (that individuals use drugs because of their positive effects on the symptoms of psychopathology) will often be relevant. The stimulus control hypothesis of addiction (that individuals use drugs to increase, decrease, and modulate the level of impinging environmental and internal stimulation) will be useful in some cases. The object relations and self experiences discussed earlier (always crucial in characterological dependence work) will be important for almost every case.

Reciprocally Reinforcing (Synergistic) Psychiatric Substance Abuse Syndromes

The synergistic syndromes may be defined as existing in those cases in which a chronic, severe psychiatric disorder is reciprocally causal and reinforcing of a substance use disorder resulting in a synergistic pathological process. One or both disorders will increase the severity and frequency of the other. One or both disorders will persist after an acute phase. One or both disorders will demonstrate cyclicity, often with the cycles between the disorders being linked in a helixical, progressive manner. Causal lines for both disorders will at times converge. Symptom clusters in the two disorders will either converge or demonstrate a complementary relationship, or an opponent process relationship. Opponent relationships or complementary relationships will often cycle alternatively between cause and effect among three major components and their subcomponents: a major mental disorder and its consequences, a personality disorder and its consequences, and an addictive disorder and its consequences. Consequences are, of course, social, cognitive, emotional, somatic, and spiritual.

CLUES TO TREATMENT STRATEGIES

The recovery process for the two disorders, of which formal treatment is only one aspect, may also be described as occurring in degrees of relatedness as in the manner outlined for the disordering processes. The proximal goal for dual diagnosis work is not to completely resolve either pathological process in itself, but to create a synergistic relationship between the two recovery processes while interrupting the synergistic relationship between the pathological processes.

To make this process more tangible, let us use an analogy taken from modern tourism and informed by pre-Socratic Greek philosophy. Heraclitus claimed that one can never step into the same river twice, pointing out the flux of nature and the pervasiveness of change within continuity. Modern tourists to Brazil spend an expensive and dangerous day on a river, actually the confluence of two mighty rivers. One of them is a bright yellow color from the mineral-rich clays that the river rakes from the highlands. The other is a dark sepia, from the rain forests thick with humus and lavish with microbial and vegetable life. The two rivers converge, and instead of mixing immediately, they flow in a parallel position for several miles before spilling into yet another river and dispersing toward the ocean. Two rivers become a third, but before doing so they remain intact, interactive, and potentiating of one another, each itself in constant change and flux. The analogy to the dual diagnosis problem is that both disorders are in constant flux, both make up one river, yet both are separate.

Since these are pathological rivers, or processes, our goal will be to go beyond marveling at their interaction and unity. We will use our understanding of their origins and interrelationships to redirect them both, make them less destructive, and, if possible, use the energy stored in them to some positive benefit to the individual. This process of marshalling these energies for life enhancement is called recovery. We will want to work on this confluence from both banks (recovery from addiction, recovery from mental illness) simultaneously, as in the parallel treatment approach cited above, but we will do so with a more informed strategy. When possible, we will ford the river at the areas that are shallowest and slowest moving, and narrowest at both banks, and those points will determine the placements of our dams and channels (interventions) to a great extent.

We may find it necessary at times to go upstream, to the sites above the confluence, to understand why they have intersected and, perhaps, to influence where they will meet to our advantage, if possible.

REFERENCES

Adams, J. W. (1978) Psychoanalysis of Drug Dependence. The Understanding and Treatment of a Particular Form of Pathological Narcissism. N.Y., Grune & Stratton.

Bandura, A. (1978) The self system in reciprocal determinism. American Psychologist, 33, 344–358.

Cantor, N., E. Smith, R. French, & J. Mizzich (1980) Psychiatric diagnosis as prototype categorization. Journal of Abnormal Psychology, 89, 181–193.

Jellinek, E. (1963) The Disease Concept of Alcoholism. New Haven, CT, Hilldale.

Klein, M. (1952) The origins of transference. In The Writings of Melanie Klein (Vol. 3): Envy, Gratitude and Other Works. London, Hogarth.

Kosten, T., & H. Kleber (1988) Differential diagnosis of psychiatric comorbidity in substance abusers. Journal of Substance Abuse Treatment, 5, 201–206.

Kuhn, T. (1970). The Structure of Scientific Revolutions. Chicago, University of Chicago Press.

Lewin, K. (1936). Principles of Topographical Psychology. New York, McGraw-Hill.

Maslow, A. (1962) Toward a Psychology of Being. New York, Harper & Row.

Maslow, A. *(1964)* Religions, Values and Peak-Experiences. *New York, Viking.*

Maslow, A. *(1970)* Motivation and Personality, *2nd ed. New York, Harper & Row.*

Maslow, A. *(1971)* The Farther Reaches of Human Nature. *New York, Viking.*

McKelvy, M., J. Kane, and K. Kellison *(1987) Substance abuse and mental illness: Double trouble.* Journal of Psychosocial Nursing and Mental Health Services, *25,* 20–25.

Minkoff, K. *(1989) An integrated treatment model for dual diagnosis of psychosis and addiction. Hospital and Community* Psychiatry, *40, 1031–1036.*

Ogden, T. H. *(1989)* The Primitive Edge of Experience. *Northvale, NJ, Jason Aronson.*

Regier, D., M. Farmer, D. Rae et al. *(1990) Comorbidity of mental disorders with alcohol and other drug abuse. Results form the Epidemiologic Catchment Area (ECA) Study.* Journal of the American Medical Association, *264, 2511–2528.*

Rychlak, J. *(1981)* Personality and Psychotherapy: A Theory-Construction Approach. *2nd ed. Boston, Houghton Mifflin.*

Sabelli, H. *(1989)* Union of Opposite: A Comprehensive Theory of Natural and Human Processes. *Lawrenceville, VA. Brunswick.*

Sabelli, H., and Carlson-Sabelli, L. *(1989) Biological priority and psychological supremacy: A new integrative paradigm derived from process theory.* American Journal of Psychiatry, *146, 1541–1551.*

Segal, H., and Bell, D. *(1991) The theory of narcissism in the work of Freud and Klein. In* Freud's On Narcissism: An Introduction. *Ed. by J. Sandler. New Haven, CT, Yale University Press.*

Solomon, R. *(1977) An opponent-process theory of acquired motivation: The affective dynamics of addiction. In* Psychopathology: Experimental Models. *Ed. by J. D. Maser and M. E. Seligman, San Francisco: Freedman.*

Solomon, R. *(1980) The opponent-process theory of acquired motivation: The costs of pleasure and the benefits of pain.* American Psychologist, *35, 691–712.*

Wilson, A., S. D. Passik, J. Faude, J. Abrams, & E. Gordon *(1989) A Hierarchical model of opiate addiction: Failures of self-regulation as a central aspect of substance abuse.* Journal of Nervous and Mental Disease, *177, 390–399.*

References

Abraham, K. 1908. *The psychological relations between sexuality and alcoholism. In* Selected Papers on Psychoanalysis. *New York: Brunner/Mazel.*

Alcoholics Anonymous World Services. 1952. Twelve Steps and Twelve Traditions. *New York: Alcoholics Anonymous World Services.*

————. 1957. Alcoholics Anonymous Comes of Age. *New York Alcoholics Anonymous World Services.*

————. 1976. Alcoholics Anonymous. *New York Alcoholics Anonymous World Services.*

Alexander, F., and T. M. French. 1946. Psychoanalytic Therapy. *New York: Ronald Press.*

American Psychiatric Association. 1980. Diagnostic and Statistical Manual of Mental Disorders. *3d ed. Washington, D.C.: American Psychiatric Association.*

————. 1994. Diagnostic and Statistical Manual of Mental Disorders. *4th ed. Washington, D.C.: American Psychiatric Association.*

Armor, D. J., J. M. Polich, and H. B. Stambul. 1978. Alcoholism and Treatment. *New York: Wiley.*

Bateson, G. 1973. Steps to an Ecology of Mind. *Frogmore, England: Pallidan.*

Bean, M. H. 1981. *Denial and the psychological complications of alcoholism. In* Dynamic Approaches to the Understanding and Treatment of Alcoholism. *Ed. M. H. Bean and N. E. Zinberg. 55–96. New York: Free Press.*

————. 1986. *Psychopathology produced by alcoholism. In* Psychopathology and Addictive Disorders. *Ed. R. E. Meyer. 334–45. New York: Guilford.*

Becker, J. T., and R. F. Kaplan. 1986. *Neurophysiological and neuropsychological concomitants of brain dysfunction in alcoholics. In* Psychopathology and Addictive Disorders. *Ed. R. E. Meyer. 263–92. New York: Guilford.*

Bell, C. M., and E. J. Khantzian. 1991. *Contemporary psychodynamic perspectives and the disease concept of addiction: Complimentary or competing models?* Psychiatric Annals *21: 273–81.*

Berthelsdorf, S. 1976. *Survey of the successful analysis of a young man addicted to heroin.* Psychoanalytic Study of the Child *31: 165–91.*

Blatt, S. J., C. McDonald, A. Sugarman, and C. Wilber. 1984. *Psychodynamic theories of opiate addiction: New directions for research.* Clinical Psychology Review *4: 159–89.*

Blume, S. B. 1983. *The disease concept of alcoholism today.* Journal of Psychiatric Treatment and Evaluation *5: 471–78.*

————. 1986. *Alcoholism rehabilitation: Getting involved—A memoir of the 60s. In* Alcohol Interventions: Historical and Sociocultural Approaches. *Ed. D. L. Strug, S. Priyadarsini, and M. M. Hyman. 75–80. New York: Haworth Press.*

————. 1987. *Compulsive gambling and the medical model.* The Journal of Gambling Behavior *3: 237–47.*

Brickman, B. 1988. *Psychoanalysis and substance abuse: Toward a more effective approach.* Journal of the American Academy of Psychoanalysis *16: 359–79.*

Brook, J. S., P. Cohen, M. Whiteman, and A. S. Gordon. 1992. *Psychosocial risk factors in the transition from moderate to heavy use or abuse of drugs. In* Vulnerability to Drug Abuse *Ed. M. Glantz and R. Pickens. 359–88. Washington, D.C.: American Psychological Association.*

Brown, B. S. 1990. *The growth of drug abuse treatment systems. In* Handbook of Drug Control in the United States. *Ed. J. A. Inciardi. 115–38. New York: Greenwood Press.*

Brown, C. L. 1950. *A transference phenomenon in alcoholics.* Quarterly Journal of Studies on Alcohol *11: 403–9.*

Brown, H. P. 1992. *Substance abuse and the disorders of the self: Examining the relationship.* Alcoholism Treatment Quarterly *9: 1–27.*

Brown, S. 1985. *Treating the Alcoholic: A Developmental Model of Recovery. New York: Wiley.*

Brunswick, A. F., P. A. Messeri, and S. P. Titus. 1992. *Predictive factors in adult substance abuse: A prospective study of African American adolescents. In* Vulnerability to Drug Abuse. *Ed. M. Glantz and R. Pickens. 419–72. Washington, D.C.: American Psychological Association.*

Byck, R., ed. 1974. Cocaine Papers by Sigmund Freud. *New York: Stonehill.*

Cadoret, R. J. 1992. *Genetic and environmental factors in initiation of drug use and the transition to abuse. In* Vulnerability to Drug Abuse. *Ed. M. Glantz and R. Pickens. 99–114. Washington, D.C.: American Psychological Association.*

Cahn, S. 1970. The Treatment of Alcoholics: An Evaluative Study. *New York: Oxford University Press.*

Chafetz, M. E. 1959. *Practical and theoretical considerations in the psychotherapy of alcoholism.* Quarterly Journal of Studies on Alcohol *20: 281–91.*

Chafetz, M. E., and R. Yoerg. 1977. *Public health treatment programs in alcoholism. In* Treatment and Rehabilitation of the Chronic Alcoholic. *Ed. B. Kissin and H. Begleiter. 593–614. New York: Plenum.*

Chan, A. W. 1991. *Multiple drug use in drug and alcohol addiction. In* Comprehensive Handbook of Drug and Alcohol Addiction. *Ed. N. S. Miller. 87–113.*

Chein, I., D. L. Gerard, R. S. Lee, and E. Rosenfeld. 1964. The Road to H: Narcotics, Delinquency, and Social Policy. *New York: Basic Books.*

Chelton, L. G., and W. C. Bonney. 1987. *Addiction, affects and self object theory.* Psychotherapy *24: 40–46.*

Chodorkoff, B. 1964. *Alcoholism and ego function.* Quarterly Journal of Studies on Alcohol *25: 292–99.*

Clark, L. P. 1919. *A psychological study of some alcoholics.* Psychoanalytic Review *6: 268–95.*

Colletti, G., T. J. Payne, and A. A. Rizzo. 1987. *Treatment of cigarette smoking. In* Developments in the Assessment and Treatment of Addictive Behaviors. *Ed. T. D. Nirenberg and S. A. Maisto. 243–75. Norwood, N.J.: Ablex.*

Cook, C. C. 1988a. *The Minnesota model in the management of drug and alcohol dependency: Miracle, method or myth? Part I: The philosophy and the programme.* British Journal of Addiction *83: 625–34.*

———. 1988b. *The Minnesota model in the management of drug and alcohol dependency: miracle, method or myth? Part II: Evidence and conclusions.* British Journal of Addiction *83: 735–48.*

Daniels, G. E. 1933. *Turning point in the analysis of a case of alcoholism.* Psychoanalytic Quarterly *2: 123–30.*

DeLeon, G. 1986. *The therapeutic community for substance abuse: Perspectives and approaches. In* Therapeutic Communities for Addictions: Readings in Theory, Research, and Practice. *Ed. G. DeLeon and J. T. Ziegenfuss. 5–18. Springfield, Ill.: Charles C. Thomas.*

———. 1990. *Treatment Strategies. In* Handbook of Drug Control in the United States. *Ed. J. A. Inciardi. 115–38. New York: Greenwood Press.*

DeSoto, C. B., W. E. O'Donnell, L. J. Allred, and C. E. Lopes, 1985. *Symptomatology in alcoholics at various stages of abstinence.* Alcoholism *9: 505–12.*

Dodes, L. M. 1988. *The psychology of combining dynamic psychotherapy and alcoholics anonymous.* Bulletin of the Menninger Clinic *52: 283–93.*

———. 1990. *Addiction, helplessness, and narcissistic rage.* Psychoanalytic Quarterly *59: 398–419.*

Dole, V. P., and M. E. Nyswander. 1967. *Heroin addiction: A metabolic disease.* Archives of Internal Medicine *120: 19–24.*

Dowling, S., ed. 1995. The Psychology and Treatment of Addictive Behavior. *Madison, Conn.: International Universities Press.*

Fillmore, K. M., and D. Kelso. 1987. *Coercion into alcoholism treatment: Meanings for the disease concept of alcoholism.* Journal of Drug Issues *17: 301–19.*

Fingarette, H. 1988. Heavy Drinking. *Berkeley: University of California Press.*

Fitzgerald, H. E., R. A. Zucker, and H. Y. Yang. 1995. *Developmental systems theory and alcoholism: Analyzing patterns of variation in high-risk families.* Psychology of Addictive Behaviors *9: 8–22.*

Freud, S. 1895. *On the grounds for detaching a particular syndrome from neurasthenia under the description anxiety neurosis. In* Standard Edition. *Vol. 3. 90–115.*

———. 1898. *Sexuality in the etiology of the neuroses. In* Standard Edition. *Vol. 3. 263–85.*

———. 1919. *Lines of advance in psychoanalytic therapy. In* Standard Edition. *Vol. 17. 159–68.*

Freudenberger, J. J. 1976. *The professional and the human services worker: Some solutions to the problems they face in working together.* Journal of Drug Issues *6: 273–82.*

Gallant, D. M. 1987. Alcoholism: A Guide to Diagnosis, Intervention and Treatment. *New York: W. W. Norton.*

Glasscote, R. M., T. F. Plaut, D. W. Hammersley, F. J. O'Neill, M. E. Chafetz, and E. Comming. 1967. *The Treatment of Alcoholism: A Study of Programs and Problems. Washington, D.C.: Joint Information Service.*

Glassman, A. H. 1993. *Cigarette smoking: Implications for psychiatric illness.* American Journal of Psychiatry *4: 546–51.*

Goodman, A. 1993. *The addictive process: A psychoanalytic understanding.* Journal of the American Academy of Psychoanalysis *21: 89–105.*

Gorski, T. 1986. Alcohol Health and Research World *11, no. 1: 11, 63.*

Graham, A., and C. Glickauf-Hughes. 1992. *Object relations and addictions: The role of "transmuting externalizations."* Journal of Contemporary Psychotherapy 22: 21–33.

Grant, B. F., and R. P. Pickering. 1996. *Comorbidity between DSM-IV alcohol and drug use disorders: Results from the National Longitudinal Alcohol Epidemiologic Survey.* Alcohol Health and Research World 20: 67–72.

Grant, I., and R. Reed. 1985. *Neuropsychology of alcohol and drug abuse. In* Substance Abuse and Psychopathology. *Ed. A. I. Alterman. 289–341. New York: Plenum.*

Greenson, R. R. 1967. The Technique and Practice of Psychoanalysis. Vol. 1. *New York: International Universities Press.*

Hall, S. M., R. F. Munoz, V. I. Reus, and K. L. Sees. 1993. *Nicotine, negative affect, and depression.* Journal of Consulting and Clinical Psychology 61: 761–66.

Hanson, M., T. H. Kramer, and W. Gross. 1990. *Outpatient treatment of adults with coexisting substance use and mental disorders.* Journal of Substance Abuse Treatment 7: 109–16.

Hayman, M. 1966. Alcoholism: Mechanism and Management. *Springfield, Ill.: Charles C. Thomas.*

Hester, R. K., and W. R. Miller, eds. 1995. Handbook of Alcoholism Treatment Approaches. 2d ed. *Boston: Allyn and Bacon.*

Hofmann, F. G. 1975. A Handbook on Drug and Alcohol Abuse: The Biomedical Aspects. *New York. Oxford University Press.*

Hubbard, R. L., M. E. Marsden, J. V. Rachal, H. J. Harwood, E. R. Cavanaugh, and H. M. Ginzburg. 1989. Drug Abuse Treatment: A National Study of Effectiveness. *Chapel Hill: University of North Carolina Press.*

Humphreys, K. 1993. *Psychotherapy and the twelve step approach for substance abusers: The limits of integration.* Psychotherapy 30: 207–13.

Imhof, J. E. 1991. *Countertransference issues in the treatment of drug and alcohol addiction. In* Comprehensive Handbook of Drug and Alcohol Addiction. *Ed. N. S. Miller. 931–46.*

Jaffe, J. H., and M. Kanzler. 1979. *Compulsive smoking—A new look at an old addiction. In* Addiction Research and Treatment: Converging Trends. *Ed. E. L. Gottheil, A. T. McLellan, K. A. Druley, and A. I. Alterman. 69–78. New York: Pergamon Press.*

Jessor, R., and S. L. Jessor. 1978. *Theory testing in longitudinal research on marihuana use. In* Longitudinal Research in Drug Use. *Ed. D. Kandel. 41–70. Washington, D.C.: Hemisphere-Wiley.*

Johnson, B. 1992. *Psychoanalysis of a man with active alcoholism.* Journal of Substance Abuse Treatment 9: 111–23.

———. 1993. *A developmental model of addictions, and its relationship to the twelve step program of alcoholics anonymous.* Journal of Substance Abuse Treatment 10: 23–34.

Jones, E. 1953. The Life and Work of Sigmund Freud. *New York. Basic Books.*

Kalb, M., and M. S. Propper. 1976. *The future of alcohology: Craft or science?* American Journal of Psychiatry 134: 641–45.

Kandel, D. B. 1978. Longitudinal Research in Drug Use. *Washington, D.C.: Hemisphere-Wiley.*

Kandel, D. B., and J. A. Logan. 1984. *Patterns of drug use from adolescence to young adulthood: I. Periods of risk for initiation, continued use, and discontinuation.* American Journal of Public Health *74: 660–666.*

Kaplan, E. H. 1977. *Implications of psychodynamics of therapy in heroin use: Borderline case. In* Psychodynamics of Drug Dependence. *NIDA Research Monograph, no. 12. Ed. J. D. Blaine and D. A. Julius. 126–41.*

Kaufman, E. 1978. *The relationship of social class and ethnicity to drug abuse. In* A Multicultural View of Drug Abuse. *Ed. D. E. Smith, S. M. Anderson, M. Buxton, N. Gottlieb, William Harvey, and Tommy Chung. 158–64. Cambridge, Mass.: G. K. Hall & Co./Schenkman.*

———. 1994. Psychotherapy of Addicted Persons. *New York: Guilford.*

Keller, D. S. 1996. *Exploration in the service of relapse prevention: A psychoanalytic contribution to substance abuse treatment. In* Treating Substance Abuse Theory and Technique. *Ed. F. Rotgers, D. S. Keller, and J. Morgenstern. 84–116. New York: Guilford.*

Keller, E. L. 1992. *Addiction as a source of perversion.* Bulletin of the Menninger Clinic *56: 221–31.*

Keller, M. 1972. *On the loss-of-control phenomenon in alcoholism.* British Journal of Addiction *67: 153–66.*

———. 1976. *The disease concept of alcoholism revisited.* Journal of Studies on Alcohol *37: 1694–1717.*

———. 1986. *The origins of modern research and responses relevant to problems of alcohol. In* Research Advances in Alcoholism and Drug Problems. *Vol. 10. Ed. L. T. Kozlowski, H. M. Annis, H. D. Cappell, F. B. Glaser, M. S. Goodstadt, Y. Israel, H. Kalant, E. M. Sellers, and E. R. Vingilis. 157–70. New York: Plenum.*

Khantzian, E. J. 1978. *The ego, the self, and opiate addiction: Theoretical and treatment considerations.* International Review of Psychoanalysis *5: 189–98.*

———. 1980. *The alcoholic patient: An overview and perspective.* American Journal of Psychotherapy *34: 4–19.*

———. 1981. *Some treatment implications of the ego and self disturbances in alcoholics. In* Dynamic Approaches to the Understanding and Treatment of Alcoholism. *Ed. M. H. Bean and N. E. Zinberg. 163–88. New York: Free Press.*

———. 1985. *Psychotherapeutic interventions with substance abusers—The clinical context.* Journal of Substance Abuse Treatment *2: 83–88.*

———. 1987. *A clinical perspective of the cause-consequence controversy in alcoholic and addiction suffering.* Journal of the American Academy of Psychoanalysis *15: 521–37.*

Khantzian, E. J., K. S. Halliday, and W. E. McAuliffe. 1990. Addiction and the Vulnerable Self: Modified Group Therapy for Substance Abusers. *New York: Guilford Press.*

Knight, R. P. 1937a. *Dynamics and treatment of chronic alcohol addicts.* Bulletin of the Menninger Clinic *1: 233–50.*

———. 1937b. The Psychodynamics of chronic alcoholism. *Journal of Nervous and Mental Disease* 86: 538–48.

———. 1938. *The psychoanalytic treatment in a sanatorium of chronic addiction to alcohol.* Journal of the American Psychoanalytic Association *3: 1443–48.*

Kohut, H. 1971. The Analysis of the Self. *New York: International Universities Press.*
———. 1977. The Restoration of the Self. *New York: International Universities Press.*
Krystal, H. 1974. *The genetic development of affects and affect regression.* Annual of Psychoanalysis 2: 98–126.
———. 1975. *Affect tolerance.* Annual of Psychoanalysis 3: 179–219.
———. 1978. *Self representation and the capacity for self care.* Annual of Psychoanalysis 6: 209–46.
Krystal, H., and H. A. Raskin. 1970. Drug Dependence: Aspects of Ego Function. *Detroit: Wayne State University Press.*
Kurtz, E. 1979. Not God: A History of Alcoholics Anonymous. *Center City, Minn.: Hazelden Educational Services.*
Laundergan, J. C. 1982. Easy Does It: Alcoholism Treatment Outcomes, Hazelden and the Minnesota Model. *Center City, Minn.: Hazelden Educational Services.*
Leeds, J., and J. Morgenstern. 1996. *Psychoanalytic theories of substance abuse.* In Treating Substance Abuse: Theory and Technique. *Ed. F. Rotgers, D. S. Keller, and J. Morgenstern. 68–83. New York: Guilford.*
Lender, M. E., and J. K. Martin. 1987. Drinking in America. *New York: Free Press.*
Levin, J. D. 1987. Treatment of Alcoholism and Other Addictions: A Self-Psychology Approach. *New York: Jason Aronson.*
Levin, J. D., and R. H. Weiss, eds. 1994. The Dynamics and Treatment of Alcoholism: Essential Papers. *Northvale, N.J.: Jason Aaronson.*
Levinson, V. R. 1985. *The compatibility of the disease concept with a psychodynamic approach in the treatment of alcoholism.* Alcoholism Treatment Quarterly 2: 7–24.
Lewis, J. A., R. Q. Dana, and G. A. Blevins. 1994. Substance Abuse Counseling. 2d ed. *Pacific Grove, Calif.: Brooks/Cole.*
Little, M. I. 1981. Transference Neurosis and Transference Psychosis. *New York: Jason Aronson.*
Mack, J. E. 1981. *Alcoholism, A.A., and the governance of the self.* In Dynamic Approaches to the Understanding and Treatment of Alcoholism. *Ed. M. H. Bean and N. E. Zinberg. 128–62. New York: Free Press.*
Mann, G. A. 1991. *History of theory of a treatment for drug and alcohol addiction.* In Comprehensive Handbook of Drug and Alcohol Addiction. *Ed. N. S. Miller. 1201–1212. New York: Marcel Dekker.*
Mannheim, J. 1955. *Notes on a case of drug addiction.* International Journal of Psychoanalysis 36: 166–73.
Margenau, E. 1984. *Resolution of a drug abuse problem in a private practice setting.* Journal of Contemporary Psychotherapy 14: 167–77.
Margolin, A., and T. R. Kosten. 1991. *Opioid detoxification and maintenance with blocking agents.* In Comprehensive Handbook of Drug and Alcohol Addiction. *Ed. N. S. Miller. 1127–41.*
Martlatt, G. A., and J. R. Gordon, eds. 1985. Relapse Prevention: Maintenance Strategies in the Treatment of Addictive Behaviors. *New York: Guilford.*
Masson, J. M. 1985. The Complete Letters of Sigmund Freud to Wilhelm Fliess, 1887–1904. *Cambridge: Harvard University Press.*
McCullough, W. E. 1952. *A two-year survey of alcoholic patients in a California state hospital.* Quarterly Journal of Studies on Alcohol 13: 240–53.

Milam, J. R., and K. Ketcham. 1981. Under the Influence: A Guide to the Myths and Realities of Alcoholism. *Seattle: Madrona Publications.*

Milhorn, H. T. 1990. Chemical Dependence: Diagnosis, Treatment, and Prevention. *New York: Springer-Verlag.*

Miller, N. S. 1991. *Nicotine addiction as a disease. In* The Clinical Management of Nicotine Dependence. *Ed. J. A. Cocores. 66–78. New York: Springer-Verlag.*

Miller, N. S., and D. Toft. 1990. The Disease Concept of Alcoholism and Other Drug Addiction *(pamphlet). Center City, Minn.: Hazelden.*

Miller, P. M. 1987. *Commonalities of addictive behaviors. In* Developments in the Assessment and Treatment of Addictive Behaviors. *Ed. T. D. Nireberg and S. A. Maisto. 9–30. Norwood, N.J.: Ablex.*

Moore, R. A. 1961. *Reaction formation as a countertransference phenomenon in the treatment of alcoholism.* Quarterly Journal of Studies on Alcohol *22: 481–86.*

Morgenstern, J., and J. Leeds. 1993. *Contemporary psychoanalytic theories of substance abuse: A disorder in search of a paradigm.* Psychotherapy *30: 194–206.*

Morgenstern, J., and B. S. McCrady. 1992. *Curative factors in alcohol and drug treatment: Behavioral and disease model perspectives.* British Journal of Addiction *87: 901–12.*

Nace, E. P. 1987. The Treatment of Alcoholism. *New York: Brunner-Mazel.*

———. 1993. *Inpatient treatment. In* Recent Developments in Alcoholism. *Vol. 11,* Ten Years of Progress. *Ed. M. Galanter. 429–51. New York: Plenum.*

Narrow, W. E., D. A. Regier, D. S. Rae, R. W. Manderscheid, and B. Z. Locke. 1993. *Use of services by persons with mental and addictive disorders.* Archieves of General Psychiatry *50: 95–107.*

Newcomb, M. D., E. Maddahian, and P. M. Bentler. 1986. *Risk factors for drug use among adolescents: concurrent and longitudinal analyses.* American Journal of Public Health *76: 525–31.*

New York State Office of Alcoholism and Substance Abuse Services. 1996. OASAS Cross-Training History Script. *New York State Office of Alcoholism and Substance Abuse Services.*

NIAAA. 1972. Alcohol and Alcoholism: Problems, Programs and Progress. *NIMH, DHEW. Publication number. HSM. 72-9127, Washington, D.C.: Government Printing Office.*

Noble, D. 1949. *Psychodynamics of alcoholism in a woman.* Psychiatry *12: 413–25.*

Nowinski, J., and S. Baker. 1992. The Twelve-Step Facilitation Handbook. *New York: Lexington.*

Orford, J. 1985. Excessive Appetites: A Psychological View of Addiction. *New York: Wiley.*

Panepinto, W. C., and L. Simmons. 1986. *Treating the illness, not the mandate: Techniques for successful referral, engagement, and treatment of alcoholic persons.* Alcoholism Treatment Quarterly *3: 37–48.*

Pattison, E. M., M. B. Sobell, and L. C. Sobell, eds. 1977. Emerging Concepts of Alcohol Dependence. *New York: Springer.*

Peele, S. 1984. *The cultural context of psychological approaches to alcoholism.* American Psychologist *39: 1337–51.*

Peele, S. 1989. Diseasing of America: Addiction Treatment Out of Control. *Boston: Houghton Mifflin.*

Pine, F. 1990. Drive, Ego, and Self. *New York: Basic Books.*

Plaut, T. F. 1967. Alcohol Problems: A Report to the Nation by the Cooperative Commission on the Study of Alcoholism. *New York: Oxford University Press.*

Radford, P., S. Wiseber, and C. Yorke. 1972. *A study of main-line heroin addiction: A preliminary report.* Psychoanalytic Study of the Child *27: 156–80.*

Radó, S. 1933. *The psychoanalysis of pharmacothymia.* Psychoanalytic Quarterly *2: 1–23.*

Rapaport, D. 1951. *The autonomy of the ego.* In The Collected Papers of David Rapaport. *Ed. M. M. Gill. 357–67. New York: Basic Books, 1967.*

Regier, D. A., W. E. Narrow, D. S. Rae, R. W. Manderscheid, B. Z. Locke, and F. K. Goodwin. 1993. *The de facto US mental and addictive disorders service system.* Archieves of General Psychiatry *50: 85–94.*

Robbins, B. 1935. *A note on the significance of infantile nutritional disturbances in the development of alcoholism.* Psychoanalytic Review *22: 53–59.*

Rogers, R. L., and C. S. McMillan. 1989. The Healing Bond: Treating Addiction in Groups. *New York: W. W. Norton.*

Rohsenow, D. J., R. Corbett, and E. Devine. 1988. *Molested as children: A hidden contribution to substance abuse.* Journal of Substance Abuse Treatment *5: 13–18.*

Rosen, A. 1981. *Psychotherapy and alcoholics anonymous: Can they be coordinated?* Bulletin of the Menninger Clinic *45: 229–46.*

Rosenfeld, H. A. 1960. *On drug addiction.* In Psychotic States. *128–43. London: Hogarth Press, 1965.*

———. 1964. *The psychopathology of drug addiction and alcoholism: A critical review of the psycho-analytic literature.* In Psychotic States. *217–52. London: Hogarth Press, 1965.*

Rotgers, F., D. S. Keller, and J. Morgenstern, eds. 1996. Treating Substance Abuse: Theory and Technique. *New York: Guilford.*

Sadava, S. W. 1987. *Interactional theory.* In Psychological Theories of Drinking and Alcoholism. *Ed. H. T. Blane and K. E. Leonard. 90–130. New York: Guilford.*

Savitt, R. A. 1954. *Extramural psychoanalytic treatment of a case of narcotic addiction.* Journal of the American Psychoanalytic Association *2: 494–502.*

Saxe, L., D. Dougherty, D. Esty, and M. Fine. 1983. The Effectiveness and Costs of Alcoholism Treatment. *Washington, D.C.: Office of Technology Assessment.*

Selzer, M. L. 1957. *Hostility as a barrier to therapy in alcoholism.* Psychiatric Quarterly *31: 301–5.*

Shea, J. E. 1954. *Psychoanalytic therapy and alcoholism.* Quarterly Journal of Studies on Alcohol *15: 595–605.*

Silber, A. 1959. *Psychotherapy with alcoholics.* Journal of Nervous and Mental Diseases *129: 477–85.*

———. 1970. *An addendum to the technique of psychotherapy with alcoholics.* Journal of Nervous and Mental Diseases *150: 423–37.*

Simmel, E. 1929. *Psychoanalytic treatment in a sanatorium.* International Journal of Psychoanalysis *10: 70–89.*

———. 1948. *Alcoholism and addiction.* Psychoanalytic Quarterly *17: 6–31.*

Simpson, D. D., and S. B. Sells. 1982. *Effectiveness of treatment for drug abuse: An overview of the DARP research program.* Advances in Alcohol and Substance Abuse *2: 7–29.*

Sobell, M. B., and L. C. Sobell. 1993. Problem Drinkers: Guided Self-Change Treatment. *New York: Guilford.*

Spiegel, E., and E. A. Mulder. 1986. *The anonymous program and ego functioning.* Issues in Ego Psychology *9: 34–42.*

Steiner, C. 1971. Games Alcoholics Play. *New York: Grove Press.*

Stone, L. 1954. *The widening scope of indications for psychoanalysis.* Journal of the American Psychoanalytic Association *2: 567–94.*

Strachan, J. G. 1971. Practical Alcoholism Programming: An Honorable Approach to Man's Alcoholism Problem. *Vancouver: Mitchell Press.*

Straus, R. 1976. *Problem drinking in the perspective of social change, 1940–1973. In* Alcohol and Alcohol Problems: New Thinking and New Directions. *Ed. W. J. Filstead, J. J. Rossi, and M. Keller. 29–57. Cambridge, Mass.: Balinger Publishing.*

Stuckey, R. F., and J. S. Harrison. 1982. *The alcoholism rehabilitation center. In* Encyclopedic Handbook of Alcoholism. *Ed. E. M. Pattison and E. Kaufman. 865–73. New York: Gardner Press.*

Tarter, R. E., and A. C. Mezzich. 1992. *Ontogeny of substance abuse: Perspectives and findings. In* Vulnerability to Drug Abuse. *Ed. M. Glantz and R. Pickens. 149–78. Washington, D.C.: American Psychological Association.*

Tiebout, H. M. 1953. *Surrender versus compliance in therapy.* Quarterly Journal of Studies on Alcohol *14: 58–68.*

———. *1954. The ego factors in surrender in alcoholism.* Quarterly Journal of Studies on Alcohol *15: 610–21.*

———. *1961. Alcoholics Anonymous—An experiment of nature.* Quarterly Journal of Studies on Alcohol *22: 52–68.*

Tournier, R. E. 1979. *Alcoholics Anonymous as treatment and ideology.* Journal of Studies on Alcohol *40: 230–39.*

Ulman, R. B., and H. Paul. 1989. *A self-psychological theory and approach to treating substance abuse disorders: The "intersubjective absorption" hypothesis. In* Dimension of Self Experience. *Progress in Self Psychology, no. 5. Ed. A. Goldberg. 121–41. Hillsdale, N.J.: Analytic Press.*

———. *1990. The addictive personality and "addictive trigger mechanisms" (ATMs): The self psychology of addiction and its treatment. In* Dimension of Self Experience. *Progress in Self Psychology, no. 6. Ed. A. Goldberg. 129–56. Hillsdale, N.J.: Analytic Press.*

U.S. Department of Health and Human Services. 1988. *The health consequences of smoking: A report of the surgeon general. Rockville, Md.: U.S. Government Printing Office.*

Vanicelli, M. 1992. Removing the Roadblocks: Group Psychotherapy with Substance Abusers and Family Members. *New York: Guilford.*

Van Schoor, E. 1992. *Pathological narcissism and addiction: A self-psychology perspective.* Psychoanalytic Psychotherapy *6: 205–12.*

Voegtlin, W. L. 1940. *The treatment of alcoholism by establishing a conditioned reflex.* American Journal of Medical Sciences *199: 803–10.*

Wallace, J. 1993. *Modern disease models of alcoholism and other chemical dependencies: The new biopsychosocial models.* Drugs and Society 8: 69–87.

———. 1996. *Theory of 12-step oriented treatment. In* Treating Substance Abuse: Theory and Technique. *Ed. F. Rotgers, D. S. Keller, and J. Morgenstern. 13–36. New York: Guilford.*

Wallerstein, R. W. 1957. Hospital Treatment of Alcoholism: A Comparative, Experimental Study. *New York: Basic Books.*

Washton, A. M., and M. S. Gold, eds. 1987. Cocaine: A Clinicians Handbook. *New York: Guilford.*

Wiener, C. L. 1981. The Politics of Alcoholism. *New Brunswick: Transaction Books.*

Wills, T. A. 1985. *Stress, coping, and tobacco and alcohol use in early adolescence. In* Coping and Substance Use. *Ed. S. Shiffman and T. A. Wills. 67–94. Orlando, Fla.: Academic Press.*

Wurmser, L. 1974. *Psychoanalytic considerations of the etiology of compulsive drug use.* Journal of the American Psychoanalytic Association 22: 820–43.

———. 1977. *Mr. Pecksniff's horse? Psychodynamics in compulsive drug use. In* Psychodynamics of Drug Dependence. *NIDA Research Monograph, no. 12. Ed. J. D. Blaine and D. A. Julius. 36–72.*

———. 1978. The Hidden Dimension: Psychodynamics in Compulsive Drug Use. *New York: Jason Aronson.*

———. 1984a. *More respect for the neurotic process: Comments on the problem of narcissism in severe psychopathology, especially the addictions.* Journal of Substance Abuse Treatment 1: 37–45.

———. 1984b. *The role of super-ego conflicts in substance abuse and their treatment.* International Journal of Psychoanalytic Psychotherapy 10: 227–58.

Yalisove, D. L. 1988. *Review of* 42 Lives in Treatment: A Study of Psychoanalysis and Psychotherapy, *by R. S. Wallerstein (New York: Guilford, 1986).* Journal of Nervous and Mental Diseases 176: 696–97.

———. 1992. *Survey of contemporary psychoanalytically oriented clinicians on the treatment of the addictions: A synthesis. In* The Chemically Dependent: Phases of Treatment and Recovery. *Ed. B. C. Wallace. 61–81. New York: Brunner/Mazel.*

Zinberg, N. E. 1984. Drug, Set, and Setting: The Basis for Controlled Intoxicant Use. *New Haven: Yale University Press.*

Zweben, J. E. 1989. *Recovery-oriented psychotherapy: Patient resistances and therapist dilemmas.* Journal of Substance Abuse Treatment 6: 123–32.

———. 1992. *Issues in the treatment of the dual-diagnosis patient. In* The Chemically Dependent: Phases of Treatment and Recovery. *Ed. B. C. Wallace. 298–309. New York: Brunner/Mazel.*

Index